ADOPTION ACT
MANUAL

AUSTRALIA
LBC Information Services
Sydney

CANADA and USA
Carswell
Toronto

NEW ZEALAND
Brooker's
Auckland

SINGAPORE and MALAYSIA
Thomson Information (S.E. Asia)
Singapore

ADOPTION ACT MANUAL

SECOND EDITION

by

Richard M. Jones, M.A., Solicitor
Consultant, Morgan Bruce, Solicitors

LONDON
SWEET & MAXWELL
1997

Published in 1997 by
Sweet & Maxwell Limited of
100 Avenue Road, Swiss Cottage
London NW3 3PF
http://www.smlawpub.co.uk
Typeset by Dataword Services Limited of Chilcompton
Printed and bound in Great Britain by
MPG Books Ltd, Bodmin, Cornwall

First edition 1988
Second edition 1997

*No natural forests were destroyed to make this product; only
farmed timber was used and replanted*

**A CIP catalogue record for this book is available from
the British Library**

ISBN 0421 520 108

PREFACE

The Adoption Act 1976 consolidated the law on adoption as found in the Adoption Acts of 1958, 1960, 1964 and 1968, and the Children Act 1975. Although it received its Royal Assent in July 1976, the Act was not brought into force until January 1988. The passing of the Children Act 1989, coupled with developments in social work practice, prompted the Conservative government to set up an inter-departmental working group to review all aspects of adoption law. This group published four discussion papers which were supported by three substantial background papers. A widespread consultation exercise followed and this led to the publication in October 1992 of the *Report to Ministers of an Inter-departmental Working Group: A Consultation Document*. The next year saw the publication of the White Paper, *Adoption — The Future*, and in 1994 separate consultation documents on *Placements for Adoption* and *The Future of Adoption Panels* were produced. Finally, the Government published its draft Adoption Bill in March 1996 as the "final phase" of the consultation process.

As the new Labour government has indicated that it is not going to give priority to taking this protracted process forward, it was decided to publish a second edition of this *Manual*. As well as incorporating the many legislative and case law developments that have occurred over the last nine years, this edition reproduces, with the permission of the Department of Health, the first 12 sections of the recently published *A Guide to Intercountry Adoption — Practice and Procedures*.

I would like to thank Victoria Jones for helping me with the preparation of the index.

Richard Jones
Penarth
September 1997

CONTENTS

TABLE OF CASES

TABLE OF CIRCULARS AND LETTERS

Entries in **bold** indicate paragraphs where text is set out in full.

PART I

ADOPTION ACT 1976

(1976 C. 36)

Supplemental

Part III

Care and Protection of Children Awaiting Adoption

Restrictions on removal of children

Protected children

Part IV

Status of Adopted Children

Part V

Registration and Revocation of Adoption Orders and Convention Adoptions

MISCELLANEOUS AND SUPPLEMENTAL

SCHEDULES

An Act to consolidate the enactments having effect in England and Wales in relation to adoption. [July 22, 1976]

GENERAL NOTE

This Act consolidates the law on adoption as found in the Adoption Acts 1958, 1960, 1964 **1–002**
and 1968, and the Children Act 1975. Adoption law is a creature of statute; there is no
procedure for adoption under the common law (*R. v. Secretary of State for the Home
Department, ex p. Brassey* [1989] 2 F.L.R. 486, DC).

ABBREVIATIONS

In the commentary the following abbreviations are used:
Bevan and Parry: Children Act 1975, H. K. Bevan and M. L. Parry (Butterworths, 1979).
Houghton: Report of the Departmental Committee on the Adoption of Children, Cmnd.
5107 (1972).

TABLE OF DERIVATIONS

The following abbreviations are used in this Table:

    1958 = The Adoption Act 1958
           (7 & 8 Eliz. 2, c.5)
    1960 = The Adoption Act 1960
           (1960 c.59)
    1964 = The Adoption Act 1964
           (1964 c.57)
    1968 = The Adoption Act 1968
           (1968 c.53)
    1975 = The Children Act 1975
           (1975 c.72)

ADOPTION ACT 1958

1958	1976
s.9(3)(4)	s.66(1)(2)(6)
(5)	(5)
19	40(1)(2)
20	50
20A	51
21(1)	Sch. 1, para. 1(1)
(4)–(6)	Sch. 1, para. 1(3)–(5)
24(1)–(3)	Sch. 1, para. 4(1)–(3)
(4)	Sch. 1, para. 2(1)
(6)	Sch. 1, para. 4(4)
(7)	Sch. 1, para. 4(6)
26(1)	s.52(1)
(2)	Sch. 1, para. 6
(3)	s.52(4)
27	Sch. 1, para. 5(1)
29(1)	s.11
(2A)	11

1958	1976
s.29(3)–(5)	s.11
32(1)	9(1)(2)
(1A)	(1)(2)
(2)	(4)
(3)	(3)
(4)	67(5)
33	10
34	27
34A	28
(7)	67(3)
35	30
36(1)	31(1)
(2)	(2)(3)
(3)	22(4)
37(1)	32(1)(2)
(3)	(3)
(4)	(4)
38	33(1)
39	(2)
40(4), (6)	35(1)
(5)	(2)
43(1)–(4)	34
44(1)(a)(b)	36(1)(a)(b)
(d)	(1)(c)

1958	1976
s.44(2)	s.36(2)
45	37(1)
46	(2)
47	(4)
48	(3)
50	57
51	58
52	56
54(1)	68
55	69
56(1)	67(1)(2)
(2)	(6)
57(1)	72(1)
(2)	(3)
(4)	(4)
Sch. 5,	
para. 5	Sch. 2, para. 8
para. 6	Sch. 2, para. 5(2)(3)
para. 7	Sch. 2, para. 5(4)
para. 10	Sch. 2, para. 4

ADOPTION ACT 1960

1960	1976
s.1(1)	s.52(2)
(3)	(4)

ADOPTION ACT 1964

1964	1976
s.1(5)	s.59(3)
2	60
3	Sch. 1, para. 2 (2)–(5)

ADOPTION ACT 1968

1968	1976
s.4(3)	s.72(2)
5(1)	59(1)
6(1)	53(1)
(3)–(5)	(2)–(5)
7	54
8(1)	Sch. 1, para. 1(2)

1968	1976
s.8(2)	Sch. 1, para. 3
(4)	Sch. 1, para. 5(2)
9(1)–(4)	s.70
(5)	40(3)
10	71(2)

1968	1976
s.11(1)	ss.71(1), 72(1)
(2)	s.72(4)
12(2)	67(1)(2)
(3)	(4)
(4)	(5)

CHILDREN ACT 1975

1975	1976
s.1	s.1
2	2
3	6
4	3
5	4
6	5
7	8
8(1)–(5)	12(1)–(5)
(7)–(8)	(6)(7)
9	13
10	14
11	15

1975	1976
s.12	s.16
13	7
14	18
(6)	59(2)
15	19
16	20
(3)(c)	59(2)
17(1)–(3)	26
18	22(1)–(3)
19	25
21(1)–(3)	64
22(1)(2)	66(3)(4)

1975	1976
s.22(3)	s.23
(4)(5)	24
23	21
24	17
25	55
30(1)–(5)	29
32	57
100(1)(2)	
(4)(a)	62(1)(2)
(5)	(3)(4)
(6)	(6)
(8)	(5)

PART I

THE ADOPTION SERVICE

The Adoption Service

Establishment of Adoption Service

1.—(1) It is the duty of every local authority to establish and maintain **1–003** within their area a service designed to meet the needs, in relation to adoption, of—

(a) children who have been or may be adopted,

(b) parents and guardians of such children, and

(c) persons who have adopted or may adopt a child,

and for that purpose to provide the requisite facilities, or secure that they are provided by approved adoption societies.

(2) The facilities to be provided as part of the service maintained under subsection (1) include—

(a) temporary board and lodging where needed by pregnant women, mother or children;

(b) arrangements for assessing children and prospective adopters, and placing children for adoption;

(c) counselling for persons with problems relating to adoption.

(3) The facilities of the service maintained under subsection (1) shall be provided in conjunction with the local authority's other social services and approved adoption societies in their area, so that help may be given in a co-ordinated manner without duplication, omission or avoidable delay.

(4) The services maintained by local authorities under subsection (1) may be collectively referred to as "Adoption Service," and a local authority or approved adoption society may be referred to as an adoption agency.

DEFINITIONS
local authority: s.72(1).
child: s.72(1).
guardian: s.72(1).
approved adoption society: s.72(1).

GENERAL NOTE

This section requires the establishment of an adoption service within the area of every local **1–004** social services authority. The authority must itself provide the requisite facilities or ensure that approved adoption societies provide them. The adoption service must act in conjunction with other social services provided by the authority, and with local approved adoption societies. It

7

must therefore be seen as a part of a comprehensive child care service. Implementation of this section has been patchy (*For Children's Sake: An SSI Inspection of Local Authority Adoption Services*; see below).

The intention behind this section "is that local authorities should establish an adoption service as an integral part of their social services provision in partnership with adoption societies operating in their area. The Act does not lay down the form that this partnership should take; it will vary according to the needs of the area—of children, prospective adopters and natural parents—and according to the adoption societies operating in the area, the particular category of clients they serve (*e.g.* whether they have to be of a particular religious faith) and the extent of which they are likely to meet the new criteria for approval. Each authority will have to consider and assess which groups are not covered by voluntary agencies; ideally, where authorities are not already acting as adopting agencies, the local authority and the voluntary service should be complementary, with the minimum of duplication or parallel working. (Some overlapping will be inevitable if natural parents and prospective adopters are to be allowed an element of choice, *e.g.* between a local authority or a voluntary society or between a local authority and a society offering a service to persons of a particular religious faith.) It will be necessary for each authority to ensure oversight of the service available in the area. This will involve at least one senior, experienced officer with a recognised executive responsibility for adoption who should have access to the Director's management team to ensure that an adequate adoption service is provided in conjunction with their other services for families and children and in liaison with voluntary agencies. The officer involved will need to have direct links with the area teams to ensure that:

    (a) the social workers are knowledgeable about the adoption service;

    (b) they receive advice and guidance; and

    (c) the service is available to local families and children, including children in care." (D.H.S.S. Circular No. LAC (76)15, para. 14).

The effect of this section is also explained in D.H.S.S. Circular No. LAC (87)8.

The Social Services Inspectorate of the Department of Health has published the following reports which focus on the adoption service provided by local authorities: *Adoption: In the Child's Best Interests* (1991), *Planning for Permanence?—Adoption Services in 3 Northern Local Authorities* (1993), *"Moving Goalposts"—A Study of Post-Adoption Contact in the North of England* (1995), *For Children's Sake: An SSI Inspection of Local Authority Adoption Services* (1996) and *For Children's Sake Part 2: An Inspection of Local Authority Post-Placement and Post-Adoption Services* (1997).

Subs. (1)

1–005   *Children:* If adopted children have problems relating to their adoption which occur after they have reached adulthood they will be entitled to a counselling service provided under subs. (2)(*c*).

May . . . be adopted . . . may adopt a child: Note the scope of this provision.

Requisite facilities: See subs. (2).

Approved adoption societies: Voluntary organisations can be approved as adoption societies under s.3.

Subs. (2)

1–006   *Part of the service maintained under subsection (1):* i.e. as part of the adoption service.

Include: The list of facilities contained in this subsection is not exhaustive. *Houghton* considered that a comprehensive service should "comprise a social work service to natural parents, whether married or unmarried, seeking placement for a child (which would include channels of communication with related community resources); skills and facilities for the assessment of the parents emotional resources, and their person and social situation; short term accommodation for unsupported mothers; general child care resources including short term placement facilities for children pending adoption placement; assessment facilities; adoption placement services; after care for natural parents who need it; counselling for adoptive families. In addition, it should have access to a range of specialised services, such as medical services (including genetic, psychiatric and psychological assessments, arrangements for the examination of children and adoptive applicants, and a medical adviser) and a legal advisory service" (paragraph 38).

Mothers: But not fathers.

Counselling for persons with problems relating to adoption: Which would include prospective adopters who are refused an adoption order and children in respect of whom an adoption order was refused. For counselling where an adult person seeks a copy of his birth certificate, see s.51.

Other social services: See s.2.   **1–007**

Co-ordinated manner: The local authority and approved adoption societies would need to work in close collaboration with each other if a truly comprehensive and co-ordinated service is to be provided.

Subs. (4)

Adoption agency: In *Re W.* (*A Minor*) (*Adoption Agency: Wardship*) [1990] 2 All E.R. 463, Sir **1–008** Stephen Brown P. held that as the adoption process has been closely regulated by Parliament, the court would not exercise its wardship jurisdiction to supervise or review the merits of a decision of an approved adoption society taken pursuant to its duties and within its powers under this Act and the regulations made thereunder. The President further held that as an approved adoption society carries out a public function pursuant to statutory powers, *prima facie* it would be open to an application for judicial review to challenge the legality of its actions in appropriate cases.

Local authorities' social services

2. The social services referred to in section 1(3) are the functions of a **1–009** local authority which stand referred to the authority's social services committee, including, in particular but without prejudice to the generality of the foregoing, a local authority's functions—

   [(a) under the Children Act 1989, relating to family assistance orders, local authority support for children and families, care and supervision and emergency protection of children, community homes, voluntary homes and organisations, registered children's homes, private arrangements for fostering children, child minding and day care for young children and children accommodated by health authorities [National Health Service Trusts] and local education authorities or in residential care, nursing or mental nursing homes or in independent schools; and

   (b) under the National Health Service Act 1977, relating to the provision of care for expectant and nursing mothers.]

AMENDMENT

The words in square brackets were substituted by the Children Act 1989, s.88, Sched. 10, **1–010** para. 1 and the National Health Service and Community Care Act 1990, s.66(1), Sched. 9, para. 17.

DEFINITIONS

local authority: s.72(1).
child: s.72(1).

GENERAL NOTE

This section defines the "social services" referred to in s.1(3), as those functions which are **1–011** referred to a local authority's social services committee under the Local Authority Social Services Act 1970. The effect of the section is set out in D.H.S.S. Circular No. LAC (87)8.
Including: The list is not exhaustive.

Adoption Societies

Approval of adoption societies

3.—(1) Subject to regulations under section 9(1), a body [which is a **1–012** voluntary organisation and desires] to act as an adoption society or, if it is already an adoption society, desires to continue to act as such may, in the manner specified by regulations made by the Secretary of State, apply to the Secretary of State for his approval to its doing so.

(2) On an application under subsection (1), the Secretary of State shall take into account the matters relating to the applicant specified in subsections (3) to (5) and any other relevant considerations, and if, but only if, he is satisfied that the applicant is likely to make, or, if the applicant is an approved adoption society, is making, an effective contribution to the Adoption Service he shall by notice to the applicant give his approval, which shall be operative from a date specified in the notice or, in the case of a renewal of approval, from the date of the notice.

(3) In considering the application, the Secretary of State shall have regard, in relation to the period for which approval is sought, to the following—

(a) the applicant's adoption programme, including, in particular, its ability to make provision for children who are free for adoption,

(b) the number and qualifications of its staff,

(c) its financial resources, and

(d) the organisation and control of its operations.

(4) Where it appears to the Secretary of State that the applicant is likely to operate extensively within the area of a particular local authority he shall ask the authority whether they support the application, and shall take account of any views about it put to him by the authority.

(5) Where the applicant is already an approved adoption society or, whether before or after the passing of this Act, previously acted as an adoption society, the Secretary of State, in considering the application, shall also have regard to the record and reputation of the applicant in the adoption field, and the areas within which and the scale on which it is currently operating or has operated in the past.

(6) If after considering the application the Secretary of State is not satisfied that the applicant is likely to make or, as the case may be, is making an effective contribution to the Adoption Service, the Secretary of State shall, subject to section 5(1) and (2), by notice inform the applicant that its application is refused.

(7) If not withdrawn earlier under section 4, approval given under this section shall last for a period of three years from the date on which it becomes operative, and shall then expire or, in the case of an approved adoption society whose further application for approval is pending at that time, shall expire on the date that application is granted or, as the case may be, refused.

AMENDMENTS

1–013   In subs. (1) the words in square brackets were substituted by the Health and Social Services and Social Security Adjudications Act 1983, s.9, Sched. 2, para. 29.

DEFINITIONS
adoption society: s.72(1).
voluntary organisation: s.72(1).
adoption service: s.1(4).
notice: s.72(1).
child: s.72(1).
local authority: s.72(1).
approved adoption society: s.72(1).

GENERAL NOTE

1–014   This section provides for the central control of the approval of voluntary adoption societies. A voluntary organisation which wishes to act as an adoption society must obtain the approval of the Secretary of State. In considering the application the Secretary of State must have regard to the matters set out in subss. (3) to (5). Approval, which can be withdrawn at any time under s.4, lasts for three years from the date specified in the notice of approval. Renewals last for three years from the date of the notice of renewal. Taking part in the management or control of an unapproved adoption society is an offence under s.11.

There is no requirement that local authority adoption services established under s.1 should be individually approved by the Secretary of State. Local authorities have from time to time chosen to have their adoption services reviewed; see *Adoption: In the Child's Best Interests* (1991) Social Services Inspectorate, Department of Health, Ch. 2.

The activities of all adoption societies are governed by the Adoption Agencies Regulations 1983 (S.I. 1983 No. 1964); see s.9. Adoption agency decisions over children in their care are amendable to judicial review; see *Re W. (A Minor) (Adoption Agency: Wardship)* [1990] 2 All E.R. 463, which is noted under s.1(3).

The Social Services Inspectorate of the Department of Health has published a report which draws on the findings of 10 voluntary adoption agency inspections: see *Overview Report: Voluntary Adoption Agencies Inspections to 31 March 1994* (1994).

Subs. (1)

Body: An unincorporated body cannot apply (S.I. 1983 No. 1964, reg. 2(2)). **1–015**

Desires to continue to act: For transitional provisions, see S.I. 1981 No. 1792, art. 3, Sched. 2, para. 5.

Apply: See S.I. 1984 No. 1964, reg. 2(1).

Subs. (2)

Shall take into account: The requirement is mandatory. **1–016**

Any other relevant considerations: Houghton, in Appendix C, specifies information which should be required of voluntary adoption societies applying for registration.

Give his approval: See subs. (6) for the procedure on the refusals of an application.

Notice: The written notice (s.72(1)) may be sent by post (s.69).

Subs. (3)

Children who are free for adoption: The society will have to show that it has the ability to find **1–017** families for children who have been freed for adoption under s.18.

Subs. (4)

"This requirement is emimently desirable because the authority will have a far clearer **1–018** appreciation of the needs and resources of its own area than will the Secretary of State, particularly in view of the duty of the authority to ensure that an effective adoption service is being provided in its area"; *Bevan and Parry*, para. 21.

Subs. (6)

The Secretary of State is not satisfied: The onus is on the society to satisfy the Secretary of **1–019** State that it will make an effective contribution to the adoption service.

Refused: No procedure has been permitted to enable an appeal against refusal to be made; see further, *Houghton*, para. 60. Judicial review could be sought where an error of law is alleged.

Subs. (7)

Date on which it becomes operative: See subs. (2). **1–020**

Withdrawal of approval

4.—(1) If, while approval of a body under section 3 is operative, it **1–021** appears to the Secretary of State that the body is not making an effective contribution to the Adoption Service he shall, subject to section 5(3) and (4), by notice to the body withdraw the approval from a date specified in the notice.

(2) If an approved adoption society fails to provide the Secretary of State with information required by him for the purpose of carrying out his functions under subsection (1), or fails to verify such information in the manner required by him, he may by notice to the society withdraw the approval from a date specified in the notice.

(3) Where approval is withdrawn under subsection (1) or (2) or expires the Secretary of State may direct the body concerned to make such arrangements as to children who are in its care and other transitional matters as seem to him expedient.

GENERAL NOTE

1–022 This section provides for the withdrawal of approval of adoption societies by the Secretary of State if it appears to him that the society is not making an effective contribution to the adoption service. The procedure to be followed is set out in s.5.

Action can be taken against inactive or defunct adoption societies under s.8.

Subs. (1)

1–023 *It appears to the Secretary of State:* The test is subjective.

Notice: The written notice (s.72(1)) may be sent by post (s.69).

Withdraw the approval: There is no appeal against the Secretary of State's decision.

Subs. (3)

1–024 *Or expires:* Note that this provision deals with expiry as well as withdrawal of approval. The approval will expire after a period of three years, or on the refusal of a further application.

May direct the body concerned: "The most important practical problem created by the withdrawal of approval of a society will be the question of the welfare of children in its care . . . One might have expected a duty to have been imposed rather than a discretion granted," *Bevan and Parry*, para. 24.

Procedure on refusal to approve, or withdrawal of approval from, adoption societies

1–025 **5.**—(1) Before notifying a body which has applied for approval that the application is refused in accordance with section 3(6) the Secretary of State shall serve on the applicant a notice—

(a) setting out the reasons why he proposed to refuse the application;

(b) informing the applicant that it may make representations in writing to the Secretary of State within 28 days of the date of service of the notice.

(2) If any representations are made by the applicant in accordance with subsection (1), the Secretary of State shall give further consideration to the application taking into account those representations.

(3) The Secretary of State shall, before withdrawing approval of an adoption society in accordance with section 4(1), serve on the society a notice—

(a) setting out the reasons why he proposes to withdraw the approval; and

(b) informing the society that it may make representations in writing to the Secretary of State within 28 days of the date of service of the notice.

(4) If any representations are made by the society in accordance with subsection (3), the State shall give further consideration to the withdrawal of approval under section 4(1) taking into account those representations.

(5) This section does not apply where the Secretary of State, after having considered any representations made by the applicant in accordance with this section, proposes to refuse approval or, as the case may be, to withdraw

approval for reasons which have already been communicated to the applicant in a notice under this section.

DEFINITIONS
notice: s.72(1).
adoption society: s.72(1).

GENERAL NOTE

This section provides for the procedure to be followed if the Secretary of State refuses to **1–026** approve an adoption society under s.3 or withdraws the approval of an adoption society under s.4. In neither case does the Act allow for an appeal against the Secretary of State's decision. Failure to comply with the terms of this section would enable an aggrieved society to apply for judicial review.

Subs. (1)

Applied for approval: In accordance with s.3(1). **1–027**
Notice: The written notice (s.72(1)) may be sent by post (s.69).

Welfare of Children

Duty to promote welfare of child

6. In reaching any decision relating to the adoption of a child a court or **1–028** adoption agency shall have regard to all the circumstances, first consideration being given to the need to safeguard and promote the welfare of the child throughout his childhood; and shall so far as practicable ascertain the wishes and feelings of the child regarding the decision and give due consideration to them, having regard to his age and understanding.

DEFINITIONS
child: s.72(1).
adoption agency: s.1(4).

GENERAL NOTE

This section provides guidance to courts and adoption agencies on the weight to be given to **1–029** the child's welfare when any decision which relates to the child's adoption has to be made. Adoption proceeding are not governed by the welfare principle set out in s.1 of the Children Act 1989 (*Re B. (Adoption Child's Welfare)* [1995] 1 F.L.R. 895).

The meaning of this provision was explained by Lord Simon of Glaisdale in *Re D. (An Infant) (Adoption: Parent's Consent)* [1977] A.C. 602 at 638 as follows: "In adoption proceedings, the welfare of the child is not the paramount consideration (*i.e.* outweighing all others)—see [Adoption Act 1976, s.6], which may well have been no more than elucidatory and confirmatory of the pre-existing law (compare Lord Reid in *O'Connor v. A and B* [1971] 1 W.L.R. 1227 at p. 1230A), though the new statutory provisions are explicit that in adoption proceedings it is the welfare of the child throughout childhood which must be considered, and not merely short-term prospects."

In *Re D. (A Minor) (Adoption Order: Injunction)* [1991] Fam. 137, the Court of Appeal held that this section does not require the court to find a benefit to the child during minority as a condition precedent to the making of an adoption order. In this case the court, in affirming an adoption order made in respect of a child who, at the date of the order, had only six days left of his childhood, approved of the following passage from the judgment of Thorpe J. who made the order:

"I am in no doubt at all that the effect of those authorities is to show that in an appropriate case the court is entitled to have regard to considerations which will inure to the benefit of the child beyond minority and for the rest of his or her life. The fact that a child may be within a very short time of attaining his or her minority is not, in my judgment, to preclude the carrying out of the balancing exercise having regard to all the circumstances of the case. Obviously, the nearer a child is to attaining majority, then the less significance is to be attached to advantages that will secure his or her care during minority. But I cannot accept [the] submission that in the present case this court is without jurisdiction to make an order. Manifestly, in my judgment, the authorities show that there is jurisdiction. The fact that this application fortuitously comes to be decided in the last days of the child's minority is only one fact that should operate on the discretionary exercise."

The High Court practice of deciding whether an adoption order (or a freeing order) is in the best interests of the child before proceeding to consider the question whether to dispense with the parent's consent to the order (*Re D. (A Minor) (Adoption: Freeing Order)* [1991] 1 F.L.R. 49, CA) should be followed in the county court (*Re E. (A Minor) (Adoption)* [1989] 1 F.L.R. 126, CA) and the magistrates' court (*Re W., The Times*, November 25, 1976). Both issues should normally be considered at one hearing (*Re K. (A Minor) (Adoption: Procedure)* [1986] 1 F.L.R. 295, CA), although separate hearings might be justified in serial number applications to courts where there could be practical difficulties in keeping the parties apart and preserving the anonymity of the prospective adopters (*Re L.S. (A Minor) (Adoption: Procedure)* [1986] 1 F.L.R. 302, CA).

In *H. (A Minor) v. Oldham M.B.C.* FC3 95/6232, August 18, 1995, CA, Waite L.J. said that the principle set out in s.1 of the Children act 1989 that delay in determining questions affecting the upbringing of a child was prejudicial to a child's welfare applied with equal, if not greater, force to adoption proceedings as to proceedings under the 1989 Act.

When considering its recommendations the adoption panel of an adoption agency must have regard to the duty placed on the agency by this section (Adoption Agencies Regulations 1983 (S.I. 1983 No. 1964), reg. 10(3)).

Adoption of Foreign Nationals

1–030   In *Re W. (A Minor)* [1986] Fam. 54, the Court of Appeal identified four considerations which must apply when a British Citizen applies to adopt a foreign national (1) the applicant should give notice of the application to the Home Office to see whether the Home Secretary wishes to be added as a party to the proceedings; (2) when the court comes to consider the application on its merits it must give first consideration to the need to safeguard and promote the welfare of the child throughout its childhood. This factor carries less weight if only a short period of that childhood remains; (3) the court should also consider whether the welfare of the child would be better, or as well, promoted by another type of order which does not have the same effect on nationality and immigration as an adoption order; and (4) the court should take into account considerations of public policy in relation to the effect of an adoption order on nationality and the right or abode, and should carry out the balancing exercise between welfare (being the first consideration) and such public policy.

Re W. was applied by the Court of Appeal in *Re K. (A Minor) (Adoption: Nationality)* [1994] 3 All E.R. 553, where it was held that:

(1) the correct approach for a court to adopt in such cases is to consider first the motive for the application and only if satisfied that the true motive was not to achieve British nationality and the consequent right of abode, rather to serve the child's general welfare, to proceed to the second stage which is to carry out a balancing exercise between public policy and the child's welfare;

(2) in carrying out the balancing exercise the court should not take into account those benefits which flow from the acquisition of British nationality; cf. *Re D. (A Minor) (Adoption Order: Injunction)*, noted above. *Per* Hobhouse L.J. at 564: "Where, as in the present case, the welfare aspect is negligible, it may be difficult for the applicant for the adoption order to find grounds which are sufficient to counterbalance the public policy considerations of not allowing a right of entry or abode to be acquire save within the scheme of the code governing immigration to the United Kingdom." In this case the child was only eight days short of her eighteenth birthday when the matter came before the court; and

(3) (a) while the subsequent annulment of an adoption order relating to a foreign child will not effect the British nationality that the child acquired by virtue of the adoption (British Nationality Act 1981, s.1(6), a successfully appeal against the order would have such an effect; and

(b) the wording of s.1(6) does not abrogate the Home secretary's right to appeal against an adoption order where he is a party to the proceedings.

The possibility that adoption may be used primarily to secure British nationality for a foreign child was given further consideration by the Court of Appeal in *Re H. (A Minor) (Adoption: Non-Patrial)* [1996] 4 All E.R. 600 where the court rejected the two stage approach which had been adopted in *Re K. (A Minor) (Adoption: Nationality)* above, and other cases. In the words of Thorpe L.J. at p. 606, the:

"Family Division judge must dispose of the adoption application by reference principally to s.6 of the Adoption Act 1976. . . . Although not referred to in the section it is an important consideration that immigation regulations and policies should be upheld. A misuse of the right to apply for adoption as a device to circumvent

14

immigation controls will always be fatal to an adoption application. Quite apart from immigration policy considerations, adults exposed in that way are likely to have forfeited the confidence in their maturity and responsibility which the judge must hold before committing to them a child on such an irrevocable basis. Nor can I conceive that in a case of blatant abuse the application might be rescued by the argument that subsequent delay has resulted in the development of circumstances justifying a submission that the refusal of the application would be contrary to the welfare consideration. In such circumstances even if the applicants have redeemed themselves to some extent as potential parents the public policy consideration is likely to outweigh the welfare consideration."

Also note Peter Gibson L.J.'s comment at 607 that the wording of s.6 "does not justify the rejection of a genuine adoption application simply on the ground that it is not primarily motivated by welfare considerations".

For the adoption of children outside the jurisdiction, see the General Note to s.17.

Any decision relating to the adoption of a child: The Court of Appeal has held that this section does not apply when the court is considering the question under s.16(2)(b), of whether a parent is unreasonably withholding consent to adoption; see *Re P. (An Infant) (Adoption: Parental Consent)* [1977] Fam. 25, not following *Re B. (An Infant) (Adoption: Parental Consent)* [1976] Fam. 161. This decision has been criticised (see, for example, *Bevan and Parry*, para. 41) and in *Re D. (An Infant) (Adoption: Parental Consent)* [1977] A.C. 602, Lord Simon referred to *Re P.* and said: "as at present advised I feel some reservation about accepting the construction put by the Court of Appeal (*obiter* I think) on [this section] . . . it is a strong thing in an Act of this sort to read 'any decision relating to the adoption of a child' in other than the ordinary and primary sense of those words." In *Re M. (A Minor)* [1980] C.L.Y. 1801, the Appeal Committee of the House of Lords refused leave to appeal in a case which questioned the ruling in *Re P.* Note, however, that the question of the child's welfare is taken into account under s.16 as a reasonable parent would consider the child's welfare in coming to a decision on whether to withhold consent to adoption; see further the note on s.16(2)(*b*).

In *Royal Borough of Kensington and Chelsea v. K. and Q.* [1989] 1 F.L.R. 399, Hollings J. held that since a decision to give leave for an adoption agency to use television to advertise for adoptive parents for a ward of court was not a "decision relating to the adoption of a child," this section does not apply; see the General Note to s.58.

Court: An authorised court as defined by s.62.

Shall have regard: This section imposes a duty on courts and adoption agencies.

All the circumstances: Which specifically include the child's welfare and his wishes and feelings; see below. They also include the interest or claims of all interested parties (*Re W. (A Minor) (Adoption)* [1984] F.L.R. 402, CA), issues of public policy, such as the enforcement of immigration controls (see above), and the status of adoption in a foreign country (*Re B. (Adoption: Child's Welfare)* 1995 1 F.L.R. 895). "The court should have before it all relevant and significant information which will assist it to make a right decision," *per* Sir Stephen Brown P, in *Re C. (A Minor) (Evidence:* Confidential Information) [1991] 2 F.L.R. 478 at 482, 483. In this case the Court of Appeal held that a doctor's evidence is admissible in adoption proceedings even though it may involve a breach of the duty of confidentiality which a doctor owes to his patient. The court should order disclosure in cases where it can be said that the public interest in the achievement of justice outweighs the public interest in confidentiality.

The welfare of the child: Unlike the Children Act 1989, this Act does not contain any direct guidance as to how the child's welfare should be assessed. The term "welfare" has been given a wide interpretation by the courts: "welfare does not mean just material welfare. It extends . . . to all factors which will affect the future of the child" (*Re D. (AN Infant) (Parents' Consent)* [1977] 1 All E.R. 145, *per* Lord Dilhorne at 56. "One must look at the whole future of the child; not to mere temporary unhappiness or grief, however acute, if it is transient, not to mere affluence later" (*Re C. (L.)* [1965] 2 Q.B. 449, *per* Diplock L.J. at 471). Relevant factors relate to "material and financial prospects, education, general surroundings, happiness, stability of home and the like", *Re B.* [1971] Q.B. 437, *per* Davies L.J. at 443, the social and psychological benefits of truly belonging to a family (*Re R. (Adoption)* [1967] 1 W.L.R. 34), and a benefit accruing after the child's majority (*Re D. (A Minor) (Adoption Order: Validity)* [1991] Fam. 137). In *Re D.* the Court of Appeal held that a benefit during childhood is not a condition precedent to the making of an adoption order. For a case where the Court of Appeal granted an adoption order in circumstances where the prospective adoptive parents were refusing to reveal to a 13-year-old child her true origins, see *Re S. (A Minor) (Adoption),* *The Times,* August 26, 1987; [1988] Fam. Law 171.

Debate about the controversial issue of transracial adoption has been conducted largely at an ideological level as there is "no empirical evidence that transracial placements lead to low self esteem or psychological problems": see I. Weyland, "Attachment and the Welfare

Principle" [1996] Fam. Law 686 at 688. This statement is confirmed by the research undertaken by R. Simon, H. Alstein and M. Melli: see *The Case for Transracial Adoption* (1994), which considers a 20-year longitudinal study of transracial adoptees and their families. The Department of Health's review of research relating to adoption states that no large scale research studies "support the fears of black social workers about the dangers of trans-racial placements . . ." (*Research which has a bearing on adoption or alternatives to adoption* (1993), 23). The current judicial approach to such placements can be identified in the following passage from Wall J.'s judgment in *Re B.* (*Adoption: Child's Welfare*) [1995] 1 F.L.R. 895 at 902:

> "In my view a child has in principle a right to be brought up by his or her parents in the way of life and in the religion practised by the parents. That principle, however, is not absolute. It is an expression of what would ordinarily be in the child's interests and falls to be displaced where the welfare of the child requires it to be displaced. The test accordingly is welfare. It follows that the weight which has to be given to what generically I may term "heritage" or "birthright" will vary from case to case. In some cases it will be of minimum importance. In others it will be of great weight if not decisive".

Also note the following remarks made by Bush J. in *Re N.* (*A Minor*) (*Adoption*) [1990] 1 F.L.R. 58 at 63: "In my view—and I have no wish to enter what is clearly a political field—the emphasis on colour rather than cultural upbringing can be mischievous and highly dangerous when you are dealing in practical terms with the welfare of children."

In *Re O.* (*Transracial Adoption: Contact*) [1995] 2 F.L.R. 597, Thorpe J. rejected the guardian *ad litem's* attempt to make the transracial placement of the child the central issue in a case where the child had been living with the prospective adopters for over four years. A further example of how such placements can lead to a dangerous loss of professional perspective is to be found in Thorpe J.'s comment in the same case, at 605, on the recommendation of a clinical psychologist with "very great specialist knowledge of transracial placements". His Lordship said that her recommendation that the child should be reunited with her family in Nigeria "fell outside the range of solutions that could be responsibly commended by a qualified expert in the field of psychological medicine".

The issue of race and culture in the family placement of children is the subject of two letters from the Chief Inspector of the Social Services Inspectorate to Directors of Social Services (refs. CI (90) 2 and CI (96) 4). Also see paras. 2.40–2.42 of the Children Act 1989 Guidance and Regulations, Vol. 3: "Family Placement". An agency policy of total prohibition of inter-racial adoptors would be unlawful as it would not be compatible with the provisions of this section.

Throughout his childhood: Which ends at the age of 18. Courts and adoption agencies should therefore take a long-term view of the child's welfare. (*Re D.* (*A Minor*) (*Adoption: Freeing Order*) [1991] 1 F.L.R. 49, 52). Also see *Re D.* (*A Minor*) (*Adoption Order: Validity*) noted under "The Welfare of the Child", above.

So far as practicable: Which will largely depend on the child's age.

Wishes and feelings: The child must attend the adoption hearing unless excused (Adoption Rules 1984, s.23(4)). Only "due consideration" has to be given to the child's "wishes and feelings." These could conflict with the course of action that either the court or the adoption agency considers most likely to promote the child's long term welfare. In *Re D.* (*Minors*) (*Adoption by Step-Parent*) (1981) 2 F.L.R. 102, the Court of Appeal considered this provision in the context of a case where two girls aged 13 and 10½ had indicated that they wished to be adopted. *Per* Ormrod L.J.: "the court . . . is required . . . to ascertain, so far as practicable, the wishes and feelings of the child regarding the decision and give due consideration to them. . . . That, to my mind, must be an important consideration when dealing with children of the age of these children. They are fully old enough to understand . . . the broad implications of adoption and, if they actively wish to be adopted, even if they cannot give a very coherent reason for that wish, to refuse an adoption order in the face of that wish does require . . . some fairly clear reason." In *Re O.* (*Transracial Adoption: Contact*), above, Thorpe J. said, at 611:

> "I think that in future it may be necessary to emphasise the importance of giving voice to a child in any hybrid proceedings or in any straightforward adoption proceedings where the wishes and feelings of the child are in conflict with the guardian's assessment of welfare and disposal".

Religious upbringing of adopted child

1–032   **7.** An adoption agency shall in placing a child for adoption have regard (so far as is practicable) to any wishes of a child's parents and guardians as to the religious upbringing of the child.

GENERAL NOTE

Under the Adoption Act 1958 a parent's consent to the making of an adoption order could **1–031** be made subject to conditions as to the religious upbringing of the child. Parental agreement to an adoption order must now be unconditional (s.16(1)(b)(i), although under this section the parent can express his "wishes" about the child's religious upbringing to the adoption agency, which must "have regard" to them.

When considering its recommendations the adoption panel of an adoption agency must have regard to the duty placed on the agency by this section (Adoption Agencies Regulations 1983, S.I. 1983 No. 1964, reg. 10(3)).

Adoption agency: It is submitted that a *court* must take account of parental wishes about the **1–033** upbringing of their child by virtue of the duty placed on it by s.6, to "have regard to all the circumstances." A court could include a condition about the child's religious upbringing in the adoption order; see s.12(6).

Have regard: First consideration being given to the welfare of the child; see s.6, above.

So far as is practicable: It is submitted that an agency should always "have regard" to parental wishes but need not comply with such wishes if this is not practicable.

Parent: Is defined in s.72(1).

Religious: "It seems to me that the two essential attributes of religion are faith and worship; faith in a God and worship of that God," *per* Dillon J. in *Barralet v. Attorney General* [1980] 3 All E.R. 918 at 924.

Supplemental

Inactive or defunct adoption societies

8.—(1) If it appears to the Secretary of State that an approved adoption **1–034** society, or one in relation to which approval has been withdrawn under section 4 or has expired, is inactive or defunct he may, in relation to any child who is or was in the care of the society, direct what appears to him to be the appropriate local authority to take any such action as might have been taken by the society or by the society jointly with the authority; and if apart from this section the authority would not be entitled to take that action, or would not be entitled to take it without joining the society in the action, it shall be entitled to do so.

(2) Before giving a direction under subsection (1) the Secretary of State shall, if practicable, consult both the society and the authority.

GENERAL NOTE

Under this section the Secretary of State can take action against an adoption society which **1–035** appears to him to be inactive or defunct by directing an appropriate local authority to take any action which the society could have taken, whether acting alone or with the authority. Before he acts the Secretary of State must, if it is practicable, consult with both the society and the authority. The Secretary of State is not required to give reasons to the society and the society does not have a right to make representations to him. There is no appeal against a direction issued under this section.

Subs. (1)

Approval . . . has expired: After a period of three years, or on the refusal of a further **1–036** application (s.3(7)).

Inactive or defunct: "When is a society inactive or defunct? A defunct society is presumably one which has ceased to exist and an inactive society is one which still exists but ceases to operate. There could therefore be a society from which approval has been withdrawn but which is neither defunct nor inactive, in which case the Secretary of State would have to rely on his powers under [s.4(3)]"; *Bevan and Parry*, para. 25.

He may: The Secretary of State is not obliged to act.

Or with the society jointly with the authority: The local authority could apply to a court for an order transferring parental responsibility from the society to itself in cases where parental rights had been vested in the society by virtue of a freeing order made under s.18.

Subs. (2)

1–037   *If practicable:* Consultation would not be practicable if the delay involved would place children at risk.

Regulation of adoption agencies

1–038   **9.**—(1) The Secretary of State may by regulations prohibit unincorporated bodies from applying for approval under section 3; and he shall not approve any unincorporated body whose application is contrary to regulations made under this subsection.

(2) The Secretary of State may make regulations for any purpose relating to the exercise of its functions by an approved adoption society.

(3) The Secretary of State may make regulations with respect to the exercise by local authorities of their functions of making or participating in arrangements for the adoption of children.

(4) Any person who contravenes or fails to comply with regulations made under subsection (2) shall be guilty of an offence and liable on summary conviction to a fine not exceeding [level 5 on the standard scale].

Definitions
    approved adoption society: s.72(1).
    child: s.72(1).
    local authority: s.72(1).

Amendment
    In subs. (4) the words in square brackets were substituted by the Criminal Justice Act 1982, ss.38, 46.

General Note

1–039   The Adoption Agencies Regulations 1983 (S.I. 1983 No. 1964) (as amended by the Adoption Agencies and Children (Arrangements for Placement and Reviews) (Miscellaneous Amendments) Regulations 1997 (S.I. 1997 No. 649)) were made under this section as originally enacted in the Adoption Act 1958, s.32. They continue in force as if made under this section by virtue of s.73(1), Sched. 2, para. 1, and are considered in Departmental Circulars LAC (84)3 and LAC (97)13.

    Although it is necessary to comply strictly with the letter of these regulations, they are intended to be directory, not mandatory. A judge is therefore entitled to take breaches of the regulations into account at the adoption hearing (*Re T.* (*A Minor*) (*Adoption: Parental Consent*) [1986] 1 All E.R. 817, CA). Although *Re T.* was concerned specifically with regs. 11(2)(a) and 12(2)(f) it is submitted that the finding applies generally and that non-compliance will not necessarily vitiate the adoption as long as there has been a substantial compliance with the regulations and the interests of the natural parents have not been prejudiced.

Subs. (1)

1–040   *Regulations:* See s.67 for the making of regulations.
    Prohibit unincorporated bodies: See reg. 2(2) of the 1983 Regulations.

Subss. (2), (3)

1–041   *Regulations:* See the Adoption Allowance Regulations 1991 (S.I. 1991 No. 2030).

Subs. (3)

1–042   *Arrangements for the adoption of children:* See s.72(3).

18

Person: Or corporation (Interpretation Act s.5, Sched. 1). For offences by corporate bodies, **1–043** also see s.68.

Inspection of books, etc. of approved adoption societies

10. [*Repealed by the Health and Social Services and Social Security* **1–044** *Adjudications Act* 1983, *s.*30(1), *Sched.* 10, *Pt. I.*]

Restriction on arranging adoptions and placing of children

11.—(1) A person other than an adoption agency shall not make **1–045** arrangements for the adoption of a child, or place a child for adoption, unless—

(a) the proposed adopter is a relative of the child, or

(b) he is acting in pursuance of an order of the High Court.

[(2) An adoption society which is—

(a) approved as respects Scotland under section 3 of the Adoption (Scotland) Act 1978; or

(b) registered as respects Northern Ireland under Article 4 of the Adoption (Northern Ireland) Order 1987,

but which is not approved under section 3 of this Act, shall not act as an adoption society in England and Wales except to the extent that the society considers it necessary to do so in the interests of a person mentioned in section 1 of the Act of 1978 or Article 3 of the Order of 1987.]

(3) A person who—

(a) takes part in the management or control of a body of persons which exists wholly or partly for the purpose of making arrangements for the adoption of children and which is not an adoption agency; or

(b) contravenes subsection (1); or

(c) receives a child placed with him in contravention of subsection (1),

shall be guilty of an offence and liable on summary conviction to imprisonment for a term not exceeding three months or to a fine not exceeding [level 5 on the standard scale] or to both.

(4) In any proceedings for an offence under paragraph (a) of subsection (3), proof of things done or of words written, spoken or published (whether or not in the presence of any party to the proceedings) by any person taking part in the management or control of a body of persons, or in making arrangements for the adoption of children on behalf of the body, shall be admissible as evidence of the purpose for which that body exists.

(5) [*Repealed by the Children Act* 1989, *s.*108(7), *Sched.* 15]

AMENDMENT

In subs. (3) the words in square brackets were substituted by the Criminal Justice Act 1982, ss.38, 46. Subs. (2) was substituted by the Children Act 1989, s.88, Sched. 10, Pt. 1, para. 2.

DEFINITIONS

adoption agency: s.1(4).
child: s.72(1).
relative: s.72(1).
adoption society: s.72(1).
body of persons: s.72(1).

GENERAL NOTE

This section attempts to prevent private adoption placements by non-relatives by making it **1–046** an offence for a person other than an adoption agency to make arrangements for the adoption of a child or place a child for adoption unless the proposed adopter is a relative of the child or he is acting in pursuance of a High Court order. Anyone who receives a child who has been placed in breach of this section also commits an offence. Although it might be expected that private adoption placements would be less successful than agency placements, the National Child Development Study (see, J. Seglow *et al., Growing Up Adopted* (1972)) found no evidence that privately placed children did any worse than those who had been placed by agencies (presumably using specialist staff).

No court has power retrospectively to authorise a placement in breach of this section (*Re G. (Adoption: Illegal Placement)* [1995] 1 F.L.R. 403, CA). Nevertheless, the fact that an offence has been committed under this section does not prevent an adoption order being made, as long as the application for adoption is made to the High Court; see *Re S. (Arrangements for Adoption)* [1985] F.L.R. 579, where the Court of Appeal confirmed that save in a situation where the proposed adopter is a relative of the child, the authority of the High Court is an essential prerequisite for the making of arrangements by any person other than an adoption agency for the adoption of a child or for placing the child for adoption.

In *Re G.*, the Court of Appeal approved the following finding by Douglas Brown J. in *Re Adoption Application (Non-Patrial: Breach of Procedures)* [1993] 1 F.L.R. 947:

> "the court hearing an adoption application where there had been a proved breach of s.11 was not prohibited from making an order notwithstanding the absence of a statutory dispensing and retrospective power. It must take the breach into account and consider whether public policy required that the order should be refused because of the applicants' criminal conduct, while giving first consideration to the welfare of the child pursuant to s.6, following the same principle properly adopted by a court considering whether to authorise a breach of s.57."

If a breach of this section is revealed during the course of proceedings in the County Court the court should exercise its powers under art. 12 of the Children (Allocation of Proceedings). Order 1991 to transfer the proceedings to the High Court (*Re G.*).

The relationship between this section and s.13(2), awaits clarification. Section 13(2) states that a child who has not been placed by an adoption agency or in pursuance of a High Court order cannot be adopted until he is 12 months old and has had his home with the applicants for 12 months. It could therefore be argued that the prohibition against private placements made by this section could be evaded if the provisions of s.13(2) were satisfied. In *Re S. (Arrangements for Adoption)*, Slade L.J. said, at 584, that he was "not as yet persuaded that the essentially restrictive provisions of [s.13(2)] are in any circumstances apt to eliminate the need for compliance with the prohibitive provisions of [s.11(1)] . . . I think it better to leave this point to be fully considered and finally decided when it calls for a decision." If those concerned with the placement of the child never intended it to be a placement for adoption then neither the foster parents nor the person who placed the child would be guilty of an offence under this section if the foster parents subsequently formed an intention to apply for adoption.

Under s.22, in cases where the child was not placed by an adoption agency the court must be provided with a report by the local authority which will specifically investigate whether the child was placed with the applicant in contravention of this section. The Act does not specify what action an adoption court should take if the local authority does report that the child has been placed illegally. The court could either adjourn the hearing of the adoption application pending the completion of criminal proceedings or proceed with the application.

This section is considered by Sandland in "Problems in the criminal law of adoption", *Journal of Social Welfare and Family Law*, 17(2) 1995: 149 and by K. O'Donnell in "Illegal Placements in Adoption", *Journal of Child Law*, 6(1) 1994: 17.

Subs. (1)

1–047   Where the mother of a child is under a disability and thus incapable both of caring properly for her child and of making fully informed decisions about the placement of the child, a third party who approaches an approved adoption agency on her behalf with a view to making arrangements for the child to be placed for adoption does not act in breach of this provision (*Re W. (A Minor) (Adoption: Mother under Disability)* [1995] 4 All E.R. 282. *Per* Wall J. at 287, 288: "In my judgment s.11(1) simply cannot be construed as rendering unlawful arrangements made between an individual and an adoption agency for the placement of a child by the latter. . . . [T]here may be cases where a mother is under a disability in which the child in question is properly placed by an adoption society for adoption without recourse to the public law provisions of the Children Act 1989. In such a case the protection against exploitation of her disability afforded to the mother is twofold: first, the fact that adoption agencies are responsible bodies approved and regulated by statute which must apply stringent criteria in the placement of any child for adoption; secondly, that adoption remains a judicial process in which an order cannot be made without the court being satisfied of the statutory criteria laid down by ss.6 and 16 of the 1976 Act in proceedings to which the mother must be a party and in which she will be represented by a guardian ad litem."

A person: Including the parents of the child. This section therefore makes it an offence for a mother to place her own child with non-relatives for adoption.

Arrangements for the adoption of a child: This phrase is defined in s.72(3). In *Re Adoption Application* 8605498/99, *Adoption and Fostering,* Vol. 12, No. 2, p. 58, it was held that assistance offered to prospective adopters by a person in England supplying a fact sheet on adoption from Brazil did not come within the scope of the definition. There are conflicting decisions on whether the commissioning of home study reports in inter-country adoption cases constitute the making of "arrangements" for adoption: see *Re An Adoption Application* [1992] 1 F.L.R. 341 (breach) and *Re Adoption Application (Non-Patrial: Breach of Procedures),* above (no breach).

Place a child for adoption: In *Re A. (Adoption: Placement)* [1988] 1 W.L.R. 229, it was held that this provision only applied where the placement of the child occurred within the jurisdiction of the United Kingdom and that there could be no placement of a child with proposed adopters until there is physical contact between them. In this case the court ruled that this section had been breached in circumstances where a child who had been brought from El Salvador was met by his prospective adoptive parents after she had passed through U.K. customs and immigration control. The section would not have been breached if the proposed adopters had met the child abroad and brought her back with them to this country. *Re A* was followed by Bracewell J. in *Re A.W. (Adoption Application)* [1993] 1 F.L.R. 62 and by Douglas Brown J. in *Re Adoption Application (Non-Patrial: Breach of Procedures),* above.

Relative: Note that the definition of relative in s.72(1) includes the father of an illegitimate child.

Subs. (3)

A person: This includes a body of persons corporate or unincorporate (Interpretation Act **1–048** 1978, s.5, Sched. 1). The management and control of the adoption of children is therefore restricted to adoption societies approved by the Secretary of State. For offences by corporations, see s.68.

Receives a child: Proof of the offence of receiving a child for the purposes of adoption under para. (c) requires evidence of the commission of the offence of making arrangements for the adoption of that child under subs. (1). The question that justices should ask themselves when considering a charge under *para.* (c) is with what real purpose did the defendants take the child into their care (*Gatehouse v. R.* [1986] 1 W.L.R. 18, DC).

PART II

Adoption Orders

The Making of Adoption Orders

Adoption orders

   12.—(1) An adoption order is an order [giving parental responsibility for **1–049** a child to] the adopters, made on their application by an authorised court.

   (2) The order does not affect [parental responsibility so far as it relates] to any period before the making of the order.

   (3) The making of an adoption order operates to extinguish—

  [(a) the parental responsibility which any person has for the child immediately before the making of the order;

 (aa) any order under the Children Act 1989]

  (b) any duty arising by virtue of an agreement or the order of a court to make payments, so far as the payments are in respect of the child's maintenance [or upbringing for any period after the making of the order.]

   (4) Subsection (3)(b) does not apply to a duty arising by virtue of an agreement—

  (a) which constitutes a trust, or

  (b) which expressly provides that the duty is not to be extinguished by the making of an adoption order.

(5) An adoption order may not be made in relation to a child who is or has been married.

(6) An adoption order may contain such terms and conditions as the court thinks fit.

(7) An adoption order may be made notwithstanding that the child is already an adopted child.

AMENDMENTS

The amendments to this section were made by the Children Act 1989, s.88, Sched. 10, Pt. 1, para. 3.

DEFINITIONS

adoption order: s.72(1).
child: s.72(1).
guardian: s.72(1).

GENERAL NOTE

1–050   This section, together with ss.39 and 41, sets out the effect of an adoption order which, in general terms, is to create between the adopter and the child a legal relationship which is almost equivalent to that between a parent and his natural legitimate child.

> "[This Act] requires that an adoption should be such that all rights, duties, obligations and liabilities of the parents or guardians of infants in relation to the future custody, maintenance and education of the infant should be extinguished and all such rights, duties, obligations and liabilities should vest in and be exercisable by and enforceable against the adopter as if the child were a child born to the adopter in lawful wedlock",

per Sir John Arnold P. in *Re H.* (*A Minor*) (*Adoption*) [1985] F.L.R. 519, 527.

The nature of an adoption order was also considered by Sir Thomas Bingham M.R. in *Re B.* (*Adoption Order: Jurisdiction to Set Aside*) [1995] 3 All E.R. 333, CA at 343:

> "The act of adoption has always been regarded in this country as possessing a peculiar finality. This is partly because it affects the status of the person adopted, and indeed adoption modifies the most fundamental of human relationships, that of parent and child. It effects a change intended to be permanent and concerning three parties. The first of these are the natural parents of the adopted person, who by adoption divest themselves of all rights and responsibilities in relation to that person. The second party is the adoptive parents, who assume the rights and responsibilities of parents in relation to the adopted person. And the third party is the subject of the adoption, who ceases in law to be the child of his or her natural parents and becomes the child of the adoptive parents."

The psychological benefits of adoption have been described as follows:

> "It is well recognised that adoption confers an extra and psychologically and emotionally important sense of 'belonging'. There is real benefit to the child/parent relationship in knowing that each is legally bound to the other and in knowing that the relationship thus created is as secure and free from interference by outsiders as the relationship between natural parents and their child. So strong and important is this sense of belonging that time and again in ordinary domestic adoption cases it is held to outweigh a natural parent's unwillingness to give his or her agreement to adoption, even when there is no question or suggestion of actually removing the child from applicants such as foster parents", *per* Holman J. in *Re H.* (*Adoption: Non-Patrial*) [1996] 1 F.L.R. 717 at 726.

In *Re H.* (*Adoption: Parental Agreement*) (1982) 3 F.L.R. 386 at 388, CA, Ormrod L.J. answered the question: "What do the adoptive parents gain by an adoption order over and above what they have already got on a long-term fostering basis?" He said:

> "To that the answer is always the same—and it is always a good one— adoption gives us total security and makes the child part of our family, and places us in parental control of the child; long-term fostering leaves us exposed to changes of view of the local authority, it leaves us exposed to applications, and so on, by the natural parent. That is a perfectly sensible and reasonable approach; it is far from being only an emotive one."

Although an adopted child of a married couple is to be treated in law as if he had been born a child of their marriage (s.39; an adopted child of a single adopter is treated as if born in wedlock, but not as a child of an actual marriage) that child's relationship with his natural family remains relevant for the purposes set out in ss.47 and 48.

As proceedings under this Act are "family proceedings" for the purposes of the Children Act 1989 (*ibid.* s.8(3)(4)), a court hearing an adoption application can make any order it considers correct, whether or not it is asked for, which is permitted by s.8 of that Act. Thus, for example, the court could make a residence order instead of an adoption order or could make a contact order as well as an adoption order; for contact orders, see the note to subs. (6).

"The court ought not to exercise its discretion under the adoption legislation for the purpose of overruling an intended exercise by the care authority of its power under the Child Care Act [1980]," *per* Sir John Arnold P. in *Re H.* (*A Minor*) (*Adoption*) (1985) F.L.R. 519, CA In this case an adoption order was refused on the ground, *inter alia*, that the real purpose of the adoption application was to frustrate the plan of the local authority to remove the children from their foster home. The principle established in this case would apply to the use of a local authority's powers under the Children Act 1989.

Where an order authorising the adoption of a minor who is not a British citizen is made by any court in the United Kingdom after January 1, 1983, he shall be a British citizen as from the date on which the order is made if the adopter or, in the case of a joint adoption, one of the adopters is a British citizen on that date (British Nationality Act 1981, s.1(5)).

The setting aside of Adoption Orders

Apart from the purposes provided for in ss.52 and 53 an adoption is irrevocable, although in **1–051** exceptional circumstances the High Court does have the power to set aside an adoption order on appeal in cases where mistake (*Re M.* (*Minors*) (*Adoption*) [1991] 1 F.L.R. 458, CA) or failures of natural justice due to procedural irregularity (*Re F.* (*R.*) [1970] 1 Q.B. 385; *Re K.* (*Adoption and Wardship*) [1997] 2 F.L.R. 221, CA, can be alleged. The courts have been willing to extend the time for appeal in such cases. *Re M.* (a case where the natural father successfully appealed out of time against the adoption order on the ground that his agreement to the adoption had been given in ignorance of his wife's terminal condition) was distinguished in *Re B.*, above, where the Court of Appeal held that the court has no interent jurisdiction to set aside a validly made adoption order by reason of a misapprehension or mistake. *Per* Sir Thomas Bingham M.R. at 344:

"An adoption order is not immune from any challenge. A party to the proceedings can appeal against the order in the usual way. The authorities show, I am sure correctly, that where there has been a failure to natural justice, and a party with a right to be heard on the application for the adoption order has not been notified of the hearing or has not for some other reason been heard, the court has jurisdiction to set aside the order and so make good the failure of natural justice. I would also have little hesitation in holding that the court could set aside an adoption order which has shown to have been obtained by fraud."

At the hearing at first instance Sir Stephen Brown P. said:

"The edifice of adoption would be gravely shaken if adoption orders could be set aside after the time for appealing had expired because (i) natural parents did not know everything about or were even misled about the adopters; and/or (ii) the adopters did not know everything about or were misled about the child; and/or (iii) the child did not like the aspects or attributes of the adopters. Once made the order is impregnable" ([1995] 1 F.L.R. 1 at 7).

Concurrent applications under the Children Act 1989 and the Adoption Act 1976

Where there are competing adoption and contact applications concerning a child, both **1–052** applications should normally be heard together in the same court: *G. v. G.* (*Children: Concurrent Applications*) [1993] 2 F.L.R. 306. *Per* Cazalet J., at 312, 313: "It is desirable that each available option should be open to the court when it is making its decision as to what the child's welfare properly requires." A similar approach should be taken to concurrent applications for adoption and residence orders.

The procedure to be adopted by a court when hearing concurrent applications, especially as it relates to the need to preserve the anonymity of the prospective adopters, was considered by Butler-Sloss L.J. in *Re S.* (*A Minor*) (*Adoption*) [1993] 2 F.L.R. 203, 209, CA:

"Although in the present case the mother has not asked for a residence order, her application for contact is clearly designed, as she said in her affidavits, to lead to rehabilitation and the return to her of her son. At the hearing of the applications, despite no application by a residence order, the judge in this case will be bound to consider the prospects of success of an application for a residence order in the future. If there is any prospect of success, the judge is likely to have to consider making a contact order. In any event, the judge would be most unlikely to proceed with the adoption application if there is the sightest possibility of a residence order being made to the mother. On the facts of this case, if there is any prospect of continuing or rather renewing contact between the mother and the child, it would be unlikely that adoption would follow since this is a confidential serial number case. In the logical progression, the judge will look first at the prospects of residence and then at the prospects of contact, and in this type of case will not consider the question of adoption until he has formed a conclusion on the first two questions. It is not until there is no real prospect of rehabilitation to the natural parent, and no advantage to the child of a contact order, that the confidential adoption of the child becomes a serious option.

At the stage of the consideration of a future residence order and the application for contact, the particular characteristics of the current carers, so long as they are suitable, are not relevant. By definition, such carers are likely to be suitable people, selected and scrutinised as they will have been by the adoption fostering panel of the local authority. The degree to which the child is attached to them and the length that the child has spent with them, and the fact that they are the providers of the child's home, are highly relevant factors. But their own special characteristics do not appear to me to be of importance in the residence and contact applications. Their attributes and the suitability of their home as a long-term placement for the child are not to be placed in the balance in considering adequacy of the mother as a parent. To do so would be to engage in social engineering, since they are almost bound to have the advantage over the mother, material and psychological. In my view, therefore, the particular physical characteristic of the prospective adoptive father is irrelevant to the first two issues which the judge has to address and the information should not be made available to the mother by the guardian *ad litem* in the Children Act applications."

In *Re C.* (*A Minor*) (*Adoption: Parental Agreement: Contract*) [1993] 2 F.L.R. 260, the Court of Appeal approved of the decision of the judge to consider concurrent applications in the following order:

(1) the parents' application for a residence order;
(2) the parents' alternative application for a contact order and the local authority's counter-application for an order that there be no contact; and
(3) the local authority's application under s.18 of the Adoption Act 1976 for a freeing order in respect of the child.

For confidentiality in the Adoption Act proceedings, see r.53(2) of the Adoption Rules 1984 and the notes thereto.

Subs. (1)

1–053   *Adoption order:* A child cannot be adopted without a court order: an informal arrangement, sometimes called a *de facto* adoption, where adults have agreed to bring up a child, does not provide the adults with parental responsibility (Children Act 1989, s.2(9)).

Vesting: The adoption order does not transfer the rights of the child's natural parents in the adopters: it extinguishes the rights of the natural parents (subs. (3)) and confers on the adopters the rights of the parents of a legitimate child (s.39).

Parental responsibility: Is defined in s.3 of the Children Act 1989 as "all the duties, powers, responsibilities and authority which by law a parent of a child has in relation to the child and his property". The exercise of parental responsibility by the adopter is not subject to supervision by the court or the adoption agency.

Adopters: Or adopter if only one person adopts (s.15).

Their application: For procedure and parties to the proceedings, see r.15 of the Adoption Rules 1984, and the Magistrates' Courts (Adoption) Rules 1984.

Subs. (2)

1–054   For the application of this subs. and subs. (3) where an order is made freeing a child for adoption, see s.18(5).

Any period before the making of the order: As the order is prospective, areas of child maintenance which arose before the order could be enforced.

Subs. (3)

1–055   *Making the order:* In *R. v. Colchester and Clacton County Court, ex p. A.D.W. and B.A.W.* [1980] 1 F.L.R. 363, following a hearing at the local county court the judge pronounced an adoption order. Subsequently, the applicants were informed, via the local authority, that the judge had reconsidered the case and had felt obliged to ask the clerk of the court not to issue the order until he had thoroughly considered the advantages of wardship proceedings. A subsequent application to perfect the order was dismissed and the applicants then applied to the High Court for judicial review. The Court held that although the judge was entitled at any time until the order was perfected to vary or alter the order he originally expressed there must be a valid reason for altering that order. The sole question in this case was whether the judge had expressed his discretion judicially. Unfortunately, the judge had expressed no reason why the child should be made a ward of court and was, therefore, not justified in making the variation. The application was granted and the judge directed to perfect his original order.

Extinguish: From the date of the order (subs. (2)). Unless there are exceptional circumstances in which the court in adoption proceedings continues an injunction, any orders made in wardship come to an end on the adoption (and presumably on the making of a freeing order) (*Re O. (Minors) (Adoption: Injunction)* [1993] 2 F.L.R. 737).

Person: This will include an adoption agency to whom parental rights have been transferred after the making of a freeing order; see. s.18(5).

Immediately before: Thus, where a freeing order has been made it will be the adoption agency that has parental responsibility, and not the natural parents.

Any order under the Children Act 1989: While this provision has the effect of extinguishing a pre-existing order made under s.8 of the Children Act 1989, it does not prevent the court making an adoption order and then adding a s.8 order.

Subs. (4)

This subsection enables a natural parent to make financial provision for a child who is to be adopted. **1–056**

Subs. (5)

Child: In exceptional circumstances an adoption order can be granted close to the child's majority; see, for example, *Re D. (A Minor) (Adoption Order: Validity)* [1991] 2 F.L.R. 66, CA, where an adoption order was made in respect of a severely mentally handicapped child six days before his eighteenth birthday. **1–057**

Married: The prohibition is not limited to marriage in this country.

Subs. (6)

Adoption order: Note that the court does not have the power to attach terms and conditions to a freeing order made under s.18. **1–058**

Terms and conditions: The court could make a contact order under s.8 of the Children Act 1989 as an alternative to attaching conditions to the adoption order: see below. Although parental agreement to adoption must be unconditional the court has a wide discretion under this provision to attach terms and conditions to the adoption order. The imposition of terms and conditions will always be subject to the general duty placed on the court by s.6. Examples of terms and conditions would be as to the religious upbringing of the child (*cf.* s.7) or allowing a member of the adopted child's natural family to have access to the child (*Re C. (A Minor) (Adoption: Conditions)* [1988] 1 All E.R. 705, HL). In *Re C.* the House of Lords held that (1) in normal circumstances it was desirable that on adoption there should be a complete break with the child's natural family; (2) where it was in the best interests of the child to have future contact with a member of the child's natural family that could be achieved by making the adoption order subject to a condition as to access; (3) such a condition would not be imposed, except in the most exceptional case, without the adopters' agreement; and (4) where no agreement was forthcoming the court would, with very rare exceptions, have to choose between making an adoption order without conditions as to access and seeking to safeguard access through other machinery. The study by M. Murch *et al.* found very little evidence of adoption orders being made with access conditions attached (*Pathways to Adoption* (1993), p. 10).

Re C. was applied by the Court of Appeal in *Re S. (A Minor) (Blood Transfusion: Adoption Order Condition)* [1994] 2 F.L.R. 416, where Waite L.J. said at 421 that the "imposition of a condition resented or objected to by the adopters may threaten the very peace and security for the child which it is the aim of adoption to achieve. It is liable, moreover, to be difficult not only to supervise such a condition, because of the confidentiality which the adoptive process requires, but also to enforce it, because it can seldom be desirable to place adopters at risk of punishment for contempt of court." In this case the court held that it was not appropriate to attach a condition to an adoption order which required adoptive parents who were Jehovah's Witnesses to institute court proceedings if their adopted child required a blood transfusion. If such a situation arose in an emergency there is a satisfactory procedure agreed between the Department of Health and the Medical Defence Union. In non-urgent situations the local authority could apply for a specific issue order; see *Re R. (A Minor) (Blood Transfusion)* [1993] 2 F.L.R. 757.

In *Re C* (*A Minor*) (*Wardship and Adoption*) [1981] 2 F.L.R. 177, CA, Roskill L.J. observed that "the court must be extremely careful to see that it is not imposing terms and conditions which are fundamentally inconsistent with the principles which underline the making of an adoption order." It would therefore not be a valid exercise of the power given by this subsection to make an order for adoption subject to the condition that the child should remain in the care and control of some person other than the adopters; see *Re J.* (*A Minor*) (*Adoption Order: Conditions*) [19713] Fam. 106. The Court of Appeal in *Re R.* (*A Minor*) (*Adoption Access*) [1991] 2 F.L.R. 78, held that it was "wholly wrong" to make an adoption order, and to leave over indefinately a question as to access by the natural father. Such a course of action would "be to invite unknown problems and could not be considered to be consistent with a proper approach to the making of an adoption order."

1–059   In *Re O.* (*Transracial Adoption: Contact*) [1995] 2 F.L.R. 597, Thorpe J. made contact a condition of the adoption, rather than leaving this to the discretion of the adopters on the ground that, in the absence of such a condition, "it becomes procedurally and as a matter of prospects very difficult for the biological parent to obtain [contact] by a subsequent applicant", (at 610). In this case the determination of the dates and venue of contact was left to the local authority. In *Re G.R.* (*Adoption: Access*) (1985) F.L.R. 643, 647, Sheldon J., said: "in my view there is nothing inconsistent with the judge refusing to make an order for access while, at the same time, saying expressly that he was not prohibiting access."

The question of whether an adoption order should be made in circumstances where a condition as to access is the underlying basis on which the order is made was considered by Oliver L.J. in *Re V.* (*A Minor*) (*Adoption: Dispersing with Agreement*) [1987] 2 F.L.R. 89 at 98, CA:

> "speaking for myself, I confess to a degree of unease about the desirability of seeking to secure stability by an adoption order in a case where the whole process is being approached on the footing that an opposing natural parent is to be accorded immediate and continuing access, not simply for the purpose of keeping her memory alive and investing the child with a sense of his own identity, but on a regular and frequent basis and where it is found as a fact that, to put it no higher, there exists a serious doubt whether she is capable of concealing her desire to have the child re-established as a member of her family. An adoption order would no doubt frustrate the realisation of that desire, but it cannot be thought realistically to eliminate it. [. . .] Once it is found [. . .], that regular and frequent access, inevitably maintaining and strengthening the family ties between the child and his mother and her other children, is so conducive to the welfare of the child that provision has to be made for it in the adoption order as the underlying basis on which the order is made at all, I find it difficult to reconcile that with the avowed purpose of the adoption of extinguishing any parental rights or duties in the natural parent. I entertain considerable reservations about whether, on the basis of continuing regular and frequent access by a natural parent who has not shown himself or herself unfit in any way to care for his or her own child, it can be right to impose an irrevocable change of status with a view simply to discouraging him or her from the hope of persuading a court in the future to alter the status quo as regards care and control."

In *Re D.* (*A Minor*) (*Adoption Order: Injunction*) [1991] 3 All E.R. 461; [1991] 2 F.L.R. 66, the Court of Appeal said at p. 470 that, "in its context, s.12(6) seems to be intended to enable the court to limit, or impose conditions upon, those parental rights and duties which would otherwise vest in the adopters, or might otherwise be extinguished in the natural parents. Thus, by imposing a condition relating to access in favour of the natural parents, the court will both qualify the parental rights conferred upon the adopters and leave to that extent unextinguished the parental rights of the natural parents. Similarly, the court may think it right to impose upon the adoption order a condition requiring access by relatives other than the actual parents, or that the child should be brought up in a particular religion; this would be to qualify the parental rights conferred upon the adopters, although not in this case leaving any residuary right in the natural parents." The court held that this provision was not intended to enable the court to grant to adopters rights far more extensive than those to which natural parents were entitled, such as the right to prevent specific third parties from having any contact with the child. Section 37(1) of the Supreme Court Act 1981 cannot be used for this purpose because injunctions issued under that provision can only be used to protect a right created by the imposition of a term under subs. (6). The court concluded its consideration of this issue by stating that if, "in any particular case, it is considered necessary to grant injunctions to restrain contact with third parties during the period of the child's minority, this can be done by following the existing practice and making the child a ward of court (if the child is not already one), and making the appropriate orders in wardship. This will be to put the adoptive parents in the same position as natural parents vis-à-vis third parties: neither better nor worse."

In *Re C.* (*A Minor*) (*Adoption Order: Condition*) [1986] 1 F.L.R. 315, the child's natural father had taken out an insurance policy in the child's favour which would mature when she was 13. The judge in making an adoption order attached a condition requiring the adoptive parents to make annual reports on the child's progress. These reports would enable the father to decide whether to extend the insurance policy to mature when the child was older. On appeal the Court of Appeal set aside the condition on the grounds that it detracted from the rights and duties of the adoptive parents and undermined the feelings of security which the adoptive parents should have and were entitled to have, and which would form the basis of the love and the feeling of security which they are able to pass onto the child. *Per* Balcombe L.J.: it is difficult to see how such a condition could promote the welfare of the child as is required under section 6 of this Act.

Compliance with any term or condition imposed by the court would, if all else failed, be enforceable by committal proceedings; *Re C.* (*A Minor*) (*Adoption: Conditions*), above.

For the findings of a study of contact after contested adoptions; see M. Ryburn, "Contact after contested adoptions," (1994) 4 *Adoption and Fostering* 30.

Adoption Orders with Contact Orders

In recent years there has been a significant and vocal lobby in favour of a move towards **1–060** more "open" adoptions, where adoptions are set up from the start to give the child two sets of continuing parents and their respective family networks. To use Martin Shaw's words: "Like much received wisdom throughout the history of adoption, enthusiasm for 'openness' appears driven more by ideology than by empirical evidence of its benefits. There is some evidence that it can be helpful to adults involved; its value for children (particularly those placed in infancy) has yet to be demonstrated" (*A Bibliography of Family Placement Literature* (1994), p. 60). In her review of the literature on open adoption Alexina McWhinnie found "no research evidence, as to its genuine long-term advisability and certainly none as to its outcome" (A. McWhinnie and J. Smith (eds.) *Current Human Delemmas in Adoption* (1994), p. 7). Also note Butler-Sloss L.J.'s comment that the view "of open adoption embraced by the experts does not seem to be shared by many prospective adopters" (*Re A* (*A Minor*) (*Adoption: Contact Order*) [1993] 2 F.L.R. 645 at 650).

As there could be problems in varying or enforcing conditions relating to contact imposed under this section, a contact order made under s.8 of the Children Act 1989 would be a better way for the court to ensure that contact takes place. It will be very rare for a contact order to be made against the wishes of the adoptive parents (*Re C.* (*A Minor*) (*Adoption: Conditions*), above) because such action would "create a potentialy frictional situation which would be hardly likely to safeguard or promote the welfare of the child", *per* Lord Ackner at 712. If the adoptive parents are agreeable to contact being maintained the court should adopt the practice outlined by Millett L.J. in *Re T.* (*Adoption: Contact*), noted below, rather than make a contact order because "it is for the benefit of the child that the adoptive parents should have the feeling that they are not under constraint in doing what they have already said they would do and everybody trusts them to do" and "if the circumstances change, they should have the flexibility to change with the circumstances and not to be tied to an order", *per* Butler-Sloss L.J. at 257.

Although a contact order made under s.8 cannot survive a subsequent adoption order, a "contact order can (in theory at least) now be imposed upon adopters after the making of the adoption order as the alternative to the making of an adoption order with conditions", *per* Butler-Sloss L.J. in *Re A* (*A Minor*) (*Adoption: Contact Order*) [1993] 2 F.L.R. 645 at 649, CA. However, since the natural parent will no longer be the child's legal parent leave to bring the proceedings must be obtained (unless the parent comes within one of the categories set out in s.10(5) of the 1989 Act) with the court applying the criteria prescribed in s.10(9) of that Act. The approach that should be adopted by the courts on hearing an application for leave brought by a natural parent has been identified by Thorpe J. in *Re C.* (*A Minor*) (*Adopted Child: Contact*) [1993] 3 All E.R. 259 and by the Court of Appeal in *Re T. and others* (*Minors*) (*Adopted Children: Contact*) [1996] 1 All E.R. 215.

In adoption cases, if the issue of contact was not raised at the adoption hearing or if the issue of contact had been raised but had been rejected by the adoption court, an application for leave by the child's former parent is unlikely to be granted in the absence of a fundamental change of circumstances. An application for indirect contact could only be made by way of a condition attached to the adoption order prior to the perfection of the order and could not be made at any time thereafter (*Re C.*). If agreement on contact had been reached by the adopters and the former parent at the time of the adoption and the adopters subsequently decide to stop contact they should give clear reasons in simple terms to explain their action. A former parent will be granted leve to apply for contact if the court considers that the adopters have acted against the best interests of the child (*Re T.*). *Per* Balcombe L.J. at 222: When dealing with an application for leave "the object is to ensure that adopters . . . are not unnecessarily worried but that at the same time the court has before it such information as it considered necessary to determine the application . . . bearing in mind that that is not the substantive application. In most cases it should be sufficient to notify the local authority, if that were the adoption agency; in some cases it may be necessary to transfer the applications to the High Court and to bring in the Official Solicitor but I see no reason why that should be the general rule."

In *Re T. Adoption: Contact)* [1995] 2 F.L.R. 251, CA, Millet L.J. said that it was "wrong in principle" to make a contact order which required the adopter to do that which they had already agreed to do. The right course was to include in the adoption order a recital that the adopting parents had stated their intention to permit the child to have contact with the mother at specified intervals and continue with the statement that the court did not find it necessary to make any order. If the judge wanted to dispense with the leave requirement for future applications by the former parent, "he did not have to make a contact order in order to achieve this; he could have done so by including 'liberty to apply' even though he had not made any substantive order," (at 258).

Where natural parents claim that assurances they received about contact were overlooked when the adoption order was made, they should either apply to the adoption court for the amendment of the adoption order or appeal the adoption order. Any attempt to revive those assurances should be made within those proceedings and not by the issue of fresh proceedings under the Children Act 1989 (*Re E. (Adopted Child: Contact: Leave)* [1995] 1 F.L.R. 57, Thorpe J.) The power of the court to amend an adoption order in these circumstances is unclear.

Subs. (7)

1–061 *Adopted child:* This provision allows for re-adoption irrespective of the country where the child was originally adopted. There is no restriction on the number of occasions or the personnel involved and it is therefore possible for a child to be re-adopted by his natural parents. See Sched. 1, para. 1(4) for the registration of a re-adoption.

Child to live with adopters before order made

1–062 **13.**—(1) Where—

(a) the applicant, or one of the applicants, is a parent, step-parent or relative of the child, or

(b) the child was placed with the applicants by an adoption agency or in pursuance of an order of the High Court,

an adoption order shall not be made unless the child is at least 19 weeks old and at all times during the preceding 13 weeks had his home with the applicants or one of them.

(2) Where subsection (1) does not apply, an adoption order shall not be made unless the child is at least 12 months old and at all times during the preceding 12 months had his home with the applicants or one of them.

(3) An adoption order shall not be made unless the court is satisfied that sufficient opportunities to see the child with the applicant, or, in the case of an application by a married couple, both applicants together in the home environment have been afforded—

(a) where the child was placed with the applicant by an adoption agency, to that agency, or

(b) in any other case, to the local authority within whose area the home is.

DEFINITIONS
adoption society: s.1(4).
adoption order: s.72(1).
child: s.72(1).
local authority: s.72(1).
relative: s.72(1).

This section sets out a number of preconditions to the making of an adoption order. They **1–063** are:

(1) Where the child is related to the adopters, or is placed with the applicants by an adoption agency or in pursuance of a High Court order, an adoption order cannot be made unless the child is at least 19 weeks old and at all times during the 13 weeks preceding the date on which the adoption order is due to be made has his home with the applicants or one of them.

(2) In all other cases an adoption order cannot be made unless the child is at least 12 months old, and at all times during the 12 months preceding the day on which the adoption order is due to be made has his home with the applicants or one of them.

(3) Whichever period applies an adoption order will not be made unless the court is satisfied that the agency which placed the child (or in non-agency cases, the relevant local authority), has had sufficient opportunities to see the child with the applicant or, in the case of an application by a married couple, both applicants together in the home environment.

In cases where the child was not placed by an adoption agency, the applicants must give notice to the local authority for their home area at least 3 months before the date of the order (s.22(11)). The child then becomes a "protected child" (s.32) and the local authority must arrange for the child to be visited (s.33).

A birth parent may be prevented from removing the child before the periods set out in this section have expired; see ss.27 and 28.

The professional assessment of prospective adopters is considered in a letter issued by the Chief Inspector, Social Services Inspectorate (ref. CI(96)4) and in paragraphs 39 to 45 of Department of Health Circular No. LAC (97) 13.

Subs. (1)

Applicant: For the position where an applicant is domiciled in England and Wales but **1–064** resident abroad, see *Re Y. (Minors) (Adoption: Jurisdiction)* [1985] 3 All E.R. 33 noted in the General Note to s.22. The conditions as to eligibility to adopt are set out in ss.14 and 15.

Parent: Is defined in s.72(1).

Placed: The Foster Placement (Children) Regulations 1991 (S.I. 1991 No. 910) do not apply to the placement of a child for adoption pursuant to this Act with a person who proposes to adopt him, *ibid.*, reg. 2(2). Such a placement is also outside the scope of the Accommodation of Children (Charge and Control) Regulations 1988 (S.I. 1988 No. 2183), *ibid.* reg. 2(3), the Arrangements for Placement of Children (General) Regulations 1991 (S.I. 1991 No. 890), *ibid.*, reg. 2(3), and the Review of Children's Cases Regulations 1991 (S.I. 1991 No. 895), *ibid.*, reg. 13A.

Had his home with the applicants: When determining with what person, or where, a child has his home, temporary absences shall be disregarded (s.72(1A)). The question of what is to be regarded as a "home" for the purposes of this Act, was considered in the following extract from Sheldon J.'s judgment in *Re Y.* above, at 36, 37:

"It is a question to which little or no assistance in finding an answer is provided by [s.72 of the 1976 Act]. Nor, in my view, unless it is to be given for any particular purpose some arbitrary statutory meaning, is the concept capable of precise definition. Nor, too, in my opinion, should such a definition be attempted beyond indicating the principal features that a 'home' may be expected to embody. Subject to that, in my judgment, it must be a question of fact in any particular case whether or not the applicant has a 'home' here within the meaning of the [1976] Act.

'Home' is defined thus in the *Shorter Oxford English Dictionary*:

'A dwelling-house, house, abode: the fixed residence of a family or household; one's own dwelling in which one habitually lives or which one regards as one's proper abode.'

It is a definition which, in my judgment, contains the essential elements of a 'home' as it is to be understood for present purposes. I have no doubt that an individual may have two homes; but each, in my judgment, to be properly so called, must comprise some element of regular occupation (whether past, present or intended for the future, even if intermittent), with some degree of permanency, based on some right of occupation whenever it is required, where, in the words of Kekewich J. in *Re Estlin, Prichard v. Thomas* (1903) 72 L.J. Ch. 687 at 689, 'you find the comforts of what is known as home', the fixed residence of a family or household. . . .

The requirement that the applicant or applicants must have a 'home' within the jurisdiction for the period specified, however, does not also import an obligation that they or the child should be living or residing there at or for any particular time or length of time. Of course the less time that any of them spend there the more difficult it is likely to be to persuade the court that it is a 'home'; but the only statutory obligation in this connection would seem to be that they should spend sufficient time there to enable the local authority concerned to see all parties together in their 'home environment' as provided by [s.13(3) of the 1976] Act and properly to investigate the circumstances as required by s.22. What that will involve in terms of residence will be a question to be decided in the light of the facts of each case."

In *Re K.T. (A Minor) (Adoption)* [1993] Fam. Law 567, Ward J. held that the child "had his home" with the applicant where the child lived during the week with his grandparents and stayed with his aunt (the applicant, who took all major decisions concerning his upbringing) at weekends and during the holidays. His Lordship said that the situation was no different from the boy being away at boarding school during the week.

Or one of them: This provides for cases where one of the adoptive parents is engaged in business abroad or is serving overseas. But note subs. (3).

Subs. (2)

1–065   On this Dr. David Owen said:

"This is a difficult issue, because we have here two aims. The first aim is to prevent the placement itself without the professional skills and safeguards which agency regulation is to provide . . . The second aim is that adoption law must also give assurance of adequate safeguards for the welfare of the child. To improve restrictions on independent placements for adoption, without making it possible for private foster parents to adopt a child, if this were in the child's interests, would be to work against the principle of protecting the child. Yet the Committee does not want to make it so wide that private placements would be encouraged. There is a balance to be struck here". (Standing Committee A on the Childrens Bill 1975, cols. 133–4.)

The balance is struck by banning independent placements and using criminal law sanctions, whilst allowing adoption where the child has had his home with the applicant for 12 months. In *Re S. (Arrangements for Adoption)* [1985] F.L.R. 579, CA. Slade L.J. indicated as a matter for guidance that he was not persuaded that the provisions of this subsection eliminated the prohibition contained in s.11 of the Adoption Act 1976; see the note on s.11.

Where subsection (1) Does not apply: e.g. where the applicants have been fostering the child.

Twelve months old: This period includes the first six weeks of the child's life (*c.f.* subs. (1)).

Months: Mean calendar months (Interpretation Act 1978, s.5, Sched. 1).

Had his home with the applicants: See the note on subs. (1).

Subs. (3)

1–066   *Sufficient opportunities:* No time limit is imposed by this provision.

Both applicants: While the child has to have his home for a fixed period with only one applicant, the court, before making the adoption order, must be satisfied that the local authority or adoption agency reporting on the application has had sufficient opportunities to see the child with both applicants (if there are two) in their home environment. This "provision would seem to exclude the making of an adoption order in favour of a married couple who were separated by the time the [adoption] application was made", *per* Johnson J. in *Re WM* [1997] 1 F.L.R. 132 at 136.

Adoption by married couple

1–067   **14.**—[(1) An adoption order shall not be made on the application of more than one person except in the circumstances specified in subsections (1A) and (1B).

(1A) An adoption order may be made on the application of a married couple where both the husband and the wife have attained the age of 21 years.

(1B) An adoption order may be made on the application of a married couple where—

   (a) the husband or the wife—

      (i) is the father or mother of the child; and

      (ii) has attained the age of 18 years;

       and

   (b) his or her spouse has attained the age of 21 years.]

    adoption order: s.72(1).
    child: s.72(1).
    Convention adoption order: s.72(1).

GENERAL NOTE

This section sets out the qualifications and restrictions concerning the eligibility of a single **1–074** person to adopt. The study by M. Murch, *et al.*, found very few applications for adoption made by single people (*Pathways to Adoption* (1993), p. 10).

Subs. (1)

One person: An adoption application can be made by a single person, whether he or she at **1–075** that time lives alone, or cohabits in a heterosexual, homosexual or even an asexual relationship with another person who it is proposed should fulfil a quasi-parental role towards the child (*Re W. (A Minor) (Adoption: Homosexual Adopter)* [1997] 3 All E.R. 620). *Per* Singer J. at 627: "Any other conclusion would be both illogical, arbitrary and inappropriately discriminatory in a context where the court's duty is to give first consideration to the need to safeguard and promote the welfare of the child throughout his childhood." Subs. (3) applies if the applicant is either the mother or father of the child.

Attained the age: See the note on s.14(1).

Para. (a)

Is not married: It is possible for an adoption order to be made in favour of one co-habitee **1–076** with a joint residence order in favour of them both: see *Re A.B. (Adoption: Joint Residence)* [1996] 1 F.L.R. 27, noted under s.14.

Para. (b)

"The policy behind this provision is clearly to avoid creating limping relationships within **1–077** marriage whereby as a result of an individual adoption order the child would become for all purposes a child of one spouse but not at all of the other"; *per* Singer J. in *Re W*, above, at 623.

Is married: In *Re WM* [1997] 1 F.L.R. 132, Johnson J. held that although there is no specific provision which bars an adoption order being made in favour of a married couple who had separated after the adoption application had been made, such an order could only be made if the requirement of s.13(3), that the local authority has had sufficient opportunity to see the child with "both applicants together in the home environment", is satisfied. "An adoption order can certainly be made in in favour of one spouse if the separation of the couple occurred after the making of the application: see *Re B. and S. (Minors) (Adoption)* [1995] 1 F.C.R. 486", *per* Johnson J. at 136.

Cannot be found: The court would need to be satisfied that all reasonable steps had been taken in an attempt to trace the spouse; see the note on s.16(2)(*a*).

His spouse is . . . incapable: Whether or not the spouse is living with the applicant.

Subs. (2)

Domicile: See the note on s.14(2).   **1–078**

Subs. (3)

Father: It is unclear whether this provision applies to the father of an illegitimate child. In **1–079** adoption law he is not a "parent" (*Re M.* [1955] 2 Q.B. 479) but is a "relative" (s.72(1)). The fact that this provision refers to the "other natural parent" rather than simply to the "other parent" suggests that the natural father of an illegitimate child is intended to be included and that an application by the mother to adopt her own illegitimate child cannot succeed unless the court is satisfied that the terms of this subsection have been complied with; see *Bevan and Parry*, para. 97. Note that under ss.4 and 12 of the Children Act 1989, an unmarried father can obtain parental responsibility for his child without ending the child's legal relationship with the mother.

Cannot be found: See the note on subs. (1).

Some other reason: Which would presumably relate to the welfare of the child. This provision is unsatisfactory as there seems to be no reason why single parent adoptions could not be dealt with by using the provisions contained in s.6 (the court to have regard to all circumstances, the child's welfare being the first consideration) and s.16 (dispensing with parental agreement). A detailed analysis of this provision is provided by *Bevan and Parry* at paras. 95 to 98.

Justifying: The burden of proof is a heavy one (*Re C.* (*A Minor*) (*Adoption by Parent*) (1986) Fam. Law 360).

Parental agreement

1–080   **16.**—(1) An adoption order shall not be made unless—

(a) the child is free for adoption by virtue of an order made
   [(i) in England and Wales, under section 18;
   (ii) in Scotland, under section 18 of the Adoption (Scotland) Act 1978; or
   (iii) in Northern Ireland, under Article 17(1) or 18(1) of the Adoption (Northern Ireland) Order 1987.];
      or
(b) in the case of each parent or guardian of the child the court is satisfied that—
   (i) he freely, and with full understanding of what is involved agrees unconditionally to the making of an adoption order (whether or not he knows the identity of the applicants), or
   (ii) his agreement to the making of the adoption order should be dispensed with on a ground specified in subsection (2).

(2) The grounds mentioned in subsection (1)(b)(iii) are that the parent or guardian—

(a) cannot be found or is incapable of giving agreement;
(b) is withholding his agreement unreasonably;
(c) has persistently failed without reasonable cause to discharge [his parental responsibility for] the child;
(d) has abandoned or neglected the child;
(e) has persistently ill-treated the child;
(f) has seriously ill-treated the child (subject to subsection (5)).

(3) Subsection (1) does not apply in any case where the child is not a United Kingdom national and the application for the adoption order is for a Convention adoption order.

(4) Agreement is ineffective for the purposes of subsection (1)(b)(i) if given by the mother less than six weeks after the child's birth.

(5) Subsection (2)(f) does not apply unless (because of the ill-treatment or for other reasons) the rehabilitation of the child within the household of the parent or guardian is unlikely.

AMENDMENTS

The amendments to this section were made by the Children Act 1989, s.88, Sched. 10, Pt. 1, para. 5.

DEFINITIONS

adoption order: s.72(1).
child: s.72(1).
Convention adoption order: s.72(1).
guardian: s.72(1).
United Kingdom national: s.72(1).
parent: s.72(1).

GENERAL NOTE

1–081   This section provides that an adoption can only be made if the child is free for adoption or the court is satisfied that each parent or guardian of the child, freely and with full understanding of what is involved, agrees unconditionally to the making of the order, unless that agreement can be dispensed with.

For a collection of papers on contested adoptions, see M. Ryburn (ed.), *Contested Adoption: Research Law, Policy and Practice* (1994).

Parent: The father of an illegitimate child is not a "parent" for these purposes unless he has parental responsibility for the child (s.72(1)). Although a care order gives a local authority parental responsibility for the child, the authority has no right to agree or to refuse to agree to the making of an adoption order (Children Act 1989, s.33(6)(b)).

Is satisfied: Where, in adoption proceedings, the mother of a child unreasonably withheld her consent, the public interest in the restricted disclosure, in furtherance of the child's interests, of relevant and material confidential information concerning the mother's medical condition might, having regard to the special circumstances, prevail over the public interest in the need to preserve confidentiality between a doctor and her patient (*Re C. (A Minor) (Evidence: Confidential Information)* [1991] 2 F.L.R. 478, CA).

Agrees: The court should not hear evidence on the parent's inability or unwillingness to consent and then adjourn the matter for decision at a later date (*Devon County Council v. B.* [1997] 1 F.L.R. 591, CA). Whilst in the ordinary case agreement is usually given in writing, that requirement is not mandatory under the rules and consent may be given and agreement may be expressed orally in the absence of any formality (*Re T. (A Minor) (Adoption: Parental Consent)* [1986] 1 All E.R. 817 and *Re WM (Adoption: Non-Patrial)* [1997] 1 F.L.R. 132). If the child has not been freed for adoption the parent must agree at the time of the making of the order. Agreement can therefore be withdrawn at any time up to the hearing. Parents should be warned, however, that time begins to run against them once consent has been given, so they may subsequently be found to be unreasonable in withholding their consent; see the comments of Ormrod L.J., in *Re H. (Infants) (Adoption: Parental Consent)* [1977] 1 W.L.R. 471, CA, noted below. For restrictions on the removal of a child by a parent once adoption has been agreed, see s.27. Payments to obtain the required agreement are prohibited by s.57. For evidence of agreement, see s.61.

The agreement is to an adoption order made by an authorised court (s.72) which, by s.62, is a court in England or Wales. In *Re WM (Adoption: Non-Patrial)*, above, Johnson J. was prepared to hold that agreement had been given for the purposes of this section in circumstances where the mother had consented to the making of an adoption order in Paraguay, and there was reason to believe that she was aware that there would be adoption proceedings in England and that she gave her consent for the purpose of the English proceedings. Compare this case with *Re G. (Foreign Adoption: Consent)* [1995] 2 F.L.R. 534, another decision of Johnson J., where his Lordship held that the agreement to adoption given by the child's mother in relation to adoption order made in Paraguay (which is not recognised by English Law) was not an agreement for the purposes of this section as nothing she had said or done in Paraguay could be construed as an agreement to an adoption order made in England.

Unconditionally: An agreement which purports to contain conditions is therefore invalid and, unless parental agreement is dispensed with, an adoption order cannot be made. The court can attach conditions to the adoption order under s.12(6). Note that a parent can express his wishes about the child's religious upbringing to the adoption agency under s.7.

Identity of the applicants: The identity of the applicants can be kept confidential by the assignment of a serial number under r.14 of the Adoption Rules 1984 and the Magistrates' Courts (Adoption) Rules 1984.

Dispensed with: The requirement of parental agreement to the adoption or a finding that the parent is unreasonably withholding consent "is for the purpose of protecting the rights of the parent; the child's welfare will already have been considered under the first stage [when s.6 of this Act is at issue]. (See *per* Lord Hailsham L.C. in *Re W. (An Infant)* [1971] A.C. 682 at 693, 694)": *Re C. (A Minor) (Adoption: Parental Agreement: Contact)* [1993] 2 F.L.R. 240 at 269, *per* Balcombe L.J. The agreement must relate to the particular adoption order that the court is being asked to make, and not to adoption generally.

As dispensing with consent is a judicial act which bears directly on the propriety of making **1–083** an adoption order, it should be recorded in the order (*S. v. Huddersfield B.C.* [1975] Fam. 113). In *Re C. (Adoption Application: Hearing)* [1982] 3 F.L.R. 95, the Court of Appeal said that where the issue of dispensing with consent arises and there is a potential controversy about it, the matter must be dealt with in a proper judicial hearing. This means that evidence must be on oath, opportunities to cross-examine must be given, and a proper note made of the proceedings so that, if asked, the Court of Appeal can reconsider the judge's decision as quickly as possible.

Where the applicant intends to ask the court to dispense with the agreement of a parent of the child on one of the grounds specified in subs. (2), the request shall be made in the originating process or application to which three copies of the statement of facts on which the applicant intends to rely shall be attached; r.19(1) Adoption Rules 1984, and the Magistrates' Courts (Adoption) Rules 1984.

The High Court practice of deciding whether an adoption order (or a freeing order) is in the best interests of the child before proceeding to consider the question whether to dispense with the parents' consent to the order (*Re D. (A Minor) (Adoption: Freeing Order)* [1991] 1 F.L.R. 48, should be followed in the county court (*Re E. (A Minor) (Adoption)* [1989] 1 F.L.R. 126, CA and the magistrates' court (*Re W., The Times,* November 25, 1976). As was pointed out in *Re E. (Adoption Child: Contact: Leave)* [1995] 1 F.L.R. 57, there are overwhelming difficulties in the county court if the High Court practice identified in *Re D.* is applied to cases where the respondent parents are in person. Rights of cross-examination available to a litigant in person inevitably breach the intended confidentiality of the applicant's identity. In this case Thorpe J. made a strong plea for progress to be made in ensuring that the necessary facilities be made available at a selected number of court centres, so that within a reasonable distance of any court of issue there would be a court of trial with the requisite facilities and equipment to enable a contested hearing to be determined at a single sitting, without risking any contact between the applicant adopters and the respondent parents. For further cases on procedure, see the General Note to s.6.

Where parents have not agreed to the making of an adoption order they should not be denied legal aid except on the basis of means (*Re C. (Adoption Application: Legal Aid)* Note [1985] F.L.R. 441, Sheldon J.).

A ground specified in subsection (2): The list is thus exclusive. The applicants are required to file a written statement of facts on which they intend to rely with their application: see rr.7.19 of the Adoption Rules 1984 and the Magistrates' Courts (Adoption) Rules 1984. A guardian *ad litem* will then be appointed to investigate the matters alleged in the application and statement of facts (*ibid.*, rr.6 and 18).

Subs. (2)

1-084   *Cannot be found:* Agreement may only be dispensed with on this ground if the court is satisfied that every reasonable step by reasonable means has been taken to trace the parent; see *Re F. (R.)* [1970] 1 Q.B. 385 and *Re An Adoption Application* [1992] 1 F.L.R. 341.

Reasonable steps could include writing to the parent's last known address, advertising in the press, enlisting the assistance of the post office, and identifying relatives who might have kept in touch with the parent. Notice must be served on each person whose consent is required.

If it is not practicable to communicate with a person whose whereabouts are known, then they "cannot be found" for the purposes of this provision; see *Re R. (Adoption)* [1967] 1 W.L.R. 34, where the parents lived in a totalitarian regime and any attempt to communicate with them could have placed them in danger.

Incapable of giving agreement: This can include mental incapacity but goes further than conditions described in the Mental Health Act 1983. It could also include someone in a coma or suffering from some other physical incapacity. This provision is concerned with the situation where the parent is not capable of expressing a view about the proposed adoption. If a parent who has a mental disorder does not agree to the making of an adoption order an application to dispense with parental agreement should be made under para. (*b*) (*Re. L. (A Minor) (Adoption: Parental Agreement)* [1987] 1 F.L.R. 400).

A finding could be made under this provision if it was probable that the parents would not be freely permitted to give their agreement; see *Re R. (Adoption),* above.

Is withholding his agreement unreasonably: The test of "unreasonableness" is an objective one. In *Re W. (An Infant)* [1971] A.C. 682 the House of Lords agreed that the following passage from Lord Denning's judgment in *Re L. (An Infant)* (1962) 106 S.J. 611, CA may now be considered to be authoritative: "In considering the matter I quite agree that: (1) the question whether [the mother] is unreasonably withholding her consent is to be judged at the date of the hearing; and (2) the welfare of the child is not the sole consideration; and (3) the one question is whether she is unreasonably withholding her consent. But I must say that in considering whether she is reasonable or unreasonable we must take into account the welfare of the child. A reasonable mother surely gives great weight to what is better for the child. Her anguish of mind is quite understandable; but still it may be unreasonable for her to withhold consent. We must look and see whether it is reasonable or unreasonable according to what a reasonable woman in her place would do in all the circumstances of the case."

The major importance of questions relating to the child's welfare in considering cases of refusal or withdrawal of consent was emphasised by their Lordships in *Re W.* and especially by Lord Hailsham when he said:

"It is clear that the test is reasonableness and not anything else. It is not culpability. It is not indifference. It is not failure to discharge parental duties. It is reasonableness, and reasonableness in the context of the totality of the circumstances. But, although welfare *per se* is not the test, the fact that a reasonable parent does pay regard to the welfare of his child must enter into the question of reasonableness as a relevant factor.

It is relevant in all cases if and to the extent that a reasonable parent would take it into account. It is decisive in those cases where a reasonable parent must so regard it."

The range of possible reasonable decisions was emphasised by Lord Hailsham in *Re W.* at 699, 700:

"[I]t does not follow from the fact that the test is reasonableness that any court is entitled simply to substitute its own view for that of the parent. In my opinion, it should be extremely careful to guard against this error. Two reasonable parents can perfectly reasonably come to opposite conclusions on the same set of facts without forfeiting their title to be regarded as reasonable. The question in any given case is whether a parental veto comes within the band of possible reasonable decisions and not whether it is right or mistaken. Not every reasonable exercise of judgment is right, and not every mistaken exercise of judgment is unreasonable. There is a band of decisions within which no court should seek to replace the individual's judgment with his own."

The facts relevant to the decision of the reasonable parent relate to the child, the natural parents, and the adopting family. Lord Reid said in *O'Connor v. A and B* [1971] 1 W.L.R. 1227 at 1229:

"I think that a reasonable parent, or, indeed, any other reasonable person, would have in mind the interests or claims of all three parties concerned—the child whose adoption is in question, the natural parents, and the adopting family. No doubt a child's interests come first and in some cases they may be paramount. But I see no reason why the claims of the natural parents should be ignored. If the mother were deeply attached to the child and had only consented in the first place to adoption because of adverse circumstances it would seem to me unjust that on a change of circumstances her affection for the child . . . should be ignored. And the adopting family cannot be ignored either. If it was the mother's action that brought them in, in the first place, they ought not to be displaced without good reason."

The test is whether at the time of the hearing (including an appellate hearing—*Re S.* [1973] 3 All E.R. 88) the agreement is being withheld unreasonably. In *Re C. (Minors) (Adoption)* [1992] 1 F.L.R. 115, the Court of Appeal said that it does not follow that a parent who is reasonably withholding his agreement at the date of the application can be said to be unreasonably withholding his consent at the date of the hearing by reason only of the delay in hearing the application. "That would be to make the welfare of the child the sole test, which Lord Hailsham in *Re W.* made clear it was not. Clearly much will depend on the age of the child concerned and the period of the delay; the younger the child and the longer the delay, the more obvious it may be that the child's welfare could be harmed by a change in the status quo, and the greater the weight this should have on the mind of a reasonable parent," *per* Balcombe L.J. at 132. Also see Ormrod L.J.'s remarks in *Re H. (Infants) (Adoption: Parental Consent)*, noted below.

In *Re C. (A Minor) (Adoption: Parental Agreement: Contact)* [1993] 2 F.L.R. 260, 272, CA, **1–085** Steyn and Hoffmann L.JJ., in a joint judgment, described the test as follows:

"[The question whether the mother is withholding her agreement unreasonably] had to be answered according to an objective standard. In other words, it required the judge to assume that the mother was not, as she in fact was, a person of limited intelligence and inadequate grasp of the emotional and other needs of a lively little girl of four. Instead, she had to be assumed to be a woman with a full perception of her own deficiencies and an ability to evaluate dispassionately the evidence and opinions of the experts. She was also to be endowed with the intelligence and altruism needed to appreciate, if such were the case, that her child's welfare would be so much better served by adoption that her own maternal feelings should take second place. Such a paragon does not of course exist: she shares with the 'reasonable man' the quality of being, as Lord Radcliffe once said, an 'anthropomorphic conception of justice'. The law conjures the imaginary parent into existence to give expression to what it considers that justice requires as between the welfare of the child as perceived by the judge on the one hand and the legitimate views and interests of the natural parent on the other".

It would seem that objective standard should be viewed from the perspective of a reasonable parent coming from the particular natural environment of the parent in question; see *Re O. (Transracial Adoption)* [1995] 2 F.L.R. 597, where Thorpe J. identified, at 609, the views of "the reasonable Nigerian mother". Also note Ormrod L.J.'s comment in *Re F. (A Minor) (Adoption: Parental Consent)* [1982] 1 All E.R. 321, 327, CA, that "in applying the objective test, the court must have regard to the practical consequences of making or refusing to make an adoption order."

In *Re H. (Infants) (Adoption: Parental Consent)* [1977] 1 W.L.R. 471, CA, Ormrod L.J. said: "The attitude of the court to the question of dispensing with consent, or holding that the consent is unreasonably withheld, has changed over the years, since adoption became possible in 1926. It has changed markedly since Lord Denning M.R.'s judgment in *Re L. (An Infant)* (1962) 106 S.J. 611 and perhaps even more markedly since the House of Lords' decision in *Re W.* and probably it will change even more in consequence of the Children Act 1975, although, at the moment, this court has said [in *Re P. (An Infant) (Adoption: Parental Consent)* [1976] 3 W.L.R. 924] that [s.6] does not apply to this particular issue. However, it is safe to say this: the relative importance of the welfare of the children is increasing rather than diminishing in relation to dispensing with consent. That being so, it ought to be recognised by all concerned with adoption cases that once the formal consent has been given or perhaps once the child has been placed with the adopters, time begins to run against the mother and, as time goes on, it gets progressively more and more difficult for her to show that the withdrawal of her consent is reasonable." Note, however, that in *Re H.; Re W. (Adoption: Parental Agreement)* [1983] 4 F.L.R. 614, CA the court held that although there has been a detectable move within the parameters set by the House of Lords in *Re W.* and in *O'Connor v. A and B* towards a greater emphasis upon the welfare of the child as a factor to be considered in dispensation cases, short of amending legislation or further consideration by the House of Lords there must be a limit to this shift. The court also held that in considering whether there were reasonable grounds for a natural parent withholding his or her consent the court must look to the attitude of that parent as one of the potentially relevant factors when assessing the attitude of the hypothetical, reasonable, natural parent. Where the natural parent presented himself or herself at the time of the hearing as someone capable of caring for the child, that was a factor which should be taken into account together with the other circumstances of the case including the ultimate welfare of the child. Where there was an inherent defect likely to persist in the natural parent, that was an important factor, but where the unsuitability of the parent could only be related to past history, unless the past history was likely to influence the future position, then it should carry little weight. The chances of a successful reintroduction or continuation of contact with the natural parent was also a critical factor in assessing the reaction of the hypothetical, reasonable parent. *Re H.; Re W.* was referred to in the following extract from the judgment of Balcombe L.J. in *Re E. (A Minor) (Adoption)* [1989] 1 F.L.R. 126, 133, CA:

"[The] balance, or tension, between the welfare of the child and justice to the parent arises constantly in cases concerning children. At one time it may have seemed that the pendulum had swung markedly in favour of the welfare test, but recent cases have shown that, while local authorities are rightly concerned solely with the welfare of the child in accordance with their statutory duties, and so also is the guardian *ad litem* concerned to represent the child's interests, the courts have the statutory duty to determine whether the parent is unreasonably withholding consent to adoption. I refer particularly to the judgment of this court in *Re H.; Re W.*"

Also see Christina Lyon in [1983] J.S.W.L. 175 and Charles Reed in the Summer 1984 issue of the Statute Law Review at pp. 124 *et seq.*

1–086 If a judge finds that continued contact with their natural mother is likely to be beneficial to the children, he would be entitled to conclude, on that finding, that the mother was not being unreasonable in withholding her agreement to the adoption: *Re M. (Minors) (Adoption: Parent's Agreement)* [1985] F.L.R. 921, CA and *Re P. (Adoption: Freeing Order)* [1994] 2 F.L.R. 100, CA. A residence order would be available as an alternative to adoption in such cases. *Re M.* and *Re P.* can be contrasted with *Re A (A Minor) (Adoption: Contact Order)* [1993] 2 F.L.R. 645, CA, where the judge believed that there should be adoption in any event, although it would be desirable that such adoption should be with contact. The agreement of the parent was dispersed with on the basis that the reasonable hypothetical parent would think that to settle the child by way of adoption was more important than to hold that there should be continuing contact. The Court of Appeal upheld the judge's order.

Whilst a mother's vacillation over whether to consent to the adoption of her child could not be conclusively held against her, it was a factor which could show that she did not possess the insight to enable her to make the judgment of the reasonable parent. Equally, the material benefit a child, whose mother lived in poor circumstances, would be likely to enjoy if adopted by middle class parents was not an element that should be allowed to weigh too heavily in the scales, given that affluence and happiness were not necessarily synonymous: *Re P. (Adoption: Parental Agreement)* [1985] F.L.R. 635, CA. Also note Ormrod L.J.'s comment in *Re W. (Adoption: Parental Agreement)* [1981] 1 F.L.R. 75, 81, that although "it is easy to understand the difficulties of the mother as a young woman, it is equally easy to be over-indulgent in approaching her problems because, once she takes the step of initiating adoption proceedings, she starts a chain reaction going which can only be stopped with great damage to some people." When considering whether or not a mother is unreasonably withholding her consent to the adoption of her child, and the mother is still bringing up another child of her own, the court must consider what weight a reasonable parent would give to the effect that the adoption would have on that other child (*Re E. (A Minor) (Adoption)* [1989] 1 F.L.R. 126, L.A.).

In *Re D (An Infant) (Adoption: Parental Consent)* [1977] A.C. 617, the House of Lords held that there could be no "general principle of dispensing with parental consent on the grounds of homosexual conduct alone", *per* Lord Wilberforce at 629. See further, R. Sandland, "Adoption, Law and Homosexuality: Can Gay People Adopt a Child?" [1993] J. Soc. Wel. & Fam. L. 321.

In *Re B. (A Minor) (Adoption: Parental Agreement)* [1990] 2 F.L.R. 383 the Court of Appeal held that in any ordinary case it would be difficult to see how a parent's sense of grievance could be of any weight for the purposes of determining whether consent was being withheld unreasonably. *Per* Ralph Gibson L.J.: "If the facts about which the feeling of grievance is felt to be relevant, and if that feeling is justified, then it will be the facts which provide the weight and not the sense of grievance. If it was a sense of grievance which explains conduct which would otherwise be relevantly held against the parent, then the grievance has served not to provide a relevant factor but to remove one." Also see *Re E. (Minors) (Adoption: Parental Agreement)* [1990] 2 F.L.R. 397, CA, where this reasoning was followed.

Guidance on the extent to which prospective adopters can assist their own applications was given by Devlin J. in *Hitchcock v. W.B. and F.E.B.* [1952] 2 Q.B. 561 at 573:

> "If they (the prospective adopters) can bring evidence before the court which shows that his (the natural father's) prospects of providing a home are quite illusory and that there is no real chance of it, that would again be a matter to be taken into consideration. Again the test is the same: a father might say, 'I want my child and I think I can find a home for it,' but if an answer, a satisfactory answer to the minds of justices is, 'You want your child but having regard to the difficulties with which you are faced and having regard to your own past record and your own situation you will never be able to provide a home for him or bring him up as you ought and you should realise as a reasonable man, that it is in his own best interests that you should part with him altogether,' then the presumption of reasonableness is displaced."

(This passage was cited with approval by Lord MacDermott in *Re W.* [1971] A.C. 682 and by Ormrod L.J. in *Re W. and W.* [1981] CA. Bound Transcript 366, [1982] J.S.W.L. 167).

The Court of Appeal has held in *Re P. (An Infant) (Adoption: Parental Consent)* [1977] 1 **1–087** W.L.R. 471, that a decision whether a parent was withholding consent unreasonably to a child's adoption was not a decision "relating to the adoption of a child," under s.6 of this Act. Ormrod L.J. dissented on this point. He said: "I think that [s.6] does apply to the decision to dispense with consent, but I do not think it materially alters the law as it stood before it came into force." And he continued: "So long as the welfare of the child is not the overriding consideration, I doubt whether there is much practical difference between applying the test established in *Re W.* and treating the welfare of the child as the first or most important consideration". Lord Simon in *Re D. (An Infant) (Adoption: Parent's Consent)* [1977] A.C. 617, agreed with Ormrod L.J. and suggested that the majority opinion in *Re P.* on the application of s.6 to this section might have been *obiter*. Although the law cannot be said to be completely settled on this point the following comments of Lord Simon in *Re D.* should be noted: "If I am right in thinking that it would only be exceptionally that a reasonable parent would not make the welfare of the child his or her foremost consideration . . . the point of construction will only exceptionally have any practical bearing."

"The conflicts involved in applications under [s.16(2)(b)] frequently call for independent representation of the minor concerned, or at least an independent report of a court welfare officer to supplement the report of the guardian *ad litem*," *Re H.*; *Re W.*, above, *per* Purchas L.J. at 625.

Has persistently failed . . . without reasonable cause to discharge . . . parental responsibility: "Obligations of a parent" (the terminology used in s.5 of the 1958 Act) were interpreted as "the natural and moral duty of a parent to show affection, care and interest towards his child; and secondly, as well, the common law or statutory duty of a parent to maintain his child in the financial or economic sense" (*per* Pennycuick J. in *Re P.* [1962] 3 All E.R. 789). "Persistently" has been interpreted to mean "permanently" (*per* Baker P., in *Re D.* [1973] 3 All E.R. 1001). In *W. v. Sunderland Borough Council* [1980] 2 All E.R. 514 Sir John Arnold P. referred to a distinction between the use of the word "persistently" in this paragraph and the word "consistently" used in s.3 of the Child Care Act 1980. This paragraph envisages more than "a temporary drifting apart", the failure must be "of such gravity, so complete, so convincingly proved, that there can be no advantage to the child in keeping continuous contact with the natural parent, who has so abrogated his duties that he for his part should be deprived of his own child against his wishes."

In *Re M. (an Infant)* (1965) 109 S.J. 574, an unmarried mother's wish to conceal the child's birth from her parents was held to be a "reasonable cause" (noted in Cretney and Masson, *Principles of Family Law* (1997), p. 928).

Abandoned: It has been held that conduct to constitute abandonment must be such as to render the parent liable to prosecution under the criminal law; see *Watson v. Nikolaisen* [1955] 2 Q.B. 286. "Abandon" in the context of the criminal law means "leave to its fate" by, *e.g.* placing a baby in a bus shelter. Under this restrictive interpretation, there can be few acts which constitute abandonment.

1–088   *Neglected:* This has been interpreted similarly to "abandoned"; see *Re W.* (1962) (unreported), referred to in *Re P.* [1962] 3 All E.R. 789, 793.

Persistently ill-treated the child: There is no authority on the words "persistently ill-treated." Bevan (*The Law Relating to Children*, p. 342) believes that it "is unlikely that a different test [from that for abandonment] would apply," though he says "it is arguable that this is a too restrictive view." Although the conduct will have to be proved, a criminal prosecution is not necessary. As the conduct must be persistent, proof of a single attack will not suffice. In *Re A. (A Minor) (Adoption: Dispensing with Agreement)* [1981] 2 F.L.R. 173, the Court of Appeal confirmed the decision of a County Court judge who found that a child who, according to the medical evidence, had been the subject of severe and repeated assaults over a period of three weeks, had been "persistently ill-treated". In *Re P.B. (A Minor) (Application to Free for Adoption)* [1985] F.L.R. 394, both parents were held to be responsible for the child's persistent and serious ill-treatment while in their charge, even though it was not possible to identify which parent had actually harmed the child.

Seriously ill-treated the child: The object of this provision is to encompass within grounds of dispensing with consent the case of the single serious attack. This ground is available only if the rehabilitation of the child within the household of the parent or guardian is unlikely (subs. (5)).

Subs. (3)

1–089   The question of consents where the application is for a convention adoption order is governed by s.17(6)(7).

Subs. (4)

1–090   "This delay is intended to ensure that [the mother] has recovered from the effects of childbirth", *per* Houghton, para. 188.

Subs. (5)

1–091   *The ill-treatment: i.e.* serious ill-treatment. "In my opinion . . . the finding required under [this provision] as a condition precedent to dispensing with consent under [s.16(2)(f)] . . . has to be approached [upon the basis set out in s.6 of this Act], *per* Sheldon J. in *Re P.B. (A Minor) (Application to Free for Adoption)*, above.

Convention adoption orders

1–092   **17.**—(1) An adoption order shall be made as a Convention adoption order if the application is for a Convention adoption order and the following conditions are satisfied both at the time of the application and when the order is made.

(2) The child—

(a) must be a United Kingdom national or a national of a Convention country, and

(b) must habitually reside in British territory or a Convention country.

(3) The applicant or applicants and the child must not all be United Kingdom nationals living in British territory.

(4) If the application is by a married couple, either—

(a) each must be a United Kingdom national or a national of a Convention country, and both must habitually reside in Great Britain, or

(b) both must be United Kingdom nationals, and each must habitually reside in British territory or a Convention country,

and if the applicants are nationals of the same Convention country the adoption must not be prohibited by a specified provision (as defined in subsection (8)) of the internal law of that country.

(5) If the application is by one person, either—

(a) he must be a national of a Convention country, and must habitually reside in Great Britain, or

(b) he must be a United Kingdom national and must habitually reside in British territory or a Convention country,

and if he is a national of a Convention country the adoption must not be prohibited by a specified (as defined in subsection (8)) of the internal law of that country.

(6) If the child is not a United Kingdom national the order shall not be made—

(a) except in accordance with the provisions, if any, relating to consents and consultations of the internal law relating to adoption of the Convention country of which the child is a national, and

(b) unless the court is satisfied that each person who consents to the order in accordance with that internal law does so with full understanding of what is involved.

(7) The reference to consents and consultations in subsection (6) does not include a reference to consent by and consultation with the applicant and members of the applicant's family (including his or her spouse), and for the purposes of subsection (6) consents may be proved in the manner prescribed by rules and the court shall be treated as the authority by whom, under the law mentioned in subsection (6), consents may be dispensed with and the adoption in question may be effected; and where the provisions there mentioned require the attendance before that authority of any person who does not reside in Great Britain, that requirement shall be treated as satisfied for the purposes of subsection (6) if—

(a) that person has been given a reasonable opportunity of communicating his opinion on the adoption in question to the proper officer or clerk of the court, or to an appropriate authority of the country in question, for transmission to the court; and

(b) where he has availed himself of that opportunity, his opinion has been transmitted to the court.

(8) In subsections (4) and (5) "specified provision" means a provision specified in an order of the Secretary of State as one notified to the Government of the United Kingdom in pursuance of the provisions of the Convention which relate to prohibitions on an adoption contained in the national law of the Convention country in question.

DEFINITIONS

    adoption order: s.72(1).
    Convention adoption order: s.72(1).
    United Kingdom national: s.72(1).
    Convention country: s.72(1).
    British territory: s.72(1).
    internal law: ss.71, 72(1).
    child: s.72(1).
    the Convention: s.72(1).
    rules: s.72(1).

GENERAL NOTE

The main purpose of this section is to implement the Hague Convention on Jurisdiction **1–093** Applicable Law and Recognition of Decrees relating to Adoptions, Cmnd. 7342. The Convention was ratified by the United Kingdom on August 24, 1978 and came into force on October 23, 1978 for the United Kingdom and for Austria and Switzerland, the only other countries which have ratified the Convention. The general purpose of the Convention is to resolve, within a limited sphere, some of the difficulties and legal conflicts which can arise in inter-country adoptions because the adopters and the child are subject to different personal laws; its aim is not, however, to promote such adoptions. Some foreign countries refuse to recognise adoptions granted in another country where the law applied is not similar in nature and effect to their own. Adoptions granted under the Convention, on the other hand, will be recognised without further formalities in all the countries in which the Convention is in force. Broadly speaking, adoptions can be granted under the Convention where the adopters and the child are nationals or habitual residents of different countries in which the Convention is in force. Jurisdiction to grant Convention adoption orders is restricted in England and Wales to the High Court (s.62(1)(2)(4)). Convention adoption orders are rarely made. Also see the Hague Convention on Intercountry Adoption which will not come into force in the United Kingdom until implementing legislation is enacted.

D.H.S.S. Circular LAC(78)19, which deals, *inter alia*, with the role of local authorities in Convention adoptions contains an explanatory memorandum on the Hague Convention.

The procedure governing Convention proceedings is set out in Part IV of the Adoption Rules 1984. A Convention adoption order may be annulled under s.53.

Adoption of children outside the jurisdiction

1–094   Adoption orders made abroad which have been designated as "overseas adoptions" are recognised in this country and a child who has been adopted in one of the designated countries need not therefore be re-adopted if he later comes to live in Great Britain; see s.72(2) and the notes thereto. Apart from Convention adoptions and overseas adoptions this Act applies to children within the jurisdiction only. "Once a child has been brought from overseas within that jurisdiction, the Act comes into full play, and the adoption court has wide powers, regardless of the child's nationality or permitted length of stay, to act in what is seen as the child's best interests—even if that would, or might, involve an infringement of our domestic immigration laws . . ." No adoption order can, however, be made in relation to a child outside the jurisdiction; both because the Act contains no such extra-territorial power, and because of the prohibition in the Act itself against making any adoption order unless the child has been with the prospective adopters for at least three months before the date of the order. There is no domestic legislation in this country regulating the terms on which, apart from [Convention adoptions and overseas adoptions], an overseas child who is not a British subject may be brought into this country for the purposes of adoption. Such children are subject to s.1(2) of the Immigration Act 1971, and can enter and remain in this country only by permission of the Home Office"; *R. v. Secretary of State for Health, ex p. Luff* [1992] 1 F.L.R. 59, *per* Waite J. at p. 63. This case contains an analysis of the procedure adopted by the Home Office in such cases. The Home Office has produced a leaflet on entry clearance in connection with intercountry adoption which is reproduced in *A Guide to Intercountry Adoption Practice and Procedures*; see Part III.

Prospective adopters of children brought from overseas can obtain a leaflet on "Adopting from Overseas", from the Department of Health (0171 972 4014).

Subs. (2)

1–095   *National:* For determination of nationality, see s.70.

Convention country: Austria and Switzerland were designated as Convention countries by the Convention Adoption (Austria and Switzerland) Order 1978 (S.I. 1978 No. 1431).

Habitually reside: "Habitually" refers to the quality of the residence rather than its duration and requires an element of intention to reside. It denotes a regular physical presence which has to endure for sometime (*Cruse v. Chittum (formerly Cruse)* [1974] 2 All E.R. 940).

Subs. (4)

1–096   *Internal law:* As to countries where there are two or more systems of law, see s.71(2).

Subs. (5)

1–097   *Great Britain:* See the note on s.56(1).

Subs. (7)

1–098   *Prescribed by rules:* See the Adoption Rules 1984, r.34.

42

Freeing child for adoption

18.—(1) Where, on an application by an adoption agency, an authorised **1–099** court is satisfied in the case of each parent or guardian of the child that—

    (a) he freely, and with full understanding of what is involved, agrees generally and unconditionally to the making of an adoption order, or

    (b) his agreement to the making of an adoption order should be dispensed with on a ground specified in section 16(2),

the court shall make an order declaring the child free for adoption.

(2) No application shall be made under subsection (1) unless—

    (a) it is made with the consent of a parent or guardian of a child, or

    (b) the adoption agency is applying for dispensation under subsection (1)(b) of the agreement of each parent or guardian of the child, and the child is in the care of the adoption agency.

[(2A) For the purposes of subsection (2) a child is in the care of an adoption agency if the adoption agency is a local authority and he is in their care.]

(3) No agreement required under subsection (1)(a) shall be dispensed with under subsection (1)(b) unless the child is already placed for adoption or the court is satisfied that it is likely that the child will be placed for adoption.

(4) An agreement by the mother of the child is ineffective for the purposes of this section if given less than 6 weeks after the child's birth.

(5) On the making of an order under this section, [parental responsibility for the child is given to] the adoption agency, and subsections (2) [to (4)] of section 12 apply as if the order were an adoption order and the agency were the adopters.

(6) Before making an order under this section, the court shall satisfy itself, in relation to each parent or guardian [of the child who can be found], that he has been given an opportunity of making, if he so wishes, a declaration that he prefers not to be involved in future questions concerning the adoption of the child; and any such declaration shall be recorded by the court.

[(7) Before making an order under this section in the case of a child whose father does not have parental responsibility for him, the court shall satisfy itself in relation to any person claiming to be the father that—

    (a) he has no intention of applying for—

        (i) an order under section 4(1) of the Children Act 1989, or

        (ii) a residence order under section 10 of that Act, or

    (b) if he did make any such application, it would be likely to be refused.

(8) Subsections (5) and (7) of section 12 apply in relation to the making of an order under this section as they apply in relation to the making of an order under that section.]

AMENDMENT

In subs. (6) the words in square brackets were substituted by the Health and Social Services and Social Security Adjudications Act 1983, s.9, Sched. 2, para. 31. The other amendments to this section were made by the Children Act 1989, s.88, Sched. 10, Pt. 1, para. 6.

adoption agency: ss.1(4), 72(1).
authorised court: s.62.
adoption order: s.72(1).
child: s.72(1).
guardian: s.72(1).
parental responsibility: s.72(1).

GENERAL NOTE

1–100   This section enables an adoption agency at a preliminary hearing to apply to the court for an order freeing the child for adoption. If the order is granted parental responsibility for the child will be transferred to the agency until either the order is revoked or an adoption order is made. A subsequent adoption order can be made without further evidence of parental consent and on such an order being made the child is treated as if he were the child of the adopters (s.39(2)).

As proceedings under this section are "family proceedings" for the purposes of the Children Act 1989, a court has the power to make a "section 8 order", including a contact order, at any time during the course of the proceedings (*ibid.*, ss.8(3), 10(1), 11(3)). A freeing order extinguishes the birth parents' parental responsibility and they become former parents with no right to apply for a section 8 order (*Re C. (Minors) (Parent: Residence Order)* [1993] 3 All E.R. 313, CA). A former parent can therefore only apply for such an order with leave of the court: see the note to s.12(6), above.

A useful summary of the freeing procedure is contained in paras. 4 to 11 of D.H.S.S. Circular No. LAC(84)2:

"[Section 18] enables an adoption agency to apply to a court for an order freeing a child for adoption with the effect that [parental responsibilities] are transferred to the agency. The existing procedure for adoption (which still continues) can be a cause of anxiety both to natural parents and to prospective adopters, because of the length of time during which the outcome is uncertain. The child's parents may be encouraged to put off making a firm decision, and the fear that parents may change their minds before the hearing may prevent some adopters from committing themselves whole-heartedly to the child. The agency will be able to plan the child's future with greater certainty once a freeing order has been made, and the child can then be placed with prospective adopters in the knowledge that the question of parental agreement has already been resolved. The agency can choose whether or not to apply for a freeing order where the child is in its care, and so can effectively pursue the adoption plan even though the parents are not happy with it.

At least one of the child's parents must consent to the agency's making the freeing application, unless the agency is applying for dispensation of both parents' agreement to adoption. If the child is *not* in the agency's care, the freeing application cannot be made without the consent of one of his parents. Because a freeing order, like an adoption order, extinguishes the natural parents' rights and duties, parental agreement to adoption must be given or dispensed with (and the mother's agreement cannot be given before the child is six weeks old). The grounds for dispensation are the same as for adoption orders, but the court may not dispense with a parent's agreement unless *either* the child is already placed for adoption *or* the court is satisfied that it is likely that he will be. The agency cannot apply for the agreement of *both* parents to be dispensed with unless the child is in the agency's care. Where the agency is applying for a parent's agreement to be dispensed with, that parent can apply for legal aid. . . .

Where the parents are willing for the child to be adopted, the freeing provisions give them the choice of relinquishing their [parental responsibilities] by giving their agreement to adoption before an adoption order has been applied for, thus enabling them to withdraw at an early stage from any further involvement if they wish. For the mother of a baby, the freeing procedure means that she can start to rebuild her life quite soon after the child's birth, free from further visits of social workers and court officers associated with the sometimes protracted adoption hearings which remind her that the future of the child has not been finalised. Where a child is 'free for adoption' (that is, the subject of a freeing order), there is no requirement to obtain parental agreement at the subsequent adoption hearing as this issue has already been dealt with in the freeing proceedings.

Agencies themselves may find the new procedures useful in a number of situations. Freeing may be appropriate where the agency has decided that adoption is in the child's best interest, despite parental opposition, and it enables the agency's view to be tested in the courts. Thus any question of dispensing with parental agreement can be resolved at an early stage, and this helps to avoid the problem of cases where a prolonged period during which the child is out of the care of his parents becomes a factor in their disfavour when the question has to be decided by the court.

The freeing procedure may also be appropriate where the child is already living with a family and the agency considers the parents are suitable adoptive parents for the child. If the natural parents are unable to accept that adoption would be in their child's best interests, the prospective adopters may be reluctant to apply for an adoption order because they do not wish to take the risk of becoming involved in a disputed case. Freeing may be useful in these circumstances, as the prospective adopters would not directly be involved in the application for a freeing order.

An application for a freeing order can only be made by an adoption agency; the adoption agencies regulations set out the action which a local authority or approved adoption society must take before deciding to make a freeing application, and the detailed procedural arrangements for freeing applications and proceedings are covered in the court rules.

Before making a freeing order, the court must be satisfied that each parent has been asked if he wishes to make a declaration that he prefers not to be involved in future questions about the child's adoption. If such a declaration has been made it must be recorded by the court, and the parent who made it will have no further involvement in the child's adoption following the making of the freeing order. The opportunity to make a declaration enables a parent to decide whether or not he wishes to be kept informed about the child's progress. If he does, it leaves open the possibility of applying for revocation after 12 months where the child has not yet been adopted or placed for adoption."

The following general comments on the freeing procedure were made by Butler-Sloss L.J. in **1–101** *Re. H. (A Minor) (Freeing Order)* [1993] 2 F.L.R. 325, 328, CA:

"Undoubtedly, the application to free for adoption is a valuable procedure and, in circumstances such as where the child is not yet placed or may have only recently been placed, it may be of particular value. It is also a procedure which . . . protects foster-parents (wishing in due course to adopt) from the, on occasions even, trauma of contested proceedings; it protects confidentiality in cases where the parents do not know, and ought not to know, the identity of the potential adopters, and saves the difficulties that have been experienced in some courts of keeping parents and prospective adopters in separate rooms and giving evidence at different times and the other devices to protect the confidentiality of an adoption of that type. One aspect of the control of the local authority adoption agency . . . is the unfettered discretion of the local authority to place the child where the local authority as the adoption agency thinks is best—not only to place but of course also to move from an existing foster placement. The application to free for adoption, valuable though it is, is not necessarily to be preferred to making an adoption application with the difficulties there may be of it being opposed, and the freeing application is not necessarily in every case the most appropriate procedure."

In this case Butler Sloss L.J. also said, at 329, that in her view the question of open adoption is one which is less suited to be considered on a freeing application than on an adoption application in a case where the natural parents knew the prospective adopters and wanted to be satisfied that the child was well settled and wanted consideration as to whether they should have continuing contact with the child.

Courts hearing an application under this section should adopt a two stage approach. It must first decide under s.6 whether an adoption order would "safeguard and promote the welfare of the child throughout his childhood". If the answer is in the affirmative, the court should then go on to the second stage under subs. (1) of this section and decide whether parental agreement has been given or should be dispensed with. If satisfied on both tests the court should make the order sought (*Re D. (A Minor) (Adoption Freeing Order)* [1991] 1 F.L.R. 48, CA and *Re. U. (Application to Free for Adoption)* [1993] 2 F.L.R. 992, CA). Where "the child has been placed (or, alternatively, prospective adopters have been identified), consideration of their personal circumstances may become relevant in assessing the reasonableness of parental opposition to adoption. Thus a hybrid situation has arises which has secured judicial approval, particularly where an assessment of the reasonableness or otherwise of parental opposition may depend upon the attitude of identified prospective adopters to, and indeed evidence from them concerning, post adoption contact with the birth family"; *per* Singer J. in *Re W. (A Minor) (Adoption: Homosexual Adopter)* [1997] 3 All E.R. 620, at 622.

The authorities in *Re E. (Minors) (Adoption: Parental Agreement)* [1990] 2 F.L.R. 397, CA **1–102** and *Re C. (Minors) (Adoption)* [1992] 1 F.L.R. 15, CA that where children are in care, but are enjoying beneficial access by their parents, it is premature to issue an application to free the children for adoption until the issue of access is first determined, are no longer applicable since the coming into force of the Children Act 1989 (*Re A. (A Minor) (Adoption: Contract Orders*) [1993] 2 F.L.R. 645, CA). *Per* Butler-Sloss L.J., at 649:

"Since the Children Act . . . a judge has the opportunity both to free but also to preserve contact between the child and the natural family pending adoption. The wider jurisdiction of the court now exists since a s.8 application, including a contact application, can be made in any family proceedings and by s.8(4)(d) this includes proceedings under the Adoption Act 1976. Although a former parent, this mother retains the right to be heard on contact. She will have the right to respond to the local authority's application to vary the existing contact order and to apply herself to vary it. The contact order cannot survive the adoption order, but a contact order can (in theory at least) now be imposed upon adopters after the making of the adoption order as an alternative to the making of an adoption order with conditions."

Her Ladyship also said, at 650, that when a contact order is made with a freeing order, it is important that directions are given to provide

"for a continuity of judicial approach in subsequent hearings to ensure that the judge hearing the adoption application is not faced with an outstanding contact order in favour of a parent who has no right to be heard on the occasion when the effect of the adoption order is to extinguish the contact order. If a freeing order is made with a s.8 contact order, the judge should give the appropriate directions to ensure that, if possible, the judge who hears the adoption application is also the judge who hears any contact application affecting the former parent."

If a local authority acting as an adoption agency considers that the level of contact established under the contact order is inappropriate, s.9(2) of the Children Act 1989 prevents it from making an application to vary the order (*Re C. (Contact Jurisdiction)* [1995] 1 F.L.R. 777, CA).

A freeing order and a contact order were made in *Re R. (A Minor) (Adoption: Contact Order)* [1994] 1 F.C.R. 104, CA, where the court said that whilst infrequent contact with the birth family of up to three times a year might be acceptable after a freeing order, monthly contact would seem incompatible with the likely views of prospective adopters.

In *Re B. (Minors) (Freeing for Adoption)* [1992] 2 F.L.R. 37, CA, a case where foster parents had cared for children who were the subject of a freeing application for nine years and where the local authority had no intention to move the children elsewhere, Butler-Sloss L.J. said, at 39, that "the decision to apply for freeing for adoption, rather than to let the foster parents make an adoption application, seems to me, as it did to the guardian *ad litem*, unnecessarily elaborate." Note, however, that research has shown that freeing is seen as having certain advantages in contested cases over a straight adoption application: it relieves the prospective adopters of some of their anxiety and the agency pays the costs of the proceedings (see N. Lowe, "Freeing for Adoption—The Experience of the 1980s" [1990] J.S.W.L. 220).

The study by N. Lowe *et al.*, found a wide disparity in the use of freeing, "with some agencies using the process relatively frequently, others not using it at all, and still others somewhere in between" (*Freeing for Adoption Provisions* (1993), p. 71).

In *W. v. Hertfordshire C.C.* [1985] 2 All E.R. 301, the House of Lords held that the fact that the relatives of a child had no right to appear in proceedings under this section was not a ground for making the child a ward of court on an application by the relatives who wished to care for the child themselves.

For procedural rules, see Part II (rr. 4 to 13) of the Adoption Rules 1984 and the Magistrates' Courts (Adoption) Rules 1984.

Subs. (1)

1–103   *Adoption agency:* Only an adoption agency can apply for a freeing order.

Authorised court: "If the hearing of the application is likely to last several days, having regard to the delays that would be likely to result from the probable difficulty of arranging that the same panel of justices should sit without any break between hearings for the whole of that period, the magistrates' court might be thought to be the least suitable tribunal," *per* Sheldon J. in *Re P.B. (A Minor) (Application to Free for Adoption)* [1985] F.L.R. 394.

Parent: The natural father of an illegitimate child who does not have parental responsibility is not a parent for these purposes, but note subs. (7). If a natural parent fails to acknowledge the receipt of the notice asking if he or she wishes to be heard in freeing proceedings in the High Court the applicant's solicitors should send the parent a notice in the form set out in *Practice Direction* [1984] 1 All E.R. 1024.

Agrees: Where the parent is present the court can ask whether such agreement is forthcoming. In the majority of cases, however, it will rely on the report of a reporting officer. The study by M. Murch, *et al.*, found that the majority of freeing applications were made without the natural mother's consent (*Pathways to Adoption* (1993), p. 11).

46

To the making of an adoption order: The agreement is to adoption generally rather than to a specific adoption application.

Unconditionally: Once the parent has agreed to the principle of adoption he no longer has any control over the identity of the prospective adopters.

Dispensed with: The court should decide whether a freeing order is in the best interests of the child before proceeding to consider whether to dispense with the parents' consent; see the General Note to this section. The consideration of the parent's inability or unwillingness to consent has to be undertaken and decided at the time when the freeing order is made (*Devon County Council v. B.* [1997] 1 F.L.R. 591, CA).

The court shall make an order: There is no provision for the inclusion of any terms or conditions in a freeing order, although the court does have the power to make a "section 8 order" under the Children Act 1989 at any stage during the freeing application: see the General Note to this section. If the court is satisfied that the provisions of para. (*a*) or (*b*) are satisfied it must proceed to make a freeing order.

Subs. (2)

Application: For restrictions on the removal of a child when an application under this **1–104** section is pending, see s.27.

Consent: The freeing process therefore involves *two* distinct acts: *agreeing* to the making of an adoption order under subs. (1) and *consenting* to the making of a freeing application under this subsection. Although a care order gives a local authority parental responsibility for the child, the authority has no right to consent or to refuse to the making of a freeing application (Children Act 1989, s.33(6)(b)). For evidence of consent, see s.61.

Care: No minimum period in care is prescribed. "In care" means that the child is in care by virtue of a care order; see s.72(1B).

Subs. (3)

"The provisions of s.18(3) . . . clearly contemplate that a child may already be placed for **1–105** adoption when a freeing order is made," *Re C.* (*Minors*) (*Adoption*), *per* Balcombe L.J. at 128.

It is likely: On the balance of probabilities. In *Re P.B.*, Sheldon J. said, at 403, that this is a "likelihood which may be thought to be beyond doubt in the case of most young children." In this connection his Lordship said that:

> "save as may be in exceptional circumstances, the local authority should issue the originating process under [this section] as soon as practicable after the decision in favour of adoption had been taken, even though they have no particular potential adopters in mind. On the other hand, I am also of the opinion that they should not be deterred by the fact that proceedings are now pending from pursuing their search for suitable candidates and thereafter from placing the child with them."

In *Re G.* (*Adoption: Freeing Order*) [1996] 2 F.L.R. 398 at 403, Butler-Sloss L.J. considered the meaning of this phrase and said, "in my view the time-scale of the Act is immediate rather than long term".

Subs. (4)

Agreement: Witnessed by a reporting officer appointed by the court; see r.5 of the Adoption **1–106** Rules 1984 and the Magistrates' Courts (Adoption) Rules 1984.

Subs. (5)

Parental responsibility: Is defined in the Children Act 1989, s.3; see the note on s.12(10). The **1–107** transfer of parental responsibility does not prevent a judge from preserving contact between the child and the natural family pending adoption by means of a contact order made under s.8 of the Children Act 1989 (*Re A.* (*A Minor*) (*Adoption: Contact*) [1993] 2 F.L.R. 645, CA). Although the contact order cannot survive the adoption order, a fresh contact order could be made on the making of the order as the alternative to the making of an adoption order with conditions: see the note on s.12(6).

Decisions relating to a freed child are governed by s.6 and the adoption agency must monitor the child's situation (Adoption Agencies Regulations 1983, reg. 13). If the agency is a local authority the child is "looked after" (Children Act 1989, s.22(1)(b)) and he will be subject to the Review of Children's Cases Regulations 1991 (S.I. 1991 No. 895) until he is placed for adoption (*ibid.*, reg. 13A).

The legal position of the child who has been freed for adoption is unsatisfactory in that, apart from the transfer of parental responsibility, this Act does not set out the effect of a freeing order on the child's legal relationship with members of his natural family; see, for example, the comment by Stephen Cretney that there is no specific provision removing a freed child from his birth family for such purposes as succession rights (*Elements of Family Law* (1992), p. 248). In *Re G. (A Minor) (Adoption: Freeing Order)* [1997] 2 All E.R. 534 at 539, HL, Lord Browne-Wilkinson described the position of the freed child in graphic terms: "Pending the making of an adoption order, [the child] has no human being as a parent: the mother is not a parent and there is no adoptive parent. [The child] is in what the Court of Appeal ([1996] 2 F.L.R. 398 at 405) described as an 'adoption limbo': a statutory orphan".

Subsections (2) to (4) of section 12: The order does not affect parental responsibilities which relate to any period before the making of the order, but otherwise extinguishes all pre-existing parental responsibilities and any duty to make payments for the child's maintenance (subject to s.12(4)).

Subs. (6)

1–108   A failure to observe the requirements of this provision will not invalidate a freeing order made under this section (*Re. C. (Minors) (Adoption)* [1992] 1 F.L.R. 155, CA).

Can be found: Reasonable steps must be taken to trace the parents.

Making . . . a declaration: If the parent decides not to make a declaration, ss.19 and 20 apply.

Subs. (7)

1–109   *Father:* The adoption agency is not required to seek out such a father, it is a matter for the agency's discretion (*Re L. (A Minor) (Adoption: Procedure)* [1991] 1 F.L.R. 71, CA).

Progress reports to former parent

1–110   **19.**—(1) This section and section 20 apply to any person ("the former parent") who was required to be given an opportunity of making a declaration under section 18(6) but did not do so.

(2) Within the 14 days following the date 12 months after the making of the order under section 18 the adoption agency [to which parental responsibility was given] on the making of the order, unless it has previously by notice to the former parent informed him that an adoption order has been made in respect of the child, shall by notice to the former parent inform him—

(a) whether an adoption order has been made in respect of the child, and (if not)

(b) whether the child has his home with a person with whom he has been placed for adoption.

(3) If at the time when the former parent is given notice under subsection (2) an adoption order has not been made in respect of the child, it is thereafter the duty of the adoption agency to give notice to the former parent of the making of an adoption order (if and when made), and meanwhile to give the former parent notice whenever the child is placed for adoption or ceases to have his home with a person with whom he has been placed for adoption.

(4) If at any time the former parent by notice makes a declaration to the adoption agency that he prefers not to be involved in future questions concerning the adoption of the child—

(*a*) the agency shall secure that the declaration is recorded by the court which made the order under section 18, and

(*b*) the agency is released from the duty of complying further with subsection (3) as respects that former parent.

DEFINITIONS
adoption agency: ss.1(4), 72(1).
adoption order: s.72(1).
child: s.72(1).
notice: s.72(1).

AMENDMENT
In subs. (2) the words in square brackets were substituted by the Children Act 1989, s.88, Sched. 10, Pt. 1, para. 7.

"Where a freeing order has been made, [this section] sets out the adoption agency's duties **1–111** towards any natural parent who has *not* made a declaration (who is referred to in the freeing provisions as 'the former parent'). In a case where one of the child's parents has made a declaration and the other has not, that other parent becomes a former parent. The agency must write to any former parent within the fortnight after the first anniversary of the freeing order, to notify him whether an adoption order has been made and, if not, whether the child has been placed for adoption. This notification does not, however, have to be sent if the agency has already notified him in writing that an adoption order has been made (it would be good practice in any case to keep the former parent informed from the start of any changes when they happen). Until the child is adopted, the agency must continue to notify the former parent of any change in the position, and he should always be invited to discuss the matter with the agency.

At any time after a freeing order has been made, a former parent can make a written declaration to the agency that he prefers not to be involved in future questions about the child's adoption. The agency must ensure that the declaration is recorded by the court, and is then no longer required to send notifications to that former parent" (D.H.S.S. Circular No. LAC (84)2, paras. 12, 13).

A natural parent, having become a "former parent" after the making of a freeing order, ceases to be a "parent" within the meaning of s.10(4) of the Children Act 1989 and is therefore not entitled to apply for a residence order in respect of the child without the leave of the court (*Re C. (Minors) (Parent: Residence Order)* [1993] 3 All E.R. 313, CA).

Subs. (1)

Former parent: This expression is used because the parental responsibility in respect of the **1–112** child have already passed to the adoption agency.

Subs. (2)

Within 14 days: The day from which the period runs is not to be counted (*Stewart v.* **1–113** *Chapman* [1951] 2 K.B. 792).

Shall: The requirement is mandatory.

By notice: Which must be in writing (s.72(1)) and may be sent by post (s.69).

Has his home: See the note on s.32 and s.72(1A).

Placed for adoption: The adoption agency must have carried out its duties under the Adoption Agencies Regulations 1983, regs 11, 12.

Subs. (3)

Duty of the adoption agency: Which is explained in para. 12 of D.H.S.S. Circular No. **1–114** LAC(84) 2.

Former parent is given notice: The former parent will have a right to apply for the revocation of the freeing order under s.20, if the notice states that the child is no longer placed for adoption.

Ceases to have his home: In *R. v. Derbyshire County Council, ex p. T.* [1990] 1 All E.R. 792, the Court of Appeal held that the test for determining whether a child had ceased to have his home with a person with whom he had been placed for adoption was what, on the facts, was the child's status or quality of placement at any particular time. Therefore, if the adoptive placement broke down with the status of the child changing from one of being placed for adoption to one of being in care, the child ceased to have his home with a person with whom he had been placed for adoption and the duty to give notice to the former parent arose, notwithstanding that he remained with the former prospective adoptive parents while new adoptive parents were arranged. *Per* Butler-Sloss L.J.:

"Section 19(3) requires notice to be given whenever a child ceases to have his home etc. What is a reasonable time may depend on the circumstances. The time scale should obviously be as short as possible. Some guidance may be gained from the time scale in s.19(2), which requires an adoption agency to give notice within 14 days. 14 days should, in my view, in the context of this legislation, be the limit of the time scale in s.19(3)."

The *Derbyshire* case is considered by Clifford Bellamy in "Revocation of Freeing Orders" [1990] Fam. Law 352. Note that the adoption agency is released from its duty to give notice to the former parent in the circumstances set out in s.20(4).

Placed for adoption: See subs. (2).

Revocation of s.18 order

1–115 **20.**—(1) The former parent, at any time more than 12 months after the making of the order under section 18 when—

(a) no adoption order has been made in respect of the child, and

(b) the child does not have his home with a person with whom he has been placed for adoption,

may apply to the court which made the order for a further order revoking it on the ground that he wishes to resume [parental responsibility].

(2) While the application is pending the adoption agency having [parental responsibility] shall not place the child for adoption without the leave of the court.

[(3) The revocation of an order under section 18 ("a section 18 order") operates—

(a) to extinguish the parental responsibility given to the adoption agency under the section 18 order;

(b) to give parental responsibility for the child to—

  (i) the child's mother; and

  (ii) where the child's father and mother were married to each other at the time of his birth, the father; and

(c) to revive—

  (i) any parental responsibility agreement,

  (ii) any order under section 4(1) of the Children Act 1989, and

  (iii) any appointment of a guardian in respect of the child (whether made by a court or otherwise),

    extinguished by the making of the section 18 order.

(3A) Subject to subsection (3)(c), the revocation does not—

(a) operate to revive—

  (i) any order under the Children Act 1989, or

  (ii) any duty referred to in section 12(3)(b),

    extinguished by the making of the section 18 order; or

(b) affect any person's parental responsibility so far as it relates to the period between the making of the section 18 order and the date of revocation of that order.]

(4) Subject to subsection (5), if the application is dismissed on the ground that to allow it would contravene the principle embodied in section 6—

(a) the former parent who made the application shall not be entitled to make any further application under subsection (1) in respect of the child and

(b) the adoption agency is released from the duty of complying further with section 19(3) as respects that parent.

(5) Subsection (4)(a) shall not apply where the court which dismissed the application gives leave to the former parent to make a further application under subsection (1), but such leave shall not be given unless it appears to the court that because of a change in circumstances or for any other reason it is proper to allow the application to be made.

AMENDMENTS

    The words in square brackets in subss. (1) and (2) and subss. (3) and (3A) were substituted by the Children Act 1989, s.88, Sched. 10, Pt. 1, para. 8.

DEFINITIONS
adoption agency: ss.1(4), 72(1).
adoption order: s.72(1).
child: s.72(1).
local authority: s.72(1).
voluntary organisation: s.72(1).

GENERAL NOTE

This section "permits the former parent to apply to resume [parental responsibility] after at **1–116**
least a year has passed since the freeing order was made. He can only apply for the freeing
order to be revoked, however, if the child has not at the time of his application either been
adopted or placed for adoption (and the agency cannot then place the child without the
court's permission whilst the application is pending). However, no application can be heard if
a declaration by that parent was recorded before the freeing order was made. Upon
revocation, [parental responsibilities] are returned to the individual(s) in whom they were
vested before the freeing order was made, but not to any local authority or voluntary
organisation which has [parental responsibilities] immediately beforehand. As the court will
have considered all the circumstances in deciding that the former parent should be allowed to
resume [parental responsibilities], any . . . order made when the child was in need of care does
not therefore automatically revive. Any duty relating to payments towards a child's
maintenance—*e.g.* by a putative father—which was extinguished by the freeing order is
automatically revived from the date when the order is revoked.

When an application by a former parent to resume [parental responsibilities] fails because
that would be detrimental to the child's welfare, he cannot make any further application
without leave of the court, and the agency is released from the duty of making progress
reports to him" (D.H.S.S. Circular No. LAC (84)2, paras. 14, 15).

This section was considered in the following passage from Butler-Sloss L.J.'s judgment in *Re
G. (Adoption: Freeing Order)* [1996] 2 F.L.R. 398 at 404–405, CA:

"Unlike the mandatory requirement to make the order under s.18 if the criteria are
met, s.20 is discretionary. The section sets out two objectives. The first is in the
application of the parent to revoke which is in order to resume parental responsibility.
It is implicit in the section that the court has to be satisfied that the parents should
resume the parental responsibility for that child. The second objective is the withdrawal
of the local authority, both by extinguishing the parental responsibility of the adoption
agency and by not reviving previous care or supervision orders. In exercising its
discretion the court is required to consider the welfare of the child and to have regard
to all the circumstances, which would no doubt include, if relevant, the basis upon
which the parental agreement was given or dispensed with and the circumstances of the
granting of the original freeing order. But the court is limited in the exercise of its
discretion. It is given, in my judgment, a stark choice—either to revoke the freeing
order or to refuse the application. If the order is revoked, the parent's resumption of
parental responsibility is unfettered."

The finding of the Court of Appeal that a court's discretion on hearing an application under **1–117**
this section is limited to the "stark choice" identified by Butler-Sloss L.J. was rejected by the
House of Lords (*Re G. (A Minor) (Adoption: Freeing Order)* [1997] 2 All E.R. 534. Lord
Brown-Wilkinson, who gave the leading speech, said there was no reason why the provisions
of this Act had to be read as a self-sufficient code. The powers it conferred in relation to
adoption could, if necessary, be used in conjunction with and supplemented by the powers of
the Children Act 1989. The position was as follows:

"Where a freeing order has been made under s.18 of the 1976 Act but at the end of
one year thereafter it is clear that no adoption is likely to take place within a short
period, the freeing order may be revoked so as to restore the parent to his or her
normal rights and to ensure that the child does not remain in an adoption limbo. Even
if the former parent is not, at the date of the revocation, fit to have sole and unfettered
responsibility, the court has jurisdiction to make the order provided that the welfare of
the child can be protected whether by making the revocation of the freeing order
conditional upon such consequential orders as are appropriate under the 1989 Act or
under the inherent jurisdiction or in some other way" (at 542).

Subs. (1)

Former parent: See s.19(1).   **1–118**
Have his home: See the note on s.19(3) and s.72(1A).

May apply: The procedure is set out in r.12 of the Adoption Rules 1984 and the Magistrates' Courts (Adoption) Rules 1984.

Order revoking it: The court is not bound to revoke the freeing order merely because the conditions set out in this subsection are satisfied. In exercising its discretion the court must give first consideration to the child's welfare (s.6). It is not possible for the former parents to ask the court to review the reasonableness of the withholding of their consent or otherwise at the revocation hearing; see further, Clifford Bellamy, "Revocation of Freeing Orders" [1990] Fam. Law 354.

On the ground: This is the only ground.

Subs. (2)

1–119 *Leave of the court:* The court being guided by the welfare principle set out in s.6.

Subs. (3)

1–120 *Parental responsibility:* See the note on s.12(1).

Subs. (4)

1–121 If the court refuses an application for the revocation of a freeing order this subsection prohibits further applications by the same person. However, subs. (5) gives the court a wide discretion to allow further applications to be made.

The former parent who made the application: The other parent is not therefore barred from making a further application.

As respects that parent: The agency is not released from its duty in respect of the other parent.

[Variation of s.18 order so as to substitute one adoption agency for another

1–122 **21.**—(1) On an application to which this section applies, an authorised court may vary an order under section 18 so as to give parental responsibility for the child to another adoption agency ("the substitute agency") in place of the agency for the time being having parental responsibility for the child under the order ("the existing agency").

(2) This section applies to any application made jointly by—

(a) the existing agency; and

(b) the would-be substitute agency.

(3) Where an order under section 18 is varied under this section, section 19 shall apply as if the substitute agency had been given responsibility for the child on the making of the order.]

AMENDMENT

This section was substituted by the Children Act 1989, s.88, Sched. 10, Pt. 1, para. 9.

DEFINITIONS

authorised court: s.72(1).
child: s.72(1).
adoption agency: s.72(1).

GENERAL NOTE

1–123 This section provides that where a court varies a freeing order so as to give parental responsibility to another adoption agency, the new agency will be deemed to have had the duties imposed under s.19, *i.e.* to make progress reports to the former parents.

Subs. (1)

1–124 *Parental responsibility:* See the note on s.12(1).

52

Supplemental

Notification to local authority of adoption application

22.—(1) An adoption order shall not be made in respect of a child who **1–125** was not placed with the applicant by an adoption agency unless the applicant has, at least 3 months before the date of the order, given notice to the local authority within whose area he has his home of his intention to apply for the adoption order.

[(1A) An application for such an adoption order shall not be made unless the person wishing to make the application has, within the period of two years preceding the making of the application, given notice as mentioned in subsection (1).

(1B) In subsection (1) and (1A) the references to the area in which the applicant or person has his home are references to the area in which he has his home at the time of giving the notice.]

(2) On receipt of such a notice the local authority shall investigate the matter and submit to the court a report of their investigation.

(3) Under subsection (2), the local authority shall in particular investigate,—

   (a) so far as is practicable, the suitability of the applicant, and any other matters relevant to the operation of section 6 in relation to the application; and

   (b) whether the child was placed with the application in contravention of section 11.

(4) A local authority which [receive] notice under subsection (1) in respect of a child whom the authority know to be [looked after by] another local authority shall, not more than seven days after the receipt of the notice, inform that other local authority in writing, that they have received the notice.

AMENDMENTS
   Subss. (1A) and (1B) and the words in square brackets in subs. (4) were inserted and substituted by the Children Act 1989, s.88, Sched. 10, Pt. 1, para. 10.

DEFINITIONS
   adoption agency: ss.1(4), 72(1).
   adoption order: s.72(1).
   child: s.72(1).
   local authority: s.72(1).
   notice: s.72(1).

GENERAL NOTE

   This section requires applicants wishing to adopt a child who was *not* placed with them by **1–126** an adoption agency to notify their local authority of their intention. The local authority will then carry out the investigations required by subss. (2) and (3) and submit a report to the court. "Local authorities will not, therefore, be notified of any intended adoption where the child was placed with the prospective adopters by an adoption agency, but they will be notified in all other cases:
   —adoption by a parent, relative, [or] step-parent . . . ;
   —adoption by foster parents who are looking after the child under private arrangements;
   —adoption by foster parents with whom the child has been boarded-out by a local authority or voluntary organisation, where the foster parents have either not sought or received that body's support for their application;
   —adoption of children from overseas" (D.H.S.S. Circular No. LAC (84)2, para. 21).
   Once notification has been given the child becomes a "protected child" and ss.32 to 37 of the Act apply. Where the child has been placed by an adoption agency, the agency will carry out the necessary investigations (s.23).

The relationship between this section and s.13, above was considered by Sheldon J. in the following passage from *Re Y. (Minors) (Adoption: Jurisdiction)* [1985] 3 All E.R. 33, 36:

> "Even though an applicant to adopt a child, or one of two joint applicants, may be domiciled in England or Wales, an adoption order cannot be made unless: (a) when giving notice of his intention to adopt (which must be at least three months before the date of the order) he had a 'home' here in the area of the local authority to which by [subs. (1) of this section], such notice had to be given; and (b) at all times during the alternative period of 13 weeks or 12 months (depending on whether the applicant or one of the applicants was a parent, step-parent or relative of the child), referred to in section [13] . . . he also provided a 'home' for the child in the area of the local authority required by that section to see all parties together in their 'home environment'."

Subs. (1)

1–127 *Placed:* It is submitted that "placed" means placed for adoption, so that this section will apply where foster parents apply to adopt a child who was originally placed with them under a fostering arrangement.

By an adoption agency: For restrictions on private placements, see s.11.

3 months: As to the period during which the child must live with the adopters before an adoption order can be made, see s.13.

Notice: By virtue of r.15(1)(d) of the Adoption Rules 1984 and the Magistrates' Courts (Adoption) Rules 1984, the local authority becomes a respondent to the application on receipt of the notice.

Local authority: Means authority in England or Wales (*Re Y.*, above.)

Had his home: See the note on s.13. In *Re Y.*, above, Sheldon J. said that para. 21 of D.H.S.S. Circular No. LAC (84)2 may be misleading in stating that "the notification requirements can only be met by applicants who are resident in this country" since "residence" here and having a "home" here may not necessarily be the same conceptually or in time and that at any given time an applicant may be "resident" here without having a "home" here, or he may have a "home" here without actually residing in it.

Subs. (2)

1–128 *Investigate:* The local authority must be given sufficient opportunities to see the child in his home environment (s.13(3)).

Submit to the court a report: The local authority's duties are amplified by r. 22 of the Adoption Rules 1984 and the Magistrates' Courts (Adoption) Rules 1984.

Subs. (3)

1–129 *In particular:* The local authority is not precluded from investigating other matters.

In contravention of section 11: Which prohibits private placements with non-relatives. If the local authority reports that the child has been placed illegally it has been suggested that the court should adjourn the hearing pending the outcome of the criminal proceedings; see *Bevan and Parry*, para. 110. The fact that the applicants have been convicted under s.11 does not prevent the court from making an adoption order as long as the adoption application is made to the High Court (*Re S. (Arrangements for Adoption)* [1985] F.L.R. 579).

Reports where child placed by agency

1–130 **23.** Where an application for an adoption order relates to a child placed by an adoption agency, the agency shall submit to the court a report on the suitability of the applicants and any other matters relevant to the operation of section 6, and shall assist the court in any manner the court may direct.

DEFINITIONS
  adoption agency: ss.1(4), 72(1).
  adoption order: s.72(1).
  child: s.72(1).

GENERAL NOTE

1–131 This section provides that where there is an agency placement the agency is responsible for submitting a report to the court and assisting the court in any manner it may direct. The procedure for submitting the report and the contents of the report are governed by r.22 and Sched. 2 of the Adoption Rules 1984 and the Magistrates' Courts (Adoption) Rules 1984.

Restrictions on making adoption orders

24.—(1) The court shall not proceed to hear an application for an **1–132** adoption order in relation to a child where a previous application for a British Adoption order made in relation to the child by the same persons was refused by any court unless—

(a) in refusing the previous application the court directed that this subsection should not apply, or

(b) it appears to the court that because of a change in circumstances or for any other reason it is proper to proceed with the application.

(2) The court shall not make an adoption order in relation to a child unless it is satisfied that the applicants have not, as respects the child, [contravened] section 57.

AMENDMENT

In subs. (2) the word in square brackets was substituted by the Health and Social Services and Social Security Adjudications Act 1983, s.9, Sched. 2, para. 32.

DEFINITIONS

adoption order: s.72(1).
British adoption order: s.72(1).
child: s.72(1).

GENERAL NOTE

Subs. (1)

Under this provision a court will not hear a second application by the same adopters for the **1–133** same child, unless the previous court exempted them from this rule, or the court finds that there has been a change in circumstances or other reason which justifies the second application.

The court shall not proceed: For procedure, see r.16 of the Adoption Rules 1984 and the Magistrates' Courts (Adoption) Rule 1984.

British adoption order: But not a Convention order.

Subs. (2)

This prohibits the making of an adoption order where the applicant has contravened the **1–134** rules relating to payments for adoption. Compare this with the effect of a contravention of s.11 (on private placements) which does not prevent an adoption order being made.

Interim orders

25.—(1) Where on an application for an adoption order the require- **1–135** ments of sections 16(1) and 22(1) are complied with, the court may postpone the determination of the application and make an order [giving parental responsibility for the child to] the applicants for a probationary period not exceeding two years upon such terms for the maintenance of the child and otherwise as the court thinks fit.

(2) Where the probationary period specified in an order under subsection (1) is less than 2 years, the court may by a further order extend the period to a duration not exceeding 2 years in all.

AMENDMENT

In subs. (1) the words in square brackets were substituted by the Children Act 1989, s.88, Sched. 10, Pt. 1, para. 11.

DEFINITIONS

adoption order: s.72(1).
child: s.72(1).
parental responsibility: s.72(1).

1–136   This section gives the court discretion to make an interim order giving parental responsibility for the child to the applicants for probationary period of up to two years. The applicants must have complied with the requirement under s.22(1) to notify the local authority of their intention to adopt, and the question of parental agreement to adoption must have been settled. An interim order is not an adoption order, and a subsequent hearing is required for the court to decide finally whether or not to make an adoption order.

Interim orders are rarely made. In *Re S.M.H. and R.M.H. Adoption and Fostering* (1979) No. 4, p. 63, the Court of Appeal said that an interim order should only be made where it is necessary to await the expiry of a probationary period in order to be satisfied about the suitability of the adopters. However, the Court of Appeal has held that the reference to a "probationary period" in the section does not mean that the power can only be used in cases where the suitability of the prospective adopters is in question as the term "probationary" implies a process of investigation or experiment in relation to all the circumstances relevant to the proposed adoption; see *S. v. Huddersfield Borough Council* [1975] Fam. 113.

In *Re C. and F. (Adoption: Removal Notice)* [1997] 1 F.L.R. 190 at 195, CA, Butler-Sloss L.J. said that this section:

> "is not intended to be an order to preserve the status quo at an early stage or to define the interim position of the children and the parties. It has a different purpose. It is there to give additional powers to the court where all the necessary matters have been dealt with at a substantive hearing of the adoption application, including the requirement as to residence and the decision about the agreement of the parent if he/ she does not consent, but there is still some doubt about the wisdom of making the final and conclusive adoption order. The minimum period of residence required by s.13 can thus be extended and the determination of the application postponed. In *S. v. Huddersfield Borough Council*, a decision based on s.8(1) of the Adoption Act 1958, this court upheld the interim order of the trial judge."

Her Ladyship was satisfied that this section "was not designed to give to a person with whom the children are not living the opportunity to qualify as a prospective adopter and then to adjourn the hearing of the adoption application until he does qualify". For further examples of cases where interim orders were made, see *Re O. (A Minor) (Adoption of Grandparents)* [1985] F.L.R. 546 and *Re A.W. (Adoption Application)* [1993] 1 F.L.R. 62. If the court has doubts about the appropriateness of adoption, it could make a residence order under s.8 of the Children Act 1989.

If the interim order expires without an adoption order being made, the child must be returned to the adoption agency (s.30(4)).

For further proceedings after an interim order has been made, see. r.25 of the Adoption Rules 1984 and the Magistrates' Courts (Adoption) Rules 1984.

Subs. (1)

1–137   *The court:* An authorised court as defined by s.62.

Postpone the determination of the application: The application remains pending during the relevant period and the restriction on removing the child contained in s.27, will apply.

Make and order: Applying the test contained in s.6.

Parental responsibility: See the note on s.12(1).

Such terms . . . as the court thinks fit: Such as a condition granting access to a natural parent of the child; *S. v. Huddersfield Borough Council*, above.

Care, etc. of child on refusal of adoption order

1–138   **26.** [*Repealed by the Children Act* 1989, *s.108(7), Sched.* 15.]

PART III

CARE AND PROTECTION OF CHILDREN AWAITING ADOPTION

Restrictions on removal of children

Restrictions on removal where adoption agreed or application made under s.18

1–139   **27.**—(1) While an application for an adoption order is pending in a case where a parent or guardian of the child has agreed to the making of the adoption order (whether or not he knows the identity of the applicant), the parent or guardian is not entitled, against the will of the person with whom the child has his home, to remove the child from the [home] of that person except with the leave of the court.

(2) While an application is pending for an order freeing a child for adoption and—

(a) the child is in the care of the adoption agency making the application, and

(b) the application was not made with the consent of each parent or guardian of the child,

no parent or guardian of the child is entitled, against the will of the person with whom the child has his home, to remove the child from the [home] of that person except with the leave of the court.

[(2A) For the purposes of subsection (2) a child is in the care of an adoption agency if the adoption agency is a local authority and he is in their care.]

(3) Any person who contravenes subsection (1) or (2) shall be guilty of an offence and liable on summary conviction to imprisonment for a term not exceeding 3 months or a fine not exceeding [level 5 on the standard scale] or both.

(4), (5) [*Repealed by the Health and Social Services and Social Security Adjudications Act* 1983, *s.*30(1), *Sched.* 10, *Pt. I.*]

AMENDMENTS

In subss. (1) and (2) the words in square brackets were substituted by the Children Act 1989, s.88, Sched. 10, Pt. 1, para. 12. Subs. (2A) was inserted by *ibid.*, para. 13.

In subs. (3) the words in square brackets were substituted by the Criminal Justice Act 1982, ss.38, 46.

DEFINITIONS

adoption agency: ss.1(4), 72(1).
adoption order: ss.55(4), 72(1).
child: s.72(1).
guardian: s.72(1).
order freeing a child for adoption: s.72(1).

GENERAL NOTE

This section makes it an offence in certain circumstances for a parent or guardian to **1–140** remove the child while an adoption or freeing application is pending. Subs. (1) provides that while an adoption order is pending and the parent or guardian has agreed to an adoption order being made he cannot remove the child against the will of the person with whom the child has his home, without the permission of the court. Subs. (2) provides that where the child is in the care of an adopting agency which has applied for an order freeing the child for adoption and the application was not made with the consent of each parent or guardian then, so long as the application is pending, no parent or guardian is entitled to remove the child against the will of the person with whom the child has his home, without the permission of the court. Note that in neither case is the consent of the adoption agency required. However if the child is the subject of a care order, the parent will not be able to remove the child against the wishes of the local authority.

If a parent changes his or her mind about agreeing to adoption after the application for the adoption has been lodged and wishes to assume the care of the child, the appropriate procedure to be followed is for the parent to apply to the court under this section for leave to remove the child from the prospective adopters' home.

For the power of the court to order the return of a child who has been removed in contravention of this section and to prohibit a suspected removal in advance, see s.29.

1–141   *Parent:* Is defined in s.72(1).

Agreed: The agreement can be given either orally or in writing (*Re T. (A Minor) (Adoption: Parental Consent)* [1986] 1 All E.R. 817). This section therefore covers informal agreements to adoption as well as formal agreements witnessed by the reported officer. In D.H.S.S. Circular No. LAC 84(3) the following passage comes under the heading "Are you willing for your child to be adopted?": "Once you have given your written agreement, you are not allowed to take your child away from his new family before the adoption hearing, unless the court says you may." This statement is incorrect in so far as it implies that if a parent has merely given an oral agreement he is entitled to remove the child without the court's permission. The prohibition contained in this provision would not be affected if the parent or guardian subsequently changed his mind and withdrew his agreement to adoption.

To the making of the adoption order: The agreement must relate to a specific adoption application and not to the idea of adoption.

Against the will of the person: The child can therefore be removed without recourse to the court if the applicants are willing.

Had his home: See the note to s.32 and s.72(1A).

Leave of the court: As a decision by the court would be a decision "relating to the adoption of a child" the court is required by s.6, to make the welfare of the child its first consideration (*Re C. (A Minor) (Adoption)* [1994] 2 F.L.R. 513, and see the note on s.30(2)). The procedure for applying for a child to be removed is set out in the Adoption Rules 1984, r.47 and the Magistrates' Courts (Adoption) Rules 1984, r.27. The relevant court is the court which will hear the adoption application.

Subs. (2)

Person with whom the child has his home: Who may not be the person who ultimately applies for the adoption order. It is the consent of the person with whom the child has his home rather than the adoption agency that is required.

Leave of the court: i.e. the court which will hear the freeing application. For procedure, see the note on subs. (1).

Restrictions on removal where applicant has provided home for 5 years

1–142   **28.**—(1) While an application for an adoption order in respect of a child made by the person with whom the child has had his home for the 5 years preceding the application is pending, no person is entitled, against the will of the applicant, to remove the child from the applicant's [home] except with the leave of the court or under authority conferred by any enactment or on the arrest of the child.

(2) Where a person ("the prospective adopter") gives notice to the local authority within whose area he has his home that he intends to apply for an adoption order in respect of a child who for the preceding 5 years has had his home with the prospective adopter, no person is entitled, against the will of the prospective adopter, to remove the child from the prospective adopter's [home], except with the leave of a court or under authority conferred by any enactment or on the arrest of the child, before—

(a) the prospective adopter applies for the adoption order, or

(b) the period of 3 months from the receipt of the notice by the local authority expires,

whichever occurs first.

[(2A) The reference in subsections (1) and (2) to an enactment does not include a reference to section 20(8) of the Children Act 1989.]

[(3) In any case where subsection (1) or (2) applies and—

(a) the child was being looked after by a local authority before he began to have his home with the applicant or, as the case may be, the prospective adopter, and

(b) the child is still being looked after by a local authority,

the authority which are looking after the child shall not remove him from the home of the applicant or the prospective adopter except in accordance with section 30 or 31 or with the leave of a court.]

(4) In subsections (2) and (3) "a court" means a court with jurisdiction to make adoption orders.

(5) A local authority which [receive] such notice as is mentioned in subsection (2) in respect of a child whom the authority know to be [looked after by another local authority] shall, not more than 7 days after the receipt of the notice, inform that other authority [. . .] in writing, that they have received the notice.

(6) Subsection (2) does not apply to any further notice served by the prospective adopter on any local authority in respect of the same child during the period referred to in paragraph (b) of that subsection or within 28 days after its expiry.

(7) Any person who contravenes subsection (1) or (2) shall be guilty of an offence and liable on summary conviction to imprisonment for a term not exceeding 3 months or a fine not exceeding [level 5 on the standard scale] or both.

(8) (9) [*Repealed by the Health and Social Services and Social Security Adjudications Act* 1983, *s.*30(1), *Sched.* 10, *Pt. I.*]

(10) The Secretary of State may by order amend subsection (1) or (2) to substitute a different period for the period of 5 years mentioned in that subsection (or the period which, by a previous order under this subsection, was substituted for that period).

AMENDMENTS
The amendments to this section were made by the Children Act 1989, s.88, Sched. 10, Pt. I, paras. 12 and 14, the Domestic Proceedings and Magistrates' Courts Act 1978, s.89(2)(a), Sched. 2, para. 50 and the Criminal Justice Act 1982, ss.38, 46.

DEFINITIONS
adoption order: ss.55(4), 72(1).
child: s.72(1).
local authority: s.72(1).
notice: s.72(1).
voluntary organisation: s.72(1).

GENERAL NOTE

This section protects the child against removal from prospective adopters with whom he has **1–143** had his home for a continuous period of five years. In such a case the court's permission is required if a person wishes to remove the child from his home against the wishes of the prospective adopters. The object of this provision is to give the foster parents the right to apply to the court for adoption without incurring the risk of the natural parent frustrating the application by suddenly removing the child. For a research study which examines the operation of this section, see Rowe, Cain, Hundleby, and Keane, *Long Term Fostering and the Children Act* (1984).

In *Re H. (A Minor) (Adoption)* [1985] F.L.R. 519, the Court of Appeal held that it was a misuse of the adoption procedure, and an adoption application may be refused, if the objective of the application was to defeat one of the statutory responsibilities of the local authority, such as the power to remove a child.

For the power of the court to order the return of a child who has been removed in contravention of this section and to prohibit a suspected removal in advance, see s.29.

Subs. (1)

The person: Who will either be a private or a local authority foster parent. **1–144**

Had his home: See the note on s.32 and s.72(1A).

No person: Unlike s.27 the prohibition contained in this provision is not limited to parents and guardians. It therefore applies to local authorities who have placed a looked-after child with foster parents. However, the local authority can still remove the child under ss.30 and 31 (subs. (3)).

5 years: This period may be altered (subs 10).

Preceding the application: The protection provided by this subsection does not apply until the adoption application has been made.

Leave of the court: Which is the court that will hear the adoption application. The decision of the court is governed by the welfare test contained in s.6 (*Re C (A Minor) (Adoption)* [1994] 2 F.L.R. 513, and see the note on s.30(2)). The procedure for applying for a child to be removed is set out in the Adoption Rules 1984, r.47 and the Magistrates' Courts (Adoption) Rules 1984, r.27.

Subs. (2)

1–145   This extends the protection given to applicants by subs. (1) to prospective adopters. Once the adoption application is made, subs. (1) continues the protection.
Notice: which must be in writing (s.72(1)) and may be given by post (s.69).
The period of three months: Subs. (6) prevents the three months being extended by subsequent notices.

Subs. (3)

1–146   *Looked after by a local authority:* see s.72(1B).

Subs. (4)

1–147   *A court with jurisdiction to make adoption orders:* See ss. 12(1) and 62.

Subs. (6)

1–148   *28 days:* The child could be removed during this period.

Return of a child taken away in breach of s.27 or 28

1–149   **29.** [(1) An authorised court may, on the application of a person from whose home a child has been removed in breach of—
    (a) section 27 or 28,
    (b) section 27 or 28 of the Adoption (Scotland) Order 1978, or
    (c) Article 28 or 29 of the Adoption (Northern Ireland) Order 1987,
order the person who has so removed the child to return the child to the applicant.

(2) An authorised court may, on the application of a person who has reasonable grounds for believing that another person is intending to remove a child from his home in breach of—
    (a) section 27 or 28,
    (b) section 27 or 28 of the Adoption (Scotland) Act 1978, or
    (c) Article 28 or 29 of the Adoption (Northern Ireland) Order 1987,
by order direct that other person not to remove the child from the applicant's home in breach of any of those provisions.]

(3) If, in the case of an order made by the High Court under subsection (1), the High Court or, in the case of an order made by a county court under subsection (1), a county court is satisfied that the child has not been returned to the applicant, the court may make an order authorising an officer of the court to search such premises as may be specified in the order for the child and, if the officer finds the child, to return the child to the applicant.

(4) If a justice of the peace is satisfied by information on oath that there are reasonable grounds for believing that a child to whom an order under subsection (1) relates is in premises specified in the information, he may issue a search warrant authorising a constable to search the premises for the child; and if a constable acting in pursuance of a warrant under this section finds the child, he shall return the child to the person on whose application the order under subsection (1) was made.

(5) An order under subsection (3) may be enforced in like manner as a warrant for committal.

AMENDMENTS
    Subss. (1) and (2) were substituted by the Children Act 1989, s.88, Sched. 10, Pt. 1, para. 15.

DEFINITION
    child: s.72(1).

GENERAL NOTE
    This section enables a court, on application by the person from whom a child has been **1–150** removed in breach of s.27 or s.28 to order the return of the child. The order can be enforced by court officers searching specified premises and returning the child to the applicant (subs. (3)) or by a magistrate issuing a search warrant authorising a policeman to search premises and to return the child (subs. (4)). The section also enables the court to forbid the removal of a child if the applicant satisfies the court that there are reasonable grounds for believing that a person is intending to remove the child in breach of s.27 or s.28. Wardship proceedings provide an alternative course of action in these circumstances.
    The procedure for making an application to the court under this section is governed by the Adoption Rules 1984, r.47 and the Magistrates' Courts (Adoption) Rules 1984, r.27.

Subs. (1)
    Authorised court: See s.62(1), (5).   **1–151**
    May . . . order: The exercise of the courts discretion is governed by s.6.
    The person who has so removed the child: who may no longer have custody of the child. The enforcement powers contained in subss. (3) and (4) can be used where the person who committed the breach has handed the child to a third party.

Subs. (2)
    May . . . order: See subs. (1).   **1–152**

Subs. (4)
    Provides an alternative enforcement procedure to that contained in subs. (3) for orders **1–153** made by the High Court or County Court, and is the only enforcement procedure available for orders made by the magistrates' court.

Return of children placed for adoption by adoption agencies

30.—(1) Subject to subsection (2), at any time after a child has been **1–154** [placed with] any person in pursuance of arrangements made by an adoption agency for the adoption of the child by that person, and before an adoption order has been made on the application of that person in respect of the child,—

(a) that person may give notice to the agency of his intention not to [give the child a home]; or

(b) the agency may cause notice to be given to that person of their intention not to allow the child to remain in his [home].

(2) No notice under paragraph (b) of subsection (1) shall be given in respect of a child in relation to whom an application has been made for an adoption order except with the leave of the court to which the application has been made.

(3) Where a notice is given to an adoption agency by any person or by an adoption agency to any person under subsection (1), or where an application for an adoption order made by any person in respect of a child placed [with him] by an adoption agency is refused by the court or withdrawn, that person shall, within 7 days after the date on which notice was given or the application refused or withdrawn, as the case may be, cause the child to be returned to the agency, who shall receive the child.

(4) Where the period specified in an interim order made under section 25 (whether as originally made or as extended under subsection (2) of that section) expires without an adoption order having been made in respect of the child, subsection (3) shall apply as if the application for an adoption

order upon which the interim order was made, had been refused at the expiration of that period.

(5) It shall be sufficient compliance with the requirements of subsection (3) if the child is delivered to, and is received by, a suitable person nominated for the purpose by the adoption agency.

(6) Where an application for an adoption order is refused the court may, if it thinks fit at any time before the expiry of the period of 7 days mentioned in subsection (3), order that period to be extended to a duration, not exceeding 6 weeks, specified in the order.

(7) Any person who contravenes the provisions of this section shall be guilty of an offence and liable on summary conviction to imprisonment for a term not exceeding 3 months or to a fine not exceeding £400 or to both; and the court by which the offender is convicted may order the child in respect of whom the offence is committed to be returned to his parent or guardian or to the adoption agency which made the arrangements referred to in subsection (1).

AMENDMENTS
In this section the words in square brackets were inserted by the Health and Social Services and Social Security Adjudications Act 1983, s.9, Sched. 2, para. 60(c) and the Children Act 1989, s.88, Sched. 10, para. 16.

DEFINITIONS
adoption agency: ss.1(4), 72(1).
adoption order: ss.55(4), 72(1).
child: s.72(1).
notice: s.72(1).

GENERAL NOTE

1–155   This section sets out the steps that must be taken if either the prospective adopters or the adoption agency wish to withdraw from the arrangement and end the placement. In both situations notice must be given and the child returned to the agency. If the adoption application has been made, the adoption agency can give notice only with leave of the court. The section also provides for the return of the child if the court refuses to make an adoption order (or if the adoption order is withdrawn) (subs. (3)) and if an interim order expires without a full order being made (subs. (4)). A contravention of the provisions of this section is an offence and the convicting court may order the child to be returned to his parents or to the adoption agency (subs. (7)).

Subs. (1)

1–156   The court has no power to intervene and review the merits of the adoption agency's decision to remove children under this provision: it can only intervene under subs. (2) (*Re C. and F. (Adoption: Removal Notice)* [1997] 1 F.L.R. 190, CA). However, the court will intervene on an application for judicial review if the agency's decision making process is flawed.

In *R. v. Devon County Council, ex p. O.* [1997] Fam. Law 390, the local authority served the prospective adopters with a notice under this provision requiring them to return the child (who had been placed with the family for over two years) within seven days of service of the notice. Scott Baker J. held that the local authority's decision was unlawful, in that: (a) there was inadequate consultation with the family, in particular that the family was not invited to the strategy meeting that had been convened to consider the placement, or to any part of it; and (b) the authority failed to give due regard to the wishes and feelings of the child in that it had looked through adult eyes at what were perceived to be the child's needs; it should have looked to the future through the child's eyes.

Notice: The written notice (s.72(1)) may be given by post (s.69).

Subs. (2)

1–157   *In respect of a child:* The fact that the child is subject to a care order does not effect the obligation to obtain leave (*Re P.* [1994] 2 F.C.R. 537).

Leave of the court: This is governed by the welfare test contained in s.6 (*Re C. (A Minor) (Adoption)* [1994] 2 F.L.R. 513, CA). In this case Butler-Sloss L.J. said, at 522, 523, that:

"a court determining a s.30(2) application by a local authority must give most careful consideration to the plan of the local authority but it has the task to decide whether that plan should go ahead or whether the child should remain with its existing carer even if the consequences of its decision may be to frustrate the local authority's arrangements. It is never the task of the court to rubber-stamp the local authority. Either it has no jurisdiction to interfere or it has the duty to decide."

She identified the following questions that the court might ask:

"Is the application a serious one or is it an abuse of the process of the court?

If it is a serious application, does the prospective adopter have a real prospect of success or it is a vain hope by, for instance, a devoted foster-mother who cannot let go but could not be regarded as a suitable adopter?

Is the care plan of the local authority of such strength in that, for instance, the prospective adopters proposed by them would be obviously better for the child than the existing carer(s)? Is there evidence that the family chosen by the local authority are not prepared to wait?

Does the guardian *ad litem*, if appointed, support the application of the current carer?"

The procedure is governed by the Adoption Rules 1984, r.47 and the Magistrates' Courts (Adoption) Rules 1984, r.27.

Subs. (3)

Within seven days: The day on which the notice is served is to be disregarded (*Stewart v.* **1–158** *Chapman* [1951] 2 K.B. 792). The court has no power to authorise the prospective adopters to retain the child pending an appeal against the court's refusal (*Re C.S.C. (An Infant)* [1960] 1 W.L.R. 304), although the court has power to extend the 7 day period under subs. (6).

Application of s.30 where child not placed for adoption

31.—(1) Where a person gives notice in pursuance of section 22(1) to the **1–159** local authority within whose area he has his home of his intention to apply for an adoption order in respect of a [child—

(a) who is (when the notice is given) being looked after by a local authority; but

(b) who was placed with that person otherwise than in pursuance of such arrangements as are mentioned in section 30(1),

that section shall apply as if the child had been placed in pursuance of such arrangements], except that where the application is refused by the court or withdrawn the child need not be returned to the local authority in whose care he is unless that authority so require.

(2) Where notice of intention is given as aforesaid in respect of any child who is [(when the notice is given) being looked after by] a local authority then, until the application for an adoption order has been made and disposed of, any right of the local authority to require the child to be returned to them otherwise than in pursuance of section 30 shall be suspended.

(3) While the child [has his home with] the person by whom the notice is given no contribution shall be payable (whether under a contribution order or otherwise) in respect of the child by any person liable under [Part III of Schedule 2 to the Children Act 1989] to make contributions in respect of him (but without prejudice to the recovery of any sum due at the time the notice is given), unless 12 weeks have elapsed since the giving of the notice without the application being made or the application has been refused by the court or withdrawn.

[(4) Nothing in this section affects the right of any person who has parental responsibility for a child to remove him under section 20(8) of the Children Act 1989].

AMENDMENTS
The amendments to this section were made by the Children Act 1989, s.88, Sched. 10, para. 17.

DEFINITIONS
adoption order: ss.55(4), 72(1).
child: s.72(1).
local authority: s.72(1).

GENERAL NOTE

1–160   This section extends the provisions of s.30 to the situation where the child is being looked after by a local authority and placed with foster parents who notify the authority of their intention to adopt. Once the notice of intention to apply for adoption has been received, the authority must comply with s.30 if it wishes to recall the child. This means that the authority will require the court's leave once the adoption application has been made. If the adoption application is either withdrawn or refused the child need not be returned to the authority unless that authority so requires, *c.f.* s.30(3). The giving of the notice of intention to apply for adoption suspends the parents' liability to contribute towards the maintenance of the child (subs. (3)). It also makes the child a "protected child" (s.32) and the local authority is given powers to ensure that the child is properly cared for; see ss.33, 34 and 37.

Subs. (1)

1–161   *Unless that authority so requires:* The local authority might wish the applicants to continue to act as foster parents.

Protected children

Meaning of "protected child"

1–162   **32.**—(1) Where a person gives notice in pursuance of section 22(1) to the local authority within whose area he lives of his intention to apply for an adoption order in respect of a child, the child is for the purposes of this Part a protected child while he has his home with that person.

(2) A child shall be deemed to be a protected child for the purposes of this Part if he is a protected child within the meaning of

[(a) section 32 of the Adoption (Scotland) Act 1978; or

(b) Article 33 of the Adoption (Northern Ireland) Order 1987.]

(3) A child is not a protected child by reason of any such notice as is mentioned in subsection (1) while—

[(a) he is in the care of any person—

(i) in any community home, voluntary home or registered children;

(ii) in any school in which he is receiving full-time education;

(iii) in any health service hospital]; or

(b) [he is—

(i) suffering from mental disorder within the meaning of the Mental Health Act 1983; and

(ii) resident in a residential care home, within the meaning of Part I of Schedule 4 to the Health and Social Services and Social Security Adjudications Act 1983;] or

(c) he is liable to be detained or subject to guardianship under [the Mental Health Act 1983].

[(d) he is in the care of any person in any home or institution not specified in this subsection but provided, equipped and maintained by the Secretary of State.]

[(3A) In subsection (3) "community home," "voluntary home," "registered children's home," "school" and "health service hospital" have the same meaning as in the Children Act 1989.]

[(4) A protected child ceases to be a protected child—

(a) on the grant or refusal of the application for an adoption order;

(b) on the notification to the local authority for the area where the child has his home that the application for an adoption order has been withdrawn;

(c) in a case where no application is made for an adoption order, on the expiry of the period of two years from the giving of the notice;

(d) on the making of a residence order, a care order or a supervision order under the Children Act 1989 in respect of the child;

(e) on the appointment of a guardian for him under that Act;

(f) on his attaining the age of 18 years; or

(g) on his marriage,

whichever first occurs.

(5) In subsection (4)(d) the references to a care order and a supervision order do not include references to an interim care order or interim supervision order.]

AMENDMENTS

The words in square brackets in subs. (1), subs. (3)(a) and subs. (4) were substituted, and the words in square brackets at the end of subs. (3) and subs. (3A) were inserted, by the Children Act 1989, s.88, Sched. 10, Pt. 1, para. 18.

Subs. (3)(b), was substituted by the Health and Social Services and Social Security Adjudications Act 1983, s.29(1), Sched. 9, Pt. I, para. 19.

In subs. (3)(c), the words in square brackets were substituted by the Mental Health Act 1983, s.148, Sched. 4, para. 45.

DEFINITIONS

adoption order: ss.55(4), 72(1).
child: s.72(1).
local authority: s.72(1).

GENERAL NOTE

This and the next four sections deal with "protected children". A protected child is a child **1–163** in respect of whom a person has given notice to the relevant local authority that he intends to apply for an adoption order. Subject to subs. (4) a child continues to be a protected child as long as he has his home with the prospective applicants. Children placed for adoption by adoption agencies do not become protected children as the agency is expected to supervise them.

Subs. (1)

Notice: Which must be in writing (s.72(1)) and may be given by post (s.69). **1–164**

Intention to apply for an adoption order: The Foster Placement (Children) Regulations 1991 (S.I. 1991 No. 910) do not apply to the placement of a child for adoption pursuant to this Act with a person who proposes to adopt him; *ibid*. reg. 2(2).

Subs. (3)

Residental care home: Now see the Registered Homes Act 1984. **1–165**

Subs. (4)

Attained the age: At the commencement of his eighteenth birthday (Family Law Reform Act **1–166** 1969, s.9(1)).

Duty of local authorities to secure well-being of protected children

33.—(1) It shall be the duty of every local authority to secure that **1–167** protected children within their area are visited from time to time by officers of the authority, who shall satisfy themselves as to the well-being of the children and give such advice as to their care and maintenance as may appear to be needed.

(2) Any officer of a local authority authorised to visit protected children may, after producing, if asked to do so, some duly authenticated document showing that he is so authorised, inspect any premises in the area of the authority in which such children are to be or are being kept.

DEFINITIONS
  protected child: s.32.
  child: s.72(1).
  local authority: s.72(1).

GENERAL NOTE

1–168   This section obliges a local authority to ensure that a protected child is visited by its officers who must be satisfied about the child's well-being and must offer advice about his care and maintenance. These officers are authorised to inspect any premises in the authority's area where the child is being kept.

A court can only order the removal of a protected child from an unsatisfactory home if the conditions for an emergency protection or care order are satisfied (Children Act 1989, ss.31 and 44).

Subs. (1)

1–169   *Well-being of the children:* This phrase encompasses every aspect of the child's welfare.

Subs. (2)

1–170   *Authorised to visit . . . inspect any premises:* It is an offence to refuse to allow the visiting of a protected child or the inspection of premises (s.36(1)(*b*)).

After producing, if asked to do so: This does not mean that the right of entry can only be exercised if there is someone to whom the document can be shown (*Grove v. Eastern Gas Board* [1952] 1 K.B. 77).

Removal of protected children from unsuitable surroundings
1–171   34. [*Repealed by the Children Act* 1989, *s.*108(7), *Sched.* 15.]

Notices and information to be given to local authorities
1–172   35.—(1) Where a person [with whom a protected child has his home] changes his permanent address he shall, not less than 2 weeks before the change, or, if the change is made in an emergency, not later than one week after the change, give notice specifying the new address to the local authority in whose area his permanent address is before the change, and if the new address is in the area of another local authority, the authority to whom the notice is given shall inform that other local authority and give them such of the following particulars as are known to them, that is to say—

(a) the name, sex and date and place of birth of a child;

(b) the name and address of every person who is a parent or guardian or acts as a guardian of the child or from whom the child was received.

(2) If a protected child dies, the person [with whom he has his home] at his death shall within 48 hours give notice of the child's death to the local authority.

DEFINITIONS
  protected child: s.32.
  child: s.72(1).
  guardian: s.72(1).
  local authority: s.72(1).
  notice: s.72(1).
  parent: s.72(1).

AMENDMENTS

The amendments to this section were made by the Children Act 1989, s.88, Sched. 10, Pt. 1, para. 19.

If a person with whom a protected child has his home changes his permanent address he **1–173** must give the local authority in whose area the child is living, written notice specifying his new address. Notice must also be given to the local authority if the child dies. Failure to take action under this section constitutes an offence under s.36(1)(a).

Subs. (1)

Notice: The written notice (s.72(1)) may be sent by post (s.69). **1–174**

Offences relating to protected children

36.—(1) A person shall be guilty of an offence if— **1–175**

(a) being required, under section 35 to give any notice or information, he fails to give the notice within the time specified in that provision or fails to give the information within a reasonable time, or knowingly makes or causes or procures another person to make any false or misleading statement in the notice of information;

(b) he refuses to allow the visiting of a protected child by a duly authorised officer of a local authority or the inspection, under the power conferred by section 33(2) of any premises;

(c) [. . .]

(2) A person guilty of an offence under this section shall be liable on summary conviction to imprisonment for a term not exceeding 3 months or a fine not exceeding [level 5 on the standard scale] or both.

Amendment

In subs. (1), para. (c) was repealed by the Children Act 1989, s.108(7), Sched. 15.
In subs. (2) the words in square brackets were substituted by the Criminal Justice Act 1982, ss.38, 46.

Definitions

protected child: s.32.
child: s.72(1).
local authority: s.72(1).
notice: s.72(1).

General Note

Subs. (1)

Person: Includes a body of persons corporate or unincorporate (Interpretation Act 1978, s.5, **1–176** Sched. 1). For further provisions relating to offences by corporations, see s.68.

Obstructs: Cases on the offence of obstructing a constable in the execution of his duty suggest that an offence under this section: (1) need not involve physical violence (*Hinchcliffe v. Sheldon* [1955] 1 W.L.R. 1207); (2) is not committed on a mere refusal to answer questions (*Rice v. Connolly* [1966] 2 Q.B. 414); and (3) might be committed if a verbal warning of an impending inspection is given (*Green v. Moore* [1982] 2 W.L.R. 671). There is also authority to support the contention that an offence is committed if the defendant's conduct makes it more difficult for an authorised person to carry out his duties; see the dictum of Lord Goddard C.J. in *Hinchcliffe v. Sheldon* at p. 1210, which was followed by the Divisional Court in *Lewis v. Cox* [1984] 3 W.L.R. 875. Note, however, that in *Swallow v. London County Council* [1916] 1 K.B. 224, a case on the Weights and Measures Act 1889, it was held that, in the absence of a legal duty to act, standing by and doing nothing did not amount to an obstruction.

Miscellaneous provisions relating to protected children

37.—(1) [. . .] **1–177**

(2) A person who maintains a protected child shall be deemed for the purposes of the Life Assurance Act 1774 to have no interest in the life of the child.

(3) [...]
(4) [...]

AMENDMENTS

Subss. (1), (3) and (4) were repealed by the Children Act 1989, s.108(7), Sched. 15.

DEFINITION

protected child: s.32.

GENERAL NOTE

Subs. (2)

1–178   *No interest:* Any policy on the life of a protected child which is for the benefit of the person who maintains that child is therefore void.

PART IV

STATUS OF ADOPTED CHILDREN

Meaning of "adoption" in Part IV

1–179   **38.**—(1) In this Part "adoption" means adoption—

(a) by an adoption order;

(b) by an order made under the Children Act 1975, the Adoption Act 1958, the Adoption Act 1950 or any enactment repealed by the Adoption Act 1950;

(c) by an order made in Scotland, Northern Ireland, the Isle of Man or in any of the Channel Islands;

(d) which is an overseas adoption; or

(e) which is an adoption recognised by the law of England and Wales and effected under the law of any other country,

and cognate expressions shall be construed accordingly.

(2) The definition of adoption includes, where the context admits, an adoption effected before the passing of the Children Act 1975, and the date of an adoption effected by an order is the date of the making of the order.

DEFINITIONS

adoption order: s.72(1).
overseas adoption: s.72(2).

Subs. (1)

1–180   *Overseas adoption:* "Where an adoption order is specified as an 'overseas adoption', it can be said to be already recognised under s.38(1)(d) of the Adoption Act 1976. However, for the avoidance of doubt, it may be better to seek a declaration that the adoption is valid", J. Rosenblatt, *International Adoption* (1995), p. 23. The procedure for obtaining such a declaration is set out in the Family Proceedings Rules 1991, rr. 3.15, 3.16. Overseas adoptions are considered in the note to s.72(2).

Subs. (2)

1–181   *Before the passing of the Children Act 1975:* The 1975 Act was passed on November 12, 1975.

Status conferred by adoption

1–182   **39.**—(1) An adopted child shall be treated in law—

(a) where the adopters are a married couple, as if he had been born as a child of the marriage (whether or not he was in fact born after the marriage was solemnized);

(b) in any other case, as if he had been born to the adopter in wedlock (but not as a child of any actual marriage of the adopter).

68

(2) An adopted child shall, subject to subsection (3), be treated in law as if he were not the child of any person other than the adopters or adopter.

(3) In the case of a child adopted by one of its natural parents as sole adoptive parent, subsection (2) has no effect as respects entitlement to property depending on relationship to that parent, or as respects anything else depending on that relationship.

(4) It is hereby declared that this section prevents an adopted child from being illegitimate.

(5) This section has effect—

(a) in the case of an adoption before January 1, 1976, from that date; and

(b) in the case of any other adoption, from the date of the adoption.

(6) Subject to the provisions of this Part, this section—

(a) applies for the construction of enactments or instruments passed or made before the adoption or later, and so applies subject to any contrary indication; and

(b) has effect as respects things done, or events occurring, after the adoption, or after December 31, 1975, whichever is the later.

DEFINITIONS
  adoption: s.38.
  child: s.72(1).

TRANSITIONAL PROVISIONS
  See s.73(1), Sched. 2, para. 6.

GENERAL NOTE

The effect of an adoption order is set out in this section, s.12 and s.41. The combined effect **1–183** of these sections is set out in the General Note to s.12.

In *Watson v. Willmott* [1991] 1 All E.R. 473, Garland J. held that although neither this section nor this Act read as a whole can extinguish a child's accrued right of action under the Fatal Accidents Act 1976, the quantification of dependency was affected because the effect of adoption, with its legal obligation on the adoptive parents to maintain the adopted child, replaced any future loss of dependency *pro tanto*.

Subs. (1)

An adopted child shall be treated: For exceptions, see ss.47, 48 and 49.   **1–184**

As if he had been born: The effect of this section is carried back to the adopted persons birth; see *Secretary of State for Social Services v. S.* [1983] 3 All E.R. 173, CA.

Subs. (4)

Prevent an adopted child from being illegitimate: Even if the child is adopted by a single **1–185** person. This provision did not prevent Ewbank J. from making a declaration of legitimacy in circumstances where the child had been legitimised by her parents' marriage which took place after her birth and before a court had unwittingly made an adoption order in their favour; see *Veasey v. Attorney-General* (1982) 3 F.L.R. 267.

The concept of legitimacy is the subject of the Family Law Reform Act 1987. The Act lays down a general principle in s.1 which states that in relation to Acts passed after April 4, 1988, and to other specified Acts, "references (however expressed) to any relationship between two persons shall, unless the contrary intention appears, be construed without regard to whether or not the father and mother of either of them, or the father and mother of any person through whom the relationship is deduced, have or had been married to each other at any time". This has the effect of removing the relevance of the distinction between legitimacy and illegitimacy. However, it is specifically provided in s.1(2), (3) of the 1987 Act that a person who is regarded as legitimate by virtue of being an adopted child within the meaning of this Part of this Act is still to be treated as being legitimate.

1–186   *January 1, 1976:* The date of commencement of the relevant provisions of the Children Act 1975.

Citizenship
1–187   **40.** [*Repealed by the British Nationality Act* 1981, *s.*52(8), *Sched* 9.].

Adoptive relatives
1–188   **41.** A relationship existing by virtue of section 39 may be referred to as an adoptive relationship, and—

   (a) a male adopter may be referred to as the adoptive father;
   (b) a female adopter may be referred to as the adoptive mother;
   (c) any other relative of any degree under an adoptive relationship may be referred to as an adoptive relative of that degree,

but this section does not prevent the term "parent", or any other term not qualified by the word "adoptive" being treated as including an adoptive relative.

DEFINITIONS
   adopter: s.38.
   relative: s.72(1).

GENERAL NOTE
1–189   This section enables the relationship between the adopted child and his adoptive parents to be described as an adoptive relationship, and a male and female adopter to be described as the adoptive father and mother. This principle extends to any other relative under an adoptive relationship.

Rules of construction for instruments concerning property
1–190   **42.**—(1) Subject to any contrary indication, the rules of construction contained in this section apply to an instrument, other than an existing instrument, so far as it contains a disposition of property.

(2) In applying section 39(1) to a disposition which depends on the date of birth of a child or children of the adoptive parent or parents, the disposition shall be construed as if—

   (a) the adopted child had been born on the date of adoption,
   (b) two or more children adopted on the same date had been born on that date in the order of their actual births,

but this does not affect any reference to the age of a child.

(3) Examples of phrases in wills on which subsection (2) can operate are—

   1. Children of A "living at my death or born afterwards."
   2. Children of A "living at my death or born afterwards before any one of such children for the time being in existence attains a vested interest and who attain the age of 21 years."
   3. As in example 1 or 2, but referring to grandchildren of A instead of children of A.
   4. A for life "until he has a child" and then to his child or children.

Note. Subsection (2) will not affect the reference to the age of 21 years in example 2.

(4) Section 39(2) does not prejudice any interest vested in possession in the adopted child before the adoption, or any interest expectant (whether immediately or not) upon an interest so vested.

(5) Where it is necessary to determine for the purposes of a disposition of property effected by an instrument whether a woman can have a child, it

70

shall be presumed that once a woman has attained the age of 55 years she will not adopt a child after execution of the instrument, and, notwithstanding section 39, if she does so that child shall not be treated as her child or as the child of her spouse (if any) for the purposes of the instrument.

(6) In this section, "instrument" includes a private Act settling property, but not any other enactment.

DEFINITIONS
adoption: s.38.
adoptive parent: s.41.
disposition: s.46.
child: s.72(1).
existing: s.72(1).

GENERAL NOTE

1–191

Subs. (2)
This subsection is concerned with the situation where a disposition depends upon the date of birth of a child of adoptive parents.

Subs. (4)
Although an adopted child loses the property rights that he would have had as a member of **1–192** his natural family, this subsection provides that certain interests will be retained by him.
Interest expectant: The right conferred by s.1 of the Inheritance (Provision for Family and Dependents) Act 1975 on children of the deceased and others to claim that reasonable financial provision is made for them out of the deceased's estate is not, in the case of an adopted child, an interest expectant which is preserved by this subsection. A person who is qualified to claim under the 1975 Act has to be qualified at the time of making an application. A child who is subsequently adopted ceases to so qualified by virtue of s.39(2) of this Act under which an adopted child is to be treated in law as if he were not the child of any person other than the adopters (*Re Collins (deceased)* [1990] 2 All E.R. 47).

Dispositions depending on date of birth

43. (1) Where a disposition depends on the date of birth of a child who **1–193** was born illegitimate and who is adopted by one of the natural parents as sole adoptive parent, section 42(2) does not affect entitlement under Part III of the Family Law Reform Act 1969 (illegitimate children).

(2) Subsection (1) applies for example where—
(a) a testator dies in 1976 bequeathing a legacy to his eldest grandchild living at a specified time,
(b) his daughter has an illegitimate child in 1977 who is the first grandchild,
(c) his married son has a child in 1978,
(d) subsequently the illegitimate child is adopted by the mother as sole adoptive parent,
and in all those cases the daughter's child remains the eldest grandchild of the testator throughout.

DEFINITIONS
adopted: s.38.
adoptive parent: s.41.
disposition: s.46.
child: s.72(1).

GENERAL NOTE
This section provides that if a disposition depends on the date of birth of an illegitimate **1–194** child, his adoption by one of his parents as sole adopter and his subsequent legitimation will not affect his entitlement.

Property devolving with peerages, etc.

1–195   **44.**—(1) An adoption does not affect the descent of any peerage or dignity or title of honour.

(2) An adoption shall not affect the devolution of any property limited (expressly or not) to devolve (as nearly as the law permits) along with any peerage or dignity or title of honour.

(3) Subsection (2) applies only if and so far as a contrary intention is not expressed in the instrument, and shall have effect subject to the terms of the instrument.

DEFINITION
   adoption: s.38.

GENERAL NOTE

1–196   This section prevents an adopted child from inheriting a peerage, dignity or title of honour, and from succeeding to property devolving with any peerage etc., unless there is a contrary intention expressed in the instrument.

Protection of trustees and personal representatives

1–197   **45.**—(1) A trustee or personal representative is not under a duty, by virtue of the law relating to trusts or the administration of estates, to enquire, before conveying or distributing any property, whether any adoption has been effected or revoked if that fact could affect entitlement to the property.

(2) A trustee or personal representative shall not be liable to any person by reason of a conveyance or distribution of the property made without regard to any such fact if he has not received notice of the fact before the conveyance or distribution.

(3) This section does not prejudice the right of a person to follow the property, or any property representing it, into the hands of another person, other than a purchaser, who has received it.

DEFINITION
   adoption: s.38.

GENERAL NOTE

1–198   This section protects trustees and personal representatives who convey or distribute property in ignorance of the making or revocation of an adoption order. The right of a person to follow the property into the hands of anyone other than a purchaser is not prejudiced.

Meaning of "disposition"

1–199   **46.** In this Part, unless the context otherwise requires,—
   "disposition" includes the conferring of a power of appointment and any other disposition of an interest in or right over property;
   "power of appointment" includes any discretionary power to transfer a beneficial interest in property without the furnishing of valuable consideration.

(2) This Part applies to an oral disposition as if contained in an instrument made when the disposition was made.

(3) For the purposes of this part, the death of the testator is the date at which a will or codicil is to be regarded as made.

(4) For the purposes of this Part, provisions of the law of intestate succession applicable to the estate of a deceased person shall be treated as if contained in an instrument executed by him (while of full capacity) immediately before the death.

(5) [*Repealed by the Trusts of Land and Appointment of Trustees Act 1996, s.25(2), Sched. 4.*]

GENERAL NOTE

This section is concerned with various matters relating to the disposition of property. **1–200**

Miscellaneous enactments

47.—(1) Section 39 does not apply for the purposes of the table of **1–201** kindred and affinity in Schedule 1 to the Marriage Act 1949 or sections 10 and 11 (incest) of the Sexual Offences Act 1956.

(2) [. . .] section 39 does not apply for the purposes of any provision of—

(a) [the British Nationality Act 1981],

(b) the Immigration Act 1971,

(c) any instrument having effect under an enactment within paragraph (a) or (b), or

(d) any other provision of the law for the time being in force which determines [British citizenship, British Dependent Territories citizenship [the status of a British National (Overseas)] or British Overseas citizenship].

(3) [*Repealed by the Social Security Act 1986, s.86(2), Sched. 11 and S.I. 1986 No. 1959*]

(4)(5) [*Repealed by the Social Security Act 1988, s.16(2), Sched. 5*]

AMENDMENT

In subs. (2) the words in square brackets were substituted by the Hong Kong (British Nationality) Order 1986, art. 8, Sched. and the British Nationality Act 1981, s.52(6), Sched. 7. The words omitted were repealed by *ibid.*, s.52(8), Sched. 9.

Subs. (1)

This subsection provides that adoption does not affect the law relating to incest and to **1–202** marriage and for these purposes an adopted child remains in his natural family. Although an adoptive person cannot marry his adoptive parent (Marriage Act 1949, Sched. 1, Pt. 1), there are not further restrictions on marrying within the adoptive family, *e.g.* a brother and sister by adoption can marry. An adopted child can ask the Registrar General to examine his birth certificate to check whether the person whom he intends to marry comes within the prohibited degrees of relationship for the purposes of the Marriage Act (s.51(2) and reg. 3 of S.I. 1991 No. 1981).

Subs. (2)

This subsection states that the general principle that an adopted child is to be treated as if **1–203** he had been born as a child of the adopters is not to apply to various statutes which deal with questions of immigration and nationality.

The British Nationality Act 1981: The exclusion of the provisions of this Act has the effect of preventing the acquisition of British nationality by adoption overseas. By virtue of s.1(5) of the 1981 Act, a child who is not a British Citizen will acquire that citizenship automatically on being adopted in this country, provided that the adopter or, in the case of a joint adoption, one of the adopters is a British citizen.

Pensions

48. Section 39(2) does not affect entitlement to a pension which is **1–204** payable to or for the benefit of a child and is in payment at the time of his adoption.

DEFINITIONS

adoption: s.38.

child: s.72(1).

1–205   This section provides that the general rule that an adopted child is to be treated as the child of the adopters does not affect his entitlement to a pension which is being paid at the time of his adoption.

Insurance
1–206   **49.** Where a child is adopted whose natural parent has effected an insurance with a friendly society or a collecting society or an industrial insurance company for the payment on the death of the child of money for funeral expenses, the rights and liabilities under the policy shall by virtue of the adoption be transferred to the adoptive parents who shall for the purposes of the enactments relating to such societies and companies be treated as the person who took out the policy.

DEFINITIONS
    adoption: s.38.
    adoptive parent: s.41.
    child: s.72(1).

GENERAL NOTE
1–207   This section explains the effect of adoption on certain policies of insurance.

PART V

REGISTRATION AND REVOCATION OF ADOPTION ORDERS AND CONVENTION ADOPTIONS

Adopted Children Register
1–208   **50.**—(1) The Registrar General shall maintain at the General Register Office a register, to be called the Adopted Children Register, in which shall be made such entries as may be directed to be made therein by adoption orders, but no other entries.

(2) A certified copy of an entry in the Adopted Children Register, if purporting to be sealed or stamped with the seal of the General Register Office, shall, without any further or other proof of that entry, be received as evidence of the adoption to which it relates and, where the entry contains a record of the date of the birth or the country or the district and sub-district of the birth of the adopted person, shall also be received as aforesaid as evidence of that date or country or district and sub-district in all respects as if the copy were a certified copy of an entry in the Registers of Births.

(3) The Registrar General shall cause an index of the Adopted Children Register to be made and kept in the General Register Office; and every person shall be entitled to search that index and to have a certified copy of any entry in the Adopted Children Register in all respects upon and subject to the same terms, conditions and regulations as to payment of fees and otherwise as are applicable under the Births and Deaths Registration Act 1953, and the Registration Service Act 1953, in respect of searches in other indexes kept in the General Register Office and in respect of the supply from that office of certified copies of entries in the certified copies of the Registers of Births and Deaths.

(4) The Registrar General shall, in addition to the Adopted Children Register and the index thereof, keep such other registers and books, and make such entries therein, as may be necessary to record and make traceable the connection between any entry in the Registers of Births which

has been marked "Adopted" and any corresponding entry in the Adopted Children Register.

(5) The registers and books kept under subsection (4) shall not be, nor shall any index thereof be, open to public inspection or search, and the Registrar General shall not furnish any person with any information contained in or with any copy or extract from any such registers or books except in accordance with section 51 or under an order of any of the following courts, that is to say—

(a) the High Court;

(b) the Westminster County Court or such other county court as may be prescribed; and

(c) the court by which an adoption order was made in respect of the person to whom the information, copy or extract relates.

(6) In relation to an adoption order made by a magistrates' court, the reference in paragraph (c) of subsection (5) to the court by which the order was made includes a reference to a court acting for the same petty session area.

(7) Schedule 1 to this Act, which, among other things, provides for the registration of adoptions and the amendment of adoption orders, shall have effect.

DEFINITIONS
  adoption order: s.72(1).
  prescribed: s.72(1).

TRANSITIONAL PROVISIONS
  See s.73(1), Sched. 2, para. 8.   **1–209**

GENERAL NOTE
  This section requires the Registrar General to maintain an Adopted Children's Register, **1–210** provides for certified copies of entries in the Register to be received as evidence, enables the public to search the indexes of the Register, and obliges the Registrar General to keep other registers and books in order that a link may be made between the entry in the Adopted Children's Register and the child's original registration of birth.

  In *Re X. (A Minor) (Adoption Details: Disclosure)* [1994] 3 All E.R. 372, CA, the local authority, supported by the child's guardian *ad litem*, applied for an order restricting the information to be placed on the Adopted Children Register by omitting the names, addresses and occupations of the adopters, on the grounds that there was a real risk that the mother, who had a severe personality disorder, would attempt to trace the child by searching the register, which was open to public inspection, and thereafter disrupt the placement of the child. The court held that while the statutory purpose of this section is clear in that it provides for the establishment and keeping of a register of adoptions and for the transmission of details contained on the register to members of the public, in a case such as this the court must regard the welfare of the child as the paramount consideration. Although it would be beyond the powers of the court to edit the entry to be made in the register, the court could exercise its inherent jurisdiction by making an order restricting the disclosure of the details entered on the register. In this case the court made an order that "during the minority of the child . . . the Registrar General should not disclose to any person without the leave of the court the details of the adoption entered in the Adopted Children Register."

Subs. (1)
  Such entries as may be directed: An entry is made in the Adopted Children's Register on **1–211** every occasion when an adoption order is made by a court in England and Wales (Sched. 1, para. 1).

Subs. (2)
  Shall . . . be received in evidence: The receipt in evidence documents receivable under Scots **1–212** law or the law of Northern Ireland is dealt with in s.60.

75

1–213   *Search:* At the General Register Office, St. Catherine's House, 10 Kingsway, London WC2.

Subs. (4)
1–214   *Make traceable the connection:* It is therefore possible to trace the original name and the natural parents of an adopted child. But note subs. (5).
Entry in the registers of births: Which will be marked "adopted" (Sched. 1 , para. 1(3)).

Subs. (5)
1–215   In *D. v. Registrar General* [1997] 1 F.L.R. 715, *sub nom. Re. L. (Adoption: Disclosure of Information)* [1997] 2 W.L.R. 747, the Court of Appeal, in holding that the presence of exceptional circumstances was necessary to persuade a court to override the statutory duty of non-disclosure imposed on the Registrar General by this provision, approved of the following statement made by Cazalet J. at first instance: the court cannot deal with an application simply upon the basis of the "understandable emotional desire in any birth relative to obtain information about an adopted adult. In my view it involves something more than the strongly held wish to know or the strong underlying curiosity to find out; there must be a need or benefit, which must relate to the adopted person rather than to the birth family." It was not sufficient for the applicant merely to establish a case of "sufficient weight and justification" as had been suggested in *Re H. (Adoption: Disclosure of Information)* [1995] 1 F.L.R. 236. In *Re H.* a woman with a treatable genetic disorder wished to trace her brother who had been adopted as a baby so that he could be screened for the disorder and receive treatement if necessary. The order was granted. In *Lawson v. Registrar General* (1956) 106 L.J. 204, disclosure was required to enable a legacy to be paid to the adopted child.

Thorpe J. made the following statement on procedural issues in his judgment in *Re H.*:
> "It seems to be quite inappropriate for applications under s.50(5) to be made *ex parte*. Seldom, if ever, will there be pressing urgency. There are many advantages in ensuring that the Registrar General has proper notice of any intended application to the court. Where any person, or organisation, wishes to invoke the court's jurisdiction then the application should be by summons issued, in the case of the High Court, out of the Principal Registry of the Family Division headed, 'In the matter of s.50(5) of the Adoption Act 1976' and joining the Registrar General as respondent. On the return date, the Registrar General will have the opportunity either of signifying his consent to the application or of appearing to oppose it."

Such other county court as may be prescribed: By rules (s.72(1)). No rules have been made.

Disclosure of birth records of adopted children
1–216   **51.**—(1) Subject to [what follows], the Registrar General shall on an application made in the prescribed manner by an adopted person a record of whose birth is kept by the Registrar General and who has attained the age of 18 years supply to that person on payment of the prescribed fee (if any) such information as is necessary to enable that person to obtain a certified copy of the record of his birth.

(2) On an application made in the prescribed manner by an adopted person under the age of 18 years, a record of whose birth is kept by the Registrar General and who is intending to be married in England or Wales, and on payment of the prescribed fee (if any), the Registrar General shall inform the applicant whether or not it appears from information contained in the registers of live births or other records that the applicant and the person whom he intends to marry may be within the prohibited degrees of relationship for the purposes of the Marriage Act 1949.

[(3) Before supplying any information to an applicant under subsection (1), the Registrar General shall inform the applicant that counselling services are available to him—

(a) if he is in England and Wales—

(i) at the General Register Office;

(ii) from the local authority in whose area he is living;

    (iii) where the adoption order relating to him was made in England and Wales, from the local authority in whose area the court which made the order sat; or

    (iv) from any other local authority;

  (b) if he is in Scotland—

    (i) from the regional or islands council in whose area he is living;

    (ii) where the adoption order relating to him was made in Scotland, from the council in whose area the court which made the order sat; or

    (iii) from any other regional or islands council;

  (c) if he is in Northern Ireland—

    (i) from the Board in whose area he is living;

    (ii) where the adoption order relating to him was made in Northern Ireland, from the Board in whose area the court which made the order sat; or

    (iii) from any other Board;

  (d) if he is in the United Kingdom and his adoption was arranged by an adoption society—

    (i) approved under section 3,

    (ii) approved under section 3 of the Adoption (Scotland) Act 1978,

    (iii) registered under Article 4 of the Adoption (Northern Ireland) Order 1987,

    from that society.

  (4) Where an adopted person who is in England and Wales—

  (a) applies for information under—

    (i) subsection (1), or

    (ii) Article 54 of the Adoption (Northern Ireland) Order 1987, or

  (b) is supplied with information under section 45 of the Adoption (Scotland) Act 1978,

it shall be the duty of the persons and bodies mentioned in subsection (5) to provide counselling for him if asked by him to do so.

  (5) The persons and bodies are—

  (a) the Registrar General;

  (b) any local authority falling within subsection (3)(a)(ii) to (iv);

  (c) any adoption society falling within subsection (3)(d) in so far as it is acting as an adoption society in England and Wales.

  (6) If the applicant chooses to receive counselling from a person or body falling within subsection (3), the Registrar General shall send to the person or body the information to which the applicant is entitled under subsection (1).

  (7) Where a person—

  (a) was adopted before November 12, 1975, and

  (b) applies for information under subsection (1),

the Registrar General shall not supply the information to him unless he has attended an interview with a counsellor by a person or body from whom counselling services are available as mentioned in subsection (3).

  (8) Where the Registrar General is prevented by subsection (7) from supplying information to a person who is not living in the United Kingdom, he may supply the information to any body which—

  (a) the Registrar General is satisfied is suitable to provide counselling to that person, and

  (b) has notified the Registrar General that it is prepared to provide such counselling.

(9) In this section—

"a Board" means a Health and Social Services Board established under Article 16 of the Health and Personal Social Services (Northern Ireland) Order 1972; and

"prescribed" means prescribed by regulations made by the Registrar General.]

AMENDMENTS
Subss. (3) to (9) were substituted by the Children Act 1989, s.88, Sched. 10, Pt. 1, para. 20.

DEFINITIONS
adoption order: s.72(1).
adoption society: s.72(1).
approved adoption society: s.72(1).
local authority: s.72(1).

GENERAL NOTE

1–217 This section gives an adopted person who is over the age of 18 the right to have the information necessary to enable him to obtain his original birth certificate. There is no corresponding provision which provides for the natural parent of an adopted person to obtain similar information which might lead to the identification of the adopted person. Those who were adopted before November 12, 1975, the date on which the Children Act 1975 was passed, are *required* to see a counsellor before they are supplied with the relevant information. Those who were adopted after that date will be *offered* the opportunity to see a counsellor, but counselling is not mandatory for this group. The section lists those who may provide counselling as, (1) the Registrar General's office, (2) the applicant's local authority, (3) the local authority in whose area the adoption order was made, and (4), the adoption society which arranged the adoption if it is an approved adoption society. See further, J. Treseliotis, *Obtaining Birth Certificates* (1984) and J. Feast, "Working in the adoption circle—outcomes of section 51 counselling", (1992) 4 *Adoption and Fostering* 46. During 1991 the total number of people who received counselling under this section was 3437 (G. Stafford (1993) 1 *Adoption and Fostering* 5).

In *R. v. Registrar General, ex p. Smith* [1991] 2 All E.R. 88, the Court of Appeal held that the absolute duty of the Registrar General under this section to provide a person with the information necessary to enable him to obtain a birth certificate was subject to the principle of public policy that the Registrar General should not comply with that duty if to do so would enable a person to benefit from a serious crime committed by him or which he intended to commit or if the circumstances were such that there was a current and justified apprehension of a significant risk that he might in the future use the information obtained to commit a serious crime. *Smith* was a case where, because of the severe disturbance of a man who had been adopted in his childhood, there was a likelihood of danger to the person who might be revealed as being his natural mother, following a search of the adoption register.

If an adopted person is under the age of 18 and intending to marry in England or Wales, this section gives him the right to require the Registrar General to inform him whether or not it appears from the records that he and his intended marriage partner may be within the degrees of relationship prohibited by Schedule 1 to the Marriage Act 1949.

For guidance to counsellors and parties to adoption on sources of information on adoption records, see G. Stafford, *Where to Find Adoption Records—A Guide for Counsellors* (BAAF, 1993). Also see DHSS Circular No. LAC (76) 21, para. 19 *et seq.* For a collection of personal accounts of those who have been involved in reunions between adopted people and their birth relatives, see *Preparing for Reunion* (The Children Society, 1994). In *Letter to Louise* (Corgi, 1993) Pauline Collins writes as a birth mother who has met with the daughter she gave up for adoption and in *The Adoption Papers* (Bloodaxe Books, 1991) Jackie Kay writes about a meeting with her birth mother.

Subs. (1)

1–218 *Application made in the prescribed manner.* See the Adopted Persons (Birth Records) Regulations 1991 (S.I. 1991 No. 1981). The address for postal applications for birth records is: The General Register Office, Postal Applications Section, Smedley Hydro, Trafalgar Road, Southport, Merseyside PR8 2HH. Persons adopted in Northern Ireland should write to: The General Register Office, Oxford House, 49–55 Chichester Street, Belfast BT1 4HL. The address for persons adopted in Scotland is: The General Register Office, Adoptions Unit, New Register House, Edinburgh EH1 3YT.

A record of whose birth: An adopted person born abroad of British parents will therefore be included.

Attained the age: See the note on s.14(1).

That person: The information can only be supplied to the adopted person.

Certified copy of the record of his birth: The information on a birth certificate includes the name of the birth mother and her address at that time; it may have her maiden name, if any, and possibly the name, address and occupation of the birth father.

Subs. (2)

Application: Which will probably only be made in circumstances where the applicant has **1–219** information to suggest that his or her intended spouse may come within the prohibited degrees of relationship. Counselling is not required or provided for in the case of an application under this subsection.

Prescribed manner: See subs. (1).

A record of whose birth: See subs. (1).

Married in England or Wales: An adopted person intending to be married abroad is not covered by this provision.

Subs. (3)

Counselling: The purpose of counselling is to "provide an opportunity for the counsellor to **1–220** bring to the attention of the adopted person the implications and possible unhappy consequences of learning his origins and, in particular, trying to trace his parents, the result of which might be to deter him from pursuing his application"; *R. v. Registrar General, ex p. Smith, per* McCowan L.J. at 97.

Advice on counselling, together with the addresses of specialist post-adoption agencies can be found in "If you are adopted", a leaflet produced by the British Agencies for Adoption and Fostering, 11 Southwark Street, London SE1 1RQ. Two informative booklets on counselling have been produced by the Registrar General. They are "Access to Birth Records—Notes for Counsellors" (A.C.R. 113) and "Access to Birth Records—Information for Adopted People in the UK" (A.C.R. 100). They can be obtained from the Adoption Section of the General Registrar Office, the address of which is given above.

Local authority: Is also under a duty to provide a counselling service by virtue of s.1(2)(c).

Subs. (5)

Adoption society: The disclosure of information identifying the agency that arranged the **1–221** adoption is permitted by the Adoption Rules 1984, r.53(3)(b)(ii) and the Magistrate's Courts (Adoption) Rules 1984, r.32(5)(b)(ii).

Subs. (7)

This provision was enacted because of concern about the position of natural parents who **1–222** had placed their children for adoption prior to the passing of the Children Act 1975 with a promise of complete confidentiality.

Subs. (8)

Not living in the United Kingdom: Two booklets for such people have been published by the **1–223** Registrar General. They are: "Access to Birth Records—Information for Adopted People Living Outside the United Kingdom" (A.C.R. 101) and "Access to Birth Records— Counselling Organisations Outside the United Kingdom" (A.C.R. 114). Both booklets can be obtained from the Adoption Section of the General Registrar Office, the address of which is given above.

[Adoption Contact Register

51A.—(1) The Registrar General shall maintain at the General Register **1–224** Office a register to be called the Adoption Contact Register.

(2) The register shall be in two parts—

(a) Part I: Adopted Persons; and

(b) Part II: Relatives.

(3) The Registrar General shall, on payment of such fee as may be prescribed, enter in Part I of the register the name and address of any adopted person who fulfils the conditions in subsection (4) and who gives notice that he wishes to contact any relative of his.

(4) The conditions are that—

(a) a record of the adopted person's birth is kept by the Registrar General; and

(b) the adopted person has attained the age of 18 years and—

    (i) has been supplied by the Registrar General with information under section 51; or

    (ii) has satisfied the Registrar General that he has such information as is necessary to enable him to obtain a certified copy of the record of his birth.

(5) The Registrar General shall, on payment of such fee as may be prescribed, enter in Part II of the register the name and address of any person who fulfils the conditions in subsection (6) and who gives notice that he wishes to contact an adopted person.

(6) The conditions are that—

(a) a record of the adopted persons's birth is kept by the Registrar General; and

(b) the person giving notice under subsection (5) has attained the age of 18 years and has satisfied the Registrar General that—

    (i) he is a relative of the adopted person; and

    (ii) he has such information as is necessary to enable him to obtain a certified copy of the record of the adopted person's birth.

(7) The Registrar General shall, on receiving notice from any person named in an entry in the register that he wishes the entry to be cancelled, cancel the entry.

(8) Any notice given under this section must be in such form as may be determined by the Registrar General.

(9) The Registrar General shall transmit to an adopted person whose name is entered in Part I of the register the name and address of any relative in respect of whom there is an entry in Part II of the register.

(10) Any entry cancelled under subsection (7) ceases from the time of cancellation to be an entry for the purposes of subsection (9).

(11) The register shall not be open to public inspection or search and the Registrar General shall not supply any person with information entered in the register (whether in an uncancelled or a cancelled entry) except in accordance with this section.

(12) The register may be kept by means of a computer.

(13) In this section—

(a) "relative" means any person (other than an adoptive relative) who is related to the adopted person by blood (including half-blood) or marriage;

(b) "address" includes any address at or through which the person concerned may be contacted; and

(c) "prescribed" means prescribed by the Secretary of State."]

AMENDMENT

This section was inserted by the Children Act 1989, s.88, Sched. 10, para. 21.

GENERAL NOTE

1–225   This section places a duty on the Registrar General to maintain an Adoption Contact Register. The Register is in two parts—one for adopted persons and one for relatives. Its purpose is to put adopted people and their birth parents or other relatives in touch with each other where this is what they both want. The Registrar General is required to register eligible applicants in the relevant register and to transmit to an adopted person on the register the name and address of any relative in respect of whom there is an entry on the register. No information about the adopted person will be given to the relative except that the Registrar General will inform the relative when his details have been sent to the adopted person. The decision about whether or not to establish contact is left to the adopted person. The register is only open to people who are at least 18 years of age, and in order to use the register, the people concerned will have to satisfy the Registrar General of the identity and, in the case of the relative, of their relationship with the adopted person. There is no provision in this section that would enable a person to register that he does not want to be contacted. An alternative method of obtaining information from the Registrar General is to be found in s.50(5).

There is no requirement for counselling under this section (c.f. s.51).

The purpose and operation of the Adoption Contact Register is described in Department of Health Circular No. LAC (91)9. Information on the Register can also be found in booklet ACR 110 produced by the Registrar General. Copies can be obtained from: Adoption Section, The General Registrar Office, Office of Population Censuses and Surveys, Smedley Hydro, Trafalgar Road, Birkdale, Southport PR8 2HH. Also see, L. Lambert, et al., "Using contact registers in adoption searches", (1992) 1 *Adoption and Fostering* 42.

In 1996 there were 7,309 adopted people on Part I of the register and 4,121 birth relatives on Part II. Since the register was established in 1991 there have been 128 "links". In the vast majority of these cases the relative has been the birth mother; see *Adoption and Fostering News*, Autumn 1996.

Subs. (1)

Registrar General: The address of the Registrar General can be found in the General Note **1–226** to this section. A similar service has been provided by Family Care, 21 Castle Street, Edinburgh EH2 3DN.

Subs. (3)

Such fee as may be prescribed: The fee payable is £9.50 (The Adopted Persons (Contact **1–227** Register) (Fees) Rules 1991 (S.I. 1991 No. 952), r.2(1)).

Subs. (5)

Such fee as may be prescribed: The fee payable is £27.50 (S.I. 1991 No. 952, r. 2(2)).   **1–228**

Revocation of adoptions on legitimation

52.—(1) Where any person adopted by his father or mother alone has **1–229** subsequently become a legitimated person on the marriage of his father and mother, the court by which the adoption order was made may, on the application of any of the parties concerned, revoke that order.

(2) Where any person legitimated by virtue of section 1 of the Legitimacy Act 1959, had been adopted by his father and mother before the commencement of that Act, the court by which the adoption order was made may, on the application of any of the parties concerned, revoke that order.

(3) Where a person adopted by his father or mother alone by virtue of a regulated adoption has subsequently become a legitimated person on the marriage of his father and mother, the High Court may, upon an application under this subsection by the parties concerned, by order revoke the adoption.

(4) In relation to an adoption order made by a magistrates' court, the reference in subsections (1) and (2) to the court by which the order was made includes a reference to a court acting for the same petty sessions area.

DEFINITIONS
  adoption order: s.72(1).
  regulated adoption: s.72(1).

GENERAL NOTE

This section provides for the revocation of the adoption order of an illegitimate child if the **1–230** subsequent marriage of his parents legitimises him.

1–231 *Subsequently become a legitimate person:* But an adopted child cannot be illegitimate (see s.39(4) and the note thereto).

Application: See the Adoption Rules 1984, r.49(1) and the Magistrate's Courts (Adoption) Rules 1984, r.28(1)(2).

Revoke that order: With the child becoming the legitimate child of both parents instead of the adopted child of one and the step-child of the other. Section 1(6) of the British Nationality Act 1981 provides that a person who becomes a British citizen by adoption after that Act came into force will not lose his citizenship if the adoption subsequently comes to an end.

Subs. (3)

1–232 *Application:* The manner of making an application is provided for in s.54.

Annulment, etc. of overseas adoptions

1–233 **53.**—(1) The High Court may, upon an application under this subsection, by order annul a regulated adoption [or an adoption effected by a Convention adoption order]—

(a) on the ground that at the relevant time the adoption was prohibited by a notified provision, if under the internal law then in force in the country of which the adopter was then a national or the adopters were then nationals the adoption could have been impugned on that ground;

(b) on the ground that at the relevant time the adoption contravened provisions relating to consents of the internal law relating to adoption of the country of which the adopted person was then a national, if under that law the adoption could then have been impugned on that ground;

(c) on any other ground on which the adoption can be impugned under the law for the time being in force in the country in which the adoption was effected.

(2) The High Court may, upon an application under this subsection—

(a) order that an overseas adoption or a determination shall cease to be valid in Great Britain on the ground that the adoption or determination is contrary to public policy or that the authority which purported to authorise the adoption or make the determination was not competent to entertain the case;

(b) decide the extent, if any, to which a determination has been affected by a subsequent determination.

(3) Any court in Great Britain may, in any proceedings in that court, decide that an overseas adoption or a determination shall, for the purposes of those proceedings, be treated as invalid in Great Britain on either of the grounds mentioned in subsection (2).

(4) An order or decision of the Court of Session on an application under subsection (3) of section 6 of the Adoption Act 1968 shall be recognised and have effect as if it were an order or decision of the High Court on an application under subsection (3) of this section.

(5) Except as provided by this section and section 52(3) the validity of an overseas adoption or a determination shall not be impugned in England and Wales in proceedings in any court.

AMENDMENTS

In subs. (1) the words in square brackets were inserted by the Domestic Proceedings and Magistrates' Courts Act 1978, s.74.

    determination: s.54(4).
    notified provision: s.54(4).
    relevant time: s.54(4).
    internal law: s.71.
    Convention adoption order: s.72(1).
    regulated adoption: s.72(1).
    overseas adoption: s.72(2).

GENERAL NOTE

This section enables the High Court to annul a Convention adoption order and to order **1–234** that an overseas adoption shall cease to be valid in Great Britain. For the setting aside of adoption orders, see the General Note to s.12.

Subs. (1)

Application: Which, except with leave of the court, cannot be made later than two years **1–235** after the date of the adoption to which it relates (Adoption Rules, r. 37(2)). Either the child or the adopters must reside in England or Wales at the time when the application is made (s.54(2)).

Annul: The provisions of s.1(6) of the British Nationality Act 1981, whereby a person acquiring British nationality as a consequence of an adoption order retained that nationality if the adoption order ceased to have effect, only applies to an order made subsequent to the adoption proceedings and not to an order made on appeal in the adoption proceedings themselves (*Re K. (A Minor) (Adoption Order: Nationality)* [1994] 2 F.L.R. 557, CA).

Notified provision: For the purpose of this section the provisions set out in the Schedule to the Convention Adoption (Miscellaneous Provisions) Order 1978, (S.I. 1978 No. 1432) are specified as the provisions relating to prohibitions on an adoption contained in the national law of the United Kingdom which have been notified by the Government in pursuance of the Convention of Jurisdiction, Applicable Law and Recognition of Decrees relating to Adoptions, Cmnd. 7342.

Internal law: As to countries where there are two or more systems of internal law, see s.71(2).

National: Provisions relating to nationality are contained in s.70.

Great Britain: See the note on s.56(1).

Subs. (2)

This subsection provides for the High Court to declare invalid in Great Britain a **1–236** determination made in a Convention country or a specified country relating to an adoption under the Hague Convention, or an overseas adoption which was not granted under the Convention but which would nevertheless otherwise be recognised in Great Britain by the Adoption (Designation of Overseas Adoptions) Order 1973 (S.I. 1973 No. 18.).

Subs. (3)

If the validity of an adoption arises as an incidental question in the course of other **1–237** proceedings, the court (*i.e.* any court) can utilise the grounds in subs. (2).

Provisions supplementary to ss.52(3) and 53

54.—(1) Any application for an order under section 52(3) or 53 or a **1–238** decision under section 53(3) shall be made in the prescribed manner and within such period, if any, as may be prescribed.

(2) No application shall be made under section 52(3) or section 53(1) in respect of an adoption unless immediately before the application is made the person adopted or the adopter habitually resides in England and Wales or, as the case may be, both adopters habitually reside there.

(3) In deciding in pursuance of section 53 whether such an authority as is mentioned in section 59 was competent to entertain a particular case, a court shall be bound by any finding of fact made by the authority and stated by the authority to be so made for the purpose of determining whether the authority was competent to entertain the case.

(4) In section 53—

"determination" means such a determination as is mentioned in section 59 of this Act;

"notified provision" means a provision specified in an order of the Secretary of State as one in respect of which a notification to or by the Government of the United Kingdom was in force at the relevant time in pursuance of the provisions of the Convention relating to prohibitions contained in the national law of the adopter; and

"relevant time" means the time when the adoption in question purported to take effect under the law of the country in which it purports to have been effected.

DEFINITIONS
   the Convention: s.72(1).
   prescribed: s.72(1).

Subs. (1)
1-239   *Prescribed manner:* See the Adoption Rules 1984, rr.37 to 41, Sched 1, Forms 9 to 11.

Subs. (4)
1-240   *Notified provision:* See the Convention Adoption (Austria and Switzerland) Order 1978 (S.I. 1978 No. 1431) and the Convention Adoption (Miscellaneous Provisions) Order 1978 (S.I. 1978 No. 1432).

PART VI

MISCELLANEOUS AND SUPPLEMENTAL

Adoption of children abroad
1-241   **55.**—(1) Where on an application made in relation to a child by a person who is not domiciled in England and Wales or Scotland [or Northern Ireland] an authorised court is satisfied that he intends to adopt the child under the law of or within the country in which the applicant is domiciled, the court may, subject to the following provisions of this section, make an order [giving him parental responsibility for the child].

(2) The provisions of Part II relating to adoption orders, except sections 12(1), 14(2), 15(2), 17 to 21 and 25, shall apply in relation or orders under this section as they apply in relation to adoption orders subject to the modification that in section 13(1) for "19" and "13" there are substituted "32" and "26" respectively.

(3) Sections 50 and 51 and paragraphs 1 and 2(1) of Schedule 1 shall apply in relation to an order under this section as they apply in relation to an adoption order except that any entry in the Registers of Births, or the Adopted Children Register which is required to be marked in consequence of the making of an order under this section shall, in lieu of being marked with the word "Adopted" or "Re-adopted" (with or without the addition of [words "(Scotland)" or "(Northern Ireland)"], be marked with the words "Proposed foreign adoption" or "Proposed foreign re-adoption," as the case may require.

(4) [. . .]

AMENDMENTS
   The amendments to this section were made by the Children Act 1989, s.88, Sched. 10, Pt. 1, para. 22 and *ibid.* s.108(7), Sched. 15.

    child: s.72(1).
    authorised court: ss.62, 72(1).
    adoption order: s.72(1).

GENERAL NOTE

Under s.56, it is an offence to take or send a child who is a British subject out of Great **1–242**
Britain to any place outside the United Kingdom with a view to the adoption of the child. This
section allows for an exception to this prohibition by enabling a "court to authorise a
proposed foreign adoption where the applicants wish to adopt the child but are not domiciled
in this country. An order authorising a proposed foreign adoption gives them [parental
responsibility] and permits them to take the child out of Great Britain for adoption in their
own country. The court must therefore be satisfied that the applicants intend to adopt the
child under their own country's law. All the usual requirements for an adoption order apply in
these cases, including the requirement for parental agreement, except that where the child has
been placed for adoption by an adoption agency he must be at least 32 weeks old and the
applicants must have cared for him throughout the 26 weeks before the order is made. The
usual restrictions on the removal of the child pending the hearing apply in these cases, and the
placing agency or local authority must supervise the placement until the case is decided,"
D.H.S.S. Circular No. LAC (84)2, para. 30.

If the child is in the care of a local authority, they may arrange for the child to emigrate,
with the approval of the court, by virtue of the Children Act 1989, Sched. 2, para. 19.

Subs. (1)

An application: See the Adoption Rules 1984, r.48.   **1–243**
Authorised court: A magistrates' court is not an authorised court for this purpose (s.62(6)).
Intends to adopt the child: The applicant does not have to satisfy the court that it is his
immediate intention to adopt the child and he cannot be compelled to adopt the child once he
has been granted parental responsibility under this section.
The applicant: Who must file expert evidence of the law of adoption in the country in which
he is domiciled (Adoption Rules 1984, r.48(3)).

Subs. (2)

This subsection states that, apart from specified exceptions, all the requirements relating to **1–244**
procedure, prerequisites and prohibitions which are applicable to an ordinary adoption
application must be satisfied before an order under this section can be made.
Section 12(1): An order made under this section does not have the effect in English law of
an adoption order.
For "19" and "13" there are substituted "32" and "26" respectively: The child, who cannot be
younger than 32 weeks, must have had his home with the prospective adopters for at least 26
weeks.

Subs. (3)

Registers of births: See Sched. 1, para. 2.   **1–245**
Adopted children register: See s.50.

Restriction on removal of children for adoption outside Great Britain

56.—(1) Except under the authority of an order under section 55, **1–246**
[section 49 of the Adoption (Scotland) Act 1978 or Article 57 of the
Adoption (Northern Ireland) Order 1987] it shall not be lawful for any
person to take or send a child who is a British subject or a citizen of the
Republic of Ireland out of Great Britain to any place outside the [United
Kingdom, the Channel Islands and the Isle of Man] with a view to the
adoption of the child by any person not being a parent or guardian or
relative of the child; and any person who takes or sends a child out of Great
Britain to any place in contravention of this subsection, or makes or takes
part in any arrangements for [placing a child with] any person for that
purpose, shall be guilty of an offence and liable on summary conviction to
imprisonment for a term not exceeding three months or to a fine not
exceeding [level 5 on the standard scale] or to both.

(2) In any proceedings under this section, a report by a British consular officer or a deposition made before a British consular officer and authenticated under the signature of that officer shall, upon proof that the officer or the deponent cannot be found in the United Kingdom, be admissible as evidence of the matters stated therein, and it shall not be necessary to prove the signature or official character of the person who appears to have signed any such report or deposition.

(3) A person shall be deemed to take part in arrangements for [placing a child with] a person for the purpose referred to in subsection (1) if—

(a) he facilitates the placing of the child [with] that person; or

(b) he initiates or takes part in any negotiations of which the purpose or effect is the conclusion of any agreement or the making of any arrangement therefor, and if he causes another person to do so.

AMENDMENT

In subs. (1) the final set of words in square brackets were substituted by the Criminal Justice Act 1982, ss.38, 46. The remaining amendments to this section were made by the Children Act 1989, s.88, Sched. 10, Pt. 1, para. 23.

DEFINITIONS

child: s.72(1).
guardian: s.72(1).
relative: s.72(1).

GENERAL NOTE

1–247   This section makes it an offence to take or send a child who is a British subject to any place outside the United Kingdom for the purpose of his being adopted by a person who is not a relative, parent or guardian, except under the authority of an order made under s.55, or under s.49 of the Adoption (Scotland) Act 1978 or Art. 57 of the Adoption (Northern Ireland) Order 1987.

Wardship proceedings cannot be used to circumvent the absolute prohibition imposed by this section (*Re M. (A Minor)* [1973] Fam. 66).

Subs. (1)

1–248   *Any person:* Or corporation (Interpretation Act 1978, s.5, Sched. 1).

Great Britain: Means England, Scotland and Wales.

United Kingdom: Means Great Britain and Northern Ireland (Interpretation Act 1978, Sched. 1).

British subject: See s.5(1) of the British Nationality Act 1981.

With a view to adoption: The prohibition imposed by this section covers cases where, although immediate adoption is not contemplated, the removal is one step in a larger process, the ultimate purpose of which is adoption (*Re M. (A Minor)* [1973] Fam. 66).

Parent: Does not include the natural father of an illegitimate child who does not have parental responsibility (s.72(1)). However, such a person is included in the definition of "relative" in s.72(1).

Guardian: In *Re C. (Minors) (Wardship: Adoption)* [1989] 1 All E.R. 395, the Court of Appeal doubted whether the court had any inherent jurisdiction to appoint guardians in the presence of an existing wardship, as this would be a derogation of the wardship jurisdiction being exercised by the court. In this case guardians had been appointed as a means of avoiding the embargo contained in this section.

Relative: The definition of this term in s.72(1) is clear and precise and does not include the great-uncle of the child; see *Re C*, above, and the note on s.72(1).

Subs. (2)

1–249   *Consular officer:* This has the meaning assigned by Art. 1 of the Vienna Convention, set out in Sched. 1 to the Consular Relations Act 1968 (Interpretation Act 1978, s.5, Sched. 1).

Prohibition on certain payments

57.—(1) Subject to the provisions of this section, it shall not be lawful to **1–250** make or give to any person any payment or reward for or in consideration of—

(a) the adoption by that person of a child;

(b) the grant by that person of any agreement or consent required in connection with the adoption of a child;

(c) the [handing over of a child by that person] with a view to the adoption of the child; or

(d) the making by that person of any arrangements for the adoption of a child.

(2) Any person who makes or gives, or agrees or offers to make or give, any payment or reward prohibited by this section, or who receives or agrees to receive or attempts to obtain any such payment or rewards, shall be guilty of an offence and liable on summary conviction to imprisonment for a term not exceeding three months or to a fine not exceeding [level 5 on the standard scale] or to both; [. . .].

(3) This section does not apply to any payment made to an adoption agency by a parent or guardian of a child or by a person who adopts or proposes to adopt a child, being a payment in respect of expenses reasonably incurred by the agency in connection with the adoption of the child, or to any payment or reward authorised by the court to which an application for an adoption order in respect of a child is made.

[(3A) This section does not apply to—

(a) any payment made by an adoption agency to a person who has applied or proposes to apply to a court for an adoption order or an order under section 55 (adoption of children abroad), being a payment of or towards any legal or medical expenses incurred or to be incurred by that person in connection with the application; or

(b) any payment made by an adoption agency to another adoption agency in consideration of the placing of a child [with] any person with a view to the child's adoption; or

(c) any payment made by an adoption agency to a voluntary organisation for the time being approved for the purposes of this paragraph by the Secretary of State as a fee for the services of that organisation in putting that adoption agency into contact with another adoption agency with a view to the making of arrangements between the adoption agencies for the adoption of a child.

In paragraph (c) "voluntary organisation" means a body, other than a public or local authority, the activities of which are not carried on for profit.]

(4)–(10) [*Repealed by the Children Act* 1989, *s.*108(7), *Sched.* 15.]

AMENDMENT

In subs. (2) the words in square brackets were substituted by the Criminal Justice Act 1982, ss.38, 46. Subs. (3A) was inserted by the Criminal Law Act 1977, s.65, Sched. 12. The remaining amendments were made by the Children Act 1989 s.88, Sched. 10, Pt. 1, para. 25 and s.108(7), Sched. 15.

DEFINITIONS

adoption agency: s.1(4).
child: s.72(1).
guardian: s.72(1).
parent: s.72(1).
place of safety: s.72(1).

1–251   Under this section it is an offence to give or receive any payment or reward in consideration of adoption. This general prohibition is subject to the exceptions set out in subs. (3) and (3A).

There are conflicting decisions on the issue of whether this section has extraterritorial effect. Bracewell J. in *Re A.W. (Adoption Application)* [1993] 1 F.L.R. 62, Lincoln J. in *Re A. (Adoption Placement)* [1988] 2 F.L.R. 133 and Douglas Brown J. in *Re Adoption Application (Non-Patrial: Breach of Procedures)* [1993] 1 F.L.R. 947 concluded that there is no extra-territorial jurisdiction. The opposite conclusion was reached by Hollings J. in *Re An Adoption Application* [1992] 1 F.L.R. 341. It is likely that Hollings J. is wrong on this issue because, as Douglas Brown J. pointed out in *Re Adoption Application* at 954, "there is an established presumption that, in the absence of clear and specific words to the contrary, a statute does not make conduct outside the jurisdiction a criminal offence".

This section is considered by Ralph Sandland in "Problems in the criminal law of adoptions", (1995) 17(2) *Journal of Social Welfare and Family Law* 149.

Subs. (1)

1–252   *Any person:* Including parents, prospective adopters and adoption agencies.

Agreement or consent: See especially ss.16(1)(*b*)(i), 17(6) and 18(1)(*a*), (2)(*a*).

Payment or reward for . . . adoption: The question of whether there had been any such payment or reward is a question of fact to be decided on the evidence. Where a couple had entered into a surrogacy agreement with a surrogate mother this provision will not be contravened if it is only after the payments had been made and the baby had been born that the parties had contemplated adoption and the legalities of the situation. (*Re An Adoption Application (Surrogacy)* [1987] 2 All E.R. 826, Latey J.; considered by S.P. De Cruz at [1987] J.S.W.L. 314 to 319). In this case Latey J. held that in order to be illegal the payment or reward has to be commercial or for profit. A contrary conclusion was reached by Bracewell J. in *Re A.W.*, above, who was "compelled to the conclusion that a commercial or profit motive is wholly irrelevant to whether a breach has actually been committed" (at 74). In *Re An Adoption Application*, above payments made for a private home study report relating to the adoption of a foreign child and payments made to foreign lawyers for arranging the adoption were held to contravene this section. A similar finding was made by Lincoln J. in *Re A. (Adoption Placement)*, above. However, in *Re A.W.*, Bracewell J., in holding that such payments were illegal, said that "whether the payment is to reimburse hospital expenses for the delivery or, at the other end of the scale, to commercially traffic and buy a child, such payment is unlawful, but the nature and purpose of the payment are crucial factors in assessing whether it is appropriate to give [dispensation under subs. (3)]" (at 74). In *Re Adoption Application (Non-Patrial: Breach of Procedures)*, above. Douglas Brown J. having reviewed the above-mentioned authorities, held that payments to professionals such as independent social workers and doctors to provide independent assessment, opinion and analysis which might or might not be favourable to the applicants were not covered by this provision because in agreeing to provide a report they were not entering into or making "any . . . agreement or arrangement for or for facilitating the adoption of the child." On the other hand payments made to a lawyer who was concerned with making arrangements for the adoption of the child were caught by this section.

Arrangements for the adoption of a child: Is defined in s.72(3).

Subs. (3)

1–253   *Authorised by the court: i.e.* any authorised court. The court has a discretion to authorise payments retrospectively. In exercising that discretion the court should balance all the circumstances of the case, with the welfare of the child as first consideration, against the degree of taint of the transaction for which authorisation is asked. (*Re An Adoption Application (Surrogacy)*, above.) In *Re Adoption Application (Non-Patrial: Breach of Procedures)*, above, Douglas Brown J. said, at 957, that once "adoption proceedings have been commenced in whatever court, it will be possible to apply for prior or retrospective authority". Note, however, that in *Re C. (A Minor) (Adoption Application)* [1993] 1 F.L.R. 87, Booth J. said that "whether or not the High Court, by an order, can retrospectively authorise an illegal placement is not, I think, altogether clear. There are two authorities which suggest that retrospective authorisation is within the terms of the statute. One is *Re A. (Adoption Placement)*, a decision of Anthony Lincoln J. . . . The second is a decision of my own, *Re Z.H.H. (Adoption Application)* [1993] 1 F.L.R. 83. . . . If such a power to authorise an illegal placement does exist, then, in my judgment, the court should exercise its discretion with great caution and only give authorisation where the placement is entirely in the interests of the child concerned, and an adoption order is also in his best interests" (at 94). In *Re C.* Booth J. refused to authorise payments that would "amount to ratifying the sale of a child for adoption" in circumstances where the applicants were unsuitable. In *Re M.W. (Adoption: Surrogacy)* [1995] 2 F.L.R. 759, Judge Calman authorised the payment to a surrogate mother of "£7,500 by way of expenses for loss of wages and otherwise". Adoption orders have been made despite breaches of this provision where the court has concluded that such an order would promote the child's welfare; see *Re An Adoption Application (Surrogacy)*, above, *Re A.W. (Adoption Application)*, above and *Re W.M. (Adoption: Non-Patrial)* [1997] 1 F.L.R. 132.

Subs. (3A)

This subsection declares the legality of three types of payment made by adoption agencies— **1–254**
- (i) payment made to adoptive parents or prospective adopters in respect of legal or medical expenses incurred by them in connection with the adoption;
- (ii) payment made to another adoption agency which has found an adoptive home for a child whose placement was sought by the paying agency;
- (iii) payment made to an approved voluntary organisation by an adoption agency which was seeking an adoptive home for a child, as a fee for the organisation's services in putting the agency in touch with another adoption agency with a view to arrangements being made for the child's adoption.

Para. (a)

"This provision, in my judgment, sanctions the payment or reimbursement of fees paid by **1–255** an applicant to . . . professional men in connection with the application in an agency adoption . . . [It] would provide a complete answer for a doctor or solicitor charged with an offence under this section in an agency adoption . . . ," *per* Douglas Brown J. in *Re Adoption Application (Non-Patrial: Breach of Procedures)*, above, at 953.

Approved: The Adoption Resource Exchange has been approved by the Secretary of State for Social Services for the purposes of paragraph (c) (D.H.S.S. Circular No. LAC (77)18, para. 8).

Not carried on for profit: It is likely that a body will not be held to be "carried on for profit" if the making of a profit is not one of its main objects, but is only a subsidiary object; *i.e.* it is only a means whereby the organisation's main objects can be furthered or achieved; see *National Deposit Friendly Society Trustees v. Skegness Urban District Council* [1959] A.C. 293, *per* Lord Denning at 319, 320.

[Permitted allowances

57A.—(1) The Secretary of State may make regulations for the purpose **1–256** of enabling adoption agencies to pay allowances to persons who have adopted, or intend to adopt, children in pursuance of arrangements made by the agencies.

(2) Section 57(1) shall not apply to any payment made by an adoption agency in accordance with the regulations.

(3) The regulations may, in particular, make provision as to—
- (a) the procedure to be followed by any agency in determining whether a person should be paid an allowance;
- (b) the circumstances in which an allowance may be paid;
- (c) the factors to be taken into account in determining the amount of an allowance;
- (d) the procedure for review, variation and termination of allowances; and
- (e) the information about allowances to be supplied by any agency to any person who is intending to adopt a child.

(4) Any scheme approved under section 57(4) shall be revoked as from the coming into force of this section.

(5) Section 57(1) shall not apply in relation to any payment made—
- (a) in accordance with a scheme revoked under subsection (4) or section 57(5)(b); and
- (b) to a person to whom such payments were made before the revocation of the scheme.

(6) Subsection (5) shall not apply where any person to whom any payments may lawfully be made by virtue of subsection (5) agrees to receive (instead of such payments) payments complying with regulations made under this section.]

AMENDMENT
This section was inserted by the Children Act 1989, s.88, Sched. 10, Pt. 1, para. 25.

DEFINITIONS
adoption agency: s.72(1).
child: s.72(1).

GENERAL NOTE

1–257   This section enables the Secretary of State to make regulations enabling adoption agencies to pay allowances to "persons who have adopted, or intend to adopt, children in pursuance of arrangements made by the agencies." The object of adoption allowances is to encourage the adoption of whole families, children with handicaps and long term foster-children, where applicants might be deterred by the expense or loss of the fostering allowance. The regulations replace the provisions contained in the repealed s.56(4) to (7) under which agencies had to submit to the Secretary of State their own allowance schemes for his approval. The Adoption Allowance Regulations 1991 (S.I. 1991 No. 2030) came into force on October 14, 1991. Guidance on the Regulations is contained in Chapter 2 of *The Children Act 1989: Guidance and Regulations*, Vol. 9 *Adoption Issues*.

The operation of adoption allowance schemes approved under s.56 is considered by L. Lambert and J. Seglow in, *Adoption Allowances in England and Wales: The Early Years* (1988). According to Government guidance this research "firmly demonstrated the importance of adoption allowances in facilitating the adoption for children who would otherwise be unlikely to have the opportunity for permanence and security which adoptions provides" (*ibid.*, para. 2.7).

Restriction on advertisements

1–258   **58.**—(1) It shall not be lawful for any advertisement to be published indicating—

(a) that the parent or guardian of a child desires to cause a child to be adopted; or

(b) that a person desires to adopt a child; or

(c) that any person (not being an adoption agency) is willing to make arrangements for the adoption of a child.

(2) Any person who causes to be published or knowingly publishes an advertisement in contravention of the provisions of this section shall be guilty of an offence and liable on summary conviction to a fine not exceeding [level 5 on the standard scale].

AMENDMENT
In subs. (2) the words in square brackets were substituted by the Criminal Justice Act 1982, ss.38, 46.

DEFINITIONS
adoption agency: s.1(4).
child: s.72(1).
guardian: s.72(1).
parent: s.72(1).

GENERAL NOTE

1–259   This section makes it an offence either for parents or for prospective adoptive parents to advertise their desire for adoption, or for anyone other than an adoption agency to advertise their willingness to make adoption arrangements. It is not an offence for an adoption agency to advertise the fact that it has a particular child who is available for adoption, as long as it does not indicate that a parent or guardian desires the child to be adopted. The use of advertisements by adoption agencies to find families for "hard to place" children is now a common practice.

In *Royal Borough of Kensington and Chelsea v. K and Q* [1989] 1 F.L.R. 399, children were the subject of wardship proceedings in which a placement with a view to adoption had been authorised. The local authority decided that it was necessary and desirable that they, as an adoption agency, should be allowed to use television for the purposes of advertising with the intention of seeking adopters for the children. The authority applied to the court for directions as to the use of television for this purpose and Hollings J. gave directions as follows:

"(1) I declare that it is lawful for a local authority to seek potential adopters for a child in their care by means of the advertisements. . . .

(2) Where the child is a ward of court, leave of the court is required.

(3) In giving leave, the court shall regard the welfare of the child the first and paramount consideration. It is not a decision relating to the adoption of a child and therefore s.6 of the Adoption Act 1976 does not apply.

(4) Where the child has already been placed in the care of the local authority and leave to place the child with long-term foster-parents has already been granted, or the child has been freed for adoption, an application for leave shall be made in the first instance to a registrar *ex parte* and in normal circumstances it would be appropriate for the registrar to deal with the application on this basis. In cases where the Official Solicitor acts on behalf of the children notice of intention to apply for such leave should be given to him. This is, of course, without prejudice to the registrar's discretion to deal with the matter *inter partes* or to refer the matter to a judge.

(5) In deciding whether or not to grant leave the court should have regard to the age and circumstance of a child, that the confidentiality of the wardship proceedings must be preserved, that the surname of the child must not be given nor may any details of the reason he is in care.

(6) In deciding whether or not to grant leave for advertising by the medium of television the court should have regard to whether or not the television company is retaining an advisor who is experienced in finding foster and adoptive homes for children, and the nature of the programme.

(7) If leave is given, the local authority continues to have a responsibility to ensure that it continues to be in the best interests of the child to appear in the programme, and the court should normally require that the local authority is able to withdraw permission for a child to appear at any time prior to transmission of the programme."

Subs. (1)

Arrangements for the adoption of a child: see s.72(3).   **1–260**

Subs. (2)

Any person: Or corporation (Interpretation Act 1978, s.5, Sched. 1).   **1–261**

[Information concerning adoption

58A.—(1) Every local authority and every approved adoption society **1–262** shall transmit to the Secretary of State, at such times and in such form as he may direct, such particulars as he may require with respect—

(a) to their performance of all or any of their functions under the enactments mentioned in subsection (2) below; and

(b) to the children and other persons in relation to whom they have exercised those functions.

(2) The enactments referred to in subsection (1) above are—

(a) the Adoption Act 1958;

(b) Part I of the Children Act 1975; and

(c) this Act.

(3) The clerk of each magistrates' court shall transmit to the Secretary of State, at such times and in such form as he may direct, such particulars as he may require with respect to the proceedings of the court under the enactments mentioned in subsection (2) above.

(4) The Secretary of State shall publish from time to time abstracts of the particulars transmitted to him under subsections (1) and (3) above.]

1–263   This section was inserted by the Health and Social Services and Social Security Adjudications Act 1983, s.9, Sched. 2, para. 35.

   approved adoption society: s.72(1).
   child: s.72(1).
   local authority: s.72(1).

1–264   This section, which came into force on May 27, 1984 (S.I. 1983 No. 1946), provides for local authorities, approved adoption societies and magistrates' clerks to submit information concerning adoption to the Secretary of State.

Subs. (1)
1–265   *Such form as he may direct:* The "Adoption Proceedings Unit Return" is set out in D.H.S.S. Circular No. LAC (84)6.

Effect of determination and orders made in Scotland and overseas in adoption proceedings

1–266   **59.**—(1) Where an authority of a Convention country or any British territory other than [United Kingdom] having power under the law of that country or territory—

   (a) to authorise or review the authorisation of a regulated adoption or a specified order; or

   (b) to give or review a decision revoking or annulling a regulated adoption, a specified order or a Convention adoption order,

makes a determination in the exercise of that power, then, subject to section 52(3) and 53 and any subsequent determination having effect under this subsection, the determination shall have effect in England and Wales for the purpose of effecting, confirming or terminating the adoption in question or confirming its termination, as the case may be.

[(2) Subsections (2) to (4) of section 12 shall apply in relation to an order freeing a child for adoption (other than an order under section 18) as if it were an adoption order; and, on the revocation in Scotland or Northern Ireland of an order freeing a child for adoption, subsections (3) and (3A) of section 20 shall apply as if the order had been revoked under that section.]

(3) Sections 12(3) and (4) and 49 apply in relation to a child who is the subject of an order which is similar to an order under section 55 and is made (whether before or after this Act has effect) in Scotland, Northern Ireland, the Isle of Man or any of the Channel Islands, as they apply in relation to a child who is the subject of an adoption order.

   The amendments to this section were made by the Children Act 1989, s.88, Sched. 10, Pt. 1, para. 26.

   adoption order: s.72(1).
   British territory: s.72(1).
   child: s.72(1).
   Convention adoption order: s.72(1).
   regulated adoption: s.72(1).
   specified order: s.72(1).

1–267   This section is concerned with the recognition of determinations made in Scotland and overseas in adoption proceedings.

Evidence of adoption in Scotland and Northern Ireland

60. Any document which is receivable as evidence of any matter—   **1–268**

(a) in Scotland under [section 45(2) of the Adoption (Scotland) Act 1978]; or

(b) in Northern Ireland under [Article 63(1) of the Adoption (Northern Ireland) Order 1987],

shall also be so receivable in England and Wales.

<small>AMENDMENTS</small>

The amendments to this section were made by the Children Act 1989, s.88, Sched. 10, Pt. 1, para. 27.

<small>GENERAL NOTE</small>

This section states that a document which is receivable as evidence under the adoption **1–269** legislation applying in Scotland and Northern Ireland, is also receivable in England and Wales. The provisions mentioned deal with certified copies of extracts from Adopted Children's Registers.

Evidence of agreement and consent

61.—(1) Any agreement or consent which is required by this Act to be **1–270** given to the making of an order or application for an order (other than an order to which section 17(6) applies) may be given in writing, and, if the document signifying the agreement or consent is witnessed in accordance with rules, it shall be admissible in evidence without further proof of the signature of the person by whom it was executed.

(2) A document signifying such agreement or consent which purports to be witnessed in accordance with rules shall be presumed to be so witnessed, and to have been executed and witnessed on the date and at the place specified in the document, unless the contrary is proved.

<small>DEFINITION</small>

rules: s.72(1).

<small>GENERAL NOTE</small>

This section deals with the documentary evidence of agreement and consent.   **1–271**

Subs. (1)

Agreement: That is an agreement by a parent or guardian to the making of an adoption **1–272** order; see ss.16(1)(*b*)(i), 18(1)(*a*). For the witnessing of agreements to adoption by reporting officers, see s.65(1)(*b*).

Consent: That is the consent by a parent or guardian to an application for a freeing order; see s.18(1)(a).

Other than an order to which section 17(6) applies: Consents under s.17(6) are governed by the provisions of s.17(7).

May be given in writing: This provision is permissive. Oral as well as written agreement is sufficient (*Re T. (A Minor) (Adoption: Parental Consent)* [1986] 1 All E.R. 817, CA)

Subs. (2)

In accordance with the rules: See r.8 of the Adoption Rules 1984 and the Magistrates' Court **1–273** (Adoption) Rules 1984.

Courts

62.—(1) In this Act, "authorised court," as respects an application for an **1–274** order relating to a child, shall be construed as follows.

(2) Subject to subsections (4) to (6), if the child is in England or Wales when the application is made, the following are authorised courts—

(a) the High Court;

(b) the county court within whose district the child is, and, in the case of an application for an order freeing a child for adoption, any county court within whose district a parent or guardian of the child is;

(c) any other county prescribed by rules made under [section 75 of the County Courts Act 1984];

(d) a magistrates' court within whose area the child is, and, in the case of an application for an order freeing the child for adoption, a magistrates' court within whose area a parent or guardian of the child is.

(3) If, in the case of an application for an adoption order or for an order freeing a child for adoption, the child is not in Great Britain when the application is made, the High Court is the authorised court.

(4) In the case of an application for a Convention adoption order, paragraphs (b), (c) and (d) of subsection (2) do not apply.

(5) Subsection (2) does not apply in the case of an application under section 29 but for the purposes of such an application the following are authorised courts—

(a) if there is pending in respect of the child an application for an adoption order or an order freeing him for adoption, the court in which that application is pending;

(b) if paragraph (a) does not apply and there is no application for an order under

[(i) section 12 or 18 of the Adoption (Scotland) Act 1978; or

(ii) Article 12, 17 or 18 of the Adoption (Northern Ireland) Order 1987],

the High Court, the county court within whose district the applicant lives and the magistrates' court within whose area the applicant lives.

(6) In the case of an order under section 55, paragraph (d) of subsection (2) does not apply.

[(7) Any court to which the proceedings on an application are transferred under any enactment is, as regards the transferred proceedings, an authorised court if it is not an authorised court under the preceding provisions of this section.]

AMENDMENT

Subs. (2)(b) was repealed by the Children (Allocation of Proceedings) (Amendment) (No. 2) Order 1994 (S.I. 1994 No. 3138), art. 6.

In subs. (2)(c) the words in square brackets were substituted by the County Courts Act 1984, s.148(1), Sched. 2, para. 58.

In subs. (5)(b) the words in square brackets were substituted by the Children Act 1989, s.88, Sched. 10, Pt. 1, para. 28.

Subs. (7) was added by the Matrimonial and Family Proceedings Act 1984, s.46(1), Sched. 1, para. 20(b).

DEFINITIONS

adoption order: s.72(1).
child: s.72(1).
Convention adoption order: s.72(1).
guardian: s.72(1).
order freeing a child for adoption: s.72(1).

GENERAL NOTE

1–275   This section identifies authorised courts for the purposes of this Act. In deciding whether, under Art. 12 of the Children (Allocation of Proceedings) Order 1991 (S.I. 1991 No. 1677), adoption proceedings concerning a child whose place of origin is outside the United Kingdom are appropriate for determination in the High Court, guidance may continue to be derived from the decision of the Court of Appeal in *Re N. and L. (Minors) (Adoption Proceedings: Venue)* [1987] 2 All E.R. 732 that transfer should be limited to those cases giving rise to issues of complexity, difficulty or gravity (*Practice Direction* [1993] 4 All E.R. 960).

In suitable cases, when leave is given to commence adoption or freeing for adoption proceedings in respect of a ward of court, the court may direct that such proceedings may be commenced in the appropriate county court; see *Practice Direction* [1986] 2 All E.R. 832.

Subs. (1)

England or Wales: The courts in England and Wales have no jurisdiction if the child was in **1–276** Scotland when the application for a freeing order or an adoption order was made.

Appeals, etc.

63.—(1) [. . .], where any application has been made under this Act to a **1–277** county court, the High Court may, at the instance of any party to the application, order the application to be removed to the High Court and there proceeded with on such terms as to costs as it thinks proper.

(2) Subject to subsections (3) [. . .], where on an application to a magistrates' court under this Act the court makes or refuses to make an order, an appeal shall lie to the High Court.

(3) [. . .], where an application is made to a magistrates' court under this Act, and the court considers that the matter is one which would more conveniently be dealt with by the High Court, the magistrate's court shall refuse to make an order, and in that case no appeal shall lie to the High Court.

(4) [No appeal shall lie to the High Court] against an order made under section 34.

AMENDMENT

In subs. (4) the words in square brackets were substituted by the Health and Social Services and Social Security Adjudications Act 1983, s.9, Sched. 2, para. 36. The words omitted in subss. (1), (2) and (3) were repealed by *ibid.*, s.30(1), Sched. 10, Pt. I.

GENERAL NOTE

This section describes appellate procedure under this Act. For the setting aside of adoption **1–278** orders, see the General Note to s.12.

Leave to appeal out of time will only be granted in wholly exceptional circumstances (*Re M. (Minors) (Adoption)* [1991] 1 F.L.R. 458, CA, noted in the General Note to s.12.

Proceedings to be in private

64. Proceedings under [this Act]—   **1–279**
   (a) in the High Court, may be disposed of in chambers;
   (b) in a county court, shall be heard and determined in camera;
   (c) [. . .]

AMENDMENTS

In this section the words in square brackets were substituted by the Domestic Proceedings and Magistrates' Courts Act 1978, s.73 and the words omitted were repealed by *ibid.*, s.89(2)(b), Sched. 3, and S.I. 1979 No. 731.

GENERAL NOTE

This section provides that proceedings under this Act may be heard is private in the High **1–280** Court and must be heard in private in the county court. Under s.69(3) of the Magistrates' Courts Act 1980 adoption applications heard in the magistrates' court must be heard in private.

Guardians *ad litem* and reporting officers

65.—(1) For the purpose of any application for an adoption order or an **1–281** order freeing a child for adoption or an order under section 20 or 55 rules shall provide for the appointment, in such cases as are prescribed—

(a) of a person to act as guardian *ad litem* of the child upon the hearing of the application, with the duty of safeguarding the interests of the child in the prescribed manner;

(b) of a person to act as reporting officer for the purpose of witnessing agreements to adoption and performing such other duties as the rules may prescribe.

(2) A person who is employed—

(a) in the case of an application for an adoption order, by the adoption agency by whom the child was placed; or

(b) in the case of an application for an order freeing a child for adoption, by the adoption agency by whom the application was made; or

(c) in the case of an application under section 20, by the adoption agency with the parental rights and duties relating to the child,

shall not be appointed to act as guardian *ad litem* or reporting officer for the purposes of the application but, subject to that, the same person may if the court thinks fit be both guardian *ad litem* and reporting officer.

DEFINITIONS

adoption agency: s.1(4).
adoption order: s.72(1).
child: s.72(1).
order freeing a child for adoption: s.72(1).
prescribed: s.72(1).
rules: s.72(1).

GENERAL NOTE

1–282   This section provides for the appointment of guardians *ad litem* and reporting officers in adoption and freeing proceedings. The guardian *ad litem* and reporting officer must be independent of the agency involved in the application (subs. (2)). Part IV of the *Manual of Practice Guidance for Guardians ad Litem and Reporting Officers* (H.M.S.O., 1992) provides guidance to guardians *ad litem* and reporting officers involved in adoption and freeing proceedings.

Guardians *ad litem* and reporting officers are appointed from panels established under s.65A and the Guardian *ad litem* and Reporting Officers (Panels) Regulations 1991 (S.I. 1991 No. 2051). In difficult and finely balanced cases it is advisable for the guardian *ad litem* to be legally represented (*Re C. (Minors) (Adoption)* [1992] 1 F.L.R. 115, CA).

Matters relating to the appointment and duties of guardians *ad litem* and reporting officers in adoption and freeing proceedings are set out in the Adoption Rules 1984 and the Magistrates' Courts (Adoption) Rules 1984; also see paras. 9 to 28 of D.H.S.S. Circular No. LAC (84)10. If a parent agrees to the making of an adoption order the court will appoint a reporting officer whose duties are set out in r.5 (for freeing proceedings) and r.17 (for adoption proceedings). Where the parent is unwilling to agree to an adoption order or if there are special circumstances the court will appoint a guardian *ad litem* whose duties are set out in r.6 (for freeing proceedings) and r.18 (for adoption proceedings).

Although the Official Solicitor will usually act as guardian *ad litem* or reporting officer in proceedings commenced in the High Court he will not normally act in either capacity if the natural parent is consenting to the proceedings (*Practice Direction* [1986] 2 All E.R. 832).

A guardian *ad litem* appointed by a magistrates' court or a county court should remain in the same capacity for the purposes of an appeal to the High Court (*Re S. (An Infant)* [1959] 1 W.L.R. 921).

The Adoption Rules state that the guardian's report shall be confidential to the court; see S.I. 1984 No. 265, r.6(10); S.I. 1984 No. 611, r.6(10); and *Re P.A. (An Infant)* [1971] 1 W.L.R. 1530. An individual who is a party to adoption proceedings may inspect references to himself in any of the confidential reports supplied to the court; see the Adoption Rules 1984, r.53(2), the Magistrates' Courts (Adoption) Rules 1984, r.32(4), and D.H.S.S. Circular No. LAC (84)10, para. 86. Under the above rules the court can order that the relevant parts of the report be not revealed to the individual. In reaching such a decision the court should adopt the approach established by the House of Lords in *Re D. (Minors) (Adoption Reports: Confidentiality)* [1995] 4 All E.R. 385, noted under r.53(2).

A guardian *ad litem* should not attempt to usurp the function of the court by giving in her report an opinion as to whether a natural parent had sufficient grounds to oppose an adoption; *per* Hollis J. in *Re M. (Adoption: Parental Consent)* [1985] F.L.R. 664, DC, at 668.

In adoption proceedings both the reporting officer and the guardian *ad litem* may at any time make an interim report to the court with a view to obtaining the directions of the court on any matter (S.I. 1984 No. 265, rr.5(5), 6(8); S.I. 1984 No. 611, rr.5(5), 6(8)), but he must not appear to take part in the court's decision (*Re B. (A Minor) (Adoption by Parent)* [1965] Fam. 127).

A guardian *ad litem* who has been appointed in care proceedings is not entitled to attend an adoption panel which is to discuss the placement of the child: see *R. v. North Yorkshire County Council, exp. N. (No. 2)* [1989] 2 F.L.R. 79, noted under reg. 10 of the Adoption Agencies Regulations 1983.

Subs. (1)

Application for an adoption order: See s.16.   **1–283**
Order freeing a child for adoption: See s.18.
Order under s.20 or 55: Which provide for the revocation of freeing orders and the adoption of children abroad.
Rules: As to the appointment of guardians *ad litem* and reporting officers, see rr.17 and 18 of the Adoption Rules 1984 and the Magistrates' Courts (Adoption) Rules 1984.
Guardian ad litem: The guardian *ad litem* has no right to a private hearing (*Re B. (A Minor) (Adoption by Parent)* [1975] Fam. 127).
Interests of the child: The court has a duty to safeguard and promote the welfare of the child under s.6.
Agreements to adoption: Agreements are required by s.16(1)(*b*)(i) or 18(1)(*a*). For evidence to agreement, see s.61.

Subs. (2)

Same person: Rule 6(3) of both sets of Rules provide for the same person to be appointed **1–284** as both guardian *ad litem* and reporting officer.

[Panels for selection of guardians *ad litem* and reporting officers

65A.—(1) The Secretary of State may by regulations provide for the **1–285** establishment of panels of persons from whom guardians *ad litem* and reporting officers appointed under rules made under section 65 must be selected.

(2) The regulations may, in particular, make provision—

(a) as to the constitution, administration and procedures of panels;

(b) requiring two or more specified local authorities to make arrangements for the joint management of a panel;

(c) for the defrayment by local authorities of expenses incurred by members of panels;

(d) for the payment by local authorities of fees and allowances for members of panels;

(e) as to the qualifications for membership of a panel;

(f) as to the training to be given to members of panels;

(g) as to the co-operation required of specified local authorities in the provision of panels in specified areas; and

(h) for monitoring the work of guardians *ad litem* and reporting officers.

(3) Rules of court may make provision as to the assistance which any guardian *ad litem* or reporting officer may be required by the court to give to it.]

[(4) The Secretary of State may, with the consent of the Treasury, make such grants with respect to expenditure of any local authority—

(a) in connection with the establishment and administration of guardian *ad litem* and reporting officer panels in accordance with section 65;

(b) in paying expenses, fees, allowances and in the provision of training for members of such panels.

as he considers appropriate.]

AMENDMENTS
This section was inserted by the Children Act 1989, s.88, Sched. 10, Pt. 1, para. 29. Subs. (4) was added by the Courts and Legal Services Act, s.116, Sched. 16, para. 7.

DEFINITION
local authority: s.72(1).

GENERAL NOTE

1–286 This section enables the Secretary of State to make regulations providing for the establishment of panels of guardians *ad litem* and reporting officers. The Guardians *ad litem* and Reporting Officers (Panels) Regulations 1991 (S.I. 1991 No. 2051) (as amended by S.I. 1997 No. 1662) came into force on October 14, 1991.

Rules of procedure

1–287 **66.**—(1) Rules in regard to any matter to be prescribed under this Act and dealing generally with all matters of procedure and incidental matters arising out of this Act and for carrying this Act into effect shall be made by the Lord Chancellor.

(2) Subsection (1) does not apply in relation to proceedings before magistrates' courts, but the power to make rules conferred by [section 144 of the Magistrates' Courts Act 1980], shall include power to make provision as to any of the matters mentioned in that subsection.

(3) In the case of—

(a) an application for an adoption order in relation to a child who is not free for adoption;

(b) an application for an order freeing a child for adoption,

rules shall require every person who can be found and whose agreement or consent to the making of the order is required under this Act to be notified of a date and place where he will be heard on the application and of the fact that, unless he wishes or the court requires, he need not attend.

(4) In the case of an application under section 55, rules shall require every parent and guardian of the child who can be found to be notified as aforesaid.

(5) Rules made as respects magistrates' courts may provide for enabling any fact tending to establish the identity of a child with a child to whom a document relates to be proved by affidavit and for excluding or restricting in relation to any facts that may be so proved the power of a justice of the peace to compel the attendance of witnesses.

(6) This section does not apply in relation to section 9, 10, 11 and 32 to 37.

AMENDMENT
In subs. (2), the words in square brackets were substituted by the Magistrates' Courts Act 1980, s.154(1), Sched. 7, para. 141.

DEFINITIONS
adoption order: s.72(1).
child: s.72(1).
guardian: s.72(1).
order freeing a child for adoption: s.72(1).

Subs. (1)

1–288 *Rules:* See the Adoption Rules 1984 (S.I. 1984 No. 265) and the Magistrates' Courts (Adoption) Rules 1984 (S.I. 1984 No. 611).

Subs. (3)

Agreement; consent: See the notes on s.61. **1–289**

Subs. (4)

Application under s.55: Which is an application made in relation to a child by a person who **1–290** is not domiciled in England, Wales or Scotland.

Orders, rules and regulations

67.—(1) Any power to make orders, rules or regulations conferred by **1–291** this Act on the Secretary of State, the Lord Chancellor or the Registrar General shall be exercisable by statutory instrument.

(2) A statutory instrument containing rules or regulations made under any provision of this Act, except section 3(1), shall be subject to annulment in pursuance of a resolution of either House of Parliament.

(3) An order under section 28(10) or 57(8) shall not be made unless a draft of the order has been approved by resolution of each House of Parliament.

(4) An order made under any provision of this Act, except section 74, may be revoked or varied by a subsequent order under that provision.

(5) Orders and regulations made under this Act may make different provision in relation to different cases or classes of cases and may exclude certain cases or classes of cases.

(6) The Registrar General shall not make regulations under section 51 or paragraph 1(1) of Schedule 1 except with the approval of the Secretary of State.

Offences by bodies corporate

68. Where an offence under this Act committed by a body corporate is **1–292** proved to have been committed with the consent or connivance of or to be attributable to any neglect on the part of, any director, manager, member of the committee, secretary or other officer of the body, he as well as the body shall be deemed to be guilty of that offence and shall be liable to be proceeded against and punished accordingly.

Service of notices, etc.

69. Any notice or information required to be given under this Act may be **1–293** given by post.

GENERAL NOTE

The service of documents is governed by the Adoption Rules 1984, r.50 and the **1–294** Magistrates' Courts (Adoption) Rules 1984, r.29.

May: Note that service by post is not mandatory.

Be given by post: Service is deemed to be effected by properly addressing, pre-paying and posting a letter containing the document and, unless the contrary is proved, to have been effected at the time at which the letter would be delivered in the ordinary course of post (Interpretation Act 1978, s.7).

Nationality

70.—(1) If the Secretary of State by order declares that a description of **1–295** persons specified in the order has, in pursuance of the Convention, been notified to the Government of the United Kingdom as the description of the persons who are deemed to possess the nationality of a particular Convention country, person of that description shall, subject to the following provisions of this section, be treated for the purposes of this Act as nationals of that country.

(2) Subject to section 54(3) and subsection (3) of this section, where it appears to the court in any proceedings under this Act, or to any court by which a decision in pursuance of section 53(3) falls to be given, that a person is or was at a particular time a national of two or more countries, then—

(a) if it appears to the said court that he is or was then a United Kingdom national, he shall be treated for the purposes of those proceedings or that decision as if he were or had then been a United Kingdom national only;

(b) if, in the case not falling within paragraph (a), it appears to the said court that one only of those countries is or was then a Convention country, he shall be treated for those purposes as if he were or had then been a national of that country only;

(c) if, in a case not falling within paragraph (a), it appears to the said court that two or more of those countries are or were then Convention countries, he shall be treated for those purposes as if he were or had then been a national of such one only of those Convention countries as the said court considers is the country with which he is or was then most closely connected;

(d) in any other case, he shall be treated for those purposes as if he were or had then been a national of such one only of those countries as the said court considers is the country with which he is or was then most closely connected.

(3) A court in which proceedings are brought in pursuance of section 17, 52(3) or 53 shall be entitled to disregard the provisions of subsection (2) in so far as it appears to that court appropriate to do so for the purposes of those proceedings; but nothing in this subsection shall be construed as prejudicing the provisions of section 54(3).

(4) Where, after such inquiries as the court in question considers appropriate, it appears to the court in any proceedings under this Act, or to any court by which such a decision as aforesaid falls to be given, that a person has no nationality or no ascertainable nationality, he shall be treated for the purposes of those proceedings or that decision as a national of the country in which he resides or, where that country is one of two or more countries having the same law of nationality, as a national of those countries.

DEFINITIONS
the convention: s.72(1).
Convention country: s.72(1).
United Kingdom national: s.72(1).

GENERAL NOTE

1–296 This section provides rules for resolving the difficulties that can arise in determining a person's nationality where that person appears to have two nationalities or to have no nationality.

Subs. (1) enables the Secretary of State to make an order specifying, in accordance with information given by the Government of a Convention country, the categories of persons which are to be treated as nationals of that country. To date, no such order has been made.

Convention country: Austria and Switzerland have been designated as convention countries by the Convention Adoption (Austria and Switzerland) Order 1978 (S.I. 1978 No. 1431).

Subs. (2) contains rules for determining the nationality of a person who is a national of two or more countries.

Subs. (4) provides that a stateless person is to be treated as a national of the country where he resides.

Internal law of a country

71.—(1) In this Act "internal law" in relation to any country means the **1–297**
law applicable in a case where no question arises as to the law in force in
any other country.

(2) In any case where the internal law of a country falls to be ascertained
for the purposes of this Act by any court and there are in force in that
country two or more systems of internal law, the relevant system shall be
ascertained in accordance with any rule in force throughout that country
indicating which of the systems is relevant in the case in question or, if
there is no such rule, shall be the system appearing to that court to be most
closely connected with the case.

Interpretation

72.—(1) In this Act, unless the context otherwise requires—   **1–298**
"adoption agency" in sections 11, 13, 18 to 23 and 27 to 32 includes an
adoption agency within the meaning of
 [(a) section 1 of the Adoption (Scotland) Act 1978; and
  (b) Article 3 of the Adoption (Northern Ireland) Order 1987.]
["adoption order"—
  (a) means an order under section 12(1); and
  (b) in sections 12(3) and (4), 18 to 20, 27, 28 and 30 to 32 and in
      the definition of 'British adoption order' in this subsection
      includes an order under section 12 of the Adoption (Scotland)
      Act 1978 and Article 12 of the Adoption (Northern Ireland)
      Order 1987 (adoption orders in Scotland and Northern Ireland
      respectively); and
  (c) in sections 27, 28 and 30 to 32 includes an order under section
      55, section 49 of the Adoption (Scotland) Act 1978 and Article
      57 of the Adoption (Northern Ireland) Order 1987 (orders in
      relation to children being adopted abroad);]
"adoption society" means a body of persons whose functions consist of
or include the making of arrangements for the adoption of children;
"approved adoption society" means an adoption society approved
under Part I,
"authorised court" shall be construed in accordance with section 62;
"body of persons" means any body of persons, whether incorporated
or unincorporated;
["British adoption order" means—
  (a) an adoption order as defined in this subsection, and
  (b) an order under any provision for the adoption of a child
      effected under the law of any British territory outside the
      United Kingdom.]
"British territory" means, for the purposes of any provision of this
Act, any of the following countries, that is to say, Great Britain,
Northern Ireland, the Channel Islands, the Isle of Man and a colony,
being a country designated for the purposes of that provision by order of
the Secretary of State or, if no country is so designated, any of those
countries;
"child," except where used to express a relationship, means a person
who has not attained the age of 18 years;
"the Convention" means the Convention relating to the adoption of
children concluded at the Hague on November 15, 1965 and signed on
behalf of the United Kingdom on that date;

101

"Convention adoption order" means an adoption order made in accordance with section 17(1);

"Convention country" means any country outside British territory, being a country for the time being designated by an order of the Secretary of State as a country in which, in his opinion, the Convention is in force;

"existing," in relation to an enactment or other instrument, means one passed or made at any time before January 1, 1976;

["guardian" has the same meaning as in the Children Act 1989;]

"internal law" has the meaning assigned by section 71;

"local authority" means the council of a county (other than a metropolitan county), a metropolitan district, a London borough or the Common Council of the City of London [. . .];

"notice" means a notice in writing;

"order freeing a child for adoption" means an order under section 18 [and in] [sections 27(2) and 59 includes an order under]—

    (a) section 18 of the Adoption (Scotland) Act 1978; and

    (b) Article 17 or 18 of the Adoption (Northern Ireland) Order 1987.]

"overseas adoption" has the meaning assigned by subsection (2);

["parent" means, in relation to a child, any parent who has parental responsibility for the child under the Children Act 1989;]

["parental responsibility" and "parental responsibility agreement" have the same meaning as in the Children Act 1989;]

[. . .]

"prescribed" means prescribed by rules;

"regulated adoption" means an overseas adoption of a description designated by an order under subsection (2) as that of an adoption regulated by the Convention;

"relative" in relation to a child means a grandparent, brother, sister, uncle or aunt, whether of the full blood or half-blood or by affinity and includes, where the child is illegitimate, the father of the child and any person who would be a relative within the meaning of this definition if the child were the legitimate child of his mother and father;

"rules" means rules made under section 66(1) or made by virtue of section 66(2) under [section 144 of the Magistrates' Courts Act 1980];

"specified order" means any provision for the adoption of a child effected under enactments similar to section 12(1) and 17 in force in [. . .] any British territory outside the United Kingdom;

"United Kingdom national" means, for the purposes of any provision of this Act, a citizen of the United Kingdom and colonies satisfying such conditions, if any, as the Secretary of State may by order specify for the purposes of that provision;

["upbringing" has the same meaning as in the Children Act 1989;]

"voluntary organisation" means a body other than a public or local authority the activities of which are not carried on for profit.

[(1A) In this Act, in determining with what person, or where, a child has his home, any absence of the child at a hospital or boarding school and any other temporary absence shall be disregarded.

(1B) In this Act, references to a child who is in the care of or looked after by a local authority have the same meaning as in the Children Act 1989.]

(2) In this Act "overseas adoption" means an adoption of such a description as the Secretary of State may by order specify, being a description of adoptions of children appearing to him to be effected under the law of a country outside Great Britain; and an order under this subsection may contain provision as to the manner in which evidence of an overseas adoption may be given.

(3) For purposes of this Act, a person shall be deemed to make arrangements for the adoption of a child if he enters into or makes any agreement or arrangement for, or for facilitating, the adoption of the child by any other person, whether the adoption is effected, or is intended to be effected, in Great Britain or elsewhere, or if he initiates or takes part in any negotiations of which the purpose or effect is the conclusion of any agreement or the making of any arrangement therefor, and if he causes another person to do so.

(4) Except so far as the context otherwise requires, any reference in this Act to an enactment shall be construed as a reference to that enactment as amended by or under any other enactment, including this Act.

(5) In this Act, except where otherwise indicated—

(a) a reference to a numbered Part, section or Schedule is a reference to the Part or section of, or the Schedule to, this Act so numbered, and

(b) a reference in a section to a numbered subsection is a reference to the subsection of that section so numbered, and

(c) a reference in a section, subsection or Schedule to a numbered paragraph is a reference to the paragraph of that section, subsection or Schedule so numbered.

AMENDMENTS

In subs. (1), the words in square brackets were substituted and inserted by the Magistrates' Courts Act 1980, s.154(1), Sched. 7, para. 142 and the Health and Social Services and Social Security Adjudications Act 1983, s.9, Sched. 2, para. 37 and the Family Law Reform Act 1987, ss.7(2), 33(1), Sched. 2, para. 68. The remaining amendments were made by the Children Act 1989, s.88, Sched. 10, Pt. 1, para. 30 and *ibid.* s.108(7), Sched. 15.

Subs. (1)

British adoption order: For "United Kingdom," see the note on s.56. **1–299**

British territory: For "Great Britain," see the note on s.56.

Child: For "attained the age," see the note on s.14. Note that there is nothing to prevent an adopted child being re-adopted (s.12(7)). An adoption order cannot be made in respect of a child who is or has been married (s.12(5)).

The Convention: The text of the Hague Convention is set out in Cmnd 7342.

Notice: Unless the contrary intention appears, writing includes other modes of representing or reproducing words in a visible form (Interpretation Act 1978, s.5, Sched. 1).

Relative: By affinity means by marriage. In *Re C. (Minors) (Wardship: Adoption)* [1989] 1 All E.R. 395, the Court of Appeal, in holding that great aunts and great uncles are not relatives for the purposes of this Act, said that the definition of relative ought to be construed precisely. A step-grandparent is a relative who comes within this definition (*Re U. (Application to Free for Adoption)* [1993] 2 F.L.R. 992, CA).

A commissioning "mother" in a surrogacy arrangement who has no biological link with the child is not a "relative" of the child (*Re M.W. (Adoption: Surrogacy)* [1995] 2 F.L.R. 759).

United Kingdom national: A citizen of the United Kingdom and colonies is defined by the British Nationality Act 1981, s.51(3)(*a*).

Voluntary organisation: For "not carried on for profit" see the note on s.57.

Subs. (2)

Overseas adoption: The Adoption (Designations of Overseas Adoptions) Order 1973 (S.I. **1–300** 1973 No. 19) specifies the overseas adoption orders which are recognised under this section and prescribes the manner in which evidence of an overseas adoption may be given. An overseas adoption has the same effect on a child's status as an adoption made in this country (s.38(1)(*d*)) and a child who has been adopted in one of the specified countries need not therefore be re-adopted if he later comes to live in Great Britain. The one exception to this general rule relates to children adopted abroad by British Citizens. Paragraph 11 of D.H.S.S. Circular LASSL (82)8 explains the position as follows:

> "Under the [British Nationality Act 1981], a child who is adopted abroad by a British citizen will have *no* automatic entitlement to British citizenship and *no* automatic right to come to the United Kingdom. This is so whether or not the adoption is recognised in our law under the Adoption (Designation of Overseas Adoptions) Order 1973. It will, however, be possible for the child to be registered as a British citizen under the Home Secretary's discretionary powers. If an application for registration is granted and the child becomes a British citizen, this will automatically give him the right of abode in the United Kingdom and entitle him to come to this country."

The British Nationality Act does not affect applications for entry clearance for a child to come to this country for adoption. The Home Office deals with such applications, and it seeks the advice of the Department of Health in each case on whether the proposed adoption is likely to be in the child's interests and whether there is a *prima facie* reason why a court in this country might not grant an adoption order; see further, the General Note to s.17.

Information and guidance to social services departments who are asked to provide services in connection with the adoption of children from overseas is contained in *A Guide to Intercountry Adoption—Practice and Procedures* (Department of Health, 1997) and in Letter No. CI(92)12 which is concerned specifically with the adoption of Romanian children. Both of these documents are produced in Part III.

In *Re K. (Adoption and Wardship)* [1997] 2 F.L.R. 221, the Court of Appeal approved the guidance concerning unaccompanied children from the former Yugoslavia offered by the Refugee Council (Tel: 0171 582 6922), which was sent to social services directors on February 18, 1993.

In *Re An Adoption Application* [1992] 1 F.L.R. 341, Hollings J. said, at 355–356, that "where a local authority is notified by prospective adopters that they have brought into the country a foreign child whom they hope to adopt, the authority should, at once, seek information from the relevant embassy or consultate as to the validity of any foreign or adoption order obtained by, or on behalf of, the proposed adopters."

Subs. (3)

1–301   *Any other person:* "An adoption agency, properly constituted under [this] Act and approved by the Secretary of State, cannot, in my view be 'any other person' within s.72(3)," *per* Wall J. in *Re W. (A Minor) (Adoption: Mother under Disability)* [1995] 4 All E.R. 282 at 287.

Transitional provision, amendments and repeals

1–302   **73.**—(1) The transitional provisions contained in Schedule 2 shall have effect.

(2) The enactments specified in Schedule 3 shall have effect subject to the amendments specified in that Schedule, being amendments consequential upon the provisions of this Act.

(3) The enactments specified in Schedule 4 are hereby repealed to the extent specified in column 3 of that Schedule.

Short title, commencement and extent

1–303   **74.**—(1) This Act may be cited as the Adoption Act 1976.

(2) This Act shall come into force on such date as the Secretary of State may by order appoint and different dates may be appointed for different provisions.

(3) This Act extends to England and Wales only.]

AMENDMENT

Subs. (3) was substituted by the Children Act 1989, s.88, Sched. 10, Pt. 1, para. 31.

Subs. (2)

1–304   This section and s.58A were brought into force on May 17, 1984 by the Children Act 1975 and the Adoption Act 1976 (Commencement) Order 1983 (S.I. 1983 No. 1946). The remainder of this Act was brought into force on January 1, 1988 by the Children Act 1975 and this Adoption Act 1976 (Commencement No. 2) Order 1987 (S.I. 1987 No. 1242).

SCHEDULE 1

REGISTRATION OF ADOPTIONS

Registration of adoption orders

1.—(1) Every adoption order shall contain a direction to the Registrar General to make in **1–305**
the Adopted Children Register an entry in such form as the Registrar General may by
regulations specify.

(2) The direction contained in a Convention adoption order in pursuance of this paragraph
shall include an instruction that the entry made in that register in consequence of the order
shall be marked with the words "Convention order."

(3) Where on an application to a court for an adoption order in respect of a child (not
being a child who has previously been the subject of an adoption order made by a court in
England or Wales under this Act or any enactment at the time in force) there is proved to the
satisfaction of the court the identity of the child with a child to whom an entry in the Registers
of Births relates, any adoption order made in pursuance of the application shall contain a
direction to the Registrar General to cause the entry in the Registers of Births to be marked
with the word "Adopted."

(4) Where an adoption order is made in respect of a child who has previously been the
subject of an adoption order made by a court in England or Wales under this Act or any
enactment at the time in force, the order shall contain a direction to the Registrar General to
cause the previous entry in the Adoption Children Register to be marked with the word "Re-
adopted."

(5) Where an adoption order is made, the prescribed officer of the court which made the
order shall cause the order to be communicated in the prescribed manner to the Registrar
General, and upon receipt of the communication the Registrar General shall cause compliance to be made with the directions contained in the order.

**Registration of adoptions in Scotland, Northern Ireland, the Isle of Man and the Channel
Islands**

2.—(1) Where the Registrar General is notified by the Registrar General for Scotland that **1–306**
an adoption order has been made by a court in Scotland in respect of a child to whom an
entry in the Registers of Births or the Adopted Children Register relates, the Registrar
General shall cause the entry to be marked "Adopted (Scotland)" or, as the case may be "Re-
adopted (Scotland)"; and where, after an entry has been so marked, the Registrar General is
notified as aforesaid that the adoption order has been quashed, or that an appeal against the
adoption order has been allowed he shall cause the marking to be cancelled.

(2) Where the Registrar General is notified by the authority maintaining a register of
adoptions in Northern Ireland, the Isle of Man or any of the Channel Islands that an order
has been made in that country authorising the adoption of a child to whom an entry in the
Registers of Births or the Adopted Children Register relates, he shall cause the entry to be
marked with the word "Adopted" or "Re-adopted", as the case may require, followed by the
name, in brackets, of the country in which the order was made.

(3) Where, after an entry has been so marked, the Registrar General is notified as aforesaid
that the order has been quashed, that an appeal against the order has been allowed or that the
order has been revoked, he shall cause the marking to be cancelled; and a copy or extract of
entry in any register, being an entry the marking of which is cancelled under this sub-
paragraph, shall be deemed to be an accurate copy if and only if both the marking and the
cancellation are omitted therefrom.

(4) The preceding provisions of this paragraph shall apply in relation to orders corresponding to orders under section 55 as they apply in relation to orders authorising the adoption of a
child; but any marking of an entry required by virtue of this sub-paragraph shall consist of the
words "proposed foreign adoption" or as the case may require, "proposed foreign re-
adoption" followed by the name in brackets of the country in which the order was made.

(5) Without prejudice to sub-paragraphs (2) and (3) where, after an entry in the Registers
of Births has been marked in accordance with this paragraph, the birth is re-registered under
section 14 of the Births and Deaths Registration Act 1953 (re-registration of births of
legitimated children) the entry made on the re-registration shall be marked in the like
manner.

Registration of overseas adoptions

1–307   **3.** If the Registrar General is satisfied that an entry in the Registers of Births relates to a person adopted under an overseas adoption and that he has sufficient particulars relating to that person to enable an entry, in the form specified for the purposes of this sub-paragraph in regulations made under paragraph 1(1), to be made in the Adopted Children Register in respect of that person, he shall—

    (a) make such an entry in the Adopted Children Register; and

    (b) if there is a previous entry in respect of that person in that register, mark the entry (or if there is more than one such entry the last of them) with the word "Re-adopted" followed by the name in brackets of the country in which the adoption was effected; and

    (c) unless the entry in the Registers of Births is already marked with the word "Adopted" (whether or not followed by other words), mark the entry with that word followed by the name in brackets of the country aforesaid.

Amendment of orders and rectification of registers

1–308   **4.**—(1) The court by which an adoption order has been made may, on the application of the adopter or of the adopted person, amend the order by the correction of any error in the particulars contained therein, and may—

    (a) if satisfied on the application of the adopter or the adopted person that within one year beginning with the date of the order any new name has been given to the adopted person (whether in baptism or otherwise), or taken by him, either in lieu of or in addition to a name specified in the particulars required to be entered in the Adopted Children Register in pursuance of the order, amend the order by substituting or adding that name in those particulars, as the case may require;

    (b) if satisfied on the application of any person concerned that a direction for the marking of an entry in the Registers of Births or the Adopted Children Register included in the order in pursuance of sub-paragraph (3) or (4) of paragraph 1 was wrongly so included, revoke that direction.

(2) Where an adoption order is amended or a direction revoked under sub-paragraph (1), the prescribed officer of the court shall cause the amendment to be communicated in the prescribed manner to the Registrar General who shall as the case may require—

    (a) cause the entry in the Adopted Children Register to be amended accordingly; or

    (b) cause the marking of the entry in the Registers of Births or the Adopted Children Register to be cancelled.

(3) Where an adoption order is quashed or an appeal against an adoption order allowed by any court, the court shall give directions to the Registrar General to cancel any entry in the Adopted Children Register, and any marking of an entry in that Register, or the Registers of Births as the case may be, which was effected in pursuance of the order.

(4) Where an adoption order has been amended, any certified copy of the relevant entry in the Adopted Children Register which may be issued pursuant to subsection (3) of section 50 shall be a copy of the entry as amended, without the reproduction of any note or marking relating to the amendment or of any matter cancelled pursuant thereto; and a copy or extract of an entry in any register, being an entry the marking of which has been cancelled, shall be deemed to be an accurate copy if and only if both the marking and the cancellation are omitted therefrom.

(5) If the Registrar General is satisfied—

    (a) that a Convention adoption order or an overseas adoption has ceased to have effect, whether on annulment or otherwise; or

    (b) that any entry or mark was erroneously made in pursuance of paragraph 3 in any register mentioned in that paragraph,

he may cause such alterations to be made in any such register as he considers are required in consequence of the cesser or to correct the error; and where an entry in such a register is amended in pursuance of this sub-paragraph, any copy or extract of the entry shall be deemed to be accurate if and only if it shows the entry as amended but without indicating that it has been amended.

(6) In relation to an adoption order made by a magistrates' court, the reference in sub-paragraph (1) to the court by which the order has been made includes a reference to a court acting for the same petty sessions area.

Marking of entries on re-registration of birth on legitimation

5.—(1) Without prejudice to section 52, where, after an entry in the Registers of Births has **1–309** been marked with the word "Adopted" (with or without the addition of the word "(Scotland)"), the birth is re-registered under section 14 of the Births and Deaths Registration Act 1953 (re-registration of births of legitimated persons) the entry made on the re-registration shall be marked in the like manner.

(2) Without prejudice to paragraph 4(5), where an entry in the Registers of Births is marked in pursuance of paragraph 3 and the birth in question is subsequently re-registered under the said section 14, the entry made on re-registration shall be marked in the like manner.

Cancellations in registers on legitimation

6. Where an adoption order, [. . .], is revoked under section 53(1) or (2) the prescribed **1–310** officer of the court shall cause the revocation to be communicated in the prescribed manner to the Registrar General who shall cause to be cancelled—
   (a) the entry in the Adopted Children Register relating to the adopted person; and
   (b) the marking with the word "Adopted" (or, as the case may be, with that word and the word "(Scotland)") of any entry relating to him in the Registers of Births;
and a copy or extract of an entry in any register, being an entry the marking of which is cancelled under this section, shall be deemed to be an accurate copy if and only if both the marking and the cancellation are omitted therefrom.

AMENDMENT
In para. 6 the words omitted were repealed by the Domestic Proceedings and Magistrates' Courts Act 1978, s.89(2)(b), Sched. 3.

DEFINITIONS
   adoption order: s.72(1).
   child: s.72(1).
   Convention adoption order: s.72(1).
   prescribed: s.72(1).
   overseas adoption: s.72(2).

Para. 1

This paragraph places a duty on the Registrar General to register adoptions in the Adopted **1–311** Children Register.

Sub-para. (1)
   Adopted children register: Which is kept under s.50.   **1–312**
   Such form: The Forms of Adoption Regulations 1975 (S.I. 1975 No. 1959) prescribe the form of the entries to be made in the Adopted Children Register.

Sub-para. (3)
   Register of births: The Registration of Births, Deaths and Marriages Regulations 1968 (S.I. **1–313** 1968 No. 2049), regs. 37, 38, provide for the marking of entries of adopted children.

Sub-para. (5)
   Prescribed manner: See the Adoption Rules 1984, r.52(1) and the Magistrates' Courts **1–314** (Adoption) Rules 1984, r.31(1).

Para. 2

Sub-para. (5)
   Entry: For regulations relating to the birth entry of an adopted child, see S.I. 1968 No. 2049, **1–315** reg. 37.

Sub-para. (1)

1–316 *The court:* Note sub-para. (6).

Application: The procedure for making an application is set out in the Adoption Rules 1984, r.49 and the Magistrates' Courts (Adoption) Rules 1984, r.28.

Correction of any error: This is a wide power to correct errors and not a mere rule for correcting slips (*R.* v. *Chelsea Juvenile Court (Re An Infant)* [1955] 1 W.L.R. 52).

Beginning with: Including the date of the order (*Hare* v. *Gocher* [1962] 2 Q.B. 641).

SCHEDULE 2

TRANSITIONAL PROVISIONS AND SAVINGS

General

1–317 1. In so far as anything done under an enactment repealed by this Act could have been done under a corresponding provision of this Act it shall not be invalidated by the repeal but shall have effect as if done under that provision.

2. Where any period of time specified in any enactment repealed by this Act is current at the commencement of this Act, shall have effect as if the corresponding provision thereof had been in force when that period began to run.

3. Nothing in this Act shall affect the enactments repealed by this Act in their operation in relation to offences committed before the commencement of this Act.

4. Any reference in any document, whether express or implied, to any enactment repealed by this Act shall, unless the context otherwise requires, be construed as a reference to the corresponding enactment of this Act.

Existing adoption orders

1–318 5.—(1) Without prejudice to paragraph 1, an adoption order made under an enactment at any time before this Act comes into force shall not cease to have effect by virtue only of a repeal effected by this Act.

(2) Paragraph 4(1) and (2) of Schedule 1 shall apply in relation to an adoption order made before this Act came into force as if the order had been made under section 12, but as if, in sub-paragraph (1)(b) of the said paragraph 4, there were substituted for the reference to paragraph 1(3) and (4) a reference—

    (a) in the case of an order under the Adoption of Children Act 1926, to section 12(3) and (4) of the Adoption of Children Act 1949,

    (b) in the case of an order under the Adoption Act 1950, to section 18(3) and (4) of that Act.

    (c) in the case of an order under the Adoption Act 1958, to section 21(4) and (5) of that Act.

(3) The power of the court under the said paragraph 4(1) to amend an order includes power, in relation to an order made before April 1, 1959, to make on the application of the adopter or adopted person any such amendment of the particulars contained in the order as appears to be required to bring the order into form in which it would have been made if paragraph 1 of Schedule 1 had applied to the order.

(4) Section 52(1) and paragraph 6 of Schedule 1 shall apply in relation to an adoption order made under an enactment at any time before this Act came into force as they apply in relation to an adoption order made under this Act.

Right relating to property

1–319 6.—(1) Section 39—

    (a) does not apply to an existing instrument or enactment in so far as it contains a disposition of property, and

    (b) does not apply to any public general Act in its application to any disposition of property in an existing instrument or enactment.

(2) Sections 16 and 17 of the Adoption Act 1958, and provisions containing references to those sections shall continue to apply in relation to disposition of property effected by existing instruments notwithstanding the repeal of those sections, and such provisions, by the Children Act 1975.

(3) Section 46 shall apply in relation to this paragraph as if it were contained in Part IV.

Payments relating to adoptions

7. Section 57(7), (8) and (9) shall not have effect if, immediately before section 57 comes **1–320** into force, there is in force in England and Wales an order under section 50(8) of the Adoption Act 1958.

Registers of adoptions

8. Any register, or index to a register kept under the Adoption Act 1958, or any register or **1–321** index deemed to be part of such a register, shall be deemed to be part of the register kept under section 50.

DEFINITIONS
  existing: s.72(1).
  adoption order: s.72(1).

Para. 5

Sub-para. (3)
  April 1, 1959: The date on which the Adoption Act 1958 came into force. **1–322**

SCHEDULES 3 AND 4

[Not reproduced.] **1–323**

PART II

DELEGATED LEGISLATION

ADOPTION (DESIGNATION OF OVERSEAS ADOPTIONS) ORDER 1973

(S.I. 1973 No. 19)

Dated January 1, 1973, and made by the Home Secretary under the Adoption Act 1968 (c. 53), s.4(3)

GENERAL NOTE

This Order designates overseas adoptions for the purposes of s.72(2) of the Adoption Act **2–001** 1976. Art. 4 concerns the manner of proof of an overseas adoption. Although these Regulations were made under the Adoption Act 1968, they remain in force by virtue of the transitional provisions contained in s.73(1), Sched. 2, para. 1 of the Adoption Act 1976.

AMENDMENTS

The amendments to this Order were made by the Adoption (Designation of Overseas Adoptions) (Variation) Order 1993 (S.I. 1993 No. 690).

1. This Order may be cited as the Adoption (Designation of Overseas **2–002** Adoption) Order 1973 and shall come into operation on February 1, 1973.

2. The Interpretation Act 1889 shall apply to the interpretation of this **2–003** Order as it applies to the interpretation of an Act of Parliament.

3.—(1) An adoption of an infant is hereby specified as an overseas **2–004** adoption if it is an adoption effected in a place in relation to which this Article applies and under the law in force in that place.

(2) [Subject to paragraph (2A) of this Article] as respects any adoption effected before the date on which this Order comes into operation, this Article applies in relation to any place which, at that date, forms part of a country or territory described in Part I or II of the Schedule to this Order and as respects any adoption effected on or after that date, this Article applies in relation to any place which, at the time the adoption is effected, forms part of a country or territory which at that time is a country or territory described in Part I or II of the Schedule to this Order.

[(2A) This Article also applies, as respects any adoption effected on or after April 5, 1993, in relation to any place which, at the time the adoption is effected, forms part of the People's Republic of China.]

(3) In this Article the expression—

"infant means a person who at the time when the application for adoption was made had not attained the age of 18 years and had not been married;

"law" does not include customary or common law.

4.—(1) Evidence that an overseas adoption had been effected may be **2–005** given by the production of a document purporting to be—

(a) a certified copy of an entry made, in accordance with the law of the country or territory concerned, in a public register relating to the recording of adoptions and showing that the adoption has been effected; or

(b) a certificate that the adoption has been effected, signed or purporting to be signed by a person authorised by the law of the country or territory concerned to sign such a certificate, or a certified copy of such certificate.

(2) Where a document produced by virtue of paragraph (1) of this Article is not in English, the Registrar General or the Registrar General of Births, Deaths and Marriages for Scotland, as the case may be, may require the production of an English translation of the document before satisfying himself of the matters specified in section 8 of the Adoption Act 1968.

(3) Nothing in this Article shall be construed as precluding proof, in accordance with the Evidence (Foreign, Dominion and Colonial Documents) Act 1933, or the Oaths and Evidence (Overseas Authorities and Countries) Act 1963, or otherwise, that an overseas adoption has been effected.

SCHEDULE

PART I

COMMONWEALTH COUNTRIES AND UNITED KINGDOM DEPENDENT TERRITORIES

2–006

Australia	Malaysia
Bahamas	Malta
Barbados	Mauritius
Bermuda	Montserrat
Botswana	New Zealand
British Honduras	Nigeria
British Virgin Islands	Pitcairn
Canada	St. Christopher, Nevis and Anguilla
Cayman Islands	St. Vincent
The Republic of Cyprus	Seychelles
Dominica	Singapore
Fiji	Southern Rhodesia
Ghana	Sri Lanka
Gibraltar	Swaziland
Guyana	Tanzania
Hong Kong	Tonga
Jamaica	Trinidad and Tobago
Kenya	Uganda
Lesotho	Zambia
Malawi	

PART II

OTHER COUNTRIES AND TERRITORIES

2–007 Austria
Belgium
Denmark (including Greenland and the Faroes)
Finland
France (including Réunion, Martinique, Guadeloupe and French Guyana)
The Federal Republic of Germany and Land Berlin (West Berlin)
Greece
Iceland
The Republic of Ireland
Israel
Italy
Luxembourg
The Netherlands (including the Azores and Madeira)
South Africa and South West Africa
Spain (including the Balearics and the Canary Islands)
Sweden
Switzerland
Turkey
The United States of America
Yugoslavia

CONVENTION ADOPTION (AUSTRIA AND SWITZERLAND) ORDER 1978

(S.I. 1978 No. 1431)

Dated September 13, 1978, *and made by the Secretary of State for Social Services under the Adoption Act* 1968, *ss.*7(4) *and* 11(1) *and the Children Act* 1975 (*c.* 72), *ss.*24(8) *and* 107(1).

Citation, commencement, extent and interpretation

1.—(1) This order may be cited as the Convention Adoption (Austria **2-009** and Switzerland) Order 1978 and shall come into operation on October 1, 1978.

(2) This order shall not apply to Scotland.

(3) The rules for the construction of Acts of Parliament contained in the Interpretation Act 1889 shall apply for the purposes of the interpretation of this order as they apply for the purposes of the interpretation of an Act of Parliament.

Designation of "convention country"

2. For the purposes of the Adoption Act 1968 and the Children Act 1975, **2-010** Austria and Switzerland are hereby designated as countries in which the Convention on Jurisdiction, Applicable Law and Recognition of Decrees relating to Adoptions concluded at the Hague on November 15, 1965, is in force.

Meaning of "notified provision" and "specified provision"

3. For the purposes of sections 6 and 7 of the Adoption Act 1968 **2-011** ("notified provision") and section 24 of the Children Act 1975 ("specified provision"), the provisions set out in Schedule 1 to this order, in relation to Austria, and in Schedule 2 to this order, in relation to Switzerland, are hereby specified as the provisions relating to prohibitions on an adoption contained in the national law of Austria and of Switzerland respectively which have been notified to the Government of the United Kingdom in pursuance of the provisions of the Convention.

PROVISIONS RELATING TO PROHIBITIONS OF AN ADOPTION CONTAINED IN THE NATIONAL LAW OF
AUSTRIA NOTIFIED UNDER ARTICLES 13, 17 AND 24 OF THE CONVENTION

1. Zum Artikel 13 Absatz 1 Buchstabe d

2–012   Nach par. 179 Abstaz 2 allgemeines burgerliches Gesetzbuch ist die Annahme eines
Wahlkindes durch mehr als eine Person, sei es gleichzeitig, sie as nacheinander, nur zulässig,
wenn die Annehmenden mit einander verheiratet sind, Daraus ergibt sich, dass das Bestehen
einer früheren Annahme des Kindes durch andere Personen nur erlaubt ist, wenn diese
andere Person der Ehegatte des Wahlvaters oder der Wahlmutter ist, sonst nicht.

2. Zum Artikel 13 Absatz 1 Buchstabe e

2–013   Nach par. 180 allgemeines bügerliches Gesetzbuch müssen die Wahletern mindestens 18
Jahre älter als das Wahlkind sien; eine geringfügige Unterschreitung dieses Zeitraums ist
unbeachtlich, wenn zwischen dem Annehmenden und dem Wahlkind bereits eine dem
Verhältnis zwischen leiblichen Eltern und Kindern entsprechende Beziehung besteht. Ist das
Wahlkind ein leibliches Kind des Ehegatten des Annehmenden oder mit dem Annehmenden
verwandt, so genügt ein Altersunterschied von 16 Jahren.

3. Zum Artikel 13 Absatz 1 Buchstabe f

2–014   Der Wahlvater muss das 30., die Wahlmutter das 28. Lebensjahr vollendet haben. Nehmen
aber Ehegatten gemeinsam an oder ist das Wahlkind ein leibliches Kind des Ehegatten des
Annehmenden, so ist eine Unterschreitung dieser Altersgrenze zulässig, wenn zwischen dem
Annehmenden und dem Wahlkind bereits eine dem Verhältnis zwischen leiblichen Eltern und
Kindern entsprechende Beziehung besteht. Eine Mindestgrenze nach unten gibt es dann nicht.

TRANSLATION

1. Article 13(d) of the Convention

2–015   Under paragraph 179(2) of the General Civil Code, the adoption of a child by more than
one person, either at the same time or at different times, is permitted only if the adopters are
married to each other. From this it follows the existence of a previous adoption by other
persons is permissible only if the other person is the spouse of the adoptive father or of the
adoptive mother.

2. Article 13(e) of the Convention

2–016   Under paragraph 180 of the General Civil Code, the adoptive parents shall be at least 18
years older than the adoptive child; if the difference in age is slightly less than 18 years, the
period by which it is less shall be disregarded provided that the relationship which has
developed between the adopter and the child corresponds to that existing between parents and
their issue. If the child is the issue of the adopter's spouse or is related to the adopter, a
difference in age of 16 years shall suffice.

3. Article 13(f) of the Convention

2–017   The adoptive father must have completed his thirtieth year and the adoptive mother her
twenty-eighth year. However, if a husband and wife are adopting a child together, or if the
adoptive child is the natural child of the spouse of the adoptive parent, these minimum age
limits do not apply provided that the relationship which has developed between the adopter
and the child corresponds to that existing between parents and their issue. In this case there is
no minimum age.

PROVISIONS RELATING TO PROHIBITIONS ON AN ADOPTION CONTAINED IN THE NATIONAL LAW OF SWITZERLAND NOTIFIED UNDER ARTICLES 13, 17 AND 24 OF THE CONVENTION

1. En ce qui concerne l'article 13, 1er alinéa, lettre e, de la convention:

Art. 265 (Code Civil Suisse)   **2–018**

IV. Age et consentement de l'enfant

1. L'enfant doit être d'au moins seize ans plus jeune que les parents adoptifs.
2. . . . .
3. . . . .

2. En ce qui concerne l'article 13, 1er alinéa, lettre f, de la convention:

Art. 264 a (Code Civil Suisse)   **2–019**

II. Adoption Conjointe

1. . . . .
2. Les époux doivent être mariés depuis cinq ans ou être âgés de trente-cinq ans révolus.
3. Un époux peut cependant adopter l'enfant de son conjoint s'il est marié avec lué depuis deux ans ou s'il est âgé de trent-cinq ans révolus.

3. En ce qui concerne l'article 13, 1er alinéa, lettre g, de la convention:

Art. 264 (Code Civil Suisse)   **2–020**

A. Adoption de mineurs

1. Conditions générales

Un enfant peut être adopté si les futurs parents adoptifs lui ont fourni des soins et ont pourvu à son éducation pendant au moins deux ans et si toutes les circonstances permettent de prévoir que l'établissement d'un lien de filiation légitime servira au bien a l'enfant sans porter une atteinte inéquitable à la situation d'autres enfants des parents adoptifs.

TRANSLATION

1. Article 13(e) of the Convention

Art. 265 (Swiss Civil Code)   **2–021**

IV. Age and consent of the child

1. The child shall be at least sixteen years younger than the adopters.
2. . . . .
3. . . . .

1. Article 13(f) of the Convention:

Art. 264(a) (Swiss Civil Code)   **2–022**

II. Joint adoption

1. . . . .
2. The spouses shall have been married for five years or shall have completed the thirty-fifth year of their lives.
3. A spouse may, however, adopt the child of his spouse if he has been married to that spouse for two years or if he has completed the thirty-fifth year of his life.

1. Article 13(g) of the Convention:

2–023

A. Adoption of minors

I. General conditions

Art. 246 (Swiss Civil Code)

A child may be adopted if the future adopters have taken care of and brought up the child for at least two years and if there is every reason to believe that the establishment of a legal filial relationship will benefit the child without unduly affecting the position of other children of the adopters.

CONVENTION ADOPTION (MISCELLANEOUS PROVISIONS) ORDER 1978

(S.I. 1978 No. 1432)

Dated September 13, 1978, *and made by the Secretary of State for Social Services under the Adoption Act* 1968, *ss.*4(3), 7(4) *and* 11(1) *and the Children Act* 1975 (*c.* 72), *s.*107(1).

GENERAL NOTE

This Order contains the definition of "convention adoption", "British territory", "specified **2–024** country" and "United Kingdom national" in relation to England and Wales for the purposes of the Adoption Act 1976 in respect of the Convention on Jurisdiction, Applicable Law and Recognition of Decrees relating to Adoptions concluded at The Hague on November 15, 1965. Article 8 of and the Schedule to this Order specify, for the purposes of the definition of "notified provision" in ss.53 and 54 of the 1976 Act, the provisions of the United Kingdom national law which prohibit adoptions and which have been notified by the United Kingdom pursuant to Articles 13 and 17 of the Convention. Also see D.H.S.S. Circular No. LAC (78) 19.

Citation, commencement and extent

1.—(1) This order may be cited as the Convention Adoption (Mis- **2–025** cellaneous Provisions) Order 1978 and shall come into operation on October 23, 1978.

(2) This order shall not apply to Scotland.

Interpretation

2.—(1) Any reference in this order to the provisions of an enactment or **2–026** statutory instrument shall be construed, unless the context otherwise requires, as a reference to that enactment or statutory instrument as amended, extended, applied or replaced by or under any other enactment.

(2) The rules for the construction of Acts of Parliament contained in the Interpretation Act 1889 shall apply for the purposes of the interpretation of this order as they apply for the purposes of the interpretation of an Act of Parliament.

Meaning of "convention adoption"

3. For the purposes of the meaning of "convention adoption" in section **2–027** 5(2) of the Adoption Act 1968 there is hereby designated an overseas adoption which is an adoption of the description specified in the Adoption (Designation of Overseas Adoptions) Order 1973 regulated by the Convention on Jurisdiction, Applicable Law and Recognition of Decrees relating to Adoptions concluded at the Hague on November 15, 1965.

Evidence of convention adoption

4.—(1) Evidence that an overseas adoption which has been effected is **2–028** regulated by the Convention may be given by the production of a document purporting to be—

119

(a) a certified copy of an entry made, in accordance with the law of the country or territory concerned, in a public register relating to the recording of adoptions and showing that the adoption is so regulated; or

(b) a certificate that the adoption is so regulated, signed or purporting to be signed by a person authorised by the law of the country or territory concerned to sign such a certificate, or a certified copy of such certificate.

(2) Where a document produced by virtue of paragraph (1) of this Article is not in English, the Registrar General may require the production of an English translation of the document before satisfying himself of the matters specified in section 8 of the Adoption Act 1968.

(3) Nothing in this Article shall be construed as precluding proof, in accordance with the Evidence (Foreign, Dominion and Colonial Documents) Act 1933, or the Oaths and Evidence (Overseas Authorities and Countries) Act 1963, or otherwise, that an overseas adoption which has been effected is regulated by the Convention.

Designation of "British territory"

2–029 **5.** For the purposes of the provisions of sections 24 and 107(1) of the Children Act 1975, the United Kingdom is hereby designated as British territory.

Designation of "specified country"

2–030 **6.** For the purposes of the provisions of section 5(1) and 11(1) of the Adoption Act 1968, Northern Ireland is hereby designated as a specified country.

Meaning of "United Kingdom national"

2–031 **7.** For the purposes of any provision of the Adoption Act 1968 or of the Children Act 1975, a United Kingdom national is a citizen of the United Kingdom and Colonies who satisfies the condition hereby specified, that is to say, he has the right of abode in the United Kingdom by virtue of section 2 of the Immigration Act 1971.

Meaning of "notified provision"

2–032 **8.** For the purposes of sections 6 and 7 of the Adoption Act 1968 ("notified provision"), the provisions set out in the Schedule to this order are hereby specified as the provisions relating to prohibitions on an adoption contained in the national law of the United Kingdom which have been notified by the Government of the United Kingdom in pursuance of the provisions of the Convention.

Article 8   SCHEDULE

PROVISIONS RELATING TO PROHIBITIONS OF AN ADOPTION CONTAINED IN THE NATIONAL LAW OF THE UNITED KINGDOM NOTIFIED UNDER ARTICLES 13 AND 17 OF THE CONVENTION

2–033 In accordance with the provisions of Article 13 and with reference to the second paragraph of Article 13 and with reference to the second paragraph of Article 17 of the Convention, the United Kingdom declares, with a view to the application of Article 4, that the provisions of its internal law prohibiting adoptions are as follows.

A: In England and Wales and Scotland:

With reference to Article 13(b) of the Convention

Under section 11(1) of the Children Act 1975 an adoption order may not be made on the **2–034** application of one person unless one of the following conditions is satisfied:—
- (a) he is not married, or
- (b) he is married and the court is satisfied that:—
  - (i) his spouse cannot be found, or
  - (ii) the spouses have separated and are living apart, and the separation is likely to be permanent, or
  - (iii) his spouse is by reason of ill health, whether physical or mental, incapable of making an application for an adoption order.

With reference to Article 13(b) and (c) of the Convention

Under section 11(3) of the Children Act 1975 an adoption order shall not be made on the **2–035** application of the mother or father of the child alone unless the court is satisfied that:—
- (a) the other natural parent is dead or cannot be found, or
- (b) there is some other reason justifying the exclusion of the other natural parent.

With reference to Article 13(f) of the Convention

Under sections 10(1), 11(1) and 107(1) of the Children Act 1975:   **2–036**
- (a) the adopter or each of joint adopters must have attained the age of 21;
- (b) the child to be adopted must be under the age of 18.

With reference to Article 13(g) of the Convention

Under section 3(1) of the Adoption Act 1958 an adoption order shall not **2–037** be made in respect of any child unless he has been continuously in the actual custody of the applicant for at least three consecutive months immediately preceding the date of the order, not counting any time before the date which appears to the court to be the date on which the child attained the age of six weeks.

B: In Northern Ireland:

With reference to Article 13(b) of the Convention

- (a) Under sections 1(2) and 4(1)(b) of the Adoption Act (Northern Ireland) 1967 an **2–038** adoption order may not be made on the application of one person unless:
  - (i) he is not married; or
  - (ii) he is married and *either* his spouse has consented to the making of the order *or* the court dispenses with the consent of the spouse on a ground specified in (b) below.
- (b) The court may dispense with the consent of the spouse of an applicant for an adoption order if it is satisfied that the person whose consent is so dispensed with cannot be found or is incapable of giving his consent or that the spouses have separated and are living apart and the separation is likely to be permanent.
- (c) Under section 2(3) of the Adoption Act (Northern Ireland) 1967 an adoption order shall not be made in respect of a child who is a female in favour of sole applicant who is a male unless the court is satisfied that there are special circumstances which justify as an exceptional measure the making of an adoption order.

With reference to Article 13(f) of the Convention

Under the provisions of sections 2(1) and (2) and 46(1) of the Adoption Act (Northern **2–039** Ireland) 1967:
- (a) In the case of a sole applicant who is not a parent of the child:
  - (i) if he is a relative of the child, the applicant must have attained the age of 21;
  - (ii) otherwise the applicant must have attained the age of 25.

(b) In the case of a joint application where neither spouse is a parent of the child:
  (i) if one of the applicants is a relative of the child, (a)(i) applies and the spouse must also have attained the age of 21;
  (ii) otherwise one of the applicants must satisfy (a)(ii) and the spouse must have attained the age of 21.
(c) The child to be adopted must be under the age of 18.

"Relative" in relation to a child means a grandparent, brother, sister, uncle or aunt, whether of the full blood, of the half-blood or by affinity, and includes—

(a) where an order authorising an adoption has been made in respect of the child or any other person under the Adoption Act (Northern Ireland) 1967 or the Adoption of Children Act (Northern Ireland) 1950 or any enactment repealed by that Act or has been made anywhere in Great Britain, the Isle of Man or any of the Channel Islands, any person who would be a relative of the child within the meaning of this definition if the adopted child were the child of the adopter born in lawful wedlock;

(b) where the child is illegitimate, the father of the child and any person who would be a relative of the child within the meaning of this definition if the child were the legitimate child of its mother and father.

With reference to Article 13(g) of the Convention

2–040 Under section 3(1) of the Adoption Act (Northern Ireland) 1967 an adoption order shall not be made in respect of any child unless he has been continuously in the care and possession of the applicant in Northern Ireland for at least three consecutive months immediately preceding the date of the order, not counting any time before the date which appears to the court to be the date on which the child attained the age of six weeks.

ADOPTION AGENCIES REGULATIONS 1983

(S.I. 1983 No. 1964)

Dated December 30, 1983, and made by the Secretary of State for Social Services and the Secretary of State for Wales under the Adoption Act 1958 (c. 5) s.32 and the Children Act 1975 (c.72) s.4(1)).

These Regulations make provision for the approval of adoption societies and for annual **2–041** reports and information to be provided by such societies (regs. 2 and 3). They provide for the establishment of adoption panels by adoption agencies and for arrangements to be made by agencies in relation to their adoption work (regs. 4–6). They specify the procedures to be followed before and after a child is placed for adoption (regs. 7–13). They make provision for the confidentiality and preservation of case records and for access to case records and disclosure of information (regs. 13A–15). They also make provision in respect of the transfer of case records between adoption agencies and progress reports to former parents of children who have been freed for adoption (regs. 16–17).

Although it is necessary to comply strictly with the letter of these regulations they are intended to be directory, not mandatory. Therefore, non compliance with the regulations does not necessarily vitiate the adoption procedure. A judge is entitled to take breaches of the regulations into account at the adoption hearing in deciding whether to make an adoption order (*Re T. (A Minor) (Adoption: Parental Consent)* [1986] 1 All E.R. 817, CA).

These Regulations, which were made under the Adoption Act 1958 and the Children Act 1975, remain in force by virtue of the transitional provisions contained in s.73(1), Sched. 2, para. 1 of the Adoption Act 1976.

GUIDANCE

Guidance on these Regulations can be found in Departmental Circulars LAC (84) 3 and **2–042** LAC (97) 13.

AMENDMENTS

The amendments to these regulations were made by the Adoption Agencies and Children **2–043** (Arrangements for Placement and Reviews) (Miscellaneous Amendments) Regulations 1997 (S.I. 1997 No. 649).

Citation, commencement, extent and interpretation

1.—(1) These regulations may be cited as the Adoption Agencies **2–044** Regulations 1983 and shall come into operation on May 27, 1984.

(2) These regulations shall not apply to Scotland.

(3) In these regulations, unless the context otherwise requires—

["the Act" means the Adoption Act 1976;]

["the Children Act" means the Children Act 1989;]

"adoption agency" means an approved adoption society or local authority;

"adoption panel" means a panel established in accordance with regulation 5;

"prospective adopter" means a person who proposes to adopt a child.

(4) Any reference in these regulations to any provision made by or contained in any enactment or instrument shall, except insofar as the context otherwise requires, be construed as including a reference to any provision which may re-enact or replace it, with or without modification.

(5) Any reference in these regulations to a numbered regulation or the Schedule is to the regulation bearing that number in or the Schedule to these regulations and any reference in a regulation or the Schedule to a numbered paragraph is a reference to the paragraph bearing that number in that regulation or the Schedule.

GENERAL NOTE

2–045   Guidance on this Regulation can be found in Circular LAC (84) 3 at para. 7.

Approval of adoption societies

2–046   **2.**—(1) An application to the Secretary of State under [section 3 of the Act] (approval of adoption societies) shall be made in writing of a form supplied by the Secretary of State.

(2) An unincorporated body of persons shall not apply for approval under [section 3 of the Act].

GENERAL NOTE

2–047   Guidance on this Regulation can be found in Circular LAC (84)3 at paras. 2–6.

Annual reports and information to be provided by approved adoption societies

2–048   **3.** Every approved adoption society shall—

(a) furnish the Secretary of State with two copies of the society's annual report as soon as is reasonably practicable after the issue thereof and with such other information as and when the Secretary of State may from time to time require;

(b) notify the Secretary of State in writing of any change in the society's name or in the address of its registered or head office within one month after such change;

(c) where the society proposes to cease, or expects to cease, to act as an adoption society, so notify the Secretary of State in writing not less than one month, or as soon as is reasonably practicable, before the date when the society will cease, or expects to cease, so to act; and

(d) where the society has ceased to act as an adoption society, notify the Secretary of State in writing that it has ceased so to act as soon thereafter as is reasonably practicable.

GENERAL NOTE

2–049   See paras. 8 and 9 of Circular LAC (84)3.

Application of regulations to certain adoption agencies

2–050   **4.** Where an adoption agency operates only for the purpose of putting persons into contact with other adoption agencies and for the purpose of putting such agencies into contact with each other or for either of such purposes, regulation 5 and, to the extent that it requires consultation with the adoption panel and the making of arrangements for the exercise of the panel's functions, regulation 6, shall not apply to such an agency.

GENERAL NOTE

2–051   See para. 10 of Circular LAC (84)3.

[Establishment of adoption panel and appointment of members

5.—(1) Subject to paragraphs (2), (3) and (6), an adoption agency shall **2–052** establish at least one panel and shall appoint no more than 10 persons, including at least one man and one woman, to be members of such a panel.

(2) The adoption agency shall appoint as chairman of an adoption panel a person who has such experience in adoption work as the agency considers appropriate. and the other members of the panel shall include:

(a) subject to paragraph (6), two social workers in the employment of the adoption agency,

(b) subject to paragrah (6), at least one member of the adoption agency's management committee where the agency is an approved adoption society or, where the agency is a local authority, at least one member of that authority's social services committee,

(c) the person nominated as the medical adviser to the adoption agency under regulation 6(4) (or one of them if more than one are appointed), for so long as that person is so nominated, and

(d) at least three other persons ("independent persons"), not being members or employees of the adoption agency, or elected members, where the agency is a local authority who shall where reasonably practicable include an adoptive parent and an adopted person who must be at least 18 years of age.

(3) The adoption agency shall appoint one of the members of the adoption panel as vice-chairman, who, where the chairman of the panel has died or ceased to hold office, or is unable to perform his duties by reason of illness, absence from England and Wales or any other cause, shall act as the chairman for so long as there is no chairman able to do so.

(4) An adoption panel shall make the recommendations specified in regulation 10 only when, subject to paragraph (6), at least six of its members meet as a panel and those members include the chairman or vice-chairman and a social worker in the employment of the adoption agency.

(5) An adoption panel shall keep a written record of any of the recommendations specified in regulation 10 which it makes and the reason for them.

(6) Any two but no more than three local authorities may establish a joint adoption panel, and where a joint adoption panel is established—

(a) the maximum number of members who may be appointed to that panel shall be increased to eleven,

(b) the chairman shall be appointed by agreement between the local authorities,

(c) one social worker in the employment of each local authority and one member of each local authority's social services committee shall be appointed to the panel,

(d) three independent persons shall be appointed to the panel by agreement between the local authorities,

(e) the vice-chairman shall be appointed from the menbers of the panel by agreement between the local authorities, and

(f) the quorum set out in paragraph (4) shall be increased to seven.]

GENERAL NOTE

This regulation requires adoption agencies to establish adoption panels and makes **2–053** provision for panel membership. In particular, it provides for the appointment of a chairman and vice-chairman, for the panel to include at least three independent persons including, where prcticable, an adoptive parent or adopted person, for a written record of the panel's reasons for its recommendations, and for the establishment of a joint panel by no more than three local authorities where this is felt to be appropriate.

Guidance on this Regulation is given in paras. 10.1 to 10.17 of Circular LAC (97)13.

Para. (1)

2–054   *Establish:* From November 1, 1997 (reg. 5B).

Appoint: There is no provision for alternatives or deputies to be appointed. Suggestions for a protocol for panel members are contained in para. 47 of Circular (97)13.

Para. (2)

2–055   *Chairman:* Note reg. 11(1A).

[Tenure of office of members

2–056   **5A.**—(1) Subject to the provisions of this regulation and regulation 5B a member of the adoption panel shall hold office for a term not exceeding three years, and may not hold office as a member of that panel for more than two consecutive terms without an intervening period of at least three years.

(2) An adoption agency shall so arrange the tensure of office of the members of the panel so that so far as possible the term of office of at least one third of its members shall expire each year.

(3) The medical adviser member of the adoption panel shall hold office only for so long as he is the medical adviser nominated under regulation 6(4).

(4) A member may resign his office at any time after appointments by giving notice in writing to that effect to the adoption agency, or if he is a member of a joint adoption panel, by giving notice to one of the local authorities whose panel it is.

(5) Subject to paragraph (6), if an adoption agency is of the opinion that a member is unfit or unable to hold office, the agency may terminate his office by giving him notice in writing with reasons.

(6) If the member whose appointment is to be terminated under paragraph (5) is a member of a joint adoption panel, his appointment may only be terminated with the agreement of all the local authorities whose panel it is.

(7) Where a member is appointed to replace a person whsoe appointment has been terminated for any reason before the expiry of the term for which he has been appointed, that member shall hold office as a member of that panel for the unexpired part of the term of the person whom he replaces, and may not hold office for more than one consecutive term after the expiry of that term without an intervening period of three years.]

GENERAL NOTE

2–057   This regulation provides for a maximum three-year term of office for panel members and for their eligibility for one consecutive re-appointment. It is considered at paras. 10.18 to 10.25 of Circular LAC (97)13.

[Establishment of new panels on November 1, 1997

2–058   **5B.**—(1) All members of an adoption panel established before November 1, 1997, shall cease to hold office on that date.

(2) With effect from November 1, 1997, an adoption agency shall establish a new adoption panel in accordance with regulations 5 and 5A.]

126

Adoption agency arrangements for adoption work

6.—(1) An adoption agency shall, in consultation with the adoption panel **2–059** and to the extent specified in paragraph (5) with the adoption agency's medical adviser, make arrangements which shall be set out in writing to govern the exercise of the agency's and the panel's functions and such arrangements shall be reviewed by the agency not less than once every three years.

(2) Subject to regulations 14 and 15, the arrangements referred to in paragraph (1) shall include provision—

(a) for maintaining the confidentiality and safekeeping of adoption information, case records and the indexes to them,

(b) for authorising access to such records and indexes or disclosure of information by virtue of regulation 15, and

(c) for ensuring that those for whom access is provided or to whom disclosure is made by virtue of regulation 15(2)(a) agree in writing before such authorisation is given that such records, indexes and information will remain confidential, so however that a child who is placed for adoption or who has been adopted and his prospective adopter or adoptive parent shall not be required to give such agreement in respect of that child's adoption.

(3) The adoption agency shall satisfy itself that social work staff employed on the agency's work have had such experience and hold such qualifications as the adoption agency considers appropriate to that work.

(4) The adoption agency shall nominate at least one registered medical practitioner to be the agency's medical adviser.

(5) The adoption agency's medical adviser shall be consulted in relation to the arrangements for access to and disclosure of health information which is required or permitted by virtue of regulation 15.

GENERAL NOTE

Guidance on this Regulation can be found in Circular LAC (84)3 at paras. 22 to 30.   **2–060**

Adoption agency's duties in respect of a child and his parents or guardian

7.—(1) When an adoption agency is considering adoption for a child it **2–061** shall either—

(a) in respect of the child, having regard to his age and understanding, and as the case may be his parents or guardian, so far as is reasonably practicable—

(i) provide a counselling service for them,

(ii) explain to them the legal implications of and procedures in relation to adoption and freeing for adoption, and

(iii) provide them with written information about the matters referred to in head (ii), or

(b) satisfy itself that the requirements of sub-paragraph (a) have been carried out by another adoption agency.

(2) Where, following the procedure referred to in paragraph (1), an adoption agency is considering adoption for a child, the agency shall—

(a) set up a case record in respect of the child and place on it any information obtained by virtue of this regulation,

(b) obtain, so far as is reasonably practicable, such particulars of the parents or guardian and having regard to his age and understanding the child as are referred to in Parts I and III to V of the Schedule

127

together with any other relevant information which may be requested by the adoption panel,

(c) arrange and obtain a written report by a registered medical practitioner on the child's health which shall deal with the matters specified in Part II of the Schedule, unless such a report has been made within six months before the setting up of the case record under sub-paragraph (a) and is available to the agency,

(d) arrange such other examinations and screening procedures of and tests on the child and, so far as is reasonably practicable, his parents, as are recommended by the adoption agency's medical adviser, and obtain a copy of the written report of such examinations, screening procedures and tests, and

(e) prepare a written report containing the agency's observations on the matters referred to in this regulation, which shall be passed together with all information obtained by it by virtue of this regulation to the adoption panel or to another adoption agency.

(3) [Where the father of a child does not have parental responsibility for the child and his identity] is known to the adoption agency, it shall so far as it considers reasonably practicable and in the interests of the child—

(a) carry out in respect of the father the requirements of paragraph (1)(a) as if they applied to him unless the agency is satisfied that another adoption agency has so complied with those requirements,

(b) obtain the particulars of him referred to in Parts III and IV of the Schedule together with any other relevant information which may be requested by the adoption panel, and arrange and obtain a copy of the written report of such examinations, screening procedures and tests on him as are recommended by the adoption agency's medical adviser, and

(c) ascertain so far as possible whether he intends to apply for custody of the child.

GENERAL NOTE
Guidance on this Regulation can be found in Circular LAC (84)3 at paras. 31 to 52.

Para. (3)

2–062   *Reasonably practicable:* Contacting the father would not be practicable if this would be detrimental to the child's welfare; see *Re P. (Adoption) (Natural Father's Rights)* [1994] 1 F.L.R. 771, noted under para. (2)(*j*) of Sched. 2 to the Adoption Rules 1994.

Adoption agency's duties in respect of a prospective adopter

2–063   **8.**—(1) When an adoption agency is considering whether a person may be suitable to be an adoptive parent, either—

(a) it shall—
   (i) provide a counselling service for him,
   (ii) explain to him the legal implications of and procedures in relation to adoption, and
   (iii) provide him with written information about the matters referred to in head (ii), or

(b) it shall satisfy itself that the requirements of sub-paragraph (a) have been carried out in respect of him by another adoption agency.

(2) Where, following the procedures referred to in paragraph (1), an adoption agency considers that a person may be suitable to be an adoptive parent, it shall—

128

(a) set up a case record in respect of him and place on it any information obtained by virtue of this regulation,

(b) obtain such particulars as are referred to in Part VI of the Schedule together with, so far as is reasonably practicable, any other relevant information which may be requested by the adoption panel,

(c) obtain a written report by a registered medical practitioner on the prospective adopter's health which shall deal with the matters specified in Part VII of the Schedule, unless such a report has been made within six months before the setting up of the case record under sub-paragraph (a) and is available to the agency,

(d) obtain a written report in respect of any premises which that person intends to use as his home if he adopts a child,

(e) obtain written reports of the interviews with two persons nominated by the prospective adopter to provide personal references for him,

(f) obtain a written report from the prospective adopter's local authority in relation to him, [. . .]

(g) [prepare a written report which shall include the agency's assessment of the prospective adopter's suitability to be an adoptive parent and any other observations of the agency on the matters referred to in this regulation,

(h) notify the prospective adopter that his application is to be referred to the adoption panel and at the same time send a copy of the agency's assessment referred to in paragraph (g) to the prospective adopter inviting him to send any observations in writing on that assessment to thea gency within 28 days, and

(i) at the end of the period of 28 days referred to in sub-paragraph (h), (or earlier if any observations made by the prospective adopter on the assessment are received before the 28 days has expired), pass the written report referred to in sub-paragraph (g) and any written observations made by the prospective adopter together with all information obtained by the agency by virtue of this regulation, to the adoption panel or to another adoption agency.]

GENERAL NOTE

See Circular LAC (84)3, paras. 53 to 65.   **2–064**

Para. (2)(h)

Copy of the agency's assessment: This means the social worker's assessment of the suitability **2–065** of the prospective adopter and not the complete home study report (Circular LAC (97)13, para. 13).

Para. (2)(i)

Written observations: See para. 14 of Circular LAC (97)13.   **2–066**

Adoption agency's duties in respect of proposed placement

9.—(1) Subject to paragraph (2), an adoption agency shall refer its **2–067** proposal to place a particular child for adoption with a prospective adopter, which it considers may be appropriate, together with a written report containing its observations on the proposal and any information relevant to the proposed placement, to its adoption panel.

(2) An Adoption agency shall refer its proposal to place a child for adoption to the adoption panel only if—

(a) any other adoption agency which has made a decision in accordance with regulation 11(1) that adoption is in the best interests of the child or that the prospective adopter is suitable to be an adoptive parent, has been consulted concerning the proposal, and

(b) any local authority or voluntary organisation [which has parental responsibility for the child by virtue of section 18 or 21 of the Act (freeing for adoption and variation of order to substitute one adoption agency for another) or in whose care the child is, has been consulted and agrees with the proposal.

(3) An adoption agency which has a proposal to place a particular child for adoption with a prospective adopter shall set up case records in respect of them to the extent that it has not already set up such records and place on the appropriate record any information, reports and decisions referred to it by another adoption agency together with any information to be passed to the adoption panel by virtue of this regulation in respect of them.

(4) An adoption agency shall obtain, so far as is reasonably practicable, any other relevant information which may be requested by the adoption panel in connection with the proposed placement.

GENERAL NOTE

2–068   Guidance on this Regulation can be found in Circular LAC (84)3 at paras. 66 to 70.

Adoption panel functions

2–069   **10.**—(1) Subject to paragraphs (2) and (3), an adoption panel shall consider the case of every child, prospective adopter and proposed placement referred to it by the adoption agency and shall make one or more of the recommendations to the agency, as the case may be, as to—

(a) whether adoption is in the best interests of a child and, if the panel recommends that it is, whether an application under section 18 of the Act (freeing child for adoption) should be made to free the child for adoption,

(b) whether a prospective adopter is suitable to be an adoptive parent, and

(c) whether a prospective adopter would be a suitable adoptive parent for a particular child.

(2) An adoption panel may make the recommendations specified in paragraph (1) at the same time or at different times, so however that it shall make the recommendation specified in paragraph (1)(c) in respect of a particular child and prospective adopter only if—

(a) that recommendation is to be made at the same meeting of the panel at which a recommendation has been made that adoption is in the best interests of the child, or

(b) an adoption agency decision has been made in accordance with regulation 11(1) that adoption is in the best interests of the child, and

(c) in either case—

(i) the recommendation specified in paragraph (1)(c) is to be made at the same meeting of the panel at which a recommendation has been made that the prospective adopter is suitable to be an adoptive parent, or

(ii) an adoption agency decision has been made in accordance with regulation 11(1) that the prospective adopter is suitable to be an adoptive parent.

(3) In considering what recommendations to make the panel shall have regard to the duties imposed upon the adoption agency by sections 6 and 7 of the Act (duty to promote welfare of child and religious upbringing of adopted child) and shall, as the case may be—

(a) consider and take into account all the information and reports passed to it by virtue of regulations 7(2)(e), 8(2)(g) and 9(1),

(b) request the adoption agency to obtain any other relevant information which the panel considers necessary,

(c) obtain legal advice in relation to each case together with advice on an application for an adoption order or, as the case may be, an application to free a child for adoption.

GENERAL NOTE

Guidance on this Regulation can be found in Circular LAC (84)3 at paras. 71 to 79.

In *R. v. North Yorkshire County Council, ex p. M (No. 2)* [1989] 2 F.L.R. 79, a guardian *ad* **2–070** *litem* had been appointed under s.32B of the Children and Young Persons Act 1969 to act for the child in care proceedings. Ewbank J. held that although the local authority had a duty both to inform the guardian of any proposed major changes in the child's circumstances (such as a placement for adoption) and to listen to the guardian's views on any such proposal, that did not imply that the guardian was entitled to decide how the local authority was to conduct its affairs. His Lordship therefore refused the guardian's application to set aside the authority's decision not to allow him to attend its adoption panel meeting where the placement of the child was to be discussed.

Para. (1)

Recommendations: The panel must keep a written record of its recommendations and the **2–071** reasons for them (reg. 5(5)).

Para. (3)(a)

All the information and reports: All of the information which has been obtained by virtue of **2–072** the regulations specified in this sub-paragraph must be made available to the panel.

Adoption agency decisions and notifications

11.—(1) An adoption agency shall make a decision on a matter referred **2–073** to in regulation 10(1)(a), [. . .] or (c) only after taking into account the recommendation of the adoption panel made by virtue of that regulation on such matter.

[(1A) No member of an adoption panel shall take part in any decision made by the adoption agency under paragraph (1).

(2) As soon as possible after making such a decision the adoption agency shall, as the case may be, notify in writing—

(a) the parents of the child, including his father if he does not have parental responsibility for the child but only where the agency considers this to be in the child's interests, or the guardian of the child, if their whereabouts are known to the agency, of its decision as to whether it considers adoption to be in the best interest of the child,

(b) the person to be notified under sub-paragraph (a), if it considers adoption to be in the best interests of the child, of its decision as to whether an application under section 18 of the Act (freeing child for adoption) should be made to free the child for adoption,

(c) [. . .]

(d) the prospective adopter of its decision that he would be suitable as such for a particular child.

131

    Guidance on this Regulation can be found in Circular LAC (84)3 at paras. 80 to 85.

Para. (1)

2–075   *Taking into account:* The ultimate decision on the matters referred to in reg. 10(1) rests with the agency and not with the panel. For agency decision making, see paras. 50 to 53 of Circular LAC (97)13.

[Adoption agency decisions and notifications—prospective adopters

2–076   **11A.**—(1) In relation to a matter referred to in regulation 10(1)(b) (panel recommendations—prospective adopters) the adoption agency shall take into account the recommendation of the adoption panel made by virtue of that regulation on that matter before making its decision.

(2) No member of an adoption panel shall take part in any decision made by the agency under paragraph (1).

(3) If the agency decide to approve the prospective adopter as suitable to be an adoptive parent, the agency shall notify the prospective adopter in writing of its decision.

(4) If the agency consider that the prospective adopter is not suitable to be an adoptive parent, the agency shall—

(a) notify the prospective adopter in writing that it proposes not to approve him as suitable to be an adoptive parent;

(b) send with that notification their reasons together with a copy of the recommendation of the adoption panel, if different; and

(c) invite the prospective adopter to submit any representations he wishes to make within 28 days.

(5) If within the period of 28 days referred to in paragraph (4), the prospective adopter has not made any representations, the agency may proceed to make its decision and shall notify the prospective adopter in writing of its decision together with the reasons for that decision.

(6) If within the period of 28 days referred to in paragraph (4) the agency receive further representations from the prospective adopter, it may refer the case together with all the relevant information to its adoption panel for further consideration.

(7) The adoption panel shall reconsider any case referred to it under paragraph (6) and make a fresh recommendation to the agency as to whether the prospective adopter is suitable to be an adoptive parent.

(8) The agency shall make a decision on the case but if the case has been referred to the adoption panel under paragraph (6) it shall make the decision only after taking into account any recommendation of the adoption panel made by virtue of paragraph (7).

(9) As soon as possible after making the decision under paragraph (8), the agency shall notify the prospective adopter in writing of its decision, stating its reasons for that decision if they do not consider the prospective adopter to be suitable to be an adoptive parent, and of the adoption panel's recommendation, if this is different from thea gency's decision.]

2–077   Under this regulation, prospective adopters whom the agency considers not suitable to be adoptive parents must be notified of the agency's reasons and given an opportunity to make representations before the agency reaches its decision. Guidance is given at paras. 16 to 22 of Circular LAC (97)13.

    In *R. v. Buckinghamshire County Council, The Times,* December 21, 1985, the Court of Appeal held that the decision of an adoption panel that the plaintiffs were not suitable as proposed adopters was a decision of the local authority pursuant to the powers and duties imposed and confirmed on it by the statutory code and the High Court was therefore precluded from reviewing the decision unders its wardship jurisdiction.

Para. (4)

Reasons: In *Re Poyser and Mills' Arbitration* [1964] 2 Q.B. 467 at 478, Megaw J. said that **2–078** where Parliament has said that reasons must be given that means that "proper, adequate reasons must be given. The reasons that are set out must be reasons which will not only be intelligible, but which deal with the substantial points that have been raised."

Placement for adoption

12.—(1) Where an adoption agency has decided in accordance with **2–079** regulation 11(1) that a prospective adopter would be a suitable adoptive parent for a particular child it shall provide the prospective adopter with written information about the child, his personal history and background, including his religious and cultural background, his health history and current state of health, together with the adoption agency's written proposals in respect of the adoption, including proposals as to the date of placement for adoption with the prospective adopter.

(2) If the prospective adopter accepts the adoption agency's proposals the agency shall—

(a) inform the child of the proposed placement for adoption with the prospective adopter where the child is capable of understanding the proposal,

(aa) notify in writing the parent or guardian of the child, if their whereabouts are known to the agency, of the proposed placement for adoption, unless the parent or guardian has made a declaration under section 18(6) or 19(4) of the Act (declaration as to no further involvement with child),

[(aaa) where the father of the child does not have parental responsibility for him and his identity is known to the agency, notify the father of the proposed placement provided the agency considers this to be in the best interests of the child,]

(b) send a written report of the child's health history and current state of health to the prospective adopter's registered medical practitioner, if any, before the proposed placement, together with particulars of the proposed placement,

(c) notify the local authority and the district health authority in whose area the prospective adopter resides in writing before the placement with particulars of the proposed placement,

(d) notify the local education authority in whose area the prospective adopter resides in writing before the placement with particulars of the proposed placement if the child is of compulsory school age within the meaning of section 35 of the Education Act 1944 or the adoption agency's medical adviser considers the child to be handicapped,

(e) place the child with the prospective adopter, so however that where the child already has his home with the prospective adopter the agency shall notify the prospective adopter in writing of the date the child is placed with him by the agency for adoption,

(f) [. . .]

(g) ensure that the child is visited within one week of the placement and on such other occasions as the adoption agency considers necessary in order to supervise the child's well-being,

(h) ensure that written reports are obtained of such visits,

133

(i) provide such advice and assistance to the prospective adopter as the agency considers necessary,

[(j) make appointments for the child to be examined by a registered medical practitioner and for a written assessment on the state of his health and his need for health care to be made—

    (i) at least once in every period of six months before the child's second birthday, and

    (ii) at least once in every period of six months before the child's second birthday, unless the child is of sufficient understanding to make an informed decision and refuses to submit to the examination, and]

[(k) review the placement for adoption of the child within four weeks of placement, and not more than three months after the review unless an application for an adoption order has been made, and at least every six months thereafter until an application for an adoption order is made.]

[(3) The agency who carry out the review referred to in paragraph (2)(k) shall—

(a) set out in writing the arrangements governing the manner in which the case of each child shall be reviewed and shall draw the written arrangements to the attention of the child, where reasonably practicable having regard to his age and understanding, to the prospective adopters, and to any other person the agency considers relevant,

(b) have regard so far as reasonably practicable to the considerations specified in Part VIII of the Schedule, and

(c) ensure that—

    (i) the information obtained in respect of a child's case,

    (ii) details of the proceedings at any meeting arranged by the agency to consider any aspect of the review of the case, and

    (iii) details of any decision made in the course of or as a result of the review,

    are recorded in writing.

(4) The agency who carry out the review shall, so far as reasonbly practicable, notify details of the result of the review and of any decision taken by them in consequence of the review to—

(a) the child where he is of sufficient age and understanding;

(b) his parents, except where a freeing order has been made under section 18 of the Act and that order has not been revoked;

(c) his father, if he does not have parental responsibility for him and his identity is known, provided that the agency considered this to be in the child's interests;

(d) the prospective adopters; and

(e) any other person whom they consider ought to be notified.]

GENERAL NOTE

2–080   Guidance on this Regulation can be found in Circular LAC (84)3 at paras. 86 to 101.

Para. (1)

2–081   *Provide the prospective adopter with written information:* No relevant information falling within the categories specified in this paragraph should be withheld from the prospective adopters. In local settlement 94/A/3720 an adoptive placement had broken down. The Local Government Ombudsman recommended that the local authority should pay compensation to the prospective adopter on the ground that she would not have accepted the placement if she had been given sufficient information about the child's history.

Para. (2)(aa)
Parent: See para. 23 of Circular LAC (97)13.   **2–082**

Paras. (2)(g), (h)
Ensure: The adoption agency could delegate its responsibilities to another adoption agency **2–083**
under an inter-agency placement agreement.

Paras. (2)(i), (j)
Considers necessary: The provision of advice and assistance and the child's health monitor- **2–084**
ing could also be delegated under an inter-agency agreement.

Review of case where no placement made within six months of freeing for adoption
13.—(1) Where a child has been freed for adoption by virtue of an order **2–085**
under [section 18 of the Act] (freeing child for adoption) and six months
have elapsed since the making of that order and the child does not have his
home with a prospective adopter, the adoption agency [which has parental
responsibility for the child by virtue of section 18 or 21 of the Act (freeing
for adoption and variation of order to substitute one agency for another)]
shall review that child's case to determine why no placement has been made
and what action if any should be taken to safeguard and promote his
welfare.

(2) A case of which paragraph (1) applies shall be subject to such a
review at intervals of not more than six months.

GENERAL NOTE
Guidance on this Regulation can be found in Circular LAC (84)3 at paras. 102 to 105.   **2–086**

[Information on adoption
13A.—As soon as practicable after the making of an adoption order in **2–087**
respect of a child, the adoption agency shall—
(a) provide the adopters with such information about the child as they
    consider appropriate; and
(b) at the same time advise the adopters that this information should be
    made available to the child at a time when they consider it is
    appropriate but not later than the child's eighteenth birthday.]

GENERAL NOTE
Guidance on this Regulation can be found in Circular LAC (84)3 at paras. 28 to 29.   **2–088**

Confidentiality and preservation of case records
14.—(1) Subject to regulation 15, any information obtained or recom- **2–089**
mendations or decisions made by virtue of these regulations shall be treated
by the adoption agency as confidential.

(2) Where a case record has been set up by an adoption agency under
regulations 7(2)(a), 8(2)(a) or 9(3) in respect of a child or a prospective
adopter, any report, recommendation or decision made by that agency by
virtue of these regulations in respect of that child or that prospective
adopter shall be placed on the record relating to that child or, as the case
may be, that prospective adopter, and any case records set up by the agency
together with the indexes to them shall be kept in a place of special
security.

(3) Subject to regulation 16(2), an adoption agency shall preserve the
indexes to all its case records and the case records in respect of those cases

135

in which an adoption order is made in a place of special security for at least 75 years and shall preserve other case records in a place of special security for so long as it considers appropriate, so however that any case records and indexes may be so preserved on microfilm or such other system as reproduces the total contents of any such record or index.

[(4) The adoption agency shall ensure that the place of special security referred to in paragraphs (2) and (3) preserved the records etc., so far as is possible, and in particular minimise the risk of damage from fire or water.]

GENERAL NOTE

2–090   Guidance on this Regulation can be found in Circular LAC (84)3 at paras. 106 to 108. For a checklist of the range of documents which should be found in a child's case record, see paras. 57 and 58 of Circular LAC (97)13.

For sources of information on adoption records, see *Where to find adoption records—A guide for counsellors* (BAAF, 1993). Advice to local authorities on the disclosure of information that they have on adoption is contained in D.H.S.S. Circular LAC (76)21, para. 19, *et seq.*

Para. (1)

2–091   *Confidential:* In *R. v. Bournemouth Justices, ex p. Grey: R. v. Same, ex p. Rodd* [1987] 1 F.L.R. 36, the mother brought affiliation proceedings against W. who denied paternity. The mother had to have corroborative evidence. She alleged that she and W had discussed the child's adoption and W had signed a form as father of the unborn child. The social worker at the adoption agency involved refused to provide the evidence on the basis that it was confidential information protected by public interest immunity. The mother obtained a magistrates' court witness summons. The social worker sought an order of certiorari to quash the witness summons. Hodgson J. held, that where justices were satisfied that a person was likely to be able to give material evidence, as in this case, and that person would not attend court voluntarily, it was mandatory for them to issue a summons. The question of immunity would be considered at court. The adoption agency's claim for public interest immunity was not justified; that type of immunity (although recently extended) was a restricted one, there was no analogy between informants to the police or the N.S.P.C.C. and the father in this case. It might be that if an application were made for discovery of all an adoption agency's records relating to one case, the agency could claim immunity, similar to the immunity successfully claimed by the N.S.P.C.C. (*Re D. (Infants)* [1970] 1 W.L.R. 599) and a local authority (*Gaskin v. Liverpool City Council* [1980] 1 W.L.R. 1549). However, in this case the evidence sought was precisely known and vital to the justice of the case. Therefore the social worker's application would be refused.

Also see *Re an Ex Parte Originating Summons in an Adoption Application* [1990] 1 All E.R. 639, noted under r.53(3) of the Adoption Rules 1984, S.I. 1984 No. 265.

Para. (2)

2–092   *Kept in a place of special security:* In Investigation No. 91/B/1262 against Birmingham City Council the Local Government Ombudsman recommended that the Council should pay the complainant the sum of £1000 in recognition of the "suffering and loss" that he experienced on being informed that his adoption file had been lost.

Access to case records and disclosure of information

2–093   **15.**—(1) Subject to paragraph (3), an adoption agency shall provide such access to its case records and the indexes to them and disclose such information in its possession, as may be required—

(a) to those holding an inquiry under [section 81 of the Child Care Act] (inquiries), for the purposes of such an inquiry,

(b) to the Secretary of State,

(c) subject to the provisions of sections 29(7) and 32(3) of the Local Government Act 1974 (investigations and disclosure), to a Local Commissioner, appointed under section 23 of that Act (Commissioners for Local Administration), for the purposes of any investigation conducted in accordance with Part III of that Act,

[(cc) to any person appointed by the adoption agency for the purposes of the consideration by the agency of any representations (including conplaints),]

(d) to the persons and authorities referred to in regulations 11 and 12 to the extent specified in those regulations,

(e) to a guardian *ad litem* or reporting officer appointed under rules made pursuant to [section 65 of the Act] (guardian *ad litem* and reporting officer) for the purposes of the discharge of his duties in that behalf, and

(f) to a court having power to make an order under the Act [. . .]

(2) Subject to paragraph (3), an adoption agency may provide such access to its case records and the indexes to them and disclose such information in its possession, as it thinks fit—

(a) for the purposes of carrying out its functions as an adoption agency, and

(b) to a person who is authorised in writing by the Secretary of State to obtain information for the purposes of research.

(3) A written record shall be kept by an adoption agency of any access provided or disclosure made by virtue of this regulation.

GENERAL NOTE

Guidance on this Circular can be found in Circular LAC (84)3 at paras. 110 to 122.   **2–094**

Although a guardian *ad litem* in care proceedings is not one of the persons to whom access is to be given, and information disclosed, under this regulation, s.42(1)(b) of the Children Act 1989 entitles the guardian to have access to, and take copies from, the local authorities case record (Form F) and to use the information so acquired in his report or evidence to the court considering the application for a care order: *Manchester City Council v. T.* [1994] 2 All E.R. 526, CA, and see the note to s.42 of the 1989 Act.

Para. (1)(cc)
See para. 31 of Circular LAC (97)13.

Para. (1)(c)

Local commissioners: In *Re A Subpoena (Adoption: Commissioner for Local Administration)*   **2–095**
[1996] 2 F.L.R. 629, the local authority claimed public interest immunity in respect of adoption records that the Local Government Ombudsman had requested to see during the course of an investigation. In dismissing the authority's appeal from the decision of the Master upholding the Ombudsman's subpoena, Carnwath J. said: "Provided the Commissioner can show that the material is bona fide required for the purpose of his investigation, and that he is able and willing to comply with the encessary restrictions on disclosure by himself and his staff (which are in any event secured by the provisions of the Act), then in my view the balance should normally come down in favour of disclosure".

Para. (2)
Carrying out its function as an adoption agency: It is submitted that an adoption agency cannot disclose copies of material that has been obtained in connection with the adoption proceedings; see r.53(3) of the Adoption Rules 1984 and r.32(5) of the Magistrates' Courts (Adoption) Rules 1984. The leave of the adoption court should be obtained before such information is disclosed.

Transfer of case records

16.—(1) Subject to paragraphs (2) and (3), an adoption agency may   **2–096** transfer a copy of a case record (or part thereof) to another adoption agency when it considers this to be in the interests of a child or prospective adopter to whom the record relates, and a written record shall be kept of any such transfer.

(2) An approved adoption society which intends to cease to act or exist as such shall forthwith either transfer its case records to another adoption agency having first obtained the Secretary of State's approval for such transfer, or transfer its case records—

(a) to the local authority in whose area the society's head office is situated, or

(b) in the case of a society which amalgamates with another approved adoption society to form a new approved adoption society, to the new society.

(3) An adoption agency to which case records are transferred by virtue of paragraph (2)(a) or (b) shall notify the Secretary of State in writing of such transfer.

GENERAL NOTE

2–097   Guidance on this Regulation can be found in Circular LAC (84)3 at paras. 123 to 124.

Progress reports under section 15 of the 1975 Act

2–098   [17. Where parental responsibility for a child who is in Great Britain has been transferred from one adoption agency ("the existing agency") to another ("the substitute agency") by virtue of an order under section 21 of the Act (variation of section 18 order), the substitute agency shall provide such information as the existing agency as that agency considers necessary for it to comply with its duty under section 19(2) and (3) of the Act.]

Revocations

2–099   **18.** The Adoption Agencies Regulations 1976 the Adoption Agencies (Amendment) Regulations 1981 are hereby revoked.

Regulations 7(2)(b)   SCHEDULE
and (2) and (3)(b),
and 8(2)(b)
and (c)

PART I

PARTICULARS RELATING TO THE CHILD

2–100   1. Name, sex, date and place of birth and address.

2. Whether legitimate or illegitimate at birth and, if illegitimate whether subsequently legitimated.

3. Nationality.

4. Physical description.

5. Personality and social development.

6. Religion, including details of baptism, confirmation or equivalent ceremonies.

7. Details of any wardship proceedings and of any court orders [, or agreement under section 4 of the Children Act, relating to parental responsibility for the child] or to his custody and maintenance.

8. Details of any brothers and sisters, including dates of birth, arrangements in respect of care and custody and whether any brother or sister is also being considered for adoption.

9. Extent of access to members of the child's natural family and, if the child is illegitimate, his father, and in each case the nature of the relationship enjoyed.

10. If the child has been in the care of a local authority or voluntary organisation, details (including dates) of any placements with foster parents, or other arrangements in respect of the care of the child, including particulars of the persons with whom the child has had his home and observations on the care provided.

11. Names, addresses and types of schools attended, with dates and educational attainments.

[12. Any special needs in relation to the child's health (whether physical or mental) and his emotional and behavioural development, and how those are to be met.]

[12A. Any educational needs which the child has and how these needs are to be met, the result of any assessment carried out in respect of any special educational needs under the Education Act 1996, and how any needs identified in the statement of special educational needs under section 324 of that Act are to be met.]

13. What, if any, rights to or interest in property or any claim to damages, under the Fatal Accidents Act 1976 or otherwise, the child stands to retain or lose if adopted.

14. Wishes and feelings in relation to adoption and, as the case may be, an application under [section 18 of the Act (freeing child for adoption)], including any wishes in respect of religious and cultural upbringing.

15. Any other relevant information which the agency considers may assist the panel.

MATTERS TO BE COVERED IN REPORT ON THE CHILD'S HEALTH

1. Name, date of birth, sex, weight and height.   **2–101**
2. A neo-natal report on the child, including—
    (a) details of the birth, and any complications,
    (b) results of a physical examination and screening tests,
    (c) details of any treatment given,
    (d) details of any problem in management and feeding,
    (e) any other relevant information which may assist the panel,
    (f) the name and address of any doctor who may be able to provide further information about any of the above matters.
3. A full health history and examination of the child, including—
    (a) details of any serious illness, disability, accident, hospital admission or attendance at an out-patient department, and in each case any treatment given,
    (b) details and dates of immunisations,
    (c) a physical and developmental assessment according to age, including an assessment of vision and hearing and of neurological, speech and language development and any evidence of emotional disorder,
    (d) for a child over five years of age, the school health history (if available),
    [(dd) how his health and medical history has affected his physical, intellectual, emotional, social or behavioural development.]
    (e) any other relevant information which may assist the panel.
4. The signature, name, address and qualifications of the registered medical practitioner who prepared the report, the date of the report and of the examinations carried out together with the name and address of any doctor (if different) who may be able to provide further information about any of the above matters.

PART III

PARTICULARS RELATING TO EACH NATURAL PARENT, INCLUDING WHERE APPROPRIATE THE FATHER OF AN ILLEGITIMATE CHILD

1. Name, date and place of birth and address.   **2–102**
2. Marital status and date and place of marriage (if any).
3. Past and present relationship (if any) with the other natural parent, including comments on its stability.
4. Physical description.
5. Personality.
6. Religion.
7. Educational attainments.
8. Past and present occupations and interests.
9. Names and brief details of the personal circumstances of the parents and any brothers and sisters of the natural parent, with their ages or ages at death.
10. Wishes and feelings in relation to adoption and, as the case may be, and application under [section 18 of the Act (freeing child for adoption)], including any wishes in respect of the child's religious and cultural upbringing.
11. Any other relevant information which the agency considers may assist the panel.

PART IV

PARTICULARS RELATING TO THE HEALTH OF EACH NATURAL PARENT INCLUDING WHERE APPROPRIATE THE FATHER OF AN ILLEGITIMATE CHILD

1. Name, date of birth, sex, weight and height.   **2–103**
2. A family health history, covering the parents, the brothers and sisters (if any) and the other children (if any) of the natural parent with details of any serious physical or mental illness and inherited and congenital disease.
3. Past health history, including details of any serious physical or mental illness, disability, accident, hospital admission or attendance at an out-patient department, and in each case any treatment given.
4. A full obstetric history of the mother, including any problems in the ante-natal, labour and post-natal periods, with the results of any tests carried out during or immediately after pregnancy.

5. Details of any present illness, including treatment and prognosis.

6. Any other relevant information which the agency considers may assist the panel.

7. The signature, name, address and qualifications of any registered medical practitioner who supplied any of the information in this Part together with the name and address of any doctor (if different) who may be able to provide further information about any of the above matters.

PART V

PARTICULARS RELATING TO A GUARDIAN

2–104 1. Particulars referred to in paragraphs 1, 6, 10 and 11 of Part III.

PART VI

PARTICULARS RELATING TO THE PROSPECTIVE ADOPTER

2–105 1. Name, date and place of birth and address.

2. Domicile.

3. Marital status, date and place of marriage (if any) and comments on stability of relationship.

4. Details of any previous marriage.

5. If a married person proposes to adopt a child alone, the reasons for this.

6. Physical description.

7. Personality.

8. Religion, and whether willing to follow any wishes of a child or his natural parents or guardian in respect of the child's religious and cultural upbringing.

9. Educational attainments.

10. Past and present occupations and interests.

11. Details of income and comments on the living standards of the household.

12. Details of other members of the prospective adopter's household (including any children of the prospective adopter even if not resident in the household).

13. Details of the parents and any brothers or sisters of the prospective adopter, with their ages or ages at death.

14. Attitudes to adoption of such other members of the prospective adopter's household and family as the agency considers appropriate.

15. Previous experience of caring for children as step-parent, foster parent, child-minder or prospective adopter and assessment of ability in this respect, together where appropriate with assessment of ability of bringing up the prospective adopter's own children.

16. Reasons for wishing to adopt a child and extent of understanding of the nature and effect of adoption.

17. Assessment of ability to bring up an adopted child throughout his childhood.

18. Details of any adoption allowance payable.

19. Names and addresses of two referees who will give personal references on the prospective adopter.

20. Name and address of the prospective adopter's registered medical practitioner, if any.

21. Any other relevant information which the agency considers may assist the panel.

PART VII

MATTERS TO BE COVERED IN REPORT ON HEALTH OF THE PROSPECTIVE ADOPTER

2–106 1. Name, date of birth, sex, weight and height.

2. A family health history, covering the parents, the brothers and sisters (if any) and the children (if any) of the prospective adopter, with details of any serious physical or mental illness and inherited and congenital disease.

3. Marital history, including (if applicable) reasons for inability to have children.

4. Part health history, including details of any serious physical or mental illness, disability, accident, hospital admission or attendance at an out-patient department, and in each case any treatment given.

5. Obstetric history (if applicable).

6. Details of any present illness, including treatment and prognosis.

7. A full medical examination.

8. Details of any daily consumption of alcohol, tobacco and habit-forming drugs.

9. Any other relevant information which the agency considers may assist the panel.

10. The signature, name, address and qualifications of the registered medical practitioner who prepared to report, the date of the report and of the examinations carried out together with the name and address of any doctor (if different) who may be able to provide further information about any of the above matters.

[PART VIII

CONSIDERATIONS TO BE INCLUDED IN REVIEW

1. The child's needs (including his educational needs), progress and development, and **2–107** whether any changes are needed to help to meet those needs or to assist his progress or development.

2. Any arrangements for contact, and whether there is need for any change in such arrangements.

3. Existing arrangements for the child's medical and dental care and treatment, and health and dental surveillance.

4. The possible need for an appropriate course of action to assist any necessary change of such care, treatment or surveillance.

5. The possible need for preventive measures, such as vaccination and immunisation, and screening for vision and hearing.]

ADOPTED PERSONS (BIRTH RECORDS) REGULATIONS 1991

(S.I. 1991 No. 1981)

Dated September 3, 1991, *and made by the Registrar General, with the approval of the Secretary of State for Health, under the Adoption Act* 1976, *ss.*51(1)(2), 67(5)(6).

GENERAL NOTE

2–108   These Regulations prescribe the manner in which an application is to be made by an adopted person for information enabling him to obtain a certified copy of the record of his birth (by reg. 2) or for information whether he and the person whom he intends to marry may be within the prohibited degrees of relationship under the Marriage Act 1949 (by reg. 3).

Citation, commencement and interpretation

2–109   **1.**—(1) These Regulations may be cited as the Adopted Persons (Birth Records) Regulations 1991 and shall come into force on 14th October 1991.

(2) In these Regulations "the Act" means the Adoption Act 1976.

Application for access to birth records

2–110   **2.** For the purposes of section 51(1) of the Act (which provides for information to be supplied to an adopted person to enable him to obtain a certified copy of the record of his birth), the adopted person shall apply to the Registrar General as follows:—

    (a) in the case of a person who was adopted before 12th November 1975, in the form set out in Schedule 1 to these Regulations; or

    (b) in the case of a person who was adopted after 11th November 1975, in the form set out in Schedule 2 to these Regulations.

Application for verification in connection with intended marriage

2–111   **3.** For the purposes of section 51(2) of the Act (which provides for an adopted person to be informed whether or not it appears that he and the person whom he intends to marry may be within the prohibited degrees of relationship for the purpose of the Marriage Act 1949), the adopted person shall apply to the Registrar General in the form set out in Schedule 3 to these Regulations.

Revocation

2–112   **4.** The Adopted Persons (Birth Records) Regulations 1976 are revoked.

1. I hereby apply for the information necessary to enable me to obtain a certified copy of **2–113** the record of my birth. I understand that before this information is given to me, I am required to attend an interview with a counsellor.

Either   A.   I am in the United Kingdom and would prefer the interview to take place at (please put a tick in the box indicating your choice):–

    (a) the General Register Office; ☐

    (b) the local authority (in England and Wales), the regional ☐ or island council (in Scotland) or the Health and Social Security Board (in Northern Ireland) in whose area I am residing;

    (c) some other local authority; regional or island council or ☐ Board (Please specify which) ....
....;
or, if known,

    (d) the adoption society approved under section 3 of the ☐ Adoption Act 1976, Section 3 of the Adoption (Scotland) Act 1978 or registered under Article 4 of the Adoption (Northern Ireland) Order 1987 which arranged my adoption. The name and address of the approved adoption society is ....
....
....
....

Or   B.   I am living outside the United Kingdom and would prefer the interview to take place with a counsellor from ....
(name, address and status of organisation willing to provide counselling).

I enclose that organisation's notification that it is prepared to provide such counselling.

2. The following are the particulars of my adoption:—

Full name and surname ....
Date of birth ....
Country of birth (if known) ....
Name of adoptive father ....
Name of adoptive mother ....
Date of adoption (if known) ....

3. Declaration

I declare that to the best of my knowledge and belief I am the adopted person to whom the above particulars relate and that my adoption is recorded at entry number† in the Adopted Children Register.

Signature: Date
Address: ....
....
....

SCHEDULE 2

FORM OF APPLICATION FOR ACCESS TO BIRTH RECORDS BY A PERSON ADOPTED AFTER
NOVEMBER 11, 1975

2–114   1. I hereby apply for the information necessary to enable me to obtain a certified copy of the record of my birth.

2. I understand, that if I am in the UK a counselling service is available to me. I wish/do not wish to see a counsellor. (Please delete as required, and if you have chosen to see a counsellor, tick one of the boxes in 3 below).

3. I would like to see a counsellor at:—

    (a) the General Register Office;   ☐

    (b) the local authority (in England and Wales), the regional or island council ☐
        (in Scotland) or the Health and Social Security Board (in Northern
        Ireland) in whose area I am residing;

    (c) some other local authority; regional or island council or Board (Please ☐
        specify which) . . . .
        . . . . ;

    or, if known,

    (d) the adoption society approved under section 3 of the Adoption Act 1976, ☐
        Section 3 of the Adoption (Scotland) Act 1978 or registered under Article
        4 of the Adoption (Northern Ireland) Order 1987 which arranged
        my adoption. The name and address of the approved adoption society
        is . . . .
        . . . .
        . . . .
        . . . .

4. The following are the particulars of my adoption:—

    Full name and surname . . . .
    Date of birth . . . .
    Country of birth (if known) . . . .
    Name of adoptive father . . . .
    Name of adoptive mother . . . .
    Date of adoption (if known) . . . .

5. Declaration

    I declare that to the best of my knowledge and belief I am the adopted person to whom the above particulars relate and that my adoption is recorded at entry number†
in the Adopted Children Register.

    Signature: Date
    Address: . . . .
                 . . . .
                  . . . .

---

† This number will be found in the column headed "No. of Entry" on a full certificate and in the bottom left hand corner of most short certificates.

FORM OF APPLICATION FOR VERIFICATION OF ANY RELATIONSHIP IN CONNECTION WITH MARRIAGE

1. I hereby apply to be informed whether or not it appears from the records of the Registrar **2–115**
General that I and the person I intend to marry may be within the prohibited degrees of
relationship for the purposes of the Marriage Act 1949.

2. I give below details of myself and the person I intend to marry:—

Myself	*My Fiancé(e)*
Name and surname	Name and surname ....
Date of birth	Date of birth ....
Country of birth	Place of birth ....
Adoptive father's name	Father's name ....
Adoptive mother's name	Mother's name and
Date of adoption	Maiden surname ....
Signature	Address ....
Date	

---

† This number will be found in the column headed "No. of Entry" on a full certificate and in the bottom left
hand corner of most short certificates.

ADOPTION ALLOWANCE REGULATIONS 1991

(S.I. 1991 No. 2030)

Dated September 9, 1991, *and made by the Secretary of State for Health under the Adoption Act*, 1976, *ss.* 9(2)(3), 57A.

GENERAL NOTE

2–116   These Regulations make provision to enable adoption agencies to pay allowances to persons who have adopted or intend to adopt a child in pursuance of arrangements made by such agencies. They replace schemes approved by the Secretary of State under s.57(4) of the Adoption Act 1976 which are revoked on the coming into force of paragraph 25 of Sched. 10 to the Children Act 1989.

Detailed guidance on these regulations can be found in Chapter 2 of *The Children Act 1989: Guidance and Regulations*, Vol. 9 *Adoption Issues* (abbreviated to *Guidance* in the notes to these Regulations).

AMENDMENTS

The amendments to these Regulations were made by the Adoption Allowance (Amendment) Regulations 1991 (S.I. 1991 No. 2130).

Citation, commencement and interpretation

2–117   **1.**—(1) These Regulations may be cited as the Adoption Allowance Regulations 1991 and shall come into force on 14th October 1991.

(2) In these Regulations unless the context otherwise requires—

"the Act" means the Adoption Act 1976;

"adopters" means the persons who have adopted or intend to adopt a child or, where there is only one such person, that person;

"adoption agency" means an approved adoption society or a local authority;

"adoption panel" means a panel established in accordance with regulation 5 of the Adoption Agencies Regulations 1983;

"attendance allowance" means an allowance under section 35 of the Social Security Act 1975;

"child benefit" means a benefit under section 1 of the Child Benefit Act 1975;

"fostering allowance" means the amount of money paid by way of maintenance for a child placed with a foster parent pursuant to section 23(2)(a) or section 59(1)(a) of the Children Act 1989 (placement with foster parents and others by local authorities and voluntary organisations);

"income support" means income support under section 20 of the Social Security Act 1986;

"mobility allowance" means an allowance under section 37A of the Social Security Act 1975;

"unemployment benefit" means unemployment benefit under section 14 of the Social Security Act 1975.

(3) In these Regulations unless the context otherwise requires, a reference to a numbered regulation is to the regulation in these Regulations bearing that number, and a reference to a numbered paragraph is to the paragraph of that regulation bearing that number.

Circumstances in which an allowance may be paid

2.—(1) Without prejudice to paragraph (3), an allowance may be paid **2–118** where one or more of the circumstances specified in paragraph (2) exists and the adoption agency—

(a) is making the arrangements for the child's adoption; and

(b) has decided—

    (i) in accordance with regulation 11(1) of the Adoption Agencies Regulations 1983 that the adoption by the adopters would be in the child's best interests, and

    (ii) after considering the recommendation of the adoption panel, that such adoption is not practicable without payment of an allowance.

(2) The circumstances referred to in paragraph (1) are—

(a) where the adoption agency is satisfied that the child has established a strong and important relationship with the adopters before the adoption order is made;

(b) where it is desirable that the child be placed with the same adopters as his brothers or sisters, or with a child with whom he has previously shared a home;

(c) where at the time of the placement for adoption the child—

    (i) is mentally or physically disabled or suffering from the effects of emotional or behavioural difficulties, and

    (ii) needs special care which requires a greater expenditure of resources than would be required if the child were not so disabled, or suffering from the effects of emotional or behavioural difficulties;

(d) where at the time of the placement for the adoption the child was mentally or physically disabled, or suffering from the effects of emotional or behavioural difficulties, and as a result at a later date he requires more care and a greater expenditure of resources than were required at the time he was placed for adoption because there is—

    (i) a deterioration in the child's health or condition, or

    (ii) an increase in his age; or

(e) where at the time of the placement for adoption it was known that there was a high risk that the child would develop an illness or disability and as a result at a later date he requires more care and a greater expenditure of resources than were required at the time he was placed for adoption because such illness or disability occurs.

(3) An allowance may be paid by the agency where before these Regulations come into force—

(a) an allowance was being paid by the agency to the adopters in respect of a child in accordance with a scheme which is revoked by section 57A(4) of the Act (revocation of schemes approved under section 57(4) of the Act) or under section 57(5)(b) of the Act (revocation of scheme by the Secretary of State) and the adopters have agreed to receive (instead of such allowance) an allowance complying with these Regulations, or

(b) the agency decided that the adopters are eligible to receive an allowance in accordance with a scheme which is revoked by section 57A(4) of the Act or under section 57(5)(b) of the Act and—

    (i) no payment has been made pursuant to that decision, and

    (ii) any conditions to which the agency's decision to pay such an allowance is subject are satisfied.

(4) In each case before an allowance is payable the adoption agency shall require the adopters to have agreed to—

   (a) inform the adoption agency immediately if—

      (i) the child no longer has his home with them (or either of them), if they have changed their address, or if the child dies, or

      (ii) there is any change in their financial circumstances or the financial needs or resources of the child; and

   (b) complete and supply the adoption agency with an annual statement of their financial circumstances and the financial circumstances of the child.

(5) An allowance may not be paid from a date before the date of placement for adoption and may be from such later date as may be determined by the adoption agency and notified to the adopters.

GENERAL NOTE

2–119   "Agencies should note that the term 'allowance' is intended to apply to a periodic or regular payment payable at intervals to be determined by the agency. Where a single lump sum or capital payment is required in connection with the child's circumstances—for example, in order to purchase special equipment or to make adaptations to the home—local authorities can assist by exercising powers available in other legislation. This applies whether an allowance is to be paid by the authority or by another adoption agency (or, of course, whether or not an allowance is paid at all). Such legislation includes the Chronically Sick and Disabled Persons Act 1970 and powers which are available in Part III of the Children Act 1989 in relation to children in need" (*Guidance*, para. 2.13).

Para. (1)

2–120   *May be paid:* The *Guidance* advises, at para. 2.34, that "entitlement to an allowance does not automatically follow if the child's circumstances satisfy one or more of the conditions specified in [para. (2)]". The adopters may be able financially to take on the added responsibility of caring for the child (see, reg. 3) or they may prefer to assume, unaided, the whole responsibility for meeting the child's needs and feel able to do so.

Para. (2)(a)

2–121   The situation described here will apply where a child has been living with foster parents who wish to adopt him but cannot afford to lose the fostering allowance which they have been receiving in respect of the child. In these circumstances, where an adoption allowance is payable, "it is recommended that payment should commence from the date of the adoption placement. This will enable the agency to evaluate the adoption placement in the circumstances which will apply after the adoption order is made and will assist in the preparation of the Schedule 2 report in connection with the adoption hearing" (*Guidance*, para. 2.22).

Para. (2)(c)

2–122   "The expression 'mentally or physically disabled' . . . is not restrictively defined and is intended to include children who are sensorily impaired . . . Payment of the allowance is intended where the child's condition is serious and long term" (*Guidance*, paras. 2.27, 2.29).

Para. (2)(d)

2–123   This paragraph enables the agency to plan for an anticipated deterioration in the child's condition by agreeing in principle to the payment of an allowance and at some future date effecting the payment if they are satisfied that the child's condition has deteriorated to make the payment of an allowance necessary and that the adopters' financial circumstances merit this: see, *Guidance*, para. 2.30. An allowance will not become payable because of a change relating to the adopters' circumstances which is unrelated to the child's condition, such as the loss of a job.

Para. (2)(e)

2–124   The circumstance described here would apply, for example, "where information relating to the child's medical or genetic history was such that there existed strong grounds for concern about the child's medical progress" (*Guidance*, para. 2.31).

Para. (3)

This should be read in conjunction with reg. 4(2)(a) and (b). **2–125**

Para. (4)

Shall require: The conditions set out in this paragraph must be agreed by the adopters **2–126** before an allowance is payable.

Financial circumstances: "The agency will need to operate with sensitivity in determining how far changes in financial circumstances or needs affect the allowance payable" (*Guidance*, para. 2.43).

Para. (5)

Date of placement: It "is recommended that the adoption allowance should commence from **2–127** the date of placement for adoption" (*Guidance*, para. 2.46).

Amount of the allowance

3.—(1) The allowance shall be of such amount as the adoption agency **2–128** determines in accordance with paragraphs (2) to (4).

(2) In determining the amount of allowance the adoption agency shall take into account—

(a) the financial resources available to the adopters including any financial benefit which would be available in respect of the child when adopted;

(b) the amount required by the adopters in respect of their reasonable outgoings and commitments (excluding outgoings in respect of the child); and

(c) the financial needs and resources of the child.

(3) In assessing the income available to the adopters the adoption agency shall disregard mobility and attendance allowance payable in respect of the child and, where the adopters are in receipt of income support, child benefit.

(4) The allowance paid by the adoption agency shall not—

(a) include any element of remuneration for the care of the child by the adopters;

(b) exceed the amount of the fostering allowance excluding any element of remuneration in that allowance which would be payable if the child were fostered by the adopters.

GENERAL NOTE

"In assessing the amount of allowance the aim is to facilitate a successful placement and to **2–129** enhance the child's well-being in the adoptive home. In undertaking its assessment, especially before the adoption placement, the agency will need to project forward and consider all the financial circumstances which are likely to apply when the child is living in the adoptive home" (*Guidance*, para. 2.50). Detailed advice on this regulation is contained in *Guidance*, paras. 2.52 to 2.58.

Procedure in determining whether an allowance should be paid

4.—(1) Subject to paragraphs (2) and (3), an adoption agency shall, **2–130** before an adoption order is made in respect of a child whose adoption they are arranging or have arranged—

(a) consider whether an allowance may be paid in accordance with paragraphs (1) and (2) of regulation 2 (circumstances in which an allowance may be paid);

(b) supply information to the adopters about allowances including the basis upon which amounts of allowances are determined;

149

(c) give notice in writing in accordance with paragraph (4) to the adopters of their proposed decision as to whether an allowance should be paid and the proposed amount, if any, which would be payable;

(d) consider any representations received from the adopters within the period specified in the notice;

(e) make a decision as to whether an allowance should be paid, determine the amount, if any, which would be payable and notify the adopters of that decision and determination.

(2) The adoption agency shall not be required—

(a) in a case where the adopters may agree in accordance with regulation 2(3)(a) to receive payments complying with these Regulations instead of payments which are made to them in accordance with a scheme revoked by section 57A(4) of the Act (revocation of schemes approved under section 57(4) of the Act) or under section 57(5)(b) of the Act (revocation of scheme by the Secretary of State)—

  (i) to comply with sub-paragraph (a) of paragraph (1),

  (ii) to comply with sub-paragraph (b) of that paragraph before the adoption order is made provided that they do so as soon as is reasonably practicable after 14 October 1991, or

  (iii) to comply with sub-paragraphs (c) to (e) of that paragraph unless and until an application is received by the [agency] for an allowance to be made under these Regulations instead of under a scheme which has been revoked; or

(b) in a case where regulation 2(3)(b) applies, to comply with either of the following—

  (i) sub-paragraph (a) of paragraph (1), or

  (ii) sub-paragraphs (b) to (e) of that paragraph before an adoption order is made provided that they do so as soon as is reasonably practicable after 14 October 1991;

(c) in a case to which regulation 2(2)(d) or (e) of these Regulations applies, to determine the amount of an allowance unless or until—

  (i) there is a deterioration in the child's health or condition, or an increase in his age, (in a case to which regulation 2(2)(d) applies) or

  (ii) the onset of the illness or disability (in a case to which regulation 2(2)(e) applies,

and as a result the child requires more care and a greater expenditure of resources than were required at the time at which he was placed for adoption.

(3) An approved adoption society which holds itself out as not being an adoption agency which normally pays allowances shall not be required to comply with sub-paragraphs (a) and (b) of paragraph (1) and need comply with sub-paragraphs (c), (d) and (e) of that paragraph as respects any adopters only if they have considered whether or not to pay an allowance to those adopters.

(4) A notice under paragraph (1)(c) shall state the period of time within which the adopters may make representations to the adoption agency concerning the proposed decision or determination and the adoption agency shall not make a decision or determination under paragraph (1)(e) until after the expiry of that period.

150

This regulation sets out the procedure which the agency should follow in order to determine **2–131** whether an allowance is payable in an individual case. The determination will result in the agency's decision under reg. 2(1)(b)(ii) whether the adoption is, or is not, practicable without payment of an allowance. Detailed advice on this regulation is contained in paras. 2.62 to 2.69 of the *Guidance*.

Information about allowances

5. After a decision has been made to pay an allowance, the adoption **2–132** agency shall notify the adopters in writing of the following—

(a) the method of the determination of the amount of the allowance;

(b) the amount of the allowance as initially determined;

(c) the date of the first payment of the allowance;

(d) the method of payment of the allowance and frequency with which and the period for which payment will be made;

(e) the arrangements and procedure for review, variation and termination of the allowance;

(f) the responsibilities of—

(i) the agency under regulation 6, and

(ii) the adopters pursuant to their agreement under paragraph (4) of regulation 2,

in respect of the allowance in the event of a change in circumstances of the adopters or the child.

Review, variation and termination of allowances

6.—(1) The adoption agency shall review an allowance—　　　　**2–133**

(a) annually, on receipt of a statement from the adopters as to—

(i) their financial circumstances;

(ii) the financial needs and resources of the child;

(iii) their address and whether the child still has a home with them (or either of them); and

(b) if any change in the circumstances of the adopters or the child, including any change of address, comes to their notice.

(2) The adoption agency may vary or suspend payment of the allowance if, as a result of a review, they consider that, the adopters' need for it has changed or ceased since the amount of the allowance was last determined.

(3) Where the adopters fail to supply the adoption agency with an annual statement in accordance with their agreement under regulation 2(4)(b), the adoption agency may deem the adopters' need for an allowance to have ceased until such time as a statement is supplied.

(4) Where payment of an allowance is suspended the agency may recommence payment if as a result of a review the adoption agency considers that the financial circumstances of the adopters have become such that an allowance should be paid.

(5) The adoption agency shall terminate payment of an allowance when—

(a) the child ceases to have a home with the adopters (or either of them);

(b) the child ceases full-time education and commences employment or qualifies for a placement on a Government training scheme;

(c) the child qualifies for income support or unemployment benefit in his own right;

(d) the child attains the age of eighteen, unless he continues in full-time education, when it may continue until he attains the age of twenty-one so long as he continues in full-time education; or

(e) any period agreed between the adoption agency and the adopters for the payment of the allowance expires.

GENERAL NOTE

2–134 "Agencies should demonstrate flexibility in responding to changes of circumstances and at the annual review. An allowance may increase or decrease as appropriate in an individual case. For example, a change of address involving higher housing costs may arise from a move to a home which is more appropriate to the needs of the adopted child. In other cases it may have no connection with the child's needs. Or a deterioration in the child's condition may necessitate additional financial assistance. Conversely, a change in circumstances may result in a lower allowance or may result in the allowance being suspended until further review. In such a case, payment may recommence if circumstances again require the need for an allowance" (*Guidance*, para. 2.73).

Para. (5)

2–135 *Terminate:* These regulations do not provide for an allowance to recommence once it has been terminated.

Confidentiality, preservation and access to records

2–136 **7.**—(1) Subject to regulation 15 of the Adoption Agencies Regulations 1983, any information obtained or recommendations received or decisions made by virtue of these Regulations shall be treated by the adoption agency as confidential.

(2) The adoption agency shall place a record of the details of each allowance in respect of a child including details of any determination under regulation 3 and review under regulation 6 on the case records that they are required to set up under the Adoption Agencies Regulations 1983.

ADOPTION RULES 1984

(S.I. 1984 No. 265)

Dated February 17, 1984, and made by the Lord Chancellor under the Adoption Act 1958 (c. 5), s.9(3) (as amended) and the Adoption Act 1968 (c. 53), s.12(1) (as amended).

GENERAL NOTE

These Rules lay down the procedure to be followed in the High Court and county courts in **2–137** all proceedings under the Adoption Act 1976, for or relating to the adoption or freeing for adoption of children.

Although these Rules were made under the Adoption Acts of 1958 and 1968 they remain in force by virtue of the transitional provisions contained in s.73(1), Sched. 2, para. 1 of the Adoption Act 1976.

Proceedings brought under the Adoption Act 1976 are "family proceeding" for the purposes of the Children Act 1989; see *ibid.*, s.8(3)(4).

For guidance on these rules, see D.H.S.S. Circular No. LAC (84) 10.

AMENDMENTS

The amendments to these Rules were made by the Adoption (Amendment) Rules 1991 (S.I. 1991 No. 1880).

PART I

INTRODUCTORY

Citation and commencement

1. These rules may be cited as the Adoption Rules 1984 and shall come **2–138** into operation on May 27, 1984.

Interpretation

2.—(1) In these rules, unless the context otherwise requires— **2–139**
["the Act" means the Adoption Act 1976;]
"adoption agency" means a local authority or approved adoption society;
"the child" means the person whom the applicant for an adoption order or an order authorising a proposed foreign adoption proposes to adopt, or, as the case may be, the person the adoption agency proposes should be freed for adoption;
"Convention proceedings" means proceedings in the High Court on an application for a Convention adoption order and proceedings in the High Court under [the 1968 Act];
"the court" means the High Court and any county court [falling within the class specified for the commencement of proceedings under the Act by an order under Part I of Schedule 11 to the Children Act 1989];
"interim order" means an order under [section 25 of the Act];
"order authorising a proposed foreign adoption" means an order under [section 55 of the Act];
"process" means, in the High Court, a summons and, in a county court, an application;

153

"proper officer" means, in the High Court, [a district judge] of the Principal Registry of the Family Division and, in a county court, the person defined as "proper officer" by Order 1(3) of the County Court Rules 1981; and

"regular armed forces of the Crown" means the Royal Navy, the Regular Armed Forces as defined by section 225 of the Army Act 1955, the Regular Air Force as defined by section 223 of the Air Force Act 1955, the Queen Alexandra's Royal Naval Nursing Service and the Women's Royal Naval Service.

[(2) Except where a contrary intention appears, a word or phrase used in these rules shall have the same meaning as in the Children Act 1989 or, where in the word or phrase does not appear in that Act, as in the Act.]

(3) In these rules [. . .] a form referred to by number means the form so numbered in Schedule 1 to these rules, or a form substantially to the like effect, with such variations as the circumstances may require.

Extent and application of other rules

2–140 **3.**—(1) These rules shall apply to proceedings in the High Court and in a county court under [the Act], and Part IV of these rules shall apply to Convention proceedings commenced on or after May 27, 1984.

(2) Subject to the provisions of these rules and any enactment, the Rules of the Supreme Court [. . .] 1965 and the County Court Rules 1981 shall apply with the necessary modifications to proceedings in the High Court [or a county court under the Act].

(3) For the purposes of paragraph (2) any provision of these rules authorising or requiring anything to be done shall be treated as if it were a provision of the Rules of the Supreme Court 1965 or the County Court Rules 1981 as the case may be.

(4) Unless the contrary intention appears, any power which by these rules may be exercised by the court may be exercised by the proper officer.

PART II

FREEING FOR ADOPTION

Commencement of proceedings

2–141 **4.**—(1) Proceedings to free a child for adoption shall be commenced—
  (a) by originating summons in Form 1 issued out of the Principal Registry of the Family Division; or
  (b) by filing in the office of [a] county court an originating application in Form 1.

(2) The applicant shall be the adoption agency and the respondents shall be—
  (a) each parent or guardian of the child;
  [(b) any local authority or voluntary organisation which has parental responsibility for, is looking after, or is caring, for the child;]
  (c) [. . .]
  (d) [. . .]
  (e) [. . .]
  (f) any person liable by virtue of any order or agreement to contribute to the maintenance of the child; and
  (g) in the High Court, the child.

(3) The court may at any time direct that any other person or body, save in a county court the child, be made a respondent to the process.

(4) On filing the originating process the applicant shall pay the appropriate fee and supply three copies of:—

(a) Form 1, together with any other documents required to be supplied, and

(b) a report in writing covering all the relevant matters specified in Schedule 2 to these rules.

Para. (3)

In *Re C. (Minors) (Adoption)* [1992] 1 F.L.R. 115, the Court of Appeal allowed an appeal **2–142** against a freeing order on the ground of the failure by the judge to direct that the prospective adopters be joined as parties. Also see the note on r.15(3).

Appointment and duties of reporting officer

5.—(1) As soon as practicable after the originating process has been filed **2–143** or at any stage thereafter, if it appears that a parent or guardian of the child is willing to agree to the making of an adoption order and is in England or Wales, the proper officer shall appoint a reporting officer in respect of that parent or guardian, and shall send to him a copy of the originating process and any documents attached thereto and of the report supplied by the applicant.

(2) The same person may be appointed as reporting officer in respect of two or more parents or guardians of the child.

(3) The reporting officer shall be appointed from a panel established by [regulations under section 41(7) of the Children Act 1989, if any,] but shall not be a member or employee of the applicant or any respondent body nor have been involved in the making of any arrangements for the adoption of the child.

(4) The reporting officer shall—

(a) ensure so far as is reasonably practicable that any agreement to the making of an adoption order is given freely and unconditionally and with full understanding of what is involved;

(b) confirm that the parent or guardian has been given an opportunity of making a declaration under [section 18(6) of the Act] that he prefers not to be involved in future questions concerning the adoption of the child;

(c) witness the signature by the parent or guardian of the written agreement to the making of an adoption order;

(d) investigate all the circumstances relevant to that agreement and any such declaration;

(e) where it is proposed to free [for adoption a child whose parents were not married to each other at the time of his birth and whose father is not his guardian] interview any person claiming to be the father in order to be able to advise the court on the matters listed [in section 18(7) of the Act]; but if more than one reporting officer has been appointed, the proper officer shall nominate one of them to conduct the interview; and

(f) on completing his investigations makes a report in writing to the court, drawing attention to any matters which, in his opinion, may be of assistance to the court in considering the application.

(5) With a view to obtaining the directions of the court on any matter, the reporting officer may at any time make such interim report to the court as appears to him to be necessary and, in particular, the reporting officer shall make a report if a parent or guardian of the child is unwilling to agree to the making of an adoption order, and in such a case the proper officer shall notify the applicant.

(6) The court may, at any time before the final determination of the application, require the reporting officer to perform such further duties as the court considers necessary.

(7) The reporting officer shall attend any hearing of the application if so required by the court.

(8) Any report made to the court under this rule shall be confidential.

GENERAL NOTE

Para. 1

2–144   *As soon as practicable:* See the note on r.17(1).

Appointment and duties of guardian *ad litem*

2–145   **6.**—As soon as practicable after the originating process has been filed, or after receipt of the statement of facts supplied under rule 7, if it appears that a parent or guardian of the child is unwilling to agree to the making of an adoption order, the proper officer shall appoint a guardian *ad litem* of the child and shall send to him a copy of the originating process, together with any documents attached thereto, the statement of facts and the report supplied by the applicant.

(2) Where there are special circumstances and it appears to the court that the welfare of the child requires it, the court may at any time appoint a guardian *ad litem* of the child, and where such an appointment is made the court shall indicate any particular matters which it requires the guardian *ad litem* to investigate, and the proper officer shall send the guardian *ad litem* a copy of the originating process together with any documents attached thereto and the report supplied by the applicant.

(3) The same person may be appointed as reporting officer under rule 5(1) in respect of a parent or guardian who appears to be willing to agree to the making of an adoption order, and as guardian *ad litem* of the child under this rule, and, whether or not so appointed as reporting officer, the guardian *ad litem* may be appointed as reporting officer in respect of a parent or guardian of the child who originally was unwilling to agree to the making of an adoption order but who later signifies his or her agreement.

(4) In the High Court, unless the applicant desires some other person to act as guardian *ad litem*, the Official Solicitor shall, if he consents, be appointed as the guardian *ad litem* of the child.

(5) In a county court and where, in the High Court, the Official Solicitor does not consent to act as guardian *ad litem*, or the applicant desires some other person so to act, the guardian *ad litem* shall be appointed from a panel established by [regulations under section 41(7) of the Children Act 1989, if any,] but shall not be a member or employee of the applicant or any respondent body nor have been involved in the making of any arrangements for the adoption of the child.

(6) With a view to safeguarding the interests of the child before the court, the guardian *ad litem* shall, so far as is reasonably practicable—
    (a) investigate—

(i) so far as he considers necessary, the matters alleged in the originating process, the report supplied by the applicant and, where appropriate, the statement of facts supplied under rule 7, and

(ii) any other matters which appear to him to be relevant to the making of an order freeing the child for adoption;

(b) advise whether, in his opinion, the child should be present at the hearing of the process; and

(c) perform such other duties as appear to him to be necessary or as the court may direct.

(7) On completing his investigations the guardian *ad litem* shall make a report in writing to the court, drawing attention to any matters which, in his opinion, may be of assistance to the court in considering the application.

(8) With a view to obtaining the direction of the court on any matter, the guardian *ad litem* may at any time make such interim report to the court as appears to him to be necessary.

(9) The court may, at any time before the final determination of the application, require the guardian *ad litem* to perform such further duties as the court considers necessary.

(10) The guardian *ad litem* shall attend any hearing of the application unless the court otherwise orders.

(11) Any report made to the court under this rule shall be confidential.

GENERAL NOTE

See the notes on r.18.

2–146

Para. 11

Confidential: See the notes on r.53.

Statement of facts in dispensation cases

7.—(1) Where the adoption agency applying for an order freeing a child **2–147** for adoption intends to request the court to dispense with the agreement of a parent or guardian of the child on any of the grounds specified in [section 12(2) of the Act], the request shall, unless otherwise directed, be made in the originating process, or, if made subsequently, by notice to the proper officer and there shall be attached to the originating process or notice three copies of the statement of facts on which the applicant intends to rely.

(2) Where the applicant has been informed by a person with whom the child has been placed for adoption that he wishes his identity to remain confidential, the statement of facts supplied under paragraph (1) shall be framed in such a way as not to disclose the identity of that person.

(3) Where a statement of facts has been supplied under paragraph (1), the proper officer shall, where and as soon as practicable, inform the parent or guardian of the request to dispense with his agreement and shall send to him a copy of the statement supplied under paragraph (1).

(4) The proper officer shall also send a copy of the statement supplied under paragraph (1) to the guardian *ad litem* and to the reporting officer if a different person.

GENERAL NOTE

Para.3

Statement of facts: See the note on r.19(3).

2–148

Agreement

2–149   **8.**—(1) Any document signifying the agreement of a person to the making of an adoption order may be in Form 2, and, if executed by a person outside England and Wales before the commencement of the proceedings, shall be filed with the originating process.

(2) If the document is executed in Scotland it shall be witnessed by a Justice of the Peace or a Sheriff.

(3) If the document is executed in Northern Ireland it shall be witnessed by a Justice of the Peace.

(4) If the document is executed outside the United Kingdom it shall be witnessed by one of the following persons—

   (a) any person for the time being authorised by law in the place where the document is executed to administer an oath for any judicial or other legal purpose;

   (b) a British consular officer;

   (c) a notary public; or

   (d) if the person executing the document is serving in any of the regular armed forces of the Crown, an officer holding a commission in any of those forces.

Notice of hearing

2–150   **9.**—(1) As soon as practicable after receipt of the originating process, the proper officer shall list the case for hearing by the judge, and shall serve notice of the hearing on all the parties, the reporting officer and the guardian *ad litem* (if appointed) in Form 3.

(2) The reporting officer and the guardian *ad litem* (if appointed), but no other person, shall be served with a copy of the originating process and the report supplied by the applicant, and that report shall be confidential.

(3) If, at any stage before the hearing of the process, it appears to the court that directions for the hearing are required, the court may give such directions as it considers necessary and, in any event, the court shall, not less than four weeks before the date fixed for the hearing under paragraph (1), consider the documents relating to the process with a view to giving such further directions for the hearing as appear to the court to be necessary.

General Note

Para. 1

2–151   *As soon as practicable:* The "fixing of a day for the hearing must depend upon the registrar's assessment, from his experience and from the documents before him, of the time that the reporting officer or the guardian *ad litem* is likely to need in preparing his report to the court, of the length of time that the hearing is likely to take, of the urgency of the matter and, as always in matters of listing, the availability of a suitable court. So far as possible, however, in my opinion, the date specified should be a realistic date to which, it is to be hoped, the parties, the reporting officer and the guardian *ad litem* will be able to adhere. I doubt, in fact, whether it will ever be necessary for it to be more than three months ahead. It should also be noted that the fixing of a date for hearing is no longer dependant, as it was by r.17 of the Adoption (High Court) Rules 1976 (now revoked), upon the receipt by the court of the guardian *ad litem*'s report" (*Re P.B. (A Minor) (Application to Free for Adoption)* [1985] F.L.R. 394 at 398, *per* Sheldon J.).

Para. 3

2–152   "In my opinion . . . the registrar, at the same time that he serves notice of the intended hearing date as provided by r.9(1), should take advantage of r.9(3) to require the much earlier attendance (say, 21 days ahead, whether before himself or a judge) of all parties . . . in order to give such preliminary directions (*e.g.* as to the filing of evidence) as may be necessary. Such a step, however, would be without prejudice to the compliance by the court with the further obligation contained in r.9(3) . . .", *per* Sheldon J. in *Re P.B.*, above, at 399.

The hearing

10.—(1) On the hearing of the process, any person upon whom notice is **2–153** required to be served under rule 9 may attend and be heard on the question whether an order freeing the child for adoption should be made.

(2) Any member or employee of a party which is a local authority, adoption agency or other body may address the court if he is duly authorised in that behalf.

(3) Where the court has been informed by the applicant that the child has been placed with a person (whether alone or jointly with another) for adoption and that person wishes his identity to remain confidential, the proceedings shall be conducted with a view to securing that any such person is not seen by or made known to any respondent who is not already aware of his identity except with his consent.

(4) Subject to paragraph (5), the judge shall not make an order freeing the child for adoption except after the personal attendance before him of a representative of the applicant duly authorised in that behalf and of the child.

(5) If there are special circumstances which, having regard to the report of the guardian *ad litem* (if any), appear to the court to make the attendance of the child unnecessary, the court may direct that the child need not attend.

(6) If there are special circumstances which appear to the court to make the attendance of any other party necessary, the court may direct that that party shall attend.

GENERAL NOTE

Para. (4)

The attendance of the child will not always be necessary; see *Re P. (Minors) (Adoption)* **2–154** [1989] 1 F.L.R. 1, CA, noted under r.23.

Proof of identity of child, etc.

11.—(1) Where the child who is the subject of the proceedings is **2–155** identified in the originating process by reference to a birth certificate which is the same, or relates to the same entry in the Registers of Births, as a birth certificate exhibited to a form of agreement, the child so identified shall be deemed, unless the contrary appears, to be the child to whom the form of agreement refers.

(2) Where the child has previously been adopted, paragraph (1) shall have effect as if for the references to a birth certificate and to the Registers of Births there were substituted respectively references to a certified copy of an entry in the Adopted Children Register and to that Register.

(3) Where the precise date of the child's birth is not proved to the satisfaction of the court, the court shall determine the probable date of his birth and the date so determined may be specified in the order freeing the child for adoption as the date of his birth.

(4) Where the place of birth of the child cannot be proved to the satisfaction of the court but it appears probable that the child was born in the United Kingdom, the Channel Islands or the Isle of Man, he may be treated as having been born in the registration district and sub-district in which the court sits, and in any other case (where the country of birth is not proved) the particulars of the country of birth may be omitted from the order freeing the child for adoption.

Application for revocation of order freeing a child for adoption

2-156   **12.**—(1) An application by a former parent for an order revoking an order freeing the child for adoption shall be made in Form 4 in the proceedings commenced under rule 4.

(2) Notice of the proceedings shall be served on all parties and on any adoption agency [which has parental responsibility for the child by virtue of section 21 of the Act], save that notice shall not be served on a party to the proceedings who was joined as a party by virtue of [rule 4(2)(b)].

(3) As soon as practicable after receipt of the application, the proper officer shall list the case for hearing by a judge and shall appoint a guardian *ad litem* of the child in accordance with rule 6(4) or (5) and shall send to him a copy of the application and any documents attached thereto.

(4) The guardian *ad litem* shall have the same duties as if he had been appointed under rule 6 but as if in that rule:—

(a) the reference to an order freeing the child for adoption was a reference to the revocation of an order freeing the child for adoption; and

(b) each reference to the report supplied by the applicant was omitted.

[Substitution of one adoption agency for another]

2-157   **13.**—(1) An application [under section 21(1) of the Act] to transfer the parental rights and duties relating to the child between themselves under section 23 of the 1975 Act shall be made in Form 5 in the proceedings commenced under rule 4.

(2) Notice of any order made under [section 21 of the Act] shall be sent by the court to the court which made the order under [section 18 of the Act] (if a different court) and to any former parent (as defined in [section 19(1) of the Act]) of the child.

PART III

ADOPTION ORDERS

Application for a serial number

2-158   **14.** If any person proposing to apply to the court for an adoption order wishes his identity to be kept confidential, he may, before commencing proceedings, apply to the proper officer for a serial number to be assigned to him for the purposes of identifying him in the proposed process and a number shall be assigned to him accordingly.

GENERAL NOTE

2-159   Once a serial number has been given the confidentiality of the applicant must be preserved; see r.23(3). A parent's right to oppose the adoption application does not entitle him or her to receive information about the prospective adopters (*Re S. (A Minor)* [1993] 2 F.L.R. 204, CA). The procedure to be followed where disclosure is an issue in adoption cases was identified in *Re K. (Adoption: Disclosure of Information)* [1997] 2 F.L.R. 74, which is noted under r.53(2).
Person proposing to apply: But not the natural parents.

Commencement of proceedings

2-160   **15.**—(1) Proceedings for an adoption order shall be commenced—

(a) by originating summons in Form 6 issued out of the Principal Registry of the Family Division; or

(b) by filing in the office of [a] county court an originating application in Form 6.

(2) The applicant shall be the proposed adopter and the respondents shall be—

(a) each parent or guardian (not being an applicant) of the child, unless the child is free for adoption;

[(b) any adoption agency having parental responsibility for the child by virtue of sections 18 or 21 of the Act];

(c) any adoption agency named in the application or in any form of agreement to the making of the adoption order as having taken part in the arrangements for the adoption of the child;

(d) any local authority to whom the applicant has given notice under [section 22 of the Act] of his intention to apply for an adoption order;

[(e) any local authority or voluntary organisation which has parental responsibility for, is looking after, or is caring for, the child;]

(f) [. . .]

(g) [. . .]

(h) any person liable by virtue of any order or agreement to contribute to the maintenance of the child;

(i) [. . .]

(j) where the applicant proposes to rely on [section 15(1)(b)(ii) of the Act], the spouse of the applicant; and

(k) in the High Court, the child.

(3) The court may at any time direct that any other person or body, save in a county court the child, be made a respondent to the process.

(4) On filing the originating process the applicant shall pay the appropriate fee and supply three copies of—

(a) Form 6, together with any other documents required to be supplied, and

(b) where the child was not placed for adoption with the applicant by an adoption agency, save where the applicant or one of the applicants is a parent of the child, reports by a registered medical practitioner made not more than three months earlier on the health of the child and of each applicant, covering the matters specified in Schedule 3 to these rules.

GENERAL NOTE

Para. (2)

Notice of the hearing must be sent to all the parties under r.21.

Each parent: The word "parent" has the same meaning as in the Children Act 1989 (r.2(2) **2–161** and s.72(1) of the Adoption Act 1976 as amended by Sched. 10, para. 30(7) of the 1989 Act). Therefore, an unmarried father who does not have parental responsibility for the child does not fall into this category (*Re C. (Adoption: Parties)* [1995] 2 F.L.R. 483). Such a person will become a respondent if he has either agreed or been ordered to contribute towards the child's maintenance (para. (h)) or if the court has exercised its discretion to make him a respondent under para. (3).

Para. (3)

This provision can be used to make the guardian *ad litem* a party to the proceedings. The **2–162** guardian would then be entitled to be legally represented (*Re C. (Minor) (Adoption)* [1992] 1 F.L.R. 115, CA).

Preliminary examination of application

16. If it appears to the proper officer on receipt of the originating process **2–163** for an adoption order that the court—

(a) may be precluded, by virtue of [section 24(1) of the Act], from proceeding to hear the application, or

(b) may for any other reason appearing in the process have no jurisdiction to make an adoption order,

he shall refer the process to the [judge or district judge] for directions.

Appointment and duties of reporting officer

2–164   **17.**—(1) As soon as practicable after the originating process has been filed or at any stage thereafter, if the child is not free for adoption and if it appears that a parent or guardian of the child is willing to agree to the making of an adoption order and is in England and Wales, the proper officer shall appoint a reporting officer in respect of that parent or guardian, and shall send to him a copy of the originating process and any documents attached thereto.

(2) The same person may be appointed as reporting officer in respect of two or more parents or guardians of the child.

(3) The reporting officer shall be appointed from a panel established by [regulations under section 41(7) of the Children Act 1989, if any,] but shall not be a member or employee of any respondent body (except where a local authority is made a respondent only under rule 15(2)(*d*)) nor have been involved in the making of any arrangements for the adoption of the child.

(4) The reporting officer shall—

(a) ensure so far as is reasonably practicable that any agreement to the making of the adoption order is given freely and unconditionally and with full understanding of what is involved;

(b) witness the signature by the parent or guardian of the written agreement to the making of the adoption order;

(c) investigate all the circumstances relevant to that agreement; and

(d) on completing his investigations make a report in writing to the court, drawing attention to any matters which, in his opinion, may be of assistance to the court in considering the application.

(5) Paragraphs (5) to (8) of rule 5 shall apply to a reporting officer appointed under this rule as they apply to a reporting officer appointed under that rule.

GENERAL NOTE

2–165   Detailed guidance on the role of Reporting Officers in adoption and freeing applications can be found in Chapter 15 of *Manuarl of Practice for Guardians ad Litem and Reporting Officers* (H.M.S.O., 1992).

Para. 1

2–166   *As soon as practicable:* As the court's functions at this stage are purely administrative, this means, save maybe in wholly exceptional circumstances, immediately and without delay; *per* Sheldon J. in *Re P.B. (A Minor) (Application to Free for Adoption)* [1985] F.L.R. 394, at 398.

Appointment and duties of guardian *ad litem*

2–167   **18.**—(1) As soon as practicable after the originating process has been filed, or after receipt of the statement of facts supplied under rule 19, if the child is not free for adoption and if it appears that a parent or guardian of the child is unwilling to agree to the making of the adoption order, the proper officer shall appoint a guardian *ad litem* of the child and shall send to him a copy of the originating process together with any documents attached thereto.

162

(2) Where there are special circumstances and it appears to the court that the welfare of the child requires it, the court may at any time appoint a guardian *ad litem* of the child and where such an appointment is made the court shall indicate any particular matters which it requires the guardian *ad litem* to investigate, and the proper officer shall send the guardian *ad litem* a copy of the originating process together with any documents attached thereto.

(3) The same person may be appointed as reporting officer under rule 17(1) in respect of a parent or a guardian who appears to be willing to agree to the making of the adoption order, and as guardian *ad litem* of the child under this rule, and, whether or not so appointed as reporting officer, the guardian *ad litem* may be appointed as reporting officer in respect of a parent or guardian of the child who originally was unwilling to agree to the making of an adoption order but who later signifies his or her agreement.

(4) In the High Court, unless the applicant desires some other person to act as guardian *ad litem*, the Official Solicitor shall, if he consents, be appointed as the guardian *ad litem* of the child.

(5) In a county court and where, in the High Court, the Official Solicitor does not consent to act as guardian *ad litem*, or the applicant desires some other person so to act, the guardian *ad litem* shall be appointed from a panel established by [regulations under section 41(7) of the Children Act 1989, if any,] but shall not be a member or employee of any respondent body (except where a local authority is made a respondent only under rule 15(2)(d)) nor have been involved in the making of any arrangements for the adoption of the child.

(6) With a view to safeguarding the interests of the child before the court the guardian *ad litem* shall, so far as is reasonably practicable—

(a) investigate—
    (i) so far as he considers necessary, the matters alleged in the originating process, any report supplied under rule 22(1) or (2) and, where appropriate, the statement of facts supplied under rule 19;
    (ii) any other matters which appear to him to be relevant to the making of an adoption order;
(b) advise whether, in his opinion, the child should be present at the hearing of the process; and
(c) perform such other duties as appear to him to be necessary or as the court may direct.

(7) Paragraphs (7) to (11) of rule 6 shall apply to a guardian *ad litem* appointed under this rule as they apply to a guardian *ad litem* appointed under that rule.

GENERAL NOTE

In *Re D. (Minors) (Adoption Reports: Confidentiality)* [1995] 4 All E.R. 385, HL, Lord **2–168** Mustill said, at 390, 391, that it would be quite inappropriate for a guardian *ad litem* to give children interviewed in adoption proceedings an unqualified promise of confidentiality, since the guardian has no power to circumscribe the discretion of the judge. Note, however, the following remarks of Butler-Sloss L.J. in the Court of Appeal at [1995] 1 F.L.R. 631, 637:

> "[However] in unusually sensitive adoption cases affecting older children it would not be unreasonable for a guardian to promise the child that he would tell the judge that the child would prefer the natural parent not to be told the details of the conversations with the guardian and any reasons which the guardian considered valid for not disclosing those details. The limits of that partial assurance must be made clear to the child and it will then be for the judge to decide what should happen to that information."

In difficult and finely balanced cases, it is advisable for the guardian *ad litem* to be legally represented (*Re C. (Minors) (Adoption)* [1992] 1 F.L.R. 115, CA).

2–169   Detailed guidance on this rule for guardians *ad litem* can be found in Chapter 14 of *Manual of Practice Guidance for Guardians ad Litem and Reporting Officers* (H.M.S.O., 1992).

Para. 1

As soon as practicable: See the note on r.17(1).

Appoint a guardian ad litem: Once a guardian *ad litem* is appointed, "there is no reason for the Schedule 2 report [made under these rules] to be awaited by the guardian before making any enquiries which it already seems ought to be made" (*Re An Adoption Application* [1992] 1 F.L.R. 341, *per* Hollings J., at 356).

Para. 2

2–170   *Special circumstances:* A guardian *ad litem* should be appointed in cases where problematic and sensitive issues arise (*Re S. (A Minor) (Blood Transfusion: Adoption Order Condition)* [1994] 2 F.L.R. 416, CA). In *Re K. (A Minor)*, July 18, 1996, CA, the failure of the judge to appoint a guardian *ad litem* in a complex case involving a Bosnian child who had been brought to this country as a refugee was one of the factors that led the court to set aside the adoption order.

Appoint a guardian ad litem: For appointments in the High Court, see Practice Direction [1986] 2 All E.R. 832.

Para. 4

2–171   *The official solicitor:* Subject to certain exceptions, the Official Solicitor is not prepared to act as guardian *ad litem* or reporting officer in uncontested cases (*Practice Direction* [1986] 2 All E.R. 832).

Para. 6

2–172   *The guardian ad litem shall . . . investigate:* The guardian *ad litem* does not have a duty to seek out the child's natural father (*Re Adoption Application No. 41/61 (No. 2)* [1963] 2 All E.R. 1082).

Any other matter: Such as the wishes of relevant extended family members and the appropriateness of making a contact order under the Children Act 1989, ss.8 and 10, alongside the adoption order.

Statement of facts in dispensation cases

2–175   **19.**—(1) Where the child is not free for adoption and the applicant for the adoption order intends to request the court to dispense with the agreement of a parent or guardian of the child on any of the grounds specified in [section 16(2) of the Act], the request shall, unless otherwise directed, be made in the originating process or, if made subsequently, by notice to the proper officer and there shall be attached to the originating process or notice three copies of the statement of facts on which the applicant intends to rely.

(2) Where a serial number has been assigned to the applicant under rule 14, the statement of facts supplied under paragraph (1) shall be framed in such a way as not to disclose the identity of the applicant.

(3) Where a statement of facts has been supplied under paragraph (1), the proper officer shall, where and as soon as practicable, inform the parent or guardian of the request to dispense with his agreement and shall send to him a copy of the statement supplied under paragraph (1).

(4) The proper officer shall also send a copy of the statement supplied under paragraph (1) to the guardian *ad litem* and to the reporting officer if a different person.

Para. 3

The statement of facts: This will not contain details of the evidence upon which the **2–174** statement is based.

Agreement

20.—(1) Any document signifying the agreement of a person to the **2–175** making of the adoption order may be in Form 7, and, if executed by a person outside England and Wales before the commencement of the proceedings, shall be filed with the originating process.

(2) If the document is executed outside England and Wales it shall be witnessed by one of the persons specified in rule 8(2), (3) or (4) according to the country in which it is executed.

Notice of hearing

21.—(1) Subject to paragraph (4), the proper officer shall list the case for **2–176** hearing by a judge as soon as practicable after the originating process has been filed, and shall serve notice of the hearing on all the parties, the reporting officer and the guardian *ad litem* (if appointed) in Form 8.

(2) In a case where [section 22 of the Act] applies, the proper officer shall send a copy of the originating process and, where appropriate, of the report supplied under rule 15(4), to the local authority to whom notice under that section was given.

(3) No person other than the reporting officer, the guardian *ad litem* (if appointed) and, in cases where [section 22 of the Act] applies, the local authority to whom notice under that section was given, shall be served with a copy of the originating process.

(4) Where [section 22 of the Act] applies, the proper officer shall list the case for hearing on a date not less than three months from the date of the notice given to the local authority under that section.

(5) If, at any stage before the hearing of the process, it appears to the court that directions for the hearing are required, the court may give such directions as it considers necessary and, in any event, the court shall, not less than four weeks before the date fixed for the hearing under paragraph (1), consider the documents relating to the process with a view to giving such further directions for the hearing as appear to the court to be necessary.

GENERAL NOTE

Para. (1)

As soon as practicable: See the note on r.9(1).   **2–177**

Shall serve: Service can be dispensed with (see *Re An Adoption Application* [1992] 1 F.L.R. 341, where there had been unsuccessful attempts at finding the natural mother) and such a decision is governed by the principle set out in s.6 of the Adoption Act 1976 (*Re G. (Foreign Adoption: Consent)* [1995] 2 F.L.R. 534). Note that in *Re B. (Adoption: Jurisdiction to Set Aside)* [1995] 2 F.L.R. 1, Swinton Thomas L.J. said at 14:

> "It is fundamental to the making of an adoption order that the natural parent should be informed of the application so that she can give or withhold consent, if she has no knowledge at all of the application then, obviously, a fundamental injustice is perpetuated."

In *Re K. (Adoption and Wardship)* [1997] 2 F.L.R. 221, CA, a failure to go through the proper steps to serve notice on the head of the Bosnian Red Cross as the guardian of a Bosnian child, was one of the factors that led the court to set aside the adoption order.

Notice of the hearing: For method of service, see r.50(1). In the High Court, if the parent has not acknowledged within 21 days receipt of a notice asking if she wishes to be heard in the proceedings, the Principal Registry will inform the applicants' solicitors, and it will be their duty to serve a further notice on her giving her a final chance to state her wish (*Practice Direction* [1986] 1 All E.R. 1024).

Parties: See r.15(2).

Para. (5)

2-178   "The language of r.21(5) does not deal specifically with directions about disclosure of reports, but is limited to 'directions for the hearing'. The matter is presently governed by the senior registrar's direction of November 15, 1985, giving the opinion of the President of the Family Division to the effect that any application for such inspection should normally be made to the judge at the actual hearing of the application for which the report has been prepared, and only in exceptional circumstances should application for inspection be made before the hearing. The President was of the opinion that, when such application was made, it might be dealt with by a registrar, who might require the application to be on notice and/or made to a judge"; *Re. S (A Minor) (Adoption or Custodianship)* [1987] 2 All E.R. 99, *per* Sir Roualeyn Cumming-Bruce at 102.

Reports by adoption agency or local authority
2-179   **22.**—(1) Where the child was placed for adoption with the applicant by an adoption agency, that agency shall supply, within six weeks of receipt of the notice of hearing under rule 21, three copies of a report in writing covering the matters specified in Schedule 2 to these rules.

(2) Where the child was not placed for adoption with the applicant by an adoption agency, the local authority to whom the notice under [section 22 of the Act] was given shall supply, within six weeks of receipt of the notice of hearing under rule 21, three copies of a report in writing covering the matters specified in Schedule 2 to these rules.

(3) The court may request a further report under paragraph (1) or (2) and may indicate any particular matters it requires such a further report to cover.

(4) The proper officer shall send a copy of any report supplied under paragraph (1) or (2) to the reporting officer and to the guardian *ad litem* (if appointed).

(5) No other person shall be supplied with a copy of any report supplied under paragraph (1) or (2) and any such report shall be confidential.

GENERAL NOTE

Para. (5)
2-180   This should be read in conjunction with r.53(2).

The hearing
2-181   **23.**—(1) On the hearing of the process, any person upon whom notice is required to be served under rule 21 may attend and be heard on the question whether an adoption order should be made.

(2) Any member or employee of a party which is a local authority, adoption agency or other body may address the court if he is duly authorised in that behalf.

(3) If a serial number has been assigned to the applicant under rule 14, the proceedings shall be conducted with a view to securing that he is not seen by or made known to any respondent who is not already aware of the applicant's identity except with his consent.

(4) Subject to paragraphs (5) and (7), the judge shall not make an adoption order or an interim order except after the personal attendance before him of the applicant and the child.

(5) If there are special circumstances which, having regard to the report of the guardian *ad litem* (if any), appear to the court to make the attendance of the child unnecessary, the court may direct that the child need not attend.

(6) If there are special circumstances which appear to the court to make the attendance of any other party necessary, the court may direct that that party shall attend.

(7) In the case of an application under [section 14(1A) or (1B) of the Act], the judge may in special circumstances make an adoption order or an interim order after the personal attendance of one only of the applicants, if the originating process is verified by an affidavit sworn by the other applicant or, if he is outside the United Kingdom, by a declaration made by him and witnessed by any of the persons specified in rule 8(4).

GENERAL NOTE

"The purpose of r.23(4)] is to ensure that a child in respect of whom an adoption order is **2–182** about to be made understands fully, as far as he or she can, the nature of the order . . . it is clearly necessary that a child who is capable of understanding should understand the nature of the order about to be made, although the attendance of a child may be unnecessary in any particular case in the light of information contained in the guardian *ad litem's* report"; *Re P. (Minors) (Adoption)* [1989] 1 F.L.R. 1, CA, *per* Waterhouse J. at 6. In this case the court held that as the judge had ample evidence before him from the guardian *ad litem* and the Sched. 2 report writer (see r.22(2)) as to the children's views and the reasons for them there was no duty placed on him to see the children before reaching a decision.

Proof of identity of child, etc.

24.—(1) Where the child who is the subject of the proceedings is **2–183** identified in the originating process by reference to a birth certificate which is the same, or relates to the same entry in the Registers of Births, as a birth certificate exhibited to a form of agreement, the child so identified shall be deemed, unless the contrary appears, to be the child to whom the form of agreement refers.

(2) Where the child has previously been adopted, paragraph (1) shall have effect as if for the references to a birth certificate and to the Registers of Births there were substituted respectively references to a certified copy of an entry in the Adopted Children Register and to that Register.

(3) Subject to paragraph (5), where the precise date of the child's birth is not proved to the satisfaction of the court, the court shall determine the probable date of his birth and the date so determined may be specified in the adoption order as the date of his birth.

(4) Subject to paragraph (5), where the place of birth of the child cannot be proved to the satisfaction of the court but it appears probable that the child was born in the United Kingdom, the Channel Islands or the Isle of Man, he may be treated as having been born in the registration district and sub-district in which the court sits, and in any other case (where the country of birth is not proved) the particulars of the country of birth may be omitted from the adoption order.

(5) Where the child is free for adoption, any order made identifying the probable date and place of birth of the child in the proceedings under [section 18 of the Act] shall be sufficient proof of the date and place of birth of the child in proceedings to which this rule applies.

Further proceedings after interim order
2–184 **25.** Where the court has made an interim order, the proper officer shall list the case for further hearing by a judge on a date before the order expires and shall send notice in Form 8 of the date of the hearing to all the parties and to the guardian *ad litem* (if appointed) not less than one month before that date.

Committal of child to care on refusal of adoption order
2–185 **26.** [. . .]

PART IV

CONVENTION PROCEEDINGS

Introductory
2–186 **27.**—(1) This Part of these rules shall apply to Convention proceedings and, subject to the provisions of this Part of these rules, Parts I, III and V of these rules shall apply, with the necessary modifications, to Convention proceedings as they apply to proceedings in the High Court under the [. . .] Act.

(2) Any reference in this Part of these rules to the nationality of a person who is not solely a United Kingdom national means that person's nationality as determined in accordance with [section 70 of the Act].

Originating process
2–187 **28.**—(1) An applicant for a Convention adoption order shall state in his originating process that he is applying for a Convention adoption order.

(2) The originating process—
  (a) need not contain paragraphs corresponding to paragraphs 2, 24 or 25 of Form 6 but
  (b) shall contain the additional information required by Schedule 4 to these rules.

Evidence as to nationality
2–188 **29.**—(1) Any document (or copy of a document) which is to be used for the purposes of satisfying the court as to the nationality of the applicant or of the child shall be attached to the originating process.

(2) Where the applicant claims that for the purposes of [section 17(2)(a), (4)(a) or (5)(a) of the Act] he or the child is a national of a Convention country, he shall attach to the originating process a statement by an expert as to the law of that country relating to nationality applicable to that person.

Statement at hearing
2–189 **30.** The requirement that the conditions in [section 17(2), (3) and (4) or (5) of the Act] are satisfied immediately before the order is made may be established by—
  (a) oral evidence at the hearing of an application for a Convention adoption order, or
  (b) a document executed by the applicant containing a statement to that effect attested in accordance with rule 44 and such a statement shall be admissible in evidence without further proof of the signature of the applicant.

Orders

31. Within 7 days after a Convention adoption order has been drawn up, **2–190** the proper officer shall by notice to the Registrar General request him to send the information to the designated authorities of any Convention country—
   (a) of which the child is a national;
   (b) in which the child was born;
   (c) in which the applicant habitually resides; or
   (d) of which the applicant is a national.

ADDITIONAL PROVISIONS FOR CASES WHERE CHILD IS NOT A UNITED
KINGDOM NATIONAL

Scope of rules 33 to 36

32. Rules 33 to 36 shall apply to any case where the child is not a United **2–191** Kingdom national, and in such a case—
   (a) the provisions in Part III of these rules, other than rules 17 and 20 (agreement to adoption), and
   (b) paragraphs 9 to 14 of Form 6.
shall apply with the necessary modifications to take account of [section 17(6)(a) of the Act].

Evidence as to foreign law relating to consents and consultations

33. The applicant shall file, with his originating process, a statement by **2–192** an expert as to the provisions relating to consents and consultations of the internal law relating to adoption of the Convention country of which the child is a national.

Form of consent, etc.

34.—(1) Any document signifying the consent of a person to, or **2–193** otherwise containing the opinion of a person on the making of, the Convention adoption order shall be in a form which complies with the internal law relating to adoption of the Convention country of which the child is a national: provided that where the court is not satisfied that a person consents with full understanding of what is involved, it may call for further evidence.

(2) A document referred to in paragraph (1) shall, if sufficiently witnessed, be admissible as evidence of the consent or opinion contained therein without further proof of the signature of the person by whom it is executed.

(3) A document referred to in paragraph (1) shall, if executed before the date of the applicant's originating process referred to in rule 28(2), be attached to that process.

Notice of hearing

35.—(1) When serving notice of the hearing on the persons specified in **2–194** rule 21, the proper officer shall also serve notice on any person:—
   (a) whose consent to the making of the order is required, not being an applicant, or
   (b) who, in accordance with the internal law relating to adoption of the Convention country of which the child is a national, has to be consulted about, but does not have to consent to, the adoption.

(2) Any person served or required to be served with notice under this rule shall be treated as if he had been served or was required to be served with notice under rule 21.

Proper officer to receive opinions on adoption

2–195   **36.** For the purposes of this rule and of [section 17(7)(*a*) of the Act], the Senior [District Judge] of the Principal Registry of the Family Division is the proper officer of the court to whom any person whose consent is required under or who is consulted in pursuance of the internal law relating to adoption of the Convention country of which the child is a national may communicate his consent or other opinion on the adoption.

[PROCEEDINGS UNDER SECTIONS 52 OR 53 OF THE ACT]

Application to annul or revoke adoption

2–196   **37.**—(1) An application for an order under [section 52(1) or 53(1) of the Act] shall be made by originating process issued out if the Principal Registry of the Family Division in Form 9; and the person filing the process shall be described as the applicant and the adopted person and any adopter, not being the applicant, shall be described as a respondent.

(2) An application under [section 53(1) of the Act] shall not, except with the leave of the court, be made later than 2 years after the date of the adoption to which it relates.

Application to declare adoption invalid or determination invalid or affected

2–197   **38.** An application for an order or decision under [section 53(2) of the Act] shall be made by originating process issued out of the Principal Registry of the Family Division in Form 10; and the person filing the process shall be described as the applicant and the adopted person and any adopter, not being the applicant, shall be described as a respondent.

Evidence in support of application

2–198   **39.**—(1) Evidence in support of an application under [section 52 or 53 of the Act] shall be given by means of an affidavit in Form 11 which shall be filed within 14 days after the issue of the originating process.

(2) Where the application is made under [section 53 of the Act] there shall be exhibited to the affidavit a statement of the facts and, subject to rule 42, there shall be filed with the affidavit expert evidence of any provision of foreign law relating to adoption on which the applicant intends to rely.

(3) The court may order any deponent to give oral evidence concerning the facts stated in, or exhibited to, his affidavit.

Guardian *ad litem*

2–199   **40.** Where the adopted person is under the age of 18 on the date on which an application under [section 52 or 53 of the Act] is made, rule 18(2) and (4) to (7) shall apply to the application as it applies to an application for an adoption order as if the references in rule 18 to the making of an adoption order were references to the granting of an application under [section 52 or 53 of the Act].

170

Notice of order made under section 6, etc.

41.—(1) Where under [section 52 or 53 of the Act] the court has ordered **2–200** that an adoption be annulled or revoked or that an adoption or a determination shall cease to be valid in Great Britain, the proper officer shall serve notice of the order on the Registrar General, and shall state in the notice—

(a) the date of the adoption;

(b) the name and address of the authority which granted the adoption; and

(c) the names of the adopter or adopters, and of the adopted person as given in the affidavit referred to in rule 39.

(2) A notice under paragraph (1) in respect of the annulment or revocation of an adoption shall request the Registrar General to send the information to the designated authorities of any Convention country—

(a) in which the adoption was granted;

(b) of which the adopted person is a national; or

(c) in which the adopted person was born.

(3) [. . .]

SUPPLEMENTARY

Evidence as to specified or notified provisions

42.—(1) Where the applicant seeks to satisfy the court as to any question **2–201** which has arisen or is likely to arise concerning a provision:—

(a) of the internal law of the Convention country of which the applicant or any other person is or was a national,

(b) which has been specified in an order—

(i) under [section 17(8) of the Act] (a "specified provision"), or

(ii) under [section 54(4) of the Act] (a "notified provision"),

expert evidence of the specified or notified provision shall, where practicable, be attached to the originating process.

(2) Paragraph (1) shall apply, in the case of a person who is or was a United Kingdom national, for the purposes of a notified provision in respect of a specified country as it applies for the purposes of a notified provision in respect of a Convention country of which a person is or was a national.

Interim order

43. Where the applicant is a national or both applicants are nationals of a **2–202** Convention country, the court shall take account of any specified provision (as defined in [section 17(8) of the Act]) of the internal law of that country before any decision is made to postpone the determination of the application and to make an interim order.

Witnessing of documents

44. A document shall be sufficiently attested for the purposes of this Part **2–203** of these rules if it is witnessed by one of the following persons—

(a) if it is executed in England and Wales, the reporting officer, a Justice of the Peace, an officer of a county court appointed for the purposes of [section 58(1)(c) of the County Courts Act 1984] or a justices' clerk within the meaning of section 70 of the Justices of Peace Act 1979; or

(b) if it is executed elsewhere, any person specified in rule 8(2), (3) or (4), according to the country in which it is executed.

Service of documents
2–204 **45.**—(1) Any document to be served for the purposes of this Part of these rules may be served out of the jurisdiction without the leave of the court.

(2) Any document served out of the jurisdiction in a country in which English is not an official language shall be accompanied by a translation of the document in the official language of the country in which service is to be effected or, if there is more than one official language of the country, in any one of those languages which is appropriate to the place in that country where service is to be effected.

Translation of documents
2–205 **46.** Where a translation of any document is required for the purposes of Convention proceedings, the translation shall, unless otherwise directed, be provided by the applicant.

PART V

MISCELLANEOUS

Application for removal, return, etc. of child
2–206 **47.**—[(1) An application—
(a) for leave under section 27 or 28 of the Act to remove a child from the home of a person with whom the child lives,
(b) under section 29(2) of the Act for an order directing a person not to remove a child from the home of a person with whom the child lives,
(c) under section 29(1) of the Act for an order for the return of a child who has been removed from the home of a person with whom the child lives,
(d) under section 30(2) of the Act for leave to give notice of an intention not to give a home to a child or not to allow a child to remain in a person's home, or
(e) under section 20(2) of the Act for leave to place a child for adoption,
shall be made in accordance with paragraph (2).]

(2) The application under paragraph (1) shall be made—
(a) if an application for an adoption order or an order under [section 18 or 20 of the Act] is pending, by process on notice in those proceedings; or
(b) if no such application is pending, by filing an originating process in the [. . .] court.

(3) [. . .]

(4) Any respondent to the originating process made under paragraph (2)(b) who wishes to claim relief shall do so by means of an answer to the process which shall be made within 7 days of the service of the copy of the process on the respondent.

(5) Subject to paragraph (6), the proper officer shall serve a copy of the process, and of any answer thereto, and a notice of the date of the hearing—

(a) in a case where proceedings for an adoption order or an order under [section 18 or 20 of the Act] are pending (or where such proceedings have subsequently been commenced), on all the parties to those proceedings and on the reporting officer and guardian *ad litem*, if any;

(b) in any other case, on any person against whom an order is sought in the application and on the local authority to whom the prospective adopter has given notice under [section 22 of the Act]; and

(c) in any case, on such other person or body, not being the child, as the court thinks fit.

(6) If in any application under this rule a serial number has been assigned to a person who has applied or who proposes to apply for an adoption order, or such a person applies to the proper officer in that behalf before filing the originating process and a serial number is assigned accordingly—

(a) the proper officer shall ensure that the documents served under paragraph (5) do not disclose the identity of that person to any other party to the application under this rule who is not already aware of that person's identity, and

(b) the proceedings on the application under this rule shall be conducted with a view to securing that he is not seen by or made known to any party who is not already aware of his identity except with his consent.

(7) Unless otherwise directed, any prospective adopter who is served with a copy of an application under this rule and who wishes to oppose the application shall file his process for an adoption order within 14 days or before or at the time of the hearing of the application under this rule, whichever is the sooner.

(8) The court may at any time give directions, and if giving directions under paragraph (7) shall give further directions, as to the conduct of any application under this rule and in particular as to the appointment of a guardian *ad litem* of the child.

(9) Where an application under paragraph (1)(a) or (d) is granted or an application under paragraph (1)(b) or (c) is refused, the judge may thereupon, if process for an adoption order has been filed, treat the hearing of the application as the hearing of the process for an adoption order and refuse an adoption order accordingly.

(10) Where an application under this rule is determined the proper officer shall serve notice of the effect of the determination on all the parties.

(11) Paragraphs (6) to (10) shall apply to an answer made under this rule as they apply to an originating process made under this rule as if the answer were the originating process.

Proposed foreign adoption proceedings
48.—(1) Proceedings for an order authorising a proposed foreign adop- **2–207** tion shall be commenced—

(a) by originating summons in Form 6 issued out of the Principal Registry of the Family Division; or

(b) by filing in the office of the county court within whose district the child is an originating application in Form 6.

(2) Subject to paragraph (3), Part III of these rules except rule 15(1) and Part V except rule 52(1)(d) shall apply to an application for an order authorising a proposed foreign adoption as if such an order were an adoption order.

(3) An applicant for an order authorising a proposed foreign adoption shall provide expert evidence of the law of adoption in the country in which he is domiciled and an affidavit as to that law sworn by such a person as is mentioned in section 4(1) of the Civil Evidence Act 1972 (that is to say a person who is suitably qualified on account of his knowledge or experience to give evidence as to that law) shall be admissible in evidence without notice.

Amendment and revocation of orders
2–208   49.—(1) An application under [paragraph 4 of Schedule 1 to the Act] for the amendment of an adoption order or the revocation of a direction to the Registrar General, or [under section 52 of the Act] for the revocation of an adoption order, may be made *ex parte* in the first instance, but the court may require notice of the application to be served on such persons as it thinks fit.

(2) Where the application is granted, the proper officer shall send to the Registrar General a notice specifying the amendments or informing him of the revocation and shall give sufficient particulars of the order to enable the Registrar General to identify the case.

Service of documents
2–209   50.—(1) Subject to rule 45 and unless otherwise directed, any document under these rules may be served—
  (a) on a corporation or body of persons, by delivering it at, or sending it by post to, the registered or principal office of the corporation or body;
  (b) on any other person, by delivering it to him, or by sending it by post to him at his usual or last known address.

(2) The person effecting service of any document under these rules shall make, sign and file a certificate showing the date, place and mode of service. If he has failed to effect service of any document, he shall make, sign and file a certificate of non-service showing the reason why service has not been effected.

Costs
2–210   51. On the determination of proceedings to which these rules apply or on the making of an interim order, the judge may make such order as to the costs as he thinks just and, in particular, may order the applicant to pay—
  (a) the expenses incurred by the reporting officer and the guardian *ad litem* (if appointed),
  (b) the expenses incurred by any respondent in attending the hearing,
or such part of those expenses as the judge thinks proper.

Notice and copies of orders, etc.
2–211   52.—(1) In proceedings to which these rules apply orders shall be made in the form indicated in this paragraph—

Description of order	*Form*
(*a*) Order under [section 18 of the Act]	12
(*b*) Order under [section 20 of the Act]	13
(*c*) Interim order	14
(*d*) Adoption order	15
(*e*) Convention adoption order	15 (with the word "Convention" inserted where appropriate)
(*f*) Order authorising a proposed foreign adoption	15 (with the words "order authorising a proposed foreign adoption" substituted for the words "adoption order" wherever they appear).

(2) Where an adoption order is made by a court sitting in Wales in respect of a child who was born in Wales (or is treated under rule 24(4) as having been born in the registration district and sub-district in which that court sits) and the adopter so requests before the order is drawn up, the proper officer shall obtain a translation into Welsh of the particulars set out in the order.

(3) Within 7 days of the making of an order in proceedings to which these rules apply, the proper officer shall send a copy of the order (and of any translation into Welsh obtained under paragraph (2)) to the applicant.

(4) Within 7 days of the making of an order to which paragraph (1)(d), (e) or (f) applies, the proper officer shall send a copy of the order (and of any translation into Welsh obtained under paragraph (2)) to the Registrar General and, in the case of a Convention adoption order, shall comply with rule 31; where a translation into Welsh under paragraph (2) has been obtained, the English text shall prevail.

(5) Where an order to which paragraph (1)(a), (b), (d), (e) or (f) applies is made or refused or an order to which paragraph (1)(c) applies is made, the proper officer shall serve notice to that effect on every respondent.

(6) [. . .]

(7) The proper officer shall serve notice of the making of an order to which paragraph (1)(a), (b), (d), (e) or (f) applies on any court in Great Britain which appears to him to have made any such order as is referred to in [section 12(8) of the Act (orders relating to parental responsibility for, and the maintenance of, the child)].

(8) A copy of any order may be supplied to the Registrar General at his request.

(9) A copy of any order may be supplied to the applicant.

(10) A copy of any order may be supplied to any other person with the leave of the court.

Custody, inspection and disclosure of documents and information

53.—(1) All documents relating to proceedings under [the Act], (or **2–212** under any previous enactment relating to adoption) shall, while they are in the custody of the court, be kept in a place of special security.

(2) A party who is an individual and is referred to in a confidential report supplied to the court by an adoption agency, a local authority, a reporting officer or a guardian *ad litem* may inspect, for the purposes of the hearing,

that part of any such report which refers to him, subject to any direction given by the court that—

(a) no part of one or any of the reports shall be revealed to that party, or

(b) the part of one or any of the reports referring to that party shall be revealed only to that party's legal advisers, or

(c) the whole or any other part of one or any of the reports shall be revealed to that party.

(3) Any person who obtains any information in the course of, or relating to, any proceedings mentioned in paragraph (1) shall treat that information as confidential and shall only disclose it if—

(a) the disclosure is necessary for the proper exercise of his duties, or

(b) the information is requested—

   (i) by a court or public authority (whether in Great Britain or not) having power to determine adoptions and related matters, for the purpose of the discharge of its duties in that behalf, or

   (ii) by the Registrar General, or a person authorised in writing by him, where the information requested relates only to the identity of any adoption agency which made the arrangements for placing the child for adoption in the actual custody of the applicants, and of any local authority which was notified of the applicant's intention to apply for an adoption order in respect of the child, or

   (iii) by a person who is authorised in writing by the Secretary of State to obtain the information for the purposes of research.

(4) Save as required or authorised by a provision of any enactment or of these rules or with the leave of the court, no document or order held by or lodged with the court in proceedings under [the Act] (or under any previous enactment relating to adoption) shall be open to inspection by any person, and no copy of any such document or order, or of an extract from any such document or order, shall be taken by or issued to any person.

GENERAL NOTE

Para. (2)

2–213　　The confidentiality of reports is provided for in rr.5(8) and 6(11). For an analysis of the meaning of confidentiality within adoption proceedings, see Judge K. Barnett, "Adoption and Confidential Information" [1997] Fam. Law 489.

The proper approach of the court when deciding whether to direct that a party referred to in a confidential report should not be entitled to inspect the part of the report which referred to him or her was established by Lord Mustill in the following passage of his speech in *Re D. (Minors) (Adoption Reports: Confidentiality)* [1995] 4 All E.R. 385, HL, at 399:

"It is a fundamental principle of fairness that a party is entitled to the disclosure of all materials which may be taken into account by the court when reaching a decision adverse to that party. This principle applies with particular force to proceedings designed to lead to an order for adoption, since the consequences of such an order was so lasting and far-reaching.

When deciding whether to direct that notwithstanding r.53(2) of the 1984 rules a party referred to in a confidential report supplied by an adoption agency, a local authority, a reporting officer or a guardian *ad litem* shall not be entitled to inspect the part of the report which refers to him or her, the court should first consider whether disclosure of the material would involve a real possibility of significant harm to the child.

If it would, the court should next consider whether the overall interests of the child would benefit from non-disclosure, weighing on the one hand the interest of the child in having the material tested, and on the other both the magnitude of the risk that harm will occur and the gravity of the harm if it does occur.

If the court is satisfied that the interests of the child point towards non-disclosure, the next and final step is for the court to weigh that consideration, and its strength in the circumstances of the case, against the interest of the parent or other party in having an opportunity to see and respond to the material. In the latter regard the court should take into account the importance of the material to the issues in the case.

Non-disclosure should be the exception and not the rule. The court should be rigorous in its examination of the risk and gravity of the feared harm to the child, and should order non-disclosure only when the case for doing so is compelling."

In *Re K. (Adoption: Disclosure of Information)* [1997] 2 F.L.R. 74, it was held that:

(1) the three stage approach set out in *Re D.*, above, is not limited to an application by a party under r.53(2) but is to be applied in any case where the disclosure of confidential information is raised in an adoption application; and

(2) the rule that applies in care proceedings that notice of an application not to disclose information should always be given to a party to the proceedings does not apply to adoption applications.

In this case. Wall J. ordered that information about the prospective adoptive father's conviction for the offence of unlawful sexual intercourse with a girl aged 12 should not be disclosed to the mother of the children, who had declined to give her agreement to their adoption.

In *Re S. (A Minor) (Adoption)* [1993] 2 F.L.R. 204, CA, the court ordered that information about the adoptive father's disability be withheld from the mother on the ground that giving the information to the mother risked identifying the placement and allowing her to destabilise it.

"As the inspection under r.53(2) is 'for the purposes of the hearing', it would seem sensible that in many cases the court should consider the extent of any inspection long enough before the hearing to enable an applicant affected by the contents of the report to give instructions on it, and to decide what evidence to give about its contents, without the necessity for an adjournment at the hearing"; *Re. S (A Minor) (Adoption or Custodianship)* [1987] 2 All E.R. 99, CA, *per* Sir Roualeyn Cumming-Bruce at 101.

Party who is an individual: But not a local authority.

Para. (3)

Adoption records kept by a local authority fall within the ambit of this provision even if they **2–214** had at all material times been in the custody and control of the authority, not the family court. A defendant in criminal proceedings is entitled to seek, but is not entitled as of right, to obtain disclosure, given their confidential nature. It is a matter for the judge having the conduct of the criminal proceedings to decide whether the documents, which prima facie attract public interest immunity, should be disclosed (*Re H. (Criminal Proceedings: Disclosure of Adoption Records)* [1995] 1 F.L.R. 964). This decision should be read alongside *Re an Ex Parte Originating Summons in an Adoption Application*, noted below.

Relating to: In *R. v. Nottingham Justices, ex p. Bostock* [1970] 1 W.L.R. 1117, the Divisional Court, while recognising that these words are capable of a wide interpretation, held that the protection provided by this rule can only take effect *after* adoption proceedings have been commenced.

Confidential: In *Re D. (Minors) (Adoption Reports: Confidentiality)*, above, Lord Mustill declined an invitation to explain the meaning of this word (at 700). The privilege of confidentiality is that of the court (*Re D. (Adoption Reports: Confidentiality)* [1995] 1 F.L.R. 631).

Proper exercise: In *Re an Ex Parte Originating Summons in an Adoption Application* [1990] 1 All E.R. 639 an adoption agency had information relating to the adoption of a child which would be relevant in criminal proceedings. The agency wished to have the assistance of the court in deciding whether the information they had ought to be disclosed and, if so, under what circumstances. An originating summons was issued by the agency *ex parte* and at the hearing Ewbank J. held that the discharge of the information to the Attorney General was necessary for the "proper exercise" of the duties of the social worker who made the discovery of the relevant information. Subsequent to this decision the Attorney General issued the following Practice Note on January 4, 1990:

"In *Re an Ex Parte Originating Summons in an Adoption Application* [1990] 1 All E.R. 639 Ewbank J. ordered that an adoption agency should forward to the Attorney General some material from its files which might be relevant to a case pending in the Criminal Division of the Court of Appeal. Following an exchange of correspondence between the Attorney General and the President of the Family Division, the President has agreed that it would be sensible and wholly appropriate in future for the court to have the assistance of counsel instructed by the Attorney General in any case where it appears that a similar order may prove to be appropriate. The President is to bring the matter to the attention of the judges of the Family Division. Accordingly, any person contemplating making a similar approach to the court in the future should be aware of the Attorney General's interest and that it has been agreed between the Attorney General and the President of the Family Division that in circumstances where it appears to the court that a similar order may be appropriate the Attorney General should first be given an opportunity to be heard through counsel," [1990] 1 F.L.R. 414.

In *Re C. (A Minor) (Disclosure of Adoption Records)* [1994] 2 F.L.R. 525, Kirkwood J. held that:

(1) the Practice Note set out above applies to circumstances in which confidential reports on adoption may be required in criminal proceedings; and

(2) it is extremely doubtful, given the terms of para. (3)(b), whether a county court which has been seized all along of matters relating to the adoption of a child required the leave of the High Court to see a report emanating from its own court.

Para.(4)

2–215   *Leave of the court:* Courts use this provision to enable adopted people to have access to information about their origins which is contained in the court's adoption file. It seems that the attitude of courts, when faced with a request for access by the adopted person, is not consistent. Judge Barnett suggest that informal requests for information should be rejected and that an application for leave should be made by way of *ex parte* originating summons or *ex parte* originating application depending on whether the order was made in the High Court or a county court; see [1997] Fam. Law 489, at 493. According to E. Haines and N. Timms this power was provided to enable adopted people to make inheritance claims (*Adoption, identity and social policy* (1985), p. 13).

Revocations

2–216   **54.** Except to the extent that they continue to apply for the purposes of the determination of an application for an adoption order, a Convention adoption order or a provisional adoption order made before the commencement date of these rules in the High Court or a county court, as the case may be, the following rules are hereby revoked:—

(i) The Adoption (High Court) Rules 1976,

(ii) The Adoption (County Court) Rules 1976,

(iii) The Convention Adoption Rules 1978,

(iv) The Adoption (County Court) (Amendment) Rules 1978,

(v) The Adoption (High Court) (Amendment) Rules 1978,

(vi) The Adoption (County Court) (Amendment) Rules 1979,

(vii) The Adoption (High Court) (Amendment) Rules 1982, and

(viii) The Adoption (County Court) (Amendment) Rules 1982.

Rule 2(2)   SCHEDULE 1

GENERAL FORMS

Form 1

Originating process for an order freeing a child for adoption

2–217   (Heading—High Court)

In the High Court of Justice
Family Division

No.   of 19

[In the matter of the Adoption Act 1976 and]
In the matter of   a child

Let   of   attend at the Royal Courts of Justice, Strand, London WC2, on a date to be fixed for the hearing of the application of
                                        of
for an order:—

1. That the said child be freed for adoption;

2. That the costs of this application be provided for;

And take notice that the grounds of the application are as follows:—

(Continue as in body of the county court originating process below, from the words "I, an authorised office . . .")

(Heading—County Court)

In the   County Court

Number of matter

In the matter of the Adoption Act 1958 and

In the matter of the Children Act 1975 and

In the matter of   a child

I, an authorised officer of the   of   being an adoption

agency wishing to free for adoption   , a child, hereby give the following

further particulars in support of the application.

1. This application is/is not made with the consent of   (and   ),

the parent(s)/guardian(s) of the child.

PARTICULARS OF THE CHILD

2. Identity etc. The child is of the   sex and is not and has not been

married. He/she was born on the   day of 19   and is the person to whom the attached

birth/adoption certificate relates (or, was bornon or about the   day

of   19 , in   ). He/she is   national.

3. Parentage, etc. The child is the child of   whose

last known address was

(or deceased) and   whose last known address was

(or deceased).

(4. The guardian(s) of the child (other than the mother or father of the child is/

are   of   (and   of

).)

(5. Parental agreement. I understand that the said   (and

) is/are willing to agree to the making of an adoption order.)

(6. I request the judge to dispense with the agreement of   on the

ground(s) that   (and   ) and there are

attached hereto three copies of a statement of the facts on which I intend to rely).

7. [Home] etc. The child is currently living with   of

and has been living there since the   day of

19   . (The child has been placed with them for adoption (and they wish

their identity to remain confidential).)

[8. The child is being looked after by   (who have parental

responsibility for the child)].

(9. Maintenance   of   is liable by

virtue of an order made by the   court at

on the   day of   19   (or by an agreement dated the

day of   19   ) to contribute to the maintenance of the

child.)

(10. I attach hereto signed by the mother/father/guardian of the child a declaration that he/

she prefers not to be involved in future questions concerning the adoption of the child.)

(11. [The child's parents were not married to each other at the time of his birth]

and   of   who

is/claims to be the father does/does not intend to apply for [an order under section 4(1)(a) of

the Children Act 1989 or for a residence order in respect] of the child.)

(12. No proceedings relating in whole or in part to the child have been completed or

commenced in any courts in England and Wales or elsewhere (except

).)

I accordingly apply on behalf of   for an order freeing the child

for adoption.

Dated this   day of   19   .

Notes

(Heading): Enter the first name(s) and surname as shown in the certificate referred to in paragraph 2; otherwise enter the first name(s) and surname by which the child is known.

If the application is made to a county court, either the child or his parent or guardian must be within the district of the county court to which the application is made.

Paragraph 2: If the application is made to a county court, it may be made to any county court which has been designated as a divorce county court under section 33 of the Matrimonial and Family Proceedings Court 1984.].

Paragraph 3: If the child has previously been adopted, give the names of his adoptive parents and not those of his natural parents. [If the child's parents were not married to each other at the time of his birth and the father has parental responsibility for the child, give details under paragraph 12 of the court order or the agreement which provides for parental responsibility.]

Paragraph 4: Enter particulars of any person appointed by deed or will in accordance with the provisions of the Guardianship of Infants Acts 1886 and 1925, or the Guardianship of Minors Act 1971, or by a court of competent jurisdiction [, or under section 5 of the Children Act 1989,] to be a guardian. Do not include any person who has the custody of the child only. Delete this paragraph if the child has no guardian.

Paragraphs 5 and 6: Enter either in paragraph 5 or 6 the names of the persons mentioned in paragraphs 3 and 4, except that in the case of [a child whose parents were not married to each other at the time of his birth] the father of the child should be entered only if he has [parental responsibility for] the child by virtue of a court order [or by agreement or he has a residence order in respect of the child]. Where it is sought to dispense with parental agreement, enter in paragraph 6 one or more of the grounds set out in [section 16(2) of the Act].

Paragraph 7: Enter the name and address of the person with whom the child has his home.

Paragraph 8: This paragraph should be completed where the child is [being looked after by] a local authority or a voluntary organisation.

Paragraph 9: This paragraph should be completed where some person or body is liable to contribute to the maintenance of the child under a court order or agreement.

Paragraph 12: State the nature of the proceedings and the date and effect of any orders made.

Agreement to an adoption order (freeing cases)

(Heading as in Form 1)

IF YOU ARE IN ANY DOUBT ABOUT YOUR LEGAL RIGHTS YOU SHOULD OBTAIN LEGAL ADVICE *BEFORE* SIGNING THIS FORM.

Whereas an application is to be/has been made by   for an order freeing   , a child, for adoption:

And whereas the child is the person to whom the birth certificate attached marked "A" relates:

And whereas the child is at least six weeks old:)

I, the undersigned   of   being a parent/guardian of the child hereby state as follows:—

(1) I consent to the application of   an adoption agency, for an order freeing the child for adoption.

(2) I understand that the effect of an adoption order would be to deprive me permanently of [parental responsibility for the child and to vest it] in the adopters; and in particular I understand that, if and when an adoption order is made, I shall have no right to see or get in touch with the child or to have him/her returned to me.

(3) I further understand that the court cannot make an order freeing a child for adoption without the agreement of each parent or guardian of the child to the making of an adoption order, unless the court dispenses with that agreement on the ground that the person concerned—

    (a) cannot be found or is incapable of giving agreement, or

    (b) is withholding his agreement unreasonably, or

    (c) has persistently failed without reasonable cause to discharge [his parental responsibility] in relation to the child, or

    (d) has abandoned or neglected the child, or

    (e) has persistently ill-treated the child, or

    (f) has seriously ill-treated the child and the rehabilitation of the child within the household of the parent or guardian is unlikely.

(4) I further understand that, when the application for an order freeing the child for adoption is heard, this document may be used as evidence of my agreement to the making of an adoption order unless I inform the court that I no longer agree.

(5) I hereby freely, and with full understanding of what is involved, agree unconditionally to the making of an adoption order.

(6) (I have been given an opportunity of making a declaration that I prefer not to be involved in future questions concerning the adoption of the child. I understand that if I make such a declaration I will not be told when the child has been adopted or whether he has been placed for adoption. I further understand that I will not be able to apply for a revocation of the order freeing the child for adoption if I make such a declaration. I hereby freely declare, with full understanding of what is involved, that I do not wish to be involved in future questions concerning the adoption of the child.)

(7) (I have been given an opportunity of making a declaration that I prefer not to be involved in future questions concerning the adoption of the child, and the effect of making such a declaration has been explained to me. I do not wish to make such a declaration.)

(8) (I have not received or given any payment or reward for, or in consideration of, the adoption of the child, for any agreement to the making of an adoption order or consent to the making of an application for an order freeing the child for adoption, for placing the child for adoption with any person or making any arrangements for the adoption of the child (other than a payment to an adoption agency for their expenses incurred in connection with the adoption).)

Signature:

This form, duly completed, was signed by the said   before me at
                             on the   day of 19   .
Signature:
Address:
Description:

Notes

(Heading): (a) Insert the name of the adoption agency applying for the order.

(b) Insert the first name(s) and surname of the child as known to the person giving agreement.

(c) If the child has previously been adopted a certified copy of the entry in the Adopted Children Register should be attached and not a certified copy of the original entry in the Registers of Births.

(d) Where two or more forms of agreement are supplied to the court at the same time they may both or all refer to a certificate attached to one of the forms of agreement.

Paragraphs 6 and 7: If the parent or guardian does not make the declaration the adoption agency must, after twelve months have passed from the making of the order freeing the child for adoption, inform the parent or guardian whether an adoption order has been made in respect of the child, and, if not, whether the child has his home with a person with whom he has been placed for adoption. Further, if no adoption order has been made in respect of the child or the child does not have his home with a person with whom he has been placed for adoption, then the parent or guardian may apply to the court for revocation of the order freeing the child for adoption.

Witness statement: In England and Wales, the document should be witnessed by the reporting officer. In Scotland, it should be witnessed by a Justice of the Peace or a Sheriff, and in Northern Ireland, by a Justice of the Peace. Outside the United Kingdom it should be witnessed by a person authorised by law in the place where the document is signed to administer an oath for any judicial or legal purpose, a British consular officer, a notary public, or, if the person executing the document is serving in the regular armed forces of the Crown, an officer holding a commission in any of those forces.

182

Notice of hearing of an application for an order freeing a child for adoption

(Heading as in Form 1)
To
of
  Whereas an application for an order freeing for adoption , a
child of the   sex born on the   day of 19   , has been
made by   of
  And whereas   (and   ) was/were
appointed reporting officer(s) (and   was appointed guardian
ad litem of the child);
Take notice:—
  1. That the said application will be heard before the judge at   on the
                    day of   19   , at   o'clock and that
you may then appear and be heard on the question whether an order freeing the child for
adoption should be made.
  2. That you are not obliged to attend the hearing unless you wish to do so or the court
notifies you that your attendance is necessary.
  3. That while the said application is pending, if the child is [being looked after by] the
applicant, then a parent or guardian of the child who has not consented to the making of the
application must not, except with the leave of the court, remove the child from the [home] of
the person with whom the child has his home against the will of that person.
  (4. That the court has been requested to dispense with your agreement to the making of an
adoption order on the ground(s) that   and the statement
of the facts on which the applicant intends to rely is attached.
  It would assist the court if you would complete the attached form and return it to me.
Dated the   day of   19   .
                                                            [District Judge]

___

To the Senior [District Judge] of the Family Division/District Judge of the
County Court.
Number   of 19   .
I received notice of the hearing of the application on the   day of
                    19   .
I wish/do not wish to oppose the application.
I wish/do not wish to appear and be heard on the question whether an order should be made.
                                                            (signature)
                                                            (address)
                                                            (date)

Notes
  Preamble: Enter the first name(s) and the surname of the child as shown in the originating
process. Enter the name of the applicant agency and the name(s) of the reporting officer(s)
(and of the guardian *ad litem*, if appointed).

Application for revocation of an order freeing a child for adoption

(Heading as in Form 1)
On the   day of   19   this court made an order
freeing   , a child, for adoption.
I/We   (and   ) of (address), the former parent(s)
of the child, apply for revocation of that order on the grounds that:—
    1. No adoption order has been made in respect of the child, and
    2. The child does not have his home with a person with whom he has been placed for adoption, and
    3. I/We wish to resume [parental responsibility]

signed
date

Notes
    (a) The application must be made to the court which made the original order, and not earlier than 12 months from the date of that order.
    (b) A parent or guardian of the child who has made a declaration (referred to in [section 18(6) of the Act] that he prefers not to be involved in future questions concerning the adoption of the child may not make application for revocation of the order.
    (c) State the reasons relied upon for the revocation of the order.

Application for substitution of one adoption agency for another

(Heading as in Form 1)
    I, an authorised officer of the   of   ,
and I, an authorised officer of the   of
         , both being adoption agencies, wishing to transfer [parental responsibility for]
         , a child, from
         to   hereby give the following further
particulars in support of our application.
    1. On the   day of   19   , the court made an order
freeing the child for adoption under [section 18 of the Adoption Act]. A copy of that order is
attached.
    2. The transfer would be in the best interests of the child because
    3. The administrative reasons why the transfer is desirable are
    (4. The former parent(s),   of   (and
         of   ), has/have been informed of the making
of this application.)

Date etc.

                  (signatures)
                  (addresses)

Notes
    Preamble: Enter the names of the two agencies concerned and enter the name of the child
as shown in the order referred to in paragraph 1.
    Paragraphs 2 and 3: State concisely the reasons it is desired to transfer the child between the
agencies.
    Paragraph 4: A former parent is a person as defined in [section 19(1) of the Adoption Act].
This paragraph should be deleted only if there are no former parents.

Form 6

Originating process for an adoption order/order authorising a proposed foreign adoption.

(Heading as in Form 1)
I/We, the undersigned,   (and   ,) wishing
to adopt   , a child, hereby give the following further
particulars in support of my/our application.

Part 1

Particulars of the Applicant(s)

1. *Name and address etc.*
Name of (first) applicant in full
Address
Occupation
Date of Birth
Relationship (if any) to the child
(Name of (second) applicant in full
Address
Occupation
Date of Birth
Relationship (if any) to the child
2. *Domicile*
I am/We are/One of us (namely   ) is domiciled in England and
Wales/Scotland/Northern Ireland/the Channel Islands/the Isle of Man.
3. *Status*
We are married to each other and our marriage certificate (or other evidence of marriage)
is attached (*or* I am unmarried/a widow/a widower/a divorcee) (*or* I am applying alone as a
married person and can satisfy the court that   .)
(4. I am applying alone for an adoption in respect of my own child and can satisfy the court
that the other natural parent   .)
(5. *Health*
A report on my/our health, made by a registered medical practitioner on the
                    day of   19   , is attached.)

Notes
(Heading): Enter the first name(s) and surname of the child as shown in any certificate
referred to in paragraph 6 below; otherwise enter the first name(s) and surname by which the
child was known before being placed for adoption.
If the application is made to the county court, either the child must be within the district of
the county court to which the application is made or it must be the divorce county court in
which a declaration has been made under section 41 of the Matrimonial Causes Act 1973.
Paragraph 1: Insert the address where the applicant has his home and the place (if different)
where documents may be served upon him.
Paragraph 2: [If the application is made to a county court, it may be made to any county
court which has been designated as a divorce court under section 33 of the Matrimonial and
Family Proceedings Act 1984].
Paragraph 3: Documentary evidence of marital status should be supplied. A married
applicant can apply alone if he or she can satisfy the court that his or her spouse cannot be
found, or that they have separated and are living apart and that the separation is likely to be
permanent, or that by reason of physical or mental ill health the spouse is incapable of making
an application for an adoption order. Any documentary evidence on which the applicant
proposes to rely should be attached to the application. The name and address (if known) of
the spouse should be supplied, and the marriage certificate (or other evidence of marriage)
should be attached.
Paragraph 4: State the reason to be relied upon *e.g.* that the other natural parent is dead, or
cannot be found, or that there is some other reason, which should be specified, justifying his
or her exclusion. Documentary evidence, *e.g.* a death certificate, should be supplied where
appropriate.
Paragraph 5: A separate health report is required in respect of each applicant, and the
report must have been made during the period of three months before the date of the
application. No report is required, however, if the child was placed for adoption with applicant
by an adoption agency, or if he is the child of the applicant or either of them.

PARTICULARS OF THE CHILD

6. *Identity etc.* 2–223
The child is of the   sex and is not and has not been married. He/she was
born on the   day of   19   and is the person to whom the
attached birth/adoption certificate relates (*or* was born on or about the   day
of   19   , in   ). He/she is a   national.
(7. *Health*
A report on the health of the child, made by a registered medical practitioner
on the   day of   19   , is attached.)

(8. The child is free for adoption pursuant to [section 18 of the Adoption Act] and I/we
attach hereto the order of the   court, dated   , to that effect
[Parental responsibility for the child was thereby vested in   (and was]
transferred to   by order of the   court under [section 21 of
the Adoption Act] on   19   ).)
*(9. *Parentage, etc.*
The child is the child of   whose last known address was

(*or* deceased) and   whose last known address was

(*or* deceased).)

(10. The guardian(3) of the child (other than the mother or the father of the child) is/are of
(and   of
).)

(11. *Parental agreement*
I/We understand that the said   (and   )
is/are willing to agree to the making of an adoption order in pursuance of my/our application.)

(12. I/We request the judge to dispense with the agreement of
(and   ) on the ground(s) that
(and   ) and there are attached hereto three copies of a statement
of the facts upon which I/we intend to rely.)

[(13. The child is being looked after by   (who have parental
responsibility for the child).]
(14. *Maintenance*
of   is liable by virtue
of an order made by the   court at   on the
day of   19   , (*or* by an agreement dated the   day
of   19   ) to contribute to the maintenance of the child.)
15. *Proposed names*
If an adoption order is made in pursuance of this application, the child is to be known by
the following names:

Surname

Other names

Notes
Paragraph 6: If the child has previously been adopted a certified copy of the entry in the
Adopted Children Register should be attached and not a certified copy of the original entry in
the Registers of Births. Where a certificate is not attached, enter the place (including the
country) of birth if known.

*[This form does not contemplate the naming of the father of an illegitimate child
(which would not necessarily be known to the applicants) unless his agreement to the
adoption was necessary under the 1976 Act. As the form is that of the proposed
adopters and not that of the adoption agency, the judge has no jurisdiction to order
the adoption agency to amend the form by adding the name of the putative father (*Re
L. (A Minor) (Adoption: Procedure)* [1991] 1 F.L.R. 171, C.A.)—R.M.J.]

Paragraph 7: The report must have been made during the period of three months before the date of the application. No report is required, however, if the child was placed for adoption with the applicant by an adoption agency, or if he is the child of the applicant or either of them.

Paragraph 8: The order made by the court freeing the child for adoption and any order made under [section 21] should be attached.

Paragraph 9: This paragraph and paragraphs 10 to 14 only apply if the child is not free for adoption. If the child has previously been adopted, give the names of his adoptive parents and not those of his natural parents. [If the parents of the child were not married to each other at the time of his birth and the father has parental responsibility for the child, give details under paragraph 19 of the court order or the agreement which provides for parental responsibility.]

Paragraph 10: Enter particulars of any person appointed by deed or will in accordance with the provisions of the Guardianship of Infants Acts 1886 and 1925, or the Guardianship of Minors Act 1971 or by a court of competent jurisdiction [, or under section 5 of the Children Act 1989,] to be a guardian. Do not include any person who has the custody of the child only. Delete this paragraph if the child has no guardian.

Paragraphs 11 and 12: Enter either in paragraph 11 or 12 the names of the persons mentioned in paragraphs 9 and 10, except that in the case of [a child whose parents were not married to each other at the time of his birth], the father of the child should be entered only if he has [parental responsibility for] the child by virtue of a court order [or by agreement or he has a residence order in respect of the child]. Where it is sought to dispense with parental agreement, enter in paragraph 12 one or more of the grounds set out in [section 16(2) of the Act].

Paragraph 13: This paragraph should be completed where the child is [being looked after by] a local authority or a voluntary organisation.

Paragraph 14: This paragraph should be completed where some person or body is liable to contribute to the maintenance of the child under a court order or agreement.

PART 3

GENERAL

2–224   16. The child has lived with me/us continuously since the day of
19   (and has accordingly had his home with me/us for the five years preceding the date of this application).

17. The child was (placed with me/us for adoption on the   day of
          19   by   , an adoption agency) (*or* received into my/our [home] in the following circumstances;

).

(18. I/We notified the   Council on the   day of
19   , of my/our intention to apply for an adoption order in respect of the child.)

19. No proceedings relating in whole or in part to the child other than as stated in paragraph 8 have been completed or commenced in any court in England and Wales or elsewhere (except   .)

20. I/We have not received or given any payment or reward for, or in consideration of, the adoption of the child, for any agreement to the making of an adoption order, the transfer of the [home] of the child with a view to adoption or the making of any arrangements for adoption (except as follows:—

).

21. As far as I/We know, the only person(s) or bod(y)(ies) who have taken part in the arrangements for the child's adoption are
(22. For the purpose of this application reference may be made to
                          of   .)
(23. I/We desire that my/our identity should be kept confidential, and the serial number of this application is   .)
(24. I/We intend to adopt the child under the law of or within   which is the country of my/our domicile, and evidence as to the law of adoption in that country is filed with this process.)
(25. I/We desire to remove the child from the British Isles for the purpose of adoption.)
I/We accordingly apply for an adoption order/an order authorising a proposed foreign adoption in respect of the child.

Dated this   day of   19   .

Signature(s)

Notes

Paragraphs 16 and 17: Under [section 13 of the Act], an adoption order cannot be made unless the child has had his home with the applicants or one of them:—
   (*a*) for at least 13 weeks if the applicant or one of them is a parent, step-parent or relative of the child or if the child was placed with the applicant by an adoption agency or in pursuance of an order of the High Court;
   (*b*) for at least 12 months in any other case.

Paragraph 18: Notice does not have to be given if the child was placed with the applicant by an adoption agency. Where notice does have to be given, no order can be made until the expiration of three months from the date of the notice.

Paragraph 19: The nature of the proceedings and the date and effect of any orders made should be stated. The court cannot proceed with the application if a previous application made by the same applicant in relation to the child was refused, unless one of the conditions in [section 24(1) of the Act] is satisfied. The court must dismiss the application if it considers that, where the application is made by a married couple of whom one is a parent and the other a step-parent of the child, or by a step-parent of the child alone, the matter would be better dealt with under [Part I of the Children Act 1989].

Paragraph 21: Enter the name and address of the adoption agency or individual who took part in the arrangements for placing the child for adoption in the [home] of the applicant.

Paragraph 22: Where the applicant or one of the applicants is a parent of the child, or a relative as defined by [section 72(1) of the Act] or the child was placed with the applicant by an adoption agency, no referee need be named.

Paragraph 23: If the applicant wishes his identity to be kept confidential, the serial number obtained under rule 14 should be given.

Agreement to an adoption order/proposed foreign adoption

(Heading as in Form 1)

IF YOU ARE IN ANY DOUBT ABOUT YOUR LEGAL RIGHTS YOU SHOULD OBTAIN LEGAL ADVICE *BEFORE* SIGNING THIS FORM.

Whereas an application is to be/has been made by   and *(or* under serial No.   ) for an adoption order or order authorising a proposed foreign adoption in respect of   a child;

And whereas the child is the person to whom the birth certificate attached marked "A" relates:

(And whereas the child is at least six weeks old:)

I, the undersigned   of being a parent/guardian of the child hereby state as follows:

(1) I understand that the effect of an adoption order/an order authorising a proposed foreign adoption will be to deprive me permanently of [parental responsibility for the child] and to vest them in the applicant(s); and in particular I understand that, if an order is made, I shall have no right to see or get in touch with the child or to have him/her returned to me.

(2) I further understand that the court cannot make an adoption order/an order authorising the proposed foreign adoption of the child without the agreement of each parent or guardian of the child unless the court dispenses with an agreement on the ground that the person concerned—

    (a) cannot be found or is incapable of giving agreement, or
    (b) is withholding his agreement unreasonably, or
    (c) has persistently failed without reasonable cause to discharge the [parental responsibility for the child], or
    (d) has abandoned or neglected the child, or
    (e) has persistently ill-treated the child, or
    (f) has seriously ill-treated the child and the rehabilitation of the child within the household of the parent or guardian is unlikely.

(3) I further understand that when the application for an adoption order/order authorising the proposed foreign adoption of the child is heard, this document may be used as evidence of my agreement to the making of the order unless I inform the court that I no longer agree.

(4) I hereby freely, and with full understanding of what is involved, agree unconditionally to the making of an adoption order/an order authorising the proposed foreign adoption of the child in pursuance of the application.

(5) As far as I know, the only person(s) or bod(y)(ies) who has/have taken part in the arrangements for the child's adoption is/are   (and   ).

(6) I have not received or given any payment or reward for, or in consideration of, the adoption of the child, for any agreement to the making of an adoption order or placing the child for adoption with any person or making arrangements for the adoption of the child (other than payment to an adoption agency for their expenses incurred in connection with the adoption).

Signature:

This form, duly completed, was signed by the said   before me at on the day of   19   .

Signature:

Address:

Description:

Notes

Preamble: Insert either the name(s) of the applicant(s) or the serial No. assigned to the applicant(s) for the purposes of the application.

Insert the first name(s) and surname of the child as known to the person giving agreement.

If the child has previously been adopted a certified copy of the entry in the Adopted Children Register should be attached and not a certified copy of the original entry in the Registers of Births.

Where two or more forms of agreement are supplied to the court at the same time they may both or all refer to a certificate attached to one of the forms of agreement.

[The father of a child who was not married to the child's mother when the child was born is not a parent for this purpose unless he has parental responsibility by virtue of a court order or an agreement or he has a residence order in respect of the child;] "guardian" also means a person appointed by deed or will in accordance with the provisions of the Guardianship of Infants Acts 1886 and 1925 or the Guardianship of Minors Act 1971, or by a court of competent jurisdiction [, or under section 5 of the Children Act 1989,] to be the guardian of the child.

Paragraph 3: Notice will be given of the hearing of the application and of the court by which it is to be heard. After the making of the application a parent or guardian who has agreed cannot remove the child from the [home] of the applicant(s) except with the leave of the court.

Paragraph 5: Enter the name and address of the adoption agency or individual who took part in the arrangements for placing the child in the [home] of the applicant(s).

Witness statement: In England and Wales the document should be witnessed by the reporting officer. In Scotland, it should be witnessed by a Justice of the Peace or a Sheriff, and in Northern Ireland by a Justice of the Peace. Outside the United Kingdom it should be witnessed by a person authorised by law in the place where the document is signed to administer an oath for any judicial or legal purpose, a British consular officer, a notary public, or, if the person executing the document is serving in the regular armed forces of the Crown, an officer holding a commission in any of those forces.

Notice of hearing of an application for an adoption order/an order authorising a proposed foreign adoption.

(Heading as in Form 1)
To   of
Whereas an application for an adoption order/an order authorising a proposed foreign adoption in respect of   , a child of the   sex born on the   day of   19   , has been made (by   (and   ) of   ) (*or* under the serial number   ) and whereas   (and   ) was/were appointed reporting officer(s) (and   was appointed guardian *ad litem* of the child);

TAKE NOTICE:—

(1. That the said application will be heard before the judge at   on the   day of   19   , at   o'clock and that you may then appear and be heard on the question whether an adoption order/an order authorising a proposed foreign adoption should be made.)

(2. That if you wish to appear and be heard on the question whether an adoption order/an order authorising a proposed foreign adoption should be made, you should give notice to the court on or before the   day of   19   , in order that a time may be fixed for your appearance.)

3. That you are not obliged to attend the hearing unless you wish to do so or the court notifies you that your attendance is necessary.

4. That while the application is pending, a parent or guardian of the child who has agreed to the making of an order must not, except with the leave of the court, remove the child from the [home] of the applicant.

(5. That the application states that the child has had his home with the applicant for the five years preceding the application and accordingly, if that is correct, no person is entitled, against the will of the applicant, to remove the child from the applicant's [home] except with the leave of the court or under authority conferred by an enactment or on the arrest of the child.)

(6. That the court has been requested to dispense with your agreement to the making of an order on the ground(s) that   and a statement of the facts on which the applicant intends to rely is attached.)

It would assist the court if you would complete the attached form and return it to me.
Dated the   day of   19   .

                                                                [District Judge]

To the Senior [District Judge] of [...] the Family Division /[District Judge] of the county court.

                                        No.

I received the notice of the hearing of the application on the   day of   19   .

I wish/do not wish to oppose the application.
I wish/do not wish to appear and be heard on the question whether an order should be made.

                                        (signature)
                                        (address)
                                        (date)

Notes
Paragraph numbers in these notes refer to the appropriate paragraph in the form.

When this form is used under rule 25(2) to give notice of a further hearing of an application it is to be amended so as to refer to a further hearing and so as to give particulars of the interim order.

Preamble: Enter the name(s) and surname of the child as shown in the originating process. Enter the name of the applicant(s) unless the applicant has obtained a serial number, in which case the second part in brackets should be completed.

Paragraphs 1 and 2: Paragraph 1 should be completed and paragraph 2 struck out where the notice is addressed to any respondent where the applicant does not wish his identity to be kept confidential. When a serial number has been assigned to the applicant and the notice is addressed to an individual respondent other than the spouse of the applicant, paragraph 1 should be struck out and paragraph 2 completed.

Paragraph 5: This paragraph should be deleted except where it appears from the originating process that the child has had his home with the applicant for five years.

Paragraph 6: Unless deleted, this paragraph should contain the grounds specified in the originating application.

Form 9

Originating process for the annulment or revocation of an adoption

In the High Court
Family Division   No.   of 19

In the Matter of

and

[In the matter of the Adoption Act 1976]

Let   of
attend at the Royal Courts of Justice, Strand, London WC2A 2LL on a date to be fixed for the
hearing of application of   of   for
an order:—

1. That the adoption which was authorised on   day of 19   at
, by which   (and
) was (*or* were) authorised to adopt the said   by annulled (*or*
revoked).

(2. That the leave of the court be granted for the purpose of making this application out of
time.)

3. That the costs of this application be provided for.

Dated this   day of   19   .

This summons was taken out by   of
, solicitor for the above named

Notes
This form is for use when the adoption is to be annulled or revoked under [section 53 of the
Act]. An application may not be made unless either the adopter or both adopters, as the case
may be, or the adopted person habitually resides in Great Britain immediately before the
application is made.
Preamble: Enter the full names by which the adopted person has been known since the
adoption.
Paragraph 1: Enter the description and address of the authority by which the adoption was
authorised.
Paragraph 2: Except with the leave of the court, an application to annul an adoption may
not be made later than two years after the date of the adoption to which it relates.

Originating process for an order that an overseas adoption or a determination cease to be valid or that a determination has been affected by a subsequent determination.

(Heading as in Form 9)

Let   of

attend at the Royal Courts of Justice, Strand, London WC2A 2LL on a date to be fixed for the hearing of the application of   of

(1. An order that an overseas adoption which was authorised on the   day of   19   at   , by which   (and   ) was (*or* were) authorised to adopt the said   do cease to be valid in Great Britain;)

(2. An order that a determination made by an authority of a Convention country (*or* a specified country) to authorise (*or* review the authorisation of) a Convention adoption (*or* an adoption order made under any enactment in force in a specified country and corresponding to [sections 12(1) and 17 of the Adoption Act 1976]) do cease to be valid in Great Britain;)

(3. An order that a determination made by an authority of a Convention country (*or* a specified country) to give (*or* review) a decision revoking (or annulling) a Convention adoption (*or* an adoption order made under any enactment in force in a specified country and corresponding to [sections 12(1) and 17 of the Adoption Act 1976]) (*or* an order made under [section 12(1) of the Adoption Act 1976] as a Convention adoption order) do cease to be valid in Great Britain;)

(4. A decision as to the extent, if any, to which a determination mentioned in paragraph 2(*or* 3) above has been affected by a subsequent determination;)

(5. An order that the costs of this application be provided for.)

Dated this   day of   19   .

This summons was taken out by   of
                         solicitor for the above named

Notes

This form is principally for use if the applicant claims that the adoption or determination is contrary to public policy or that the authority which purported to authorise the adoption or make the determination was not competent to entertain the case. The applicant should delete the paragraphs which are not relevant.

Paragraph 1: [An overseas adoption is one occurring in a place, under the law of that place, listed in the Schedule to the Adoption (Designation of Overseas Adoptions) Order 1973;] a Convention adoption is an overseas adoption of a description designated in such an order as that of an adoption regulated by the Hague Convention on the Adoption of Children 1965.

Paragraphs 2 and 3: A Convention country means a country designated by an order of the Secretary of State as a country in which the Hague Convention on the Adoption of Children 1965 is in force ([section 72(1) of the 1975 Act]). A specified country means [those countries listed in the Schedule to the Adoption (Designation of Overseas Adoptions) Order 1973].

195

Affidavit in support of application under [sections 52 and 53 of the Adoption Act 1976]

(Heading as in Form 9)
I/We   of
hereby make oath and say that the particulars set out in this affidavit are true

1. Name of (first adopter in full
   Address

(2. Name and second adopter in full
   Address

3. Name of adopted person in full

(4. The said   (and the said
habitually reside(s) in Great Britain.)

5. The adopted person is of the   sex, is a national of
and was born at   on the   day of   19   .

6. On the   day of   19   the said
(and   ) was (*or* were) authorised to adopt the said
            by   at   and those persons are the persons to whom the certified
copy of an entry in a public register (or other evidence of adoption) which is exhibited to this
affidavit relates.

(7. At the time at which the adoption was authorised the said
was a national of   and resided in   (the
said   was a national of   and resided in   ) and the adopted
person was a national of   and resided in   ).
or

(7. *For other applications details of the marriage or, as appropriate, of the determination or determinations should be given and any necessary documentary evidence relating thereto supplied.*)
(8. A statement of the facts is exhibited to this affidavit.)
Sworn, etc.
This affidavit is filed on behalf of the applicant(s).

Notes
Paragraph 3: Enter the name(s) by which the adopted person has been known since the adoption.
Paragraph 4: This paragraph is not required for applications made under [section 53(2) of the Adoption Act 1976]. Where this paragraph is required, no application may be made to the court unless the adopter or, as the case may be, both adopters or the adopted person habitually reside in Great Britain immediately before the application is made. Therefore, the name(s) of either the adopter(s) or the adopted person should be entered.
Paragraph 6: Enter the description and the full address of the authority which authorised the adoption. Evidence of the adoption may be given either by a certified copy of an entry in a public register relating to adoptions or by a certificate that the adoption has been effected signed by a person who is authorised by the law of the country concerned to do so.
Paragraph 7: This paragraph should be completed where the application is made under [section 53(1) of the Adoption Act 1976]. Enter the name of the first adopter and of the second adopter, if applicable.
Paragraph 8: A statement of facts is not required for an application to revoke a convention adoption under [section 52(1) of the Adoption Act 1976]. Expert evidence as to notified provisions may be necessary. In that or any other case where the applicant intends to rely on any provision of foreign law relating to adoption, any accompanying affidavit thereon must be sworn by a person who is suitably qualified on account of his knowledge or experience to give evidence as to the law concerned.

Order freeing a child for adoption

(Heading as in Form 1)

Whereas an application has been made by   of
, being an adoption agency, for an order freeing for adoption
, a child of the   sex, the child of   (and
);

It is ordered that the child be freed for adoption and that [parental responsibility for the child] be vested in the applicant;

(and as regards costs it is ordered that   ;)

(and whereas the precise date of the child's birth has not been proved to the satisfaction of the court but the court has determined the probable date of his/her birth to be the   day of   19   ;)

(and whereas it has been proved to the satisfaction of the court that the child was born in
(country);)

(and whereas the place of birth of the child has not been proved to the satisfaction of the court (but it appears probable that the child was born in the United Kingdom, the Channel Islands or the Isle of Man, the child is treated as having been born in the registration district of   and sub-district of
            in the county of   );)

(and whereas it has been proved to the satisfaction of the court that the child is identical with
                                    to whom the entry numbered
            made on the   day of   19   ,
in the Register of Births for the registration district of   and
sub-district of   in the county of   relates
(*or with*   to whom the entry numbered   and dated the
            day of   19   , in the Adopted Children
Register relates);)

It is directed that this order is sufficient proof of the above particulars for the purposes of any future adoption application in respect of the child.

And it is further recorded that   (and   )
being a parent or guardian of the child made a declaration [. . .] that he/she prefers not to be involved in future questions concerning the adoption of the child.

Dated this   day of   19   .

197

Order revoking an order freeing a child for adoption/dismissing an application to revoke an order freeing a child for adoption

(Heading as in Form 1)

Whereas an application has been made by   of
                        (and   of   ) for an order
revoking an order freeing for adoption   , a child of the
                        sex, the child of   (and   ),
such order having been made by the   court on the
day of   19   ;

It is ordered that the said order be revoked and that [parental responsibility for the child]
be vested in   (and   );

(and it is ordered that   of   do make
periodical payments to the child in the sum of £   payable
                        ;)

(it is ordered that the application be dismissed (and that the applicant(s) shall not make
further application under [section 20 of the Adoption Act 1976]);)

(and it is ordered that   , the adoption agency which obtained the
order under [section 18 of the Adoption Act 1976] is released from the duty of complying
further with [section 19(3) of that Act] as respects the applicant(s).)

(And as regards costs is ordered that
                        .)

Dated this   day of   19   .

Interim order

(Heading as in Form 1)

Whereas an application has been made by   of
                              (and   ) for an adoption order in respect of
                    a child of the   sex, the child/adopted child of
                              (and   );
   It is ordered that the determination of the application be postponed and that the
applicant(s) do have the [parental responsibility] of the child until the
day of   19   , by way of a probationary period (*or* that the determination
of the application be postponed to the   day of   19   ,
and that the applicant(s) do have the [parental responsibility] of the child until that day by way
of a probationary period) (upon the following terms, namely
                    );

(and as regards costs it is ordered that   ;)

(and it is ordered that the application be further heard before the judge at
on the   day of   19   , at   o'clock.)

Dated this   day of   19   .

(Convention) adoption order/order authorising a proposed foreign adoption

(Heading as in Form 1)

Whereas an application has been made by   of
whose occupation is   (and
whose occupation is   ) for an adoption
order/an order authorising a proposed foreign adoption/a Convention adoption order in
respect of   , a child of the   sex, the child/adopted
child of   (and   );

It is ordered that (the applicant(s) do adopt the child) (*or* the applicant(s) be authorised to
remove the child from Great Britain for the purpose of adopting him/her under the law of or
within the country in which the applicant is/applicants are domiciled, and that [parental
responsibility for the child]) be vested in the applicant(s).

(And as regards costs, it is ordered that   );

(And it is recorded that the   , being an adoption agency, placed
the child for adoption with the applicant(s)/the   Council was notified of
the applicant(s) intention to adopt the child;)

(And whereas the child was freed for adoption by the   court
on the   day of   19   ;)

(And whereas the precise date of the child's birth has not been proved to the satisfaction of
the court but the court has determined the probable date of his/her birth to be the   day of
19   ;)

(And whereas it has been proved to the satisfaction of the court that the child was born in
(country);)

(And whereas the place of birth of the child has not been proved to the satisfaction of the
court (but it appears probable that the child was born in the United Kingdom, the Channel
Islands or the Isle of Man, the child is treated as having been born in the registration district
of   and sub-district of   in
the county of   );)

(And whereas it has been proved to the satisfaction of the court that the child was born on
the   day of   19   (and is identical with
to whom the entry numbered   made on the
day of   19   , in the Register of Births for
the registration district of   and sub-district of
in the country of   relates) (*or* with   to whom
the entry numbered   and dated the   day of
19   , in the Adopted Children Register relates);)

(And whereas the name or names and surname stated in the application as those by which
the child is to be known are

;)

It is directed that the Registrar General shall make in the Adopted Children Register an
entry in the form specified by regulations made by him recording the particulars set out in this
order (and that the entry shall be marked with the words "Convention order");

(And it is further directed that the aforesaid entry in the Register of Births/Adopted
Children Register be marked with the words "adopted"/"readopted"/"proposed foreign
adoption"/"proposed foreign readoption").

Dated this   day of   19

MATTERS TO BE COVERED IN REPORTS SUPPLIED UNDER RULES 4(4), 22(1) OR 22(2)

So far as is practicable, the report supplied by the adoption agency or, in the case of a report **2–234** supplied under rule 22(2), the local authority shall include all the following particulars:—

1. The child

    (a) Name, sex, date and place of birth and address;   **2–235**
   [(b) whether the child's parents were married to each other at the time of his birth and, if not, whether he was subsequently legitimated;]
    (c) nationality;
    (d) physical description;
    (e) personality and social development;
    (f) religion, including details of baptism, confirmation or equivalent ceremonies;
    (g) details of any wardship proceedings and of any court orders [relating to parental responsibility for the child or to maintenance and residence;]
    (h) details of any brothers and sisters, including dates of birth, arrangements [concerning with whom they are to live] and whether any brother or sister is the subject of a parallel application;
    (i) extent of [contact with] members of the child's natural family and, [if the child's parents were not married to each other at the time of his birth], his father, and in each case the nature of the relationship enjoyed;
    (j) if the child has been in the care of a local authority or voluntary organisation, [or is in such care, or is being, or has been, looked after by such an authority or organisation,] details (including dates) of any placements with foster parents, or other arrangements in respect of the care of the child, including particulars of the persons with whom the child has had his home and observations on the care provided;
    (k) date and circumstances of placement with prospective adopter;
    (l) names, addresses and types of schools attended, with dates, and educational attainments;
   (m) any special needs in relation to the child's health (whether physical or mental) and his emotional and behavioural development and whether he is subject to a statement under the Education Act 1981;
    (n) what, if any, rights to or interests in property or any claim to damages, under the Fatal Accidents Act 1976 or otherwise, the child stands to retain or lose if adopted;
    (o) wishes and feelings in relation to adoption and the application, including any wishes in respect of religious and cultural upbringing; and
    (p) any other relevant information which might assist the court.

2. Each natural parent [. . .]

    (a) Name, date and place of birth and address;   **2–236**
    (b) marital status and date and place of marriage (if any);
    (c) past and present relationship (if any) with the other natural parent, including comments on its stability;
    (d) physical description;
    (e) personality;
    (f) religion;
    (g) educational attainments;
    (h) past and present occupations and interests;
    (i) so far as available, names and brief details of the personal circumstances of the parents and any brothers and sisters of the natural parent, with their ages or ages at death;
    (j) wishes and feelings in relation to adoption and the application, including any wishes in respect of the child's religious and cultural upbringing;
    (k) reasons why any of the above information is unavailable; and
    (l) any other relevant information which might assist the court.

GENERAL NOTE

Para. (1)(o)

  For a study which examines the content of this aspect of Schedule 2 reports, see J. Selwyn, **2–237** "Ascertaining children's wishes and feelings in relation to adoption", (1996) 3 *Adoption and Fostering* 14.

2–238 The opening words of this Schedule require agencies "so far as is practicable" to, *inter alia*, obtain the particulars set out in this paragraph. In *Re P. (Adoption) (Natural Father's Rights)* [1994] 1 F.L.R. 771, Ewbank J. held that when considering whether a course of action is practicable it is permissible to look at the end result. If the consequences of ascertaining the wishes and feelings of an unmarried father, who was unaware of the child's birth, would be detrimental to the child, the court would be prepared to say that it was not practicable to obtain them.

3. Guardian(s)

2–239 Give the details required under paragraph 2(*a*), (*f*), (*j*) and (*l*).

4. Prospective adopter(s)

2–240
    (a) Name, date and place of birth and address;
    (b) relationship (if any) to the child;
    (c) marital status, date and place of marriage (if any) and comments on stability of relationship;
    (d) details of any previous marriage;
    (e) if a parent and step-parent are applying, the reasons why they prefer adoption or [a residence order];
    (f) if a natural parent is applying alone, the reasons for the exclusion of the other parent;
    (g) if a married person is applying alone, the reasons for this;
    (h) physical description;
    (i) personality;
    (j) religion, and whether willing to follow any wishes of the child or his parents or guardian in respect of the child's religious and cultural upbringing;
    (k) educational attainments;
    (l) past and present occupations and interests;
    (m) particulars of the home and living conditions (and particulars of any home where the prospective adopter proposes to live with the child, if different);
    (n) details of income and comments on the living standards of the household;
    (o) details of other members of the household (including any children of the prospective adopter even if not resident in the household);
    (p) details of the parents and any brothers or sisters of the prospective adopter, with their ages or ages at death;
    (q) attitudes to the proposed adoption of such other members of the prospective adopter's household and family as the adoption agency or, as the case may be, the local authority considers appropriate;
    (r) previous experience of caring for children as step-parent, foster parent, child-minder or prospective adopter and assessment of ability in this respect, together where appropriate with assessment of ability in bringing up the prospective adopter's own children;
    (s) reasons for wishing to adopt the child and extent of understanding of the nature an effect of adoption;
    (t) any hopes and expectations for the child's future;
    (u) assessment of ability to bring up the child throughout his childhood;
    (v) details of any adoption allowance payable;
    (w) confirmation that any referees have been interviewed, with a report of their views and opinion of the weight to be placed thereon; and
    (x) any other relevant information which might assist the court.

5. Actions of the adoption agency or local authority supplying the report

2–241
    (a) Reports under rules 4(4) or 22(1):—
        (i) brief account of the agency's actions in the case with particulars and dates of all written information and notices given to the child, his natural parents and the prospective adopter;
        (ii) details of alternatives to adoption considered;
        (iii) reasons for considering that adoption would be in the child's best interests (with date of relevant decision); and
        (iv) reasons for considering that the prospective adopter would be suitable to be an adoptive parent and that he would be suitable for this child (with dates of relevant decisions) or, if the child has not yet been placed for adoption, reasons for considering that he is likely to be so placed.

OR
(b) Reports under rule 22(2):—
    (i) confirmation that notice was given under [section 22 of the Act], with the date of that notice;
    (ii) brief account of the local authority's actions in the case; and
    (iii) account of investigations whether child was placed in contravention of [section 11 of the Act].

6. Generally

(a) Whether any respondent appears to be under the age of majority or under a mental **2–242** disability; and

(b) whether, in the opinion of the body supplying the report, any other person should be made a respondent (for example, a person claiming to be the father of [a child whose parents were not married to each other at the time of his birth], a spouse or ex-spouse of a natural parent, a relative of a deceased parent, or a person with [parental responsibility]).

7. Conclusions

(This part of the report should contain more than a simple synopsis of the information **2–243** above. As far as possible, the court should be given a fuller picture of the child, his natural parents and, where appropriate, the prospective adopter).

(a) Except where the applicant or one of them is a parent of the child, a summary by the medical adviser to the body supplying the report, of the health history and state of health of the child, his natural parents and, if appropriate, the prospective adopter, with comments on the implications for the order sought and on how any special health needs of the child might be met;

(b) opinion on whether making the order sought would be in the child's best long-term interests, and on how any special emotional, behavioural and educational needs of the child might be met;

(c) opinion on the effect on the child's natural parents of making the order sought;

(d) if the child has been placed for adoption, opinion on the likelihood of full integration of the child into the household, family and community of the prospective adopter, and on whether the proposed adoption would be in the best long-term interests of the prospective adopter;

(e) opinion, if appropriate, on the relative merits of adoption and [a residence order]; and

(f) final conclusions and recommendations whether the order sought should be made (and, if not, alternative proposals).

Rules 15(4)   **SCHEDULE 3**

REPORTS ON THE HEALTH OF THE CHILD AND OF THE APPLICANT(S)

This information is required for reports on the health of a child and of his prospective **2–244** adopter(s). Its purpose is to build up a full picture of their health history and current state of health, including strengths and weaknesses. This will enable the local authority's medical adviser to base his advice to the court on the fullest possible information, when commencing on the health implications of the proposed adoption. The reports made by the examining doctor should cover, as far as practicable, the following matters.

1. The child

Name, date of birth, sex, weight and height.   **2–245**

(A.) A health history of each natural parent, so far as is possible, including:—
    (i) name, date of birth, sex, weight and height;
    (ii) a family health history, covering the parents, the brothers and sisters and the other children of the natural parent, with details of any serious physical or mental illness and inherited and congenital disease;
    (iii) past health history, including details of any serious physical or mental illness, disability, accident, hospital admission or attendance at an out-patient department, and in each case any treatment given;

(iv) a full obstetric history of the mother, including any problems in the ante-natal, labour and post-natal periods, with the results of any tests carried out during or immediately after pregnancy;

(v) details of any present illness including treatment and prognosis;

(vi) any other relevant information which might assist the medical adviser; and

(vii) the name and address of any doctor(s) who might be able to provide further information about any of the above matters.

(B.) A neo-natal report on the child, including:—

    (i) details of the birth, and any complications;

    (ii) results of a physical examination and screening tests;

    (iii) details of any treatment given;

    (iv) details of any problem in management and feeding;

    (v) any other relevant information which might assist the medical adviser; and

    (vi) the name and address of any doctor(s) who might be able to provide further information about any of the above matters.

(C.) A full health history and examination of the child, including:—

    (i) details of any serious illness, disability, accident, hospital admission or attendance at an out-patient department, and in each case any treatment given;

    (ii) details and dates of immunisations;

    (iii) a physical and developmental assessment according to age, including an assessment of vision and hearing and of neurological, speech and language development and any evidence of emotional disorder;

    (iv) for a child over five years of age, the school health history (if available);

    (v) any other relevant information which might assist the medical adviser; and

    (vi) the name and address of any doctor(s) who might be able to provide further information about any of the above matters.

(D.) The signature, name and address and qualifications of the registered medical practitioner who prepared the report, and the date of the report and of the examinations carried out.

2. The applicant

2–246 (If there is more than one applicant, a report on each applicant should be supplied covering all the matters listed below.)

A. (i) name, date of birth, sex, weight and height;

    (ii) a family health history, covering the parents, the brothers and sisters and the children of the applicant, with details of any serious physical or mental illness and inherited and congenital disease;

    (iii) marital history, including (if applicable) reasons for inability to have children;

    (iv) past health history, including details of any serious physical or mental illness, disability, accident, hospital admission or attendance at an out-patient department, and in each case any treatment given;

    (v) obstetric history (if applicable);

    (vi) details of any present illness, including treatment and prognosis;

    (vii) a full medical examination;

    (viii) details of any daily consumption of alcohol, tobacco and habit-forming drugs;

    (ix) any other relevant information which might assist the medical adviser; and

    (x) the name and address of any doctor(s) who might be able to provide further information about any of the above matters.

B. The signature, name, address and qualifications of the registered medical practitioner who prepared the report, and the date of the report and of the examinations carried out.

Rule 28(2)(b)   SCHEDULE 4

MODIFICATION TO FORM 6 FOR THE PURPOSES OF CONVENTION PROCEEDINGS

2–247 Form 6 shall contain the following additional paragraphs after paragraph 25:—

Part IV

Additional Information Required for a Convention Adoption Application

26. *The child.*

The child— **2–248**
    (a) is a United Kingdom national (*or* a national of   which is a Convention country) and
    (b) habitually resides at   which is in British territory (*or* a Convention country).

27. *The applicants*

We are applying together, in reliance on [section 17(4)(*a*) of the Act], and the first applicant **2–249** is a United Kingdom national (*or* a national of   which is a Convention country) and the second applicant is a United Kingdom national (*or* a national of   which is a Convention country) and we habitually reside at   which is in Great Britain.

(*or*

27. *The applicants*

We are applying together in reliance on [section 17(4)(*b*) of the Act], and are both United **2–250** Kingdom nationals, and we are habitually resident at   which is in British territory (*or* a Convention country).)

(*or*

27. *The applicant*

I am applying alone in reliance on [section 17(5)(*a*) of the Act], and am a United Kingdom **2–251** national (*or* a national of   which is a Convention country) and habitually reside at   which is in Great Britain.)

(*or*

27. *The applicant*

I am applying alone in reliance on [section 17(5)(*b*) of the Act], and am a United Kingdom **2–252** national and habitually reside at   which is in British territory (*or* a Convention country).)

28. *Specified provisions*

We are both (*or* I am), accordingly, nationals of the same (*or* a national of a) Convention **2–253** country, namely   and there are no specified provisions in respect of that country (*or* there are no relevant specified provisions in respect of that country because   ).

Notes

Paragraphs 26 and 27: Documentary evidence of nationality should be exhibited. Where a **2–254** child or an applicant is a national of a Convention country, evidence as to the law of the country relating to nationality applicable to that person should be supplied. Where the child is not a United Kingdom national, evidence as to the provisions relating to consents and consultations of the internal law relating to adoption of the Convention country of which the child is a national should be supplied. Any affidavit on foreign law must be sworn by a person who is suitably qualified on account of his knowledge or experience to give evidence as to the law concerned. British territory is defined in [section 72(1) of the Act].

Paragraph 28: "Specified provision" is defined in [section 17(8) of the Act]. Expert evidence as to specified provisions may be necessary; if so any affidavit on foreign law must be sworn by a person who is suitably qualified on account of his knowledge or experience to give evidence as to the law concerned.

MAGISTRATES' COURTS (ADOPTION) RULES 1984

(S.I. 1984 No. 611)

Dated April 24, 1984, *and made by the Lord Chancellor under the Magistrates' Courts Act* 1980 (*c.* 43), *s.*114.

GENERAL NOTE

2–255   These Rules consolidate with amendments the Magistrates' Courts (Adoption) Rules 1976, the Magistrates' Courts (Adoption) (Amendment) Rules 1979 and the Magistrates' Courts (Adoption) (Amendment) Rules 1981. They are considered in Home Office Circular No. 36/1984.

Proceedings brought under the Adoption Act 1976 are "family proceedings" for the purposes of the Children Act 1989; see *ibid.*, s.8(3)(4).

AMENDMENTS

2–256   The amendments to these Rules were made by S.I. 1989 No. 384, S.I. 1991 No. 1991 and S.I. 1992 No. 709.

PART I

INTRODUCTORY

Citation, operation and revocations

2–257   **1.**—(1) These Rules may be cited as the Magistrates' Courts (Adoption) Rules 1984 and shall come into operation on May 27, 1984.

(2) The Magistrates' Courts (Adoption) Rules 1976, the Magistrates' Courts (Adoption) (Amendment) Rules 1979 and the Magistrates' Courts (Adoption) (Amendment) Rules 1981 are hereby revoked; but where an application for an adoption order has been made before May 27, 1984 and has not been determined by that date, the provisions of the said Rules continue to apply in connection with that application and nothing in these Rules affects those provisions.

Interpretation

2–258   **2.**—(1) In these Rules, the following expressions shall, unless the context otherwise requires, have the meaning hereby respectively assigned to them, that is to say:—

["the 1976 Act" means the Adoption Act 1976];
["the 1989 Act" means the Children Act 1989];
[. . .];
"adoption agency" means a local authority or approved adoption society;
"the child" means the person whom the applicant for an adoption order proposes to adopt or, as the case may be, the person the adoption agency proposes should be freed for adoption;
"interim order" means an order under [section 25 of the 1976 Act];
"regular armed forces of the Crown" means the Royal Navy, the regular forces as defined by section 225 of the Army Act 1955, the regular air force as defined by section 223 of the Air Force Act 1955,

the Queen Alexandra's Royal Naval Nursing Service and the Women's Royal Naval Service.

[(2) Expressions which are used in these Rules which are used in the 1976 Act and the 1989 Act have the same meaning as in those Acts.]

(3) In these Rules, unless the context otherwise requires, any reference to a rule or to a Schedule shall be construed as a reference to a rule contained in these Rules or to a Schedule hereto, and any reference in a rule to a paragraph shall be construed as a reference to a paragraph of that rule.

(4) In these Rules, any reference to a form shall be construed as a reference to the form so numbered in Schedule 1 to these Rules or to a form substantially to the like effect, with such variations as the circumstances may require.

Extent

3. [These Rules shall apply only to proceedings under the 1976 Act.]   **2–259**

PART II

FREEING FOR ADOPTION

The application

4.—(1) An application to free a child for adoption shall be in Form 1 and   **2–260** shall be made to a [family proceedings] court acting for the area within which either the child or a parent or guardian of the child is at the date of the application by delivering it, or sending it by post to that court, together with all documents referred to in the application.

(2) The applicant shall be the adoption agency and the respondents shall be—

(a) each parent or guardian of the child;

[(b) any local authority or voluntary organisation which has parental responsibility for, is looking after, or which is caring for, the child;] [. . .] and

(f) any person liable by virtue of any order or agreement to contribute to the maintenance of the child.

(3) The court may at any time direct that any other person or body, except the child, be made a respondent to the application.

(4) The applicant shall supply to the justices' clerk three copies of—

(a) Form 1, together with any other documents required to be supplied, and

(b) a report in writing covering all the relevant matters specified in Schedule 2.

Appointment and duties of reporting officer

5.—(1) As soon as practicable after the application has been made or at   **2–261** any stage thereafter, if it appears that a parent or guardian of the child is willing to agree to the making of an adoption order and is in England or Wales, the court shall appoint a reporting officer in respect of that parent or guardian, and shall send to him a copy of the application and any documents attached thereto and of the report supplied by the applicant.

(2) The same person may be appointed as reporting officer in respect of two or more parents or guardians of the child.

(3) The reporting officer shall be appointed from a panel established in accordance with [any regulations made by the Secretary of State under s.41(7) of the Children Act 1989] but shall not be a member or employee of the applicant or any respondent body nor have been involved in the making of any arrangements for the adoption of the child.

(4) The reporting officer shall—

(a) ensure so far as is reasonably practicable that any agreement to the making of an adoption order is given freely and unconditionally and with full understanding of what is involved;

(b) confirm that the parent or guardian has been given an opportunity of making a declaration under [section 18(6) of the 1976 Act] that he prefers not to be involved in future questions concerning the adoption of the child;

(c) witness the signature by the parent or guardian of the written agreement to the making of an adoption order;

(d) investigate all the circumstances relevant to that agreement and any such declaration;

(e) where it is proposed to free [a child whose mother and father were not married at the time of his birth] for adoption and his father is not his guardian, interview any person claiming to be the father in order to be able to advise the court on the matters listed in [section 18(7) of the 1976 Act]; but if more than one reporting officer has been appointed, the court shall nominate one of them to conduct the interview; and

(f) on completing his investigations make a report in writing to the court, drawing attention to any matters which, in his opinion, may be of assistance to the court in considering the application.

(5) With a view to obtaining the directions of the court on any matter, the reporting officer may at any time make such interim report to the court as appears to him to be necessary; and in particular, the reporting officer shall make a report if a parent or guardian of the child is unwilling to agree to the making of an adoption order, and in such a case the justices' clerk shall notify the applicant.

(6) The court may, at any time before the final determination of the application, require the reporting officer to perform such further duties as the court considers necessary.

(7) The reporting officer shall attend any hearing of the application if so required by the court.

(8) Any report made to the court under this rule shall be confidential.

(9) The powers of the court to appoint a reporting officer under paragraph (1), to nominate one reporting officer to conduct an interview under paragraph (4)(e), to give directions following the making of an interim report in accordance with paragraph (5) and to require the reporting officer to perform further duties under paragraph (6) shall also be exercisable, before the hearing of the application, by a single justice or by the justices' clerk.

GENERAL NOTE

2–262   See the notes r.17 of the Adoption Rules 1984.

Appointment and duties of guardian *ad litem*

6.—(1) As soon as practicable after the application has been made, or **2–263** after receipt of the statement of facts supplied under rule 7, if it appears that a parent or guardian of the child is unwilling to agree to the making of an adoption order, the court shall appoint a guardian *ad litem* of the child and shall send to him a copy of the application, together with any documents attached thereto, the statement of facts and the report supplied by the applicant.

(2) Where there are special circumstances and it appears to the court that the welfare of the child requires it, the court may at any time appoint a guardian *ad litem* of the child, and where such an appointment is made the court shall indicate any particular matters which it requires the guardian *ad litem* to investigate, and the court shall send the guardian *ad litem* a copy of the application, together with any documents attached thereto, and the report supplied by the applicant.

(3) The same person may be appointed as reporting officer under rule 5(1) in respect of a parent or guardian who appears to be willing to agree to the making of an adoption order, and as guardian *ad litem* of the child under this rule; and, whether or not so appointed as reporting officer, the guardian *ad litem* may be appointed as reporting officer in respect of a parent or guardian of the child who originally was unwilling to agree to the making of an adoption order but who later signifies his or her agreement.

(4) The guardian *ad litem* shall be appointed from a panel established in accordance with [any regulations made by the Secretary of State under section 41(7) of the Children Act 1989] but shall not be a member or employee of the applicant or any respondent body nor have been involved in the making of any arrangements for the adoption of the child.

(5) With a view to safeguarding the interests of the child before the court, the guardian *ad litem* shall, so far as is reasonably practicable—

    (a) investigate—
        (i) so far as he considers necessary, the matters alleged in the application, the report supplied by the applicant and, where appropriate, the statement of facts supplied under rule 7, and
        (ii) any other matters which appear to him to be relevant to the making of an order freeing the child for adoption;
    (b) advise whether, in his opinion, the child should be present at the hearing of the application; and
    (c) perform such other duties as appear to him to be necessary or as the court may direct.

(6) On completing his investigations the guardian *ad litem* shall make a report in writing to the court, drawing attention to any matters which, in his opinion, may be of assistance to the court in considering the application.

(7) With a view to obtaining the directions of the court on any matter, the guardian *ad litem* may at any time make such interim report to the court as appears to him to be necessary.

(8) The court may, at any time before the final determination of the application, require the guardian *ad litem* to perform such further duties as the court considers necessary.

(9) The guardian *ad litem* shall attend any hearing of the application unless the court otherwise orders.

(10) Any report made to the court under this rule shall be confidential.

(11) The powers of the court to appoint a guardian *ad litem* under paragraph (1) or (2), to require the performance by the guardian *ad litem*

209

of particular duties in accordance with paragraph (2), (5)(c) or (8), and to give directions following the making of an interim report in accordance with paragraph (7) shall also be exercisable, before the hearing of the application, by a single justice or by the justices' clerk.

GENERAL NOTE
2–264   See the notes on r.18 of the Adoption Rules 1984.

Statement of facts in dispensation cases
2–265   **7.**—(1) Where the adoption agency applying for an order freeing a child for adoption intends to request the court to dispense with the agreement of a parent or guardian of the child on any of the grounds specified in [section 16(2) of the 1976 Act], the request shall, unless otherwise directed, be made in the application, or, if made subsequently, by notice to the justices' clerk, and there shall be attached to the application or notice three copies of the statement of facts on which the applicant intends to rely.

(2) Where the applicant has been informed by a person with whom the child has been placed for adoption that he wishes his identity to remain confidential, the statement of facts supplied under paragraph (1) shall be framed in such a way as not to disclose the identity of that person.

(3) Where a statement of facts has been supplied under paragraph (1), the justices' clerk shall, where and as soon as practicable, inform the parent or guardian of the request to dispense with his agreement and shall send to him a copy of the statement supplied under paragraph (1).

(4) The justices' clerks shall also send a copy of the statement supplied under paragraph (1) to the guardian *ad litem* and to the reporting officer if a different person.

Agreement
2–266   **8.**—(1) Any document signifying the agreement of a person to the making of an adoption order may be in Form 2, and, if executed by a person outside England and Wales before the commencement of the proceedings, shall be filed with the application.

(2) If the document is executed in Scotland it shall be witnessed by a Justice of the Peace or a Sheriff.

(3) If the document is executed in Northern Ireland it shall be witnessed by a Justice of the Peace.

(4) If the document is executed outside the United Kingdom it shall be witnessed by one of the following persons:—
   (a) any person for the time being authorised by law in the place where the document is executed to administer an oath for any judicial or other legal purpose;
   (b) a British consular officer;
   (c) a notary public; or
   (d) if the person executing the document is serving in any of the regular armed forces of the Crown, an officer holding a commission in any of those forces.

Notice of hearing
2–267   **9.**—(1) As soon as practicable after the application has been made, the justices' clerk shall fix a time for the hearing of the application and shall serve notice of the hearing on all the parties, the reporting officer and the guardian *ad litem* (if appointed) in Form 3.

(2) The reporting officer and the guardian *ad litem* (if appointed), but no other person, shall be served with a copy of the application and the report supplied by the applicant, and that report shall be confidential.

The hearing

10.—(1) On the hearing of the application any person upon whom notice **2–268** is required to be served under rule 9 may attend and be heard on the question whether an order freeing the child for adoption should be made.

(2) Any member or employee of a party which is a local authority, adoption agency or other body may address the court if he is duly authorised in that behalf.

(3) Where the court has been informed by the applicant that the child has been placed with a person (whether alone or jointly with another) for adoption and that person wishes his identity to remain confidential, the proceedings shall be conducted with a view to securing that any such person is not seen by or made known to any respondent who is not already aware of his identity except with his consent.

(4) Subject to paragraph (5), the court shall not make an order freeing the child for adoption except after the personal attendance before the court of a representative of the applicant duly authorised in that behalf and of the child.

(5) If there are special circumstances which, having regard to the report of the guardian *ad litem* (if any), appear to the court to make the attendance of the child unnecessary, the court may direct that the child need not attend.

(6) If there are special circumstances which appear to the court to make the attendance of any other party necessary, the court may direct that that party shall attend.

Proof of identity of child, etc.

11.—(1) Where proof of the identity of the child is required for any **2–269** purpose, any fact tending to establish his identity with a child to whom a document relates may be proved by affidavit.

(2) Where any such fact is proved by affidavit, the attendance of a witness at the hearing to prove that fact shall not be compelled unless the fact is disputed or for some special reason his attendance is required by the court.

(3) Where the precise date of the child's birth is not proved to the satisfaction of the court, the court shall determine the probable date of his birth and the date so determined may be specified in the order freeing the child for adoption as the date of his birth.

(4) Where the place of birth of the child cannot be proved to the satisfaction of the court but it appears probable that the child was born in the United Kingdom, the Channel Islands or the Isle of Man, he may be treated as having been born in the registration district and sub-district in which the court sits, and in any other case (where the country of birth is not proved) the particulars of the country of birth may be omitted from the order freeing the child for adoption.

Application for revocation of order freeing a child for adoption

12.—(1) An application by a former parent for an order revoking an **2–270** order freeing the child for adoption shall be made in Form 4 to the court which made the order to which the application relates by delivering it, or

211

sending it by post to that court, together with all documents referred to in the application.

(2) Notice of the application shall be served on all persons who were parties to the proceedings in which the order freeing the child for adoption was made and on any adoption agency [which has parental responsibility for the child by virtue of section 21 of the 1976 Act], save that notice shall not be served on a party to the earlier proceedings who was joined as a party by virtue of rule 4(2)(b) [. . .].

(3) As soon as practicable after the application has been made, the justices' clerk shall fix a time for the hearing of the application and the court (or a single justice or the justices' clerk) shall appoint a guardian *ad litem* of the child in accordance with rule 6(4) and shall send to him a copy of the application and any documents attached thereto.

(4) The guardian *ad litem* shall have the same duties as if he had been appointed under rule 6 but as if in that rule:—

(a) the reference to an order freeing the child for adoption was a reference to the revocation of an order freeing the child for adoption; and

(b) each reference to the report supplied by the applicant was omitted.

[Joint application for parental responsibility by adoption agencies]

2–271   **13.**—(1) An application by two adoption agencies under section 21(1) of the 1976 Act shall be made in the appropriate form prescribed in Schedule 1 to these Rules to a court acting for the area within which the child is at the date of the application by delivering it, or sending it by post, to that court, together with all documents referred to in the application.

(2) Notice of any order made under section 21 of the 1976 Act shall be sent by the court to the court which made the order under section 18 of the 1976 Act (if a different court) and to any former parent (as defined in section 19(1) of the 1976 Act) of the child.]

PART III

ADOPTION ORDERS

Application for a serial number

2–272   **14.** If any person proposing to apply to a domestic court for an adoption order wishes his identity to be kept confidential, he may, before making his application, apply to the justices' clerk for a serial number to be assigned to him for the purposes of identifying him in connection with the proposed application, and a number shall be assigned to him accordingly.

GENERAL NOTE

2–273   Once a serial number has been given the confidentiality of the applicant must be preserved; see r.19(3). A parent's right to oppose the adoption application does not entitle him or her to receive information about the prospective adopters (*Re S. (A Minor)* [1993] 2 F.L.R. 204, CA).

The application

2–274   **15.**—(1) An application for an adoption order shall be in Form 6 and shall be made to a [family proceedings] acting for the area within which the child is at the date of the application by delivering it, or sending it by post to that court, together with all documents referred to in the application.

(2) The applicant shall be the proposed adopter and the respondents shall be—

(a) each parent or guardian (not being an applicant) of the child, unless the child is free for adoption;

(b) [any adoption agency having parental responsibility for the child by virtue of section 18 or 21 of the 1976 Act;]

(c) any adoption agency named in the application or in any form of agreement to the making of the adoption order as having taken part in the arrangements for the adoption of the child;

(d) any local authority to whom the applicant has given notice under [section 22 of the 1976 Act] of his intention to apply for an adoption order;

[(e) any local authority or voluntary organisation which has parental responsibility for, is looking after, or is caring for, the child;] [. . .] and

(j) where the applicant proposes to rely on [section 15(1)(b)(ii) of the 1976 Act], the spouse of the applicant.

(3) The court may at any time direct that any other person or body, except the child, be made a respondent to the application.

(4) The applicant shall supply to the justices' clerk three copies of—

(a) Form 6, together with any other documents required to be supplied, and

(b) where the child was not placed for adoption with the applicant by an adoption agency, save where the applicant or one of the applicants is a parent of the child, reports by a registered medical practitioner made not more than three months earlier on the health of the child and of each applicant, covering the matters specified in Schedule 3.

GENERAL NOTE

Para. (2)(a)
Each parent or guardian: See the note on r.15(2) of the Adoption Rules 1984. **2–275**

Preliminary examination of application
16. If it appears to the justices' clerk on receipt of the application for an **2–276** adoption order that the court—

(a) may be precluded, by virtue of [section 24(1) of the 1976 Act], from proceeding to hear the application, or

(b) may for any other reason appearing in the application, have no jurisdiction to make an adoption order,

he shall bring the relevant matter to the attention of the court and the application shall not be proceeded with unless the court gives directions as to the further conduct of the application.

Appointment and duties of reporting officer
17.—(1) As soon as practicable after the application has been made or at **2–277** any stage thereafter, if the child is not free for adoption and if it appears that a parent or guardian of the child is willing to agree to the making of an adoption order and is in England and Wales, the court shall appoint a reporting officer in respect of that parent or guardian, and shall send to him a copy of the application and any documents attached thereto.

(2) The same person may be appointed as reporting officer in respect of two or more parents or guardians of the child.

(3) The reporting officer shall be appointed from a panel established in accordance with [any regulations made by the Secretary of State under s.41(7) of the Children Act 1989] but shall not be a member or employee of any respondent body (except where a local authority is made a respondent only under rule 15(2)(d)) nor have been involved in the making of any arrangements for the adoption of the child.

(4) The reporting officer shall—

(a) ensure so far as is reasonably practicable that any agreement to the making of the adoption order is given freely and unconditionally and with full understanding of what is involved;

(b) witness the signature by the parent or guardian of the written agreement to the making of the adoption order;

(c) investigate all the circumstances relevant to that agreement; and

(d) on completing his investigations make a report in writing to the court, drawing attention to any matters which, in his opinion, may be of assistance to the court in considering the application.

(5) Paragraphs (5) to (8) of rule 5 shall apply to a reporting officer appointed under this rule as they apply to a reporting officer appointed under that rule; and paragraph (9) of rule 5 shall apply in relation to the appointment of a reporting officer under this rule as it applies in relation to such an appointment made under that rule.

GENERAL NOTE

2–278   See the notes on r.17 of the Adoption Rules 1984.

Appointment and duties of guardian *ad litem*

2–279   **18.**—(1) As soon as practicable after the application has been made, or after receipt of the statement of facts supplied under rule 19, if the child is not free for adoption and if it appears that a parent or guardian of the child is unwilling to agree to the making of the adoption order, the court shall appoint a guardian *ad litem* of the child and shall send him a copy of the application together with any documents attached thereto.

(2) Where there are special circumstances and it appears to the court that the welfare of the child requires it, the court may at any time appoint a guardian *ad litem* of the child and where such an appointment is made the court shall indicate any particular matters which it requires the guardian *ad litem* to investigate and the court shall send the guardian *ad litem*, a copy of the application together with any documents attached thereto.

(3) The same person may be appointed as reporting officer under rule 17(1) in respect of a parent or guardian who appears to be willing to agree to the making of the adoption order, and as guardian *ad litem* of the child under this rule; and, whether or not so appointed as reporting officer, the guardian *ad litem* may be appointed as reporting officer in respect of a parent or guardian of the child who originally was unwilling to agree to the making of an adoption order but who later signifies his or her agreement.

(4) The guardian *ad litem* shall be appointed from a panel established in accordance with [any regulations made by the Secretary of State under section 41(7) of the Children Act 1989] but shall not be a member or employee of any respondent body (except where a local authority is made a respondent only under rule 15(2)(d)) nor have been involved in the making of any arrangements for the adoption of the child.

(5) With a view to safeguarding the interests of the child before the court the guardian *ad litem* shall so far as is reasonably practicable—

(a) investigate—
    (i) so far as he considers necessary, the matters alleged in the application, any report supplied under rule 22(1) or (2) and, where appropriate, the statement of facts supplied under rule 19;
    (ii) any other matters which appear to him to be relevant to the making of an adoption order;
(b) advise whether, in his opinion, the child should be present at the hearing of the application; and
(c) perform such other duties as appear to him to be necessary or as the court may direct.

(6) Paragraphs (6) to (10) of rule 6 shall apply to a guardian *ad litem* appointed under this rule as they apply to a guardian *ad litem* appointed under that rule; and paragraph (11) of rule 6 shall apply in relation to the appointment of a guardian *ad litem* under this rule as it applies in relation to such an appointment made under that rule.

GENERAL NOTE

See the notes on r.18 of the Adoption Rules 1984.　　　　　　　　　**2–280**

Statement of facts in dispensation cases

19.—(1) Where the child is not free for adoption and the applicant for **2–281** the adoption order intends to request the court to dispense with the agreement of a parent or guardian of the child on any of the grounds specified in [section 16(2) of the 1976 Act], the request shall, unless otherwise directed, be made in the application or, if made subsequently, by notice to the justices' clerk and there shall be attached to the application or notice three copies of the statement of facts on which the applicant intends to rely.

(2) Where a serial number has been assigned to the applicant under rule 14, the statement of facts supplied under paragraph (1) shall be framed in such a way as not to disclose the identity of the applicant.

(3) Where a statement of facts has been supplied under paragraph (1), the justices' clerk shall, where and as soon as practicable, inform the parent or guardian of the request to dispense with his agreement and shall send to him a copy of the statement supplied under paragraph (1).

(4) The justices' clerk shall also send a copy of the statement supplied under paragraph (1) to the guardian *ad litem* and to the reporting officer if a different person.

GENERAL NOTE

See the notes on r.19 of the Adoption Rules 1984.　　　　　　　　　**2–282**

Agreement

20.—(1) Any document signifying the agreement of a person to the **2–283** making of the adoption order may be in Form 7, and, if executed by a person outside England and Wales before the commencement of the proceedings, shall be filed with the application.

(2) If the document is executed outside England and Wales it shall be witnessed by one of the persons specified in rule 8(2), (3) or (4), according to the country in which it is executed.

Notice of hearing

2-284 **21.**—(1) Subject to paragraph (4), as soon as practicable after the application has been made the justices' clerk shall fix a time for the hearing of the application and shall serve notice of the hearing on all the parties, the reporting officer and the guardian *ad litem*, (if appointed) in Form 8.

(2) In a case where [section 22 of the 1976 Act] applies, the justices' clerk shall send a copy of the application and, where appropriate, of the report supplied under rule 15(4), to the local authority to whom notice under that section was given.

(3) No person other than the reporting officer, the guardian *ad litem* (if appointed) and, in cases where [section 22 of the 1976 Act] applies, the local authority to whom notice under that section was given, shall be served with a copy of the application.

(4) Where section [22 of the 1976 Act] applies, the justices' clerk shall fix a time for the hearing so that the hearing takes place on a date not less than three months from the date of the notice given to the local authority under that section.

GENERAL NOTE

Para. (1)
2-285 See the notes on r.21(1) of the Adoption Rules 1984.

Reports by adoption agency or local authority

2-286 **22.**—(1) Where the child was placed for adoption with the applicant by an adoption agency, that agency shall supply, within six weeks of receipt of the notice of hearing under rule 21, three copies of a report in writing covering the matters specified in Schedule 2.

(2) Where the child was not placed for adoption with the applicant by an adoption agency, the local authority to whom the notice under [section 22 of the 1976 Act] was given shall supply, within six weeks of receipt of the notice of hearing under rule 21, three copies of a report in writing covering the matters specified in Schedule 2.

(3) The court may request a further report under paragraph (1) or (2) and may indicate any particular matters it requires such a further report to cover.

(4) The justices' clerk shall send a copy of any report supplied under paragraph (1) or (2) to the reporting officer and to the guardian *ad litem* (if appointed).

(5) No other person shall be supplied with a copy of any report supplied under paragraph (1) or (2) and any such report shall be confidential.

The hearing

2-287 **23.**—(1) On the hearing of the application any person upon whom notice is required to be served under rule 21 may attend and be heard on the question whether an adoption order should be made.

(2) Any member or employee of a party which is a local authority, adoption agency or other body may address the court if he is duly authorised in that behalf.

(3) If a serial number has been assigned to the applicant under rule 14, the proceedings shall be conducted with a view to securing that he is not seen by or made known to any respondent who is not already aware of the applicant's identity except with his consent.

(4) Subject to paragraphs (5) and (7), the court shall not make an adoption order or an interim order except after the personal attendance before the court of the applicant and the child.

(5) If there are special circumstances which, having regard to the report of the guardian *ad litem* (if any), appear to the court to make the attendance of the child unnecessary, the court may direct that the child need not attend.

(6) If there are special circumstances which appear to the court to make the attendance of any other party necessary, the court may direct that that party shall attend.

(7) In the case of an application under [section 14(1A) or (1B) of the 1976 Act], the court may in special circumstances make an adoption order or an interim order after the personal attendance of one only of the applicants, if the application is verified by a declaration made by the applicant who does not attend and witnessed by a justice of the peace, a justices' clerk within the meaning of section 70 of the Justices of the Peace Act 1979, or, if made outside the United Kingdom, by any of the persons specified in rule 8(4).

GENERAL NOTE

See the note on r.23(4) of the Adoption Rules 1984.   **2–288**

Proof of identity of child, etc.

24.—(1) Where proof of the identity of the child is required for any **2–289** purpose, any fact tending to establish his identity with a child to whom a document relates may be proved by affidavit.

(2) Where any such fact is proved by affidavit, the attendance of a witness at the hearing to prove that fact shall not be compelled unless the fact is disputed or for some special reason his attendance is required by the court.

(3) Subject to paragraph (5), where the precise date of the child's birth is not proved to the satisfaction of the court, the court shall determine the probable date of his birth and the date so determined may be specified in the adoption order as the date of his birth.

(4) Subject to paragraph (5), where the place of birth of the child cannot be proved to the satisfaction of the court but it appears probable that the child was born in the United Kingdom, the Channel Islands or the Isle of Man, he may be treated as having been born in the registration district and sub-district in which the court sits, and in any other case (where the country of birth is not proved) the particulars of the country of birth may be omitted from the adoption order.

(5) Where the child is free for adoption, any order made identifying the probable date and place of birth of the child in the proceedings under [section 18 of the 1976 Act] shall be sufficient proof of the date and place of birth of the child in proceedings to which this rule applies.

Further proceedings after interim order

25. Where the court has made an interim order, the justices' clerk shall **2–290** fix a time for the further hearing of the application, such hearing to be on a date before the order expires, and shall send notice in Form 8 of the date of the hearing to all the parties and to the guardian *ad litem* (if appointed) not less than one month before that date.

Committal of child to care on refusal of adoption order

2–291   26. [. . .]

PART IV

[Application for removal, return, etc. of child

2–292   27.—(1) An application—

    (a) for leave under section 27 or 28 of the 1976 Act to remove a child from the home of a person with whom the child lives,

    (b) under section 29(1) of the 1976 Act for an order for the return of a child who has been removed from the home of a person with whom the child lives,

    (c) under section 29(2) of the 1976 Act for an order directing a person not to remove a child from the home of a person with whom the child lives,

    (d) under section 30(2) of the 1976 Act, for leave to give notice of an intention not to allow a child to remain in a person's home, or

    (e) under section 20(2) of the 1976 Act, for leave to place a child for adoption,

shall be made in accordance with paragraph (2).

(2) The application under paragraph (1) above shall be made by complaint—

    (a) if an application for an adoption order or an order under section 18 or 20 of the 1976 Act is pending, to the family proceedings court in which the application is pending; or

    (b) if no such application is pending, to the family proceedings court in whose area the applicant lives or, in the case of an application made under section 28 of the 1976 Act, the court in whose area the child is:

    Provided that if an application is pending under paragraph (1) above, any further application concerning the home of the child shall be made to the family proceedings court in which that original application is pending.]

(3) The respondents shall be—

    (a) in a case where proceedings for an adoption order or an order under [section 18 or 20 of the 1976 Act] are pending (or where such proceedings have subsequently been commenced), all the parties to those proceedings;

    (b) in any other case, any person against whom an order is sought in the application and the local authority to whom the prospective adopter has given notice under [section 22 of the 1976 Act]; and

    (c) in any case, such other person or body, not being the child, as the court thinks fit.

(4) If in any application under this rule a serial number has been assigned to a person who has applied or who proposes to apply for an adoption order, or such a person applies to the justices' clerk in that behalf before making that application and a serial number is assigned accordingly—

    (a) the justices' clerk shall ensure that a summons directed to any of the respondents does not disclose the identity of that person to any

218

respondent to the application under this rule who is not already aware of that person's identity, and

(b) the proceedings on the application under this rule shall be conducted with a view to securing that he is not seen by or made known to any party who is not already aware of his identity except with his consent.

(5) The justices' clerk shall serve notice of the time fixed for the hearing on the reporting officer and guardian *ad litem* (if any), together with a copy of the complaint; and on the hearing of the application the reporting officer and guardian *ad litem* may attend and be heard on the question of whether the application made should be granted.

(6) Unless otherwise directed, any prospective adopter who is a respondent under this rule and who wishes to oppose the application shall make his application for an adoption order within 14 days of the service upon him of the summons or before or at the time of the hearing of the application under this rule, whichever is the sooner.

(7) The court may at any time give directions, and if giving directions under paragraph (6) shall give directions, as to the conduct of any application under this rule and in particular as to the appointment of a guardian *ad litem* of the child.

(8) Any member or employee of a party which is a local authority, adoption agency or other body may address the court at the hearing of an application under this rule if he is duly authorised in that behalf.

(9) Where an application under paragraph 1(a) or (d) is granted or an application under paragraph (1)(b) or (c) is refused, the court may thereupon, if application for an adoption order has been made, treat the hearing of the application as the hearing of the application for an adoption order and refuse an adoption order accordingly.

(10) Where an application under this rule is determined the justices' clerk shall serve notice of the effect of the determination on all the parties.

(11) A search warrant issued by a justice of the peace under [section 29(4) of the 1976 Act] (which relates to premises specified in an information to which an order made under the said [section 29(1)] relates, authorising a constable to search the said premises and if he finds the child to return the child to the person on whose application the said order was made) shall be in [a warrant form as per section 102 of the 1989 Act] (warrant to search for or remove a child) or a form to the like effect.

Amendment and revocation of orders

28.—(1) Any application made under [paragraph 4 of Schedule 1 to the 1976 Act] for the amendment of an adoption order or the revocation of a direction to the Registrar General, or under [section 52 of, and Schedule 2 to, the 1976 Act] for the revocation of an adoption order, shall be in Form 9, and shall be made to a [family proceedings] court acting for the same petty sessions area as the [family proceedings] court which made the adoption order, by delivering it or sending it by post to the clerk to the justices. **2-293**

(2) Notice of the application shall be given by the justices' clerk to such persons (if any) as the court thinks fit.

(3) Where the application is granted, the justices' clerk shall send to the Registrar General a notice specifying the amendments or informing him of the revocation and shall give sufficient particulars of the order to enable the Registrar General to identify the case.

Service of documents

2–294 **29.**—(1) Unless otherwise directed, any document under these rules may be served—

    (a) on a corporation or body of persons, by delivering it at, or sending it by post to, the registered or principal office of the corporation or body;

    (b) on any other person, by delivering it to him, or by sending it by post to him at his usual or last known address.

(2) A note of service or non-service shall be endorsed on a copy of Form 3 or Form 8.

(3) In the case of a document sent by post to a person's usual or last known address in accordance with paragraph (1)(b), the court may treat service as having been effected notwithstanding that the document has been returned undelivered.

Costs

2–295 **30.**—(1) On the determination of an application or on the making of an interim order, the court may make such order as to the costs as it thinks just and, in particular, may order the applicant to pay—

    (*a*) the expenses incurred by the reporting officer and the guardian *ad litem* (if appointed), and

    (*b*) the expenses incurred by any respondent in attending the hearing, or such part of those expenses as the court thinks proper.

(2) Determination of an application in this rule includes a refusal to proceed with the application or withdrawal of the application.

Notice and copies of orders, etc.

2–296 **31.**—(1) In applications to which these rules apply orders shall be made in the form indicated in this paragraph—

Description of order	Form
(a) Order under [section 18 of the 1976 Act]	10
(b) Order under [section 20 of the 1976 Act]	11
(c) Interim order	12
(d) Adoption order	13

(2) Where an adoption order is made by a court sitting in Wales in respect of a child who was born in Wales (or is treated under rule 24(4) as having been born in the registration district and sub-district in which that court sits) and the adopter so requests before the order is drawn up, the justices' clerk shall supply a translation into Welsh of the particulars set out in the order.

(3) Within 7 days of the making of an order in an application to which these rules apply, the justices' clerk shall send a copy of the order (and of any translation into Welsh required to be supplied under paragraph (2)) to the applicant.

(4) Within 7 days of the making of an adoption order, the justices' clerk shall send a copy of the order (and of any translation into Welsh supplied under paragraph (2)) to the Registrar General; where a translation into Welsh under paragraph (2) has been supplied, the English text shall prevail.

(5) Where an order to which paragraph 1(a), (b) or (d) applies is made or refused or an order to which paragraph 1(c) applies is made, the justices' clerk shall serve notice to that effect on every respondent.

(6) [. . .]

(7) The justices' clerk shall serve notice of the making of an order to which paragraph 1(a), (b) or (d) applies on any court in Great Britain which appears to him to have made any such order as is referred to in [section 12(3) of the 1976 Act (orders relating to parental responsibility for, and the maintenance of, the child).]

(8) A copy of any order may be supplied to the Registrar General at his request.

(9) A copy of any order may be supplied to the applicant.

(10) A copy of any order may be supplied to any other person with the leave of the court.

Keeping of registers, custody, inspection and disclosure of documents and information

32.—(1) Such part of the register kept in pursuance of rules made under 2–297 the Magistrates' Courts Act 1980 as relates to proceedings under [Part II of the 1976 Act] shall be kept in a separate book and shall contain the particulars shown in Form 14 and the book shall not contain particulars of any other proceedings except proceedings under the 1976 Act (or under any previous enactment relating to adoption).

(2) Any declaration by a parent or guardian or a former parent of a child that he prefers not to be involved in future questions concerning the adoption of the child which is required to be recorded by the court in accordance with [section 18(6) or 19(4) of the 1976 Act] shall be recorded in the book kept in pursuance of paragraph (1).

(3) The book kept in pursuance of paragraph (1) and all other documents relating to proceedings mentioned in that paragraph shall, while they are in the custody of the court, be kept in a place of special security.

(4) A party who is an individual and is referred to in a confidential report supplied to the court by an adoption agency, a local authority, a reporting officer or a guardian *ad litem* may, for the purposes of the hearing, be supplied with a copy of that part of any such report which refers to him, subject to any direction given by the court that—

(a) no part of one or any of the reports shall be revealed to that party, or

(b) the part of one or any of the reports referring to that party shall be revealed only to that party's legal advisers, or

(c) the whole or any other part of one or any of the reports be revealed to that party.

(5) Any person who obtains any information in the course of, or relating to, any proceedings mentioned in paragraph (1), shall treat that information as confidential and shall only disclose it if—

(a) the disclosure is necessary for the proper exercise of his duties, or

(b) the information is requested—

(i) by a court or public authority (whether in Great Britain or not) having power to determine adoptions and related matters, for the purpose of the discharge of its duties in that behalf, or

(ii) by the Registrar General, or a person authorised in writing by him, where the information requested relates only to the identity of any adoption agency which made the arrangements for placing the child for adoption in the actual custody of the applicants, and of any local authority which was notified of the applicant's intention to apply for an adoption order in respect of the child, or

(iii) by a person who is authorised in writing by the [Lord Chancellor] to obtain the information for the purposes of research.

(6) Save as required or authorised by a provision of any enactment or of these Rules or with the leave of the court, no document or order held by or lodged with the court in proceedings under the 1976 Act or [...] (or under any previous enactment relating to adoption) shall be open to inspection by any person, and no copy of any such document or order, or of an extract from any such document or order, shall be taken by or issued to any person.

GENERAL NOTE

2–298   See the General Note to r.53 of the Adoption Rules 1984.

Proceedings to be by way of complaint, etc.

2–299   **33.** Save in so far as special provision is made by these Rules, proceedings on an application shall be regulated in the same manner as proceedings on complaint, and accordingly for the purposes of this rule the application shall be deemed to be a complaint, the applicant to be a complainant, the respondents to be defendants and any notice served under these rules to be a summons; but nothing in this rule shall be construed as enabling a warrant of arrest to be issued for failure to appear in answer to any such notice.

SCHEDULE 1

FORMS

Form 1   **Rule 4(1)**

Application for an order freeing a child for adoption

To the   ....Domestic Court **2-300**

I, an authorised officer of the   of   being an
adoption agency wishing to free for adoption   , a child, hereby give
the following further particulars in support of the application.

1. This application is/is not made with the consent of   (and
                        ), the parent(s)/guardian(s) of the child.

PARTICULARS OF THE CHILD

2. Identity etc. The child is of the   sex and is not and has not been
married. He/she was born on the   day of 19   and is the person to
whom the attached birth/adoption certificate relates (*or* born on or about the
                 day of 19   , in   ). He/she is a   national.

3. Parentage etc. The child is the child of   whose last known address was
                 (*or* deceased) and   whose last known address was
        (*or* deceased).

(4. The guardian(s) of the child (other than the mother or father of the child) is/
are   of   (and   of   ).)

(5. Parental agreement. I understand that the said   (and   )
is/are willing to agree to the making of an adoption order.)

(6. I request the court to dispense with the agreement of   on the ground(s)
that   (and   ) and there are attached hereto three copies of a
statement of the facts on which I intend to rely.)

7. Care, etc. The child is currently living with   of   and has
been living there since the   day of   19   . (The child has been
placed with them for adoption (and they wish their identity to remain confidential).)

(8. The child [is looked after by]   (who have the powers and duties of
the parent or guardian of the child) (*or* the parental rights and duties in respect of the child).)

(9. Maintenance   of   is liable, by virtue of an order
made by the   court at   on the   day of   19
(*or* by an agreement dated the   day of   19   ), to contribute to
the maintenance of the child.)

(10. I attach hereto signed by the mother/father/guardian of the child a declaration that he/
she prefers not to be involved in future questions concerning the adoption of the child.)

[(11. The father and mother of the child were not married to each other at the time of his
birth and   of   who is/claims to be
the father—

    (i) [does/does not intend to apply for an order under section 4(1)(*a*) of the 1989 Act,
    (ii) does/does not intend to apply for a residence order.)]

(12. No proceedings relating in whole or in part to the child have been completed or
commenced in England and Wales or elsewhere (except   ).)

I accordingly apply on behalf of   for an order freeing the child for
adoption.

Dated this   day of   19   .

Notes

An application to a [family proceedings] court must be made to a court within the area in
which either the child or his parent or guardian is.

Introduction: Enter the first name(s) and surname as shown in the certificate referred to in paragraph 2; otherwise enter the first name(s) and surname by which the child is known.

Paragraph 2: If the child has previously been adopted, a certified copy of the entry in the Adopted Children Register should be attached and not a certified copy of the original entry in the Registers of Births. Where a certificate is not attached, enter the place, including the country, of birth if known.

[Paragraph 3: If the child has previously been adopted, give the names of his adoptive parents and not those of his natural parents. If the father and mother of the child were not married to each other at the time of his birth, and a court has made an order giving the father [parental responsibility for] the child [. . .], give details of the court order under paragraph 12.]

Paragraph 4: Enter particulars of any person appointed [under section 5 of the 1989 Act] to be a guardian. Do not include any person who has the custody of the child only. Delete this paragraph if the child has no guardian.

[Paragraphs 5 and 6: Enter either in paragraph 5 or 6 the names of the persons mentioned in paragraphs 3 and 4, except that if the father and mother of the child were not married at the time of his birth the father of the child should be entered only if a court had made an order giving him [parental responsibility for] the child [. . .]. Where it is sought to dispense with parental agreement, enter in paragraph 6 one or more of the grounds set out in [section 16(2) of the 1976 Act].

Paragraph 7: Enter the name and address of the person with whom the child has his home.

Paragraph 8: This paragraph should be completed where the child is [being looked after by] a local authority or a voluntary organsation.

Paragraph 9: This paragraph should be completed where some person or body is liable to contribute to the maintenance of the child under a court order or agreement.

Paragraph 12: State the nature of the proceedings and the date and effect of any orders made.

Agreement to an adoption order (freeing cases)

IF YOU ARE IN ANY DOUBT ABOUT YOUR LEGAL RIGHTS YOU SHOULD
OBTAIN LEGAL ADVICE *BEFORE* SIGNING THIS FORM

Whereas an application is to be/has been made by   for an order **2–301**
freeing   , a child, for adoption:

And whereas the child is the person to whom the birth certificate attached marked "A"
relates:

(And whereas the child is at least six weeks old:)

I, the undersigned   of   being a parent/guardian of the child
hereby state as follows:—

(1) I consent to the application of   an adoption agency, for an order
freeing the child for adoption.

(2) I understand that the effect of an adoption order would be to deprive me permanently
of [parental responsibility for] the child and to vest [that] in the adopters: and in particular I
understand that, if and when an adoption order is made, I shall have no right to see or get in
touch with the child or to have him/her returned to me.

(3) I further understand that the court cannot make an order freeing a child for adoption
without the agreement of each parent or guardian of the child to the making of an adoption
order, unless the court dispenses with that agreement on the ground that the person
concerned—

    (a) cannot be found or is incapable of giving agreement, or

    (b) is withholding his agreement unreasonable, or

    (c) has persistently failed without reasonable cause to discharge [his parental respon-
sibility] in relation to the child, or

    (d) has abandoned or neglected the child, or

    (e) has persistently ill-treated the child, or

    (f) has seriously ill-treated the child and the rehabilitation of the child within the
household of the parent or guardian is unlikely.

(4) I further understand that, when the application for an order freeing the child for
adoption is heard, this document may be used as evidence of my agreement to the making of
an adoption order unless I inform the court that I no longer agree.

(5) I hereby freely, and with full understanding of what is involved, agree unconditionally to
the making of an adoption order.

(6) (I have been given an opportunity of making a declaration that I prefer not to be
involved in future questions concerning the adoption of the child. I understand that if I make
such a declaration I will not be told when the child has been adopted or whether he has been
placed for adoption. I further understand that I will not be able to apply for a revocation of
the order freeing the child for adoption if I make such a declaration. I hereby freely declare,
with full understanding of what is involved, that I do not wish to be involved in future
questions concerning the adoption of the child.)

(7) (I have been given an opportunity of making a declaration that I prefer not to be
involved in future questions concerning the adoption of the child, and the effect of making
such a declaration has been explained to me. I do not wish to make such a declaration.)

(8) I have not received or given any payment or reward for, or in consideration of, the
adoption of the child, for any agreement to the making of an adoption order or consent to the
making of an application for an order freeing the child for adoption, for placing the child for
adoption with any person or making any arrangements for the adoption of the child (other
than a payment to an adoption agency for their expenses incurred in connection with the
adoption).

Signature:

This form, duly completed, was signed by the said   before me at
     on the   day of   19 .

Signature:

Address:

Description:

Notes
(Heading: (a) Insert the name of the adoption agency applying for the order.

(b) Insert the first name(s) and surname of the child as known to the person giving agreement.

(c) If the child has previously been adopted a certified copy of the entry in the Adopted Children Register should be attached and not a certified copy of the original entry in the Register of Births.

(d) Where two or more forms of agreement are supplied to the court at the same time they may both or all refer to a certificate attached to one of the forms of agreement.

Paragraphs 6 and 7: If the parent or guardian does not make the declaration the adoption agency must, after twelve months have passed from the making of the order freeing the child for adoption, inform the parent or guardian whether an adoption order has been made in respect of the child, and, if not, whether the child has his home with a person with whom he has been placed for adoption. Further, if no adoption order has been made in respect of the child or the child does not have his home with a person with whom he has been placed for adoption, then the parent or guardian may apply to the court for revocation of the order freeing the child for adoption.

Paragraph 8: Any such payment or reward is illegal, except payment to an adoption agency in respect of their expenses incurred in connection with the adoption.

Witness statement: In England and Wales, the document should be witnessed by the reporting officer. In Scotland, it should be witnessed by a Justice of the Peace or a Sheriff, and in Northern Ireland, by a Justice of the Peace. Outside the United Kingdom it should be witnessed by a person authorised by law in the place where the document is signed to administer an oath for any judicial or legal purpose, a British consular officer, a notary public, or, if the person executing the document is serving in the regular armed forces of the Crown, an officer holding a commission in any of those forces.

Notice of hearing of an application of an order freeing a child for adoption

.............Domestic Court **2–302**

To

of

Whereas an application for an order freeing for adoption , a child of the
sex born on the day of 19 has been made by
of
And whereas (and) was/were appointed reporting officer(s) (and
was appointed guardian *ad litem* of the child);

TAKE NOTICE:—

1. That the said application will be heard before the court at on the
day of 19 , at o'clock and that you may then appear and be heard on the
question whether an order freeing the child for adoption should be made.

2. That you are not obliged to attend the hearing unless you wish to do so or the court
notifies you that your attendance is necessary.

3. That while the said application is pending, if the child is [being looked after by] the
applicant, then a parent or guardian of the child who has not consented to the making of the
applcation must not, except with the leave of the court, remove the child from the [home] of
the person with whom the child [lives] against the will of that person.

(4. That the court has been requested to dispense with your agreement to the making of an
adoption order on the ground(s) that and the statement of the facts on which the
applicant intends to rely is attached.)

It would assist the court if you would complete the attached form and return it to me
by

Dated the day of 19 .

Justices' Clerk

___

To the Clerk to the Justices.

Freeing for adoption: (*state name of child*)

I received notice of the hearing of the application on the day of 19 .

I wish/do not wish to oppose the application.

I wish/do not wish to appear and be heard on the question whether an order should be made.

(signature)

(address)

(date)

Notes
 Preamble: Enter the first name(s) and the surname of the child as shown in the application.
Enter the name of the applicant agency and the name(s) of the reporting officer(s) (and of the
guardian *ad litem*, if appointed).

Application for revocation of an order freeing a child for adoption

2–303 To the

...........Domestic Court

On the   day of   19   this court made an order freeing   , a child,
for adoption.

I/We   (and   ) of (*address*), the former parent(s) of the child, apply
for revocation of that order on the grounds that:—

1. No adoption order has been made in respect of the child, and

2. The child does not have his home with a person with whom he has been placed for
adoption, and

3. I/We wish to resume [parental responsibility for the child] because (*state the reasons relied
upon for the revocation of the order*)

Signed

Dated

Notes
- (a) The application must be made to the court which made the original order, and not
earlier than 12 months from the date of that order.
- (b) A parent or guardian of the child who has made a declaration referred to in [section
18 of the 1976 Act] that he prefers not to be involved in future questions concerning
the adoption of the child may not make application for revocation of the order.

Application for transfer of parental responsibility between adoption agencies

To the ....Domestic Court **2–304**

I, an authorised officer of the   of   , and I, an authorised officer of the   of   , both being adoption agencies, wishing to transfer [parental responsibility for]   , a child, from   to   hereby give the following further particulars in support of our application.

1. On the   day of   19   , the court made an order freeing the child for adoption under [section 18 of the 1976 Act]. A copy of that order is attached.

2. The transfer would be in the best interests of the child because

3. The administrative reasons why the transfer is desirable are

(4. The former parent(s)   of   (and   of   ), has/have been informed of the making of this application.)

Dated etc.

(signatures)

(addresses)

Notes

Preamble: Enter the names of the two agencies concerned and enter the name of the child as shown in the order referred to in paragraph 1.

Paragraphs 2 and 3: State concisely the reasons it is desired to transfer the child between the agencies.

Paragraph 4: A former parent is a person as defined in [section 19(1) of the 1976 Act]. This paragraph should be deleted only if there are no former parents.

Application for an adoption order

2–305 To the ....Domestic Court

I/We, the undersigned, (and ,) wishing to adopt , a child,
hereby give the following particulars in support of my/our application.

PART 1

PARTICULARS OF THE APPLICANT(S)

1. *Name and address etc.*

2–306 Name of (first) applicant in full

Address

Occupation

Date of birth

Relationship (if any) to the child

Name of (second) applicant in full

Address

Occupation

Date of Birth

Relationship (if any) with the child

2. *Domicile*

I am/we are/one of us (namely) is domiciled in England and
Wales/Scotland/Northern Ireland/the Channel Islands/the Isle of Man.

3. *Status*

We are married to each other and our marriage certificate (or other evidence of marriage)
is attached (*or* I am unmarried/a widow/a widower/a divorcee) (*or* I am applying alone as a
married person and can satisfy the court that).

(4. I am applying alone for an adoption order in respect of my own child and can satisfy the
court that the other natural parent .)

(5. *Health*

A report on my/our health, made by a registered medical practitioner on the
day of 19 , is attached.)

Notes

The application must be made to a [family proceedings] court within whose area the child
is.

Introduction: Enter the first name(s) and surname of the child as shown in any certificate
referred to in paragraph 6 below; otherwise enter the first name(s) and surname by which the
child was known before being placed for adoption.

Paragraph 1: Insert the address where the applicant has his home and the place (if different)
where documents may be served upon him.

Paragraph 3: Documentary evidence of marital status should be supplied. A married
applicant can apply alone if he or she can satisfy the court that his or her spouse cannot be
found, or that they have separated and are living apart and that the separation is likely to be
permanent, or that by reason of physical or mental ill health the spouse is incapable of making
an application for an adoption order. Any documentary evidence on which the applicant
proposes to rely should be attached to the application. The name and address (if known) of
the spouse should be supplied, and the marriage certificate (or other evidence of marriage)
should be attached.

Paragraph 4: State the reason to be relied upon *e.g..* that the other natural parent is dead, or
cannot be found, or that there is some other reason, which should be specified, justifying his
or her exclusion. Documentary evidence, *e.g..* a death certificate, should be supplied where
appropriate.

Paragraph 5: A separate health report is required in respect of each applicant, and the report must have been made during the period of three months before the date of the application. No report is required, however, if the child was placed for adoption with the applicant by an adoption agency, or if he is the child of the applicant or either of them.

PART 2

PARTICULARS OF THE CHILD

6. *DENTITY ETC.*
  The child is of the   sex and is not and has not been married. He/she was **2–307**
born on the   day of   19   and is the person to whom the attached
birth/adoption certificate relates (*or* was born on or about the   day of
19 , in   ). He/she is a   national.

7. *Health*
  A report on the health of the child, made by a registered medical practitioner on the
              day of   19   , is attached.)
  8. The child is free for adoption pursuant to [section 18 of the 1976 Act], and I/we attach
hereto the order of the   court, dated   , to that effect. The [parental
responsibility for] the child [was] thereby vested in   (and [was] transferred to
              by order of the   court under [section 21 of the 1976 Act] on
19).)

(9. *Parentage, etc.*
  The child is the child of   whose last known address was (*or* deceased)
and   whose last known address was   (*or* deceased).)
  (10. The guardian(s) of the child (other than the mother or the father of the child) is/are
          of   (and   of   ).)

(11. *Parental agreement*
  I/We understand that the said   (and   ) is/are willing to agree to the
making of an adoption order in pursuance of my/our application.)
  (12. I/we request the court to dispense with the agreement of   (and
) on the ground(s) that   (and   ) and there are
attached hereto three copies of a statement of the facts upon which I/we intend to rely.)

[(13. *Persons by whom child looked after*
  The child is being looked after by (who have parental responsibility for him).]

(14. *Maintenance*
  of   is liable by virtue of an order made by the
  court at   on the   day of   19   , (*or* by an agreement
  dated the   day of   19   ) to contribute to the maintenance of the child.)

15. *Proposed names*
  If an adoption order is made in pursuance of this application, the child is to be known by
the following names:

Surname

Other names

Notes
  Paragraph 6: If the child has previously been adopted a certified copy of the entry in the Adopted Children Register should be attached and not a certified copy of the original entry in the Registers of Births. Where a certificate is not attached, enter the place (including the country) of birth if known.
  Paragraph 7: The report must have been made during the period of three months before the date of the application. No report is required, however, if the child was placed for adoption with the applicant by an adoption agency, or if he is the child of the applicant or either of them.
  Paragraph 8: The order made by the court freeing the child for adoption and any order made under [section 21 of the 1976 Act] should be attached.

231

Paragraph 9: This paragraph and paragraphs 10 to 14 only apply if the child is not free for adoption. If the child has previously been adopted give the names of his adoptive parents and not those of his natural parents. [If the father and mother of the child were not married to each other at the time of his birth, and a court has made an order giving the father [parental responsibility for] the child, [. . .], give details of the order under paragraph 19.].

Paragraph 10: Enter particulars of any person appointed [under section 5 of the 1989 Act] to be a guardian. Do not include any person who has the custody of the child only. Delete this paragraph if the child has no guardian.

[Paragraphs 11 and 12: Enter either in paragraph 11 or 12 the names of the persons mentioned in paragraphs 9 and 10, except that if the father and mother of the child were not married at the time of his birth the father of the child should be entered only if a court has made an order giving the father [parental responsibility for] the child [. . .]].

[Paragraph 13: This paragraph should be completed where the child is [being looked after by] a local authority or a voluntary organisation.

Paragraph 14: This paragraph should be completed where some person or body is liable to contribute to the maintenance of the child under a court order or agreement.

PART 3

GENERAL

2–308 16. The child has lived with me/us continuously since the   day of 19   (and has accordingly had his home with me/us for the five years preceding the date of this application).

17. The child was (placed with me/us for adoption on the day of   19 by   , and adoption agency) (*or* received into my/our [home] in the following circumstances:

(18. I/we/one of us (namely   ) notified the   Council on the day of   19   , of my/our intention to apply for an adoption order in respect of the child.)

19. No proceedings relating in whole or in part to the child other than as stated in paragraph 8 have been completed or commenced in any court in England and Wales or elsewhere (except   ).

20. I/we have not received or given any payment or reward for, or in consideration of, the adoption of the child, for any agreement to the making of an adoption order, the transfer of the [home] of the child with a view to adoption or the making of any arrangements for adoption (except as follows:—

21. As far as I/we know, the only person(s) or bod(y)(ies) who have taken part in the arrangements for the child's adoption are

(22. For the purpose of this application reference may be made to   of .)

(23. I/we desire that my/our identity should be kept confidential, and the serial number of this application is   .)

I/we accordingly apply for an adoption order in respect of the child.

Dated this   day of   19

Signature(s)

Notes

Paragraphs 16 and 17: Under [section 13 of the 1976 Act] an adoption order cannot be made unless the child has had his home with the applicants or one of them:—

(a) for at least 13 weeks if the applicant or one of them is a parent, step-parent or relative of the child or if the child was placed with the applicant by an adoption agency or in pursuance of an order of the High Court;

(b) for at least 12 months in any other case.

Paragraph 18: Notice does not have to be given if the child was placed with the applicant by an adoption agency. Where notice does have to be given, no order can be made until the expiration of three months from the date of the notice.

Paragraph 19: The nature of the proceedings and the date and effect of any orders made should be stated. The court cannot proceed with the application if a previous application made by the same applicant in relation to the child was refused, unless one of the conditions of [section 24 of the 1976 Act] is satisfied. The court must dismiss the application if it considers that, where the application is made by a married couple of whom one is a parent and the other a step-parent of the child, or by a step-parent of the child alone, the matter would be better dealt with under [Part 1 of the 1989 Act].

232

Paragraph 21: Enter the name and address of the adoption agency or individual who took part in the arrangements for placing the child for adoption in the [home] of the applicant.

Paragraph 22: Where the applicant or one of the applicants is a parent of the child, or a relative as defined by [section 72 of the 1976 Act] or the child was placed with the applicant by an adoption agency, no referee need be named.

Paragraph 23: If the applicant wishes his identity to be kept confidential, the serial number obtained under rule 14 should be given.

Agreement to an adoption order

IF YOU ARE IN ANY DOUBT ABOUT YOUR LEGAL RIGHTS YOU SHOULD OBTAIN LEGAL ADVICE *BEFORE* SIGNING THIS FORM

2–309   Whereas an application is to be/has been made by   and   (*or* under serial No.   ) for an adoption order in respect of   , a child;

And whereas the child is the person to whom the birth certificate attached marked "A" relates:

(And whereas the child is at least six weeks old:)

I, the undersigned   of   being a parent/guardian of the child hereby state as follows:

(1) I understand that the effect of an adoption order will be to deprive me permanently of [parental responsibility for] the child and to vest [that] in the applicant(s); and in particular I understand that, if an order is made, I shall have no right to see or get in touch with the child or to have him/her returned to me.

(2) I further understand that the court cannot make an adoption order without the agreement of each parent or guardian of the child unless the court dispenses with an agreement on the ground that the person concerned—

    (a) cannot be found or is incapable of giving agreement, or

    (b) is withholding his agreement unreasonably, or

    (c) has persistently failed without reasonable cause to discharge the parental duties in relation to the child, or

    (d) has abandoned or neglected the child, or

    (e) has persistently ill-treated the child, or

    (f) has seriously ill-treated the child and the rehabilitation of the child within the household of the parent or guardian is unlikely.

(3) I further understand that when the application for an adoption order is heard this agreement may be used as evidence of my agreement to the making of the order unless I inform the court that I no longer agree.

(4) I hereby freely, and with full understanding of what is involved, agree unconditionally to the making of an adoption order in pursuance of the application.

(5) As far as I know, the only person(s) or bod(y)(ies) who has/have taken part in the arrangements for the child's adoption is/are   (and   ).

(6) I have not received or given any payment or reward for, or in consideration of, the adoption of the child, for any agreement to the making of an adoption order or placing the child for adoption with any person or making arrangements for the adoption of the child (other than payment to an adoption agency for their expenses incurred in connection with the adoption).

Signature:

This form, duly completed, was signed by the said   before me at   on the   day of   19   .

Signature:

Address:

Description:

Notes

Preamble: Insert either the name(s) of the applicant(s) or the serial No. assigned to the applicant(s) for the purposes of the application.

Insert the first name(s) and surname of the child as known to the person giving agreement.

If the child has previously been adopted a certified copy of the entry in the Adopted Children Register should be attached and not a certified copy of the original entry in the Registers of Births.

Where two or more forms of agreement are supplied to the court at the same time they may both or all refer to a certificate attached to one of the forms of agreement.

[A father who was not married to the mother of a child at the time of his birth is not a parent for this purpose, but is a guardian if a court has made an order giving him [parental responsibility for] the child [. . .];] "guardian" also means a person appointed [under section 5 of the 1989 Act] to be the guardian of the child.

Paragraph 3: Notice will be given of the hearing of the application and of the court by which it is to be heard. After the making of the application a parent or guardian who has agreed [to the making of an adoption order cannot remove the child from the applicant's home without leave of the court.]

Paragraph 5: Enter the name and address of the adoption agency or individual who took part in the arrangements for placing the child in the actual custody of the applicant(s).

Witness statement: In England and Wales the document should be witnessed by the reporting officer. In Scotland, it should be witnessed by a Justice of the Peace or a Sheriff, and in Northern Ireland by a Justice of the Peace. Outside the United Kingdom it should be witnessed by a person authorised by law in the place where the document is signed to administer an oath for any judicial or legal purpose, a British consular officer, a notary public, or, if the person executing the document is serving in the regular armed forces of the Crown, an officer holding a commission in any of those forces.

Notice of hearing of an application for an adoption order

2–310
                                  ....Domestic Court

To   of

Whereas an application for an adoption order in respect of   , a child of the sex born on the   day of   19   , has been made (by (and   ) of   ) (*or* under the serial number) and whereas   (and   ) was/were appointed reporting officer(s) (and   was appointed guardian *ad litem* of the child):

TAKE NOTICE:—

(1. That the said application will be heard before the court at   on the   day of   19   , at   o'clock and that you may then appear and be heard on the question whether an adoption order should be made.)

(2. That if you wish to appear and be heard on the question whether an adoption order should be made, you should give notice to the court on or before the   day of   19   , in order that a time may be fixed for your appearance.)

3. That you are not obliged to attend the hearing unless you wish to do so or the court notifies you that your attendance is necessary.

4. That while the application is pending, a parent or guardian of the child who has agreed to the making of an order must not, except with the leave of the court, remove the child from the [home] of the applicant.

(5. That the application states that the child has had his home with the applicant for the five years preceding the application and accordingly, if that is correct, no person is entitled, against the will of the applicant, to remove the child from the applicant's [home] except with the leave of the court or under authority conferred by an enactment or on the arrest of the child.)

(6. That the court has been requested to dispense with your agreement to the making of an order on the ground(s) that   and a statement of the facts on which the applicant intends to rely is attached).

It would assist the court if you would complete the attached form and return it to me by

Dated the   day of   19   .

                                     Justices' Clerk

To the Clerk to the Justices.

Application for an adoption order: (*state name of child*)

I received the notice of the hearing of the application on the   day of 19   .

I wish/do not wish to oppose the application.

I wish/do not wish to appear and be heard on the question whether an order should be made.

                              (signature)

                              (address)

                              (date)

Notes

When this form is used under rule 25 to give notice of a further hearing of an application it is to be amended so as to refer to a further hearing and so as to give particulars of the interim order.

Preamble: Enter the name(s) and surname of the child as shown in the application. Enter the name of the applicant(s) unless the applicant has obtained a serial number, in which case the second part in brackets should be completed.

Paragraphs 1 and 2: Paragraph 1 should be completed and paragraph 2 struck out where the notice is addressed to any respondent where the applicant does not wish his identity to be kept confidential. When a serial number has been assigned to the applicant and the notice is addressed to an individual respondent other than the spouse of the applicant, paragraph 1 should be struck out and paragraph 2 completed.

Paragraph 5: This paragraph should be deleted except where it appears from the application that the child has had his home with the applicant for five years.

Paragraph 6: Unless deleted, this paragraph should contain the grounds specified in the application.

Application to amend or revoke adoption order

2–311 To the ....Domestic Court

1. Identification of the adoption order to be amended or revoked

Name of adopters:

Date of adoption order:

Name of child adopted:

2. Particulars of applicant

Name:

Address:

Relationship (if any) to the child (*or* if no such relationship, state reason for application):

If application is made under [section 50 of the 1976 Act], state the amendments desired and the facts relied on in support of the application:

If application is made under [section 52 of the 1976 Act] [. . .], state the facts relied on in support of the application:

I apply for the adoption order to be amended or revoked in accordance with this application.

Dated this   day of   19 .

                                                                        Signature

Order freeing a child for adoption

............Domestic Court **2–312**

Whereas an application has been made by   of   , being an adoption agency, for an order freeing for adoption   , a child of the   sex, the child of (and   );

It is ordered that the child be freed for adoption and that [parental responsibility for] the child be vested in the applicant;

(and as regards costs it is ordered that   ;)

(and whereas the precise date of the child's birth has not been proved to the satisfaction of the court but the court has determined the probable date of his/her birth to be the   day of   19   ;)

(and whereas it has been proved to the satisfaction of the court that the child was born in (*country*);)

(and whereas the place of birth of the child has not been proved to the satisfaction of the court (but it appears probable that the child was born in the United Kingdom, the Channel Islands or the Isle of Man, the child is treated as having been born in the registration district of   and sub-district of   in the county of   );)

(and whereas it has been proved to the satisfaction of the court that the child is identical with   to whom the entry numbered   made on the   day of   19   , in the Register of Births for the registration district of   and sub-district of   in the county of   relates (*or* with   to whom the entry numbered   and dated the   day of   19   , in the Adopted Children Register relates);)

It is directed that this order is sufficient proof of the above particulars for the purposes of any future adoption application in respect of the child.

And it is further recorded that   (and   ) being a parent or guardian of the child made a declaration under [section 18(6) of the 1976 Act] that he/she prefers not to be involved in future questions concerning the adoption of the child.

Dated this   day of   19   .

Justice of the Peace
[*or* By order of the Court
Clerk of the Court]

Order revoking an order freeing a child for adoption/dismissing an application to revoke an order freeing a child for adoption

2–313

..........Domestic Court

Whereas an application has been made by   of   (and   ) for an order revoking an order freeing for adoption   , a child of the   sex, the child of   (and   ), such order having been made by the   court on the   day of   19 ;

It is ordered that the said order be revoked and that   [parental responsibility for] the child be vested in   (and   );

(and it is ordered that   of   do make periodical payments to the child in the sum of £   payable   ;)

It is ordered that the application be dismissed (and that the applicant(s) shall not make further application under [section 20 of the 1976 Act];

(and it is ordered that   , the adoption agency which obtained the order under [section 18 of the 1976 Act], is released from the duty of complying further with [section 19(3)] of that Act as respects the applicant(s).)

(And as regards costs is ordered that
.)

Dated this   day of   19 .

Justice of the Peace
[*or* By order of the Court
Clerk of the Court]

Interim order

...........Domestic Court **2–314**

Whereas an application has been made by   of   (and   ) for an
adoption order in respect of   a child of the   sex, the child/adopted
child of   (and   );
It is ordered that the determination of the application be postponed and that the
applicant(s) do have [parental responsibility for] the child until the   day of
                19   , by way of a probationary period (*or* that the determination of the
application be postponed to the   day of   19   , and that the applicant(s)
do have the legal custody of the child until that day by way of a probationary period) (upon
the following terms, namely   );
(and as regards costs it is ordered that   );
(and it is ordered that the application be further heard before the court at
on the   day of   19   , at   o'clock.)

Dated this   day of   19   .

Justice of the Peace
[*or* By order of the Court
Clerk of the Court]

Adoption order

2–315

............Domestic Court

Whereas an application has been made by   of   whose occupation is
          (and   whose occupation is   ) for an adoption order in
respect of   , a child of the   sex, the child/adopted child of
          (and   );
It is ordered that the applicant(s) do adopt the child and that [parental responsibility for]
the child [. . .] be vested in the applicant(s).
(And as regards costs, it is ordered that   ;)
(And it is recorded that the   , being an adoption agency, placed the child for
adoption with the applicant(s)/the   Council was notified of the applicant(s)
intention to adopt the child;)
(And whereas the child was freed for adoption by the   court on the
          day of   19 ;)
(And whereas the precise date of the child's birth has not been proved to the satisfaction of
the court but the court has determined the probable date of his/her birth to be the
day of   19 ;)
(And whereas it has been proved to the satisfaction of the court that the child was born in
          (*country*);)
(And whereas the place of birth of the child has not been proved to the satisfaction of the
court (but it appears probable that the child was born in the United Kingdom, the Channel
Islands or the Isle of Man, the child is treated as having been born in the registration district
of   and sub-district of   in the county of   );)
(And whereas it has been proved to the satisfaction of the court that the child was born on
the   day of   19   (and is identical (with   to whom the
entry numbered   made on the   day of   19   , in the
Register of Births for the registration district of   and sub-district of
in the county of   relates (*or* with   to whom the entry numbered
          and dated the   day of   19 , in the Adopted Children
Register relates);)
(And whereas the name or names and surname stated in the application as those by which
the child is to be known are   ;)
It is directed that the Registrar General shall make in the Adopted Children Register an
entry in the form specified by regulations made by him recording the particulars set out in this
order,
(And it is further directed that the aforesaid entry in the Register of Births/Adopted
Children Register be marked with the words "adopted" "readopted").

Dated this   day of   19 .

Justice of the Peace
[*or* By order of the Court
Clerk of the Court]

Form 14

Register of adoptions

In the [county of   ] [Petty Sessional Division of   ].

No.	Date of decision	Name and address of applicant	Name of child prior to adoption	Sex of child	Age of child	Name of child after adoption	Minute of decision	Signature of justice adjudicating

MATTERS TO BE COVERED IN REPORTS SUPPLIED UNDER RULES 4(4), 22(1) OR 22(2)

2–317 So far as is practicable, the report supplied by the adoption agency or, in the case of a report supplied under rule 22(2), the local authority shall include all the following particulars:—

1. The child

2–318
    (a) Name, sex, date and place of birth and address;
    [(b) whether the child's father and mother were married to each other at the time of his birth;]
    (c) nationality;
    (d) physical description;
    (e) personality and social development;
    (f) religion, including details of baptism, confirmation or equivalent ceremonies;
    (g) [details of any wardship proceedings and of any court orders relating to parental responsibility for the child or to maintenance and residence].
    (h) details of any brothers and sisters, including dates of birth, arrangements [concerning with whom they are to hire] and whether any brother or sister is the subject of a parallel application;
    (i) extent of [contact with] members of the child's natural family and, [if the father and mother of the child were not married to each other at the time of his birth], his father, and in each case the nature of the relationship enjoyed;
    (j) if the child has been [looked after by or is in the care of a local authority or has been cared for by a] voluntary organisation, details (including dates) of any placements with foster parents, or other arrangements in respect of the care of the child, including particulars of the persons with whom the child has had his home and observations on the care provided;
    (k) date and circumstances of placement with prospective adopter;
    (l) names, addresses and types of schools attended, with dates, and educational attainments;
    (m) any special needs in relation to the child's health (whether physical or mental) and his emotional and behavioural development and whether he is subject to a statement under the Education Act 1981;
    (n) what, if any, rights to or interests in property or any claim to damages, under the Fatal Accidents Act 1976 or otherwise, the child stands to retain or lose if adopted;
    (o) wishes and feelings in relation to adoption and the application, including any wishes in respect of religious and cultural upbringing; and
    (p) any other relevant information which might assist the court.

[2. Each natural parent, including where appropriate the father who was not married to the child's mother at the time of his birth.]

2–319
    (a) Name, date and place of birth and address;
    (b) marital status and date and place of marriage (if any);
    (c) past and present relationship (if any) with the other natural parent, including comments on its stability;
    (d) physical description;
    (e) personality;
    (f) religion;
    (g) educational attainments;
    (h) past and present occupations and interests;
    (i) so far as available, names and brief details of the personal circumstances of the parents and any brothers and sisters of the natural parent, with their ages or ages at death;
    (j) wishes and feelings in relation to adoption and the application, including any wishes in respect of the child's religious and cultural upbringing;
    (k) reasons why any of the above information is unavailable; and
    (l) any other relevant information which might assist the court.

GENERAL NOTE

2–320 See the General Note to para. 2 of Sched. 2 to the Adoption Rules 1994.

3. Guardian

Give the details required under paragraph 2(*a*), (*f*), (*j*), and (*l*). **2–321**

4. Prospective adopter

2–322

(a) Name, date and place of birth and address;
(b) relationship (if any) to the child;
(c) marital status, date and place of marriage (if any) and comments on stability of relationship;
(d) details of any previous marriage;
(e) if a parent and step-parent are applying, the reason why they prefer adoption to [a residence order];
(f) if a natural parent is applying alone, the reasons for the exclusion of the other parent;
(g) if a married person is applying alone, the reasons for this;
(h) physical description;
(i) personality;
(j) religion, and whether willing to follow any wishes of the child or his parents or guardian in respect of the child's religious and cultural upbringing;
(k) educational attainments;
(l) past and present occupations and interests;
(m) particulars of the home and living conditions (and particulars of any home where the prospective adopter proposes to live with the child, if different);
(n) details of income and comments on the living standards of the household;
(o) details of other members of the household (including any children of the prospective adopter even if not resident in the household);
(p) details of the parents and any brothers or sisters of the prospective adopter, with their ages or ages at death;
(q) attitudes to the proposed adoption of such other members of the prospective adopter's household and family as the adoption agency or, as the case may be, the local authority considers appropriate;
(r) previous experience of caring for children as step-parent, foster parent, child-minder or prospective adopter and assessment of ability in this respect, together where appropriate with assessment of ability in bringing up the prospective adopter's own children;
(s) reasons for wishing to adopt the child and extent of understanding of the nature and effect of adoption;
(t) any hopes and expectations for the child's future;
(u) assessment of ability to bring up the child throughout his childhood;
(v) details of any adoption allowance payable;
(w) confirmation that any referees have been interviewed, with a report of their views and opinion of the weight to be placed thereon; and
(x) any other relevant information which might assist the court.

5. Actions of the adoption agency or local authority supplying the report

2–323

(a) Reports under rules 4(4) or 22(1):—
  (i) brief account of the agency's actions in the case, with particulars and dates of all written information and notices given to the child, his natural parents and the prospective adopter;
  (ii) details of alternatives to adoption considered;
  (iii) reasons for considering that adoption would be in the child's best interests (with date of relevant decision); and
  (iv) reasons for considering that the prospective adopter would be suitable to be an adoptive parent and that he would be suitable for this child (with dates of relevant decisions) or, if the child has not yet been placed for adoption, reasons for considering that he is likely to be so placed;
OR (b) Reports under rule 22(2):—
  (i) confirmation that notice was given under [section 22 of the 1976 Act], with the date of that notice;
  (ii) brief account of the local authority's actions in the case; and
  (iii) account of investigations whether child was placed in contravention [section 11 of the 1976 Act].

6. Generally

2–324

(a) Whether any respondent appears to be under the age of majority or under a mental disability; and

(b) whether, in the opinion of the body supplying the report, any other person should be made a respondent (for example, a person [who was not married to the mother of the child at the time of his birth and who claims to be the father of the child], a spouse or ex-spouse of a natural parent, a relative of a deceased parent, or a person with [parental responsibility].

7. Conclusions

2–325 (This part of the report should contain more than a simple synopsis of the information above. As far as possible, the court should be given a fuller picture of the child, his natural parents and, where appropriate, the prospective adopter.)

(a) Except where the applicant or one of them is a parent of the child, a summary by the medical adviser to the body supplying the report, of the health history and state of health of the child, his natural parents and, if appropriate, the prospective adopter, with comments on the implications for the order sought and on how any special health needs of the child might be met;

(b) opinion on whether making the order sought would be in the child's best long-term interests, and on how any special emotional, behavioural and educational needs of the child might be met;

(c) opinion on the effect on the child's natural parents of making the order sought;

(d) if the child has been placed for adoption, opinion on the likelihood of full integration of the child into the household, family and community of the prospective adopter, and on whether the proposed adoption would be in the best long-term interests of the prospective adopter;

(e) opinion, if appropriate, on the relative merits of adoption and [a residence order]; and

(f) final conclusions and recommendations whether the order sought should be made (and, if not, alternative proposals).

Rule 15(4)   SCHEDULE 3

REPORTS ON THE HEALTH OF THE CHILD AND OF THE APPLICANT(S)

2–326 This information is required for reports on the health of a child and of his prospective adopter(s). Its purpose is to build up a full picture of their health history and current state of health, including strengths and weaknesses. This will enable the local authority's medical adviser to base his advice to the court on the fullest possible information, when commenting on the health implications of the proposed adoption. The reports made by the examining doctor should cover, as far as practicable, the following matters.

1. The child

2–327 Name, date of birth, sex, weight and height.

A. A health history of each natural parent, so far as is possible, including:

(i) name, date of birth, sex, weight and height;

(ii) a family health history, covering the parents, the brothers and sisters and the other children of the natural parent, with details of any serious physical or mental illness and inherited and congenital disease;

(iii) past health history, including details of any serious physical or mental illness, disability, accident, hospital admission or attendance at an out-patient department, and in each case any treatment given;

(iv) a full obstetric history of the mother, including any problems in the ante-natal, labour and post-natal periods, with the results of any tests carried out during or immediately after pregnancy;

(v) details of any present illness including treatment and prognosis;

(vi) any other relevant information which might assist the medical adviser; and

(vii) the name and address of any doctor(s) who might be able to provide further information about any of the above matters.

B. A neo-natal report on the child, including:—

(i) details of the birth, and any complications;

(ii) results of a physical examination and screening tests;

(iii) details of any treatment given;

(iv) details of any problem in management and feeding;
(v) any other relevant information which might assist the medical adviser; and
(vi) the name and address of any doctor(s) who might be able to provide further information about any of the above matters.
C. A full health history and examination of the child, including:—
(i) details of any serious illness, disability, accident, hospital admission or attendance at an out-patient department, and in each case any treatment given;
(ii) details and dates of immunisations;
(iii) a physical and developmental assessment according to age, including an assessment of vision and hearing and of neurological, speech and language development and any evidence of emotional disorder;
(iv) for a child over five years of age, the school health history (if available);
(v) any other relevant information which might assist the medical adviser; and
(vi) the name and address of any doctor(s) who might be able to provide further information about any of the above matters.
D. The signature, name, address and qualifications of the registered medical practitioner who prepared the report, and the date of the report and of the examinations carried out.

2. The applicant

(If there is more than one applicant, a report on each applicant should be supplied covering **2–328** all the matters listed below.)
A. (i) name, date of birth, sex, weight and height;
(ii) a family health history, covering the parents, the brothers and sisters and the children of the applicant, with details of any serious physical or mental illness and inherited and congenital disease;
(iii) marital history, including (if applicable) reasons for inability to have children;
(iv) past health history, including details of any serious physical or mental illness, disability, accident, hospital admission or attendance at an out-patient department, and in each case any treatment given;
(v) obstetric history (if applicable);
(vi) details of any present illness, including treatment and prognosis;
(vii) a full medical examination;
(viii) details of any daily consumption of alcohol, tobacco and habit-forming drugs;
(ix) any other relevant information which might assist the medical adviser; and
(x) the name and address of any doctor(s) who might be able to provide further information about any of the above matters.
B. The signature, name, address and qualifications of the registered medical practitioner who prepared the report, and the date of the report and of the examinations carried out.

PART III

GOVERNMENT CIRCULARS AND GUIDANCE

CIRCULAR No. LAC (84)3

Dated January 16, 1984, and issued by the Department of Health and Social Security.

ADOPTION AGENCIES REGULATIONS 1983

SUMMARY

This circular gives guidance on the Adoption Agencies Regulations 1983.

Introduction

1. A copy is enclosed of the Adoption Agencies Regulations 1983, which come into **3–001** operation on 27 May 1984. Further adoption provisions of the Children Act 1975 come into force on the same date, as well as new court rules for adoption proceedings. Separate circulars are being issued on the new provisions and the court rules, and these should be referred to where necessary for guidance. In particular, circular LAC(84)2 advises adoption agencies about the action they should take before 27 May 1984 to ensure that their adoption work can go forward smoothly after that date under the new regulations. The following paragraphs of this circular contain detailed guidance on the provisions of the new regulations.

Regulation 1: Citation, Commencement, Extent and Interpretation

2. **Regulation 1(1)** gives the title of the regulations and the date from which they operate, 27 **3–002** May 1984, and **regulation 1(2)** confines their application to England and Wales. There are separate regulations for Scotland governing the approval of adoption societies and the exercise by adoption agencies of their adoption functions.

3. **Regulation 1(3)** defines some of the terms used in the regulations. No definition is needed of the many terms which are already defined in the (1975 Act or the Adoption Act 1958 (such as "adoption order", "child", and "local authority"). There is also no need for the regulations to cover general matters which are dealt with in the Interpretation Act 1978, for example, references in the regulations to a prospective adopter as "he" do not prevent the provision concerned applying, as appropriate, to a woman or to a married couple. It is also by virtue of the Interpretation Act that the regulations apply in the same way whether the adoption arrangements are intended to result in an "ordinary" adoption order, in an order (under section 25 of the 1975 Act) authorising a proposed foreign adoption, or in a Convention adoption order (under section 24 of the 1975 Act). It might be appropriate to place a child (including a child who is free for adoption) for adoption with prospective adopters from abroad if, for example, he has established close links with them or is related to them.

4. The definition of "adoption agency" includes *all* local authorities, even those which do not provide an adoption service as such. Those local authorities need not set up an adoption panel (though they must comply with the regulations in carrying out any adoption work they do undertake). Every local authority should have arrangements for ensuring that the appropriateness of adoption is considered for any child in care who is unlikely to return to his own family, but a local authority which does not provide an adoption service cannot itself place the child for adoption. The child can only be placed for adoption if that authority asks another adoption agency (either another local authority or an approved adoption society) to arrange this, and that adoption agency must follow all the requirements of the regulations in making the adoption arrangements. If, for example, a child boarded-out by such a local authority is to be adopted by his foster parents, the placement only becomes a placement "by an adoption agency"" (for the purposes of sections 9(1) and 22(3) of the 1975 Act) if he is placed in accordance with the regulations: the placement decision must be made by an adoption agency after taking into account the placement recommendation of its adoption panel. It is similarly not possible for a local authority which does not itself provide an adoption service to apply for a freeing order for a child in its care, because an adoption agency's decision to free a child can only be made after taking into account the recommendation of its adoption panel.

5. The definition of "prospective adopter" is wide enough to include the foster parents of a child boarded-out with them under the Boarding-Out of Children Regulations 1955, where their wish to adopt the child is considered in accordance with these regulations. It is possible for the foster parents of a boarded-out child to apply to the court direct for an adoption order, without involving an adoption agency in the arrangements, but the requirements of sections 9(2) and 18(1) of the 1975 Act would then apply: an adoption order could not be made unless the child had lived with them continuously throughout the previous 12 months, and unless they had notified their local authority at least 3 months before the date of the order of their intention to apply for it.

6. **Regulation 1(4)** recognises that legal provisions referred to in the regulations may be changed after the regulations have come into operation, and ensures that such references would then be to those provisions as amended. **Regulation 1(5)** is technically necessary to give the correct reference to regulations and the schedule, and to numbered paragraphs.

Regulation 2: Approval of Adoption Societies

3–003   7. **Regulation 2(1)** requires the application form issued by Children's Division of DHSS to be used by voluntary adoption societies wishing to apply for the Secretary of State's approval (or renewal of approval) under section 4 of the 1975 Act. The effect of **regulation 2(2)** is that all adoption societies applying for approval must be incorporated bodies. They must also, by virtue of an amendment made to section 4 of the 1975 Act by the Health and Social Services and Social Security Adjudications Act 1983, be voluntary organisations (ie not profit-making bodies).

Regulation 3: Annual Reports and Information to be Provided by Approved Adoption Societies

3–004   8. **Regulation 3(a)** requires every approved adoption society to send the Secretary of State two copies of its annual report each year. One copy is for Children's Division of DHSS, and the other will be needed by Social Work Service of DHSS when the society's application for renewal of approval is being considered. This regulation also requires an approved adoption society to supply any other information the Secretary of State might require, as and when he requires it. This might be, for example, in the case of a very small society, particulars of any changes in the social work staff. Notification of any change in the name or address of an approved adoption society is dealt with separately under **regulation 3(b)**, which requires the society to let the Secretary of State know of the change within a month.

9. **Regulation 3(c)** requires an approved adoption society to give the Secretary of State advance notice (of at least a month, if possible) if it proposes to close down or cease doing adoption work. The Secretary of State may then need to consider using his powers under section 7 of the 1975 Act to make any necessary arrangements for children in the society's care. Once the society has closed down or ceased doing adoption work, **regulation 3(d)** requires it to let the Secretary of State know as soon as possible. (Regulation 16 provides for the transfer of case records in these circumstances).

Regulation 4: Application of Regulations to Certain Adoption Agencies

3–005   10. **Regulation 4** recognises that the adoption work of some adoption agencies does not extend to making decisions under the regulations about whether adoption is in a particular child's best interests, whether particular prospective adopters are suitable to be adoptive parents, or whether particular prospective adopters are suitable adoptive parents for a particular child. Such agencies are generally either local authorities which do not themselves provide a full range of adoption services and which therefore refer clients to other adoption agencies, or an adoption agency like British Agencies for Adoption and Fostering which does not itself arrange adoption placements. These agencies are not required to set up adoption panels or to follow the requirements of the regulations in respect of adoption placements (regulations 7 to 13), if they only operate as adoption agencies for the purpose of putting clients in touch with other adoption agencies or adoption agencies in touch with each other (or both). But they must comply with the other requirements of the regulations in respect of their arrangements for adoption work (regulation 6), the confidentiality, preservation and transfer of their case records (regulations 14 and 16), and access to the records and disclosure of information (regulation 15).

Regulation 5: Establishment of Adoption Panel and Appointment of Members

3–006   11. **Regulation 5(1)** requires the agency to set up an adoption panel right away. The panel should normally be set up by the management committee in the case of an approved adoption

252

society and by the social services committee in the case of a local authority, and will be accountable to that committee. The membership specified in the regulations means that a local authority's adoption panel is not a sub-committee of the social services committee. The maximum number of members of a panel is 10, and the minimum is 7 (the 6 members described in regulation 5(3) as well as the chairman), and there must be at least one man and at least one woman, in recognition of the contribution which both sexes should make to decisions about the welfare of children.

12. An agency may set up more than one adoption panel if it wishes, since this may suit the way the agency organises its adoption work. The membership of each panel must, however, be in accordance with the requirements of the regulations. This means, for example, that if the agency has only one medical adviser, he must be appointed a member of each adoption panel.

13. **Regulation 5(2)** requires the agency to appoint a chairman of the panel. His role is crucial in ensuring that the panel's work is carried out efficiently and sensitively, and agencies must therefore select with great care the best person for this important appointment. His personal qualities and his experience of adoption work need to be such that he commands the respect of the other panel members and can chair the panel's meetings effectively. The regulations do not specify the amount or type of experience in adoption work which the chairman must have, and this is left to agencies to decide. Although it is generally preferable for the chairman to be a professionally qualified social worker, this is not essential and, for example, a member of the management committee who has previously chaired a panel may have acquired considerable experience of adoption work in that way.

14. **Regulation 5(3)(a)** requires two of the panel members to be social workers employed by the agency. These need not be adoption caseworkers, but could include, for example, a member of senior management or of the agency's residential child care staff. In making these appointments, agencies should bear in mind the type of adoption work undertaken by the agency, as well as the availability of suitable staff with experience of work with families and children.

15. **Regulation 5(3)(b)** requires at least one management representative to be appointed as a panel member. In the case of an approved adoption society, this must be a member of the management committee, and in the case of a local authority it must be a member of the social services committee. This appointment acknowledges the agency's overall responsibility for the provision of adoption services and for decisions on matters considered by the panel.

16. **Regulation 5(3)(c)** requires the agency's medical adviser to be appointed to the panel. He needs to be actively involved in every case because of the possible significance of health factors. These cannot be assessed in isolation but need to be considered in the wider context which the panel's discussion of a case allows.

17. **Regulation 5(3)(d)** requires at least two of the panel members to be independent of the agency. These should be people with a special contribution to make the panel's work, and agencies should make these appointments imaginatively. Depending on the type of adoption work undertaken by the agency, examples of these appointments might be:

— a representative of an ethnic minority group;
— a handicapped person;
— an adoptive or an "ordinary" parent;
— a lawyer (perhaps the agency's legal adviser if he is not an employee of the agency);
— a doctor with a special interest in child health;
— a health visitor;
— a teacher or an educational psychologist;
— a probation officer;
— a social worker from another adoption agency.

18. **Regulation 5(4)** permits the agency to fix a member's term of appointment to the panel, as well as any other conditions of appointment such as the payment of expenses and the provision of support services. Agencies may make appointments for whatever period seems appropriate and can appoint different members for different periods, bearing in mind the need to allow for the development and continuity of expertise. It is suggested that appointments should not normally be made for more than three years at a time (with the agency reserving the right to terminate the appointment without notice). Agencies can then, if they wish, re-appoint members for a further term of office.

19. **Regulation 5(5)** requires the panel's functions under the regulations to be carried out by its members meeting as a panel, in recognition of the collective nature of the panel's work. This means that the panel cannot conduct its business by correspondence (though papers for meetings can of course be circulated in advance under confidential cover). The quorum for panel meetings is 5, which must include one of the social workers employed by the agency. The quorum of 5 allows some flexibility to take account of individual members being ill or on holiday, or otherwise unavailable for a particular meeting. An absent member can in these

circumstances send comments in writing for the panel's consideration at its meeting. The social workers involved in a case (including, where relevant, the child's residential worker) should normally be in attendance during the panel's discussion of that particular case, and the agency's legal adviser should be invited to attend panel meetings as a matter of course.

20. The regulations make no special provision for deputies or substitutes for panel members, but the powers of appointment allow an appointment to be made for a particular occasion where necessary. Agencies must, however, ensure that the maximum panel membership of 10 is not exceeded and that the required categories of members (as set out in regulation 5(2) and (3)) are maintained.

21. **Regulation 5(6)** requires the panel to keep a written record of its recommendations.

Regulation 6: Adoption Agency Arrangements for Adoption Work

3–007

22. The effect of **regulation 6(1)** is to require agencies to have written policy and procedural instructions for their adoption work and for the adoption panel's functions. These instructions must be drawn up in consultation with the panel, and the agency's medical adviser must be consulted about the arrangements for disclosing health information. The policy and procedural instructions must be reviewed periodically, at least every three years, so that their continuing appropriateness can be checked. This enables changes to be made to take account of developments in service provision and in professional practice.

23. **Regulation 6(2)** sets out some of the matters which must be covered by the agency's policy and procedural instructions. They are mainly concerned with the confidentiality of adoption information, and this regulation must be read in conjunction with the detailed requirements in regulation 14 for the confidentiality and preservation of case records, and in regulation 15 for access to the records and disclosure of information.

24. **Regulation 6(2)(a)** requires the policy and procedural instructions to cover arrangements for maintaining the confidentiality and safekeeping of adoption information and the adoption case records and their indexes. This includes ensuring the physical security of manual records and the security of any computerised information.

25. **Regulation 6(2)(b)** requires the policy and procedural instructions to cover arrangements for authorising access to the adoption case records and their indexes, and for authorising the disclosure of adoption information. Access and disclosure is *only* permitted in the circumstances set out in regulation 15, but it is important that there should be clear rules for authorising access or disclosure in those circumstances. Even though, for example, requests for access or disclosure under regulation 15(1) *must* be complied with, staff need to be aware that they themselves are not individually responsible for verifying the authenticity of such requests (unless that is what the agency's arrangements provide). The arrangements should normally provide for these requests to be referred to the Director of Social Services in a local authority or to the equivalent senior manager in an approved adoption society, so that he is not only aware of the request but can satisfy himself that the request is properly made and, where necessary, can verify the credentials of the person making the request. Similar arrangements are needed for requests under regulation 15(2)(b) from authorised researchers, though in such cases the agency is free to decline such requests if it does not wish to participate in the research.

26. It is equally important for the agency's policy and procedural instructions to cover the circumstances where it might wish to make records or information available under regulation 15(2)(a), *both within and outside the agency*, for the purposes of its functions as an adoption agency. All staff need to know how requests for such access or disclosure are dealt with, and who is empowered to authorise them. **Regulation 6(2)(c)** contains an important safeguard for ensuring the confidentiality of adoption information disclosed under regulation 15(2)(a). Anyone within or outside the agency (including the agency's own members and employees, and members of its adoption panel) to whom the agency wishes to make case records or information available under the regulation must first agree in writing that the information will remain confidential, and disclosure cannot be authorised unless such agreement has been given. The agency's policy and procedural instructions must therefore include provision for explaining to those concerned that adoption information is confidential and that whatever is disclosed to them must remain confidential, and for obtaining their written agreement to this.

27. This requirement to obtain written agreement that confidentiality will be preserved does not, however, apply to the child himself or to the adopters, as they might be unnecessarily intimidated by the formality of having to give a written undertaking. They should not be inhibited from talking naturally about the adoption within their own family circles, although the confidential nature of any adoption information disclosed to the child (perhaps, when he is an adult, in the context of "birth records" counselling) or to the adopters should nevertheless be explained to them.

28. **Regulation 6(3)** requires the agency to consider what experience and qualifications its social work staff should have, and to satisfy itself that each member of the social work staff has such experience and/or qualifications. Wherever possible, staff employed on adoption work should be professionally qualified and have skills and expertise in working with families and children. The regulation permits the agency, if it wishes, to attach different requirements to different posts, and even to have very limited requirements if that seems appropriate, such as in the case of a student doing a restricted range of work under proper supervision.

29. **Regulation 6(4)** requires the agency to have a qualified medical adviser, because of the importance of the health aspects of adoption work. This is increasing with the growing numbers of older children and children with special health needs who are being adopted. The medical adviser must be a member of the agency's adoption panel, and his principal function is to evaluate the health information available to the panel and to advise them about its implications in relation to adoption. (It is recommended that the medical report forms produced by British Agencies for Adoption and Fostering should be used for obtaining health information, as they cover all the health matters listed in the schedule to the regulations). The medical adviser also needs to be involved in the agency's arrangements for meeting the requirements of the regulations for the agency to:

— disclose health information only in accordance with arrangements about which the medical adviser has been consulted — regulation 6(5);
— obtain health information about each natural parent — regulation 7(2)(b);
— obtain a report on the child's health — regulation 7(2)(c);
— arrange any other examinations, screening procedures and tests on the child and his parents which the medical adviser recommends — regulation 7(2)(d);
— obtain a report on each prospective adopter's health — regulation 8(2)(c);
— provide the prospective adopters before the placement with information about the child's health — regulation 12(1);
— send a report on the child's health to the prospective adopters' GP before the placement — regulation 12(2)(b);
— notify the prospective adopters' district health authority before the placement — regulation 12(2)(c);
— notify the prospective adopters' local education authority before the placement if the child is of school age or the medical adviser considers him to be handicapped — regulation 12(2)(d);
— monitor the child's health during the placement to the extent that the medical adviser considers necessary — regulation 12(2)(j).

Because of the importance of the medical adviser's role, he should be suitably qualified and should be expected to carry out his functions personally. Agencies may wish to approach their district health authority for advice on a suitable appointment, and agencies which are local authorities should arrange with the district health authority through the joint collaborative machinery for the nomination of a medical adviser and the provision of health services and advice under section 26 of the National Health Service Act 1977.

30. **Regulation 6(5)** requires the agency to consult its medical adviser when drawing up its policy and procedural instructions for the disclosure of health information. This reflects the particular sensitivity of health information, and enables the medical adviser to ensure that the arrangements accord with his profession's ethical practice. Health information can be disclosed under the regulations *only* in accordance with the arrangements about which the medical adviser has been consulted.

Regulation 7: Adoption Agency's Duties in Respect of a Child and his Parents or Guardian

31. **Regulation 7** sets out the action which an adoption agency must take before it can **3–008** decide whether or not adoption is in the best interests of a particular child. Under **regulation 7(1)(a)**, the agency must first provide a counselling service for the child and his parents or guardian (though counselling for the child will depend on his age and understanding). The purpose of counselling is to ensure that the parents are aware of their rights and responsibilities, that alternatives to adoption are realistically explored, and that the nature and implications of adoption are fully discussed. This gives the parents the opportunity to express their views and discuss their anxieties. The agency must carefully assess and discuss with them the various ways in which the child's future care may be provided for. They should be helped to understand the child's needs, and should be involved in planning jointly with the agency for his future care. In appropriate cases, the parents should be referred to other adoption agencies which might be able to meet their wishes about the child's religious or cultural upbringing.

32. The agency is also required by regulation 7(1)(a) to explain the legal requirements and procedures of adoption and freeing orders, including the choice of procedure for giving

agreement to adoption which the freeing provisions offer the parents. Discussion of these matters provides a useful opportunity to clarify the parents' wishes. If they need advice on the legal implications, they should be encouraged to consult a lawyer as soon as possible so that they can decide what action to take, especially where they are unhappy with the proposed adoption. The parents (and the child, if he is old enough to understand) should be told what information the agency is required to obtain about them, and the purpose of this should be explained. They should also be informed about the confidentiality provisions and about the circumstances in which the agency may need to disclose information.

33. All the matters explained to the child and his parents under regulation 7(1)(a) must be set out in writing, and the agency should present the information as simply and straightforwardly as possible. Annex A to this circular provides a specimen information note for natural parents which agencies could use as a model for the purposes of this regulation; it should be adapted as appropriate for particular cases and for use with the child. The agency may wish to ask the child and his parents to acknowledge in writing that they have received the written information, and a formal report should be made for the case record of any refusal to accept it. They should always be asked to confirm in writing their agreement that information about them may be obtained and used in accordance with the regulations, and any refusal to give this agreement should be similarly noted for the case record.

34. The requirements of regulation 7(1)(a) apply whether it is the parent or the agency which takes the initiative in suggesting adoption for the child. This has the effect of ensuring that a natural parent's request to an agency to arrange the child's adoption is not put into action until the parent (and the child, if appropriate) has been properly counselled and the reasons for seeking adoption established, as it would be wrong for an agency simply to meet the parent's request uncritically. The agency should consider and discuss with the parent what support might be available from various sources, and should have access to relevant facilities and services.

35. The requirements of regulation 7(1)(a) also mean, for example, that where a local authority concludes — perhaps following a statutory review — that adoption should be considered for a child in care, the first step must be, if possible, to discuss the proposal with the child's parents and counsel them (and the child, if appropriate) about adoption. The same would apply if the child's foster parents approached the authority, wishing to adopt him, and the authority wanted to explore whether that would be in the child's best interests. Local authorities should bear in mind that children in care who would otherwise come within the scope of sections 12A to 12F of the Child Care Act 1980 are not excluded if they are placed for adoption. A local authority cannot terminate or refuse to make arrangements for access to such a child without first serving notice on the parents (or guardian), who have the right to apply to the juvenile court for an access order. Similarly, where a parent has obtained an access order, the order remains in force as long as the child is in care or until it is varied or discharged by a court. In most cases, it will be appropriate for the local authority to apply to the juvenile court for the access order to be discharged, at the same time as the application is made for a freeing or adoption order. The authority's proposals regarding access should be discussed with the parents and their legal rights explained to them. The question of parental access after the child has been placed for adoption may be especially important where the parents are not in agreement with the plans for the child's adoption.

36. When the agency prepares its report for the court on an application it is making for a freeing order or on an adoption placement it has made, the court rules require the report to include details of the alternatives to adoption which were considered, as well as the agency's opinion about the effect of adoption on the child's parents. Agencies therefore need to ensure that the preliminary work required by regulation 7(1)(a) is done thoroughly and sensitively. In cases where a parent is under the age of majority or is mentally incapable of acting for himself, the court will consider whether it is necessary for him to have his own guardian ad litem for the adoption proceedings.

3–009   37. If freeing for adoption is being considered, the agency may find that it needs to provide more intensive help to the child's parents within a shorter period than under the other adoption procedures. This is because freeing takes place at an earlier stage than full adoption and is designed to resolve the question of parental agreement, in suitable cases, with the minimum of delay. When the adoption panel is considering whether to recommend that a child should be freed for adoption, it must take the parents' wishes into account and, if they object to adoption, the panel must consider the need to enable the child's welfare to be secured by adoption despite parental opposition. If the agency does decide that the child should be freed for adoption, sensitive regard must be given to the needs of his parents, especially those who have not given their agreement to adoption. Many will need support to cope with the sense of loss of their child, and the agency should consider whether such help would be better provided by some other body.

38. It would only be appropriate to use the freeing procedure in the case of young mothers of new-born babies if there have been adequate opportunities before the confinement to discuss with the mother the options available to her for the care of her baby. If this has not been possible, sufficient time should be given following the birth to allow her to make up her mind. It is part of the reporting officer's functions in freeing and adoption proceedings to ensure that parental agreement to adoption is given freely and with full understanding of what is involved, and agencies should therefore recognise the importance of adequate counselling.

39. Where freeing for adoption is being considered, the agency should explain to the parents that a freeing order can be revoked after at least a year has passed since it was made, if the parent then wants to resume his parental rights and duties and the court is satisfied that this would safeguard and promote the child's long-term welfare. The parent can only apply for revocation if the child has not by then been adopted or placed for adoption, since the purpose is to allow the parent to resume his parental rights and duties only in the exceptional case where the agency has been unable to arrange the child's adoption. At the stage where freeing for adoption is being considered, the agency must explain to each parent that he can, if he wishes, make a formal declaration that he does not want to be further involved in questions about the child's adoption. If the parent does make such a declaration, he will not be kept informed by the agency about the child's position and will not be entitled to apply for revocation of the freeing order.

40. **Regulation 7(1)(b)** takes account of inter-agency work by permitting an agency to follow the subsequent procedures set out in regulation 7(2) even where it has not itself done the preliminary work required by regulation 7(1)(a) — the provision of counselling, explanations about adoption, and written information — provided it is satisfied that this has been done by another adoption agency. This might be the case, for example, where the parent has been referred to a denominational agency after the preliminary work has been carried out by another agency.

41. When the preliminary work under regulation 7(1)(a) has been carried out (whether by itself or another agency) and the agency is considering adoption as a possible plan for the child, it must then take the action set out in regulation 7(2). The agency should bear in mind throughout that it has a statutory duty (under section 3 of the 1975 Act) to give first consideration to the need to safeguard and promote the child's welfare throughout his childhood, and also to ascertain the child's own wishes and feelings and give them due consideration according to his age and understanding. If at any stage the agency decides that a plan other than adoption should be pursued, it is not required to complete all the procedures under regulation 7(2).

42. **Regulation 7(2)(a)** requires the agency, as a first step, to set up a case record for the child. The agency must file on this case record all the information it obtains about the child and his parents (including all medical reports and other health information) as well as its own reports to the adoption panel, the panel's recommendations, and a full record of the agency's actions and decisions in the case. The first document in the case record will normally be a note of the action taken under regulation 7(1), but where the child is already in the care of the agency, any relevant information from the existing case record should be copied to the adoption case record when it is set up. Under regulation 14, the adoption case record and its contents are confidential and must be kept in a place of special security.

43. **Regulation 7(2)(b)** requires the agency to obtain, as far as it can, the particulars about the child and his parents which are listed in the schedule to the regulations. This covers personal, family, social and (for parents) health information, but agencies should not regard it as an exhaustive list which will provide all the relevant information for every case. Health information on the natural parents should be sought from a doctor who knows the parent and has access to the relevant records, which will usually be the GP. He and others approached for information under this regulation (such as teachers and those currently caring for the child) should be advised of the confidentiality requirements. The agency should explain to the parents why the fullest possible background information about the child and his family (including health information about the parents) is needed to help the agency, the adoptive parents and the child himself.

44. If the adoption panel, when it comes to consider the case, feels that it has insufficient information, or that the information it has is inadequate or out-of-date, it must request the agency under regulation 10(3)(b) to obtain further relevant information, and this regulation requires the agency to meet such requests as far as it can.

45. **Regulation 7(2)(c)** is designed to ensure that the agency has available a recent report on **3–010** the child's health, covering his health history and a full medical examination as set out in the schedule to the regulations. If such a report has not been made within the previous six months (strictly, within the six months before the case record was set up), the agency must obtain one. The agency's written procedural instructions under regulation 6(1) should cover the arrange-

ments for obtaining these reports, and they should normally be requested by the agency's medical adviser (if he does not himself carry out the examination and make the report). The medical adviser's request to the examining doctor should indicate that the purpose of the report is to help build up a full picture of the child's health history and current state of health, including strengths and weaknesses, so that the medical adviser can properly assess the health implications of adoption and advise the agency accordingly. In obtaining this report and any other health information on the child or his parents, the medical adviser should advise those approached about the confidentiality requirements.

46. The medical adviser should also arrange for any other available health information to be obtained. This includes approaching the child's GP if he was not the examining doctor for the report under regulation 7(2)(c), the district health authority for information from the community health services (including health visitors) and, where appropriate, the school health service. The medical adviser might also wish in relevant cases to obtain further information from consultants who are (or have been) treating the child.

47. When the medical adviser has considered the report on the child's health and any other available health information, he must recommend the number and timing of any further examinations or screening tests which he feels are necessary in order to provide adequate and up-to-date health information about the child for the adoption panel. In recommending developmental tests and screening procedures in accordance with current good practice, the medical adviser should take into account all the relevant social, epidemiological and local environmental factors, as well as the child's age and race and the health history. **Regulation 7(2)(d)** requires the agency to arrange any examinations or screening tests on the child which the medical adviser recommends, and to obtain written reports of them. This regulation similarly requires the agency to arrange, as far as it can, any examinations or screening tests on the child's parents which the medical adviser recommends after considering the health information about them which the agency has obtained under regulation 7(2)(b). This might include, for example, obtaining an up-to-date report on the development of an inherited disease.

48. When the agency has obtained all the information about the child and his parents which it is required to obtain under regulation 7(2)(b) to (d), it must then assess the information and set out its views in a written report. This should identify the sources of the agency's information, and should include assessments of the child's relationship with members of his family and other people who have close links with him, of his emotional and physical needs, and of the best way of safeguarding and promoting his long-term welfare. It should also include a summary by the medical adviser of the health history and state of health of the child and his parents, with comments on the implications for adoption and on how any special health needs of the child might be met. Although the views set out in the report will necessarily indicate which way the social workers involved in the case are thinking, the report must not pre-judge the issues which are for the adoption panel to consider. **Regulation 7(2)(e)** requires this report and all the information the agency has obtained to be passed to the adoption panel or, in an inter-agency case, to another adoption agency instead. Transferring information to another adoption agency at this stage may save time and avoid duplication of effort where a possible inter-agency placement is being considered, since only one agency need refer the case to its panel and make a decision in accordance with regulation 11(1).

49. Where the agency has itself received from another agency a report and information which that agency has passed to it under this regulation, the agency must ensure that all the requirements of regulation 7 have been carried out. To the extent that they have not already been carried out by the other agency, the agency must do so itself. In any event, it must set up its own case record for the child and must prepare its own written report before referring the case to its adoption panel. This report can be very short if the agency has nothing to add to the first agency's report except to comment on the circumstances of the inter-agency referral.

50. Although a child's case cannot be referred to the adoption panel under regulation 7(2)(e) until all the prior work under regulation 7(1) and (2) has been carried out, the agency may wish to ask the panel to discuss informally the case of a natural parent's expected child (and perhaps to give preliminary consideration to a possible placement with particular prospective adopters). This will enable the formal consideration of the case to be carried out more speedily once the child is born so that, in appropriate cases, there will be a minimum of delay in arranging the placement.

51. **Regulation 7(3)** is concerned with the father of an illegitimate child, and imposes the same duties on the agency in relation to him (where his identity is known) as it has in relation to other natural parents. The agency is not required to carry out these duties, however, if this does not seem to be both practicable and in the child's interests (though it will always be desirable to obtain as much health information as possible). An example of circumstances where the agency would be justified in not involving the putative father might be where the child was conceived as the result of rape.

258

52. **Regulation 7(3)(a)** requires the agency to carry out with the putative father the same preliminary counselling and information-giving work as for other natural parents under regulation 7(1)(a), unless another adoption agency has already done this work. This enables the agency to inform the putative father of his parental rights and responsibilities, and gives him the opportunity to express his views about his role. If he is married, the agency should consider whether it would be desirable, with his permission, to establish his wife's views. **Regulation 7(3)(b)** requires the agency to obtain the same information about the putative father as for other natural parents under regulation 7(2)(b) and (d), and **regulation 7(3)(c)** requires the agency, in addition, to find out whether he intends to apply for legal custody of the child. In seeking information from or about the putative father, the agency will need (as with all natural parents) to balance the child's needs and interests against the parent's right to privacy.

Regulation 8: Adoption Agency's Duties in Respect of a Prospective Adopter

53. **Regulation 8** sets out the action which an adoption agency must take before it can **3–011** decide whether a person is suitable to be an adoptive parent. This applies whether or not the agency has a particular child in mind (which might be the case, for example, with the child's existing foster parents, or if the couple have responded to a recruitment campaign for a specific child). Under **regulation 8(1)(a)**, the agency must first provide a counselling service, reflecting the need for adequate education and preparation for adoptive parents. Counselling should help to ensure that the prospective adopters fully understand the nature and effect of adoption and what is involved in bringing up someone else's child as one's own, and it also enables the agency to explore with the prospective adopters such crucial matters as their attitude to illegitimacy, heredity and infertility.

54. As well as providing a counselling service, the agency must explain the legal requirements and procedures of adoption and must set this out in writing. The prospective adopters should be told what information the agency is required to obtain about them and what enquiries it has to make under the regulations, and the purpose of this should be explained. They should also be informed about the confidentiality provisions and about the circumstances in which the agency may need to disclose information. They should be asked to confirm in writing their agreement that information about them may be obtained and used in accordance with the regulations.

55. **Regulation 8(1)(b)** takes account of inter-agency work by permitting an agency to follow the subsequent procedures set out in regulation 8(2) even where it has not itself done the preliminary work required by regulation 8(1)(a), provided it is satisfied that this has been done by another adoption agency.

56. When the preliminary work under regulation 8(1)(a) has been carried out (whether by itself or another agency) and the agency wishes to consider the suitability of the prospective adopter, it must then take the action set out in regulation 8(2). The requirement for preliminary work to be carried out first under regulation 8(1)(a) means that it is not necessary for the agency to start taking the detailed action under regulation 8(2) in response to every initial enquiry. Some applicants might not wish to pursue the possibility of adoption once they have received the counselling and explanation required under regulation 8(1)(a). Only after the prospective adopter has been counselled and the agency considers that he may be suitable to be an adoptive parent does the screening process begin. Once action under regulation 8(2) has started, if either the agency or the prospective adopter subsequently decides that his wish to adopt should not be pursued further, the agency is not required to complete all the procedures under that regulation.

57. When the agency does consider that the prospective adopter may be suitable, **regulation 8(2)(a)** requires it, as a first step, to set up a case record for him. In the case of a married couple, a single case record for them both can be set up. The agency must file on this case record all the information it obtains about the prospective adopter (including all medical reports and other health information) as well as its own reports to the adoption panel, the panel's recommendations, and a full record of the agency's actions and decisions in the case. The first document in the case record will normally be a note of the action taken under regulation 8(1). Under regulation 14, the case record and its contents are confidential and must be kept in a place of special security.

58. **Regulation 8(2)(b)** requires the agency to obtain the particulars about the prospective adopters which are listed in the schedule to the regulations. This covers personal, family and social information, but agencies should not regard it as an exhaustive list which will provide all the relevant information for every case. If the adoption panel, when it comes to consider the case, feels that it has insufficient information or that the information it has is inadequate or out-of-date, it must request the agency under regulation 10(3)(b) to obtain further relevant information, and this regulation requires the agency to meet such requests as far as it can.

259

59. **Regulation 8(2)(c)** requires the agency to obtain a report on the prospective adopter's health, covering his health history and a full medical examination as set out in the schedule to the regulations. The agency's written procedural instructions under regulation 6(1) should cover the arrangements for obtaining these reports, and they should normally be requested by the agency's medical adviser from the prospective adopter's GP, since he will know the prospective adopter and have access to the relevant records. (In cases where the prospective adopter is not registered under the NHS — such as where a foreign serviceman wishes to take a child abroad for adoption — the request should be sent to his medical practitioner). The medical adviser's request should indicate that the purpose of the report is to build up a full picture of the prospective adopter's health history and current state of health, including strengths and weaknesses, so that the medical adviser can properly assess the health implications of adoption and advise the agency accordingly whether there are any known health reasons why the prospective adopter would be unlikely to care adequately for a child until the age of independence. The medical adviser should consider whether any other relevant health information needs to be obtained to complement the health report, and he may wish, for example, to approach the district health authority for information from the community health services. In obtaining the health report and any other health information he considers necessary, the medical adviser should advise those approached about the confidentiality requirements.

3–012   60. The agency does not have to obtain a current report on the prospective adopter's health under this regulation if it already has available such a report made within the previous six months (strictly, within the six months before the case record was set up). This avoids unnecessary effort and expense where, for example, a report was obtained recently under this regulation by another adoption agency.

61. **Regulation 8(2)(d)** requires the agency to obtain a written report on the prospective adopter's home. This report should include general comment on the accommodation, living conditions and home environment, and also the accessibility of schools, churches and other neighbourhood facilities. If it is possible that the placement of a child with special educational or health needs might be considered for this prospective adopter, the availability and accessibility of suitable services should be covered in the report. The agency need not itself prepare this report on the prospective adopter's home, if it would be more convenient to ask someone else, perhaps another adoption agency, to do so. In the case of a proposed foreign adoption, the agency must arrange to obtain a report on the prospective adopter's home in his own country.

62. The particulars about the prospective adopter which the agency is required to obtain under regulation 8(2)(b) include the names and addresses of two personal referees. **Regulation 8(2)(e)** requires the agency to take up these references by obtaining a report of interviews with the referees. They should preferably be from different households (ie not a married couple) and should be people who know the prospective adopters well as a family but are not related to them. The referees must be interviewed, as this enables the agency to assess how well they know the prospective adopters and also the weight to be placed on their views. If the prospective adopters and also the weight to be placed on their views. If the prospective adopters do subsequently apply for an adoption order, the agency's report to the court must include its opinion of the weight to be placed on the referees' views, and the agency should therefore also cover this in its report to its adoption panel under regulation 8(2)(g).

63. **Regulation 8(2)(f)** requires the agency to consult the prospective adopter's local authority and obtain a written report. On receipt of such a request the local authority should make the usual enquiries of the police, but the district health authority need not be approached as this should have been done, where appropriate, by the agency's medical adviser. The local authority's report to the adoption agency should include any relevant information from its own records, particularly in relation to any previous experience the prospective adopter has had in caring for other people's children as a foster parent, childminder or prospective adopter, and any criminal convictions under child care law. This report is required even where the local authority is itself the adoption agency requesting the report, because it is still necessary to have a formal record of the outcome of the police enquiries and of any other relevant information held by the authority.

64. When the agency has obtained all the information about the prospective adopters which it is required to obtain under regulation 8(2)(b) to (f), it must then assess the information and set out its views in a written report. This should identify the sources of the agency's information, and should include an assessment of the prospective adopters' ability to cope with a child as he grows into adulthood. It should also include a summary by the medical adviser of the health history and state of health of the prospective adopters, with comments on the implications for adoption. Although the views set out in the report will necessarily indicate which way the social workers involved in the case are thinking, the report must not pre-judge

the issues which are for the adoption panel to consider. **Regulation 8(2)(g)** requires this report and all the information the agency has obtained to be passed to the adoption panel or, in an inter-agency case, to another adoption agency instead. Transferring information to another adoption agency at this stage may save time and avoid duplication of effort where a possible inter-agency placement is being considered, since only one agency need refer the case to its panel and make a decision in accordance with regulation 11(1).

65. Where the agency has itself received from another agency a report and information which that agency has passed to it under this regulation, the agency must ensure that all the requirements of regulation 8 have been carried out. To the extent that they have not been carried out by the other agency, the agency must do so itself. In any event, It must set up its own case record for the prospective adopter and must prepare its own written report before referring the case to its adoption panel. This report can be very short if the agency has nothing to add to the first agency's report except to comment on the circumstances of the inter-agency referral.

Regulation 9: Adoption Agency's Duties in Respect of Proposed Placement

66. **Regulation 9(1)** requires an adoption agency to refer every proposed placement to the **3–013** adoption panel for its consideration. (In an inter-agency case, the proposed placement can be referred by the other adoption agency to its panel instead, which enables the agencies to agree between themselves which should make the placement decision). The panel must be given a written report of the agency's views on the proposed placement, which should include the agency's reasons for considering that those prospective adopters might be able to meet that particular child's needs and might therefore be suitable adoptive parents for him. The report must not, however, pre-judge the issues which are for the panel to consider. The agency must also give the panel all the information which is relevant to the proposed placement, and should identify the sources of any information which has not previously been passed to the panel. This will be information which the agency has obtained (perhaps from another adoption agency) since the decisions were made that adoption is in the best interests of that child and that those prospective adopters are suitable to be adoptive parents (unless recommendations on those matters have just been made by the panel at the same meeting at which the placement decision is being considered). Such information might include, for example:
— the natural parents' response to the formal notification under regulation 11(2)(a) of the agency decision that adoption is in the child's best interests (this response might, for example, lead the panel to reconsider its earlier recommendation that a freeing order should *not* be applied for);
— the care arrangements made for the child since that decision (including information about any adoption placement which has disrupted);
— if the agency has applied for a freeing order, the outcome of the application;
— the action taken to prepare the child for placement;
— where appropriate, the child's wishes and feelings about the possible placement;
— any necessary updating of the information previously passed to the panel (for example, any further reports which the medical adviser has recommended should be obtained on the health of the child or the prospective adopters, so that he can confirm to the panel that the health information is adequate and up-to-date):
— if the child has special educational or health needs, the availability and accessibility of suitable services (about which it may have been necessary to consult the prospective adopters' local education authority or district health authority);
— the views of any bodies consulted under regulation 9(2).
67. The placement of a baby direct from hospital should be considered only where the mother has had time to reflect on her pre-birth decision and remains firm in her intention about adoption, and where the medical adviser confirms that he has no reservations about an early placement because of health risks or peri-natal complications. If there are any particular risk factors in such a case, the medical adviser will need to ensure that their implications are carefully explained to the prospective adopters.
68. **Regulation 9(2)** prohibits the agency from referring a proposed placement to its panel unless certain bodies have first been consulted. This is necessary because the regulations allow for a great deal of flexibility in inter-agency cases, and do not require a particular adoption agency to make the placement decision in a given case. The first type of organisation which must be consulted about the proposed placement is any other adoption agency which decided that adoption is in that child's best interests or that those prospective adopters are suitable to be adoptive parents (linking agencies need not therefore, be formally consulted). The other type of organisation which must be consulted is any local authority or voluntary organisation

in whose care the child is (whether voluntarily or under a court order) or, if he has been freed for adoption, which has parental rights and duties under section 14 or 23 of the 1975 Act. Any such body must not only be consulted but must also *agree with* the proposed placement, in recognition of its legal responsibility towards the child. This provision ensures, for example, that a local authority which has asked another adoption agency to arrange the adoption of a child in its care (perhaps because it does not itself have an adoption panel) can prevent a possible placement about which it may have misgivings.

69. **Regulation 9(3)** requires the agency dealing with a proposed placement to set up a case record for the child or prospective adopter if it does not already have one. This will be necessary in an inter-agency case where the other agency has already decided that adoption is in that child's best interests or that those prospective adopters are suitable to be adoptive parents. That other agency will have transferred under regulation 16 a copy of all or part of its own case record (including information, reports and decisions), which must be filed on the case record set up by the agency dealing with the proposed placement. Any information about the proposed placement which is passed to the adoption panel must also be filed on the case record.

70. If the adoption panel considers that it has insufficient information about a proposed placement which the agency has referred to it, or that the information provided by the agency is inadequate or out-of-date, it must request the agency under regulation 10(3)(b) to obtain any other relevant information which it thinks is necessary, and the agency has a duty under **regulations 9(4)** to obtain that information as far as it can.

Regulation 10: Adoption Panel Functions

3–014   71. **Regulation 10(1)** requires the adoption panel to consider all the cases referred to it by the adoption agency, subject to the provisions of regulations 10(2) about the timing of the panel's recommendations and the provisions of regulation 10(3) about how cases must be considered. Where a child's case is referred, the panel must recommend to the agency under **regulation 10(1)(a)** whether adoption is in the child's best interests and, if so, whether he should be freed for adoption. Where a prospective adopter's case is referred, the panel must recommend to the agency under **regulation 10(1)(b)** whether he is suitable to be an adoptive parent, and where a proposed placement is referred, the panel must recommend to the agency under **regulation 10(1)(c)** whether the prospective adopter would be suitable adoptive parent for that particular child. The panel's functions need not, however, be limited to the matters set out in regulation 10(1). The agency might, for example, wish to ask the panel to make recommendations about fostering as well as adoption placements.

72. Annex B to this circular sets out the steps involved in a placement decision. A child cannot be placed for adoption unless the adoption agency has first taken account of its panel's recommendation about the proposed placement and has decided that those prospective adopters would be suitable adoptive parents for that particular child. But **regulation 10(2)** ensures that the panel cannot in the first place make a recommendation to the agency about a proposed placement unless the question has already been resolved:

— that adoption is in that child's best interests, and
— that those prospective adopters are suitable to be adoptive parents.

This regulation takes account of the fact that one or both of these issues may only have come before the panel at the same meeting at which it wishes to consider a proposed placement. Unless that is the case, however, the panel cannot make a recommendation about a proposed placement unless there has already been an adoption agency decision in accordance with regulation 11(1) about both these issues (or about the one which the panel is not considering earlier at the same meeting).

73. The adoption agency decision in accordance with regulation 11(1) need not have been made by the panel's agency. Only one decision is required under the regulations on each of the matters set out in regulation 10(1), to avoid the need for duplication of decisions in inter-agency cases. When a possible inter-agency placement comes to be considered, therefore, the agencies should agree in advance between themselves which panel the case should be referred to under regulation 9(1). The agency which decides that the prospective adopters are suitable adoptive parents for that child is responsible for the placement duties under regulation 12(2): these include the duty of placing the child with the prospective adopters, and it is therefore that agency which has placed the child for adoption for the purposes of section 22(3) of the 1975 Act and which must make the statutory report to the court. (The position is slightly different, however, where an inter-agency case involves an adoption agency in Scotland: since a Scottish agency *cannot* make a decision in accordance with regulations which do not apply to Scotland, the English agency must first follow the requirements of regulation 7 or 8 (depending on whether the Scottish agency has referred the child or the prospective adopter),

and that issue must be considered by the adoption panel before it considers the proposed placement).

74. Regulation 10(2) permits the panel to make its recommendations in a particular case on all three of the matters set out in regulation 10(1) either at the same time or at different times. Occasions when all three recommendations are made at the same time in respect of a particular child and particular prospective adopters are likely to be rare, except in the case of existing foster placements, but it will not be uncommon for two recommendations to be made at one panel meeting. This might happen, for example, where the panel has previously discussed informally the possible placement of a natural parent's expected child with particular prospective adopters for whom there has already been an agency decision that they would be suitable to be adoptive parents. When the child has been born, the panel might then at its next meeting recommend both that adoption would be in his best interests (and possibly that he should be freed for adoption) and also that those prospective adopters would be suitable adoptive parents for him. Or, if the prospective adopters have been recruited for a specific child (and it has already been decided that adoption is in his best interests), the panel might at the same meeting recommend both that they are suitable to be adoptive parents and also that they would be suitable adoptive parents for that child.

75. The restriction in regulation 10(2) about the timing of the panel's recommendations does not apply to its recommendation that a child should be freed for adoption. This is because circumstances can change after the decision has been made that adoption is in the child's best interests — perhaps even after he has been placed for adoption — which mean that the question of freeing ought to be reconsidered.

76. **Regulation 10(3)** requires the panel, when it is considering what recommendations to **3–015** make to the agency on the matters set out in regulation 10(1), to bear in mind the following statutory obligations on the agency.
— the agency's duty under section 3 of the 1975 Act to have regard to all the circumstances when making any decision about a child's adoption, to give first consideration to the need to safeguard and promote his welfare throughout his childhood, to ascertain his wishes and feelings as far as it can and to give these due consideration in the light of his age and understanding;
— the agency's duty under section 13 of the 1975 Act to have regard as far as it can, when placing a child for adoption, to any wishes of his parents or guardian about his religious upbringing.

77. **Regulation 10(3)(a)** requires the panel, when it is considering what recommendations to make to the agency on the matters set out in regulation 10(1), to consider and take into account all the information and reports which have been passed to it by the agency. If the panel feels that it has insufficient information about the case, or that the information is inadequate or out-of-date, regulation 10(3)(b) requires it to request any other relevant information which it thinks is necessary. This might, for example, concern the father of an illegitimate child, if the panel is not satisfied with the extent of any work done with him, or with the reasons given in the agency's report why information about him has not been obtained. If the panel does think any additional information is needed, it has no discretion to decide *not* to ask the agency for the information, since this provision is mandatory.

78. **Regulation 10(3)(c)** requires the panel, when it is considering what recommendations to make to the agency on the matters set out in regulation 10(1), to obtain legal advice on the case generally and on an application for an adoption or freeing order. This will include advice as to whether there are any possible problems with the legal requirements for an adoption or freeing order, as well as advice on wider legal aspects if, for example, the child is in care or is a ward of court, or if his legal status is relevant in some other way. An adoption agency's legal adviser needs to be well-experienced in family and child care law and in adoption work, and it is desirable for him to be in attendance at the meeting when the adoption panel considers a complicated case, so that he can explain the issues more fully to the panel.

79. It is important that all cases should be seen by the legal adviser, as even an apparently straightforward case may contain legal snags which his early advice can help prevent from becoming major obstacles to securing a desirable adoption. He needs to scrutinise with particular care the agency's evidence to support a request for parental agreement to adoption to be dispensed with, and other matters on which his advice may be needed include:
— where the agency may wish to free a child for adoption, the likely outcome of the putative father's application for custody;
— where a proposed foreign adoption is being considered, the prospective adopters' ability to meet the legal requirements for adoption in their own country;
— where an application is pending for revocation of a freeing order, the desirability of seeking leave of the court to place the child for adoption;
— when Part II of the 1975 Act is in force, the relative merits of adoption and custodianship in the particular case.

Regulation 11: Adoption Agency Decisions and Notifications

3–016   80. An adoption agency's decisions about adoption are, in law, the responsibility of the agency itself and must therefore be made by the agency. The adoption panel can only make *recommendations* on the matters set out in regulation 10(1), and it is for the agency then to make *decisions* on those matters. But regulation 11(1) recognises the panel's vital and expert role in giving detailed consideration to the matters concerned, by prohibiting the agency from making any decision on them unless it has first taken the panel's recommendations into account are its decisions about:
  — whether adoption is in the best interests of a particular child and, if so, whether he should be freed for adoption;
  — whether particular prospective adopters are suitable to be adoptive parents;
  — whether particular prospective adopters would be suitable adoptive parents for a particular child.

81. Although it is the agency's responsibility to make these decisions, the agency may wish to exercise any legal powers it has to delegate them. In the case of a local authority, this can for example, under the powers governing the delegation of social services functions, be to an adoption sub-committee of the social services committee or to a local authority officer such as the Director of Social Services. In the case of an approved adoption society, delegation may perhaps be to a sub-committee of the management committee or to an officer of the society, depending on what the agency's constitution allows.

82. When the agency has decided whether adoption is in the best interests of a particular child, regulation 11(2)(a) requires the agency to give the child's parents or guardian written notification of the decision as soon as possible (if the agency knows their whereabouts). This requirement must be followed whatever the agency's decision is, and notification must therefore be given of a decision that adoption is *not* in the child's best interests. The putative father must be notified under this regulation if the agency considers that doing so would be in the child's interests. If a parent is known to be unhappy about the idea of adoption, a notification that adoption *is* in the child's best interests should normally, as a matter of good practice, be given to the parent in the course of a counselling interview in which the reasons for the agency's decision are explained to him. The agency should keep a copy of every notification under this regulation, for production to the court if required.

83. **Regulation 11(2)(b)** requires the agency to notify the child's parents or guardian similarly about its decision whether the child should be freed for adoption, if it has been decided that adoption is in his best interests. There may possibly be more than one decision about freeing, if the question is reconsidered because of a change in circumstances. In such a case, each decision must be notified to the parents or guardian, so that they are kept fully informed about the agency's plans for the child.

84. When the agency has decided whether a particular prospective adopter is suitable to be an adoptive parent, **regulation 11(2)(c)** requires the agency to give him written notification of the decision as soon as possible. If the agency's decision is that he is *not* suitable, the reasons for the decision should be fully recorded in the case record (and, if health factors are involved, the agency's medical adviser should inform the prospective adopters' GP in confidence). In these cases, it is normally appropriate, as a matter of good practice, for the formal written notification required by this regulation to be given to the prospective adopter in the course of a counselling interview at which the reasons for the agency's decision are, wherever possible, explained to him. This may not be possible if, for example, information about health or criminal offences is known to one spouse but not the other.

85. **Regulation 11(2)(d)** requires the agency to give the prospective adopter written notification as soon as possible of a decision that he is suitable as an adoptive parent for a particular child. The agency may wish to give this formal notification to the prospective adopters at the same time as they are given details of the child and of the agency's proposals for the adoption, under regulation 12(1). The requirement to notify the prospective adopter of the decision about a possible placement does not apply to the decision *not* to place a particular child with him. If, however, the prospective adopter has been aware that the possibility of placing a particular child with him was being considered, the agency should let him know of the decision not to do so, even though a formal notification under this regulation is not required.

Regulation 12: Placement for Adoption

3–017   86. When an adoption agency has decided that particular prospective adopters are suitable adoptive parents for a particular child, **regulation 12(1)** requires the agency to give them written information about the child and about the agency's proposals for the adoption. This must be done before the child is placed for adoption. The details which must be provided about the child must cover his personal history and background, including his religious and cultural background. It should be explained to the prospective adopters that the information is provided not only to help them bring up the child but also on behalf of the child himself. They should be reminded of the importance of his need, over the years, for knowledge about his natural family. This would also be an appropriate opportunity for the agency to remind the prospective adopters about general matters that will already have been discussed with them, and Annex C to this circular provides a specimen information note which agencies may wish to use as a model for this.

87. The details which the prospective adopters must be given under this regulation also include the child's health history and current state of health, and the agency's medical adviser should arrange for them to be advised about the child's health needs and for any health problem to be fully discussed with them. If the placement of a baby direct from hospital is being proposed, the medical adviser should ensure that it is carefully explained to the prospective adopters that only preliminary health screening and assessment has so far been possible; he should also ensure that the implications of any particular risk factors are explained. It is essential for the prospective adopters to receive these explanations, so that they can decide whether they wish to go ahead with the placement, and so that any risk of their understaking more than they feel they can manage is minimised.

88. The agency should include in its written proposals for the adoption, as well as the proposed date of placement, such matters as the approximate length of time the agency considers will be needed before it would be appropriate for the prospective adopters to apply for an adoption order, any plans for periodic review of the placement, details of any adoption allowance that would be paid, confirmation of the agency's support if the case is contested (including the payment of legal fees, if necessary), and details of any proposed continuing contact with the child's natural family. The prospective adopters should also be told about the notifications which will be sent under regulation 12(2), if they accept the agency's proposals, to their GP and to the local authority, district health authority and (if relevant) the local education authority.

89. **Regulation 12(2)** sets out the action which the agency must take if the prospective adopters accept its proposals for placing a particular child with them. The prospective adopters' acceptance of the agency's proposals does not have to be given in writing, but this would obviously be preferable. (If the proposals are *not* accepted, the agency should retrieve from the prospective adopters the written information about the child which they were given under regulation 12(1)). **Regulation 12(2)(a)** requires the agency to inform the child in advance about the proposed placement, if he is able to understand the proposal. The agency should also ensure that he has been appropriately prepared for placement. If he is old enough, the agency should consider whether to give him a copy of the background information which was given to the prospective adopters under regulation 12(1).

90. **Regulation 12(2)(b)** requires the agency to send the prospective adopters' GP, in advance of the proposed placement, a written report of the child's health history and current state of health. This helps to avoid any hiatus in the arrangements for the health care of the child. When giving the GP particulars of the proposed placement (including the date), the agency should remind him to treat the information as confidential. The child's proposed new name should be given, and his present name need not be mentioned unless it appears that the GP already knows it (which might be the case, for example, if the child is already registered with that GP because he has been boarded-out for some time with the prospective adopters).

91. **Regulation 12(2)(c)** requires the agency to send advance written notification of the proposed placement to the prospective adopters' local authority and district health authority. The notification should include the child's proposed new name and the date of the proposed placement, and, in the case of the district health authority, the name and address of the GP to whom the report on the child's health has been sent under regulation 12(2)(b). The notification should also remind the authorities to treat the information notified to them as confidential. If the child is handicapped, the local authority's attention should be drawn to the possible need for services under the Chronically Sick and Disabled Persons Act 1970. If the child is handicapped or under 5, the district health authority's attention should be drawn to the need to alert the health visitor to the proposed placement so that the desirability of an early visit can be considered.

92. **Regulation 12(2)(d)** requires the agency to send advance written notification of the proposed placement to the prospective adopters' local education authority, in cases where the child is of compulsory school age or is considered by the agency's medical adviser to be handicapped. This enables the authority to make any necessary administrative arrangements, and to ensure continuity of the arrangements for the child's education if he has special educational needs under the Education Act 1981. The agency's notification should include the

child's proposed new name and the date of the proposed placement, and should remind the authority to treat the information notified to them as confidential.

93. **Regulation 12(2)(e)** requires the agency to place the child for adoption with the prospective adopters, after the duties in regulation 12(2)(a) to (d) have been carried out. Where the child is already living with the prospective adopters, the agency must give them written notification of the date on which the agency is placing the child with them for adoption. This applies, for example, where the agency has decided that the foster parents with whom the child has been boarded-out up to now are suitable adoptive parents for him. In such a case, the child ceases to be boarded-out with effect from the date notified under this regulation. From that date, the legal status of the placement changes and the Boarding-Out of Children Regulations 1955 will no longer apply to the placement (but, until an adoption order is made, the child will continue to be in the care of a local authority or voluntary organisation if he was in their care before being placed for adoption). It will therefore be appropriate to consider whether boarding-out allowances should also cease. Any adoption allowance which the agency has decided to pay the prospective adopters can be paid from the date the child is placed for adoption, if the agency's approved adoption allowance scheme permits this.

3–018   94. The agency should at this stage give the prospective adopters form FP58B (supplies can be obtained from the local Family Practitioner Committee after March 1984), and should arrange for the child's medical card, if available, to be destroyed. The child can then be registered without delay with the prospective adopters' GP in his proposed new name, provisionally. This registration will automatically supersede any previous NHS registration once the Registrar General is notified by the court that an adoption order has been made, but it would be helpful if agencies would send identifying particulars of any placement which does *not* result in an adoption order, in confidence, to:

> NHS Central Register
> Smedley Hydro
> Southport
> Merseyside PR8 2HH

so that the new registration can be cancelled.

95. Wherever possible, the agency should also at the time of placement give the prospective adopters written authority to consent to medical treatment for the child during the placement period. The agency can only do so, however, if it has parental rights in respect of the child or if the person with parental rights (usually either a local authority or the child's parents or guardian) has agreed to this in writing.

96. **Regulation 12(2)(f)** requires the agency, after the child has been placed, to notify his parents or guardian of this in writing (if the agency knows their whereabouts). The putative father must also be notified if the agency considers that doing so would be in the child's interests. If the child has been freed for adoption, however, the agency must not notify any parent or guardien who has made a statutory declaration that he does not want to be further involved in questions about the child's adoption. Any notification sent by the agency under this regulation should not indicate the child's whereabouts or the identity of the prospective adopters, and the agency should keep a copy of every notification for production to the court if required.

97. **Regulation 12(2)(g)** requires the agency to visit the child periodically in order to supervise his well-being. The first visit must be made within a week of placement, to give the prospective adopters early reassurance at a time when they are often very vulnerable. Subsequent visits must be made at whatever intervals the agency feels is necessary in that particular case, and visits should continue until the adoption order is made or until the child ceases to live with the prospective adopters. Agencies should bear in mind that, in an adoption placement too, a child can be at risk of abuse, and child abuse procedures might therefore be applicable.

98. **Regulation 12(2)(h)** requires the agency to ensure that written reports are made of the visits carried out under regulation 12(2)(g). These visits provide the agency with opportunities to see the child with the prospective adopters in the home environment, and the agency will need to let the court know about them in due course so that the court can be satisfied (under section 9(3) of the 1975 Act) that the agency has had sufficient opportunities for this.

99. **Regulation 12(2)(i)** requires the agency, after the child has been placed, to provide any necessary advice and assistance to the prospective adopters. The need for this should be identified in the course of the visits carried out under regulation 12(2)(g).

100. **Regulation 12(2)(i)** requires the agency to monitor the child's health during the placement to the extent that the medical adviser considers necessary. This should include the normal health surveillance programme to check the child's developmental progress, and might

also include further examinations and tests if there is a particular health problem. It is important for the agency to keep itself informed about the child's current state of health as part of its supervision of his well-being, so that it has up-to-date information at the time when the prospective adopters apply to the court for an adoption order. The court rules do not require them to supply any separate health reports, and the agency's report to the court must include a summary by the medical adviser of the child's health history and state of health (as well as that of his parents and the prospective adopters), with comments on the implications for the proposed adoption and how any special health needs of the child might be met.

101. **Regulation 12(2)(k)** requires the agency to review the placement if an adoption order has not been applied for within three months. There may be good reason why an application has not yet been made (and for some children with special needs, for example, a lengthy placement may have been envisaged at the outset), but this requirement gives the agency the opportunity to take stock of the situation and satisfy itself that the placement is progressing well. This regulation also requires the placement to be reviewed subsequently at whatever intervals the agency feels is necessary in that particular case. If the child is in the care of a local authority, it will normally be appropriate for the subsequent reviews under this regulation to coincide with the periodic reviews required under section 27 of the Children and Young Persons Act 1969.

Regulation 13: Review of Case Where no Placement Made Within Six Months of Freeing for Adoption

102. **Regulation 13(1)** requires an agency to review the case of a child whom it freed for **3–019** adoption six months earlier if he is not currently in an adoption placement. The regulation describes the purpose of the review as being to decide why no placement has been made and what action (if any) should be taken to safeguard and promote the child's welfare. This reflects the agency's statutory duty under section 3 of the 1975 Act. Where the parental rights and duties have been transferred to another adoption agency by an order under section 23 of the 1975 Act, it is that agency which must review the child's case under this regulation.

103. In making the order freeing the child for adoption, the court will have endorsed the agency's view that adoption is in the child's best interests. Although there may be good reason why he is not living with prospective adopters six months later, the requirement to review the case gives the agency the opportunity to satisfy itself that all appropriate action, such as advertising or referral to a linking service, is being taken. The agency will need to consider whether any further action is necessary, though this will obviously not be so if, for example, a possible placement is shortly to be considered by the adoption panel, or if a previous placement has only very recently broken down.

104. Since the freeing order has vested the parental rights and duties in the agency, this empowers the agency to make whatever arrangements it considers appropriate for the child's care, maintenance and accommodation before he is placed for adoption. The agency must, however, be satisfied that the arrangements it makes are in the child's best interests — the welfare principle in section 3 of the 1975 Act applies to all the decisions an adoption agency makes about a child who has been freed for adoption.

105. **Regulation 13(2)** requires the case of a freed child to be reviewed as under regulation 13(1) at six-monthly intervals or more frequently, for as long as he has not been placed for adoption. (Once a year has elapsed since the freeing order was made, the agency may have a statutory duty under section 15 of the 1975 Act to keep a former parent of the child informed about the child's placement and adoption).

Regulation 14: Confidentiality and Preservation of Case Records

106. **Regulation 14(1)** states that the adoption agency must treat as confidential any **3–020** information obtained by virtue of the regulation, as well as any recommendations and decisions made under the regulations. The confidential information may concern the child or his parents or the prospective adopters, and includes all reports, letters and other documents. The only exceptions to this confidentiality requirement are set out in regulation 15.

107. **Regulation 14(2)** requires all reports, recommendations and decisions made about the child or the prospective adopters to be filed on the relevant case record. It also requires all adoption case records and their indexes to be kept in a place of special security, whether or not they are in active use, so that they are not accessible to anyone who has no right to see them. Adoption requires natural parents and adopters to disclose intensely personal information, and adoption case records contain a great deal of very sensitive information about their behaviour and personal histories, including police and health reports. Clients therefore need the assurance of a truly confidential service. The general principle governing the con-

fidentiality of adoption information is that it should not be possible for the child or his natural or adoptive parents to be identified, or for the child's pre- and post-adoption identity to be linked.

108. **Regulation 14(3)** requires the indexes to all adoption case records to be kept in a place of special security for at least 75 years and, where the case concerns a placement which resulted in an adoption order being made, the case record too must be kept securely for at least 75 years. Other case records must be kept for as long as seems appropriate in each particular case. The agency's written policy and procedural instructions under regulation 6(1) may include time limits for the preservation of general categories of case records. Examples might be cases where prospective adopters were not considered suitable to be adoptive parents, where a natural parent kept or reclaimed the child, where the court refused to make an order, or where a freed child was never placed for adoption. When adoption case records and their indexes are destroyed, they should be treated as confidential waste and disposed of accordingly.

109. This regulation permits the case records and their indexes to be preserved on microfilm (or by a similar system) if the agency wishes, provided the system reproduces the total record or index. Where a case record is to be microfilmed and then destroyed, the agency should first extract any documents which would be better preserved as originals, such as photographs or letters from a natural parent.

Regulation 15: Access to Case Records and Disclosure of Information

3–021
110. **Regulation 15(1)** sets out the circumstances in which access to adoption case records *must* be provided or information *must* be disclosed. If a request for access to case records or disclosure of information falls within this regulation, the agency has no discretion to refuse it, nor to offer merely to disclose information when it is access to the case records which has been requested. The agency should, however, satisfy itself about the genuineness of a request made under this regulation, and its written policy and procedural instructions under regulation 6(1) must include arrangements for authorising such access or disclosure.

111. **Regulation 15(1)(a)** requires access or disclosure to be provided on request to the persons who are holding a statutory inquiry under section 76 of the Child Care Act 1980.

112. **Regulation 15(1)(b)** requires access or disclosure to be provided on request to the Secretary of State. This gives general authority for the provision of statistical information on the adoption unit return, and the usual circumstances in which specific requests for access or disclosure are made are:
— where Children's Division of DHSS ask a local authority to supply a home study report on prospective adopters who are seeking to bring a child to this country from abroad for adoption here, so that the Home Office can be advised about the immigration application;
— where Social Work Service of DHSS wish to inspect some of an adoption society's case records in connection with the society's application under section 4 of the 1975 Act for the Secretary of State's approval.
If an adoption agency receives a request for access or disclosure under regulation 15(1)(b) other than from Children's Division or Social Work Service of DHSS, the request should be referred urgently to Children's Division for advice.

113. **Regulation 15(1)(c)** requires access or disclosure to be provided on request to a Local Commissioner (the "local government ombudsman") for the purposes of an investigation under the Local Government Act 1974. This provision can therefore only apply to an adoption agency which is a local authority, since the Commissioner has no power to investigate complaints against approved adoption societies (whose approval can be withdrawn, if appropriate, by the Secretary of State).

114. The Commissioner may be expected to respect the confidential nature of any records or information made available to him, and only exceptionally is the need to consider serving a statutory notice on him (under section 32(3) of the 1974 Act) likely to arise. Such a notice would preclude him from disclosing to anyone else any information which has been disclosed to him during the course of an investigation. A local authority can also, under section 29(7) of the 1974 Act, refuse to disclose information to the Commissioner where the authority would not be required to disclose it to the High Court.

115. **Regulation 15(1)(d)** authorises the agency to disclose the information which regulations 11 and 12 require it to give to the child and his parents, to the prospective adopters and their GP, and to the local authority, district health authority and local education authority.

116. **Regulation 15(1)(e)** requires access or disclosure to be provided on request to a guardian ad litem or reporting officer appointed in adoption proceedings concerning the child.

If the guardian ad litem or reporting officer refers to the information in his report to the court, the confidentiality of the information will still be preserved because the adoption court rules provide that these reports are confidential.

117. **Regulation 15(1)(f)** requires access or disclosure to be provided on request to the court dealing with the adoption proceedings concerning the child. The adoption court rules safeguard the confidentiality of the information by providing that anyone (a court officer obtaining information under this regulation, for example) who obtains any information in the course of adoption proceedings, or relating to adoption proceedings, must treat it as confidential and must only disclose it in the limited circumstances set out in the rules.

118. **Regulation 15(2)** sets out the two circumstances in which an adoption agency may, at its discretion and to the extent it considers desirable, provide access to its case records or disclose adoption information. **Regulation 15(2)(a)** permits access or disclosure for the purposes of the agency's functions as an adoption agency, in circumstances where the agency considers this to be appropriate. This covers access and disclosure within the agency as well as to outside individuals or bodies, and the agency's written policy and procedural instructions under regulation 6(1) must cover the arrangements for authorising such access or disclosure and for obtaining the prior written agreement of the person to whom the information is to be made available that it will remain confidential. The instructions should set out any tests of need and motive which are to be applied in considering requests for access or disclosure under this regulation, and should indicate how such requests are to be authorised. In authorising the disclosure of information under this regulation, the agency should always consider whether the provision of anonymised information would be sufficient.

119. *Within the agency* itself, information should as a general principle only be made available to those who need to know in order to participate in providing a service to clients. It is usually appropriate to give an unfettered right of access to the case records to the social work staff who are employed on adoption work and to the members of the adoption panel, and they should be requested, on appointment, to give the written agreement required under regulation 6(2)(c) that they will maintain the confidentiality of adoption information. Other internal matters which the agency's policy and procedural instructions should cover are the circumstances in which case records or information can be made available to:

— members of the management committee or any of its sub-committees or in the case of a local authority, elected members of the authority itself or of its social services committee or sub-committee;
— members of the management staff;
— members of the clerical and secretarial support staff;
— members of staff of other sections of the agency who might need the information, for example, for statistical returns or research projects, or for financial purposes such as the payment of an adoption allowance, or in order to cross-reference a fostering record, or to microfilm the adoption case record.

120. The agency's discretionary power to make case records or information available for the purposes of its functions as an adoption agency applies also to disclosure *outside the agency*. The sort of external circumstances which agencies may wish to provide for in their policy and procedural instructions might include:

— giving information to another adoption agency, including one providing a linking service, which is taking part in the adoption arrangements (where this involves sending the other agency a copy of all or part of a case record, regulation 16(1) requires a record of this transfer to be kept);
— making information available to the agency's legal and medical advisers;
— giving information to specialist health advisers whose help is needed in assessing the health implications of the proposed adoption;
— giving a natural parent information about the child's progress, without disclosing his new identity or his whereabouts;
— giving an adopted person background information about himself or the circumstances of his adoption (though not the information recorded on his original birth certificate, as disclosure of this is provided for separately in section 20A of the 1958 Act);
— giving background information about the adoption to the General Register Office or to a local authority, where they are undertaking the statutory "birth records" counselling;
— giving information or making case records available for the purposes of a child abuse enquiry.

Where the information concerned is health information, it can only be disclosed in accordance with the arrangements about which the medical adviser has been consulted under regulation 6(5).

121. **Regualtion 15(2)(b)** permits discretionary access or disclosure to a researcher authorised by the Secretary of State. It is entirely for the agency to decide whether it wishes to

participate in the research, as the Secretary of State cannot commit any agency to research activity. A specimen of the Secretary of State's authority is attached for information at Annex D to this circular, and agencies may not lawfully make information available to an outside researcher unless he holds such a valid authority in respect of that research project. Before the Secretary of State's authority is given, the research proposals are examined in detail by DHSS to assess whether the potential value of the research justifies a breach of the confidentiality principle and whether the methodology proposed will properly safeguard the confidentiality of the information which the researcher obtains. Authorised researchers are required by DHSS to sign an undertaking to use the information only for the purposes of the research not to publish anything which might enable any individual involved in a particular adoption to be identified, and to submit to DHSS for advance clearance any material which is to be published as a result of the research.

122. **Regulation 15(3)** requires the agency to keep a written record of any access provided or disclosure made under regulation 15(1) or (2).

3–022   **Regulation 16(1)** allows an adoption agency to pass a copy of a case record, or a copy of some of the information in it, to another adoption agency. It can only do so where it considers that this would be in the interests of the child or the prospective adopter concerned, and it must keep a written record of all transfers made under this regulation. This provision covers the sharing of information in inter-agency cases, and the referral of clients to linking services.

124. The only circumstance in which *original* case records can be transferred is where an approved adoption society ceases to operate, and this is dealt with in **regulation 16(2)**. If the Secretary of State has given his approval for the arrangement, the case records may be transferred to another adoption agency which is able and willing to provide a locally-based service to current and former clients of the society which is ceasing to operate. If the society is closing down because it is amalgamating with another approved adoption society, it must transfer its case records to the new society formed by the amalgamation. In all other cases, the records must be transferred to the local authority in whose area the society's head office is situated. In the latter two circumstances (transfer to a new society on amalgamation, and transfer to the relevant local authority), the new society or local authority is required by **regulation 16(3)** to notify the Secretary of State in writing that the records have been transferred.

Regulation 17: Progress Reports under Section 15 of the 1975 Act

3–023   125. **Regulation 17** deals with the situation where a child has been freed for adoption and the parental rights and duties have subsequently been transferred to another adoption agency by an order under section 23 of the 1975 Act. This includes the transfer of parental rights and duties from a Scottish adoption agency to an agency in England and Wales. If the agency which freed the child was under a statutory duty to keep a former parent of the child informed when the child was placed for adoption or when an adoption order was made, it still has this duty even though it no longer has the parental rights and duties: in other words, the duty in respect of a former parent is not transferred to the new agency by the section 23 order. This regulation takes account of this by requiring the agency which now has the parental rights and duties to keep the original agency informed about the child's placement and adoption, so that the original agency can comply with its residual statutory duty to inform the former parent.

Regulation 18: Revocations

3–024   126. **Regulation 18** revokes the regulations which were in operation until 27 May 1984: the Adoption Agencies Regulations 1976 and the Adoption Agencies (Amendment) Regulations 1981.

ANNEX A

INFORMATION FOR PARENTS ABOUT ADOPTION

What is Adoption?

Adoption is a way of providing a new family for a child when living with his own family is **3–025**
not possible. Because we are an adoption agency, we are legally allowed to arrange adoptions
by placing children with suitable families, but we cannot make the arrangement legally
binding. Only a court can do that, by making an adoption order. This ends the child's legal
relationship with his original family and gives him new legal parents. He becomes a full
member of his adoptive family as if he had been born to the adopters.

So adoption means changing parents, permanently. This is such an important thing to
happen in a child's life that the law requires adoption agencies and courts to put the child's
long-term welfare first when they make decisions about his adoption.

If your child is adopted, you will no longer have any legal rights over him, and you will not
be entitled to see him again or claim him back. This means that you need to think very
carefully about the idea of your child being adopted. If you have any worries or doubts or
questions, we are ready and willing to help you all we can. You may find it helpful to talk
things over with your family and friends too. Or you might want to consult someone like your
doctor, clergyman or solicitor.

Knowing About You

Before we can arrange an adoption, we are required by law to ask for a lot of information **3–026**
about you and your child. This information is so very personal that the law says we must treat
it as confidential (though we have explained to you that there are some circumstances where
we might need to pass some of it on to other people). We need all this information so that we
will have the fullest possible picture of your child and his family background and can make the
best decision about his future. You can help us with this by telling us as much as you can
about yourself and your family, and by understanding why we will be asking your doctor about
the family's health.

It will also be helpful for your child's new parents to know something about his background,
and over the years your child himself will want to know about his origins. Information about
the family's health can be very important too, especially when the child grows up.

Choosing a Family

We are required by law to make very thorough enquiries about adopters. We ask them for **3–027**
all sorts of information about themselves and their background, and we try to make sure we
understand what kind of upbringing they would offer your child. We have to be certain in our
own minds that they will be able to meet your child's needs, and we are not allowed to place
him for adoption without first considering whether that will be in his long-term interests. We
hope you will find it reassuring to know that so much thought goes into choosing the right
family.

Please let us know if there is anything special you would like us to have in mind when
choosing a family for your child. You might, for example, want him to have a particular
religious or cultural upbringing (and we can give you the names of any agencies which might
be able to meet your wishes about this). Or you might be anxious that he should not be the
only child in his new family, or that he should have the opportunity to develop any special
interest, such as a talent for singing. We cannot promise to do as you wish, because we must
always put your child's interests first when choosing a family for him, but we will certainly take
your wishes into account and do our very best to meet them.

Adoption by Foster Parents

Perhaps your child has been looked after for a while by foster parents, and they would now **3–028**
like to adopt him. This does not make any difference to our task — we have to make the same
thorough enquiries about the foster parents as we would about any other adopters. And we
still have to be quite sure that it would be best for your child to be adopted by that family,
before we can support the arrangements.

If your child has lived with his foster parents for at least five years, you are not allowed to
take him away from them before the adoption hearing, unless the court says you may.

Freeing for adoption

3–029   Adoption can be carried out in one stage or two. You can choose to wait until we have found a suitable family for your child, and then give your agreement to that adoption. You may feel happier to know something about the family we have chosen to be your child's new parents (though we will not tell you their identity, of course, because adoption arrangements are always confidential for everyone involved). They will ask the court to make an adoption order, and this will transfer your rights as parent to them, the adopters.

Or, if you would rather have things settled more quickly, you can ask us to consider "freeing" your child for adoption. This procedure lets you agree at an early stage to your child's eventual adoption, usually before a family has been found, and the "freeing" order which the court makes transfers your rights as a parent to us, the agency. Later on, when we have found a suitable family and they apply for an adoption order, the court transfers the parental rights from us to the new parents.

If we apply to the court for a freeing order, we will ask you to decide at that stage whether you would like us to let you know afterwards when we have placed your child with a suitable family and when he has been adopted. If you do want to be kept in touch, and if we have been unable to find a suitable family within a year of the freeing order, you will be able to apply to the court to resume your legal rights and duties as the child's parent.

Are you willing for your child to be adopted

3–030   If you are, the court will ask a social worker independent of this agency (known as a reporting officer) to visit you and make sure that you understand what adoption involves. He will need to be sure that you are willing to agree to your child's adoption quite freely and without any conditions. If he is happy that you have thought about it carefully and know what you are doing, he will ask you to sign a formal document giving your agreement. He will sign it too, as a witness. He will then give this form to the court, and report to them that you do understand what is involved.

Once you have given your written agreement, you are not allowed to take your child away from his new family before the adoption hearing, unless the court says you may. If you do change your mind about agreeing to adoption, you should tell the court right away that you are withdrawing your agreement. Parents naturally have mixed feelings about their child being adopted, and the courts are very sympathetic to this. But although they understand why parents sometimes change their minds, their first concern must be the child's welfare. This means that if you have been happy to let the arrangements for your child's adoption get quite far advanced, the court may not think it reasonable for you to change your mind at such a late stage. So they could dispense with your agreement and make an adoption order anyway. All this will make it clear to you how important it is for you to think very carefully and discuss the matter fully before giving your written agreement.

Are you unhappy about the idea of your child being adopted?

3–031   Then it is most important for you to have legal advice as soon as possible. Do please consult a solicitor straight away — your local Citizens' Advice Bureau may know the names of solicitors who specialise in child care cases. You may be entitled to legal advice and assistance (under the Green Form scheme) and to legal aid — your solicitor will be able to advise you about this.

One of two things must happen before a court can take away your rights as a parent, so that your child can be adopted: *either* you must agree to this *or* the court must decide to dispense with the need for you to agree. But it can only do so if one of the circumstances set out in the law applies in your case, and the court will need to have satisfactory evidence of this. The court will send you a copy of the statement of evidence they are given, and you should discuss it with your solicitor as soon as you can.

The court will also ask a social worker independent of this agency (known as a guardian *ad litem*) to visit you. His job is to safeguard your child's interests on behalf of the court, so he will want you to tell him why you do not think it is a good idea for your child to be adopted. He will report your views to the court, because it is very important for them to know how you feel about your child's future. You will also have an opportunity to go to the court yourself if you want to, to explain why you are not willing to agree to your child's adoption. An adoption order cannot be made unless the court is sure it would be in your child's best interests for him to be adopted, and they will have to take account of your views in deciding this.

If you are objecting to this agency's application for a freeing order, you are not allowed to take the child away from where he is living at the moment, unless the court says you may.

272

LAC (84)3
HC (84)1

ANNEX B

BRIEF GUIDE TO AN ADOPTION AGENCY'S PLACEMENT DECISION

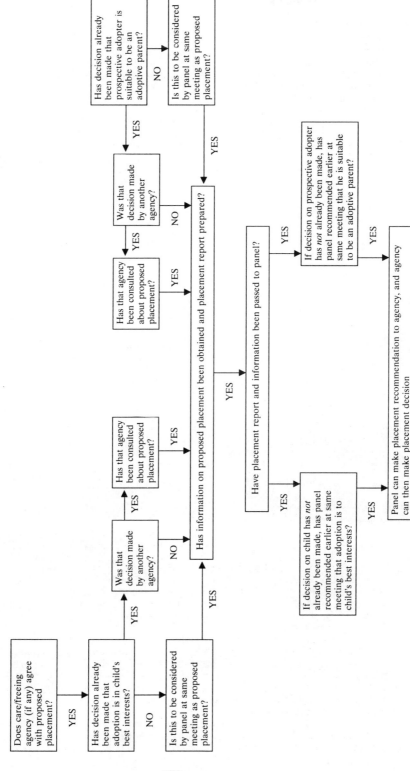

273

When your child grows up

3–033   Adopters often change the child's first name as well as his surname, and they get an adoption certificate from the Registrar General which shows the child's new name only and shows the adopters as his parents. This certificate takes the place of a birth certificate for all legal purposes. But when your child reaches 18, he will be legally entitled, if he wants to, to get a copy of his original birth certificate. This will show his original name, and will also tell him your name, and the address you were living at when his birth was registered. So you must understand that adoption cannot guarantee that your child will never know your identity or the facts of his birth and adoption.

ANNEX C

INFORMATION FOR ADOPTERS

What is adoption?

Adoption is a way of providing a new family for a child when living with his own family is **3–034**
not possible. The arrangement becomes legally binding when the court makes an adoption
order. This ends the child's legal relationship with his original family and makes you his new
legal parents. His original parents no longer have any legal rights over him, and they are not
entitled to see him again or claim him back. Your child becomes a full member of your family,
and you have the same rights and responsibilities as if he had been born to you. This means,
for example, that if you or a close relative were to die without leaving a will, your adopted
child would inherit just as he would if he had been a child of your marriage.

Bringing up a child is mutually rewarding and great fun, as well as being hard work and a
big responsibility. This is especially so when you choose to bring up a child who was not born
to you. You will have thought very carefully before adopting your child, but this certainly does
not mean there will be no problems for you in the future, as there are in all families. We shall
always be available to help in any way we can, but you may like to keep in touch in any case —
we will be particularly pleased to hear from you about how the family is getting on.

Child benefit

Child benefit can be paid to anyone who is responsible for a child — usually the person the **3–035**
child is living with. This means you can get child benefit as soon as the child comes to live with
you, and you do not have to wait until the adoption order is made. After the adoption, of
course, your child is treated for benefit purposes as if he had been born to you. Leaflet CH1
will give you further information about child benefit and how to claim it. If you are a lone
parent, you should also read leaflet CH11 (which explains about one-parent benefit). You can
get these leaflets from your local social security office.

If you have been fostering your child up to now on behalf of a local authority or a child care
organisation, you cannot get child benefit for any weeks when you were getting a boarding-out
allowance.

NHS Registration

We shall be sending your doctor a report on your child's health, so that he can take over the **3–036**
health care as soon as the child comes to live with you. You will probably want the doctor to
know your child by his proposed new name, so there are special arrangements for registering
children who have been placed for adoption. We shall give you the appropriate form to fill in
and take to your doctor. You will then get a medical card in your child's proposed new name.

Adoption orders and certificates

The court will send you a copy of the adoption order. This shows your child's original name **3–037**
as well as his new name, and also shows the names of his original parents.

The Registrar General is required by law to keep a record of all adoptions. He will send you
a short certificate which shows only your child's new name, and he will explain how you can
get a full certificate if you want one. This has details of the adoption order and shows you as
your child's adoptive parents. These adoption certificates take the place of birth certificates for
all legal purposes.

British nationality

If you are a British citizen but your child is not, he will become one automatically when the **3–038**
adoption order is made.

Telling your child about his adoption

All adopted children need to be brought up to know about their adoption from an early age. **3–039**
If you are adopting a baby, you will probably find it easier to start telling him when he begins
to show interest in his own or other children's origins. Then he will never remember a time
when he did not know about his adoption. Older children also need to be aware of their

275

adoption from the start — if you are adopting an older child, the court will want to know whether he understands what adoption is about, and they will need to consider his own wishes and feelings about it.

Explaining should be a continuing process, so that your child will gradually come to understand as he grows older. We are giving you a written note of background information about your child and his original family, so that you have this written reminder available for whenever you or your child want to talk about his past.

Your child will want to ask you questions about his adoption and his original family — this is quite natural and most children go through stages of being very curious about their origins. He needs honest and sympathetic answers, and it really is important for him to feel free to discuss these things will you. If he does not ask, this does not necessarily mean that he does not want to know. He might feel his questions would upset you. So it is a good idea to make time occasionally to talk about him about adoption. The more open and straightforward you are with him, the easier it will be for him to talk about the things that puzzle him, and the more secure your relationship is likely to be.

When your child reaches 18, he will be legally entitled, if he wants to, to get a copy of his original birth certificate. He can get one at an earlier age, of course, once you have told him what his original name was.

If you would like to talk to us again at any time about telling your child about his adoption, please do get in touch. We will be glad to help. We are also here to help with anything else you or your child might wish to talk over with us.

OBTAINING OF CONFIDENTIAL ADOPTION INFORMATION FOR THE PURPOSES OF RESEARCH

Title of project: **3–040**
....

I hereby authorise ....
to obtain, for the purposes of the above research, information which is required to be treated
as confidential under the Adoption Agencies Regulations 1983, the Adoption Rules 1984 and
the Magistrates' Courts (Adoption) Rules 1984.

This authority is valid until ....

Signed on behalf of the
Secretary of State for Social Services ....

....
Children's Division

....

CIRCULAR No. LAC (84)10

Dated April, 1894, and issued by the Department of Health and Social Security

ADOPTION COURT RULES

Summary

3–041   This Circular gives guidance on the court rules for adoption proceedings.

Introduction

3–042   1. This circular contains detailed guidance on the provisions of the Adoption Rules 1984 (see index at Annex A to this circular), which apply to adoption proceedings in county courts and the High Court. The Magistrates' Courts (Adoption) Rules 1984 make equivalent provision for adoption proceedings in domestic courts (there will be no separate circular on those rules). Both sets of rules come into operation on 27 May 1984. A copy of the Adoption Rules 1984 is enclosed. Other changes in adoption law and procedures take effect on the same date, and have been explained in these recent circulars:

LAC (83)2	Panels of guardians *ad litem* and reporting officers
LAC (84)2	Children Act 1975: Implementation of further adoption provisions
LAC (84)3	Adoption Agencies Regulations 1983
LAC (84)6	Adoption statistics

In particular, circular LAC (84)2 gives detailed guidance on the new "freeing for adoption" provisions.

Part I

Introductory

Rule 1: Citation and commencement

3–043   2. **Rule 1** gives the title of the rules and the date from which they operate, 27 May 1984.

Rule 2: Interpretation

3–044   3. **Rule 2(1)** defines some of the terms used in the rules. No definition is needed of the many terms which are already defined in the Adoption Acts 1958 and 1968 (such as "adoption order" and "guardian"). There is also no need for the rules to cover general matters which are dealt with in the Interpretation Act 1978: for example, references in the rules to an applicant for an adoption order as "he" do not prevent the provision concerned applying, as appropriate, to a woman or to a married couple. There are no longer separate adoption rules for the High Court and county courts, and several of the terms defined in rule 2(1) (such as "process" and "proper officer") are needed in order to take account of this. **Rule 2(2)** provides that terms used in the Children Act 1975 (such as "local authority") have the same meaning in the rules, and **rule 2(3)** is technically necessary to give the correct reference to numbered rules and forms.

Rule 3: Extent and application of other rules

3–045   4. **Rule 3(1)** applies the rules to all adoption proceedings which are started in the High Court and county courts on or after 27 May 1984. **Rule 3(2) and (3)** provide that the general procedural rules which apply to all proceedings in the High Court and county courts are also to apply to adoption proceedings in those courts. **Rule 3(4)** enables the proper officer of the court (as defined in rule 2(1)) to exercise the powers which the rules give to the court itself, unless that is clearly not intended by any particular rule.

PART II

FREEING FOR ADOPTION

Rule 4: Commencement of proceedings

5. Freeing proceedings enable an adoption agency to apply to a court for an order freeing a **3–046** child for adoption with the effect that parental rights and duties are transferred to the agency. **Rule 4(1)** requires freeing proceedings to be started by lodging a completed application form (Form 1) with the court. In addition to the usual courts with adoption jurisdiction, a freeing application can be made to a parent or guardian's local county court. **Rule 4(2)** requires the application to be made by the adoption agency which wishes to free the child for adoption, and it lists the individuals and bodies who are respondents in the proceedings: these include the child's parents (or guardian), and any local authority or voluntary organisation which is involved with the care of the child. In the High Court the child too is a respondent, as this is traditionally the case in High Court proceedings.

6. The court is empowered by **rule 4(3)** to make other individuals or bodies respondents (except the child in county court cases). This could include, for example, a person claiming to be the father of an illegitimate child, or a natural parent's spouse (the adoption agency is required to draw attention in its report to the court to the desirability of making any such person a respondent).

7. **Rule 4(4)** requires the adoption agency which is applying for the freeing order to lodge with the court three copies of the completed application form (Form 1) and the required enclosures (such as the child's birth certificate), and to pay the set fee. The agency must also lodge three copies of a written background report for the court covering, as far as possible, the matters set out in Schedule 2 to the rules. Details about the child (paragraph 1) will be known in all cases, and details about his parents or guardian (paragraphs 2 and 3) will usually be available, though information about the prospective adopters (paragraph 4) will only be known if the child has already been placed for adoption. The information requested in these paragraphs of Schedule 2 will already have been obtained by the agency in accordance with the Adoption Agencies Regulations 1983. The agency is also required to explain its actions and decisions in the case (paragraph 5), to cover two general points about respondents (paragraph 6), and to set out its opinions and conclusions for the court (paragraph 7). The report should cover the required matters under the headings set out in Schedule 2, in order to simplify the process of making parts of the report available for inspection under rule 53(2).

8. When lodging its report with the court, the agency should also let the court have the "Adoption proceedings unit return" with parts A to E completed to give the required statistical information about the case. When the case is decided, the court will complete part F and forward the return to the Registrar General.

Rule 5: Appointment and duties of reporting officer

9. **Rule 5(1)** requires the proper officer of the court to appoint a reporting officer for each **3–047** parent or guardian of the child who appears to be willing to agree to the child's adoption. The agency's application form (Form 1) indicates whether or not the parent is willing to agree, and the appointment of a reporting officer for a willing parent will normally be made as soon as the application has been lodged. The proper officer of the court can, however, appoint a reporting officer for a parent at a later stage — perhaps if a parent who was originally unwilling to agree to the child's adoption later changes his mind. When a reporting officer is appointed, he must be sent a copy of the adoption agency's application form, of the required enclosures (such as the child's birth certificate), and of the agency's background report for the court.

10. A reporting officer will only be appointed if the parent or guardian is in one of the countries in which the rules apply, England and Wales. If the parent lives elsewhere, a reporting officer will not be appointed, and one of the persons listed in rule 8 must instead witness the parent's written agreement to the child's adoption.

11. Because a reporting officer must carry out *personally* his duty of witnessing parental agreement to adoption, he can neither delegate this duty nor arrange for an agent to undertake it on his behalf. The court will therefore normally appoint as reporting officer someone from the parent's area of residence in England or Wales. The court will need to consult the administering local authority for the area concerned (which may be outside the court's own area) about the availability of persons who might be appointed from the local panel for guardians *ad litem* and reporting officers.

12. If there is more than one person whose agreement to the child's adoption is required (for example, both the parents of a legitimate child, or a widowed parent and a guardian appointed by the dead parent), a reporting officer is needed for each parent or guardian. **Rule 5(2)**, however, permits the same person to be appointed as reporting officer in respect of more than one parent or guardian, where this is practicable. This will obviously be so, for example, if they both live together or in the same area. **Rule 5(3)** requires the reporting officer to be appointed from a panel set up under the Guardians *Ad Litem* and Reporting Officers (Panels) Regulations 1983, but prohibits the appointment of a person who is connected with the adoption agency applying for the freeing order or with any other body involved with the care of the child. Anyone who has been personally involved in the adoption arrangements is also prohibited from being appointed. The person approached by the court for appointment as reporting officer will need to check whether any of these legal bars apply to him, and also whether there might be reasons of professional ethics for declining the appointment because of previous work with the parent or child.

13. **Rule 5(4)** sets out the detail of the reporting officer's duties. His principal duty (in accordance with section 20 of the 1975 Act) is to witness the parent's signature on Form 2, the written agreement to adoption, but he must first ensure that the parent fully understands what adoption involves and is willing to give his agreement freely and without conditions. The adoption agency which is applying for the freeing order will have explored these issues thoroughly in counselling the parent, and will have given him written information about the legal implications of adoption and freeing and about the relevant procedures. The reporting officer must confirm that the agency has also explained to the parent that he can, if he wishes, make a formal declaration that he does not want to be involved in future questions about the child's adoption. The written agreement to adoption (Form 2) allows the parent either to make this declaration or to state that he does not wish to do so.

14. If the child is illegitimate and his father does not have a custody order, the reporting officer (or one of the reporting officers if there are two) must interview anyone who claims to be the father. This is because the court is required under section 14(8) of the 1975 Act to satisfy itself, before making a freeing order, either that the putative father has no intention of applying for the custody of the child or that, if he did so, his application would be likely to be refused. The reporting officer is therefore required to advise the court on this, so that the putative father's rights to apply for custody can be fully explored before a child is freed for adoption.

15. When he has finished his investigations, the reporting officer must make a written report to the court, and this must draw attention to any significant matters. He should aim to lodge his report at least a month before the hearing date, so that it is available for the court's scrutiny of all the case documents under rule 9(3). The reporting officer may also, under **rule 5(5)**, make an interim report if he wishes to have the court's directions on any particular point, and he *must* make an interim report if the parent turns out to be unwilling to give his agreement (in which case the proper officer of the court will notify the adoption agency which is applying for the freeing order, since the agency will then need to consider requesting the court to dispense with the parent's agreement). As far as the separate issue of the parent's consent to the agency's freeing application is concerned, this is a relevant requirement only at the point when the agency lodges its application with the court (so, if the parent has changed his mind *before* the agency's application was lodged, the agency would have needed to examine whether it could still comply with section 14(2) of the 1975 Act).

16. The reporting officer may be required by the court under **rule 5(6)** to carry out further duties, and rule 5(7) requires him to attend the hearing if the court wishes him to. **Rule 5(8)** provides that any report he makes to the court is confidential, though the parent may be able under rule 53(2) to inspect references to himself in the report.

Rule 6: Appointment and duties of guardian *ad litem*

3–048   17. **Rule 6(1)** requires the proper officer of the court to appoint a guardian *ad litem* for the child if any parent or guardian of the child appears to be unwilling to agree to his adoption. The agency's application form (Form 1) indicates whether or not each parent is willing to agree, and the guardian *ad litem* will normally be appointed as soon as the application has been lodged. If, however, the application does not enclose the statement of facts supporting the agency's request for the parent's agreement to be dispensed with (perhaps because the parent was originally willing to agree but changes his mind after the application is lodged), then the proper officer of the court will appoint the guardian *ad litem* once the statement of facts is received. When a guardian *ad litem* is appointed, he must be sent a copy of the adoption agency's application form, of the required enclosures (such as the child's birth certificate), of the statement of facts, and of the agency's background report for the court.

18. A guardian *ad litem* will be appointed in *every* contested case, but there may exceptionally be special circumstances in uncontested cases where the child's welfare makes a guardian *ad litem* necessary. If the court thinks this is so a guardian *ad litem* will be appointed under **rule 6(2)** and the court will indicate what particular matters it wants him to investigate. He must be sent copies of the same documents as a guardian *ad litem* appointed in a contested case, except that there will be no statement of facts.

19. **Rule 6(3)** permits the same person to be appointed as reporting officer and as guardian *ad litem*. This might happen where the agency's application form shows that one of the child's parents is willing to agree to his adoption (so that a reporting officer is appointed for him under rule 5(1)) but the other parent is not (so that a guardian *ad litem* is appointed for the child). It might in any case turn out, whether or not a reporting officer has already been appointed for a willing parent, that an unwilling parent changes his mind after the guardian *ad litem* has been appointed. This might become known, for example, in the course of an interview between the guardian *ad litem* and the parent, but the guardian *ad litem* would not be able, in that capacity, to witness the parent's signing of the written agreement to adoption, since that is the duty of a reporting officer. This rule therefore permits the guardian *ad litem* to be appointed as a reporting officer for that parent.

20. In such a case, it will usually be appropriate for the agreement to be signed on a subsequent occasion so that the parent has time to reflect on his change of mind and to consider seeking legal advice; the guardian *ad litem*, in his capacity as reporting officer when witnessing the agreement, would have to be sure that the parent fully understood what adoption involved and was willing to give his agreement freely and without conditions. In the interval between the two interviews, therefore, the guardian *ad litem* can make an interim report to the court and ask to be appointed as reporting officer. If he has learned of the parent's change of mind through an agent because the parent lives some distance away, the guardian *ad litem* may wish to ask for someone local to be appointed as reporting officers, and the court will then need to consult the administering local authority for the area concerned about the availability of persons who might be appointed from the local panel for guardians *ad litem* and reporting officers. If the guardian *ad litem's* agent is on that local panel, it would be sensible to draw this to the court's attention, so that the court can consider appointing him as reporting officer.

21. There may be cases where an unwilling parent makes it clear in the course of an interview with the guardian *ad litem* that he has changed his mind *and*, exceptionally, the guardian *ad litem* wishes to secure his written agreement without delay. In such a case, the court may be willing to appoint the guardian *ad litem* as reporting officer for that parent right away if the circumstances are explained by telephone to the proper officer of the court.

22. The Official Solicitor is normally appointed as the guardian *ad litem* of any child involved in any proceedings in the High Court. **Rule 6(4)** therefore provides that, if he consents, he is to be appointed the child's guardian *ad litem* in freeing proceedings in the High Court, unless the adoption agency applying for the freeing order wants someone else to be appointed.

23. In the county court (and in High Court cases where the Official Solicitor is not appointed), **rule 6(5)** requires the guardian *ad litem* to be appointed from a panel set up under the Guardians *Ad Litem* and Reporting Officers (Panels) Regulations 1983. A person cannot be appointed, however, if he is connected with the adoption agency applying for the freeing order or with any other body involved with the care of the child, or if he has been personally involved in the adoption arrangements. The person approached by the court for appointment as guardian *ad litem* will need to check whether any of these legal bars apply to him, and also whether there might be reasons of professional ethics for declining the appointment because of previous work with the child or his parents or with the prospective adopters.

24. **Rule 6(6)** sets out the detail of the guardian *ad litem's* duties. His principal duty is to safeguard the child's interests before the court, and the particular duties set out in this rule are directed to that. It is not his task to gather background information on behalf of the court, as the adoption agency applying for the freeing order will have supplied this in its report to the court. The guardian *ad litem* must look into what is said in the agency's application form and the background report and, in a contested case, in the statement of facts. He is only required to do this to the extent he considers necessary, because it is not intended that he should cover all the same ground again as a matter of course. There is no point in his repeating enquiries which have already been satisfactorily concluded by the adoption agency. On the other hand, he cannot be fettered if he is to fulfil his function of safeguarding the child's interests, and so he must bear in mind the possible need to check and verify any aspect of the application.

25. The guardian *ad litem* will therefore need to read the documents carefully and critically, and he should always interview the agency's caseworker and inspect the relevant case records. This may identify gaps in the information, conflicting professional judgments, or statements

which appear to be questionable. It may thus provide leads to *necessary* matters for further or direct enquiry, and enable the guardian *ad litem* to decide which particular aspects he should investigate further. The overall approach of the guardian *ad litem* to his duties should be that he is satisfying himself that this or that is as stated, on the basis of being reasonably assured rather than certain; and that, where he has occasion for doubt, he will take active steps to enquire into any relevant matter. It may be more practicable for some of the enquiries to be made through an agent.

26. In a contested case, there is a conflict of views between the agency and the parent about whether adoption is in the child's best interests, and the court will look to the guardian *ad litem's* report to help it reach a decision on this. The guardian *ad litem* should not have preconceived notions about what might be best for the child, and he will need to test the agency's case for adoption as well as examining the unwilling parent's views. He should check that the parent has sought legal advice, and then discuss fully with him why he is objecting to adoption and what alternative way of providing for the child's future care he can offer. The adoption agency which is applying for the freeing order should have explored these issues thoroughly in counselling the parent, and should have given him written information about the legal implications of adoption and freeing and about the relevant procedures. It is not the guardian *ad litem's* task to explain these matters again, but he may be able to clarify points which the parent has misunderstood; some natural parents, for example, mistakenly believe that if the application is *refused* in a case where the prospective adopters have asked for their identity to be kept confidential, then their identity will be made known and the parent may even have a right to meet them.

27. Rule 6(6) also requires the guardian *ad litem* to investigate any other matters which seem relevant, and to carry out any further duties which he feels are necessary or which the court directs. In addition, he must advise the court whether, in his view, the child should be present at the hearing.

28. When he has finished his investigations, the guardian *ad litem* must make a written report to the court under **rule 6(7)**, and this must draw attention to any significant matters. He should aim to lodge his report at least a month before the hearing date, so that it is available for the court's scrutiny of all the case documents under rule 9(3). The guardian *ad litem* may also, under **rule 6(8),** make an interim report if he wishes to have the court's directions on any particular point. He may be required by the court under **rule 6(9)** to carry out further duties, and **rule 6(10)** requires him to attend the hearing (since his duty is to safeguard the child's interests before the court) unless the court says he need not. **Rule 6(11)** provides that any report he makes to the court is confidential, though a parent (or the child, in High Court cases) may be able to inspect references to himself in the report, under rule 53(2). It would therefore be helpful if the report dealt, as far as possible, with individual parties in separate sections.

Rule 7: Statement of facts in dispensation cases

3–049   29. If the adoption agency applying for the freeing order wishes the court to dispense with a parent's agreement to adoption, **rule 7(1)** requires the agency to request this in its application form (Form 1). When lodging the application, the agency must also attach three copies of the statement of facts supporting its request. The application will not, however, include a request for dispensation of a parent's agreement if that parent had originally appeared to be willing to agree to the child's adoption but changes his mind after the application is lodged. The reporting officer will report this to the court, and the proper officer of the court will then notify the adoption agency. If the agency decides to continue with its application for a freeing order, it must notify the proper officer of the court in writing that it requests the court to dispense with the parent's agreement, and must attach three copies of the statement of facts supporting its request.

30. In some freeing cases, the child may already have been placed for adoption. If the agency's freeing application is being contested by a natural parent, the prospective adopters may understandably not wish their identity to be disclosed to the parent if he does not already know it. Where the prospective adopters have told the agency that they do wish their identity to remain confidential, **rule 7(2)** requires the agency to draft the statement of facts for the court in such a way that the prospective adopters' identity is not disclosed.

31. Once the court has received a statement of facts, **rule 7(3)** requires the proper officer of the court to let the parent concerned know as soon as possible that the agency has requested the court to dispense with his agreement. He must also send a copy of the statement of facts to the parent and, under **rule 7(4),** to the guardian *ad litem* and the reporting officer.

Rule 8: Agreement

32. **Rule 8(1)** allows Form 2 to be used for a parent's written agreement to adoption. If the **3–050** parent is in England and Wales, a reporting officer will be appointed for him after the application has been lodged, and it will be the reporting officer's duty to witness the parent's signature on Form 2. If the parent lives elsewhere and gives his written agreement before the application has been lodged, this rule requires the agreement to be sent to the court with the application. An agreement which is signed by the parent outside England and Wales cannot be witnessed by a reporting officer, and **rule 8(2), (3) and (4)** set out the requirements for witnessing in Scotland, Northern Ireland, and countries outside the United Kingdom.

Rule 9: Notice of hearing

33. The proper officer of the court is required by **rule 9(1)** to fix a hearing date as soon as **3–051** he can after the application has been lodged. He must send notice of the hearing (Form 3) to the adoption agency applying for the freeing order, to all the respondents, and to the reporting officer and guardian *ad litem*. Under **rule 9(2)**, no-one except the reporting officer and the guardian *ad litem* may be sent a copy of the adoption agency's application form and its background report for the court. This rule also provides that the agency's report is confidential, though a parent or a prospective adopter (or the child, in High Court cases) may be able to inspect references to himself in the report, under rule 53(2).

34. **Rule 9(3)** allows the court to give any directions it thinks necessary, at any stage before the hearing. Whether or not this has been done, the court is required to go through all the case documents at least four weeks before the hearing date, so that any necessary further directions can be given. This will minimise the risk of the hearing having to be adjourned (which is time-wasting and expensive for all concerned) because of "loose ends" which could have been dealt with earlier if they had been spotted in good time.

Rule 10: The hearing

35. **Rule 10(1)** permits anyone who has received notice of the hearing (Form 3) to attend **3–052** the hearing and address the court about the adoption agency's application for a freeing order. This applies to the adoption agency itself, all the respondents, the reporting officer and the guardian *ad litem*. Some natural parents will be reluctant to attend and the court will not normally require this, as it can proceed in the parent's absence and accept written evidence of his agreement to adoption. (Where a parent does not wish to attend, it is important that the adoption agency should give the parent a written report of the outcome of the hearing and should offer to discuss the parent's future plans, as part of the social worker's normal counselling role.) In the case of the adoption agency and any local authority or voluntary organisation which is a respondent, any member or employee of the body concerned is permitted by **Rule 10(2)** to address the court if that body has authorised him to do so.

36. The adoption agency's application may have informed the court that the child has been placed for adoption and that the prospective adopters want their identity to be kept confidential. If that is so, **rule 10(3)** requires the proceedings to be conducted so that no respondent who does not already know the prospective adopters' identity is made aware of it, except with their consent. **Rule 10(4)** prohibits the judge from making a freeing order unless the hearing has been attended by an authorised representative of the adoption agency, and agencies will need to consider the appropriate level of staff for this responsibility. The child must also attend the hearing (and would normally be accompanied by the person responsible for his everyday care), unless the court has directed under **rule 10(5)** that this is unnecessary. It will only do so if there are special circumstances, because the court is under a statutory duty to ascertain the child's own wishes and feelings and to give them due consideration (having regard to his age and understanding) in reaching its decision. When considering whether the child should attend, the court will take into account any available reports including, in particular, that of the guardian *ad litem*: one of his duties is to advise the court whether, in his view, the child should be present at the hearing. The court can also, under **rule 10(6)**, require any respondent to attend the hearing if this seems necessary because of special circumstances.

Rule 11: Proof of identity of child, etc.

37. **Rule 11(1)** is technically necessary to link the child referred to in the adoption agency's **3–053** application with the child referred to in a parent's written agreement to adoption. If the birth certificates attached to the application and the agreement are the same, the child is assumed

to be the same person in each case. If the child has previously been adopted, **rule 11(2)** substitutes references to certificates from the Adopted Children Register.

38. In some cases, the child's precise date of birth cannot be proved. The court is then required by **rule 11(3)** to decide the probable date of birth (and will take account of whatever medical or other evidence is available), and this date will be shown in the freeing order as the child's date of birth. **Rule 11(4)** makes similar provision for cases where the child's place of birth cannot be proved: if he was probably born within the United Kingdom, Channel Islands or Isle of Man, he can be treated as having been born in the court's area and in other cases the freeing order will not show a country of birth.

Rule 12: Application for revocation of order freeing a child for adoption

3–054   39. A former parent of a child who is free for adoption (*i.e.* a parent who decided that he *did* wish to be involved in future questions about the child's adoption) may want to apply for a freeing order to be revoked if the child has not been adopted or placed for adoption a year after the freeing order was made. If so, **rule 12(1)** requires the former parent to lodge a completed application form (Form 4) with the court to re-open the original freeing proceedings, so that the court can consider (under section 3 of the 1975 Act) whether the child's long-term welfare would be safeguarded and promoted by allowing the former parent to resume his parental rights and duties.

40. Under **rule 12(2)**, the court must send notice of the proceedings to all the original parties, except any local authority or voluntary organisation which was previously involved with the care of the child (because their legal position in relation to the child will not be affected by the outcome of the revocation application). But *every* other parent or guardian of the child must be notified, even if that parent has made a formal declaration that he does *not* want to be involved in future questions about the child's adoption, because revocation of the freeing order would vest the parental rights and duties once more in the original parents and guardians and would revive any previous maintenance obligations. If the parental rights and duties have been transferred to another adoption agency since the freeing order was made, that agency too must be notified of the revocation proceedings.

41. The proper office of the court is required by **rule 12(3)** to fix a hearing date as soon as he can after the application has been lodged. He must appoint a guardian *ad litem* for the child (wherever possible, this will be the same person who was appointed as guardian *ad litem* in the original freeing proceedings) and must send him a copy of the former parent's application and any enclosures. **Rule 12(4)** gives the guardian *ad litem* in revocation proceedings essentially the same duties as a guardian *ad litem* in freeing proceedings, with the necessary technical changes of reference.

Rule 13: Transfer of parental rights and duties between adoption agencies

3–055   42. If two adoption agencies want to transfer between themselves the parental rights and duties relating to a child who is free for adoption. **rule 13(1)** requires them to lodge a completed application form (Form 5) with the court to re-open the original freeing proceedings (This can include a transfer to or from an adoption agency in Scotland, provided the child is in England or Wales when the application is made.) If the court makes an order under section 23 of the 1975 Act authorising the transfer, it is required by **rule 13(2)** to notify the court which made the freeing order (if that is a different court) as well as any former parent of the child.

PART III

ADOPTION ORDERS

Rule 14: Application for a serial number

3–056   43. If a prospective adopter wants his identity to be kept confidential in the adoption order proceedings, he can apply to the proper office of the court under **rule 14** for a serial number before he lodges his application. A serial number will then be allocated so that he can be identified by it in the proceedings.

44. **Rule 15(1)** requires adoption order proceedings to be started by lodging a completed **3–057** application form (Form 6) with the court. **Rule 15(2)** requires the application to be made by the prospective adopter, and it lists the individuals and bodies who are respondents in the proceedings: these include the child's parents (or guardian) if he is not free for adoption, except a parent who is an applicant for the adoption order, and any adoption agency which is responsible for a freed child or is involved in the adoption arrangements. The respondents also include any local authority or voluntary organisation which is involved with the care of the child, and any local authority which has been notified of the proposed adoption if the child was not placed for adoption by an adoption agency. In the High Court the child too is a respondent, as this is traditionally the case in High Court proceedings.

45. **Rule 15(3)** corresponds to rule 4(3) for freeing proceedings (see paragraph 6), and empowers the court to make other individuals or bodies respondents (except the child in county court cases). This might include the Home Secretary in a case where the child is a foreign national, if it appears to the court that entry clearance to come to this country was given for a purpose other than adoption (*i.e.* if the child's passport does not contain a United Kingdom visa or entry certificate endorsed "for adoption"). Making the Home Secretary a respondent will enable him to intervene if it seems that the application is being made primarily to evade the provisions of the immigration control.

46. **Rule 15(4)** requires the prospective adopter to lodge with the court three copies of the completed application form (Form 6) and the required enclosures (such as the child's birth certificate), and to pay the set free. Some prospective adopters are also required to lodge health reports, but this applies only where the child was not placed for adoption by an adoption agency and where he is not the child of one of the prospective adopters. Agency placements are excluded from this requirement because the agency will already have obtained all the relevant health information in accordance with the Adoption Agencies Regulations 1983 (and will include in its report to the court under rule 22(1) a health summary and comments by its medical adviser). Parent/step-parent cases are excluded because the child will almost certainly continue to live in that household whether or not an adoption order is made, whatever the state of health of those concerned.

47. The cases where health reports are required are therefore:
— applications by relatives or custodians;
— applications by foster parents who are looking after the child under private arrangements;
— applications by foster parents with whom the child has been boarded-out by a local authority or voluntary organisation, where the foster parents have either not sought or not received that body's support for their application;
— application in respect of children from overseas.

A separate report is required on the health of each of the prospective adopters and on the child's health, and each report must have been made not more than 3 months previously. The reports must be made by a registered medical practitioner (this will usually be the prospective adopters' GP), and Schedule 3 sets out the matters that the reports must cover (this corresponds to the health requirements in the Schedule to the Adoption Agencies Regulations 1983). It is for the prospective adopters to meet the cost of obtaining these reports, and three copies of each report must be lodged with the court. The court itself is not concerned with the clinical information in the reports, but needs to have them so that copies can be sent to the local authority which has been notified of the proposed adoption. The authority's report to the court under rule 22(2) must include a health summary and comments by the authority's medical adviser, based on the health reports supplied under this rule.

Rule 16: Preliminary examination of application

48. When the application is lodged, **rule 16** requires the proper officer of the court to check **3–058** whether the court might be debarred from hearing the case or making an adoption order. This might be so if the prospective adopters have previously had an adoption application in respect of the same child refused (unless one of the conditions in section 22(4)(a) and (b) of the 1975 Act applies), or for some other reason such as their failure to meet the legal requirements of age, domicile or marital status. In any such case, the proper officer of the court must pass the case documents to the judge to obtain his directions.

Rule 17: Appointment and duties of reporting officer

3–059 49. **Rule 17** corresponds to rule 5 for freeing proceedings (see paragraphs 9 to 16), with the following differences:

— the applicant in adoption order proceedings is the prospective adopter and not, as in freeing proceedings, an adoption agency, and the application form is Form 6, not Form 1;

— no reporting officer is appointed in adoption order proceedings if the child is free for adoption, since the question of parental agreement will have been settled in the freeing proceedings;

— the documents sent to the reporting officer by the court in adoption order proceedings cannot include a copy of "the report supplied by the applicant", because that refers in rule 5 to the background report lodged by the adoption agency in freeing proceedings;

— the prohibition on appointing as reporting officer anyone connected with a respondent body does not apply in adoption order proceedings if that body is a local authority whose only connection with the case is that it was notified of the proposed adoption (where the child was not placed for adoption by an adoption agency);

— parents are not asked in adoption order proceedings whether they want to be involved in future questions about the child's adoption (because, if an adoption order is made, they cannot subsequently resume the parental rights and duties) and the reporting officer is therefore not required to deal with this in adoption order proceedings;

— no special enquiries are necessary in adoption order proceedings about the putative father's custody intentions;

— the form of written agreement in adoption order proceedings is Form 7, not Form 2.

50. Where the child was not placed for adoption by an adoption agency, the local authority which was notified of the proposed adoption will have interviewed the parent in the course of its investigations and will have explored the relevant issues with him, including his understanding of what adoption involves and the possible need for legal advice. If it seems to the reporting officer that the parent needs any further counselling, he should draw this to the authority's attention.

Rule 18: Appointment and duties of guardian *ad litem*

3–060 51. **Rule 18** corresponds to rule 6 for freeing proceedings (see paragraphs 17 to 28) with the following differences:

— the applicant in adoption order proceedings is the prospective adopter and not, as in freeing proceedings, an adoption agency, and the application form is Form 6, not Form 1;

— the automatic appointment of a guardian *ad litem* in a contested case cannot apply in adoption order proceedings if the child is free for adoption, since the question of parental agreement will have been settled in the freeing proceedings;

— the court nevertheless has a discretionary power in adoption order proceedings to appoint a guardian *ad litem* for a freed child, if exceptionally there are special circumstances where the child's welfare makes a guardian *ad litem* necessary (and in such a case the guardian *ad litem* may wish to ask the court for sight of the case documents from the freeing proceedings);

— the documents sent to the guardian *ad litem* by the court in adoption order proceedings cannot include a copy of "the report supplied by the applicant", because that refers in rule 5 to the background report lodged by the adoption agency in freeing proceedings;

— the guardian *ad litem* will instead be sent a copy of the report supplied under rule 22 by the adoption agency which placed the child for adoption or, where the child was not placed for adoption by an adoption agency, by the local authority which was notified of the proposed adoption, and it is this report which he must include in his investigations;

— the prohibition on appointing as guardian *ad litem* anyone connected with a respondent body does not apply in adoption order proceedings if that body is a local authority whose only connection with the case is that it was notified of the proposed adoption (where the child was not placed for adoption by an adoption agency).

Rule 19: Statement of facts in dispensation cases

52. **Rule 19** corresponds to rule 7 for freeing proceedings (see paragraphs 29 to 31), with the **3–061**
following differences:
— the applicant in adoption order proceedings is the prospective adopter and not, as in
freeing proceedings, an adoption agency, and the application form is Form 6, not
Form 1;
— if the prospective adopter wishes his identity to be kept confidential in the adoption
order proceedings, he will, as the applicant, have obtained a serial number under rule
14.

Rule 20: Agreement

53. **Rule 20** corresponds to rule 8 for freeing proceedings (see paragraph 32), except that **3–062**
the form of written agreement in adoption order proceedings is Form 7, not Form 2. Parental
agreement is not required, of course, if the child is free for adoption, since the question of
parental agreement will have been settled in the freeing proceedings.

Rule 21: Notice of hearing

54. **Rule 21** corresponds to rule 9 for freeing proceedings (see paragraphs 33 and 34), with **3–063**
the following differences:
— the prescribed form of notice in adoption order proceedings is Form 8, not Form 3;
— in a serial number case, Form 8 enables arrangements to be made for the natural
parent to be heard separately (though he need not attend unless he wants to or the
court requires it);
— rule 21 contains no reference to "the report supplied by the applicant", because that
refers in rule 9 to the background report lodged by the adoption agency in freeing
proceedings;
— where the child was not placed for adoption by an adoption agency, the proper officer
of the court must send a copy of the application form (Form 6) to the local authority
which was notified of the proposed adoption, together with any health report
supplied by the applicant under rule 15(4);
— in a non-agency case, the hearing date must not be fixed earlier than 3 months from
the date on which the local authority was notified of the proposed adoption.
This last requirement is included in the rules because section 18 of the 1975 Act prohibits the
court from making an adoption order in a non-agency case unless the applicant has notified
his local authority at least 3 months before the date of the order. There are other statutory
time limits relevant to the making of adoption orders. Convention adoption orders, and orders
authorising proposed foreign adoptions, and Annex B to this circular sets these all out in a
flow-chart.

Rule 22: Reports by adoption agency or local authority

55. If the child was placed for adoption by an adoption agency, rule 22(1) requires the **3–064**
agency to let the court have three copies of a written report within 6 weeks of receiving notice
of the hearing (Form 8). The report must cover the matters set out in Schedule 2 to the rules.
These include the personal, family and social information about the child (paragraph 1) his
parents or guardian (paragraphs 2 and 3) and the prospective adopters (paragraph 4) which
the agency will already have obtained in accordance with the Adoption Agencies Regulations
1983. The agency is also required to explain its actions and decisions in the case (paragraph 5)
to cover two general points about respondents (paragraph 6), and to set out its opinions and
conclusions for the court (paragraph 7). The agency should put in hand the preparation of the
report once the child has been placed for adoption, so that it can be completed in good time
(and see also paragraphs 63 to 66 below).
56. If the child was not placed for adoption by an adoption agency, **rule 22(2)** requires the
local authority which was notified of the proposed adoption to let the court have three copies
of a written report within 6 weeks of receiving notice of the hearing (Form 8). The report
must cover the matters set out in Schedule 2 to the rules, which include details about the child
(paragraph 1), his parents or guardian (paragraphs 2 and 3) and the prospective adopters
(paragraph 4). The local authority is also required to explain its actions in the case and
investigations of whether the placement was lawful (paragraph 5) to cover two general points
about respondents (paragraph 6), and to set out its opinions and conclusions for the court
(paragraph 7).

57. The local authority will be aware of the case before it receives notice of the hearing, because it will have been notified in writing by the prospective adopters (under section 18 of the 1975 Act) of their intention to make an adoption application. This notification makes the child a protected child and the local authority becomes responsible for supervising his well-being while the adoption is pending. When it receives the notification, the local authority should acknowledge it formally: Annex C to this circular provides a specimen acknowledgment which local authorities may wish to use as a model for this. It is suggested that the authority should enclose with the acknowledgement an information note about relevant aspects of adoption because, now that local authorities have to be notified of all proposed adoptions other than agency placements, the court will no longer issue an explanatory memorandum to prospective adopters.

58. Section 18 of the 1975 Act requires the local authority to investigate the proposed adoption on receipt of the notification, and the necessary enquiries should therefore be put in hand right away, without waiting for notice of the hearing, so that the report for the court can be prepared in good time. (If, exceptionally, it seems that the report may not be completed within the six weeks required under this rule, because, for example, a parent or prospective adopter is seriously ill, the court should be informed as soon as possible and asked to agree a later date for receipt of the report).

59. The authority should arrange for the report to be prepared by one of its social work staff experienced in adoption work. Most of the enquiries which the authority needs to make are the same as those which, as an adoption agency, it is required to make under the Adoption Agencies Regulations 1983 when arranging an adoption, and many of the authority's written policy procedural instructions for its adoption work can be adapted for work in this similar context with the prospective adopters and the child and his parents. Much of the guidance in circular LAC (84)3 is relevant, and the authority should, for example:

— set up a case record and ensure its safe-keeping;
— explain to both the natural parents and the prospective adopters the legal requirements and procedures for an adoption order;
— counsel them to ensure that they fully understand the implications of the proposed
   adoption;
— suggest, where this seems appropriate, that they should seek legal advice;
— explain what enquiries the authority is required to make (including the usual
   enquiries of the police about the prospective adopters) and why, and its particular
   duty to investigate whether the placement was lawful;
— ensure that all the information obtained is filed on the case record and treated as
   confidential;
— preserve the case record for as long as seems appropriate, bearing in mind the
   possible need to provide "birth records" counselling for the child in later years.

It would be helpful if the authority would also give the prospective adopters form FP58B, so that the child can be registered with their GP in his proposed new name, provisionally (and cases which do not subsequently result in an adoption order should be notified in confidence to the NHS Central Register as requested in circular LAC(84)3.

3–065   60. Counselling will be particularly important in the case of parent and step-parent applications. Those prospective adopters are usually unaware that there may be a legal prohibition on the adoption (under section 10(3) or 37(1) of the 1975 Act), if the court thinks the child's welfare would be better secured by custody arrangements. They may need help to understand that it is the child's long-term welfare, and not their own wishes, which must be the court's first consideration; it may, for instance, be in the child's interests to maintain any links he has with the other half of his natural family.

61. In some cases (see paragraph 46), the local authority's report to the court must include a health summary and comments by the authority's medical adviser based on the health reports supplied by the prospective adopters under rule 15(4) (which must cover the matters set out in Schedule 3 to the rules). It is suggested that the authority's acknowledgment of the formal notification of intended adoption in these cases should ask for the name and address of the prospective adopters' GP and should explain that the authority's medical adviser will be getting in touch with him about the legal requirement for health reports. The medical adviser's letter to the GP can then explain that the purpose of the reports is to build up a full picture of the health history and current state of health (including strengths and weaknesses) of the child and the prospective adopters. This will enable the medical adviser to base his advice to the court on the fullest possible health information, when commenting on its implications for the proposed adoption. The letter could also invite the GP to contact the medical adviser if he wishes to discuss any aspect of the reports (such as any difficulty in obtaining the health information required).

62. It is recommended that the medical report forms produced by British Agencies for Adoption and Fostering should be used, as they cover all the health matters listed in Schedule

3, and the medical adviser may therefore wish to enclose copies for the GP's use. He should also explain that, although it is technically necessary for the reports to be lodged with the court, the court will send copies to the authority for the medical adviser's use. Should the medical adviser then wish to ask the GP for further information, this would be covered by the patient's written authority for disclosure which was obtained when the local authority acknowledged his notification of intended adoption (see Annex C to this circular).

63. In preparing a report under rule 22(1) or (2) the placing agency or local authority should bear in mind the statutory requirement for the report to cover the suitability of the prospective adopters and any other matters relevant to the operation of the welfare principle in section 3 of the 1975 Act (including the child's own wishes and feelings). The agency or authority will need to plan its work and visits so that the prospective adopters and the child are seen separately as well as together. The court is prohibited (by section 9(3) of the 1975 Act) from making an adoption order if it is not satisfied that there have been sufficient opportunities for the agency or authority to see the family group of the child and both applicants together in the home environment.

64. The report should cover the required matters under the headings set out in Schedule 2 to the rules, in order to simplify the process of making parts of the report available for inspection under rule 53(2). If the child is free for adoption, the agency might wish to ask the court whether it may provide the court with a copy of the report supplied under rule 4(4) in the freeing proceedings and cover only additional and updating information in the report required under this rule. When lodging its report with the court under this rule, the placing agency or local authority should also let the court have the "Adoption proceedings unit return" with parts A to E completed to give the required statistical information about the case. When the case is decided, the court will complete part F and forward the return to the Registrar General.

65. When the court has received the report supplied by the placing agency or the local authority, it may wish to have a further report on some particular aspect of the case. **Rule 22(3)** empowers the court to request further reports and to indicate what particular matters it wants the further report to cover.

66. The proper officer of the court is required by **rule 22(4)** to send the reporting officer and the guardian *ad litem* copies of any reports supplied under this rule. **Rule 22(5)** prohibits copies being sent to anyone else and provides that the reports are confidential, though a parent or a prospective adopter (or the child, in High Court cases) may be able to inspect references to himself in the report, under rule 53(2).

Rule 23: The hearing

67. **Rule 23** corresponds to rule 10 for freeing proceedings (see paragraphs 35 and 36), with **3–066** the following differences:
- the applicant in adoption order proceedings is the prospective adopter and not, as in freeing proceedings, an adoption agency;
- the prescribed form of notice in adoption order proceedings is Form 8, not Form 3;
- if the prospective adopter wishes his identity to be kept confidential in the adoption order proceedings, he will, as the applicant, have obtained a serial number under rule 14;
- the prohibition on the making of an order unless the applicant and the child have personally attended the hearing applies also in adoption order proceedings to the making of an interim order (in a case where the child was not placed for adoption by an adoption agency);
- if the applicants are a married couple, the judge can in special circumstances make an order in adoption order proceedings despite the attendance of only one spouse, if the absent spouse formally verifies the application form in the way set out in rule 23(7).

Rule 24: Proof of identity of child, etc.

68. **Rule 24(1) to (4)** correspond to rule 11 for freeing proceedings (see paragraphs 37 and **3–067** 38). In the case of a child who is free for adoption and whose probable date or place of birth was decided in the freeing proceedings, **rule 24(5)** allows what the freeing order shows as his date and place of birth to apply without further enquiry in the adoption order proceedings.

Rule 25: Further proceedings after interim order

3–068 69. If the court makes an interim order in a case where the child was not placed for adoption by an adoption agency, **rule 25** requires the proper officer of the court to fix a further hearing for a date before the interim order expires. At least a month before the hearing date, he must send notice of the hearing (Form 8) to all the parties and to the guardian *ad litem*. (The reporting officer does not need to be notified, because the court will have decided the question of parental agreement before making the interim order).

Rule 26: Committal of child to care on refusal of adoption order

3–069 70. As **rule 26(1)** explains, this rule applies where the court has refused an adoption application and proposes to commit the child to local authority care. If the relevant local authority is a respondent in the adoption order proceedings and has an authorised representative present at the hearing when the order is refused, **rule 26(2)** allows the court to hear right away any points the authority's representative wishes to put to the court about the making of a care order or a supplementary order requiring the child's parents to make maintenance payments to the authority.

71. **Rule 26(3)** requires the hearing to be adjourned if the local authority is not a respondent or does not have an authorised representative present, or if the authority requests the court to order maintenance payments from the parents. The proper officer of the court must then fix a further hearing date and, at least 14 days beforehand, must send notice of the hearing (Form 8) to the local authority, the prospective adopters, the child's parents and the guardian *ad litem*. If the local authority is not a respondent in the proceedings, the proper officer of the court must also send the authority copies of all the earlier notices of hearing.

PART IV

CONVENTION PROCEEDINGS

3–070 72. **Rules 27 to 46** set out the special procedural rules for Convention proceedings. These proceedings are very rare, and are restricted to the High Court. They concern either adoptions under the Hague Convention on Adoption (a treaty on inter-country adoptions involving, at present, only the United Kingdom, Austria and Switzerland) or foreign adoptions whose validity in this country is under question. Circular LAC (78)19 deals with the requirements and procedures for Convention proceedings.

PART V

MISCELLANEOUS

Rule 47: Application for removal, return, etc. of child

3–071 73. Adoption law contains a number of restrictions on the removal of a child from where he is living except with the leave of the court. There is a similar restriction prohibiting an adoption agency, except with the leave of the court, from placing a child for adoption if he is free for adoption and a revocation hearing is pending. **Rule 47(1)** lists the statutory references to these various restrictions and related provisions, and requires any relevant application to be made in accordance with **rule 47(2)**: the application must be made by process or notice in any adoption proceedings which have already been started, and must otherwise be made by starting fresh proceedings in the appropriate court. This is defined in **rule 47(3)** as the High Court or the applicant's local county court: it also includes the prospective adopters' local county court in a case where the child has lived with them for five years and they have notified their local authority that they intend to adopt him, and the applicant is seeking the court's leave to remove him.

74. If the application under this rule has been made by starting fresh proceedings (because no adoption proceedings had already been started), any respondent who wants to contest the application is required by **rule 47(4)** to put his reasons in writing in answer to the application to the court within 7 days of receiving the copy of the application.

75. **Rule 47(5)** requires the proper officer of the court to send copies of any application under this rule to all the parties in any pending adoption proceedings and to the reporting officer and guardian *ad litem*; if no proceedings are pending he must send copies to the prospective adopters and to the local authority which has been notified of the proposed adoption. He must send to each recipient of the application a copy of any answer under rule 47(4) contesting it and a notice of the hearing date, and he must also send these documents to anyone else the court thinks should be involved. In a case where the prospective adopters have been given a serial number, the proper officer is required by **rule 47(6)** to ensure that the documents he sends out preserve the confidentiality of their identity, and the proceedings under this rule must be conducted accordingly.

76. If a prospective adopter who has not yet applied for an adoption order receives a copy of an application under this rule and wants to oppose it, **rule 47(7)** requires him to lodge his application for an adoption order within 14 days or, if the hearing date for the application under this rule is less than 14 days away, by the time of that hearing. **Rule 47(8)** empowers the court to give directions at any time for the conduct of an application under this rule, and to appoint a guardian *ad litem* for the child. If the court decides, on hearing the application, that the child should no longer live with the prospective adopters, **rule 47(9)** allows the judge to refuse their application for an adoption order (if they have lodged one) at the same hearing. **Rule 47(10)** requires the proper officer of the court to let all parties know the outcome of the case, and **rule 47(11)** is technically necessary to cover the procedures in a contested case.

Rule 48: Proposed foreign adoption proceedings

77. Where prospective adopters who are not domiciled in this country wish to obtain an order authorising them to take a child out of Great Britain for adoption in their own country, **rule 48(1)** requires the proceedings to be started by lodging a completed application form (Form 6) with the court. **Rule 48(2)** applies to such proceedings all the rules relating to adoption orders (rules 15 to 26, except the provision for starting adoption order proceedings, and rules 47 to 53, except the prescribed form of adoption order), and **rule 48(3)** requires the prospective adopters to provide the court with expert evidence of the adoption law in their own country.

3–072

Rule 49: Amendment and revocation of orders

78. In certain limited circumstances, an adoption order can be amended or revoked or the marking of an entry in the Registers of Births or the Adopted Children Register can be changed. **Rule 49(1)** permits such applications to be made without there having to be respondents in the proceedings, but the court has power to require anyone it thinks fit to be notified of the application. If such an application is granted, **rule 49(2)** requires the proper officer of the court to send details to the Registrar General.

3-073

Rule 50: Service of documents

79. **Rule 50(1)** sets out how documents can be served under the rules on bodies of persons and on individuals, and **rule 50(2)** requires the person responsible for serving a document to lodge with the court a certificate giving details of the service or non-service.

3–074

Rule 51: Costs

80. **Rule 51** empowers the judge to make an order about the costs of a case once the case is decided (or when an interim order is made). In particular, the applicant can be ordered to pay all or part of the out-of-pocket expenses incurred by the reporting officer or the guardian *ad litem*, or by any respondent in attending the hearing.

3–075

Rule 52: Notice and copies of orders, etc.

81. **Rule 52(1)** requires Forms 12 to 15 to be used for the main orders which the court can make in adoption proceedings, and **rule 52(2)** requires the proper officer of the court to obtain a Welsh translation of the particulars in an adoption order made by a Welsh court in respect of a child born in Wales, if the adopter requests this before the order is drawn up.

82. The proper officer of the court is required by **rule 52(3)** to send the applicant within 7 days a copy of any order the court makes (and any Welsh translation). He must also, under **rule 52(4)**, send the Registrar General within 7 days a copy of any adoption order. Convention

3–076

adoption order, or order authorising a proposed foreign adoption, and must enclose any Welsh translation (though the English text will prevail) and the notice needed with a Convention adoption order. The Registrar General will also be sent, when any case is decided, the "Adoption proceedings unit return" with part F duly completed by the court.

83. **Rule 52(5)** requires the proper officer of the court to notify every respondent of the court's decision when any of the orders mentioned in rule 52(1) is made or an order applied for is refused, and **rule 52(6)** requires the notice to include details of any care order made where an adoption order was refused. The making of any order except an interim order must also, under **rule 52(7)**, be notified to any British court which has made any order about the parental rights and duties of the child's maintenance.

84. **Rule 52(8)** allows the court to send the Registrar General a copy of any order he requests, and the person who applied for any order the court has made may be supplied with a copy of that order under **rule 52(9)**. Anyone else can only be supplied with a copy of an order if the court uses its power under **rule 52(10)** to authorise this.

Rule 53: Custody, inspection and disclosure of documents and information

3–077 85. **Rule 53(1)** requires the court to keep in a place of special security all case documents relating to current or past adoption proceedings.

86. **Rule 53(2)** enables any individual who is a party to adoption proceedings (this will usually be a natural parent or a prospective adopter) to inspect references to himself in any of the confidential reports supplied to the court. This is so that he can be made aware of matters in a report which are critical of him, to enable him to deal with the criticisms at the hearing. The reports concerned might be the report made by the guardian *ad litem* or reporting officer, or the background report supplied by the adoption agency which is applying for a freeing order, or the report made by the placing agency or local authority in an adoption order case. When the person applies to the court to be allowed to inspect relevant parts of a report, the court will consider whether he should be allowed to see other parts of the report as well as perhaps none of it, or whether the parts which refer to him should be shown only to his lawyers. It should not generally prove a problem for the court to isolate the parts of a report which refer to the individual concerned: reports on the matters in Schedule 2 will follow the order of the Schedule, the reporting officer's report will be concerned only with the natural parent, and the guardian *ad litem* should as far as possible deal in his report with the individual parties separately.

87. **Rule 53(3)** requires anyone with any information about adoption proceedings to treat the information as confidential. It can only be disclosed in the following limited circumstances:
— if it is necessary for the proper exercise of that person's duties for him to disclose that information;
— if the information is requested by any court or public authority which needs the information in connection with an adoption case it is dealing with (it might be appropriate in some cases to make the court file available);
— if the information is requested by the Registrar General (or the authorised social worker who is undertaking "birth records" counselling), but only to the extent of disclosing which adoption agency placed the child for adoption or which local authority was notified of the proposed adoption (see paragraph 88 for disclosure of other information);
— if the information is requested by a researcher who has the Secretary of State's authority to obtain that information for the purposes of a particular research project.

88. **Rule 53(4)** prohibits anyone from inspecting or copying any document or order the court has which relates the current or past adoption proceedings. Inspection or copying is permitted, however, if any enactment or the rules themselves authorise or require this, or if the court gives permission. A social worker undertaking "birth records" counselling of an adult adopted person under section 20A of the 1958 Act might, for example, wish to seek the court's permission to have a copy of the guardian *ad litem's* report if no other background information about the adoption is available (which might be the case with a privately arranged adoption or where no agency records exist).

Rule 54: Revocations

3–078 89. **Rule 54** revokes all the rules which were in operation for adoption proceedings in the High Court and county courts until 27 May 1984. For proceedings which are pending on that date, however, the old rules continue to apply until the case is decided.

ADOPTION RULES 1984: INDEX

3–080 STATUTORY TIME LIMITS FOR MAKING ADOPTION ORDERS, CONVENTION ADOPTION ORDERS, AND ORDERS AUTHORISING PROPOSED FOREIGN ADOPTIONS

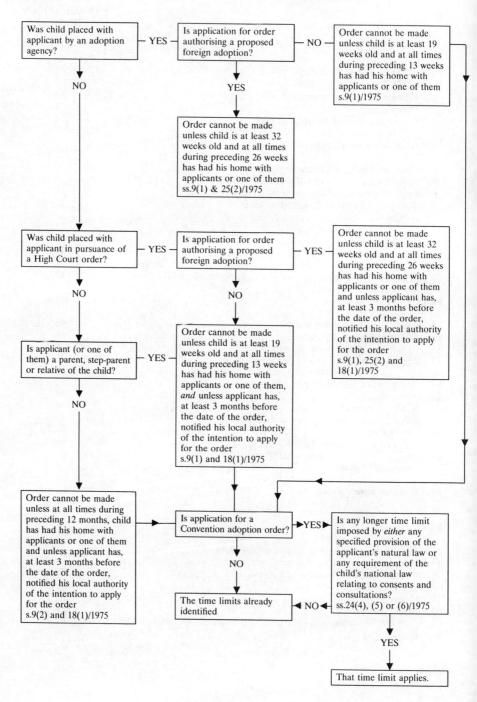

ACKNOWLEDGEMENT OF NOTIFICATION OF INTENDED ADOPTION   **3–081**

Thank you for your letter of .... in which you notified the Council that you intend to apply for an adoption order in respect of .... [As it is legally necessary for *both* of you to notify us, please arrange for your husband/wife to send us a similar letter as soon as possible.] If the court decides to make an adoption order in your case, the order cannot be made until at least three months after the date of [your] [your husband's/wife's] letter.

We are now responsible in law for supervising the child's welfare while the adoption is pending. We also required by law to prepare a detailed report for the court about the proposed adoption, because the court has to put the child's long-term welfare first when it makes decisions about his adoption. This means that it needs to know a great deal about you and the child, to help it make the best decision about the child's future. So, to prepare our report for the court we have to make thorough enquiries. We shall arrange for one of our social workers to visit you, and he will ask you for a lot of information about you and the child and your family background. We need to be sure that you understand what adoption involves, and we shall want to discuss with you what kind of upbringing you would offer the child, so that we can consider whether this would meet his needs and be in his long-term interests. And we shall need to know what the child himself thinks about the idea of being adopted. I hope you will understand that all this is necessary for the child's sake. [The court also needs to know about your health and the child's, as this could have implications for the proposed adoption. Please let us have the name and address of your doctor, so that our medical adviser can get in touch with him about the health reports which have to be supplied to the court. Please also let us have your written authority for your doctor to disclose information about your health to our medical adviser (who would of course treat it in confidence) if necessary.]

I am enclosing an information note about relevant aspects of adoption. [*The authority should adapt for this purpose the note at Annex C of Circular LAC (84)3.*] Please don't hesitate to talk to our social worker about anything else you would like to know or discuss.

CIRCULAR No. 36/1984

Dated May 11, 1984, and issued by the Home Office

MAGISTRATES' COURTS (ADOPTION) RULES 1984

3–082 1. I am directed by the Secretary of State to send you the attached copy of the Magistrates' Courts (Adoption) Rules 1984, which will come into force on May 27, 1984, on the same date as the implementation of further adoption provisions of the Children Act 1975. The Rules take account of the changes to adoption law and procedure introduced by these provisions and also replace and consolidate the Magistrates' Courts (Adoption) Rules 1976 and the associated amendment rules of 1979 and 1981.

2.–4. [Not reproduced.]

The rules

3–083 5. The rules are divided into four parts: Part I is general introductory material; Part II prescribes the procedures governing the new freeing process under sections 14 to 16 of the 1975 Act; Part III covers adoption proceedings and Part IV a number of miscellaneous matters. In substance most of Parts I, III and IV re-enacts the content of the present rules. Only Part II is entirely new. It will be seen, however, that the procedure to free a child for adoption under Part II is very similar to the adoption procedure itself under Part III and there is, in consequence, a close correspondence between the rules in the two parts.

Part I — Introductory

3–084 6. *Rules 1 to 3* contain the necessary interpretation and extent provisions. By virtue of rule 1(2), these rules will not apply to adoption proceedings already pending on May 27, for which the 1976 Rules as amended will continue to apply.

Part II — Freeing for adoption

3–085 7. Freeing proceedings enable an adoption agency to apply to a court for an order freeing a child for adoption with the effect that parental rights and duties are transferred to the agency. Under *rule 4* an adoption agency seeking a freeing order must make its application on *Form 1* and supply any required documents (such as the child's birth certificate) and a background report covering the matters set out in *Schedule 2* to the rules. In addition to the usual courts with adoption jurisdiction, a freeing application can be made to a parent or guardian's local court. Rule 4(2) lists the possible respondents to the application; a parent must be made a respondent even if he has already made a declaration under section 14(7) of the 1975 Act that he prefers not to be involved in future questions concerning the child's adoption. Under rule 4(3) the court is also empowered to make other individuals or bodies respondents (except the child). This could include, for example, a person claiming to be the father of an illegitimate child or a natural parent's spouse (the adoption agency is required to draw attention in its report to the court to the desirability of making any such person a respondent).

8. *Rule 5* requires the justices' clerk as soon as practicable to appoint a Reporting Officer for each parent or guardian of the child in England or Wales, who appears from the adoption agency's application form to be willing to agree to the child's adoption. A reporting officer can, however, also be appointed at a later stage, perhaps because a parent who was originally unwilling to agree to adoption changes his mind. If there is more than one person whose agreement to a child's adoption is required, a reporting officer is needed for each of them but the same person may be appointed as reporting officer for each parent or guardian where this is practicable, for example because they live in the same area. Because a reporting officer must carry out *personally* his duty of witnessing parental agreement to adoption, he can neither delegate this duty nor arrange for an agent to undertake it on his behalf. The court will therefore normally appoint as reporting officer someone from the parent's area of residence in England or Wales. The court will need to consult the administering local authority for the area concerned (which may be outside the court's own area) about the availability of persons who might be appointed from the local panel of guardians *ad litem* and reporting officers.

9. The details of the reporting officer's duties are prescribed in rule 5(4) and having submitted his report to the court he will attend the hearing only if required to do so by the court (rule 5(7)). When his report is received it should be checked to ensure that the parents' consent has been given, for if agreement is not forthcoming the applicant agency has to be informed. The applicant may then apply to the court to dispense with the consent, in which case a guardian *ad litem* for the child must be appointed. By virtue of rule 5(9) the court's powers in relation to the appointment of the reporting officer and the performance of his duties are exercisable before the hearing by a single justice or the justices' clerk.

10. *Rule 6* provides for the appointment of a guardian *ad litem* in every contested case where a parent or guardian appears unwilling to agree to the child's adoption and in uncontested cases where there are special circumstances and the welfare of the child requires it. At the discretion of the court the reporting officer and the guardian *ad litem* may be the same person in the circumstances set out in rule 6(3). Rule 6(5) details the guardian *ad litem's* duties: he is not required to gather all the background information already supplied by the adoption agency but nor is he fettered as to the issues he can investigate if the child's interest so demands or the court directs. He will then submit his report and attend the hearing unless the court says he need not. His report will need to be checked before the hearing to see if there is any recommendation that the child need not attend. As with rule 5(9), the court's powers in relation to the guardian *ad litem* may be exercised before the hearing by a single justice or the justices' clerk (rule 6(11)).

11. If the applicant adoption agency wishes the court to dispense with a parent's agreement to adoption *rule 7* requires the agency to request this in its application (or by notice to the justices' clerk subsequently) and to supply a statement of facts supporting its request. The justices' clerk must notify the parent concerned as soon as possible and supply copies of the statement to the parent, the guardian *ad litem* and the reporting officer. In cases where a parent agrees to adoption, *rule 8* allows *Form 2* to be used in record that written agreement. If the parent is in England or Wales it is the reporting officer's duty to witness if the parent's signature on the form. The rule also prescribes the appropriate witness if the parent is elsewhere. These two rules are very similar in content to rule 6 and 12 of the Magistrates' Courts (Adoption) Rules 1976 (the 1976 Rules).

12. *Rule 9* requires the justices' clerk to fix a hearing date as soon as practicable after the **3–086** application has been lodged, and notice of the hearing is sent in *Form 3* to all concerned in the case. Only the reporting officer and the guardian see a copy of the agency's application form and background report. *Rule 10* permits anyone who has received the notice in Form 3 to attend the hearing and address the court. A representative of the applicant agency must attend, as must the child unless the court directs that this is unnecessary. The identity of any prospective adopter must be kept confidential if he so wishes. *Rule 11* provides for proof of the child's identity and for courts to determine the child's probable date or place of birth if these cannot be proved. This provision re-enacts the substance of rule 19 of the 1976 Rules.

13. It is suggested that it would be helpful and sensible if, about a month before the hearing, a check is made of the case papers to determine whether any special directions are needed, for example, concerning the attendance of the child (under rule 10(5)) or the attendance of other parties (rule 10(6)). It may also be necessary at this stage to finalise any arrangements, where the child has been placed for adoption, to ensure the confidentiality of the proceedings under rule 10(3). Such a check will minimise the risk of the hearing having to be adjourned (which is time-consuming and expensive for all concerned) because of loose ends which could have been dealt with earlier if they had been spotted in good time.

14. *Rule 12* prescribes the procedure whereby a former parent of a child who is free for adoption (*i.e.* a parent who decided that he *did* wish to be involved in future questions about the child's adoption) may apply for the revocation of the freeing order if the child has not been adopted or placed for adoption a year after the freeing order was made. An application form is prescribed in *Form 4*. Notice of the proceedings is sent to all the parties involved in the original freeing proceedings except any local authority or voluntary organisation which was previously involved in the child's care (because their position is not affected by the outcome of the revocation application by virtue of section 16 of the Children Act 1975). However, every parent or guardian of the child must be notified even if that parent has made a formal declaration that he does *not* want to be involved in future questions about the child's adoption. This is because revocation of the freeing order would vest the parental rights and duties once more in the original parents or guardians and would revise any previous maintenance obligations. A guardian *ad litem* must be appointed and it may be convenient and helpful to appoint the person who acted as guardian *ad litem* in the original freeing proceedings.

15. *Rule 13* supplements section 23 of the 1975 Act by laying down the procedure whereby two adoption agencies can transfer between themselves the parental rights and duties in

respect of a child who is free for adoption. This can include a transfer to or from an agency in Scotland provided the child is in England or Wales when the application is made. A joint application is made by both agencies concerned in *Form 5* and if the transfer is authorised by the court it is required to notify the court which made the freeing order an any former parent.

Part III — Adoption orders

3–087 16. This part of the rules covers adoption order proceedings and many of the procedures closely parallel the freeing process and re-enact the content of the 1976 Rules.

17. *Rule 14* concerns a prospective adopter who wants his identity to be kept confidential to apply to the court for a serial number by which to be identified. It re-enacts the substance of rule 5 of the 1976 Rules.

18. *Rule 15* covers the making of the application (*in Form 6*) and is very similar in content to rules 4 and 7 of the 1976 Rules. However, the respondent will not include the child's parents or guardians where a child has been freed for adoption. In such a case the adoption agency in whom parental rights and duties rest is a respondent. As with the 1976 Rules, medical reports (which must cover the matters set out in *Schedule 3*) are not required if the child is the offspring of one of the applicants. Adoption agency placements are also exempt from this requirement because the agency will cover health issues in its report to the court under rule 22. As with rule 4(3) for freeing proceedings the court may make other individuals or bodies respondents. This might include, for example, the Home Secretary in a case where the child is a foreign national, if it appears to the court that entry clearance to come to this country was given for a purpose other than adoption. Making the Home Secretary a respondent will enable him to intervene if it seems that the application is being made primarily to evade the provisions of the immigration control.

19. When the application for an adoption order is lodged, *rule 16* requires the justices' clerk to check whether the court might be debarred from hearing the case or making the order. This might be so if the prospective adopters have previously had an application in respect of the same child refused (unless one of the conditions in section 22(4)(*a*) and (*b*) of the 1975 Act applies) or for some other reasons such as their failure to meet the legal equivalent of age, domicile or parental status. In any such case the justices' clerk must bring the case to the attention of the court. It will be noted that this rule repeats rule 8 of the 1976 Rules except that there is now no preliminary examination of whether the court may be required to dismiss the application pursuant to section 10(2) or 11(4) of the 1975 Act. These sections relate to adoption by step-parents and require the court to dismiss such an adoption application if it felt that the matter would be better dealt with by means of a custody order under the divorce jurisdiction. The operation of the present rule has caused serious disquiet because of the wide variation in practice between courts. A number of decisions in the High Court has further eroded the restriction of the present rule 8 by requiring the court to give precedence to the child's wishes and feelings under section 3 of the 1975 Act and emphasising that the court must be satisfied that a custody order would be a *better* solution before dismissing the adoption application. This approach requires a full hearing of the matter with the benefit of a report from a guardian *ad litem* and this part of the old rule 8 is accordingly omitted.

20. *Rule 17* covers the appointment and duties of the reporting officer and corresponds to rule 5 for freeing proceedings. No such appointment is required if the child is already free for adoption since the issue of parental consent will have been settled in the freeing proceedings. The reporting officer's report should be checked to ensure that parental consent has been forthcoming for if it has not the applicants must be told. They may then apply to dispense with consent in which case a guardian *ad litem* must be appointed. *Rule 18* corresponds to rule 6 for freeing proceedings with regard to the appointment and duties of a guardian *ad litem*. There is automatic appointment of a guardian *ad litem* if the child has not been freed for adoption and the case is contested. In all other cases, the court nevertheless has a discretionary power to appoint one where the child's welfare so demands. The guardian *ad litem's* report should be checked to see if there is any reason why the child need or should not attend the hearing.

3–088 21. *Rule 19* covers dispensation of parental agreement and corresponds to rule 7 of the freeing process. *Rule 20* prescribed *Form 7* to record parental agreement for adoption and corresponds to rule 8 for freeing proceedings. The content of these two rules also corresponds closely to rules 6 and 12 of the 1976 Rules.

22. *Rule 21* on the notice to be given of the hearing (*in Form 8*) corresponds to rule 9 for freeing proceedings. If the child was not placed with the applicants by an adoption agency, section 18 of the Children Act 1975 provides that the applicant must give notice to his local authority at least three months before the hearing of his intention to apply for an adoption order. Courts' attention is also drawn to the other statutory time limits relevant to the making of adoption orders which occur in section 9(1) and (2) of the 1975 Act. In addition, when

fixing the date of the hearing, sufficient time should be allowed for the guardian *ad litem* (where one is appointed) to prepare his report. This should take account of the fact that he can only begin his investigations when he has received the adoption agency or local authority report under rule 22, which allows a maximum of six weeks' preparation time from receipt of the notice of hearing.

23. As with freeing proceedings, see paragraph 13 above, the practice is commended of scrutinising the case papers a month before the hearing to finalise the arrangements and to ensure that any special directions can be given in advance with regard to the attendance of the child (rule 23(5)) or any other parties (rule 23(6)).

24. If the child has been placed for adoption by an adoption agency, *rule 22* requires the agency to supply the court with a written report covering the matters set out in *Schedule 2*. In any other case, a report is supplied by the local authority to whom the prospective adopter gave notice of intention to adopt under section 18 of the 1975 Act. *Rule 23* deals with the hearing and corresponds to rule 10 for freeing proceedings and rules 13 to 16 of the 1976 Rules. *Rule 24* corresponds to rule 11 for freeing proceedings and rule 19 of the 1976 Rules, with the difference that where a child has previously been freed for adoption, the details of his probable date and place of birth shown on the freeing order will suffice for the adoption proceedings. *Rule 25* corresponds to rule 21 of the 1976 Rules in providing for a further hearing after an interim order is made, whilst *rule 26* on the committal of a child to care where an adoption order is refused re-enacts rule 20 of the 1976 Rules.

Part IV — Miscellaneous

25. *Rule 27* deals with applications to remove a child from a person's custody where **3–089** adoption or freeing proceedings are pending or intended and where removal without the court's leave would therefore be unlawful. It also covers applications for the return of a child unlawfully removed or for an order prohibiting removal. It re-enacts as one rule the content of rules 28 and 29 of the 1976 Rules. Because these proceedings are rare, the use of prescribed forms for making applications under the rule has been replaced with the standard procedure by way of complaint.

26. *Rule 28* on the amendment of adoption orders or the revocation of a direction to the Registrar General re-enacts in a slightly simpler form the content of rule 27 of the 1976 Rules.

27. *Rule 29* on the service of documents repeats the content of rule 34 with the addition of a provision which will enable the court to treat service on a person as having been effected notwithstanding that the documents have been returned undelivered. Courts will be aware of the importance of ensuring that all possible efforts to effect service are made but the provision makes clear the court's jurisdiction to proceed with the case where a respondent is untraceable.

28. *Rule 30* on costs repeats the content of rule 30 of the 1976 Rules. *Rule 31* on notice and copies of orders re-enacts the substance of rules 22 to 26 of the 1976 Rules. It prescribes forms for a freeing order, an order revoking a freeing order, an interim order and an adoption order; provides for a Welsh translation of an adoption order to be supplied at the adopter's request; provides for a copy of an adoption order to be sent to the Registrar General and for notice of the outcome of a freeing or adoption case to be served on every respondent and other interested parties where appropriate. Copies of orders may be supplied to the Registrar General or the applicant on request and to any other person with the court's leave. It will be noted that the form of the Adoption Order (Form 13) has been simplified and the schedule and appendix to the 1976 form of the Order have been deleted. The new form 13 will be issued both to the applicants and to the Registrar General. For the benefit of courts sitting in Wales a Welsh translation of form 13 is provided at Annex A.

29. *Rule 32* covers the same ground as rules 31, 32, 33 of the 1976 Rules and regulates the keeping of a special court register for adoption proceedings, the security of documents and the disclosure of information about adoption proceedings. There are two new features in the rule. Paragraph (2) requires a declaration by parent or guardian that he does not wish to be involved in future questions of a child's adoption to be recorded in the adoption register. Paragraph (4) gives a person a right to inspect references to himself in any of the confidential reports supplied to the court. The court retains a discretion, however, to restrict the individual's right of access to a report. It should not generally prove a problem to isolate the parts of a report which refer to the individual concerned. DHSS guidance to local authorities and adoption agencies (in LAC(84) 10 which is being copied to the Probation Service) stresses that reports prepared under rules 4 and 22 should cover the required matters under the headings in Schedule 2 in order to simplify the process of making parts of the report available to individuals under this rule; the reporting officer's report will be concerned only with the natural parents and the guardian *ad litem* is urged as far as possible to deal in his report with the individual parties separately.

30. *Rule 33* re-enacts rule 35 to attract the complaint and summons procedure to proceedings on an application made under these rules.

Statistics

3–090   31. DHSS Circular LAC (84)6 informed courts of the introduction of a new system for collecting adoption statistics from May 27, based on the completion of a unit return for each case. As explained in that circular, Parts A to E of the return will be completed by the social worker in the placing agency or local authority and submitted to the court with his report. Part F is to be completed by a court official after the final disposal of all adoption or freeing applications and sent to the Registrar General together with, in appropriate cases, the copy of the adoption order. Final disposal includes dismissals and withdrawals but *not* adjournments or interim orders. For the purposes of this return an application is "not proceeded with" if the court is debarred from hearing the case or making an order by virtue of rule 16 and section 22 of the 1975 Act. It should be noted that in relation to question 26 in section F of the return, the heading "adoptive mother/father"" above the boxes should in fact read "natural mother/father".

32.–33. [Not reproduced.]

ANNEX A

3–091   <div align="center">FFURFLEN</div>   **Rheol 31(1)**

Gorchymyn mabwysiadu

Llys Domestig ....

Gan fod cais wedi ei wneud gan   o   sy'n   wrth
ei (g)alwedigaeth (a   syn'n   wrth ei (g)alwedigaeth) am
orchymyn mabwysiadu ar gyfer   , sef plentyn   , sy'n
blentyn/plentyn mabwysiedig   (a   );

Gorchmymnir i'r mabwysiadwr (mabwysiadwyr) fabwysiadu'r plentyn a bod yr hawliau a'r dyletswyddau rhieni yn ymwneud â'r plentyn (gan gynnwys cadwraeth gyfreithiol y plentyn) i gael eu thoi i'r ymgeisydd (ymgeiswyr).

(Ac ynglŷn â chostau, gorchmynnir bod   ;)

(A chofnodir bod   sy'n asiantaeth mabwysiadu, wedi rhoi'r plentyn i'w fabwysiadu i'r ymgeisydd (ymgeiswyr)/bod Cyngor   wedi ei hysbysu am fwriad yr ymgeisydd (ymgeiswyr) i fabwysiadu'r plentyn;)

(A chan fod y plentyn wedi ei ryddhau i'w fabwysiadu gan lys   ar y
        dydd o fis   19   );

(A chan ei fod wedi ei brofi'n ddigonol i fodloni'r i fodloni'r llys i'r plentyn gael ei eni yn
        (*gwlad*);)

(A chan fod lle gen'ir plentyn heb ei brofi'n ddigonol i fodloni'r llys (ond ei bod yn ymddagngos yn debygol i'r plentyn gael ei eni yn y Deyrnas Gyfunol, Ynysoedd y Sianel neu Ynrs Manaw, caiff y plentyn ei drin fel pe bai wedi ei eni yn nosbarth cofrestru   ac is-ddosbarth   yn sir   );)

(A chan ei fod wedi ei brofi'n ddigonol llys i'r plentyn gael ei eni ar y
        dydd o fis   19   (ac yntau'n union yr un fath (â
y mae'r cofnod rhif   a wnaed ar y   dydd o fis
19   yn y Gofrestr Genedigaethau ar gyfer dosbarth cofrestru   ac is-
ddosbarth   ya' sir   yn ymwneud ag ef (hi)) (*neu* â
        y mae'r cofnod rhif   a wnead ar y   dydd o fis
        19   yn y Gofrestr Plant Mabwysiedig yn ymwneud ag ef (hi);)

(A chan mai'r enw neu'r enwau a'r cyfenw a nodir yn y cais fel enwau'r plentyn
yw   ;)

Cyfarwyddir y Cofrestrydd Cyffredinol i wneud yn y Gofrestr Plant Mabwysiedig gofnod yn y ffurf beenir gan reolau a wneir ganddo yn cofnodi'r manylion a nodir yn y gorchymyn hwn;

300

(A chyfarwyddir ymhellach fod y cofnod uchod yn y Gofrestr Genedigaethau/ Cofrestr Plant Mabwysiedig i gael ei farcio â'r geiriau "mabwysiadwyd"/"ail-fabwysiadwyd").

Dyddiedig y dydd hwn o fis 19

Ynad Heddwch
[*neu* Drwy orchywyn y Llys
Clerc y Llys]

CIRCULAR No. LAC (87)8

Dated June 1987, and issued by the Department of Health and Social Security

ADOPTION ACT 1976: IMPLEMENTATION*

Summary

3–092   This Circular explains the effect of the implementation of the Adoption Act 1976 and in particular Section 1 and 2 (statutory adoption service).

Commencement

3–093   1. A commencement order is shortly to be made bringing into force the whole of the Adoption Act 1976 with effect from 1 January 1988.

Introduction

3–094   2. The law relating to adoption is consolidated in the Adoption Act 1976 which with the exception of Section 58A has not been brought into force. Sections 1 and 2 provide for each local authority to establish and maintain an adoption service within its area. Local authorities may either provide the necessary facilities themselves or secure that they are provided by approved adoption societies. In view of the fact that almost all local authorities are now providing such a service and the process by which the Secretary of State has considered each voluntary adoption society for approval is complete, the Secretary of State has decided he will make a commencement order to bring into force the whole of the 1976 Act with effect from 1 January 1988. On commencement, the whole of the Adoption Acts of 1958, 1960, 1964 and 1968, and Part I of the Children Act 1975 are repealed. Local authorities are advised to order in good time from HMSO sufficient copies of the 1976 Act. Amendments to the Act which have been introduced since 1976 are set out in Annex 1.

Approval of adoption societies

3–095   3. The Secretary of State has approved 36 societies which are listed in Annex 2. Approval is for a period of three years from the original date of approval. Local authorities will be informed of any changes in the list.

Adoption statistics

3–096   4. A new system for collecting statistics was introduced on 27 May 1984. This was designed to provide a coordinated and comprehensive picture of the adoption service, which would serve as an effective aid to policy making at national and local level. The system depends on the completion of the Adoption Unit Return by the adoption agency (the local authority in the case on non-agency placements) and by the court. Clerks of magistrates courts are required by Section 58A of the 1976 Act, which came into force on 27 May 1984, to submit particulars of proceedings as required by the Secretary of State. At the same time the Lord Chancellor's Department agreed that officers of County Courts and the High Court should also complete and submit the Unit Return.

5. The value of the system is being seriously undermined by the failure to submit Returns. *Directors of Social Services* and *heads of adoption societies* are therefore asked to ensure that all adoption caseworks complete parts A to E of the Unit Return and forward the Return to the court with the agency's report to the court. *Clerks to magistrates* and *officers of County*

Courts and the *High Court* are asked in every case to check that a completed return has been provided by the agency; to complete part F of the Return when the application has been decided, and to forward the Return to the Register General *together with*, where an order has been made, a copy of the adoption or freeing order. More detailed guidance is available in circular LAC (84)6.

The adoption service

6. Section 1 of the 1976 Act provides that the service should meet the needs of children who **3–097** have been or may be adopted, parents and guardians of such children, and persons who have adopted or may adopt a child. Section 1(2) speicfies that the adoption service is to include:
   (a) temporary board and lodging where needed by pregnant women, mother or children;
   (b) arrangements for assessing children and prospective adopters, and for placing children for adoption; and
   (c) counselling for persons with problems relating to adoption.

7. Section 1(3) requires authorities to provided the adoption service in conjunction with the authority's other social services and with approved adoption societies so as to avoid "duplication, omission or avoidable delay". This requirement for collaboration with voluntary societies acknowledges the vital role and achievements of the societies in adoption work and points to the value of partnership between the statutory and voluntary sectors in providing a full range of services and facilities most effectively and efficiently.

8. Section 2 sets out the main social services functions in relation to children and their families so as to set adoption in the context of child care services as a whole. The full integration of adoption into the mainstream of services for children should help to ensure that the possibility of adoption is not overlooked in any case where it would be in the best interest of a child and that the necessary facilities are available; and, conversely and equally important, that all those concerned with adoption work are aware of other options and facilities and have access to them.

9. Annex 3 to this circular contains an outline of the services in relation to adoption which each local authority should aim to provide in its area. The list includes the essential components of the adoption service which must be provided to meet the requirements of Section 1, having regard to local needs. It also drews on requirements elsewhere in the 1976 Act, 1983 Regulations and the Adoption Rules which lay duties on adoption agencies generally or local authorities specifically and prescribe the way in which these duties are to be performed; and on practice developments which may go beyond the statutory requirements and depend on the availability of resources, for example the development of post adoption services which offer more than counselling.

10. In areas where a component of the service as required by Section 1, is not available the local authority must, by commencement, provide the service or arrange for it to be provided by an approved society. Financial arrangements will vary according to local preference, as at present, and may take the form of a general grant; or inter-agency fees for specific placements and other services; or a combination of those methods. Nearly all authorities now provide all or most elements of an adoption service either directly or through an approved society. Any additional resources required should not therefore be significant and should be balanced by the scope for economies through more effectively coordinated services. It is suggested that before commencement each authority should review its services and, in cooperation with the voluntary societies in its area, the services available from the voluntary sector, to identify the extent to which needs are already met. Authorities and voluntary societies can then plan and work together over time to develop a coordinated, and where necessary improved, adoption service as local circumstances require and resources permit.

11. Adoption services must be provided within the framework of the Adoption Agencies **3–098** Regulations 1983. The Regulations apply equally to voluntary societies and to local authorities acting as adoption agencies. An authority which does more than refer people to other adoption agencies must comply with the Regulations — it must, for example, set up an adoption panel. Guidance on the operation of the panel is in LAC (84)3.

12. In addition to the requirements of Sections 1 and 2 of the Act, local authorities remain responsible for the supervision of protected children and the provisions of reports to the courts in non-agency placements in accordance with Court Rules. These duties cannot be fulfilled by a voluntary society.

13. It is suggested that before commencement those authorities which have not already done so should consider whether to introduce an Adoption Allowance Scheme, to facilitate the adoption of children who need adoptive families but who cannot readily be adopted without some financial assistance to the adopters.

14. Even where authorities decide to provide most or all elements of the adoption service themselves, voluntary societies will continue to offer a vital contribution to the service. The

requirement in Section 1 to avoid duplication of services does not preclude the provision of choice where this is desirable. Societies also have strengths, experience and expertise to offer in specialised areas. Examples of these are:
— specialist services such as family-finding, preparation of children for family placement, rehabilitation of child with own family;
— developing and testing innovative practice, *e.g.* post-adoption support, services including family-finding for particular ethnic groups;
— service for particular groups, *e.g.* parents and children of a particular religious denomination, or children with special needs.

15. Authorities and societies should explore opportunities of joint action. A few examples from current practice:
— joint training programmes;
— arrangements for cross-membership of adoption panels;
— joint publicity and information services;
— joint arrangements for birth records counselling;
— joint monitoring arrangements and research projects;
— sharing or exchange of specialist staff.

16. Authorities should also bear in mind the need for and the value of cooperation with other services and agencies in the statutory and voluntary sectors, for example: with health authorities, so that adoption is not overlooked as an option for children in long stay hospitals who need to return to the community; with education authorities, so that the educational needs of children and the views of their teachers can be taken into account, and so that the availability of special educational facilities can be taken into account; and with local support groups for adoptive parents and families.

ANNEXES 1 AND 2

3–099 [Not reproduced.]

ANNEX 3

Services for children

3–100 1. Identifying children in need of long term substitute family care and those who might benefit from being adopted.

2. Working with natural parents in deciding the type of care likely to be most suitable for the individual child.

3. Referring to other services for help with the child for whom adoption is not thought to be appropriate.

4. Counselling children, working with children and preparing them for adoption.

5. Arranging for the care of children awaiting adoption, including those who are free for adoption.

6. Identifying and assessing the type of adoptive family required by the child, involving him where possible in the planning and ascertaining his wishes and feelings.

7. Finding a suitable adoptive family for the child.

8. Arranging a smooth and well prepared transition into the adoptive home for the child.

9. Supervising the child in the adoptive home.

10. Arranging for the care and counselling of a child on the refusal of an adoption order or the withdrawal of the application.

11. In co-operation with the adoptive family, providing the child with continuing support after adoption, including referral to other services such as child guidance where necessary, and counselling him if he has problems relating to his adoption.

Services for adult people

3–101 1. Counselling those with questions or problems relating to their adoptions.

2. Birth records counselling.

Services for natural parents or guardians

3–102 1. Counselling parents and guardians with problems relating to the child's care, and providing information and advice on his needs, including health needs.

2. Providing short term accommodation for pregnant women and for mothers with children, where this is needed in connection with adoption.

3. Planning with parents for the future care of the child, discussing the available choices of future care, including the possibility of his remaining with his parents or being rehabilitated with them, and helping them to reach a realistic decision. This applies to parents of children in the care of a local authority as well as to parents who contact the adoption service independently.

4. Advising parents on the meaning and implications of adoption including the legal process.

5. Arranging for other services to parents, such as day care services, where it is decided that adoption is not the right choice.

6. Referring parents to denominational or other specialist agencies where this is appropriate.

7. Preparing parents for separation from the child.

8. As far as is practicable and where there is no conflict with the child's welfare, complying with parents' wishes regarding the child's religious upbringing and other preferences in relation to the adoptive family.

9. Providing parents with continuing counselling and support where it is needed after the child has been adopted.

Services for prospective adopters and adoptive parents

1. Publicising the adoption service, educating and informing the public about adoption, and **3–103** recruiting prospective adopters.

2. Counselling prospective adopters, including discussion of problems such as infertility; explaining what adoption will require of them; informing them about the availability of children for adoption; counselling those who wish to adopt from overseas and giving information about the procedures; counselling those who cannot be accepted for assessment as adopters or with whom there is no prospect of a child being placed.

3. Providing information and advice to those who wish to adopt but for whom custodianship or joint custody may be more appropriate, such as step parents and relatives.

4. Recruiting suitable adoptive parents, with special initiatives where necessary, for example, for children with special needs or requiring parents from a particular ethnic group, and providing support where necessary before the child is placed.

5. Preparing the adoptive parents to receive the child, supplying background information about him including information about his medical history and needs, and providing support after placement.

6. Preparing foster parents for the change of role when they become adoptive parents.

7. Providing continuing support for adoptive families, including help and advice on problems relating to the adoption, and referring them where necessary to other services or other sources of help.

Note

The provision of *information leaflets* aimed at prospective adopters, parents, older children and adopted people will help to make people aware of the services available and diminish the need for interviews and counselling where enquirers need information only. Consideration should be given to producing leaflets in languages which reflect the composition of local communities.

LETTER No. CI(90)2

Dated January 20, 1990, and issued by the Chief Inspector, Social Services Inspectorate, Department of Health.

ISSUES OF RACE AND CULTURE IN THE FAMILY PLACEMENT OF CHILDREN

Introduction

3–104   1. **This Letter sets out the principles which should inform the practice of Social Services Departments in the family placement of children.** It enlarges on passages of special relevance in the Handbook of Guidance on the Boarding-Out of Children and points out where a similar approach is called for in adoption work and decisions. The Letter must be read, however, in the context of all the guidance contained in the Handbook, since it applies to all children who are fostered, whatever their ethnic origin.

2. Directors are asked to make the content of this Letter known to all managers and practitioners who are providing services for children and families; and to ensure that all such managers and practitioners are familiar with the Handbook of Guidance on the Boarding-Out of Children.

3. Copies of this Letter go to Heads of approved adoption societies and voluntary child care agencies to assist them in the adoption and family placement work of their agencies.

Providing child care services in a multi-racial society

3–105   4. **Social Services must address and seek to meet the needs of children and families from all groups in the community.** Society is made up of people of many different ethnic and racial origins and of different religious affiliations. The provision of services which will reach all members of the community calls for the development within social services departments of awareness, sensitivity and understanding of the different cultures of groups in the local community; and an understanding of the effects of racial discrimination on these groups. Necessary experience and expertise should be provided for in staffing of services and through relationships with other professions and services and with the community. In some areas the local community may include too great a variety of ethnic groups to be reflected fully in the composition of staff. In others, departments may be called on only rarely to provide a service for a child or family from a minority ethnic group. In both these circumstances, departments will need to identify sources of advice and help so that the necessary experience, expertise and resources are available when needed. These principles apply to services to help children to remain within their own families as well as to services for children in care and their families, so that children are not admitted to care through lack of appropriate and effective social work support for the family. This is especially important in the light of indicators that children from certain minority ethnic groups are over-represented among children in care.

5. **Where placements are needed or likely to be needed for children from minority ethnic groups or for children of particular religious affiliation, sustained efforts may be needed to recruit a sufficient number and range of foster parents and prospective adopters from those groups and of that religion. Such efforts are essential if all children who need substitute families are to have the opportunity of placement with families which share their ethnic origin and religion.** The development and planning of fostering and adoption services should aim to ensure that the resources of the service, including the arrangements for the recruitment, assessment, approval, preparation and support of a pool of foster parents, are responsive to the demands on the service. This calls for forward planning to identify the range and estimated numbers of foster homes which are likely to be required. Publicity and recruitment campaigns, resource networks and exchange arrangements must aim to reach all groups in the community and to increase awareness and understanding generally of the needs of children. Appropriate assessment and training must be available for all foster parents.

6. **In assessing a child's needs social workers should strive for a real understanding of the child's cultural background and religion and guard against simplistic assumptions of similarity between different ethnic groups.** Clients have a right to expect the understanding, knowledge and sensitivity which are essential if their interests are to be served. Assessment

must identify and advertisements explain a child's ethnic origins, religion and family experience in such a way as to provide as helpful a guide as possible to the child's needs. Care is needed so that the terms "black" and "black family" are not used in isolation in such a way as to obscure characteristics and needs which are of particular importance to groups and to individuals. An insufficiently precise message may not reach people of the particular group at which it is aimed; and other prospective carers who could have much to offer a child of a different ethnic origin or of mixed ethnic origin, by virtue of particular knowledge, language, understanding and family or neighbourhood links, may be discouraged from coming forward or be rejected out of hand. A white family which has adopted or is fostering a child of minority ethnic origin or mixed ethnic origin should not be told that placement of another such child cannot be considered solely on the grounds of general policy. Each case must be considered on its merits, having regard to the needs of children requiring placement. A family with some members of minority ethnic origin may be well placed to meet the needs of a child or another child of similar ethnic origin.

The legal framework

7. **Directors should ensure that practitioners and their managers observe the framework of 3–106 statutory requirements, regulations and Department of Health guidance within which their departments operate: In particular, the requirement in child care and adoption legislation to promote and safeguard the welfare at each child throughout childhood, taking into account the child's wishes and feelings, having regard to his age and understanding.** The Boarding-Out of Children (Foster Placement) Regulations 1988 require agencies to be satisfied that a child's needs arising from his racial origin and cultural background are met in a foster placement, so far as is practicable; and to ensure that a child is placed with a foster parent who is of the same religion, or if that is not practicable, with a foster parent who undertakes that the child will be brought up in that religion. While there are currently no corresponding specific statutory requirements in relation to adoption, it is of equal or greater importance that the same considerations should be applied. When the Children Act 1989 comes into force, agencies will be required, in all decisions in respect of a child they are looking after, to have regard to the child's religious persuasion, cultural and linguistic background and racial origin; and to the wishes and feelings of parents and other adults who have played a significant part in the child's life as well as to the wishes and feelings of the child. Local authorities will be required, in making arrangements for day care and fostering services, to have regard to the racial groups to which children needing the services belong. These requirements will formalise in relation to **child care** an approach which should already be an indispensable element in both **child care** and **adoption** practice.

8. **All factors relevant to the welfare of the individual child must be taken into account in assessing the child's needs and making decisions about the child's welfare. None of the separate factors involved should be abstracted and converted into a general pre-condition which overrides the others or causes any of them to be less than fully considered. The only general policy that is acceptable in making decisions about placing children in adoptive or foster homes is that all relevant factors should be considered.** Different factors will obviously vary in importance in relation to different children or in relation to the same child at different times. It will be right in those circumstances to weigh different factors differently. But it is not right to define any factor as of such general significance or primacy that it overrides or qualifies the duty to consider all factors bearing on the welfare of the child as an individual. Such a rule applied in respect of a decision affecting an individual child could expose the authority (or adoption agency) to judicial challenge.

Placement decisions

9. **Within this framework, a child's ethnic origin, cultural background and religion are 3–107 important factors; it may be taken as a guiding principle of good practice that, other things being equal and in the great majority of cases, placement with a family of similar ethnic origin and religion is most likely to meet a child's needs as fully as possible and to safeguard his or her welfare most effectively.** Such a family is most likely to be able to provide a child with continuity in life and care and an environment which the child will find familiar and sympathetic and in which opportunities will naturally arise to share fully in the culture and way of life of the ethnic group to which he or she belongs. Where the aim of a foster placement is to re-unite the child with his or her own family, contact and work with the family will in most cases be more comfortable for all and carry a greater chance of success if the foster parents are of similar ethnic origin. Families of similar ethnic origin are also usually best placed to prepare children for life as members of an ethnic minority group in a multi-

racial society, where they may meet with racial prejudice and discrimination, and to help them with their development towards independent living and adult life.

10. **Guiding principles are valuable only insofar as they are applied with proper consideration for the circumstances of the individual case. There may be circumstances in which placement with a family of different ethnic origin is the best choice for a particular child. In other cases such a placement may be the best available choice.** For example, a child may have formed strong links with prospective foster parents or adopters or be related to them. Siblings or step siblings who are not all of the same ethnic origin may need placement together. A child may prefer and need to remain close to school, friends and family even though foster parents of the same ethnic origin cannot be found in the locality. A child with special needs may require carers with particular qualities or abilities, so that choice is limited. The importance of religion as an element of culture should never be overlooked: to some children and families it may be the dominant factor, so that the religion of foster parents or adopters may in some cases be more important than their ethnic origin.

11. **All children should be encouraged and helped to understand, enjoy and take a pride in their ethnic origins and cultural heritage. This principle applies to all children for whom services are provided and to all children in care in any placement. Special care is needed where placement with a family of different ethnic origin is being considered, for whatever reason, including of course white children placed with families or minority ethnic origin.** What is the extent of the family's understanding and experience of the child's culture? Do they live near or among people of similar origin and background to the child? Are there relatives or friends and neighbours of the child's ethnic origin who can help and advise the foster parents or adopters and take on the responsibility of a significant role in the child's life? Will the child have the opportunity of going to school and enjoying friendships with children and young people who share his or her culture? Practitioners must satisfy themselves that all a child's needs will be addressed, in such a way that the child will not feel cut off from his or her origins or culture and his or her choices in later life will be preserved.

12. **For a child whose parents are of different ethnic groups, placement in a family which reflects as nearly as possible the child's ethnic origins is likely to be the best choice in most cases. But choice will be influenced by the child's previous family experience and, as with all placement decisions, by the child's wishes and feelings.** In discussing and exploring these with a child, practitioners should be ready to help the child with any confusion or misunderstandings about people of different ethnic groups which may have arisen through previous family or placement experience. Children of mixed ethnic origin should be helped to understand and take a pride in both or all elements in their cultural heritage and to feel comfortable about their origins. Foster parents and adopters must be able to provide this, with the help and support of others where necessary. This applies equally whether a child is placed with a minority ethnic family or with a white family or a family including members of differing ethnic origins.

13. **The choice of the most suitable placement for any child presents a difficult task in assessing and reconciling a child's needs. Requirements in respect of a child's welfare must be met within practical limitations of choice which mean that the ideal placement may not be available. Optimum choices for each child are more likely to be available within a fostering service run on the lines set out in the Handbook of Guidance and summarised in respect of fostering and adoption services in this Letter.**

The importance of planning, monitoring and reviews

3–108   14. **Planning is of vital importance. Planned admission** to care will allow more opportunity for the child's needs to be carefully assessed and a plan developed before placement. Hasty, emergency placements should be avoided as far as possible. **Clear agreements with foster parents** on the aim of a placement can serve to avoid the frustration arising from mistaken, confused or disappointed expectations, but only if the agreement is honoured by the agency. **Careful reviews** of each child, following the requirements of the Boarding-Out of Children (Foster Placement) Regulations, should consider whether the placement continues to be appropriate and whether the child's needs, including needs arising from racial origin, cultural background and religious persuasion are being met in the placement. Otherwise, steps must be taken to remedy any deficiencies identified in the review and to make any necessary changes. Children should not be removed from placements which are otherwise satisfactory solely because the ethnic origin of the foster parents does not accord with the requirements of general policies. Such a decision should be made only after assessment of the needs of the child and review of the placement in each case. **Monitoring, planning and decision making should not, of course, be restricted to statutory reviews. Short term and interim placements, in particular, must be kept under continuous and careful scrutiny to ensure that they are**

being properly used. A child must not be left indefinitely in an interim placement, or, even worse, a succession of interim placements, while a permanent placement is sought. The plan for the child must include limits of time, which will vary with individual children and their circumstances, within which progress towards objectives is reviewed and the plan revised where necessary.

CIRCULAR No. LAC (91)9

Dated April, 1991, and issued by the Department of Health

CHILDREN ACT 1989: ADOPTION CONTACT REGISTER

Summary

3–109 This Circular advises you of the introduction on May 1, 1991 of the Adoption Contact Register under The Children Act 1989. An outline of the Register is described. Also attached* to this Circular, for information, is:

    (i) "The Adoption Contact Register: information for adopted people and their relatives" (ACR 110);

    (ii) revised copy of the leaflet "Access to Birth Records: information for adopted people" (ACR 100);

    (iii) application forms for those wishing to use the Register (ACR 105 and ACR 108).

Commencement

3–110 1. The Adoption Contact Register comes into effect from May 1, 1991 by virtue of Schedule 10, paragraph 21 of the Children Act 1989 which introduces Section 51A of the Adoption Act 1976 and the Children Act 1989 (Commencement and Transitional Provisions) Order 1991 (S.I. 1991/829).

Action

3–111 2. The Register will be operated on behalf of the Registrar General by the Office of Population Censuses and Surveys (OPCS). Adoption agencies should be prepared to give information and advice about the Register, especially within the context of existing counselling services which they are now required to provide under sections 1 and 51 of the Adoption Act 1976. Leaflet ACR 110 includes details of voluntary organisations which have agreed to provide counselling and intermediary services for the purpose of the Register. There is no requirement for adoption agencies to allow their addresses to be used for entry on the Register or to provide intermediary services. Agencies may decide to refer enquirers to a voluntary organisation or to a similar regional service. Some agencies may wish themselves to provide these services, as described in paragraphs 5 and 6.

The Adoption Contact Register

3–112 13. The purpose of the Adoption Contact Register is to make easier the possibility of contact between adopted adults and their birth parents or other relatives whilst ensuring that responsibility for initiating contact rests solely with the adopted person. The Register applies generally to adopted adults who were born and adopted in England or Wales and to their relatives as defined in Section 72(1) of the Adoption Act 1976. The Register will operate from: —

    Office of Population Censuses and Surveys
    The General Register Office
    Adoptions Section
    Smedley Hydro
    Trafalgar Road
    Birkdale
    Southport PR8 2HH

4. The Register is in two parts. Subject to the conditions in Section 51A(4), the Registrar General will enter in Part 1 the name, the current address and the details relating to the birth of an adopted person who wishes to contact his or her birth parent or other natural relatives. Subject to the conditions in Section 51A(6), the Registrar General will enter in Part II the name, the current address and the identifying details of a relative who wishes to contact an

adopted person, either directly or through an intermediary. The Registrar General will send to the registered adopted person the name of any relative who has also registered together with the address which the relative has supplied. No information about the adopted person will be given to the relative except that the Registrar General will inform the relative when his or her details have been passed to the adopted person. A fee is payable for entry on both parts of the Register. As at May 1, 1991, the fee for entry on Part I is BP 5. Section 51A(13) of the Adoption Act 1976 (extended definition of address) enables a relative of an adopted person to enter on the Register a third party address for initial contact by the adopted person — for example, receiving correspondence. Relatives may also request a third party to act as an intermediary for contact with the adopted person. The person wishing to use an intermediary should, of course, have obtained the agreement of the intermediary before putting forward their details. We would expect the intermediary to be skilled and experienced in adoption counselling and intermediary work and sensitive to the range of consequences which can arise from entry on the Register. Adoption agencies have considerable expertise in adoption counselling. All local authorities are required to provide adoption counselling services under the arrangements in Section 1 of the Adoption Act 1976. Authorities and adoption societies may also provide counselling services as specified in Section 51 of the Adoption Act.

6. Some Directors of Social Services and Secretaries of approved adoption societies may wish to offer their services as an intermediary. If so, it is suggested that any contact address should not include details relating to an individual counsellor or social worker. In some cases some considerable time may pass before the adopted person attempts to reach his or her relative, if at all. Agencies may, however, prefer to refer enquirers to reputable regional bodies (such as post-adoption centres) willing to provide counselling and intermediary services, or to one of the voluntary organisations listed in leaflet ACR 110. These organisations also provide counselling.

7. The introduction of the Register does not affect existing arrangements in Section 51 of the Adoption Act 1976 relating to the disclosure of birth records of adopted people. Statutory counselling will continue to apply to anyone who was adopted before November 12, 1975 who wishes to receive information about his or her birth. The arrangements are described in the attached revised leaflet "Access to Birth Records: information for adopted people living in the UK" (ACR 100). A similar leaflet for people living outside the UK will appear later this year in connection with the introduction on October 14, 1991 of Section 51 counselling provisions for adopted people living abroad.

Enquiries

8. Any enquiries about this Circular should be addressed to Community Services Division **3–113** (CS3B). Room B1404, Department of Health, Alexander Fleming House, Elephant and Castle, London SE1 6BY (telephone 071 972 4083). Enquiries about the Register should be directed to the Office of Population Censuses and Surveys whose address is given in paragraph 3 above.

LETTER No. C1 (92)12*

Dated April 9, 1992, and issued by the Chief Inspector, Social Services Inspectorate

ADOPTION OF ROMANIAN CHILDREN: AGREEMENT WITH THE ROMANIAN COMMITTEE FOR ADOPTIONS

3–114   1. This letter advises directors of local authority social services of the Agreement between the United Kingdom and the Romanian Committee for Adoptions. The Agreement regulates the adoption of Romanian children by prospective adopters domiciled in the United Kingdom. This letter also sets out the implications of the Agreement for local authority social services and adopters.

2. The Romanian Committee for Adoptions is the body formally established by the Romanian Senate in July 1991, following changes to the Romanian law on adoption, with responsibility for registering children at present cared for in children's homes and other institutions and who, for whatever reason, are available for adoption. The Committee is also responsible for processing all applications from prospective adopters living abroad who seek to adopt these children.

3. The Agreement with the Committee was signed on 19 March 1992 on behalf of the health departments in England, Scotland, Wales and Northern Ireland and comes into effect on 5 May 1992. From this date the Committee will accept applications to adopt Romanian children from prospective adopters meeting the conditions set out in the Agreement and domiciled in the United Kingdom.

A copy of the Agreement is attached at Appendix A to this letter.

4. The Agreement was drawn up by the Romanian Committee for Adoptions and is similar to agreements signed by other countries. Without this Agreement, adoption of children from Romania could not take place.

5. The Agreement introduces a number of amendments to existing guidance, but only in respect of the adoption of Romanian children, set out in Chief Inspector Letters CI(90)17 and CI(91)14 concerning the adoption of children from overseas. This letter contains advice about the amendments.

Copies of this letter go to Heads of approved adoption societies.

The agreement

3–115   6. Summary of the main elements:

(a) The Department of Health becomes the sole agency for the United Kingdom in all matters with the Romanian Committee for Adoptions concerning the adoption of children from Romania.

(b) The Department of Health will process applications received from local authorities in England and act as agent for the health departments in Scotland, Wales and Northern Ireland in processing applications approved by them.

(c) The Romanian Committee for Adoptions will be responsible for matching children to prospective adopters.

(d) Prospective adopters must be married to each other for at least three years.

(e) Prospective adopters must not have more than two children.

(f) Prospective adopters must be no more than [40] years older (for the mother) and [45] years older (for the father) than the child to be adopted. (But see paragraph 12 of this letter.)

(g) Prospective adopters will not be given a second choice to be matched with another child if they should not accept the first child offered to them by the Committee. (But see paragraphs 33 and 34 of this letter.)

(h) The conditions set out in paragraph 12 of the Agreement will not apply to adopters wishing to adopt a sibling to a child already adopted, children with special needs or those over 10 years of age.

---

* [This letter is reproduced as amended by Letter No. CI(93)15—R.M.J.]

(i) Reports on the progress of Romanian children brought to the United Kingdom for adoption will be forwarded to the Committee at regular intervals.

(j) The role of the Home Office concerning entry clearance requirements remains unchanged.

Children available for adoption

7. Adoptions in Romania carried out by private arrangement between Romanians and other **3–116** nationalities are illegal according to the new Romanian law on adoptions passed by the Romanian Senate on July 17, 1991. Prospective adopters can no longer travel to Romania with the expectation of identifying a child for adoption and returning to the United Kingdom to begin the adoption process.

8. *Only children being cared for in children's homes and other institutions and registered with the Romanian Committee for Adoptions will be made available for adoption by adopters living abroad.*

9. Once placed on the register, children are made available for adoption for a period of six months exclusively to Romanian citizens domiciled in Romania. At the end of that time, if the children have not been adopted by Romanians, they may then become available for adoption by people living abroad.

Eligible applicants

10. Paragraph 12 of the Agreement sets out the conditions which enable prospective **3–117** adopters to be eligible to adopt a Romanian child. These conditions apply to "normal" children. Included in this group are children who, in the view of the Romanian Committee for Adoptions, have experienced developmental delays attributable to institutional care. The Committee fully expects that good parental and health care will compensate for these delays.

11. The Committee has advised the "no more than two children" should be calculated as children born to the family or coming to the family as a result of previous marriages or adopted children. The Committee has taken the view that children do not cease to be children once they reach the age of 18 years. According to the Committee, therefore, children born to a family who have since married and moved away must still be counted among the adopters' children.

12. The Committee, however, intends to apply less stringent conditions to adopters of children with special needs or those over the age of 10 years. This means that the Committee is prepared to consider applications to adopt such children from single adopters or couples who have been married less than three years or those who are no more than 40 years older (for the mother) and 45 years older (for the father) than the child to be adopted [whom the Department of Health is prepared to support]. However, the condition relating to adopters having no more than two children remains.

13. The Committee has not been explicit about what factors constitute "special needs" but has confirmed that they are likely to be children with severe mental, emotional and physical disabilities.

14. Exceptions to paragraph 12 of the Agreement concerning the adoption of siblings will be restricted to a brother or sister who was born before the Romanian adoption order was made in respect of the child already adopted. The Committee has placed no limit on the number of siblings able to join their brother or sister as adopted children.

15. If there is any doubt about eligibility concerning the age of prospective adopters, the local authority should consult the Department of Health before proceeding to prepare a home study report. All enquiries concerning the Agreement should be addressed to:

Department of Health
Section CS3B
Wellington House
133-155 Waterloo Road
London SE1 8UG.

Tel: 0171 972 4347

Home study reports

16. As a result of the Agreement, a number of minor changes to existing guidance are **3–118** necessary for the preparation of a home study report for the adoption of Romanian children. Significantly, most of these changes are to the numbers and types of documents rather than the content itself.

17. Attention of social workers carrying out home study reports should be drawn to the list of subjects contained in paragraph 14 of the Agreement setting out basic information requirements for each adoption application, most of which can be incorporated in the social worker's report. The following are required to be presented in the form of statements separate from the home study:

(i) police statement obtained by a local authority confirming that the adopters have no record of criminal convictions;

(ii) a statement from the adoption agency's designated representative, written on the agency's letter-headed paper, that the applicants are approved as prospective adopters and that they are eligible to adopt according to the adoption laws of the United Kingdom.

18. Social workers are advised that the Committee has taken an uncompromising line regarding prospective adopters and police records. The Committee has informed officials that it will not accept any application which contains a court conviction for a criminal offence, no matter how minor the offence or how young the age of the applicant when the offence was committed.

19. Comments on the health of the other members of the household are required by the Committee. This should already be supplied by the use of the recently amended BAAF Form F. Adopters are asked to supply recent coloured photographs of themselves and any children born to them and also any others living in the same household. This request has been made by members of the Committee to help them in their work of matching children to adopters.

20. Once the local authority has prepared the home study report along the lines of the Agreement, the documents should be forwarded to the Department of Health in the usual way. The Department will examine the application and if it is able to support the recommendation of the local authority, will arrange to send the documents for translation into Romanian. The translation will be at the expense of the adopters — see paragraphs 22–25 below.

21. Social services departments are reminded of the advice contained in Chief Inspector Letter CI(91)14 of June 7, 1991 concerning the timescale for the provision of reports. SSDs should continue to apply the same timescale for the preparation of home study reports under these new arrangements as set out in paragraph 9 of the letter.

Translation of documents

3–119 22. The Committee requires all documents to be translated into Romanian before considering an adoption application from another country. In order to assist prospective adopters in this task, the Department of Health, with the assistance of the School of Slavonic and East European Studies at the University of London, has prepared a list of translators of Romanian who are prepared to take on the work in connection with Romanian adoptions.

The list of translators is at Appendix B to this letter.

23. The Department of Health has provided this list as a facilitating measure. The translators put forward by the University have been made aware of the sensitive nature of the documents and the need for confidentiality. Prospective adopters should understand that they will be responsible for negotiating the translation fee direct with the translator they have selected.

24. The Department of Health can take no responsibility for the quality of the work carried out by the translators or any fault, loss of material or breach of any agreement made between the adopters and the translators. Adopters are not obliged to choose a translator from the list and are free to make their own arrangements.

25. When the prospective adopters have identified a translator and agreed terms, they should contact the Department of Health direct so that their documents can be forwarded to the translator without delay — see paragraph 15 above for the address. Upon completion of the work, the translator will be required to return all documents to the Department. Translators have been instructed not to provide copies of either the English or Romanian documents to the adopters.

Certification of documents

3–120 26. The Committee has requested that all documents sent to them from the local authority must be certified as a true copy of the original documents by a solicitor registered in the United Kingdom. This is necessary to comply with the requirements of Romanian courts. In most cases the solicitors will be those employed by the local authority and acting as legal advisers on adoption matters.

27. The attention of social workers should be drawn to the advice contained in paragraph 29 of Chief Inspector Letter CI(90)17 and dated September 28, 1990 concerning the handling of home study reports. The address of the Department of Health to which reports should be sent has changed and is given at paragraph 15 above.

The matching process

28. The Romanian Committee for Adoptions will be responsible for matching children to **3–121** prospective adopting parents. The Committee is unable to give any indication how long the matching process is likely to take or how long adopters will have to wait before they are informed of a matching. Also, information about how this part of the process is to operate have not been made clear to the Department of Health. It is most important, therefore, that as much information as possible is provided to the Committee in the home study report to help them in this difficult process.

29. Once the Committee have matched a child to adopters it will provide the Department of Health with the documents and other information referred to in paragraph 15 of the Agreement. This information, which will be in English, will provide the basis upon which prospective adopters will be asked to decide whether they wish to proceed to adopt the child offered to them. This will then be forwarded to the social services department to be discussed with the prospective adopters.

30. The Department of Health will examine the Romanian documents in the first instance to ensure that the files are complete before passing them on to the local authorities concerned or to the relevant departments of health in Scotland, Wales and Northern Ireland.

31. The Department of Health will also take the opportunity to make observations about the information contained in the documents concerning the child offered for adoption which should be brought to the attention of the adopters by the social services department.

Child referral

32. Once these documents have been received by the local authorities, social workers should **3–122** make arrangements to counsel the adopters about the child matched to them and discuss the implications of adopting that particular child.

33. Adopters will have to consider their position in the light of any counselling received before making their decision known to the local authority. If the adopters decide not to accept the child offered, the local authority is asked to let the Department of Health know the reasons for non-acceptance so that the Committee can be informed. Again, this information will prove valuable to the Committee in its work of matching children to adopting parents. [Prospective adopters of a special needs child (which includes all children over the age of 10 years) will be offered a further child within the range of disabilities for which the adopters have been approved should an earlier offer of a child not be accepted.]

34. In order that any acceptance together with the signed Declaration of Intent to Adopt is forwarded by the Department to the Committee within the 60 days of receipt of the papers by the Department from the Committee (see paragraph 16 of the Agreement), it is likely that adopters will have about five weeks in which to make their decision.

35. Social workers are asked to make a point of advising prospective adopters at an early stage that, except in very special circumstances, they will not be offered a second choice if they do not accept the child first offered by the Committee. Special circumstances might include, for example, information about the child which is at variance with the recommendation of the local authority and which might lead to inappropriate matching.

36. In such cases, social service departments will be asked to set out for the Committee their reasons why the information about the particular child offered does not make a suitable match with the prospective adopters. This information together with the original documents should be sent to the Department of Health requesting a supportive statement to accompany the documents returned to the Committee.

Child acceptance

37. If the child is accepted by the prospective adopters, they will be asked to sign a form to **3–123** be known as a "Declaration of Intent to Adopt". This form is provided by the Romanian Committee for Adoptions. It is not a legal document and does not bind the prospective adopters in any way to a legal undertaking, including adoption.

38. Once the Declaration of Intent to Adopt has been sent to the Department of Health to be recorded, it will be forwarded to the Committee. Prospective adopters will then have 30

days from the date of signing the Declaration to make arrangements to travel to Romania and visit the child. The adopters can then arrange to complete the adoption process.

39. The Committee has given the Department of Health its assurance that it will honour recommendations contained in home study reports which specify the sex of the child to be matched to the prospective parents.

40. Both adopting parents will be required to travel to Romania to visit the child with whom they have been matched. The adopters should be advised to allow themselves sufficient time in Romania within the 30 day period to become aquainted with the child before finally coming to a decision. Adopters will be required to confirm their acceptance and intention to adopt with the local authority. This confirmation may be made by telephone.

41. Following receipt of this confirmation and subject to the final recommendation of the social services department, the local authority should inform the Department of Health of the prospective adopters' wish to adopt the child offered. The Department of Health will then recommend to the Home Office that entry clearance should be given to the child who has been offered to the adopters concerned. This information will enable the adopters to make application to the British Embassy in Bucharest for entry clearance for the particular child.

Meeting with the Romanian Committee for Adoptions

3–124   42. The couple will be required to meet representatives of the Romanian Committee for Adoptions in Bucharest, once they have made the decision to adopt the child, in order to clarify any points either side may wish to raise. It will be at this meeting that the parents will be requested to send at agreed intervals to the Committee reports on the progress of the child following the making of the adoption order in the United Kingdom. This request is set out in paragraph 17 of the Agreement and paragraphs 49 and 50 of this letter.

The address of the Committee is:

> Comitetul Roman Pentu Adoptii
> Sediul: Bd. Iancu de Hunedoara
> Nr 1–5 Sector 1
> Bucharest.

> Tel: (Bucharest) 14 34 00

Romanian court process

3–125   43. Courts in Romania are not permitted to hear applications for adoption orders made by foreign adopters unless the court has received the necessary documents from the Romanian Committee for Adoptions which will allow the court to make such an order.

44. Although it is not necessary, prospective adopters may wish to engage the services of a lawyer practicing in Romania. To this end, the adopters should be advised to contact the Romanian Bar Association in the district in which the child to be adopted is living.

The address of the local association can be obtained from:

> Mr. Nicholae Cerveni,
> Romanian Bar Association,
> Dr. Reureanu Str. No. 3,
> Sector 5, Bucuresti, Romania.

> Tel: 010 400 15 45 38

45. Prospective adopters should be advised that under Romanian law, an adoption is not made final until 15 days have elapsed after the adoption order has been made, during which time the birth parent can still withdraw consent. This period is a "cooling off" period for both parties to the adoption. In effect, however, judges have been known to waive some or all of this period, but there can be no guarantee on this point.

Entry clearance process

3–126   [46. Romanian adoption orders are not recognised in the United Kingdom. Entry clearance must therefore be applied for and obtained from the British Embassy in Bucharest in order to allow the child to travel to the United Kingdom for the purposes of adoption. Once the prospective adopters have arrived in Romania and completed the adoption process, an appointment should be made with the Visa Section at the British Embassy.

The Section's opening hours are 09.30–12.30 Monday to Friday.

47. Before entry clearance is granted, the Entry Clearance Officer will need to be satisfied that the adoption involves a genuine transfer of parental responsibility on the grounds of the

original parents inability to care for the child; that the adoption is not simply a means to facilitate the child's admission to the UK and that the child can be adequately maintained and accommodated by the adopting parents without recourse to public funds. If these requirements are met, entry clearance may be authorised.

48. The Entry Clearance Office will be advised of the impending visit of prospective adopters who have been matched with a child in Romania. The Officer will already have certain documents and other information about the proposed adoption and will be expecting the adopters to make contact with the Embassy to apply for entry clearance for the child. When applying for entry clearance, the adopters should have with them the Romanian Adoption Order and a Romanian passport for the child, obtainable from the Romanian Passport Office in Bucharest. A Romanian passport is usually issued within 24–48 hours.

Once the adoption process has been completed and a passport for the child has been issued, the British Embassy will place the entry clearance visa into the child's passport.

Upon arrival in the United Kingdom the child will normally be admitted for a period of 12 months.

49. All Romanian citizens, regardless of age, require a visa to enter the United Kingdom. It is a breach of UK Immigration Rules for a Romanian citizen to travel to the UK without a visa. An Immigration Officer at a UK port of entry may exercise his right to refuse entry to a Romanian child without a valid visa. In these circumstances the child may be required to return to Romania until a visa has been issued.]

50. The British Embassy in Bucharest has advised that their role in relation to the adoption of Romanian children is limited to dealing with applications for entry clearance and cannot assist adopters with difficulties arising from the process of adopting a child under Romanian law.

51. Before the child's period of leave to enter expires, an application should be made to the Home Office Immigration Department for extension of the child's stay. The Home Office Address is:

Immigration Department
Luna House,
40, Wellesley Road,
Croydon,
Surrey CR9 2YB.

Tel: 0181 686 0688

52. The application should include documents confirming that an application for an adoption order has been lodged with a court in the UK. The child's passport should also be sent at this time.

53. When an adoption order has been made in the UK the child's passport should be sent to the Immigration Department once more, together with a copy of the adoption order, so that the passport can be endorsed to show that the child can stay in the UK indefinitely.

54. Following an adoption order in the United Kingdom, if at least one of the adopters is a British citizen, the child will automatically become a British citizen from the date of the adoption order and an application may be made to the nearest Passport Office for a British passport for the child.

Reports to the committee

55. The Committee has asked for reports to be supplied at regular intervals on the child's **3–127** progress for two years following the child's entry into the United Kingdom. These reports should be brief and relevant to the child's progress in adjusting to the new family and can include photographs illustrating the child's progress.

56. For the provision of these reports it is suggested that:
   (i) up to the time an adoption order is made in the United Kingdom, the review reports carried out by local authorities as part of their statutory function in looking after the interests of the "protected" child can be used for this purpose;
   (ii) for the remainder of the two years, following an adoption order, these reports can be made by the parents of the child.

57. The Committee regards these reports as important feed-back relating to its work in the matching process as well as being assured that the children's best interests are being served. The reports, whether from social services departments or adopters, should be sent to the Department of Health who will forward them to the Committee. These reports will not require translation into Romanian.

Fees in Romania

3–128 58. Prospective adopters should be advised that there will be a number of fees to be paid by adopters in Romania, mainly in connection with the administrative process, and will include the following:

    (i) [$1250] payable to the Romanian Department of Health for completion of the child's medical form.

    (ii) $700–$1,000 court fees. This fee includes the services of a court lawyer. If the adopters have made private arrangements to have their own lawyer, the court fee will be correspondingly reduced.

    (iii) $80 payable to the British Embassy in Bucharest for processing the visa application. This fee is payable in local currency.

    (iv) £1.50, payable in local currency (about 500 Lei), to the Romanian Passport Office for providing the adopted child with a Romanian passport.

59. The above fees, which are approximate and also liable to fluctuation, apply as of Spring 1992.

60. The Romanian Committee for Adoptions has pointed out that Romanian law does not permit directors of children's homes and other institutions which care for children to receive or accept any payment or fee from prospective adopters in connection with the adoption of children.

Action by social services

3–129 61. Local authorities will shortly be receiving home study reports of prospective adopters living within their area which had been submitted to the Department under the old arrangements and which appear to meet the conditions of the Romanian Committee for Adoptions. These home studies will, in most cases, need to be brought up-to-date. Social workers may also wish to counsel adopters about the conditions contained in the Agreement and have the opportunity of adding to the home study report if appropriate.

62. In any case, all these home studies will require amending in order to comply with the conditions set out in paragraph 14 of the Agreement. This includes prospective adopters providing recent coloured photographs of themselves, their children and other members of the household as well as separate statements following police enquiries and comments on the health of members of their household.

63. Local authorities should be aware that the Committee is able to process a maximum of five applications from the United Kingdom at any time. [Applications from prospective adopters seeking to adopt a child with special needs will be processed separately. There is to be no delay, therefore, in processing which may be sent to the Committee as soon as they are received from the local authority and processed by the Department of Health. Such applications should be as specific as possible about the range or type of special needs child whom the prospective adopters wish to adopt.] When these applications have been processed, the Committee will ask the Department of Health to send a further five applications. This system applies to all countries with whom the Committee has an Agreement. It is based on a practical consideration, namely, that the Committee do not have the room, staff or facilities to handle large volumes of applications sent from around the world at the same time.

Private home study reports

3–130 64. This letter takes forward earlier advice to directors of social services departments contained in C1(90)17 concerning privately commissioned home study reports. A recent judgment in the Family Division of the High Court has given the Department reason to believe that privately commissioned home study reports are unlawful, being in breach of section 11 (as extended by section 72(3)) of the Adoption Act 1976 — restrictions on making arrangements for adoption — and payments for them are in breach of section 57.

AGREEMENT ON THE WORKING ARRANGEMENTS FOR THE CO-ORDINATION OF INTERCOUNTRY
ADOPTION BETWEEN THE ROMANIAN COMMITTEE FOR ADOPTIONS AND THE UNITED KINGDOM

Introduction

1. This agreement is not a legal document but has been prepared to reflect current **3–131** legislation governing the adoption of children in Romania and within the United Kingdom.

2. The Agreement is the basis for a working arrangement between the countries of the United Kingdom and the Romanian Committee for Adoptions concerning the processing of applications from those domiciled in the UK to adopt children from Romania who have been identified as being available for adoption by the Romanian Committee for Adoptions.

3. The Department of Health in England will act as agent for the Health Departments of Scotland, Wales and Northern Ireland in processing applications from prospective adopters.

General principles

4. The guiding principles for this working arrangement are those set out in the United **3–132** Nations Convention on the Rights of the Child, adopted by the General Assembly on November 20, 1989.

5. These principles recognise that:
   (a) intercountry adoption may be considered as an alternative means of child care if the child cannot be placed with foster parents or with an adoptive family or cared for in a suitable manner in the child's country of origin;
   (b) in all actions concerning children, the best interests of the child shall be a primary consideration;
   (c) the child who is the subject of intercountry adoption should enjoy safeguards and standards equivalent to those existing in the case of a national adoption;
   (d) the placement of a child should be arranged by competent authorities in Romania and the United Kingdom;
   (e) subject to paragraph "f" below, no payment shall be made in relation to arrangements for adoptions;
   (f) bona fide payments in respect of expenses and fees may be made.

Guidelines

6. Intercountry adoption of Romanian children must be performed according to Romanian **3–133** and United Kingdom laws governing adoption.

7. The Department of Health will only forward applications for the adoption of Romanian children on behalf of those domiciled in the United Kingdom and received from the relevant local authority for the area in which the applicants live.

8. In respect of developing detailed procedures and requirements for the adoption of Romanian children, the Department of Health will co-operate exclusively with the Romanian Committee for Adoptions which is the authorised body in Romania responsible for identifying and listing children who may be available for adoption by people living abroad.

9. The Romanian Committee for Adoptions will accept only from the Department of Health applications for the adoption of Romanian children from those domiciled in the UK, including Romanian citizens domiciled in the United Kingdom.

10. The Department of Health and the Romanian Committee for Adoptions will develop detailed procedures and requirements for the adoption of Romanian children by those domiciled in the United Kingdom and Romanian citizens domiciled in the United Kingdom. These procedures shall include those specified in the Annex to this document which is to be regarded as an integral part of the Agreement.

Amendment provision

11. The working arrangements may be amended at any time with the approval in writing of **3–134** both parties. Either the Department of Health or the Romanian Committee for Adoptions may terminate the Agreement by giving three months notice in writing. Termination of the

Agreement will not affect the completion of adoptions procedures already in progress at the time termination is to take effect.

Concluded today, Thursday 19 March, 1992.

Michael Brennan
(Signed)

Dr A. Zugravescu
(Signed)

FOR THE DEPARTMENTS OF HEALTH OF THE UNITED KINGDOM

ROMANIAN COMMITTEE FOR ADOPTIONS

BUCURESTI
ROMAN

[The Committee confirmed their agreement to the concession obtained in June 1992 that prospective adopters who could show evidence that they had received the notarised consent of the birth parent(s) to the adoption of their child before July 17, 1991 would not be subject to the conditions set out in the Agreement.

(The only other pre-condition which permits exemption from the conditions of the Agreement is where the prospective adopting parents can provide evidence of a court allocation number which confirms that they had registered for a court hearing in Romania before July 17, 1991.)—Letter No. CI(93)15]

ANNEX TO THE WORKING ARRANGEMENTS BETWEEN THE ROMANIAN COMMITTEE FOR ADOPTIONS AND THE UNITED KINGDOM

PROCEDURES AND REQUIREMENTS FOR THE ADOPTION OF ROMANIAN CHILDREN

ELIGIBLE APPLICANTS

12. Eligible applicants will: **3–135**
    (a) be couples married to each other for at least three years. Exceptionally, couples married less than three years and single people may be considered in respect of children with special needs or children over 10 years of age.
    (b) be a minimum of 21 years of age and no more than [40] years older (for the adopting mother) and [45] years older (for the adopting father) than the child to be adopted. Exceptionally, where the applicants wish to adopt a child with special needs, or a child over 10 years of age, the mother will be no more than 40 years older and the father no more than 45 years older than the child to be adopted;
    (c) have no more than two children.

ELIGIBLE CHILDREN

13. Eligible children are those who are registered with the Romanian Committee for **3–136** Adoptions who could not be entrusted or adopted in Romania within at least six months from their date of registration.

PROCEDURES

A. Application

14. An application to adopt a Romanian child will include the following documents which **3–137** will be forwarded to the Romanian Committee for Adoptions by the Department of Health:
    (a) a statement from the applicants expressing their desire to adopt a Romanian child. (This statement can be incorporated in the home study report.)
    (b) copies of birth and marriage certificates;
    (c) police statement of enquiries made, providing details (if any) of criminal convictions recorded in respect of each applicant;
    (d) full reports on the health of applicants and comments on the health of other members of their household;
    (e) statement of family income; (This statement can be incorporated in the home study report.)
    (f) recent colour photographs of applicants and of any children born to the applicants or living in the applicants household;
    (g) home study reports prepared by the local authority in whose area the applicant lives. The report should include reference to:
        (i) the applicant's motivation for adoption;
        (ii) psychosocial history;
        (iii) family dynamics;
        (iv) attitude of children in the household towards the possible adoption;
        (v) knowledge of and attitudes towards Romanian culture;
        (vi) attitudes of the immediate community;
        (vii) other information of interest (*e.g.* religion).
The home study should also include a statement from the local authority in whose area the applicant lives indicating their opinion regarding the capability of the applicants to adopt a Romanian child, confirming that the applicants may adopt in accordance with the relevant domestic law in the United Kingdom. This statement is to be provided by the head of the adoption agency on letter-headed paper of the agency.
    All documents must be certified by a solicitor registered in the United Kingdom as a true copy of the original documents and translated into Romanian.

B. Child referral

15. The Romanian Committee for Adoptions will review applications and register the **3–138** applicants on their waiting list. As children become available for adoption the Committee will select the family they deem most appropriate for the child and forward the following documents to the Department of Health:

(i) child's social case history including the circumstances surrounding his/her becoming available for adoption, having regard to the wishes and feelings of the child, taking into account the child's age and understanding;

(ii) child's medical history and current health status;

(iii) recent photograph of the child;

(iv) social and medical history of the child's birth parents, if available.

(v) child's certificate of birth;

(vi) notarised statement from the birth parents, or from the person having parental responsibility for the child, that consent for the child to be adopted has been freely given.

C. Child acceptance

3–139   16. If the child identified for the prospective adopters is accepted, the couple will be asked to sign a "Declaration of Intent to Adopt" which must be forwarded to the Romanian Committee for Adoptions by the Department of Health within 60 days of its receipt in the Department.

Exceptionally, the Department of Health will make representation to the Romanian Committee for Adoptions to extend the period of 60 days.

17. The Romanian Committee for Adoptions will be provided with follow-up reports for two years following the child's entry into the United Kingdom, describing the adjustment of the child into the family. These reports will be prepared by social workers approved by the local authority at regular intervals up to the time the adoption order is made in the United Kingdom.

The provision thereafter of follow-up reports for the remainder of the two years will be by agreement of the applicants and the Romanian Committee for Adoptions. These reports will be forwarded to the Romanian Committee for Adoptions by the Department of Health.

18. The applicants will travel to Romania within 30 days from the date of signing the "Declaration of Intent to Adopt" in order to complete the adoption process in Romania.

19. If the child matched to the adopters is not accepted, the Romanian Committee for Adoptions will not offer that couple a second choice. The local authority will set out for the Committee the reasons why the child has not been accepted.

D. Other provisions

3–140   20. The Romanian Committee for Adoptions will provide the applicants or their legal representatives with confirmation that the child could not be entrusted or adopted in Romania within at least six months from the date of his/her registration, as well as the file containing the documents regarding the applicants, referred to in section 15 of this Annex.

21. Applicants wishing to retain the services of a lawyer should make enquiries of the Romanian Bar Association in the district in which the child is resident.

22. In the event of a breakdown of the adoption placement or abandonment of the child in the UK, the local authority for the area in which the child resides is responsible for providing for the protection or placement of the child in accordance with the relevant domestic law in the United Kingdom.

23. The Department of Health is obliged to bring to the notice of the Romanian Committee for Adoptions all cases of breakdown of adoption placements in the United Kingdom involving a Romanian child which come to its attention.

24. The Romanian Committee for Adoptions and the Department of Health, working in close co-operation, will encourage the training of personnel with a view to improving the intercountry adoption programme.

25. The Department of Health will inform the Romanian Committee for Adoptions of cultural research programmes or other studies concerning children adopted from Romania.

Bucuresti
Roman

March 19, 1992

APPENDIX B

The following list of translators has been supplied to the Department through the School of **3–141** Slavonic and East European Studies, University of London.

Before providing the information to prospective adopters, the attention of social workers should be drawn to paragraphs 22–25 of this guidance.

Yvonne Alexandrescu
Lloyd Baker House
Lloyd Baker Street
London WC1

Tel: 0171 278 5512

Dan Vespasian Antal
37 Kinsale Road
Peckham Rye
London SE15 4HJ

Tel: 0171 358 9747

Adrian Morris
Lauriston
Weycombe
Haslemere
Surrey GU27 1EL

Tel: 014286 54494

Michaela Wolf
17 Arvon Road
Highbury
London N5 1PS

Tel: 0171 607 6905

LETTER No. CI (96)4

Dated February 1, 1996, and issued by the Chief Inspector, Social Services Inspectorate, Department of Health

ADOPTION

Introduction

3–142 1. This letter contains further guidance to local authority social services on certain issues relating to adoption practice as well as advocating a more positive approach to adoption.

2. Directors are asked to make the content of this letter known to all managers and practitioners providing adoption services for children and families. The content of this guidance does not depend on proposed changes to existing legislation or subsequent regulations.

Benefits of Adoption

3–143 3. Since the first adoption legislation was passed in 1926, thousands of children have benefitted from the commitment of adoptive families. Adoption continues to be an important service for children, offering a positive and beneficial outcome for many children, providing them with a unique opportunity of a fresh start as permanent members of new families, enjoying a sense of security and well-being so far denied them in their young lives. For many children, adoption may be their only chance of experiencing family life.

4. For some children adoption will sometimes be considered where other alternatives including rehabilitation have been tried, sometimes over a long period, but has proved to be unsuccessful. There may be some instances where adoption may never be considered a suitable option in meeting the best interests of particular children. For many children, however, it will be clear to social workers at an early stage that adoption is the only practical long-term solution likely to meet their particular needs.

5. Without any loss of the careful and balanced assessment essential in all child placements, adoption and adoptive families should be regarded positively as an important child care resource, providing new homes for children who have experienced forms of disruption so severe that it is no longer possible for them to live with their birth parents.

Assessment of Prospective Adopters

Age

3–144 6. Age is one consideration among many in assessing the suitability of prospective adopters. Agencies need to satisfy themselves that adopters have a reasonable expectation of retaining health and vigour to be able to meet the many and varied demands of children during their formative years but should bear in mind that many parents are now starting their families at a later age.

7. Adoption agencies are advised, however, that the age of prospective adopters should not be made the main or sole determinant to be applied in assessing their suitability to adopt. Agencies are expected to look at the qualities which prospective adopters have to offer children, many of whom would benefit from living with more mature adopters. In this context, older prospective adopters are likely to be established in their employment; they bring the advantage of a greater experience of life. Many have already brought up children of their own and have developed good parenting skills.

Other factors

3–145 8. It is a matter of concern that too often cases are drawn to the attention of the Department about unfair and distressing experiences of some prospective adopters who have felt that they have been dealt with in an insensitive and discourteous manner. This is clearly unacceptable. It is equally unacceptable for prospective adopters to be ruled out because the adoption agency considers them to have received too high a level of education, have time consuming jobs or an income above a certain level.

9. The Government do not intend to make changes to existing legislation which allows **3–146** adoption applications from married couples or single individuals. The Government's continued prohibition on unmarried couples making joint adoption applications is in line with Article 6.1 of the 1967 European Convention on the Adoption of Children.

10. Most children in the United Kingdom are brought up within a family comprising a father and a mother whose relationship and commitment are recognised in marriage and who have legal responsibilities towards each other. There is a strong presumption that for most children, such a structure offers the best chance for successful development into adulthood through a stable and enduring relationship with two parents.

11. There may be circumstances, however, when adoption agencies consider that the particular needs of a child can best or only be met by being placed with a single person or one no longer married; for example, where an adoptive parent is a successful long term foster carer or where a person has special skills to meet the particular needs of a child. In such cases the Department's view is that such a children should not be deprived of the opportunity to join a loving home environment where a suitable single adopter can be found.

12. Where an adoption application from a single person is being considered, adoption agencies will be expected to pay careful attention to particular aspects of the applicant's home circumstances. Among the many areas to be covered in the assessment process is for example, whether or not there are other people living in the household likely to have significant contact with the child. Information about all persons in the household must be included in the home study assessment and taken into account by the agency's adoption panel when deciding whether or not to make a favourable recommendation.

Race and Culture in Placements

Domestic adoptions

13. Issues of race, language, culture and religion are important considerations in deciding **3–147** the most suitable placement for a child in a multi-racial society. The principles set out in the Chief Inspector Letter of 29 January 1990 to Directors of Social Services (CI(90)2) continue to apply. Agencies are also reminded of the guidance contained in paragraphs 2.40–2.42 of the Children Act 1989 Guidance and Regulations, Volume 3: "Family Placement" in which the issues of race and culture in the placement of children are set out. *Other things being equal*, placement with a family sharing the same ethnic origin and religion may well be most likely to best meet a child's needs. If such a placement is not available which meets the required standards, it is appropriate for the agency to place the child with a family of mixed or different ethnic or religious background.

14. It is sometimes the case, however, that children from ethnic, cultural and religious minorities have been allowed to drift within the care system because local authorities have held out unrealistic hopes of finding adopters who could meet the child's ethnic, cultural or religious needs. It should be a guiding principle that no child should be allowed to remain in the care of the local authority without attempts to find a family placement where this is in the child's best interests.

15. Long-term plans for such children should not exclude placement with families who do not share the child's heritage but who could otherwise offer him or her a safe, warm and loving home. Such families should be willing to help these children to understand and take pride in their particular racial and cultural identities.

Intercountry adoptions

16. Applications to adopt children living abroad, where the prospective adopters share none **3–148** of the cultural, religious or ethnicity of the country from which they have chosen to adopt, present additional issues which must be faced. In many countries, particularly in South America, South East Asia and Eastern Europe, children are unable to be cared for by their birth parents or extended family and the welfare authorities are unable to find substitute parents for them. Many countries within these areas are prepared to allow such children to be adopted by families living abroad whether or not they have a connection with the child's country of birth, on the principle that it is better for the child to live with a new family abroad than no family at all. It would be quite wrong, therefore, for adoption agencies to refuse to process an adoption application on the grounds that the applicants cannot furnish strong personal links with their country of choice.

17. The 1993 Hague Convention on Protection of Children and Co-operation in Respect of Intercountry Adoption was signed by the United Kingdom in January 1994; the Government

intends to ratify as soon as the necessary legislation is in place. This Convention permits intercountry adoption when this is approved by the appropriate adoption authorities in the child's country of origin.

18. The Convention, therefore, recognises the need of such children to be found new families; it also recognises that families are prepared to respond to that need and offer these children a new start in another country.

19. The United Nations Convention on the Rights of the Child also recognises that intercountry adoption may be considered as an option when appropriate arrangements cannot be made in the child's country of origin.

20. Adoption agencies will need to be satisfied that prospective adopters of children from overseas have made reasonable efforts to acquaint themselves with the culture and history of the country of their choice so that they can provide information to the child about his or her background and the traditions of his or her country or origin.

21. Agencies are reminded that the guidance contained in the Chief Inspector letter of June 1991 on adoption of children from overseas — CI(91)14 — continues to apply and includes important advice on assessments, timescales, health matters, the role of the adoption panel and special considerations.

Contact

3–149 22. Contact involves adopted children keeping in touch (by meeting, letters, phone calls, either on a regular basis or infrequently such as cards on birthdays and at Christmas) with their birth families and other relevant members of the child's life prior to adoption. Contact is a relatively recent concept based on the principles of the Children Act 1989; although its application is increasing little is known about its long-term effects.

23. Agencies are reminded that issues of contact should always be handled with great care and sensitivity so that the proposed arrangements are serving the best interests of the adopted child and offer no threat to a successful adoption by the child's new family.

24. Before a child is placed for adoption, the placing agency should have discussed the question of contact with the child (where appropriate), his family and prospective adopters and the form it might take. Contact arrangements should therefore only proceed with the prior agreement of the parties involved. The interests of each child will need to be considered; arrangements made must be sufficiently flexible to allow for changing needs and circumstances. The extent and type of contact proposed will undoubtedly vary with each placement, taking account of both the short and long-term needs of the child.

25. A need to know about one's origins, birth parents and relatives and to be aware of cultural, ethnic and racial heritage is a basic need in children and adults alike. However, equating a need to know as synonymous with a need for some form of contact is an unsafe assumption. Current trends, which promote the value of maintaining contact and also ideas about the benefits of greater openness in adoption, are in danger of giving support to the concept that all contact is good and that the greater the move toward direct contact (meetings) between child and birth parent, the better. Such an assumption ignores the possibility that some children may prefer not to have direct contact but will find it difficult to express their views through guilt or a misplaced sense of responsibility for their birth parents.

Preparation and assessment

3–150 26. Essential to the process of preparing and assessing prospective adopters is the development of a two-way exchange of information in a sympathetic and friendly atmosphere designed to foster mutual confidence and trust. Preparation and assessment is one of the most intense and sensitive areas of the adoption process; prospective adopters are asked to reveal personal and intimate information about themselves and their families, often raising deep emotional feelings.

27. Social workers are therefore reminded of the importance of adopting a sensitive approach to this particular aspect of the process. Prospective adopters should not be made to feel that they are being interrogated and they should never be subjected to the personal views of social workers.

28. Adoption managers are reminded of the need to pay careful attention to preparation programmes, both the intended purpose and their content. Preparation has been a particular subject of complaint by some prospective adopters who have experienced a distinct lack of respect and even humiliation during the process. Managers should review from time to time all aspects of their preparation programmes and satisfy themselves that their content contributes to the proper assessment of applicants.

29. Prospective adopters should be given a full explanation about the purpose and objective of each phase of the programme and what is expected of them; they should be given the option whether or not to participate in a particular session. Where prospective adopters decide not to participate in part of the programme (and this may well reflect its appropriateness in the programme), social workers should not regard their refusal as a reason for not recommending them as suitable to adopt.

30. It is recommended that the work of interviewing prospective adopters as part of the preparation and assessment process be entrusted only to experienced social workers skilled in such work and also in placing children away from their birth families. Those new to the task should receive sufficient training and supervision by an experienced colleague until the adoption manager is satisfied about their level of competence. This is particularly important if they have not brought up children of their own, whether by birth or by adoption.

Action

31. Local authority social service departments and approved voluntary adoption agencies **3–151** are asked to review their current adoption policies and practices in the light of this guidance.

Copies of this letter are being sent to directors of approved adoption agencies and voluntary organisations to assist them in the adoption and family placement work of their agencies.

CIRCULAR No. LAC (97) 13

Dated April 23, 1997, and issued by the Department of Health

CHILDREN AND YOUNG PERSONS

ADOPTION AGENCIES AND CHILDREN (ARRANGEMENTS FOR PLACEMENT AND REVIEW) (MISCELLANEOUS AMENDMENTS) REGULATIONS 1997

Summary

3–152   1. This circular announces changes to the Adoption Agencies Regulations 1983 (1983 Regulations) proposed in the White Paper ADOPTION: THE FUTURE which was presented to Parliament in November 1993. A further consultation on proposals for amending the 1983 Regulations took place in July 1994: THE FUTURE OF ADOPTION PANELS. The Adoption Agencies and Children (Arrangements for Placement and Review) (Miscellaneous Amendments) Regulations 1997 (1997 Regulations) amend and supplement the 1983 Regulations. Part of these regulations come into force on **1 July 1997** and the remainder on **1 November 1997**. This Circular also provides additional guidance for consideration by adoption agencies when implementing these Regulations. The Welsh Office has prepared a bi-lingual edition of this circular for Wales.

2. To the extent that the Regulations bear on local authority functions, this guidance is issued under the terms of Section 7 of the Local Authority Social Services Act 1970 which places a duty on local authorities to act under the general guidance of the Secretary of State.

3. Adoption agencies are reminded that at the time when they came into force, the 1983 Regulations were made under Section 32 of the Adoption Act 1958; consequently, statutory references in those regulations relate to amendments made in Part 1 of the Children Act 1975. The 1983 Regulations, with guidance in Local Authority Circular LAC(84)3, continue in force as if made under the terms of Section 9 of the Adoption Act 1976 by virtue of Section 73(1) and Schedule 2 of that Act (transitional provisions) which were implemented on 1 January 1988.

Main changes

3–153   4. Changes to the 1983 Regulations affect three main areas:

4.1 **Adoption panels**: improvements are made to adoption panels to ensure that the advice they give to adoption agencies is more independent and informed. To achieve this there will be a better balance between professionals and independent members and the overall membership should be more representative of the local community. Panels will include, where practicable, people with direct experience of adoption. Members will be appointed for a fixed term to ensure freshness of approach.

4.2 **Prospective adopters**: people applying to be adoptive parents will have the option to comment on the assessment made by the social worker before the report is submitted to the adoption panel. The Regulations introduce procedures for adoption agencies to notify prospective adopters of the decision. Also, where the agency is minded not to accept their application, there will be an opportunity for the prospective adopters to make representation to the adoption agency and have their application reviewed before a final decision is made.

4.3 **Adoptive parents and adopted children**: adoption agencies are required to provide information to adoptive parents to be passed on to the child before his 18th birthday. This information will not identify birth parents or relatives but will help the child to know about his background and the circumstances which made his adoption necessary; it will also assist adoptive parents in the sensitive task of telling the child about his adoption. These Regulations also provide for agencies to make an assessment of the needs, including health and educational needs, of children placed for adoption and consider how those needs are to be met.

5. These amendments also remove children placed for adoption from the requirements of the Arrangements for Placement of Children (General) Regulations 1991 and the Review of Children's Cases Regulations 1991.

6. The statutory references in the 1983 Regulations are brought up-to-date so that they refer to the appropriate sections of the Adoption Act 1976 and the Children Act 1989. Also, all references to "the father of an illegitimate child" are to be read as "the father if he does not have parental responsibility for the child" in line with the Children Act 1989.

Action

7. Directors of Social Services and Directors of voluntary adoption societies are asked to ensure that the 1997 Regulations and the contents of this Circular are brought to the attention of managers and social work staff with responsibility for placing children for adoption and to ensure that the new arrangements are in place by the appointed dates. **3–154**

Regulation 1: citation and commencement

8. **Regulation 1(2)** gives the date from which the amendments to the 1983 Regulations will come into effect: **1 July 1997** for all regulations except regulation 2(4) insofar as it inserts regulations 5(1) to (4) and (6), 5(A) and 5(B) which come into force on **1 November 1997**. The coming into effect on 1 November of regulations concerning the establishment of adoption panels and appointment of members allows time for local authorities to make the necessary preparations for ensuring that new members are available for appointment from that date. **3–155**

Regulation 2: amendment of the adoption agencies regulations 1983

9. **Regulation 2(1)** requires the 1983 Regulations to be amended as set out in regulations 2(2) to 2(20). For ease of reference, this Circular is accompanied by a copy of the 1997 Regulations and copies of the 1983 Regulations and also the substantive guidance issued in 1984 under the cover of LAC(84)3 which continues to apply subject to the changes announced in this Circular. **3–156**

It is therefore essential that the 1997 Regulations are read in conjunction with the 1983 Regulations and the guidance which accompany them.

10. **Regulation 2(4)** substitutes new regulations 5, 5A and 5B for regulation 5 of the 1983 Regulations which make provisions for the establishment of an adoption panel and appointment of members. There are a number of important changes to the original regulations which need to be noted and action taken.

Establishment of adoption panel and appointment of members

10.1 **Regulation 5(1)** continues to provide for adoption agencies to establish at least one adoption panel and appoint no more than 10 members. This provision is subject to paragraphs (2) and (3) and also to paragraph (6) which permits an increase of membership to a maximum of eleven members where up to three local authorities decide to set up a joint adoption panel. **3–157**

10.2 **Regulation 5(2)** concerns the appointment of a panel chairman. The role of chairman of the adoption panel is crucial to the success and quality of the panel's work. In preparing for each meeting it is expected that the chairman will discuss and agree with senior agency staff details about who will attend the meeting in addition to the panel members and for which agenda items. The presence of non-panel members can pose limitations which may inhibit the proper working of an adoption panel. Agencies should therefore restrict attendance to those who can assist the panel in its deliberations. While recognising the benefits of observers attending, these occasions should be kept to a minimum.

10.3 During meetings the chairman should ensure that each panel member has an opportunity to raise questions or offer comments on each matter to be decided. Some members may need encouragement to participate fully; the chairman should encourage their participation so that they do not feel constrained by not having an adoption background or professional qualifications. Each panel member should be asked whether or not he supports a proposed recommendation. There is, however, no role for formal voting on recommendations; the chairman should allow the panel to reach a consensus.

10.4 Unanimity of panel members may not always be possible. An evenly divided panel for example suggests that there is serious doubt sufficient to prevent the panel making a confident recommendation. At such times, the balance of the panel's recommendation should always favour the best interests of the child. Where there is a serious difference of opinion among members, the chairman may ask for more information to be made available to the panel before a recommendation is made. Serious reservations expressed by individual panel members about a particular recommendation should be recorded in the panel minutes for consideration by the agency decision maker.

10.5 In some agencies it has been common practice for the chairman of the adoption panel to be the agency's decision maker. Regulation 2(9) now makes a clear distinction between the function of the chairman of a panel and the agency's responsibility for decisions. It provides that no member of the adoption panel may take part in any decisions on behalf of the agency relating to matters which have been considered by that panel under regulation 10 of the 1983 Regulations, as amended.

10.6 **Regulation 5(2)(a) and (b)** concerns the appointment of two social workers in the employment of the adoption agency and at least one member of the management committee where the agency is an approved adoption society, or at least one member of an authority's social services committee where the adoption agency is a local authority; these two paragraphs are essentially unchanged from the 1983 Regulations except that they are both subject to new paragraph (6) relating to joint panel arrangements.

10.7 As a matter of good practice, one of the two social workers appointed to the panel should be currently engaged in agency social work involving the placement of children for adoption; the other social worker should be a senior manager with broad experience in the management of social services for children, including adoption.

10.8 Management committee members or elected representatives appointed to serve as adoption panel members should operate on a full and equal basis as other panel members. There should be no question, for example, of balancing political representation of the local authority within the membership of the adoption panel.

3–158 10.9 **Regulation 5(2)(c)** concerns the appointment of a medical adviser. The inclusion of a medical adviser on the adoption panel remains as originally stated in the 1983 regulations and guidance. He is not subject to a fixed term of appointment from 1 November 1997, unlike other panel members. Recognising the ensuing difficulties of appointing a medical adviser for a fixed term, he is to be appointed to serve on an adoption panel for so long as he is nominated by the adoption agency.

10.10 As a panel member, the agency medical adviser should be expected to make a full contribution to the wider work of the adoption panel. In the past, the function of some medical advisers had been limited to providing advice and comment on medical issues. Restricting the contribution of medical advisers to their specialist knowledge does not make best use of their personal and professional skills.

10.11 **Regulation 5(2)(d)** requires at least three other persons (independent members) instead of two to be members of an adoption panel, not being members or employees of the adoption agency, or elected members, where the agency is a local authority. These shall where reasonably practicable include an adoptive parent and an adopted person who must be at least 18 years of age and reflect as wide a range of perspectives as possible.

10.12 In the selection of panel members it is important for adoption agencies to include a strong element of independence in the composition of its membership. As well as panel members who are elected members or are employed by the authority or agency, or appointed as professional advisers, membership should include representatives of the wider community. The addition of a third independent member is to include people who have personal experience of adoption as adopted persons, adoptive parents or as birth parents whose children have been placed for adoption. Agencies should also ensure that the independent membership of their adoption panels reflects the composition of the local communities which they serve.

When appointing new panel members, therefore, the authority or agency should approach individuals, organisations and institutions in their locality which take an active interest in child and family matters from which independent members might be nominated.

Guidance in paragraph 17 of LAC (84)3 which accompanied the 1983 Regulations may be helpful here.

10.13 **Regulation 5(3)** provides for the appointment of a vice chairman; this is a new requirement. The appointment from within the panel membership of a vice-chairman of the panel is required so that he or she may act in the absence of the chairman. This would be particularly important if urgent issues involving recommendations for the placement of a child occurred between meetings — see paragraph 48 of this Circular, Additional Guidance — Urgent Placements. Like the chairman, the personal qualities and experience of adoption work require that the vice-chairman commands the respect of other panel members and is effective in chairing meetings. The amount or range of experience in adoption work expected of the vice-chairman continues to be left for agencies to determine. It may be preferable, for example, for the vice-chairman to be a qualified social worker with supervisory or management experience, although this is not essential.

10.14 **Regulation 5(4)**, subject to paragraph (6) about joint arrangements, increases the quorum from 5 to least 6 panel members for a meeting of the adoption panel. The quorum must include the chairman or vice-chairman and a social worker in the employment of the adoption agency.

10.15 **Regulation 5(5)** requires an adoption panel to maintain a written record of the panel's recommendations and reasons for them. As a measure of good practice the written record may be made by a member of the panel or by a person who is not a panel member but appointed to keep such a record; the chairman should be satisfied that the record is an accurate reflection of the panel's considerations.

10.16 **Regulation 5(6)** makes special provision for local authorities who decide they wish to join together to establish a joint adoption panel for up to three local authorities. Where they do, the maximum number of members who may be appointed is increased to eleven. It will be necessary for local authorities wishing to establish a joint panel to agree the appointment of a panel chairman and vice-chairman and to decide which of their nominated medical advisers shall sit on the panel. They will also need to agree which of the authorities is to make the appointment. In each case, one social worker in the employment of each local authority is to be appointed to the panel and also one member from each local authority social services committee. Local authorities should ensure so far as is practicable that the appointment of social workers reflects the skill mix referred to above in paragraph 10.7.

10.17 In the case of the appointment of independent members however, this is to be done by agreement between the local authorities; this arrangement will assist those local authorities which might otherwise experience difficulty appointing an independent member. The quorum of a joint adoption panel is to be increased from 6 to 7 members, subject to there being present at the adoption panel meeting the chairman or vice-chairman and a social worker in the employment of each agency.

Tenure of office of members

10.18 **Regulation 5A** is a new provision which limits the length of time a member of the **3–159** adoption panel may hold office to a term not exceeding three years; the same person may not hold office as a member of that panel for more than two consecutive terms without an intervening period of at least three years.

10.19 Where an existing panel member leaves the panel before the expiry of his current term, this new provision requires agencies to appoint a replacement panel member; in such cases, the first period of appointment for the new member should be for the unexpired portion of the former member's appointment.

10.20 **Regulation 5A(2)** requires adoption agencies to arrange the tenure of office of adoption panel members so that so far as possible the term of at least one third of its members shall expire each year. This is to ensure that new members are introduced into adoption panels at regular intervals. To meet the requirements of this provision, adoption agencies will need to be pro-active in maintaining programmes of recruiting and training new members to adoption panels. (In this context, BAAF has published, "Handbook for Members of Adoption Panels" which may be helpful.)

10.21 **Regulation 5A(4)** provides that where a panel member wishes to resign his office, he may do so at any time after his appointment; the notice of resignation is to be made in writing to the adoption agency which appointed him. In the case of joint panel arrangements, he may give notice to any one of the local authorities which set up the joint panel.

10.22 **Regulation 5A(5)** provides for the termination of appointment of a panel member before the expiry of the term of appointment if the agency gives written notice to the panel member that it considers him or her unfit, unwilling or unable to continue. Written notice in such cases should set out the reasons why the agency intends to terminate the appointment. It is likely that the grounds of unfitness will mainly concern issues of competence and are therefore likely to be raised by others.

10.23 The role of the adoption panel chairman in such cases is crucial. Where lack of competence is observed, or where a member's effectiveness decreases, the chairman will want to discuss this fully and in private with the member concerned. It may be that words of encouragement or access to training opportunities may be all that is required. Should these steps prove unsuccessful, the member may welcome an opportunity to resign. The work of the adoption panel is of such importance that it should not be expected to "carry", ineffective or disruptive members.

10.24 Where difficulties are incapable of informal and early resolution, the panel chairman, after discussion with at least one other panel member, should raise the matter urgently with the Director of Social Services or Director of the approved adoption society who will then prepare a report and make recommendations to the appropriate Social Services Sub-committee or Management Committee, allowing the panel member an opportunity to make observations. There may be exceptional circumstances in which individual members of the panel will need to speak directly with the agency's Director without first discussing matters with the panel chairman.

10.25 Adoption agencies are advised to set out in writing for each panel member, prior to their appointment, the agency's expectation of them, to include areas such as regular attendance at panel meetings and training days and also the importance of confidentiality and the security of papers sent to them.

Further advice is given in paragraph 47 of this Circular under the heading of Additional Guidance, Adoption Panels — Protocol for Panel Members.

Establishment of new panels on 1 November 1997

3–160 10.26 **Regulation 5B** is new, requiring all members of adoption panels established before 1 November 1997 to cease to hold office on that date. With effect from the same date, every adoption agency shall establish a new adoption panel in accordance with regulations 5 and 5A. In the meantime, adoption agencies are advised to consider how best to recruit, train and carry out the necessary checks on those whom they wish to consider appointing as members of an adoption panel on 1 November.

11. **Regulation 2(6)(b)** amends regulation 8(2) by replacing sub-paragraph (g) and introducing two new sub-paragraphs: (h) and (i). New sub-paragraph (g) specifically requires an adoption agency to produce an assessment of the prospective adopter's suitability to be an adoptive parent which must be included in the written report together with any other observations on any matter referred to in regulation 8.

12. New sub-paragraph (h) requires the agency to inform the prospective adopter that his application is to be referred to the adoption panel and to send him a copy of the assessment of his suitability to be an adoptive parent. In sending the copy of the assessment to the prospective adopter, the adoption agency's letter should notify him of the following:

(a) that his application is to be considered by an adoption panel;
(b) that he will have up to 28 days within which to make any observations on the contents of the assessment, and
(c) that his observations, together with the agency's report, will be considered by the adoption panel.

13. **Adoption agencies should note that it is not appropriate for a prospective adopter to be given the complete home study report (which includes the response of referees) but only the social worker's assessment of his suitability to be an adoptive parent.**

14. New sub-paragraph (i) of regulation 8(2) provides that at the end of 28 days (earlier if any observations have been received from the prospective adopter before the 28 days has expired), the adoption agency shall pass the written report and written observations of the prospective adopter to their adoption panel or, where appropriate, to another adoption agency. It may be the case that the prospective adopter does not wish to make written

observations but asks to make an oral representation. Adoption agencies should consider such requests sympathetically. Where an oral representation is made, the agency will wish to ensure that an accurate note of the main issues is taken at the time.

15. **Regulation 2(9)** amends regulation 11 of the 1983 Regulations (adoption agency decisions and notifications) so that it applies only to decisions on recommendations whether it is in the best interests of a particular child to be adopted and whether a prospective adopter is suitable to be an adoptive parent for a particular child. It inserts a new paragraph (1A) to the effect that no member of an adoption panel shall take part in any decision made by the adoption agency under regulation 11(1).

Adoption agency decisions and notifications — prospective adopters

16. **Regulation 2(10)** inserts a new paragraph 11A to deal with decisions about and **3–161** notifications to a prospective adopter. Before making its decision about whether a prospective adopter is suitable to be an adoptive parent, the adoption agency is required by regulation 11A(1) to take into account the recommendation of the adoption panel. Where an application is considered by the adoption panel, regulation 11A(2) provides that no member of that panel may take part in any decision made by the agency on the panel's recommendation. Where the adoption agency decides to approve a prospective adopter as suitable to be an adoptive parent, regulation 11A(3) directs the agency to notify the prospective adopter in writing of its decision.

17. However, if the agency is minded not to approve a prospective adopter as suitable to be an adoptive parent, regulation 11A(4) requires the agency to:

   (a) notify the prospective adopter in writing that it is proposed not to approve him as suitable to be an adoptive parent;

   (b) send with the notification its reasons together with a copy of the recommendation of the adoption panel if that recommendation is different from the agency's. The agency should not however provide a copy of the panel's deliberations or give any details about these other than the recommendation made;

   (c) invite the prospective adopter to submit any representation he wishes to the agency within 28 days.

18. It will normally be the case that the reasons for the agency decision maker not to approve a prospective adopter will be the same as those submitted by the agency's adoption panel and which accompanied their recommendation not to approve; it is these reasons therefore which are to be supplied to the prospective adopter under regulation 11A(4)(b). Where, exceptionally, this is not the case, the adoption agency must provide the prospective adopter with its own reasons with the notification. If no representation is made by the prospective adopter within 28 days, regulation 11A(5) permits the adoption agency to proceed to make its decision and notify the prospective adopter in writing of its decision and the reasons for it.

19. Where however the prospective adopter makes a representation within 28 days, regulation 11A(6) provides that the adoption agency may refer the case together with all the relevant information to its adoption panel for further consideration and the panel may make a fresh recommendation to the agency as to whether the prospective adopter is suitable to be an adoptive parent under regulation 11(A)7.

20. The agency may consider referring the case to another adoption panel instead where the agency has more than one panel or has arrangements with another local authority or adoption agency. Adoption agencies are under no obligation to enter into reciprocal arrangements with other local authorities or adoption agencies; however, where they have done so, an adoption agency may be able to use these arrangements to refer such cases to a different panel which may reassure a prospective adopter that his case will be genuinely reconsidered.

21. Where the adoption agency decides to refer the case back to its adoption panel, regulation 11A(8) requires the agency to take into account the recommendation of the panel before making its decision. As soon as the adoption agency has made its decision, regulation 11A(9) requires the agency to notify the prospective adopter in writing of its decision, and to give its reasons if the agency does not consider the prospective adopter suitable to be an adoptive parent. At the same time, the agency must also send a copy of the panel's recommendation if this is different from the agency's decision.

22. Adoption agencies should note that this process is not an appeals procedure and that requests for re-assessment should be treated as a new application. In this context, there is no obligation on the adoption agency to carry out a further assessment on an applicant who has been unsuccessful in an earlier application, unless in the meantime the agency is aware of significant changes to the applicant's circumstances which would be likely to help him meet the criteria of the agency.

23. **Regulation 2(11)** makes a number of important changes to regulation 12 of the 1983 Regulations. New requirements have been inserted into paragraph (2) of regulation 12. New sub-paragraph 12(2)(aa) requires the adoption agency to notify in writing a parent or guardian of the proposed placement of the child for adoption before the child is placed rather than afterwards as was previously the case. This is required in all cases unless the parent or guardian has made a formal declaration seeking no further involvement with the child (section 18(6) or 19(4) of the 1976 Act — freeing for adoption). Adoption agencies should also consider notifying an unmarried father who has not acquired parental responsibility (under section 4 of the 1989 Act), so long as the agency considers this to be in the best interests of the child and his identity is known to the agency. Where, of course, the proposed placement does not take place, the adoption agency should inform the parent or guardian accordingly.

24. Although the Review of Children's Cases Regulations 1991 will no longer apply to children "looked after" by the local authority who are subsequently placed for adoption, the relevant parts of those regulations have been incorporated in these regulations by amending regulation 12(2) and adding a new Part VIII to the Schedule. New paragraphs (2)(j) and (k) of regulation 12 have been substituted. In essence, these arrangements for reviewing the placement up to the time the adoption order is made, still reflect the requirements of the 1989 Act. New paragraph (2)(j) concerning the monitoring of the health of a child placed for adoption is essentially the same as regulation 6 of the Review of Children's Cases Regulations 1991; new paragraph (2)(k), concerning the review of an adoption placement, is based on regulation 3 of the 1991 Review Regulations.

25. Regulation 12(2)(k) requires that adoption placements be reviewed at least as frequently as follows:
— within four weeks of placement;
— not more than three months after that review unless an application for an adoption order has been made;
— at least every six months thereafter until an application for an adoption order is made.

Adoption agencies are reminded that once an application has been made for an adoption order, they are required to continue to review adoption placements up to the time an adoption order is made. Details of reviews are to be recorded in writing.

26. Two new paragraphs are inserted in regulation 12 of the 1983 Regulations — paragraphs (3) and (4) — which are concerned with the manner in which the review of the placement is to be carried out and also who should be notified about the results of such reviews. New paragraph (3) brings together the requirements of regulations 4(1) and 10 and Schedules 2 and 3 of the Review of Children's Cases Regulations 1991, adapted where appropriate. New paragraph (4) is based on regulation 7(3) of the same 1991 Regulations, taking account of the range of interested parties in adoption who may require to be notified of the results of the review and any decision taken in consequence of the review.

27. In any event, correspondence about the result of the review and any decision taken should be carefully summarised so as not to identify, for example, the prospective adopter or his address when this would be contrary to the best interests of the child placed for adoption. In this context, "parent" includes an unmarried father who has acquired parental responsibility under the terms of section 4 of the 1989 Act. Additionally, an unmarried father who has not acquired parental responsibility shall be included, provided the agency is satisfied that this is in the child's best interests and his identity in known.

Information on adoption

3–162
28. **Regulation 2(13)** inserts a new regulation 13A in the 1983 Regulations concerning information on adoption. Once the adoption order is made, the adoption agency is required to provide the adopter with information about the child where this was not provided at the time the child was placed — for example, "later life letters" for the child or completed life story book. Adoption agencies are advised to obtain a receipt for the information provided. This information is to be made available to the child by his eighteenth birthday. However, the adoption agency should advise each adoptive parent of the benefits of imparting knowledge about adoption to their child at as early a stage as possible, taking account of the wishes and feelings of the child and having regard to his age and understanding. Ideally, an adoptive parent will take suitable opportunities from time to time during the normal course of the child's development to tell him of his adoption and provide general information about his background. In the context of post adoption support services, adoption agencies may wish to assure adoptive parents of the availability of future consultation, as and when needed.

29. The Regulations do not specify the type or form of information adoption agencies are to give to an adoptive parent. Clearly, this will vary in each case, according to the circumstances

of the adoption and the range of information available. In giving consideration to this issue, adoption agencies may find it helpful to refer to paragraph 57 of the Additional Guidance attached to this Circular which sets out a checklist of documents to be included in the child's case records. Adoption agencies should be able to pass on to the adoptive parent much of this material, suitably edited where appropriate, except where material has been supplied to the agency on a confidential basis.

30. **Regulation 2(14)** amends regulation 14 of the 1983 Regulations — confidentiality and preservation of case records. The amendment reinforces the importance of adoption agencies reviewing their arrangements to ensure the safe storage of adoption records; this amendment is made in the light of incidents in recent years where fire and water damage has resulted in the total destruction of some files, to the disadvantage of adopted persons and their relatives. Also, as a matter of good practice, adoption agencies should consider any Health and Safety aspects of storage, such as the proximity of asbestos.

31. **Regulation 2(15)** makes changes to regulation 15(1) of the 1983 Regulations — access to case records and disclosure of information — by inserting after sub-paragraph (c) a new paragraph; this will expressly permit a person appointed by the adoption agency to deal with any representations, including complaints, to have access to case records to the extent necessary to carry out the responsibilities of that appointment. Clearly, such a person could not have carried out his functions properly without such access, and the disclosure as made part of the provision of a complaints procedure which is one of an adoption agency's functions; nevertheless, it is considered that the addition of an express provision is helpful.

32. **Regulation 2(17)** amends the Schedule to the 1983 Regulations. Paragraph 12 of Part I is replaced by a new paragraph to provide that any special health or educational needs of the child must be identified and for consideration to be given to how those needs are to be met. A new paragraph is inserted — paragraph 12A — to provide that the particulars relating to the child are to include any educational needs which the child now has and how those needs are to be met, including any assessment of special educational needs carried out and identified under the Education Act 1996.

33. **Regulation 2(18)** amends Part II of the Schedule — matters to be covered in report on the child's health, inserting an extra sub-paragraph (dd) to cover how the child's health and medical history has affected his physical, intellectual, emotional, social or behavioural development. All these matters were previously covered by Schedules 2 and 3 of the Arrangements for Placement of Children (General) Regulations 1991.

PART VIII OF THE SCHEDULE: CONSIDERATIONS TO BE INCLUDED IN REVIEW

34. **Regulation 2(20)** introduces an additional part to the Schedule — Part VIII — **3–163** considerations to be included in review, and is largely derived from regulation 4(1) and Schedules 2 and 3 of the Review of Children's Cases Regulations 1991, adapted as appropriate.

Amendment of Arrangements for Placement of Children (General) Regulations 1991

35. **Regulation 3** amends the Arrangements for Placement of Children (General) Regu- **3–164** lations 1991 so they will not apply in the case of a child who is placed for adoption under the Adoption Act 1976.

Amendment of the Review of Children's Cases Regulations 1991

36. **Regulation 4** amends the Review of Children's Cases Regulations 1991 so that they will **3–165** not apply in the case of a child who is placed for adoption under the Adoption Act 1976.

37. These regulations made under the provisions of the 1989 Act are not considered wholly appropriate to the placement for adoption of children "looked after" by the local authority but this is not intended to imply that the basic philosophies of the 1989 Act should be ignored. Adoption agency placement procedures should continue to focus, as appropriate, on the issues involved in the "welfare check list" in Part 1 of the 1989 Act.

ADDITIONAL GUIDANCE

38. The addition of further guidance to this Circular is partly the result of enquiries received **3–166** from time-to-time by this Department and, although not directly associated with the amending provisions of the 1997 Regulations, nevertheless is pertinent to an assessment of the wider considerations which adoption agencies will wish to take on board to make improvements to the service they provide.

3–167   39. Preparation and assessment of an applicant who seeks to become an adoptive parent is a protracted procedure, involving social workers and other staff over many months. For adoption agencies, this is likely to be the most expensive part of the process leading to the decision by the agency whether or not an applicant is suitable to be an adoption parent. The following paragraphs set out graduated stages of assessment and are offered to adoption agencies as one way of avoiding unnecessary expenditure in manpower and other resources.

40. The **first stage** forms the introductory element of the assessment process, designed to provide prospective adopters with as much information as is practicable about the nature of adoption, the process involved, range of areas covered in the home study assessment, the nature and purpose of investigations, likely timescale envisaged, the kind of children needing new parents and the implications of taking an unrelated child into their home, making him a new member of their family. Presentation of this information will take various forms according to the needs of each applicant but could be through the medium of information packs, general guidance, preliminary counselling or participation in preparation groups.

41. This stage will provide the best opportunity for expert advice to be given to prospective adopters concerning the benefits of adoption for children and their new families. The degree of pre-assessment preparation during this first stage will undoubtedly influence the efficient progress of the applicants in the remaining stages.

42. The **second stage** introduces the completion of pre-assessment checks at an earlier stage in the adoption process. Before an application for a full home study can be accepted, all medical and other checks should be completed and the police checks begun. Written references from named referees should also be obtained at this time. Subsequent requests for advice on specific issues revealed by these checks should be made to the agency's medical and legal advisors as appropriate and to seek more information. This stage, like the first, also provides an opportunity for applicants to decide not to pursue their application or be advised by the agency that to continue would be likely to end in disappointment. Applicants should be informed at an early stage that these checks will be completed before their application is considered by the adoption panel.

43. The **third stage** will only apply in cases when pre-assessment checks have been completed and reveal information likely to prejudice the outcome of an application. Adoption panels should be asked by the agency to consider such cases at as early opportunity as possible before a full home study is undertaken. The adoption panel could advise either:

    (a) on the basis of the information provided, they would be unlikely to be able to recommend approval of the applicant, notwithstanding any favourable features which might subsequently arise after further enquiries had been made. In such cases the adoption agency should take the necessary steps to reject the application; or

    (b) recommend that they would like to receive a full home study report which might additionally serve to explore the significant facets revealed in the earlier checks and which could be offset by other features, to the advantage of the applicant.

44. The **fourth stage** will follow the third only when the adoption agency is satisfied that no further obstacle exists to continuing to process the application and complete a full home study assessment, including visits to the personal referees. However, in cases where pre-assessment checks at stage two reveal nothing to prejudice an application, the adoption application can proceed directly to stage four. Consideration of the adoption application by the agency's panel will follow after completion of this final stage.

45. Time invested on the first three stages will assist agencies to make the best use of their manpower resources by avoiding unnecessary work in completing time-consuming home study assessments where not appropriate.

2. Work of Adoption Panels

3–168   46. The 1997 Regulations make no change to the considerations required to be undertaken by adoption panels set out in regulations 10(1)(a)–(c) of the 1983 Regulations as to:

    "(a) whether adoption is in the best interests of a child and, if the panel recommends that it is, whether an application under 14 of the 1975 Act (freeing child for adoption) should be made to free the child for adoption,

    (b) whether a prospective adopter is suitable to be an adoptive parent, and

    (c) whether a prospective adopter would be a suitable adoptive parent for a particular child."

As part of their deliberations, where an adoption panel is considering whether adoption is in the best interests of a child, the panel is expected to consider all other possible options for that child and be satisfied that the agency's proposal was arrived at once those options had been explored and discounted.

47. The following is suggested as a guide to adoption agencies for a protocol for adoption **3–169** panel members which should be adapted as the agency considers appropriate:
   (a) All panel members are required to sign a confidentiality bond in accordance with the requirements on confidentiality in Regulation 6(2)(c) of the 1983 Regulations.
   (b) An annual joint training day will be arranged by the agency; there is a clear expectation that panel members will attend. Members will be consulted on the content and format of the training day.
   (c) Panel members who are not employed by the statutory bodies are entitled to claim for expenses for travel, mileage, parking fees and child care costs.
   (d) It is possible for a panel member to have some knowledge, either in a personal or professional capacity, of a case under consideration. In such circumstances a member should declare an interest and inform the chairman or vice-chairman of the panel accordingly.
   (e) An information package will be provided to adoption panel members who will also have the opportunity of observing an adoption panel and meet senior officers responsible for the placement of children.
   (f) There is an expectation that panel members will attend a minimum of 75% of meetings in a year.

4. URGENT PLACEMENTS

48. In addition to the above guidance, adoption agencies are reminded that the Children **3–170** Act 1989 established the principle that any delay in child care proceedings is likely to prejudice the welfare of the child. Exceptionally, the need may arise for the agency to seek the recommendation of an adoption panel before the next planned panel meeting in order to proceed, for example, with a placement without delay. Each agency should devise an appropriate "urgent procedure".
49. Common features of such a procedure will include:
   — discussion between senior agency staff and the panel chairman (or designated deputy in his or her absence) to determine that the matter cannot wait for the next panel meeting;
   — assemble a quorum of panel members (at least six of its members or seven if it is a joint panel).

5. ADOPTION AGENCY DECISIONS AND NOTIFICATIONS

50. The Social Services Inspectorate carry out routine inspections of voluntary adoption **3–171** societies who have applied to Secretary of State for approval to operate as adoption agencies. The Inspectorate also makes inspections of local authority adoption services. A consistent finding in these inspections has been that there continues to be some confusion about the distinction between adoption panel recommendations and agency decisions in cases referred to the panel. This circular provides the opportunity to restate the requirements.
51. A decision of an adoption agency about adoption is, in law, the responsibility of the agency itself and therefore must be made by the agency, not by the adoption panel. The adoption panel can only make *recommendations* on the matters set out in Regulation 10(1) of the 1983 Regulations; it is for the agency to make *decisions* on those matters, informed by the panel's recommendations. Regulation 11(1) recognises the panel's role in giving detailed and expert consideration on the matters concerned; this prohibits the agency from making a decision before taking account of the panel's recommendation.
52. The agency should establish a discrete procedure for making decisions on matters on which the adoption panel has made recommendations. The agency should act within its legal powers to establish an appropriate scheme of delegation for this purpose. In the case of a local authority, for example, under powers governing the delegation of social services functions, this could be the Director of Social Services or a senior officer authorised by the Director. It could also be a cases sub-committee of the social services committee. Within an approved adoption society, delegation could be to an officer of the society or to a sub-committee of the management committee, depending on provisions of the agency's constitution. In any event the decision making process should be a measured procedure taken only after careful consideration of the panel's recommendations.
53. Where the role of the agency decision making is delegated to an individual officer, it may be appropriate for that officer to attend the adoption panel meeting. His or her role

would, however, be restricted to that of a non-participating observer. It would, furthermore, be wholly inappropriate for the agency's decisions on cases presented at a panel meeting to be taken immediately following that meeting.

6. OUTCOMES OF ADOPTION PANEL'S WORK

3–172   54. The changing nature of adoption — the placement of older children and children with multiple disabilities — imposes additional challenges upon adoption panels. Planning for such children sometimes requires extended timetables for implementing the various components of the placement arrangements. Placement of these children may quite properly take place several weeks or even months following consideration of the case by the panel.

55. It is suggested that adoption agencies should make available to their panel members information about the progress of individual cases. Such progress reports are an effective means of informing panels of the outcome of their work.

56. Also, due to the more frequent placement of children for adoption who have been in local authority care for a large period of their lives, panel recommendations are often made on the assurance that expensive resources are to be provided, for example — skilled staff, placement support, adoption allowances, cost of contested hearings, etc. It is helpful for adoption panels to know what part their work plays in the context of a comprehensive adoption service and children's services plans for their area.

7. CONTENTS OF CASE RECORDS

3–173   57. As a result of enquiries received by the Department in recent years concerning the contents of a child's case records, adoption agencies may find it helpful to have recourse to a checklist when giving consideration to the range of documents which should be found in such records. As a matter of good practice, a considerable degree of care will need to be exercised in compiling the information. The following is a list contains most of the documents which should be included in case records but is by no means exhaustive.

58. The intention is to provide the adopted person with as much information as possible about his social and personal history and the reason for the adoption. Painful or unpleasant information should not necessarily be "glossed over". The identification of such material may, indeed, prove to be the basis for future post adoption support and service contingencies. Care must nevertheless be taken to anonymise the material and exceptionally, exclude confidential information about third parties, or information provided "in confidence and not for wider dissemination".

— Front sheet/checklist for key biographical information and record of key action taken resulting in an adoption order;
— birth details (time, place, weight, term, type of delivery, etc.) with supporting evidence if available;
— description/details (including genogram) of the family of origin and household;
— summary of retrospective paediatric record;
— detailed chronology of child's early development and social history;
— details of any substitute (eg foster) carers prior to adoption;
— Medical Form A (or extracts) for birth parents;
— BAAF Developmental Assessment Forms or equivalent;
— record of social work with child about his adoption;
— details of siblings and any decisions taken to place brothers or sisters separately;
— BAAF Form E (or equivalent);
— adoption panel minutes and recommendations;
— case review (statutory) records since the identification of adoption as the child care plan;
— summary of steps taken to find suitable adopters for the child and a copy of the child's "profile" records used for this purpose;
— adoption panel minutes and recommendation in respect of matching the child with prospective adopters;
— BAAF Form H — Inter-agency Agreement (where appropriate);
— key correspondence to and from members of the chid's birth family;
— placement agreement with adopters;
— details of any pre-adoption contact arrangements with members of birth family or former carers and plans, if any, for post adoption order contact arrangements;
— reports on social work visits to child in adoption placement;
— open letter from social worker describing how and why adoption plans became the plan for the child;

- photographs, certificates, personal mementos of every years;
- correspondence between the agency and birth family about the emerging plans for the adoption of the child;
- photographs, cards, open letters supplied specifically by birth family members for the child;
- Schedule 2 report (Adoption Rules 1984);
- copy of the Adoption Order.

ENQUIRIES

59. Enquiries about this Circular and its enclosures should be made to: **3—174**

Mrs Pat Phillips,
Department of Health,
Room 121
Wellington House,
Waterloo Road
London SE1 8UG.

Telephone: 0171 972 4082.

A GUIDE TO INTERCOUNTRY ADOPTION PRACTICE AND PROCEDURES

Contents

[Paras. 13 to 15 are not reproduced here — R.M.J.]

1. Introduction

3–176   1.1 Continued interest in intercountry adoption is partly a consequence of the decline in the number of very young children available for adoption in the United Kingdom. Many prospective adopters are childless and in seeking to found a family look to areas where many young children, for whatever reason, may be in need of a home; others too are motivated by altruistic and humanitarian concerns. Interest in intercountry adoption was stimulated in

January 1990 by the plight of children in Romanian children's homes; while the level of interest may fluctuate and the countries of individual choice change, as witnessed by the present interest in China, intercountry adoption will continue to provide a viable option for some families.

1.2 Most local authorities have had some involvement in providing advice, counselling and assessments for prospective intercountry adopters. Although the degree of involvement can vary between social services departments, each local authority should have clear written policies and procedures for this area of work. This guidance in the form of a handbook is designed to inform local authorities social services, voluntary adoption societies and individual social workers to assist them in their work in intercountry adoption.

1.3 In each case where an application is made to adopt a child from overseas, there are two sets of laws and procedures which have to be met: those of the country in which the prospective adopter is resident and those of the country in which the child is living. The intercountry adoption process, therefore, takes account of the requirements of both countries. So far as the requirements of England and Wales are concerned, this includes guidance issued by the Department of Health in connection with the following:

Adoption Act 1976
Adoption (Designation of Overseas Adoptions) Order 1973
Adoption Agencies Regulations 1983
Adoption Agencies and Children (Arrangements for Placement and Reviews)
(Miscellaneous Amendments) Regulations 1997.

1.4 This guidance brings together and updates previously issued guidance, taking into account developments and experience of recent years, and replaces CI(90)14 and CI(91)17. Guidance still extant includes LAC (87)8, CI(92)12, CI(93)15 and CI(96)4.

1.5 This handbook has been produced for retention in a ring binder for ease of reference and to facilitate the introduction of any amendments and additions that may be required from time to time, including issues of Intercountry Adoption News. The handbook comprises the following guidance together with information produced by the Home Office (a leaflet on Intercountry Adoption) about adoptive parents obtaining authority for their adopted child to enter the United Kingdom, the Department of Health leaflet AO1(97) to assist enquirers about intercountry adoption and the three previous editions of the Department's Intercountry Adoption Newsletter. Also included is information on 20 countries concerning their particular adoption legislation and other requirements.

1.6 The handbook will be brought up-to-date to keep pace with new information and developments as they arise.

2. Principles

2.1 The Department of Health's approach to intercountry adoption is underpinned by **3–177** provisions of the Adoption Act 1976, the principles of the Children Act 1989 and international agreements to which the United Kingdom is party, in particular:

(1) 1986 United Nations Declaration on Social Legal Principles relating to the Protection and Welfare of Children;
(2) 1989 United Nations Convention on the Rights of the Child — ratified by the United Kingdom in December 1991;
(3) 1993 Hague Convention on the Protection of Children and Co-operation in Respect of Intercountry Adoption — signed by the United Kingdom in January 1994;
(4) European Parliament resolution of December 1996 to protect children in intercountry adoption.

2.2. These international agreements provide that:

a. intercountry adoption may be considered as an alternative means of providing a family for a child who cannot be cared for in any suitable manner in his or her own country;
b. that intercountry adoptions take place in the best interests of the child and with respect for his or her fundamental rights as recognised in international law; and,
c. safeguards and standards equivalent to those which apply in domestic adoption are to be applied in intercountry adoption to protect the welfare of the child concerned.

2.3 Where adoption in the child's country of origin is not possible, intercountry adoption can provide the only opportunity for some children to belong to a permanent family. There are certain factors and risks associated with intercountry adoption which call for particular care in its management — measures intended to prevent abuses such as child trafficking. It is therefore essential that local authority social services and approved adoption agencies consider prospective adopters suitable for and equal to the responsibilities they plan to take on, particularly where a child may have experienced severe early disadvantage and be in particular need of care, security and stability.

2.4 Intercountry adoption procedures are necessarily thorough: the standards and safeguards to be applied in intercountry adoption are equivalent to those which apply in domestic adoption; there can be no question of operating a two-tier adoption service, applying a lower standard to overseas adoptions. A person who cannot be recommended as suitable to adopt a child living in the United Kingdom cannot be recommended to adopt a child living overseas. This principle must be clearly explained to all prospective adopters and anyone seeking information and counselling about intercountry adoption.

3. The Process

Introduction

3–178   3.1 Social Services Departments (SSD) have an essential role to play in safeguarding the welfare of children who come from overseas for adoption. This includes:
  a. providing information, advice and counselling for people considering adopting from overseas;
  b. making a written assessment on the suitability of prospective adopters to be adoptive parents to a child living overseas;
  c. where a child enters the United Kingdom from a non-designated country for the purposes of adoption, supervising placements, preparing reports and making recommendations to the courts;
  d. arranging post placement services.

Staffing and management

3–179   3.2 Intercountry adoption work calls for experience and skill and Directors are asked to ensure that such work is undertaken by social workers who are regularly engaged in adoption and family placement work. It is important that workers who are engaged on a contractual basis to augment the resources of SSDs should also have appropriate skills and recent experience in these fields.

3.3 Experience shows that there are difficult and stressful issues associated with intercountry adoption work. Social workers are particularly in need of support and supervision from management. Directors are asked to nominate senior staff to manage and supervise the work of a social worker engaged on a sessional or contractual basis.

Information, advice and counselling

3–180   3.4 Local Authority Circular LAC(87)8 (Annex 3) — Services for Prospective Adopters and Adoptive Parents — makes clear that the requirement in section 1 of the 1976 Act for each local authority to provide an adoption service to meet the needs of people who may adopt a child includes counselling and providing information to people wishing to adopt from overseas. SSDs should also take the opportunity to provide advice and information to enquirers about children available for adoption who are already known to the SSD.

Preparation of prospective adopters

3.5 The preparation stage is a most important part of the process in preparing prospective adopters to take on the responsibility of adopting a child from overseas. In their enthusiasm to adopt a child, some prospective adopters find it difficult to accept that there are issues peculiar to intercountry adoption over and above those to relating to domestic adoption which need to be carefully considered. Prospective adopters should be advised of the reasons why a thorough assessment is essential in order to safeguard the welfare of a child in adoption.

3.6 Prospective adopters will be required to consider what it means for a child to be adopted by a person from another country, having a different culture and possibly a different racial and religious background; this is certainly so in respect of older children. It is equally important for prospective adopters to think about what adopting a child from overseas will mean for them, in both the short and longer term, particularly a child who shares few or none of the racial, cultural or linguistic inheritance of the family and who may have suffered considerable early disadvantage. Also, prospective adopters should be aware that they may have to make decisions about whether they wish to adopt a particular child having little or no information about the child's social background or medical history. **For this reason, preparation of prospective adopters in the form of sound professional advice and counselling is essential.**

342

3.7 Experience has reinforced the Department's view that whenever possible prospective adopters of children from overseas should be counselled, assessed and prepared *before* a child is identified or provisionally placed with them. Local authorities are expected to facilitate people wishing to adopt from abroad and provide services to prepare and assess prospective adopters, in advance of their identifying a child, including provision of a home study report and recommendation to the Department of Health. Assessment should begin:

— after counselling and discussion with the SSD, when prospective adopters have formed an intention of adopting from a particular country and are able to supply or be provided with material issued by the authorities in that country setting out its requirements and procedures;

— when the prospective adopter intends to adopt through an authorised overseas adoption agency or statutory authority in the child's country which operates proper safeguards and controls and which will not release a child until the requirements of both countries have been met;

— where there are arrangements for handling intercountry adoption applications at agency or government level.

3.8 The advantages in assessing couples at an early stage are now well established. Countries are imposing more effective controls over intercountry adoption and will not accept applicants for consideration as prospective adopters without a social work report and recommendation that is supported by a Central Authority of the applicant. The number of such countries continues to grow as more states come forward to sign or ratify the 1993 Hague Convention on intercountry adoption. Prospective adopters should be encouraged to adopt from countries whose arrangements for the protection of children *and* prospective adopters are more strictly controlled, where only reports from a statutory agency are acceptable and where compliance with the procedures of both countries is assured.

3.9 Where a child from a non-designated country is admitted to the United Kingdom for the purposes of adoption, it is advantageous to SSDs to take the opportunity of influencing arrangements at the earliest possible stage since they will be responsible for supervision of the placement and for preparing a Schedule 2 reports for the court. If the child is from a designated country this is equally important since the home study assessment process is the only opportunity for the approved authorities in the UK to provide support and guidance in relation to the proposed adoption.

3.10 The process of assessment serves not only as a check on the suitability of prospective adopters, but to explore their motivation and their capacity to deal with a range of difficulties in placements which are likely to occur; assessment and preparation can proceed more effectively when prospective adopters are not already committed to a particular child where there is pressure to complete the process because an early decision is needed.

3.11 Where prospective adopters are found to be unsuitable, the authorities overseas can be notified, if necessary. Where a decision is reached that approval cannot be given it will bear harder on all parties if the adoption process has already started in the child's country of origin.

3.12 From time to time it may be necessary for the Department of Health to advise prospective adopters against adopting from certain countries; prospective adopters should always be strongly advised *not* to engage in making arrangements to adopt a child through intermediaries who are not authorised. Reports should not be prepared to help people to proceed in defiance of such advice. Information and advice is available to adoption agencies from the Department of Health and the Social Services Inspectorate in the regions where individual cases of difficulty arise.

3.13 It is important that reports prepared by SSDs are not misused to enable people to bring a child into the country in possible breach of the 1976 Act and Entry Clearance procedures. This can happen when the prospective adopters present a report to secure custody of a child in his country of origin and bring the child home without making an application for Entry Clearance or before Entry Clearance is granted. This is not a formality which can be omitted because the prospective adopters have been found generally suitable to adopt a child from overseas. Investigation of the circumstances of the adoption arrangements and of the particular child's background and history is also vital and is an important part of the Entry Clearance procedure.

3.14 Assessment reports should be undertaken by social workers experienced in adoption and child placement work. The Department of Health commends the use of BAAF Form F as a basis for preparing the report. The content of the report and associated police and health checks and interviews with referees should follow the pattern established by good practice in respect of any other adoption. Recommendations should specify the age group and characteristics (health and social) of a child which the couple might be suitable to adopt. It is also important to indicate the length of time for which the report is valid which would normally be for a period of no more than two years.

3.15 Reports should include an assessment of suitability to adopt a child from another country and, where appropriate, from a different culture and/or racial background. The principles set in paragraph 11 of CI(90)2 — Issues of Race and Culture in the Family Placement of Children — are a helpful guide, bearing in mind that intercountry adoption arrangements are made because no other suitable form of care is available for the child. However, advice and assistance on all the issues raised by intercountry adoption should be fully available.

Age of prospective adopters

3–182 3.16 Arbitrary rules regarding the age of prospective adopters should not be applied; in this context, adoption agencies are referred to paragraphs 6 and 7 of CI(96)4. However, some sending countries do apply age restrictions and this may be a relevant factor for some prospective adopters to establish as they consider their options.

Health considerations

3–183 3.17 The agency medical adviser plays an important role in the assessment process, both in considering medical reports on individual applicants and in advising and contributing to the work of the adoption panel. A medical report received in the Department of Health which has not been completed by the agency medical adviser will be returned to the local authority for comment and signature.

3.18 Investigation of each prospective adopter's health and consideration of any health risks, including those associated with life style, should follow domestic adoption practice. Involvement of the medical adviser is essential, both in considering individual medical reports and in contributing to panel discussions on the complete report. Medical advisers should feel free, if they wish, to discuss any particular case of difficulty at an early stage with a Senior Medical Officer in the Department of Health.

3.19 The possibility of health, developmental and cultural problems arising in children, particularly those adopted from overseas, is an important consideration and should feature prominently in the preparation of prospective adopters. Health issues concerning children are discussed more fully in part 7 below.

Financial status

3–184 3.20. The financial status of an applicant should be established and referred to in the report, both before and after placement if there is likely to be a change. Some countries require applicants to provide documentary evidence of income, savings and property value.

Adoption of more than one child

3.21 Prospective adopters should be recommended for placement of one child only unless, exceptionally, they have been assessed as suitable to adopt siblings. The Department of Health is concerned that some couples have sought to adopt more than one unrelated child from overseas at the same time. Some prospective adopters may be influenced by factors of expense or fear that a second child may not be available later. Others may believe that two children will provide support and company for each other in a strange environment. However, there can be very few circumstances where this can be shown to be in the interests of the children concerned.

3.22 SSDs should not depart from the established good practice of approving the placement of no more than one unrelated child at one time. Subsequent plans to adopt a second child after an interval call for further assessment in accordance with normal practice, ie not until the adoption order for the first child has been made in a UK court and until approximately 12 months have passed since the child began to live with the adopters. This practice is firmly based on the interests of all the children concerned and of the adoptive family as a whole.

Visit to a child's country by prospective adopters

3–185 3.23 It essential that *each* adopter is advised of the necessity for them to travel to their country of choice to meet the child before he or she comes to the UK for the purposes of adoption or before an adoption order is made in the child's country of residence. In some cases SSDs have reported that where there is a joint application only the prospective adoptive mother or the father intends to visit the country concerned. Prospective adopters should not be recommended on the basis of such plans. The need for each prospective parent to meet the child and to make a joint decision and a joint commitment to the child should feature in the course of counselling.

Counselling of unsuccessful applicants

3.24 People whom the local authority is unable to recommend as suitable to be an adoptive **3–186** parent should be offered sympathetic counselling to help them deal with their disappointment; this service is provided for under section 1 of the Adoption Act 1976. Arrangements may be made for counselling from another adoption agency if the applicants make such a request.

Complaints

3.25 There may be occasions when a prospective adopter is dissatisfied with the service **3–187** received from a local authority, adoption agency or social worker. It is therefore helpful to clarify any complaints or review process at the outset as part of the information provided. Adoption agencies should have in place a process for dealing with complaints from prospective adopters. When agencies are contracted to undertake the home study assessment it will be necessary to clarify their complaints procedures *and* the expectations of both the contracted agency and the SSD in considering complaints and how they might be resolved. In this context, attention of adoption agencies is drawn to the Adoption Agencies and Children (Arrangements for Placement and Reviews) (Miscellaneous Amendments) Regulations 1997.

Adoption panels

3.26 There is no statutory requirement for adoption panels to make a recommendation in **3–188** respect of intercountry adoption applications. However, adoption panels have a valuable role to play in intercountry adoption and referral of *all* cases to them is strongly recommended. The advantages of referral include:

— provision of a valuable resource, providing experience, expertise and objectivity;
— development and application of common standards in all cases, including intercountry adoption;
— consideration by the panel contributes to a recommendation which is, and is seen by all to be, a *collective* rather than an *individual* recommendation, and
— support for management and social workers in this specific area of work.

3.27 It should be clearly understood that the adoption panel's role in intercountry adoption **3–189** cases is *advisory and consultative* and relates to the suitability of prospective adopters. This should not be confused with the wider role conferred on a panel by paragraph 10(1) of the Adoption Agencies Regulations 1983, as amended, which prescribe a panel's statutory functions in connection with agency placements.

Agency approval

3.28 The agency decision maker is required to make a decision whether or not to approve **3–190** an intercountry adoption application after taking account of the panel's recommendation. Only applications which have been approved by the agency decision maker should be forwarded to the Department of Health for further action.

3.29 The agency decision maker should be someone who has not been involved in the direct management or assessment of any applicant involved nor, where the application is considered by their adoption panel, a member of the adoption panel. The decision maker should understand the intercountry adoption process and have sufficient standing in the agency to endorse or challenge a panel's recommendation. This is equally relevant where a Schedule 2 report is required; it may also be relevant where work has been contracted out.

Handling home study reports

3.30 Adoption agencies will need to take account of the Adoption Agencies and Children **3–191** (Arrangements for Placement and Reviews) (Miscellaneous Amendments) Regulations 1997 which amend the Adoption Agencies Regulations 1983. From 1 July 1997, these Regulations provide for the prospective adopter to be given a copy of that part of the home study report which concerns the social worker's assessment of his suitability to be an adoptive parent. Completed home study reports should not be given to prospective adopters but, where the agency is able to recommend a prospective adopter as suitable to adopt a child from overseas, should be sent, together with completed medical reports, original police check forms (where required), agency decision maker's written approval and panel minutes, direct to
Department of Health
Children's Services — Adoption (SC3B)
Room 121, Wellington House
133–155 Waterloo Road
London SE1 8UG.

3–192   3.31 Once the SSD has decided to accept an adoption application and the criteria described above have been met, Directors are asked to provide reports within a four month period.

3.32 In general, *a total maximum period of six months* should be the aim and expectation for the preparation counselling and assessment of prospective adopters, the provision of a home study report, recommendation of the panel and decision by the agency decision maker. The likely timescale and the ground to be covered should always be explained and discussed with prospective adopters so that they know what to expect and are not caused frustration and anxiety on account of uncertainty.

3.33 Less time may be required in some cases where prospective adopters have already been approved by an adoption agency. In some cases there may exceptionally be circumstances which require a longer period of assessment and consideration with prospective adopters. There may also be rare occasions when a particular authority has received so many applications that people must be asked to wait a little longer but such delays must be kept to a minimum and prospective adopters should be given clear indications of possible start dates which should be adhered to.

3.34 SSDs should exercise care in advising prospective adopters of the outcome of assessment and recommendation. *It should be explained that while the recommendation is a vital part of the adoption process it does not complete the process, nor does it constitute a final decision.* While this also applies to domestic adoptions the intercountry adoption process differs in that responsibilities for different stages of the process fall on different authorities including, of course, the overseas authorities who will decided whether a child can be placed with particular applicants.

3.35 These reservations do not in any way undermine the importance of a SSD's home study report and recommendation. Nor do they diminish the responsibility which falls on a SSD to exercise the same level of care, experience and judgement as they bring to domestic adoption work. Thorough preparation of prospective adopters will assist them in the later stages of the adoption process and help avoid unnecessary delay and expense.

Linking

3–193   3.36 It is the nature of intercountry adoption that while counselling, preparation and assessment of adopters are the responsibility of the authorities in the "receiving" country, the linking of prospective adopters and children takes place in the children's country of origin. *SSDs have no opportunity, apart from the home study report, to influence these decisions taken overseas.* It is therefore of particular importance that, for the guidance of those who have the task of making or authorising placements, recommendations should be clear and specific about the age range and any particular characteristics of a child for whom the prospective adopters would be suitable.

3.37 It is important for SSDs to recognise that when the application is in respect of a child from a designated country (eg China), the effects of the adoption order made in the "designated" country are recognised in law within the United Kingdom. Consequently, the child's placement will not be required to be supervised pending an application for an adoption order to a UK court. Therefore the home study assessment process is the only opportunity to ensure that the responsibilities of adoption are fully understood by the applicants.

3.38 Where a report has been prepared in advance by a SSD and an application for Entry Clearance is made for a particular child, the Department of Health will pass on to the SSD information about the child received from the child's country of origin. The local authority will discuss the information with the prospective adopters and amend or confirm the recommendation in the light of the specific placement proposed.

3.39 At this stage the Department of Health will decide whether they can recommend to the Home Office that, so far as can be judged, the proposed adoption would be in the child's best interests *and* that the Department find no *prima facie* reason why a court in the United Kingdom would not made an adoption order. In reaching this judgement, the Department of Health will have regard to all available information about the child, the prospective adopters, the circumstances of the proposed adoption and the requirements of the British Court (see para. 6.6). The Department's Social Services Inspectorate (SSI) provides professional advice at all stages of the process. Reports and recommendations supplied by SSDs are examined by the SSI who will, if necessary, contact the authors for further clarification or discussion.

Post Placement

3–194   3.40 When a child residing in a non-designated country is subsequently given leave by the Home Office to enter the United Kingdom for the purposes of adoption, an adoption application should be made to a UK court at the earliest opportunity by the prospective adopters so that the child becomes a protected child under the 1976 Act. In the meantime, the Department recommends that the placement should be treated as a private fostering arrangement under section 69 of the Children Act 1989.

3.41 This process applies equally where a child has been brought into the United Kingdom without prior Entry Clearance, provided the SSD is satisfied that the circumstances do not require action to be taken under child protection legislation. The Department will see that the SSD is advised of such cases as soon as notification is received from the Home Office. SSDs are asked to notify the Department (at the address in paragraph 3.30 above) of any such cases which are brought to their attention other than by the Department of Health.

Responsibilities of Organisations Involved in the Process

4.1 Various central and local government departments and adoption agencies have a role to **3–195** play in the intercountry adoption process; the following is an indication of those likely to be involved.

Local Authorities and Approved Adoption Societies

4.2 The work of adoption agencies in handling applications from prospective adopters who **3–196** wish to adopt a child from overseas is essentially no different from that of a domestic adoption application up to the stage of the agency making a decision about the application. Consequently, this work is carried out under provisions of the 1976 Act and the relevant other legislation set out in paragraph 1.3 above.

Department of Health

4.3 As the central authority, administrative staff within the Department are responsible for **3–197** ensuring that applications meet the criteria of the country concerned and are presented in a form acceptable to the relevant country; confirming (by the issue of the Department's Certificate) that an applicant has been approved by an appropriate body; liaison with other countries and other official parties, and co-ordinating the Department of Health process.

4.4 Social Services Inspectorate are responsible for ensuring that intercountry adoption applications meet the professional standards required, advising local authority staff on specific issues and ensuring at the entry clearance stage that the child matched with the applicants meets the recommended criteria of the application.

4.5 It may be necessary for SSI to seek additional clarification from local authorities or suggest that further issues need to be addressed; this may lead to a delay in completing the process. SSI wish to be supportive to adoption agencies and be seen as a useful source for professional advice; in this context it is often helpful if adoption agencies contact SSI at an early stage once areas of concern become apparent.

4.6 The Department's medical adviser examines all medical reports received in respect of children coming to the UK for the purposes of adoption (*e.g.* non-designated countries) and offers appropriate advice to Department of Health staff. The Department's medical adviser is also available to advise adoption agency medical advisers on specific issues and cases. In this context, adoption agencies are referred to part 7 of this guidance which deals with issues of child health.

Foreign and Commonwealth Office (FCO)

4.7 The Legalisation Department of the FCO legalise all papers required by the adoption **3–198** authorities abroad. This entails the issue of a legalisation certificate and the embossing of all related and securely attached papers. The current charge (August 1996) for each FCO certificate is £12. FCO also provide the Department of Health with intelligence and advice concerning changes of law, governments, etc. abroad where these might have an impact on intercountry adoption.

Embassy/Consulate/High Commission of the child's Country of Origin in the UK

4.8 The Embassy/Consulate/High Commission of the child's country of residence will always **3–199** have some involvement in processing intercountry adoption applications although the extent can vary between countries. They may offer advice on their respective country's law and requirements, will usually confirm the "legality" of the FCO certificate, for which a charge is levied, will in some cases arrange for the translation of documents and may forward applications direct to their home country on the applicants behalf.

British Embassy/Consulate/High Commission abroad

3–200   4.9 It is the British Embassy/Consulate/High Commission based in or with responsibility for the child's country of residence to which an application for an entry clearance visa should be made. The Entry Clearance Officer (ECO) at the Embassy will ensure that immigration requirements are met and that additional evidence required by the Department of Health (*e.g.* child's birth certificate, medical report on child, valid parental consent, permission from relevant authorities for the child to leave) is also provided. The ECO will interview any child aged seven or over to ascertain their views on the proposed adoption.

4.10 British Embassy staff are willing to assist British subjects so far as they are able; however, they cannot influence or intervene in judicial, political or policy decisions of the country concerned and this should be clearly understood by prospective adopters.

Central Authority or Approved Agency/Agent in the sending country

3–201   4.11 All countries have Central Government Authorities responsible for child care but delegation of adoption related duties to national bodies, directors of children's homes or lawyers is common. The Department of Health may be able to advise on particular countries but it is for the prospective adopters to provide confirmatory evidence to the local authority that the approach they are taking is recognised by the Central Authorities concerned.

Courts in the sending country

3–202   4.12 In some countries adoption orders are made by administrative process rather than by the courts. Courts in sending country will grant an order on the basis of evidence provided. Such orders can include entrustment, guardianship, a residence order, an interim adoption order, a simple adoption order or a full adoption order. The courts will be aware that the child will eventually travel to the United Kingdom where a new permanent home will be provided and orders may be granted on the basis that interim welfare reports will be provided by the appropriate authority in the UK.

4.13 Procedures vary from country to country but awareness of possible post placement requirements is advised. The effects of an adoption order granted in a "**designated**" country are recognised within the UK. Where the country is "**non-designated**" the child will be brought to the UK for the purposes of adoption, requiring the prospective adopters to make application to a UK court as described in paragraph 3.38 above. Designated countries are specified in the Adoption (Designation of Overseas Adoptions) Order 1973 and set out in Appendix 2 of the Home Office leaflet on Intercountry Adoption (formerly circular RON 117).

Home Office — Immigration and Nationality Directorate (IND)

3–203   4.14 Applications to bring children to the United Kingdom for adoption are governed by the entry clearance process, operated by the Home Office, with the assistance of the Health Departments. IND has responsibility for immigration matters. It will establish whether or not immigration criteria have been met in respect of the entry clearance application made on behalf of the child. More detailed guidance about the functions of the Home Office relating to intercountry adoption is contained in part 6.

Courts in the United Kingdom

3–204   4.15 When an order is made in a child's country of residence giving care of that child to prospective adoptive parents and the country is non-designated, the prospective adopters on return to the United Kingdom will make an application to a UK court to adopt the child. The court will give the same considerations to the application as it would in a domestic application. An important effect of an adoption order made in the UK is that the child will automatically receive British citizenship provided that at least one of the adoptive parents is a British citizen at the time the UK adoption order is made.

4.16 It is therefore important that prospective adopters are aware of the UK legal requirements from the time they begin the adoption process and ensure that all necessary evidence about the adoption made in the child's country is obtained before the child comes to the UK and while contact with agents and authorities in that country is still ongoing. It is not usually possible to obtain information after the adoption action in the child's country is completed.

5. Privately Commissioned Home Study Reports

5.1 It remains the Department's view that privately commissioned home study reports are in **3–205** breach of Section 11 as extended by Section 72(3) of the Adoption Act 1976 and also in breach of Section 57 of the Act concerning prohibition on certain payments for any arrangements for the adoption of a child.

5.2 In some case, prospective adopters have commissioned home study reports from social workers acting in a private capacity. SSDs have sometimes been asked to "endorse" such privately commissioned reports. Reports and recommendations on the suitability of prospective adopters are required from local authorities because of their statutory duties in connection with adoption. These include duties under sections 1 and 2 of the Adoption Act 1976 and, if a child is admitted to the UK for adoption, supervision of the welfare of the child; support to the family pending adoption in the UK; and making reports and recommendations to the court hearing an adoption application (courts cannot accept a privately commissioned report as a substitute).

5.3 If, sadly, things go wrong, the duty of protecting the child and providing services to the family will also fall on the local authority. The findings and opinion of a private social worker, commissioned by a prospective adopter cannot, therefore, be substituted for the judgement of the authority. Such social workers take no responsibility for the circumstances in which their recommendations are used nor are they accountable to anyone for consequences which may flow from that use. Private reports are provided solely as a service to *prospective adopters*. Adoption agencies, including local authorities, are part of the Statutory Adoption Service and under a duty to give first consideration to the child's interests.

5.4 There can, therefore, be no "endorsement" or "validation" by local authorities of privately commissioned reports. It is for each SSD to decide whether they can or are prepared to make some use of a privately commissioned report in their own assessment of, and work with, prospective adopters. SSDs should bear in mind that some reports can be superficial with little evidence of professional evaluation. Caution is advised. In any case, the SSD must always carry out their own investigation and evaluation of the facts on which the private report appears to be based. Assessment of a prospective adopter must include a medical report; investigations must also include a police check which cannot be obtained by social workers acting in a private capacity. Statements issued to individuals under the Data Protection Act are not a substitute for police checks undertaken at the request of a local authority.

5.5 If a SSD decides to incorporate some part of a privately commissioned report into their own report, it is important that no letterhead of a private social worker or group of private social workers appears in the final report. The practice of adding covering letters to privately commissioned reports has led to some private social workers making unfounded and potentially misleading claims that they enjoy some measure of official support or recognition. Contrary to any such claims that may have been made, there is no group of private social workers which is recommended or "recognised" by the Department. Nor is there any statutory provision for such recognition. Such claims are confusing both to prospective adopters and overseas authorities to whom only reports from statutory or approved sources are acceptable and who have been given lists of approved adoption societies and local authorities. Directors should also note that some local authority social workers and guardians ad litem provide home study reports in a private capacity; these reports do not always state clearly that they are provided in the writer's private capacity and not in his or her official capacity.

5.6 The Department of Health has advised overseas authorities that official home study reports will always:
   a. be sent direct to the overseas agency or authority by the Department of Health;
   b. be accompanied by the Department's certificate confirming verifying approval of the prospective adopter by a particular statutory authority in compliance with UK regulations; or
   c. if the application is to a country on the designated list *not* requiring central authority involvement, be sent *directly* to the overseas agency or authority by the local authority:
   and will not
   d. be given to prospective adopters for presentation to an overseas body.

5.7 Directors are asked not to advise prospective adopters, in any circumstances, to commission reports from private social workers. Instead, SSDs should consider whether, after counselling, assessment and preparation of a report can be undertaken by their authority. Arrangements outlined in paragraphs 31 to 32 can be considered, where necessary.

3–206   6.1 This section deals with the role and responsibilities of the Home Office and how they link with the Department of Health. The Home Office has the responsibility for deciding whether to grant an entry clearance application which enables a child to enter the United Kingdom for the purposes of adoption or to reside permanently with his adoptive parents. Details are set out in the Home Office leaflet on intercountry adoption (formerly RON 117), a copy of which is included with this guidance. Directors are asked to ensure that people seeking advice are given the Home Office leaflet on intercountry adoption about information on entry clearance procedures; in some cases it may also be necessary for a prospective adopter to contact the Home Office.

6.2 In their role of counselling on intercountry adoption, social workers should ensure that prospective adopters are aware of and understand the content of the Home Office leaflet and also any particular requirements of their country of choice. Where there may be difficulties, prospective adopters should be advised to contact the Immigration and Nationality Directorate of the Home Office — details of which are contained in the leaflet. Counselling on this issue will also vary according to whether or not a child has been identified, if there is a family or other connection with the child. In such cases there may be other options that will provide a more appropriate solution to safeguard the child's future.

6.3 Where a child is related to the prospective adopters it is particularly important that they are aware of the the Immigration Rules which govern the admission of minor dependent relatives at an early stage in the process. This will avoid difficulties and possible distress at a later stage. The Rules are set out in Appendix 1 of the Home Office leaflet on Intercountry Adoption (included with this Guidance). Prospective adopters should understand that a child is only likely to be granted entry clearance to come to the United Kingdom if s/he cannot be cared for by his/her original family. If necessary, prospective adopters can contact the Home Office Telephone Enquiry Bureau on 0181 686 0688 for advice.

6.4 If the Home Office is satisfied that there are no immigration grounds for refusing an entry clearance application, ie. that the proposed adoption involves a genuine transfer of parental responsibility on the grounds of the parents' inability to care for the child, they will look to the Department of Health for advice on welfare aspects of the proposed adoption.

6.5 As part of the process for entry clearance, the Department of Health is asked by the Home Office whether an adoption order is likely to be granted to the sponsor(s) in respect of the named child. The recommendation to the Home Office by the Department of Health is based on the content of the home study report, additional specified information in respect of the child and confirmation that *both* prospective adopters, where there is a joint application, have met the child.

6.6 In giving such advice the Department of Health's central concern is to give first consideration to the welfare of the child. This is the test in section 6 of the Adoption Act 1976 which requires the court in reaching any decision relating to the adoption of a child to give first consideration to the child's welfare. The Department therefore needs to be satisfied on the following matters:

    a. the reasons for the proposed adoption; evidence of the child's identity and as much information about his circumstances, history and background as can be discovered, including a health report preferably on the British Agencies for Adoption and Fostering (BAAF) Intercountry Medical Form;

    b. evidence that the child is legally available for adoption and that the appropriate authorities support the adoption plans and have authorised the children's departure from the country of origin for the purposes of adoption;

    c. there is either a valid consent to the adoption of the child by the child's parent or guardian, in a form acceptable to a UK court — namely, that consent was not given until the child is at least six weeks old, that it was freely given and with full understanding of the effects of a UK adoption order ie. that such an order severs all legal links with the birth family and is irrevocable. Where the child has been abandoned, an official certificate that the child has been genuinely abandoned and the parents cannot be found is acceptable;

    d. the prospective adopters are approved by their Social Services Department as suitable adopters for the child.

    e. that the child's views, on the proposed adoption, commensurate with his age and understanding, have been obtained and the child is not opposed to the making of an adoption order.

6.7 The Department of Health relies on reports from the authorities in the child's country of origin, supplemented where necessary by enquiries made by the Entry Clearance Officer in that country, and in some cases on information provided by prospective adopters, in order to be satisfied about a, b, c and e above.

7. Child Health Issues

3–207

7.1 As part of the Entry Clearance procedures prospective adopters must arrange for a medical report on the child to be provided, ideally on the BAAF Intercountry Adoption Medical Form. This report is scrutinised by a Senior Medical Officer in the Department, who will ask for additional information if necessary. Information about the health and development of children proposed for adoption in the United Kingdom is *not* a condition upon which a child is given leave to enter and live permanently in the United Kingdom. It is an essential part of UK adoption practice — and a legal requirements in relation to placements in UK — that information is provided about the health and development of children proposed for adoption.

7.2 Prospective adopters need to be fully aware of any significant birth or early life experience that may affect the physical, emotional or mental development of the child so that they understand the associated responsibilities. Some children proposed for intercountry adoption face health and developmental difficulties; others may require active treatment and many will need compensatory nurture; in others, harmful experiences may lead to permanent physical or mental impairment.

7.3 Many children available for intercountry adoption have been abandoned or placed for adoption by parents who provide little background or medical information about themselves or the child and prospective adopters should be aware of this. They should also establish which medical conditions are likely to be endemic in the child's country of origin, for example, tuberculosis is a particular risk for children from China, whilst HIV and Hepatitis B is more likely to be of concern if children are to be adopted from Romania.

7.4 Prospective adopters should also be aware that infants with a HIV negative test result may actually be developing antibodies and convert to HIV positive later. Other infants with positive tests may be carrying maternal antibodies which are later shed. Thus the HIV test in infants may give a flawed result. The accuracy of tests performed in some countries from which children may be adopted may be questionable and could give rise to a false sense of security. It has also been suggested that the child could be put at risk of acquiring the infection merely by being tested. It is important, therefore, that social workers should explore the prospective adopters' attitudes towards these risks and their capacity to deal with them.

7.5 Prospective adopters need time to consider these risks, to understand the implications for the child's carers and to be able to demonstrate that they have the capacity to deal with health and developmental deficiencies should they emerge at a later stage, and with the uncertainties that there will be about the child's future development.

7.6 Prospective adopters should be made aware that the Department of Health has no control over the quality of medical information contained in any medical report received from abroad and in some cases information on which to base advice is severely lacking. Prospective adopters should also be aware that there is no guarantee that the child will be free of serious health and developmental problems, even with a high level of care and nurture in the new home.

7.7 Information on the child's health should be discussed in the first instance with the GP who may recommend immunisation, or wish to consult the local consultant in communicable disease control, or if the child does have hepatitis may recommend a full assessment by a hepatologist.

8. Contractual Arrangements

3–208

8.1 Local Authorities may contract out the home study assessment work to either an individual social worker or an approved voluntary adoption society (VAA). If this approach is taken the contractual arrangements should be clearly established and understood by all the parties involved, including for example, matters of payment of fees by prospective adopters and provision of post placement work if required. The local authority in which the prospective adopters reside remains responsible for the application and the decision; it therefore follows that the policies and procedures of the agency undertaking the work should be compatible with that authority.

8.2 If a sessional social worker is contracted to undertake the assessment on behalf of the local authority, that authority's adoption panel should consider the application. If it is decided to contract the work out it is important to recognise that the local authority retains responsibility for the standards of the applications and any decisions made. Care should therefore be taken in the choice of agency/individual.

Fees

3–209   9.1 Prospective adopters can be asked to meet the costs of the preparation and assessment report. This will sometimes enable an authority to contract a social worker with experience of adoption and child placement work who is known to them and in whom they have confidence to do the work. In these circumstances the report will be considered by the relevant adoption panel and the agency decision maker who will need to approve the report and ensure that health and police checks are carried out in the normal way by that authority. Where a report has been prepared by or on behalf of an adoption agency there will be no risk of a breach of sections 11 and 72 of the 1976 Act by the parties concerned.

9.2 Local authorities may, of course, arrange for assessment and reports to be undertaken by an approved adoption society, in accordance with the spirit of sections 1 and 2 of the Adoption Act 1976. A number of approved voluntary adoption agencies now undertake assessment and preparation of prospective intercountry adopters. Reports and recommendations prepared on behalf of an authority in this way must be acceptable to the authority and in line with its own policies, procedures and standards and this must be established before the work is undertaken. This is because supervision of any subsequent placement and the duty of making a Schedule 2 report to the court will fall to the authority, not the adoption society, unless the placement has been arranged by the society in accordance with the Adoption Agencies Regulations 1983.

10. Checklist

3–210   On receipt of an intercountry adoption application the Department of Health will check the following;

the application meets the requirements of the Adoption Agencies Regulations 1983 (as amended),

the home study report has been completed and has been signed as appropriate,

the medical report on each prospective adopter is attached and has been seen and signed by the agency medical adviser,

the original police check form on each prospective adopter is attached where required e.g. China, Philippines,

the referral of the adoption application to the DH is by the agency decision maker,

a second opinion visit, where made, has been reported upon,

applications have taken account of Home Office Immigration Legislation,

references have been obtained from two non-family members and a report addressing parenting capacity completed,

the adoption panel recommendation is recorded and the panel minutes attached,

medical advice on medical and psycho-social issues have been addressed in the report and considered by the adoption panel,

the report confirms that policies and likely placements of the applicant's country of choice have been addressed, that the applicants' expectations concerning the age of the child, disabilities, contact arrangements etc are realistic and have been discussed with them,

the report addresses reasons for wanting to adopt, cultural issues, parenting capacity, relationship issues, disability issues, age of applicants in relation to that of child to be adopted, preparation for placement, post placement, care and alternate care arrangements etc.,

where a specific child has already been identified, that information in respect of parental consent or abandonment has been confirmed,

The list is not exhaustive and will vary between applications.

11. Aide memoire for the intercountry adoption process

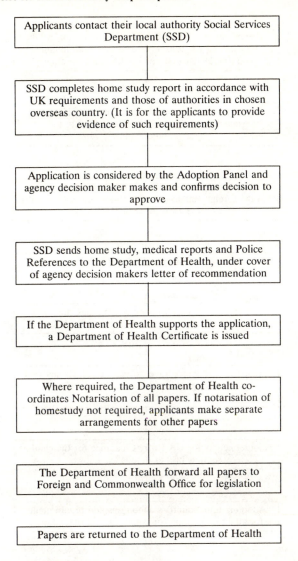

Applicants contact their local authority Social Services Department (SSD)

SSD completes home study report in accordance with UK requirements and those of authorities in chosen overseas country. (It is for the applicants to provide evidence of such requirements)

Application is considered by the Adoption Panel and agency decision maker makes and confirms decision to approve

SSD sends home study, medical reports and Police References to the Department of Health, under cover of agency decision makers letter of recommendation

If the Department of Health supports the application, a Department of Health Certificate is issued

Where required, the Department of Health co-ordinates Notarisation of all papers. If notarisation of homestudy not required, applicants make separate arrangements for other papers

The Department of Health forward all papers to Foreign and Commonwealth Office for legislation

Papers are returned to the Department of Health

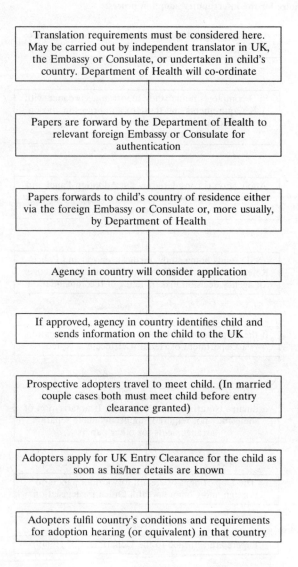

Translation requirements must be considered here. May be carried out by independent translator in UK, the Embassy or Consulate, or undertaken in child's country. Department of Health will co-ordinate

Papers are forward by the Department of Health to relevant foreign Embassy or Consulate for authentication

Papers forwards to child's country of residence either via the foreign Embassy or Consulate or, more usually, by Department of Health

Agency in country will consider application

If approved, agency in country identifies child and sends information on the child to the UK

Prospective adopters travel to meet child. (In married couple cases both must meet child before entry clearance granted)

Adopters apply for UK Entry Clearance for the child as soon as his/her details are known

Adopters fulfil country's conditions and requirements for adoption hearing (or equivalent) in that country

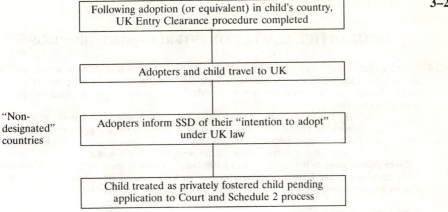

"Non-designated" countries

Following adoption (or equivalent) in child's country, UK Entry Clearance procedure completed

Adopters and child travel to UK

Adopters inform SSD of their "intention to adopt" under UK law

Child treated as privately fostered child pending application to Court and Schedule 2 process

HOME OFFICE LEAFLET ON INTERCOUNTRY ADOPTION

3–214 This leaflet explains the provisions for children who are not British citizens or nationals of the European Economic Area to join their adoptive or prospective adoptive parent(s) in the United Kingdom. While the leaflet is only a guide, it aims to answer the questions which are most likely to arise.

- If the child is the natural child of, or is otherwise related to, one of the adoptive parents or prospective adoptive parents, please turn to Appendix 1 *unless* the child has been adopted in a country listed in Appendix 2 in which case you should follow the instructions in the main body of the leaflet.

Every child coming to live in the United Kingdom permanently must obtain entry clearance *before* travelling to the United Kingdom. You are strongly advised *not* to book a flight to the United Kingdom for your adoptive child until entry clearance has been issued.

What is entry clearance?

3–215 Entry clearance is a visa or entry certificate issued for the purpose of travel to the United Kingdom. Applications for entry clearance must be made to the British Embassy, High Commission or other Diplomatic Mission (collectively known as British Diplomatic Posts) which is nearest to the child's normal place of residence and designated to issue entry clearance. Details of the Posts which are designated for this purpose, fees, information on how to apply for entry clearance and entry clearance application forms may be obtained either from the British Diplomatic Post concerned or by writing to the:

> Migration & Visa Division Correspondence Unit
> Foreign & Commonwealth Office
> 1 Palace Street
> London SW1E 5HE.

Details of the time it will take an Entry Clearance Officer to process an application may be obtained from the relevant Post.

What are the immigration requirements?

3–216 You must be able to show that:

- you are present and settled in the United Kingdom, ie. living here lawfully with no time limit on your stay; and
- you are able to maintain and accommodate the child adequately without recourse to public funds.

You or the child must show that:

- he is under 18 years old; and
- he is not leading an independent life, is unmarried and has not formed an independent family unit; and
- he was adopted when both parents were resident together abroad or either was settled in the United Kingdom; and
- he has the same rights and obligations as any other child of the adoptive parent(s); and
- he was or is to be adopted due to the inability of the original parent(s) to care for him and there has been a genuine transfer of parental responsibility; and
- he has broken his ties with his family of origin; and
- it is not an adoption of convenience arranged to facilitate the child's entry to the United Kingdom.

What are public funds?

3–217 For immigration purposes, public funds currently means:

- housing under the homeless legislation
- attendance allowance, severe disablement allowance, invalid care allowance and disability living allowance

- income support
- family credit
- Council tax benefit
- disability working allowance
- housing benefit
- child benefit
- Jobseeker's allowance

Please note that the list of public funds which are taken into account for immigration purposes may change.

How long can the child stay?

The period for which the child is admitted will depend on which basis entry clearance is **3–218** granted. It might also be dependent on any limitations on the stay of the adoptive parents. A child may be admitted:

- as an **adopted child** — a child who is the subject of a full adoption order recognised under United Kingdom law (see Appendix 2).
- as a **de facto dependant** — a child who has been adopted, not necessarily legally, by a person or persons who have been ordinarily resident abroad for a substantial period of time. The child will be so integrated in the family that he can be considered to be an adopted child.
- as a **child who is the subject of an interim adoption order** — the order must have been made in a country or territory (as listed in Appendix 2) which will convert it into a full adoption order recognised under United Kingdom law at a later date.
- **for adoption in the United Kingdom** — this will normally be where a child has been adopted in a country whose adoption orders are not recognised under United Kingdom law (ie. a country *not* listed in Appendix 2) by a person or persons who live permanently in the United Kingdom. A child may also be admitted on this basis where the intention is to adopt only in the United Kingdom courts.

Adopted children and de facto dependants will normally be admitted for an indefinite period.

Children who are the subject of interim adoption orders and children coming for adoption will be admitted for a period of 12 months to allow the adoption to be finalised. An application may be made to the Immigration and Nationality Directorate for the time limit on the child's stay to be removed on completion of the adoption proceedings.

What documents do I need to provide?

You must provide *all* of the following documents which should be *in original form*. Those which are not in English must be accompanied *by certified translations*.

- settlement application forms IM2A and IM2B, the child's passport, 2 recent passport sized photographs and the appropriate fee
- the child's original birth certificate showing his name at birth
- a contemporary report from the overseas equivalent of the social services department which details the child's parentage and history, the degree of contact with the original parent(s), the reasons for the adoption, the date, reasons and arrangements for the child's entry into an institution or foster placement and when, how and why the child came to be offered to the adoptive parent(s) — where no legal adoption has taken place, or where a legal adoption has taken place and the adoptive parent(s) were previously related to the child and for this reason the social services department did not complete a report, a full written account which covers these points should be provided by the adoptive or prospective adoptive parent(s)
- where the child has been abandoned, a certificate of abandonment from the authorities previously responsible for the child's care
- the adoption order (where applicable)
- passport(s) of the adoptive parent(s) or other evidence to show settled status such as a birth certificate, registration or naturalisation certificate
- bank statements and an accountant's letter or pay slips which show the monthly incomings and outgoings of the adoptive parent(s) and details of the accommodation of the adoptive parent(s) in the United Kingdom
- you may be asked to provide further documents.
- it may be necessary for the Entry Clearance Officer to interview some or all of the parties involved.

- if an entry clearance application is refused, there will be a right of appeal to the Independent Appellate Authorities.

Additional information for children coming for adoption

3–219   Where the child will be coming to the United Kingdom for adoption *and* the Entry Clearance Officer is satisfied that the immigration requirements listed on page 2 have been met, he will seek the advice of the relevant territorial health department on the proposed adoption before issuing entry clearance. Before the territorial health department can give advice, they will need to see the following *additional* documents. You should lodge these with the Entry Clearance Officer:
- the 2 forms marked Appendix 3 and 4
- a BAAF ICA medical form for the child
- if there is no adoption order, written permission from the authorities responsible for the child's care in his country of origin that they are content for the child to come to the United Kingdom to be adopted by you
- the written consent of the child's natural parent(s), or those with legal responsibility for the child, to the adoption and confirmation that the meaning of an adoption order granted in the United Kingdom, i.e. it is irrevocable and severs all legal ties with the birth family, is understood; to be valid, the consent should be given freely when the child is at least six weeks old and it should be notarised in the child's own country.

and these with the relevant territorial health department:
- medical forms for you (and your spouse)
- an up-to-date home study approved by your local social services or social work department
- The territorial health departments' advice is that you approach your local social services or social work department and ask them for a home study report before you identify a child. If you do not, you may find yourself in a situation where you have to leave the child for several months and return to the United Kingdom while a home study report is completed. Also, you may not be recommended as suitable to adopt.
- Provided you have lodged all of the above documents (with translations where necessary) with the Entry Clearance Officer and the territorial health department, the territorial health departments will normally be able to respond to the Entry Clearance Officer within 6 weeks.
- Please note that the Department of Health require that before a child can be brought to the United Kingdom for adoption it must have been visited abroad by both its adoptive parents.

Will my adopted child be a British Citizen?

3–220   If your child was adopted by order of a court in the United Kingdom (including, for this purpose, the Channel Islands and the Isle of Man) or in the Falkland Islands and at least one of the adoptive parents was a British citizen at the time the adoption order was made, then the child will automatically become a British citizen.

Adoption elsewhere will not result in the adopted child acquiring British citizenship automatically. The child's only avenue to citizenship will be by way of a successful application for registration under section 3(1) of the British Nationality Act 1981. Registration under this section is entirely at the discretion of the Home Secretary. An application will normally be approved if the following criteria are satisfied:
- one of the adoptive parents or the sole adopter is a British citizen otherwise than by descent (ie. by virtue of his or her birth, adoption, registration or naturalisation in the United Kingdom); and
- the adoptive parent(s) have signified their consent to the registration; and
- we are satisfied that the adoption is not one of convenience arranged to facilitate the child's admission to or stay in the United Kingdom; and
- either the adoption was made under the laws of one of the countries listed in Appendix 2 or we are satisfied that there has been a genuine transfer of parental responsibility on the grounds of the original parents' inability or unwillingness to care for the child.

Application forms are available from the Nationality Directorate (address on page 7) or from any British Diplomatic Post. If the applicant, ie. the adopted child, is in the United Kingdom on the date of application, the application should be sent direct to the Nationality Directorate. If the child is abroad, the application should be made to the nearest Diplomatic Post.

HOME OFFICE

For information about immigration matters:

Home Office
Immigration and Nationality Directorate
Lunar House
40 Wellesley Road
CROYDON
CR9 2BY
Tel: 0181 686 0688

For information about nationality matters:

Home Office
Nationality Directorate
3rd Floor
India Buildings
Water Street
LIVERPOOL
L2 0QN
Tel: 0151 237 5200

TERRITORIAL HEALTH DEPARTMENTS

For information about adoption law and procedures:

England:
Social Care Group 3B
Department of Health
Wellington House
133 Waterloo Road
LONDON
SE1 8UG
Tel: 0171 972 4347/4084

Scotland:
Social Work Services Group
(Division 3–1)
The Scottish Office
James Craig Walk
EDINBURGH
EH1 3BA
Tel: 0131 244 5480

Wales:
Children and Families Unit
Welsh Office
Cathays Park
CARDIFF
CF1 3NQ
Tel: 01222 823145

Northern Ireland:
Adoption Unit
Department of Health and Social Services
Dundonald House
Upper Newtownards Road
BELFAST
BT24 3SF
Tel: 01232 524769

BRITISH AGENCIES FOR ADOPTION AND FOSTERING (BAAF)

For medical forms and information about adoption:

British Agencies for Adoption and
Fostering (BAAF)
Skyline House
200 Union Street
LONDON SE1 0LY
Tel: 0171 593 2000

Requirements for a child to join a parent or relative

3-222   You or the child must show that he:
- is seeking leave to enter to join a parent or relative in one of the following circumstances:
- one parent is present and settled in the United Kingdom and the other parent is dead; *or*
- one parent is present and settled in the United Kingdom and has had sole responsibility for the child's upbringing; *or*
- one parent or a relative is present and settled in the United Kingdom and there are serious and compelling family or other considerations which make exclusion of the child undesirable and suitable arrangements have been made for the child's care; and
- is under the age of 18; and
- is not leading an independent life, is unmarried and has not formed an independent family unit; and
- can and will be maintained and accommodated adequately without recourse to public funds in accommodation which the parent owns or occupies exclusively.

Entry clearance for admission in this capacity is mandatory. For details on how to apply for entry clearance, please see page 1.

If the requirements are met, entry clearance will be granted. Relatives who wish to adopt the child under United Kingdom law should discuss their plans with their social services or social work department after the child's arrival in the United Kingdom.

If the requirements are not met, then an application may be considered on the basis that the child is coming to the United Kingdom for adoption. However, you and the child would still need to meet all the requirements set out on page 2.

APPENDIX 2

Only adoptions made by order of a court in the United Kingdom or Islands or in one of the countries or territories listed below are recognised under United Kingdom statutory law.

a. Commonwealth countries

Anguilla
Australia
Bahamas
Barbados
Belize
Bermuda
Botswana
British Virgin Islands
Canada
Cayman Islands
Cyprus
Dominica
Fiji
Ghana
Gibraltar
Guyana
Hong Kong
Jamaica
Kenya
Lesotho
Malawi

Malaysia
Malta
Mauritius
Montserrat
Namibia
New Zealand
Nigeria
Pitcairn Island
St Christopher and Nevis
St Vincent
Seychelles
Singapore
South Africa
Sri Lanka
Swaziland
Tanzania
Tonga
Trinidad and Tobago
Uganda
Zambia
Zimbabwe

b. Foreign countries

Austria
Belgium
China (but only where the child was adopted on or after 5 April 1993 and will be living in England or Wales or on or after 10 July 1995 and will be living in Scotland or on or after 19 February 1996 and will be living in Northern Ireland)
Denmark (including Greenland and the Faroes)
Finland
France (including Reunion, Martinique, Guadeloupe and French Guyana)
Germany
Greece
Iceland
The Republic of Ireland
Israel
Italy

Luxembourg
The Netherlands (including the Antilles)
Norway
Portugal (including the Azores and Madeira)
Spain (including the Balearics and Canary Islands)
Surinam
Sweden
Switzerland
Turkey
United States of America
Yugoslavia (but none of the states which make up the former Yugoslavia)

UNDERTAKING BY INTENDING ADOPTERS

Names of intending adopters:

....

....

Address: ....

....

....

Name of the child:

....

We, the undersigned, agree that if entry clearance is granted for the above-named child to come to the United Kingdom for adoption by us we will, as soon as the child arrives in the United Kingdom, inform the social services department of our local authority* of our intention to apply to the court for an adoption order in respect of that child, and that we will make such application to the court.

We also agree to accept full financial responsibility for the child while the child is in the United Kingdom.

Signed: (1) ....

       (2) ....

Date: ....

---

* —in Northern Ireland, the Health and Social Services Board.
   — in Scotland, the Social Work Department of the Regional or Islands Council.

Home Office reference number:

Please submit this form and the documents requested when you apply for entry clearance for a child being adopted from abroad.

The information requested on this form includes many of the details that will be required by a court hearing an adoption application. This form and the documents that you enclose with it will be treated as confidential and only passed to the territorial health department and the local authority undertaking the home study report. In some cases we may need to ask for further information.

DETAILS ABOUT THE CHILD

Surname:

Other names:

Nationality:

Sex:

Passport number:
Date of birth:

(Please enclose birth certificate or a signed and attested statement giving the date of birth)

Name and address of person currently looking after the child overseas:

Is this person a relative of the child?

If Yes, state relationship:

Has the child attended school?

If Yes, how many years has he attended school?
has he passed any examinations? (give details)

If the child has any brothers or sisters give:

Name: Date of birth: name of person
                                                                 caring for
                                                                 them:

PLEASE ATTACH A COPY OF THE MEDICAL REPORT ON THE CHILD. THIS SHOULD BE ON A BAAF ICA FORM OBTAINABLE FROM BRITISH AGENCIES FOR ADOPTION AND FOSTERING (See page 7 for address)

IF THE CHILD HAS BEEN CARED FOR BY A PUBLIC OR OTHER ORGANISATION

Name and address of the body:

Date child came into their care:

DETAILS ABOUT THE CHILD'S PARENTS

	Mother	Father

Surname:
Other names:
Date of birth:
Place of birth:
Marital status:
Date of marriage:

DETAILS ABOUT YOU

	Mother	Father

Surname:
Other names:
Date of birth:
Relationship to child:
Your home address:

Have you ever previously applied to adopt or foster a child?

Have you recently had a home study report prepared?

If you have answered yes to either of these questions, give name of local authority or agency or individual concerned:

Please give the names and addresses of two personal referees who know you both well:
1.   2.

Please state how the child came to be offered to you for adoption

Have you any other children?

If yes please give names and dates of birth

I certify that this information is true and correct to the best of my knowledge.

Signed: (1) ....

(2) ....

366

BIRTH RECORD,
adopted person, of, 2–108 *et seq.*
disclosure of, 1–216 *et seq.*
BRITISH ADOPTION ORDER,
meaning of, 1–298
BRITISH NATIONALITY,
adoption securing, 1–030
BRITISH TERRITORY,
meaning of, 1–298
designation of, 2–029

CASE RECORDS. *See,* RECORDS
CHILD. *Also see,* ADOPTED CHILD AND
PROTECTED CHILD
abandonment of, 1–080, 1–087
adopted, financial provision for,
1–056
adopted abroad, 1–241
adoption agency, placement by,
1–130
adoption agency's duties in respect
of, 2–061, 3–008
applicant having home with, 1–062
et seq.
assessment of, 1–003
case record of, 2–061
ceasing to have home with
prospective adopters, 1–114
contact by, 3–149
contact with natural parent, 1–086
freeing of, for adoption, 1–099
et seq.
ill-treatment of, 1–080, 1–088,
1–091
jurisdiction, outside the, 1–094
living with prospective adopters for
five years, 1–142
maintenance of, 1–054, 1–160
married, prohibition on making
adoption order, 1–049
meaning of, 1–298
medical report on, 2–101, 2–061,
2–245, 2–327
neglect of, 1–080, 1–088
placement, end of, 1–154
placement of, 1–003, 1–031, 1–062
et seq., 1–125, 2–079, 3–013,
3–104 *et seq.,* 3–146 *et seq.*
placement of, restrictions on, 1–045
et seq.
placement where mother under a
disability, 1–047
private placement of, 1–045 *et seq.*
proof of identity of, 2–183
proof of identity of, 2–269, 2–289,
3–053, 3–067
protected. *See* Protected child

CHILD—*cont.*
race of, 1–031, 3–014 *et seq.,* 3–147
re-adoption of, 1–061
religious upbringing of, 1–031,
1–032, 1–033
removal abroad for adoption, 1–246
removal of, 1–149
removal of, application for, 2–206,
2–292, 3–071
report on, 2–100, 2–101
restriction on removal of, 1–139
et seq., 1–142 *et seq.*
return of, 1–154
return of, application for, 2–206,
2–292, 3–071
return of wrongfully removed,
1–149
Romanian, adoption of, 3–114
et seq.
search for, 1–149
search warrant for, 1–149
services for, 3–100
welfare of the, 1–028 *et seq.,* 1–031
welfare of the, consent to adoption
and the, 1–085
wishes and feelings of, 1–029, 1–031
CHILD MAINTENANCE,
adoption order, effect on, 1–049
CHILD ACT 1989,
concurrent applications with
Adoption Act 1976, 1–052
orders, adoption extinguishing,
1–055
CITIZENSHIP,
adoption, and, 1–203
intercountry adoption and, 3–221
CO-HABITEES,
adoption applicants, as, 1–068
COMMON LAW,
adoptions, 1–002
CONCURRENT APPLICATIONS, 1–052
CONDITIONS,
adoption order with, 1–049 *et seq.*
CONFIDENTIALITY,
public interest in, 1–030, 1–082
records, of, 2–089
CONSENT. *Also see,* AGREEMENT
dispensing with, 1–082, 1–084 *et seq.*
evidence of, 1–270
unreasonable withholding of, 1–082,
1–084 *et seq.*
vacillation about, 1–086
CONTACT, 3–149. *Also see,* CONTACT
ORDER
condition of adoption order, 1–058
et seq.
indirect, 1–060
natural parent, with, beneficial to
child, 1–086

368

369

REVOCATION—*cont.*
freeing order, of, 3–054
ROMANIAN CHILD,
adoption of, 3–114 *et seq.*

SCHEDULE 2 REPORT, 2–234 *et seq.*,
2–317 *et seq.*
SCOTLAND,
adoption proceedings, and, 1–266
evidence of adoption proceedings
in, 1–268
SEARCH WARRANT,
child, for, 1–149
SECRETARY OF STATE,
adoption society, approval of, 1–012
inactive or defunct, action
against, 1–034 *et seq.*
refusal to approve, 1–025 *et seq.*
withdrawal of approval of, 1–021
et seq., 1–025 *et seq.*
information for, 1–262
SERIAL NUMBER,
application for a, 2–158, 2–272,
3–056
SETTING ASIDE,
adoption orders, of, 1–051
SINGLE PERSON,
adoption application by, 1–072
et seq.
SPECIFIED COUNTRY,
designation of, 2–030

SPECIFIED ORDER,
meaning of, 1–298
STATISTICS,
adoption, 3–096
STEP-PARENT ADOPTION, 1–062 *et seq.*,
1–070
SURROGACY,
payments for adoption, and, 1–252

TELEVISION,
advertisement seeking potential
adopter, 1–259
TRANSRACIAL ADOPTION, 1–031

UNITED KINGDOM NATIONAL,
meaning of, 1–298, 2–031

VOLUNTARY ORGANISATION,
meaning of, 1–298

WELFARE,
child, of the, 1–031
consent to adoption and the,
1–085
WILL,
adopted child named in, 1–193
WOMAN,
pregnant, accommodation for,
1–003